Handbook for Teaching Statistics and Research Methods

Second Edition

Edited by

Mark E. Ware
Creighton University

Charles L. Brewer
Furman University

LAWRENCE ERLBAUM ASSOCIATES, PUBLISHERS

1999   Mahwah, New Jersey   London

Lawrence Erlbaum Associates, Inc., Publishers
10 Industrial Avenue
Mahwah, New Jersey 07430

Library of Congress Cataloging-in-Publication Data

Handbook for teaching statistics and research methods /
  edited by Mark E. Ware, Charles L. Brewer. -- 2nd ed.
      p.   cm.
   Includes bibliographical references and index.
   ISBN 0-8058-3049-9 (pbk. : alk. paper)
   1. Statistics--Study and teaching. 2. Research--
Study and teaching.   I. Ware, Mark E. II. Brewer,
Charles L.
QA276.18.H36   1998
001.4'2--dc21   98-33522
                                             CIP

Books published by Lawrence Erlbaum Associates are printed
on acid-free paper, and their bindings are chosen
for strength and durability.

Printed in the United States of America

10 9 8 7 6 5 4 3 2 1

Table of Contents

5. Evaluating Success in Statistics

Section II: Research Methods

1. Reducing Students' Fears

2. Evaluating Ethical Issues

3. Teaching Ethics

4. Reviewing the Literature

5. Using Computers

6. Implementing Teaching Strategies

7. Demonstrating Systematic Observation and Research Design

8. Teaching Writing and Critical Thinking

9. Emphasizing Accuracy in Research

10. Fostering Students' Research and Presentations

Appendix   285

Subject Index   287

Preface

In the preface to this book's first edition, we underscored the importance of data analysis and research methodology to empirical disciplines. We further noted our desire in preparing the book to assist those who teach courses whose contents contain statistics and research methodology.

Since the first edition in 1988, several events have emphasized the value of pedagogy for statistics and research methods courses. Events included the National Conference on Enhancing the Quality of Undergraduate Education in Psychology. In the book that resulted from the conference (McGovern, 1993), one of us (CLB) identified statistics and research methods as two of three courses in the methodology domain of the undergraduate psychology curriculum; psychometrics was the third course. Furthermore, he wrote that the skills derived from methodology courses "can transcend isolated research findings . . . and . . . can enhance lifelong learning" (p. 173). Thus, we conclude that effective teaching of statistics and research methods courses is as important now as it was a decade ago.

Teaching of Psychology (*ToP*) is the official journal of The Society for the Teaching of Psychology, Division 2 of the American Psychological Association. A review of *ToP* issues since the first edition of the book revealed two recurring themes, developing students' acquisition of skills and their sensitivity to ethical issues. The importance of nurturing students' writing and critical-thinking skills was reflected in special issues of the journal that appeared in 1990 and 1995, respectively. Beginning in 1989, a new section in *ToP*, Computers in Teaching, recognized the important role of computers in teaching and learning. Does anyone at the end of the 20th century doubt the impact of computer skills for psychology teachers and their students?

These events provide a context for and anticipate many of the themes in the present edition. In the following paragraphs, we list the topics in the second edition and summarize the similarities and differences between the two editions.

We organized the 92 articles into two main sections, Statistics and Research Methods. Articles in the first section appear under 5 headings: (a) generating data sets, (b) illustrating statistical concepts, (c) examining statistical tests, (d) developing students' skills, and (e) evaluating success in statistics. Articles in the second section appear under 10 headings: (a) reducing students' fears, (b) evaluating ethical issues, (c) teaching ethics, (d) reviewing the literature, (e) using computers, (f) implementing teaching strategies, (g) demonstrating systematic observation and research design, (h) teaching writing and critical thinking,

(i) emphasizing accuracy in research, and (j) fostering students' research and presentations.

Both editions of the book contain numerous articles about teaching statistical concepts and tests, as well as techniques for generating data sets. Moreover, readers will find that both editions emphasize approaches to teaching about the literature review and research design, as well as to using computers and promoting students' scholarly production. Differences consist of using computers for more than "number crunching" and developing writing skills in the statistics course. Among articles about teaching research methods, the present edition contains considerably more articles than the first edition about ethics in research and teaching ethics. Emphasis on developing writing and critical-thinking skills has increased to such an extent that the present edition required a separate heading. Although the second edition has a heading about using computers, computer use is frequently incorporated in articles listed under other headings. Thus, the role of computers in teaching research methods is greater than might appear at first glance.

All articles in this volume were previously published in *ToP*, but none of them appeared in the earlier edition. Although the first edition had a 1988 copyright, the most recent articles were published in 1986. We included in this edition five articles from 1985 and 1986 that we had overlooked. We excluded from consideration the many excellent articles about teaching psychology that were not directly related to courses in statistics and research methods. In addition, we excluded at least two dozen statistics and research methods articles that addressed unusual topics or described graduate level uses that had little application to undergraduate education. The final selection provides a convenient and helpful source of valuable information for teachers of courses containing information about statistics and research methods.

ToP published its first issue in October 1974. Robert S. Daniel was the editor for 10 years and, in 1984, was given the honorific title of Founding Editor. This volume celebrates Bob's outstanding work and the silver anniversary of the journal that he established and nurtured during its critical first decade.

All royalties from the sale of this book will be paid directly to the Society and earmarked for promoting the laudable activities of its Fund for Excellence. If this handbook increases the zest with which teachers and students approach statistics and research methods, then our efforts will have been adequately reinforced.

Mark E. Ware
Charles L. Brewer

McGovern, T. V. (Ed.). (1993). *Handbook for enhancing undergraduate education in psychology.* Washington, DC: American Psychological Association.

SECTION I
STATISTICS

Curriculum studies sponsored by the American Psychological Association have repeatedly affirmed the importance of statistics in undergraduate psychology education. By one estimate, almost 75% of the undergraduate psychology departments in the United States require their majors to complete an introductory statistics course. Despite, or perhaps because of, its pervasiveness, the statistics course has been a major trouble spot in the psychology curriculum. One report indicated that students often rate the material as poorly presented and uninteresting.

The articles we selected for this section contain suggestions for (a) generating data sets, (b) illustrating statistical concepts, (c) examining statistical tests, (d) developing students' skills, and (e) evaluating success in statistics. These articles can help mitigate some of the obstacles statistics teachers encounter.

1. GENERATING DATA SETS

Students in Burt Thompson's statistics class at Niagara University used the Student Information Questionnaire (SIQ) to produce a realistic data set for testing a variety of student-generated hypotheses. The instructor provided a skeleton form of the SIQ, and students customized the form to their interests. Evaluations of the technique suggested that students found such data more interesting than artificial data and more helpful for learning statistics.

John Walsh at Fordham University developed an SAS program, which is reproduced in the article, to provide students with simulated questionnaire-style data for use in courses in statistics and experimental design. The program produces data that approximate the distributions of nominal or categorical variables, rating scale data, and normally distributed scores. The data sets provide a simulated research experience that can incorporate student-generated research items and statistical analyses.

To facilitate calculating statistics by hand, Bernard Beins at Ithaca College wrote a BASIC computer program to generate different sets of random numbers having integer means and variances. Users can select either the biased or unbiased formula for the standard deviation. The article also describes the program's uses and limitations.

A challenging test for students' understanding of statistical concepts consists of evaluating nonnormal data sets. John Walsh from Fordham University designed a FORTRAN program that allows instructors to construct distributions having nonnormal shapes (e.g., truncated and skewed distributions) by modifying the familiar standard unit normal distribution. Instructors can immediately use or adapt values in the program to produce distributions with different shapes.

In an unusual approach to generating data sets, Todd Riniolo from the University of Maryland, College Park designed a computer-based simulation, which is based on tenets of the central limit theorem, illustrating the consequences of excluding nonsignificant findings from published literature. The article describes a step-by-step procedure for conducting a class demonstration. The demonstration points out that exclusion of nonsignificant findings positively biases research interpretation and that smaller sample sizes are prone to greater bias when nonsignificant results are excluded from research interpretation.

Making Data Analysis Realistic: Incorporating Research Into Statistics Courses

W. Burt Thompson
Niagara University

As psychologists, we are often motivated to collect, analyze, and interpret data because we want to answer an interesting question. I believe this same motive must drive students who are learning applied statistics. This article describes one way instructors can increase their students' desire to learn by using realistic, rather than artificial, data that the students collect in a simple research project. This project yields data that create an immediate desire to learn statistics based on the students' fascination with psychology.

Most statistics textbooks contain practice problems based on artificial data. Instructors also frequently create hypothetical data for use in class, and several articles in *Teaching of Psychology* describe how to generate artificial data for the statistics course (e.g., Beins, 1989; Cake & Hostetter, 1986). The use of hypothetical data is an important part of any statistics course, but one negative consequence is that these data sets may arouse minimal student interest. After all, why would students who want to learn about human behavior care about two columns of numbers labeled X and Y? An even bigger problem is that artificial data sets remove students from the data-collection process and thus create or reinforce an artificial separation of research and data analysis, two processes that are in practice inseparable (Singer & Willett, 1990).

There are many ways to increase the realism of data. For example, Beins (1985) suggested that instructors have students test advertising claims by obtaining and analyzing research reports on which the claims are based. Hettich (1974) suggested that instructors have students complete two questionnaires (to assess study habits and test anxiety) and provide information such as height, academic major, and number of completed psychology courses (Jacobs, 1980, described a similar procedure). However, Hettich's suggestion produces only a small data set that limits the hypotheses that can be tested. More important, although the techniques suggested by Hettich and Beins do yield real data, students do not select which factors to measure or which hypotheses to test, and they do not assist in data collection. To derive full benefit from real data, students must be the researchers (not the subjects in the study), and they must collect the data themselves or assist in the design of the data-collection instrument.

Generating Realistic Data: The Student-Designed Student Information Questionnaire

Because questionnaires are widely used in psychological research and can easily produce a large data set, I have Students use a Student Information Questionnaire (SIQ) that they help construct. The SIQ taps variables that are of interest to students; it also provides a variety of measures useful in teaching an introductory statistics course. Students can test many different hypotheses because the SIQ measures many variables (one class's SIQ measured 19 variables); indeed, each student can generate a unique list of hypotheses to investigate.

Instructors can modify the SIQ to fit their pedagogical needs. However, each new group of students should modify the questionnaire to fit particular interests. When students customize the SIQ, it becomes their survey (rather than the instructor's survey) and gives them a legitimate feeling of ownership for the data. In contrast, in Hettich's (1974) proposal, the instructor assumes the role of researcher, and the students are subjects in the study. My students assume the role of researchers, and the survey is treated as a research project they conduct.

I provide the class with a skeleton form of the SIQ that includes questions about common activities, such as studying and television viewing, and it asks each respondent for a self-rating on several characteristics (e.g., friendliness, creativity, and shyness). Students in one of my classes added questions to find out if the respondents lived in a dormitory or in off-campus housing and whether they paid for their own tuition. Students later examined the relation between these two factors and how seriously the respondents approached their university studies (indexed by the amount of time spent in activities such as studying and television viewing). Another class was interested in study habits; they added questions to the SIQ such as "When you study, how much noise and activity do you prefer to have going on around you?" and "What time of day do you prefer to study?"

Early in the semester (typically during the second class meeting) my students decide how they would like to change the survey, and I guide their writing of new items. We discuss what variables to measure and the best kind of question for measuring each factor, given the constraints that the SIQ must be short and easy to complete. It is important for students to state each hypothesis as explicitly as possible to facilitate the writing of useful and unbiased items. Students must be continually asked "Will the answers given to this question allow you to test your hypothesis?"

Survey items can be written during class or as homework. I give copies of the final SIQ to instructors who have agreed to distribute it in their classes.[1] Because the SIQ can be completed in a few minutes, I have never encountered problems getting other instructors to distribute it. Typically between 100 and 150 students from a variety of courses complete the SIQ. This procedure provides enough variability and large enough subsamples to allow students to test hypotheses with predictor variables such as gender or college class. The SIQ should be distributed several weeks after the beginning of the term, although the timing depends on the questions. Waiting until the third week of classes will yield meaningful answers to the question about the amount of time spent studying each week and other questions that deal with routine aspects of college life. However, avoid waiting too long because much of the SIQ material is useful for teaching about descriptive statistics during the first part of the course.

Classroom Uses for SIQ Data

Once the surveys are returned, I devote part of one class meeting to data coding. Students working in small groups transfer the information from the completed SIQs to summary sheets that I have prepared in advance (each group is given a copy of the coding sheet). Each student codes several surveys. Because I typically have 30 students in my class (15 students in each of two sections) and 100 to 150 completed SIQs, each student must code four or five surveys. It takes about 20 min to explain how to use the coding sheet and for the students to record the data. After class, I enter the data into a computer spreadsheet and give a copy to each student. (Instructors who use computers in their classes may want the students to enter the data.)

Next, the students generate hypotheses about group differences, relations between variables, and point estimates. Students are usually interested in comparing men to women (and freshman to seniors) on such factors as how much they study, exercise, smoke, or drink. Students also make predictions about the relations between pairs of variables (e.g., self-ratings of aggression and friendliness). For point esti-

---

[1] I do not have my students assist in the actual data collection because I usually have about 30 students and the survey is distributed in only five or six classes. Although my students do not distribute and collect the SIQs, I consider them to be researchers because they design the study and create the survey. The students decide with hypotheses to test, which variables to measure, and which questions to ask to measure those variables. Students can be required to assist in the actual data collection if an instructor believes such experience would be beneficial.

mates, the students make predictions, such as the proportion of students who smoke or the average number of hours college students exercise each week. The students record their hypotheses and refer to them as new statistical procedures are presented.

The SIQ is useful in the classroom and is also an excellent source for homework assignments. Students can easily perform most analyses using calculators. I deal with large problems (e.g., computing the correlation between height and weight for all SIQ respondents) in one of two ways. One method is to divide the work among groups of students; each group might compute the quantities needed for Pearson correlation coefficients (e.g., ΣXY and ΣX) for 20 subjects. The quantities can then be combined to complete the calculation. However, once students have mastered the computations using fewer subjects, I prefer to do the calculations on the computer and let students concentrate on interpretation.

As each new topic is covered, students apply the new procedures and concepts to the SIQ data. For example, at the beginning of the course, I have students create separate frequency tables and histograms to summarize how much time men and women spend in activities such as studying and exercising. Later, the students compute descriptive statistics for these variables, and still later they compute a *t* test or one-way analysis of variance to test the reliability of the observed differences. Many pairs of variables on the SIQ can be used to teach correlation and regression. For example, Pearson correlation coefficients can be computed for pairs of variables such as height and weight as well as studying and watching television. My students also write brief conclusions based on their data analyses as part of homework assignments. This approach reminds students that statistics is not a set of isolated procedures but is a tool to help them answer questions and make discoveries based on the information they have helped collect.

Student Evaluation of SIQ Data

I have used a version of the SIQ for the past 6 years in my statistics courses. Students in my two most recent sections ($N = 28$) completed a brief survey comparing the artificial data sets and data from the SIQ that had both been used in class. When asked "Which kind of data would you prefer the instructor to use when teaching about new statistical concepts and procedures?," 92% selected SIQ data over hypothetical data sets. Most of my students also indicated that SIQ data were more interesting to work with than artificial data (see Table 1). Finally, I asked students if they thought the use of SIQ data made it easier to learn statistics compared to hypothetical data. Only 13% responded "no" to this question; 71% said "yes" (the remaining 16% selected the "I don't know" response). These data suggest that the majority of my students find the SIQ data fairly engaging and perceive them to be an aid to learning.

Table 1. Student Interest Ratings for SIQ Data and Artificial Data Sets

	How Interesting Was it to Work With This Kind of Data?			
	Very	Moderately	A Little	Not At All
SIQ data	36	54	11	0
Artificial data	0	29	46	25

Conclusion

I argued that students should learn statistics by working with real data. Two desirable consequences of using data from studies designed by students, rather than artificial data, are (a) real data are more interesting to students, and (b) students learn firsthand that data analysis is an integral part of the research process rather than a separate enterprise. Research makes the statistics course more effective and enjoyable because it gives students the chance to ask meaningful psychological questions and learn how statistics can help find the answers. From the instructor's perspective, I enjoy working with real data much more than artificial data; I become as eager as the students to see the results of a study, and this eagerness helps generate enthusiasm in my students.

The SIQ produces descriptive and correlational data. Because many other types of experiments can be performed quickly in class or by students as part of their homework, I suggest that instructors supplement SIQ data with other research studies. My students conduct several true experiments (involving manipulation of an independent variable) during the semester. Many suitable studies can be found in instructor's manuals or created from descriptions of studies in journals and books. (Interested readers may write for descriptions and copies of the materials for several studies that I have used with success.) Hypothetical data sets will remain an important part of the statistics course, but they can be supplemented with real data from studies designed by students.

References

Beins, B. (1985). Teaching the relevance of statistics through consumer-oriented research. *Teaching of Psychology, 12,* 168–169.

Beins, B. C. (1989). A BASIC program for generating integer means and variances. *Teaching of Psychology, 16,* 230–231.

Cake, L. J., & Hostetter, R. C. (1986). DATAGEN: A BASIC program for generating and analyzing data for use in statistics courses. *Teaching of Psychology, 13,* 210–212.

Hettich, P. (1974). The student as data generator. *Teaching of Psychology, 1,* 35–36.

Jacobs, K. W. (1980). Instructional techniques in the introductory statistics course: The first class meeting. *Teaching of Psychology, 7,* 241–242.

Singer, J. D., & Willett, J. B. (1990). Improving the teaching of applied statistics: Putting the data back into data analysis. *The American Statistician, 44,* 223–230.

Note

I thank Donna Fisher Thompson, Timothy Osberg, Ruth Ault, and two reviewers for their comments on an earlier version of this article.

Crafting Questionnaire-Style Data: An SAS Implementation

John F. Walsh
Fordham University

In teaching a course in statistics and experimental design, I have found the examples in textbooks to be deficient vehicles for teaching the integration of statistical analysis with the interpretation of results. Textbook material gives the student practice in mastering the specific concept in a section of a chapter, and these examples provide adequate drill and practice. As an alternative, giving students realistic data sets provides a means for integrating statistical analysis with the interpretation of data.

Table 1 lists the SAS program that produces data of three types–nominal, ordinal, and interval. The program is written in BASE SAS, version 6.07 (SAS Institute, Inc., 1990) and was developed in the VAX/VMS computing environment (Digital Equipment Corporation, 1990). The lines of the program are numbered for reference purposes only; the numbers are not part of the SAS code. As shown in Table 1, the program generates 35 different data sets. Each set simulates the responses of 50 subjects to a 20-item questionnaire. Three types of response alternatives are developed: nominal, which includes dichotomous and categorical types; ordinal; and interval. There are five items for each of these four data types. The various item types are scattered throughout the 20 items so as to approximate an actual protocol; they are Lines 9, 14, 27, and 31 in Table 1.

The program in Table 1 is a shell or template for the construction of questionnaire-style data. Questionnaires can be developed using some or all of the techniques.

The program can be modified using the editor supplied with the computer system or with a word processing program that saves the file. Both WordPerfect (WordPerfect Corporation, 1989) and Word (Microsoft Corporation, 1990) allow you to save files in text or ASCII format. In WordPerfect, one uses the ctrl/F5 key and Option 1 (DOS text). In Word, one uses the sequence, transfer save, and the option "text only with line breaks" that appears under the line where you type the filename of the document.

The program uses two SAS random number functions, RANUNI and RANNOR, to generate unit uniformly and normally distributed random values, respectively. RANUNI (see Lines 17, 21, and 29 in Table 1) is used to generate three data types: dichotomous, categorical, and Likert.

The dichotomous data are called YESNO in the program; see Lines 14–19. Different proportions of alternatives are achieved by dividing a uniformly distributed variable according to the proportion specified. For example, a 70:30 split between women and men can be achieved by entering .7 as the cut point.

Categorical-type data are generated using the discrete cumulative distribution technique (Kennedy & Gentle, 1980). As implemented in the program listed in Table 1, the cumulative distribution technique uses two arrays. The technique is implemented in Lines 20–26.

One array, CP, stores the cumulative probability distribution that is to be modeled. The difference between the successive values represents the proportion of the sampled values selected. For example, consider a five-element array, CP, that stores the elements .20, .60, .70, .95, and 1. This cumulative distribution indicates that the proportion of sampled values in each category should be .20, .40, .10, .25, and .05. The second array, LOC, stores the category value-sassociated with each element in the array CP; LOC serves as a pointer array. Specifically, using the following values in the array LOC, 3, 2, 4, 5, and 1, in conjunction with the values in CP will produce a data set in which the item will have the value of three 20% of the time, the value of two 40% of the time, the value of four 10% of the time, and so on for the remaining values of the variable.

Table 1. Listing of SAS Program

```
*    Program to generate questionnaire type data
*    nsets=number of students in clas=35
*    nsubj=number of subjects in the study=50
*    To modify either use an editor to change line(s)
*    The number of items in the questionnaire is 20;
1    filename out 'questnre.dat';
*    name of the output file that contains the data;
2    data one;
3    infile cards n=5;
*    order of cards: cutpoints for yesno items
*    cumulative prob for scale items
*    corresponding frequency values
*    means for normally distributed items
*    sds for normal items;
4    input div1-div5/p1-p5/sc1-sc5/xb1-xb5/sd1-sd5;
6    file out;
7    nsets=35;
8    nsubj=50;
9    array categ{5} q1 q3 q5 q7 q9;
10   array cp{5} p1-p5;
11   array loc{5} sc1-sc5;
12   do m=1 to nsets;
13   do k=1 to nsubj;
*    code for dichotomous variables;
14   array yesno{5} q2 q4 q6 q8 q10;
15   array div{5} div1-div5;
16   do i1= 1 to 5;
17   y=ranuni(0);
18   if y ge div{i1} then yesno{i1}=1;
else yesno{i1}=2;
19   end;
*    code for categorical items;
20   do j=1 to 5;
21   y=ranuni(0);
22   do i2=1 to 5;
23   if cp{i2} ge y then goto sub;
24   end;
25   sub: categ{j}=loc{i2};
26   end;
*    code for likert type data, 1-7 inclusive;
27   array likert{5} q12 q14 q16 q18 q20;
28   do i3=1 to 5;
29   likert{i3}=int(7*ranuni + 1);
30   end;
*    code for normally distributed variables;
31   array norm{5} q11 q13 q15 q17 q19;
32   array xbx{5} xb1-xb5;
33   array sdx{5} sd1-sd5;
34   do i4=1 to 5;
35   norm{i4}=xbx{i4} + int(sdx{i4}*rannor(0));
36   end;
*    output a response "card" per questionnaire,
m=different sets, k=individual subjects;
37   put (m k) (2.) +1 (q1-q20) (3.);
38   end;
39   end;
40   cards;
41   .2 .6 .7 .95 1.
42   3 2 4 5 1
43   50 50 100 40 18
44   8 8 16 6 2
45   .4 .5 .6 .35 .55
;
run;
```

More generally, the array CP can be kept constant, thereby fixing the profile of proportions that will be used. The instructor manipulates the values in the array LOC to produce different configurations of responses.

The program produces Likert-type values that are uniformly distributed across the rating scale. Values of 1 through 7 are generated using the technique described by Knuth (1981); see Lines 27–30 in Table 1.

Normally distributed data are generated by the function RANNOR. The $N(0,1)$ values produced are scaled to produce distributions with varying means and standard deviations; see lines 31–36 in Table 1.

The numerical specifications that craft the items are entered as part of the program. Five lines of data are included after the CARDS statement; see Line 40, at the end of the program listing in Table 1. As can be seen from Table 1, the data are entered in list format that requires a blank space between consecutive values. Line 41 gives the cumulative proportion of alternatives for each of the five dichotomous items. Program Lines 42 and 43 provide the cumulative proportions and numerical values of the alternatives of the frequencies, respectively. The last two input lines, 44 and 45, have the values for the means and standard deviations used in rescaling the $N(0,1)$ values produced by the SAS function RANNOR. To produce questionnaires with different attributes, one edits these five input lines that configure the questionnaire.

A completed data set has variables that could function as independent variables with levels that are either nominally or ordinally scaled. Examples of such variables are sex, ethnicity, marital status, and education. Other items in the questionnaire can be viewed as dependent variables (DV) that consist of frequencies, ranks, and scores. When approached in this way, the set of values produced by the program in Table 1 provides a vehicle for discussing the analysis and interpretation of data that approximate actual studies.

In the second semester of a two-semester undergraduate course in statistics and experimental design, the class designed a study to determine the variables involved in juvenile suicide. Consideration was given to family variables, peer and social relationships, academic performance, and standardized tests. The data dictionary developed through class discussion is shown in Table 2.

A printed listing and the SAS code for statistical analysis are given to each student. This code is presented in Table 3. The individual data sets are copied electronically by each student from the course directory.

Although the data analysis is done individually, a printout of the results is discussed in class to orient students to the formatting by the SAS system. During this time, the relations between hypotheses and statistical test are reviewed.

Because students were involved in designing the items and their alternatives, the connection between type of DV (i.e., frequency, rank, and score) and statistical analysis is usually direct. Analyses included chi-square, t test, and correlation.

Table 2. Data Dictionary for Juvenile Suicide Project

Columns	Content
1-2	Subject number, 01,02 . . . .
3	Group: 1=experimental, 2=control
4-5	Age in years
6	Hospitals used: 1=Bronx State 2=Cornell
7	Schools: 1=north bronx, 2=westchester
8	Sex: 1=female 2=male
9	Family config: 1 both natural 2 single widowed 3 single div 4 adoptive 5 extended
10-11	family cohesion: mother's perception
12-13	father's perception
14-15	subject's perception
16-17	Depression: N(50,10)
18-19	Suicide(MMPI): N(50,10)
20-21	Internality/externality sc: (0-22)
22	Critical event recently: 1=yes 2=no Involvement with others;
23	school activites: 0, one, two, three, 4+
24	after school: 1=friends 2=sports 3=work 4=study 5=other 6=no activity
25	Rating self esteem: 1 high 5 low
26-27	GPA
28	Use of drugs: 1 regularly 5 never
29	Use of alcohol: 1 regularly 5 never

Table 3. SAS Code for Analyzing Project Data

```
filename raw 'suicide.dat';
data one;
infile raw;
input grp 3 age 4-5 (hosp sch sex famc) (1.) (cohm cohf
cohs deprssn suicide ie) (2.) (crevnt schact schpost)
(1.) selfest 1. gpa 4.2 usedrgs 1. usealch 1.;
proc ttest;
class grp;
var age cohm--ie gpa;
proc freq;
tables grp* (hosp sch sex famc crevnt schact schpost
selfest usedrgs usealch)/chisq;
proc sort;
by grp;
proc corr;
var cohm cohf cohs;
by grp;
endsas;
```

Using simulated data sets is preferable to having students collect data themselves. Strangely enough, the simulated case is more realistic. Research studies that students would design for actual data collection would be simpler, have subjects that were not randomly selected, and use fewer data-collection instruments.

Students have no difficulty understanding that this is a classroom experience, and no student has questioned the ethics of the project. They are familiar with simulations from high school and college courses in economics and history.

The simulated research experience provides an opportunity to integrate concepts from statistics and experimental design. Because this course precedes the experimental laboratory courses, writing a report introduces students to APA style and format. Feedback from students indicates that the simulation experience provides skills that are helpful in the experimental laboratory courses.

References

Digital Equipment Corporation. (1990). *VMS DCL concepts, Version 5.0.* Maynard, MA: Author.

Kennedy, W. J., Jr., & Gentle, J. E. (1980). *Statistical computing.* New York: Dekker.

Knuth, D. E. (1981). *The art of computer programming: Semi-numerical algorithms* (2nd ed.). Reading, MA: Addison-Wesley.

Microsoft Corporation. (1990). *Word 5.1* [Computer program]. Redmond, WA: Author.

SAS Institute, Inc. (1990). *SAS language: Reference, Version 6.* Cary, NC: Author.

WordPerfect Corporation. (1989). *WordPerfect 5.1* [Computer program]. Orem, UT: Author.

A BASIC Program for Generating Integer Means and Variances

Bernard C. Beins
Ithaca College

Small data sets are useful in statistics classes because the calculations can be done by hand. Earlier articles described data sets having integer means and standard deviations computed with N rather than $N - 1$ in the denominator (Dudek, 1981; McGown & Spencer, 1980).

The computer program described in this article generates data sets with integer means and variances; however, the user can specify whether the variance is calculated using N or $N - 1$ in the denominator. In addition, any sample size can be selected. The program is written in Applesoft BASIC and will run on any Apple II family computer equipped with a printer; the program can be listed and altered at the user's convenience. The program length is 80 lines, including 11 statements that are useful for programming but may be omitted when running it.

There are three options in the program. (a) The user can either choose a sample size and obtain three data sets for that selection or use the automatic selection option whereby the program generates one number set for each of several sample sizes. (b) The user can decide whether to include N or $N - 1$ in the denominator; the former is useful in teaching descriptive statistics, the latter in inferential statistics. (c) The user can specify the range of scores.

The program prints the information as each data set is generated. When the program ends, the screen goes blank until any key is pressed. This will prevent casual observers from seeing the data.

Uses and Limitations

The program is useful for generating relatively small sets of data. For example, to generate three sets of 10 numbers could require as little as 15 s, although it may take several minutes. The reason for the variability is that the program generates a group of random numbers and evaluates the number set for integer values. The process iterates until integral values are obtained. For data sets of 5 to 8 numbers, the output of three sets will typically take 2 min or less. The

Table 1. Example of Output Generated by the Program

```
Trial # 39
  10  3  2  3  4  4  4  10
  MEAN = 5
  VAR(N) = 8.75                        S(N) = 2.96
  VAR(N − 1) = 10                      S(N − 1) = 3.16
  SUM OF X = 40
  SUM OF X-SQUARED = 270
  N = 8

Trial # 25
   2  3  1  10  6  9  7  2
  MEAN = 5
  VAR(N) = 10.5                        S(N) = 3.24
  VAR(N − 1) = 12                      S(N − 1) = 3.46
  SUM OF X = 40
  SUM OF X-SQUARED = 284
  N = 8

Trial # 109
  10  10  2  6  4  7  7  2
  MEAN = 6
  VAR(N) = 8.75                        S(N) = 2.96
  VAR(N − 1) = 10                      S(N − 1) = 3.16
  VAR(N) = 8.75                        S(N) = 2.95
  VAR(N − 1) = 10                      S(N − 1) = 3.16
  SUM OF X = 48
  SUM OF X-SQUARED = 358
  N = 8
```

Note. This data set, generated on an Apple IIe for $N = 8$ and a range of 1 to 10, required about 160 s to complete. (A similar data set with the faster Apple IIgs took 80 s.) The trial number indicates the number of iterations required to generate each data set.

program is useful in generating small samples very quickly and large samples if one is willing to let it run for several hours or overnight. One can also use the data sets provided by Dudek (1981) for such applications (i.e., $N = 15$ to 50), although those integer values of the standard deviation are based only on the so-called biased estimator of the standard deviation. The extant number sets are helpful in situations such as classroom exercises when students may not ha calculators and must analyze the data by hand; the data sets and the range of scores can be made small enough for hand calculations.

Example output appears in Table 1. The program took 100 s to produce these data. The sample size selected for this example was 8; the range was 1 to 10. The variance was 1 to 10. The variance was calculated using $N - 1$ in the denominator. The output table contains the raw data, mean, variances, and standard deviations using both N and $N - 1$ in the denominator. The output table contains the raw data, mean, variances, and standard deviations using both N and $N - 1$. The sum of X values and sum of squares are also printed. Once a data set is obtained, one can always add a constant to each value to change the mean but keep the variance the same; the new sum of X will increase by Nc, and the sum of squares will increase by $2c\Sigma X + Nc$. This latter expression is simply derived from the rules of summation. Multiplying each score by a constant will increase the mean by a factor of that constant and will increase the variance by the square of that constant.

References

Dudek, F. J. (1981). Data sets having integer means and standard deviations. *Teaching of Psychology, 8,* 51.

McGown, W. P., & Spencer, W. B. (1980). For statistics classes: Data sets with integer means and standard deviations. *Teaching of Psychology, 7,* 63.

A Simple Procedure for Generating Nonnormal Data Sets: A FORTRAN Program

John F. Walsh
Fordham University

In teaching courses in statistics and experimental design, it is often helpful to use nonnormal data sets as instructional tools. Such data sets enable the student to see how statistical measures vary dramatically as a function of the data. For example, showing how the size of the standard deviation changes as a function of the shape of the distribution provides a basis for the student to infer that experimental outcomes may result from erroneous or atypical data.

For most researchers, the ability to detect anomalous results is grounded in experience; students can gain this experience through assignments and simulated research. The program described herein allows the instructor to construct a wide range of distributions by modifying the familiar standard unit normal distribution.

The procedure for modifying the distribution is based on the technique of linearly transforming values from one scale to another. A familiar example of linear transformation is the conversion of Fahrenheit to Celsius temperatures.

Specifically, the idea is to take segments of the unit normal distribution and map them into different regions, thereby producing a nonnormal distribution. Functionally, an area of the unit normal curve is defined in terms of z scores (from −3.00 to 3.00) that define the lower and upper end-points of the area. The interval is rescaled into a new location, which is also defined by two z scores for its lower and upper endpoints. The values from the original curve are thus redistributed into the new target region.

The FORTRAN program that implements the rescaling procedures can be viewed as having three components. Table 1 contains the source listing of the program.

The first section works interactively to allow the instructor to label the output file, specify the number of cases, and select the mean and standard deviation that will be developed by the program.

The second component is a subroutine that generates values for the unit normal distribution using the Polar technique (Knuth, 1981). Although there are many techniques for generating normally distributed variables (Kennedy & Gentle, 1980; Knuth, 1981), the Polar method is reliable, easily coded, and uses only standard FORTRAN library functions that are portable to both mainframe and PC FORTRAN compilers. This subroutine uses the RAN pseudorandom number generator that is part of VAX FORTRAN (Digital Equipment Corporation, 1988). If the version of FORTRAN being used does not support a random number generator, code for a portable pseudorandom number generator is given by Wichman and Hill (1982).

The last component is a subroutine that performs the transformation. The code for this mapping uses the cumulative distribution technique (Kennedy & Gentle, 1980). The user is first prompted to enter the number of intervals to be relocated. Then a prompt requests the actual pairs of values (z scores) that determine the segments of the unit normal distribution. A third prompt requests the pairs of values (z scores) that define the target location to be used in rescaling.

To use the program, the instructor need only think in terms of the familiar z scores and the areas associated with them. Table 2 provides the mapping relations for three non-normal distributions that I have found useful in the classroom: a "tails only" set of data that consists of extreme values with no middle, a truncated distribution with a middle and no tails, and a positively skewed distribution.

As an example, to produce a distribution that has values in the tails and no middle values, two intervals would be used. The lower half of the unit normal distribution designated by the z score values of −3 and 0 would be mapped into the new interval fixed by the z score values of −3 and −1.645. In that way, 50% of the area of the original distribution is mapped into the lower 5% of the curve. Similar values corresponding to the upper half of the unit normal distribution would also be entered.

Less drastic modifications can be produced as well. By selecting pairs of endpoint values for the transformed distribution that deviate from the values of the unit normal distribution, the instructor can produce unimodal, symmetric curves that vary in kurtosis.

More generally, sketching the shape of the nonnormal distribution is helpful as a preliminary step to using the program. The visual representation gives an estimate of the areas involved in the regions. The pairs of values used in the mapping reflect the lengths of the areas in z-score units.

I have used the program to provide data sets and graphs when discussing the selection of independent variables (IVs) and dependent variables (DVs). For example, students are asked to evaluate the "tails only" graph as the distribution of both an IV and a DV in an experiment. Students focus on the distance between the tails as showing a real separation between the levels of the IV. The external validity of the underlying psychological variable is not considered as important (i.e., how typical are "tails only" variables?). Students interpret the visual separation as a large effect on the DV. What students do not appreciate is that the spread between locations will increase the standard error and decrease the power of the experiment. In this example, the crafted data set enables students to see some of the trade-offs that take place in designing experiments.

Instructors can use the program to produce a variety of data sets that enhance student discussion of how and when to use statistical procedures.

Table 1. Listing of FORTRAN Program for Generating Nonnormal Data

```
        real y (1000)
        character*20 outfil
        type '(a,$)', 'Enter output filename: '
        accept '(a)', outfil
        open (unit=7, file=outfil, status='unknown')
        type '(a,$)', ' Enter number of values (max=1000): '
        accept *, n
        type '(a,$)', 'Enter mean and sd for new
1       distribution: '
        accept *, xm, s
        call norm (n,y)
        call shape (n,y)
        do 10 i=1,n
        y (i)=xm + y(i)*s
10      write (7,11) y(i)
11      format (F6.2)
        close (7)
        end
        subroutine norm (n,y)
        real y(1)
        type '(a,$)', 'Enter seed value:'
        accept *, ix
        do 5 i=1, n
        u1=ran (ix)
        yx=sqrt (−2.*alog(u1))
        u2=ran (ix)
        th=2.*3.141593*u2
        y(i)=yx*cos(th)
5       continue
        return
        end
        subroutine shape (n,y)
        real y (1), cp (6), cps (6)
        type '(a,$)', 'Number of intervals: '
        accept *, k
        k=2*k
        type '(a,$)', 'Lower−upper limits in pairs for unit
1       normal distribution: '
        accept *, (cp(i), i=1, k)
        type '(a,$)', 'Lower−upper limits for new distrib:'
        accept *, (cps(i), i=1, k)
        do 5 i=1, n
        do 10 j=2, k, 2
        if ( y(i) .ge. cp (j−1) .and. y(i) .le. cp(j)) goto 15
10      continue
15      b=cps (j)−cps(j−1)
        a=cp(j)−cp(j−1)
        y(i)=cps(j−1)+((y(i)−cp(j−1))*b)/a
5       continue
        return
        end
```

Table 2. Sample z Values to Produce Nonnormal Data Sets

Outcome	Intervals	Original z	New z
Trials only	2	−3.00, 0.00	−3.00, −1.65
		0.00, 3.00	1.65, 3.00
Middle only	1	−3.00, 3.00	−0.38, 0.38
Positively skewed	3	−3.00, 0.00	−1.20, 0.00
		0.00, 0.80	0.00, 0.80
		0.80, 3.00	0.80, 6.00

References

Digital Equipment Corporation. (1988). *Programming in VAX FORTRAN.* Maynard, MA: Author.

Kennedy, W. J., Jr., & Gentle, J. E. (1980). *Statistical computing* (Vol. 33). New York: Dekker.

Knuth, D. E. (1981). *The art of computer programming: Semi-numerical algorithms* (2nd ed.). Reading, MA: Addison-Wesley.

Wichman, B. A., & Hill, I. D. (1982). An efficient and portable pseudo-random number generator: Algorithm AS 183. *Applied Statistics, 311,* 188–190.

Publication Bias: A Computer-Assisted Demonstration of Excluding Nonsignificant Results From Research Interpretation

Todd C. Riniolo

Department of Human Development
University of Maryland, College Park

Publication bias is an impairment to accurate interpretation of published literature. Publication bias, the increased likelihood of publication of a manuscript describing significant rather than nonsignificant findings, can arise either from researchers' failure to submit nonsignificant results for publication or journal reviewers' rejection of articles based on nonsignificant findings. Recent evidence suggests that publication bias can pose a serious impediment to accurate interpretation of research results (Berlin, Begg, & Louis, 1989; Easterbrook, Berlin, Gopalan, & Matthews, 1991; Simes, 1986) and can alter meta-analytic results designed to estimate effect sizes from published studies (Dear & Begg, 1992). Although formal studies have shown that the majority of articles published in journals are filled with positive results (Bozarth & Roberts, 1972; Sterling, 1959), introductory research methods textbooks (e.g., Graziano & Raulin, 1989; Ray, 1993) often fail to alert students that published research findings may be a biased representation of true population differences.

The cumulation of individual studies to derive an accurate interpretation of the literature is tied intimately to the Central Limit Theorem (CLT). First, the CLT states that drawing repeated samples from a given population (or differences between populations) will yield a nearly normal sampling distribution of means when the sample sizes are approximately 25 or larger for both normal and nonnormal parent populations (Hopkins & Glass, 1978). From this sampling distribution of means, the mean of the sampling distribution is an accurate estimate of the true population mean. If the full range of results from repeated sampling is not available, such as when nonsignificant findings are not published, the CLT does not accurately reflect the true population mean. Similarly, if the researcher does not have access to the full range of results because of publication bias, interpretation of the literature occurs from a biased sample. Second, the CLT states that as sample size increases, the variability (i.e., the standard error) of the sampling distribution of means decreases according to the function: $\sigma/\sqrt{N}$. A decrease in the standard error as sample size increases results in greater statistical precision to detect differences (i.e., greater statistical power) because the individual distributions being compared constrict, resulting in a smaller distributional overlap between groups.

The purpose of this article is to provide a computer-based simulation, based on tenets of the CLT, of the effects of excluding nonsignificant findings from research interpretation. The concept of publication bias may seem abstract to the student at the introductory level, and a classroom demonstration can provide a concrete and visual example to supplement class lecture and discussion.

Method

Procedure

I obtained results in this article from 10,000 trials; however, you can use 1,000 or 100 trials for the class exercise when quick processing time is essential. Processing time requires less than 5 min for 1,000 trials and less than 1 min for 100 trials on a 486-based personal computer (16MB RAM) running at 66MHz.

I performed a power analysis (desired power level as a function of effect size, significance level, and sample size) using the power function in Sigmastat 1.0 (Jandel Scientific, 1994) to approximate a 25%, 50%, and 80% chance of reaching statistical significance for two-tailed t tests (α = .05) between Group 1 ($M = 106.36$, $SD = 10$) and Group 2 ($M = 100$, $SD = 10$). The population difference between groups corresponds to $d = .636$ (Cohen, 1988). Results used for this demonstration are as follows: (a) $1 - \beta = .245$ ($n = 9$ for each group), (b) $1 - \beta = .5$ ($n = 20$ for each group), and (c) $1 - \beta = .802$ ($n = 40$ for each group). The numbers used in this demonstration can change, but are conceptually easy to interpret and understand (e.g., differences between populations on IQ scores).

The demonstration consists of the following series of steps:

1. Provide the class with a refresher of the CLT.
2. Run the simulation with the various samples sizes starting with $1 - \beta = .50$, $1 - \beta = .245$, and $1 - \beta = .802$. Record the mean results comparing the full range of results with significant results only. Print the graph after each simulation or use the figures from this article for illustration.
3. Lead a discussion of the results.

4. Instruct the class to browse through recent journals comparing significant versus nonsignificant findings to provide students with firsthand experience of the proportion of positive versus negative findings in the journals.

You may change the effect size difference between populations or sample sizes associated with this demonstration. For example, you may wish to compare the effects of publication bias on small, medium, and large effect size differences (Cohen, 1988) in the population while maintaining a constant sample size.

Programming

I created the program for this demonstration in Matlab 4.0 (Math Works, 1995) with Statistics Toolbox (Math Works, 1996). The logic of the program was to use a "for" loop to draw random samples from a given population (i.e., a normal distribution) for 2 groups and to perform t tests. The random number generator is a scalar whose value changes each time it is referenced and transforms values of a uniform generator according to the algorithm described by Forsythe, Malcolm, and Moler (1977). I then labeled results as being significant or nonsignificant, allowing for easy access to compare the full distribution versus significant results only. The program appears in Table 1.

Table 1. Publication Bias Program

```
SAM=input('Input number of samples to be drawn from a population:   ');
SUB=input('Input number of subjects in each group:   ');
MEAN_=input('Input the Mean for group 1:   ');
ES=input('Input the Population Mean difference between groups:   ');
STD_=input('Input the Standard Deviation for both groups:   ');
for n=1:SAM              %for loop to generate # of trials
GRP1=(randn(SUB,1)*STD_)+MEAN_;
GRP2=(randn(SUB,1)*STD_)+MEAN_+ES;
[h(n,1)]=ttest2(GRP1,GRP2);      %independent t-tests
Mean_dif(n,1)=mean(GRP2) - mean(GRP1);
   if h(n,1) == 1;            %flagging significant results
   reject_(n,1)=Mean_dif(n,1);
   else;
   reject_(n,1)= (abs(MEAN_*STD_+10000))*(-1);
   end;
end;
MIN_1=min(Mean_dif);MAX_1=max(Mean_dif);MM1=MIN_1:MAX_1;
%setting graph axis
R=sort(reject_);K=find(R(abs(MEAN_*STD_+10000))*(-1));
P=K(1,1);E=max(K);reject_2=R(P:E,1);
subplot(2,1,1); hist(Mean_dif,MM1);title('Full Distribution');ylabel('Frequency');
subplot(2,1,2); hist(reject_2,MM1);
title('Significant Results Only');ylabel('Frequency');
total_rej=sum(h);mean_diff=mean(Mean_dif);
std_diff=std(Mean_dif);reject_a=mean(reject_2);
reject_std=std(reject_2);
fprintf('Number of "Significant" Trials          =    %6.3f\n',total_rej);
fprintf('Mean Difference using the Full Distribution =  %6.3f\n',mean_diff);
fprintf('Standard Deviation of the Full Distribution =   %6.3f\n',std_diff);
fprintf('Mean Difference of "Significant" Trials     =   %6.3f\n',reject_a);
fprintf('Standard Deviation of "Significant" Trials  =   %6.3f\n',reject_std);
clear;
```

13

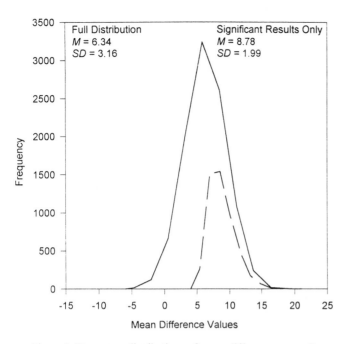

Figure 1. Frequency distributions of mean difference scores for the full distribution (solid line) and significant results only (dashed line) with 1 − ß = .500.

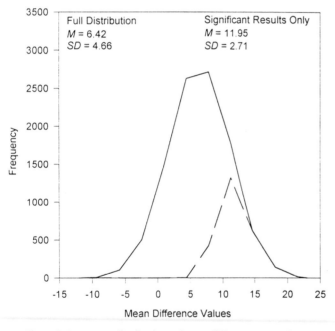

Figure 2. Frequency distributions of mean difference scores for the full distribution (solid line) and significant results only (dashed line) wiht 1 − ß = .245.

Results

Figure 1 (solid line) illustrates the full range of mean difference scores from Group 1 and Group 2 with power set at .5, giving an equal chance of obtaining significant or nonsignificant results. Findings are consistent with the CLT

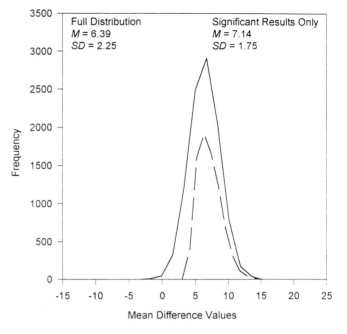

Figure 3. Frequency distributions of mean difference scores for the full distribution (solid line) and significant results only (dashed line) wiht 1 − ß = .802.

(M = 6.34, SD = 3.16), which predicts an accurate estimation of the true difference between groups (6.36 as defined by the random number generator) from the mean of the sampling distribution. Figure 1 (dashed line) illustrates the distribution of significant results only. Of the 10,000 trials, 4,996 were significant (M = 8.78; SD = 1.99). As shown by Figure 1, exclusion of negative findings produces a positively biased distribution, which results in the biased estimation of the between groups difference.

Figure 2 (solid line) shows that despite low power (.245), the full range of results still provides an accurate estimate of group differences (M = 6.42; SD = 4.66). However, when significant results only (n = 2,532) are examined (M = 11.95; SD = 2.71), a large overestimation of the true difference occurs from the limited distribution (Figure 2, dashed line). With power raised (.802), the full range of results (Figure 3, solid line) also provides an accurate estimate of true group differences (M = 6.39; SD = 2.25). Although overestimating the true difference (M = 7.14; SD = 1.75; n = 8042), this power level provided the least biased estimate of the true difference using only significant results (Figure 3, dashed line).

Discussion

Results from this demonstration are consistent with the CLT. First, inclusion of the full range of results accurately estimates the true difference between groups (i.e., an accurate interpretation of the literature derived from an unbiased sample). As shown in Figures 1, 2, and 3, exclusion of nonsignificant results biases the available distribution, impairing the interpretation by the researcher. For example, exclusion of nonsignificant results may result in a treatment (e.g., a new drug therapy for hypertension) or a group difference (e.g., gender) being represented by the literature as a greater difference than exists in the population. Second, results based on smaller samples are prone to a greater bias when nonsignificant results are excluded because of the reduction of statistical precision resulting in an increase in distributional overlap.

This demonstration provides an important lesson for psychology students that is often absent in introductory research textbooks and provides a vehicle for discussion of the more philosophical issues associated with the evolution of publication bias. Perhaps publication bias has arisen from the dichotomous nature of hypothesis testing that allows researchers to interpret only significant findings. As Hedges (1984) pointed out, when a study fails to reach statistical significance, interpretation is difficult, often resulting in unpublished manuscripts or published manuscripts with incomplete reporting of nonsignificant findings. Additionally, the ability to interpret only significant results may have contributed to the widespread overconfidence of social scientists about the probability that statistically significant findings will replicate (Cohen, 1994; Oakes, 1986; Tversky & Kahneman, 1971). Shaver (1993) recommends philosophical discussions as one method to reduce strictly mechanical application of statistics and research methodology by students and to stimulate critical analysis of research interpretation.

This computer program also works with fewer trials (e.g., 30) to simulate more realistic numbers of studies associated with a literature review of a specific research question. Additionally, this demonstration provides a transition to discuss not only philosophical issues of research methodology, but applied material such as (a) proposed methods to control and identify publication bias, (b) sample size and the probability of replication of results, and (c) the use of power analysis to determine appropriate sample sizes. By experiencing the consequences of excluding nonsignificant results from research interpretation, students will gain an invaluable lesson to aid research interpretation.

References

Berlin, J. A., Begg, C. B., & Louis, T. A. (1989). An assessment of publication bias using a sample of published clinical trials. *Journal of the American Statistical Association, 84,* 381–392.

Bozarth, J. D., & Roberts, R. R. (1972). Signifying significant significance. *American Psychologist, 27,* 774–775.

Cohen, J. (1988). *Statistical power analysis for the behavioral sciences* (2nd ed.). Hillsdale, NJ: Lawrence Erlbaum Associates, Inc.

Cohen, J. (1994). The earth is round ($p < .05$). *American Psychologist, 49,* 997–1003.

Dear, K. B. G., & Begg, C. (1992). An approach for assessing publication bias prior to performing a meta-analysis. *Statistical Science, 7,* 237–245.

Easterbrook. P. J., Berlin, J. A., Gopalan, R., & Matthews, D. R. (1991). Publication bias in clinical research. *The Lancet, 337,* 867–872.

Forsythe, G. E., Malcolm, M. A., & Moler, C. B. (1977). *Computer methods for mathematical computations.* Englewood Cliffs, NJ: Prentice Hall.

Graziano, A. M., & Raulin, M. L. (1989). *Research methods: A process of inquiry.* New York: Harper & Row.

Hedges, L V. (1984). Estimation of effect size under non-random sampling: The effects of censoring studies yielding statistically insignificant mean differences. *Journal of Educational Statistics, 9,* 61–85.

Hopkins, K. D., & Glass, G. V. (1978). *Basic statistics for the behavioral sciences.* Englewood Cliffs, NJ: Prentice Hall.

Matlab 4.0 [Computer program]. (1995). Natick, MA: Math Works.

Oakes, M. (1986). *Statistical inference: A commentary for the social and behavioral sciences.* New York: Wiley.

Ray, W. J. (1993). *Methods toward a science of behavior* (4th ed.). Monterey, CA: Brooks/Cole.

Shaver, J. P. (1993). What statistical significance testing is, and what it is not. *Journal of Experimental Education, 61,* 293–316.

Sigmastat 1.0 [Computer program]. (1994). San Rafael, CA: Jandel Scientific.

Simes, R. J. (1986). Publication bias: The case for an international registry of clinical trials. *Journal of Clinical Oncology, 4,* 1529–1541.

Statistics Toolbox [Computer program]. (1996). Natick, MA: Math Works.

Sterling, T. C. (1959). Publication decisions and their possible effects on inferences drawn from tests of significance or vice versa. *Journal of the American Statistical Association, 54,* 30–34.

Tversky, A., & Kahneman, D. (1971). Belief in the law of small numbers. *Psychological Bulletin, 76,* 105–110.

Notes

1. This article is dedicated to the memory of the late Brian J. Riniolo, my brother.
2. Special thanks to John Jeka for his eloquent teaching of computer skills and to Jane Doussard-Roosevelt for her helpful suggestions in writing this manuscript.

2. Illustrating Statistical Concepts

David Pittenger from Marietta College provided teachers with resources for overcoming the shortcomings in many statistics books about graphing techniques. This article describes several books and articles about the elements of graphing. Students can benefit by mastering these methods early in their education.

Students in Kenneth Weaver's statistics class at Emporia State University learned about the concepts of variability, null hypothesis testing, and confidence intervals from simple exercises involving exclamations, circus and cartoon characters, and falling leaves, respectively. Have you tried increasing your students' comprehension by using such everyday experiences?

To clarify and illustrate complex concepts, such as distributions of sample means, differences between independent sample means, mean difference scores, and raw score populations, Dominic Zerbolio from the University of Missouri-St. Louis developed a bag of tricks using imaginary marbles and chips. Once students learn to answer probability questions for each sampling distribution, they are primed to generalize to hypothesis testing procedures. Instructors with a flair for the dramatic will find appealing applications for teaching statistical concepts.

Michael Strube at Washington University used a BASIC program to demonstrate the influence of sample size and reliability on study outcome. Instructors can use the program to demonstrate the impact of reliability on the correlations between variables and, thus, the impact of reliability on inferences drawn from study outcomes. Readers are advised that this technique is used with students who have completed statistics and are enrolled in a research methods course.

Teaching Students About Graphs

David J. Pittenger
Marietta College

Preparing graphs is an essential part of data analysis and representation. Graphs allow one to examine the data for trends and effects that may be missed using descriptive and inferential statistics. Well designed graphs also help the researcher present complex data in a coherent and memorable manner. Although graphs are an important part of psychological research, relatively little information on the construction or perception of graphs is available to the undergraduate psychology student.

The *Publication Manual of the American Psychological Association* (American Psychological Association, 1994) and most texts on statistics and research methods provide only a brief review of graphing techniques. These references describe the general attributes of a graph and review the more common graph forms, including bar graphs, histograms, and line graphs. There is not, however, a substantive discussion of the qualities that make a good graph.

There may be several reasons why most statistics and research methods textbooks provide short reviews of graphs. The primary reason appears to be that psychologists have written little about the construction or perception of graphs. Indeed, most of the research on perception and use of graphs has been published by statisticians in their professional journals. For example, the American Statistical Association publishes a newsletter titled *Statistical Computing & Graphs* that includes original research and review articles on graphing techniques. Information about the newsletter and other services provided by the association may be obtained from the American Statistical Association, 1429 Duke Street, Alexandria, VA 22314-3402.

There are several reasons why instructors of statistical and research methods should consider providing students with a more comprehensive review of graphical techniques. First, as noted earlier, graphs serve an essential role in data analysis and presentation. Many authors (e.g., Cleveland, 1994; Loftus, 1993; Smith & Prentice, 1993; Tukey, 1977; Wainer & Thissen, 1993) emphasized that various graphing techniques are essential components of data analysis. As Tukey (1977) noted, "the greatest value of a picture is when it *forces* us to notice what we never expected to see" (p. vi). Therefore, graphs can be used to help discover unexpected results, confirm expected results, plan appropriate data analysis, and summarize the results of one's research.

Second, students need to learn the foundations of graph construction used in the sciences. Tufte (1983) coined the term *chartjunk* to refer to elements of a graph that are not essential for the representation of the data. Students are probably most familiar with graphs that contain much chart-junk. There are many bad examples of graphs in the popular press (e.g., *USA Today*) that provide students with models for inefficient graphing techniques.

Also, some popular computer software programs (e.g., spreadsheets and graphics programs) provide intriguing embellishments that are superfluous to the unambiguous presentation of information. For example, these programs afford many options, including three-dimensional axes, color, pictographs, and other nonessential decorations. These programs also include graph formats that are difficult to interpret, including stacked histograms, pie charts, and area charts. Students should learn to avoid chartjunk.

Finally, many principles used to describe graph construction and perception are familiar to psychologists. Graphs and their interpretation can be understood by referring to principles of perception and psychophysics. As demonstrated in the next section, reviewing principles and theories of perception can help students learn how to produce effective graphs.

Elements of a Graph

Cleveland is the most prolific contemporary researcher to examine the construction and interpretation of graphs (Cleveland, 1984a, 1984b, 1994; Cleveland, Diaconis, & McGill, 1982; Cleveland & McGill, 1984, 1985, 1986). Specifically, he has examined the efficiency of various elements of a graph. Elements of a graph refer to the geometric figures used to represent quantitative information. In the typical scatter plot, the position of the reference points is the element that represents the data. A pie chart contains two elements, the angle of lines for each category and the area of that wedge.

Cleveland and McGill (1984) showed that the accuracy of a subject's perception of a graph can be described by Stevens's (1975) power law. Although all graphs are subject to some error of interpretation, their research shows that line graphs are interpreted with much greater accuracy than pie charts and area graphs. Based on their research, Cleveland and McGill (1984, 1986; see also Cleveland, 1994) ranked graphic elements from the most to least accurate (a) position along a common scale; (b) position along non-aligned scales; (c) length, direction, and angle; (d) volume and curvature; and (e) shading and color saturation.

Cleveland (1984a, 1984b, 1994) recommended that researchers use position along a common scale as the sole element of a graph. He argued that graphs with a common scale (e.g., line graphs, scatter plots, and dot charts) are easier to interpret and that they produce less perceptual distortion than other graphing techniques. For example, he contended that the conventional bar graph and histogram are relatively inefficient ways to present data. According to Cleveland, when looking at these graphs the viewer must decode the position of the top of the bar and the area of the bar. This decoding task becomes more difficult if many independent variables are presented in the same graph. These graphs may also mask the presence of nonlinear trends. According to Cleveland, data presented with bar graphs, histograms, or pie charts can be presented more efficiently using line graphs and dot charts.

Other principles of perception can be applied to a discussion of graph construction. The Gestalt laws of perception can be used, for example, to prescribe various techniques in graphing. A review of continuity, proximity, and similarity can easily be incorporated into a discussion of effective graphical techniques. Furthermore, a review of information-processing limitations suggests that individual graphs should contain a limited number of perceptual groups (Kosslyn, 1989).

Students should also be shown that many embellishments, such as three-dimensional effects, make graphs difficult to interpret. Several researchers (Barfield & Robless, 1989; Carswell, Frankenberger, & Bernhard, 1991) found that two-dimensional graphs are interpreted faster, with less error, and with greater confidence than the same data presented in three-dimensional graphs.

Books on Graphing

Table 1 presents a list of texts on preparing statistical graphs. There is no comprehensive text on graphing for the behavioral and social sciences, but there are several general texts. Although there are many books on statistical graphs, only a few are appropriate as an undergraduate text, but each is a good general reference for the instructor. *Exploratory Data Analysis* (Tukey, 1977) is a classic. The style of writing is oblique, but the information and techniques presented are interesting and useful. Tufte's (1983, 1990) books, *The Visual Display of Quantitative Information* and *Envisioning Information,* offer an interesting history of graphs, many lucid examples of poorly drawn and misleading graphs, and suggestions for preparing attractive and useful graphs. Cleveland's (1994) *The Elements of Graphing Data* provides the most technical and statistical information for the creation of graphs, ranging from simple line graphs to complex multivariable graphs. The book contains many examples of traditional as well as new graphing techniques and is an excellent resource for the researcher-teacher. Kosslyn (1985) reviewed other specialized texts on graphing.

Bowen (1992) wrote a book on graphing for undergraduates. Following Cleveland's (1994) lead, Bowen presented the steps for preparing a good line graph. Alternative graphs, such as box and whisker graphs or scatter plots, are not reviewed.

Table 1. Selected Texts and Chapters on Graphing Techniques

Bertin (1983)
Bowen (1992)
Chambers, Cleveland, Kleiner, and Tukey (1983)
Cleveland (1994)
Fisher (1982)
Henry (1995)
Hoaglin, Mosteller, and Tukey (1991)
Kosslyn (1994)
Schmidt (1983)
Smith and Prentice (1993)
Tufte (1983)
Tufte (1990)
Tukey (1977)
Wainer and Thissen (1993)

Table 2. Selected Articles on Various Graphing Techniques

Topic	Article
Box-and-whisker graphs	
	Frigge, Hoaglin, and Iglewicz (1989)
	Gouvier, Jackson, Stuss, and Stethem (1992)
	Stock and Behrens (1991)
	Stuss, Stethem, and Pelchat (1988)
General and review	
	Butler (1993)
	Cleveland (1984a, 1984b)
	Cox (1978)
	Henry (1993)
	Kosslyn (1985)
	Loftus (1993)
	Spence and Lewandowsky (1991)
Pie charts, bar graphs, and histograms	
	Croxton (1927)
	Croxton and Stryker (1927)
	Ellis (1926)
	Von Huhn (1927)
Scatter plots	
	Cleveland et al. (1982)
Single-subject designs	
	Furlong and Wampold (1982)
	Morley and Adams (1991)
	Ottenbacher (1986, 1990)
Theory of graph perception	
	Cleveland and McGill (1984, 1985, 1986)
	Kosslyn (1989)
Three-dimensional graphs	
	Barfield and Robless (1989)
	Carswell et al. (1991)

Kosslyn's (1994) book is easy to read and provides a visually engaging presentation of various graphing techniques and recommendations for creating graphs. This book may be more suitable for those in the graphic arts because it contains many examples of graphical techniques (e.g., pictographs, color shading, and pictorial background images) and graphing techniques (e.g., stacked histogram) that are inappropriate for scientific graphs. Indeed, many of Kosslyn's recommendations conflict with Tufte's (1983) suggestion to remove such chartjunk from the graph. The book contains a fascinating account of perceptual principles and psychophysics that may be comprehensible to undergraduates.

Articles on Graphing

Table 2 provides a list of older as well as more recent research articles on graphs. Several of these merit additional discussion. Two articles (Cleveland, 1984b; Cleveland & McGill, 1984) are easy to read and provide a brief summary of graph theory; these could be used in an undergraduate course. Kosslyn's (1989) article includes a lengthy discussion of how graphs may be evaluated from the perspective of various principles in cognitive psychology along with detailed analyses of two graphs. For those who stress the use of single-subject designs, Morley and Adams (1991) and Ottenbacher (1986, 1990) reviewed problems associated with interpreting time series graphs and recommended solutions. Loftus (1993) discussed the role of graphs in the analysis of behavioral data. He proposed that graphs are superior to conventional inferential statistics for presenting and interpreting data. Loftus further noted that the advent of computer-based graphics programs should facilitate greater use of graphic techniques as a means of data analysis.

Summary

Cleveland (1994) and Tufte (1983) noted that the goals of writing and creating a graph are the same—accuracy, brevity, and clarity. To obtain these ends, there are systematic rules that govern the expression of ideas. If these conventions are followed, misrepresentations and misun-derstandings are decreased. A small body of research makes clear that some graphing techniques are more effective at presenting complex quantitative information than others. Students studying the foundations of data analysis will benefit by learning these methods early in their education.

References

American Psychological Association. (1994). *Publication manual of the American Psychological Association* (4th ed.). Washington, DC: Author.

Barfield, W., & Robless, R. (1989). The effects of two- and three-dimensional graphics on the problem-solving performance of experienced and novice decision makers. *Behaviour and Information Technology, 8,* 369–385.

Bertin, J. (1983). *Semiology of graphs* (W. J. Berg, Trans.). Madison: University of Wisconsin Press.

Bowen, R. W. (1992). *Graph it!* Englewood Cliffs, NJ: Prentice Hall.

Butler. D. L. (1993). Graphics in psychology: Pictures, data, and especially concepts. *Behavior Research Methods, Instruments, & Computers, 25,* 81–92.

Carswell, C. M., Frankenberger, S., & Bernhard, D. (1991). Graphing in depth: Perspectives on the use of three-dimensional graphs to represent lower-dimensional data. *Behaviour and Information Technology, 10,* 459–474.

Chambers, J. M., Cleveland, W. S., Kleiner, B., & Tukey, P. A. (1983). *Graphical methods for data analysis.* Belmont, CA: Wadsworth.

Cleveland, W. S. (1984a). Graphs in scientific publications. *The American Statistician, 38,* 261–269.

Cleveland, W. S. (1984b). Graphical methods for data presentation: Full scale breaks, dot charts, and multibased logging. *The American Statistician, 38,* 270–280.

Cleveland, W. S. (1994). *The elements of graphing data* (rev. ed.). Summit, NJ: Hobart.

Cleveland, W. S., Diaconis, P., & McGill, R. (1982). Variables on scatter plots look more highly correlated when the scales are increased. *Science, 216,* 1138–1141.

Cleveland, W. S., & McGill, R. (1984). Graphical perception: Theory, experimentation, and application to the development of graphical methods. *Journal of the American Statistical Association, 79,* 531–554.

Cleveland, W. S., & McGill, R. (1985). Graphical perception and graphical methods for analyzing scientific data. *Science, 229,* 828–833.

Cleveland, W. S., & McGill, R. (1986). An experiment in graphical perception. *International Journal of Man-Machine Studies, 25,* 491–500.

Cox, D. R. (1978). Some remarks on the role of statistics of graphical methods. *Applied Statistics, 27,* 4–9.

Croxton, F. E. (1927). Further studies in the graphic use of circles and bars II: Some additional data. *Journal of the American Statistical Association, 22,* 36–39.

Croxton, F. E., & Stryker, R. E. (1927). Bar charts versus circle diagrams. *Journal of the American Statistical Association, 22,* 473–482.

Ellis, W. C. (1926). The relative merits of circles and bars for representing component parts. *Journal of the American Statistical Association, 21,* 119–132.

Fisher, H. T. (1982). *Mapping information.* Cambridge, MA: Abt Books.

Frigge, M., Hoaglin, D. C., & Iglewicz, B. (1989). Some implementations of the boxplot. *The American Statistician, 43,* 50–54.

Furlong, M. J., & Wampold, B. E. (1982). Intervention effects and relative variation as dimensions in experts' use of visual inference. *Journal of Applied Behavior Analysis, 15,* 415–421.

Gouvier, W. D., Jackson, W. T., Stuss, D. T., & Stethem, L. L. (1992). Rapid visual data analysis in neuropsychological research: Box graphs. *The Clinical Neuropsychologist, 6,* 92–97.

Henry, G. T. (1993). Using graphical displays for evaluation data. *Evaluation Review, 17,* 60–78.

Henry, G. T. (1995). *Graphing data: Techniques for display and analysis.* Thousand Oaks, CA: Sage.

Hoaglin, D. C., Mosteller, F., & Tukey, J. W. (1991). *Fundamentals of exploratory analysis of variance.* New York: Wiley.

Kosslyn, S. M. (1985). Graphs and human information processing: A review of five books. *Journal of the American Statistical Association, 80,* 499–512.

Kosslyn, S. M. (1989). Understanding charts and graphs. *Applied Cognitive Psychology, 3,* 185–226.

Kosslyn, S. M. (1994). *Elements of graph design.* New York: Freeman.

Loftus, G. R. (1993). A picture is worth a thousand *p* values: On the irrelevance of hypothesis testing in the microcomputer age. *Behavior Research Methods, Instruments, & Computers, 25,* 250–256.

Morley, S., & Adams, M. (1991). Graphical analysis of single-case time series data. *British Journal of Clinical Psychology, 30,* 97–115.

Ottenbacher, K. J. (1986). Reliability and accuracy of visually analyzed graphed data from single-subject designs. *The American Journal of Occupational Therapy, 40,* 464–469.

Ottenbacher, K. J. (1990). Visual inspection of single-subject data: An empirical analysis. *Mental Retardation, 28,* 283–290.

Schmidt, C. F. (1983). *Statistical graphics.* New York: Wiley.

Smith, A. F., & Prentice, D. A. (1993). Exploratory data analysis. In G. Keren & C. Lewis (Eds.), *A handbook for data analysis in the behavioral sciences: Statistical issues* (pp. 349–390). Hillsdale, NJ: Lawrence Erlbaum Associates, Inc.

Spence, I., & Lewandowsky, S. (1991). Displaying proportions and percentages. *Applied Cognitive Psychology, 5,* 61–77.

Stevens, S. S. (1975). *Psychophysics.* New York: Wiley.

Stock, W. A., & Behrens, J. T. (1991). Box, line, and midgap plots: Effects of display characteristics on the accuracy and bias of estimates of whisker length. *Journal of Educational Statistics, 16,* 1–20.

Stuss, D. T., Stethem, L. L., & Pelchat, G. (1988). Three tests of attention and rapid information processing: An extension. *The Clinical Neuropsychologist, 2,* 395–400.

Tufte, E. R. (1983). *The visual display of quantitative information.* Cheshire, CT: Graphics Press.

Tufte, E. R. (1990). *Envisioning information.* Cheshire, CT: Graphics Press.

Tukey, J. W. (1977). *Exploratory data analysis.* Reading, MA: Addison-Wesley.

Von Huhn, R. (1927). Further studies in the graphic use of circles and bars I: A discussion of Ellis' experiment. *Journal of the American Statistical Association, 22,* 31–36.

Wainer, H., & Thissen, D. (1993). Graphical data analysis. In G. Keren & C. Lewis (Eds.), *A handbook for data analysis in the behavioral sciences: Statistical issues* (pp. 391–457). Hillsdale, NJ: Lawrence Erlbaum Associates, Inc.

Elaborating Selected Statistical Concepts With Common Experience

Kenneth A. Weaver
Emporia State University

Introductory statistics textbooks usually describe *statistics* as a "new way of thinking about and learning about the world" (Glenberg, 1988, p. v). By including news items and cartoons, textbook authors use well-known information to illustrate new concepts. In this article, I show how exclamations, circus and cartoon characters, and falling leaves can be used to elaborate statistical concepts, such as variability, null hypothesis testing, and confidence interval.

Variability

After demonstrating how to compute the standard deviation, I present an exclamation and ask students to evaluate the statistical information it contains. For example, a visiting grandmother remarks, "My, how you've grown!" Understanding this exclamation requires comparing one's sense of a child's average growth with the amount of growth since grandmother's last visit. The greater the difference, the more unusual is the amount of growth, and the louder is the exclamation. Familiar exclamations include Jackie Gleason's refrain "How sweet it is!" and the line from the opening song of the play *Oklahoma* (Rodgers & Hammerstein, 1942), "Oh, what a beautiful morning!"

As a class exercise, students generate their own exclamations. After learning about z scores, students convert their exclamations to an approximate z score. Selected students present their z scores to class members, who evaluate the sign and size.

I also suggest that one's intuition about averageness and difference can be intentionally manipulated for a dramatic effect. Dr. Jekyll and Mr. Hyde and Popeye before and after eating spinach exemplify obvious and extreme variation. In contrast, more subtle is the variation of selected behaviors by the same character, such as the ferocity of King Kong except for its gentleness with Ann Redman.

Testing the Null Hypothesis

After lecturing about probability, the critical region, and the null hypothesis, I talk about circus or cartoon characters that have unusual characteristics corresponding to measures in the tails of the appropriate distribution. These unusual scores (and unusual characters) can help teach students about the statistical (and social) rejection associated with such deviations from the norm.

I rhetorically ask the class: What makes circus attractions like the bearded lady or a midget so popular? My answer is that these individuals are so unusual, relative to the rest of the population, that they belong in the extremes of the distribution for that attribute. I remind students that the extreme area of the distribution is labeled the critical or *alpha* region and contains cases so different that they are not accepted as part of the group.

Adjectives such as *rare, abnormal,* and *bizarre* describe cases in the critical area. Not being accepted as a member of a particular distribution becomes increasingly likely the more unusual the individual. For example, Pinnochio's nose length, Flash's speed, and a witch's beauty (or lack of it) produce measurements that fall in the critical area and are thus rejected as members of the "regular" group.

I use the single sample t test to connect the logic of rejecting extremes with making statistical decisions. If the sampling error converted to standard deviations falls in the t distribution's critical region, then the error is not accepted as belonging to the population of "normal"-sized errors, and the null hypothesis is rejected.

Students have previously been told that *alpha* specifies the degree to which chance can be an explanation for the results. They also have been warned that *alpha* is not a measure of effect size. Thus, characterizing a result as being "highly" or "very" or "marginally" significant, based on the value of *alpha,* is inappropriate (Harcum, 1989).

Confidence Interval

For this exercise, I describe the following scene:

Imagine a wind-sheltered orchard of trees during autumn. As the trees shed their leaves, piles form around the trunks. Each pile is tallest next to the tree and decreases in height farther away from the tree. Note the similarity between the shape of each pile and the outline of the standard normal distribution. Imagine standing next to a tree's trunk and picking up a leaf from the pile. How sure are you that the particular leaf fell from the tree under which you are standing? Now imagine moving 60 ft away and picking up a leaf from the same pile. How sure are you that this leaf came from the same tree and not a neighboring one?

Invariably, students respond that they are much more confident that the leaf near the trunk belongs to that tree. I continue the discussion by saying that as distance from the tree increases, a point is ultimately reached beyond which any leaf on the ground would more confidently be considered as coming from another tree. Then I associate the trunk with the estimated population mean, the leaves with sample means, and the confidence points with 1 − alpha and say that the confidence points form the interval's two endpoints within which the population mean has a 1 − alpha probability of being located.

Conclusion

This article describes how common experiences can be used to elaborate selected statistical concepts. Students have been intrigued by the notion that the thinking they use during the exercises overlaps with the technical principles being presented in the course. They generally indicate that the exercises increase their comprehension of the related text material or, if not, provide a perspective from which to ask meaningful questions. I would appreciate knowing how other statistics instructors use commonplace experiences in their courses.

References

Glenberg, A. M. (1988). *Learning from data: An introduction to statistical reasoning.* New York: Harcourt Brace Jovanovich.

Harcum, E. R. (1989). The highly inappropriate calibrations of statistical significance. *American Psychologist, 44,* 964.

Rodgers, R., & Hammerstein, O., II. (1942). *Oklahoma.* New York: Williamson Music Corporation.

Note

I thank Charles L. Brewer and three anonymous reviewers for their comments on an earlier draft.

A "Bag of Tricks" for Teaching About Sampling Distributions

Dominic J. Zerbolio, Jr.
University of Missouri-St. Louis

To solve statistical problems, one uses more logic than math skills. Unfortunately, many students believe statistics is mathematics, and their beliefs restrict how they approach learning statistics. Too often, this means students adopt a *plug and chug approach* (i.e., fill in the numbers and arrive at a correct numerical answer), which works and provides the correct answer, as long as someone tells them what numbers to plug into what formulas. With the plug and chug approach, students typically fail to grasp the meaning and logic behind statistical procedures and, therefore, rapidly forget what they have been taught. If students could see and understand some of the key concepts and distributions, they might not so readily adopt and restrict themselves to plug and chug.

A key concept in understanding how statistics work is the notion of sampling distributions, an idea that seems to escape many students. Students grasp the idea of measures of central tendency, variability, and probability with raw score distributions, but often have difficulty generalizing these concepts to sampling distributions. Because understanding sampling distributions is central to understanding hypothesis testing, a little extra effort to help students conceptualize sampling distributions seems reasonable.

For several terms, I have been using a lecture procedure that helps students understand and differentiate sampling distributions. The procedure involves teaching students to imagine marbles and chips as various kinds of theoretical distributions and relies only on the instructor's flair for the dramatic. Once the various distributions are depicted as bags of marbles and/or bags of chips, students more easily grasp not only the plug and chug mechanics but also the underlying nature of statistical distributions. This grasp aids teaching both the logic and generality of statistical procedures.

The first step is teaching students to visualize raw score distributions. Referring to a commonly recognized distribution, like the Stanford–Binet IQ distribution, helps because most students know the average IQ is 100, and some even know its standard deviation is 16. Depicting the distribution involves describing each score in it as a "marble with a number on it." The population of raw scores becomes a "bag containing all the marbles." During the presentation, the imaginary bag is held high with one hand while the other hand points to the bag. Using marbles and bags to demonstrate the probabilities of scores in a distribution provides repetition and facilitates visualization.

Probabilities are taught by reaching into the bag (with appropriate hand and body gestures) and drawing a marble. With the imaginary marble held high in the free hand, students are asked, "What is the probability that this marble has a 120 or higher on it?" Calculating z scores for marbles (scores) and translating the z scores into probability statements quickly become routine. After a few draws, students readily accept the bag and marbles as a population of raw scores. Once the marbles and bag are established, the generation of sampling distributions becomes fairly easy.

The One-Sample Case Sampling Distribution

The one-sample case sampling distribution is the distribution of means of equal-sized samples. Two steps are required to establish this sampling distribution and distinguish it from the raw score population. In Step 1, students are asked to visualize a large number of drinking glasses. With appropriate motions, a glassful of marbles is scooped out of the raw score population bag. Each glassful of marbles represents a random sample of marbles and, by implication, is a random sample of raw scores. Additional glasses are filled with the same number of marbles as the first until the population of marbles (raw scores) is exhausted. This procedure creates a population of glassfuls, each containing the same number of marbles.

Step 2 is to create the distribution of sample means. A mean is calculated for each glass and written on a chip. All of the chips are gathered into a new or second bag. Once all the chips are put into the second bag, the new bag is held aloft and students are asked, "What's in this new bag?"

Most students recognize that the bag of chips is different from the original bag of marbles, which establishes a distinction between the raw score population and a distribution of sample means. This distinction can be enhanced by pouring all the marbles back into their own bag and holding the bag of chips in one hand and a bag of marbles in the other. I taught students earlier that they need two parameters to describe any normal distribution (a mean and a measure of variability), so a classroom discussion of the mean and standard error necessary to describe the bag of chips can be initiated. As an option, the normal shape of the chip distribution can be defended by introducing the central limit theorem at this point.

With the mean and standard error of the bag of chips established, a single chip can be drawn from the bag of chips, and students are asked, "What is the probability that the value on the chip is 105 or higher?" Most students realize the solution requires the calculation of a z score. The contrast between the proper error terms (standard deviation for the bag of marbles and standard error for the bag of chips) becomes obvious. With the proper mean and standard error term for the bag of chips understood, students easily see how to calculate z scores for chips and, using a z table, translate their z values into probability statements. With the z-score procedure for a distribution of sample means in hand, the probability of a mean (or chip) being drawn from a distribution of means (or chips) with a specific population average can be established. At this point, it is a relatively short step to the one-sample hypothesis testing procedure.

The Difference Between Independent Sample Means Case

The distribution of the differences between independent sample means seems to cause problems because students initially confuse it with the difference between the means of two independent distributions of sample means. The distribution of differences between independent sample means has an infinite number of values whereas the difference between the means of two independent sampling distributions of means has only one value. Demonstrating the distribution of differences between independent sample means to students requires a two-step process.

Step 1 is to have students visualize two glasses, one red and one blue. Each glass is filled from a bag of marbles (or population), and then the two glasses are taped together. Additional pairs are filled and taped, with the same number of marbles as in the first pair, until the original marble population is exhausted. Once all possible pairs of red and blue glasses are filled, the second step can begin.

In Step 2, the means for each pair of red and blue glasses are calculated, and the difference between the means (red mean – blue mean) is determined. Each difference is written on a chip, and the chip is placed in another bag. When the population of paired red and blue glasses is exhausted, the bag of chips, which represents the distribution of differences between sample means, can be dealt with.

A chip is drawn from the bag and students are asked, "What's on the chip?" Of course, each chip represents a difference between independent sample means and has no relation to the original sample means. Emphasizing the chip contains no information about the original means can be accomplished by asking what original means led to the number on the chip. Most students see that chips have no information about the original sample means, but represent a different kind of population, a difference between populations.

Once the difference between distribution is established, students see that describing it requires a measure of central tendency and variability. An explanation of the mean and standard error of the distribution of differences between independent sample means ensues. With the mean and standard error in hand, one can draw a single chip from the "bag of differences between" and ask about the probability of its occurrence.

Note that I referred to the distribution as the "difference between" rather than the "difference between two sample means." My experience suggests that omitting the words *sample means* enhances students' grasp of the distinction between distributions of sample means and distributions of differences between sample means. Presented this way, more students see that the "difference between" is what is important and that the actual values of the sample means are incidental. As before, once the mean, standard error, and probability characteristics of the "difference between" distribution are established, generalizing to the hypothesis testing procedure is easier. Note that red and blue glasses can be used later to denote different treatment conditions.

The Difference Between Correlated Sample Means Case

Analyzing the distribution of the differences between correlated sample means requires all the work in analyzing the distribution of differences between independent samples means plus the computation of a correlation coefficient. To reduce the computational burden, most texts use an alternative, the *direct difference method*. The direct difference method's sampling distribution is the distribution of mean differences between paired scores, known as the *bar D*-distribution, which can be demonstrated with a three-step procedure.

Step 1 uses a chip to represent both the X and Y values of a pair of raw scores. With an X value on one side and a Y value on the other, the population of paired X, Y scores becomes immediately obvious to most students. With the bag (population) of chips established, the second step begins.

In Step 2, a chip, marked with its X and Y scores, is drawn. The difference between its X and Y scores is written on a marble. This procedure is repeated for all chips, and

all the marbles are put in another bag. Then, the bag of marbles, which is the difference score distribution, can be held aloft and distinguished from the original bag of chips.

Step 3 is filling glasses with marbles. As in the one-sample case, each glass has the same number of marbles. A mean is calculated for the marbles in each glass, each mean is written on a chip, and the chips placed in another bag. However, this second bag of chips is different from the first because only one value, the mean of a sample of difference scores (or bar D), appears on each chip. As before, students are asked how to describe the bag of mean difference scores. By this point, most students realize that they need a specific mean and standard error term to characterize the bar-D distribution and often ask for them before they are presented. Once the mean and standard error term for the bar-D distribution are specified, single chips can be drawn from the bag and questions about the probability of specific bar-D values asked. Students typically generalize the entire z-score procedure immediately. Once the mechanism for determining probabilities is established, it is a short step to the hypothesis testing procedure.

Some students see the similarity between the bar-D distribution and the one-sample mean distribution. When they do, it is easy to show that the only mechanical (plug and chug) difference between the two statistical procedures is using a difference score (D) in place of a raw score (X). Noting the similarity helps some students see the generality of the statistical procedure. For the remainder, it probably means one less formula to learn. If and when the similarity is shown, the instructor must be careful to maintain a clear distinction between what the D and X scores represent.

The value of these procedures depends on the way the instructor presents the bags of marbles and chips. If bags are presented with panache, students not only seem to grasp the distinctions between various distributions more quickly, but learn the nature of the underlying sampling distributions as well. Once sampling distributions are clearly differentiated from raw score distributions, the generality of the procedures for determining probabilities can be seen, and the entire hypothesis testing procedure is much easier to show. Further, by depicting sampling distributions, students begin to see the conceptual logic and generality of statistical procedures, rather than restricting themselves to learning a series of superstitiously performed plug and chug procedures. Student reaction to the technique is good. Many find the presentation amusing, which also serves to hold their attention. More important, more students have commented that they understand sampling distributions with the bag procedure than with any other lecture technique I have tried. This understanding is often seen in our Statistics Lab sections wherein students ask more questions about sampling distributions than about plug and chug mechanics. Even more reassuring, when the same students take my Research Methods course, many see the application of the statistics and sampling distributions to research data more readily than students taught with other procedures. I have even seen Research Methods students instructing their less knowledgeable classmates about statistical comparisons using the "bag" analogy.

As a closing remark, I would not recommend using real bags, marbles, or chips, because that necessarily implies a finite limit to theoretical populations. It is important for students to see populations and sampling distributions as logical or abstract entities. The procedure works without real props.

Demonstrating the Influence of Sample Size and Reliability on Study Outcome

Michael J. Strube
Washington University

Two important concepts in any research design course are the influences of sample size and reliability on study outcome (e.g., Neale & Liebert, 1986). For example, small samples produce highly variable estimates of population parameters. This relation between sample size and the precision of estimates produces the familiar decrease in statistical power that occurs as sample size decreases. Similarly, measurement error hampers estimation of population values. Unreliable measures limit the magnitude of the correlation that can be obtained in a sample, with that upper limit being less than the population correlation. This relation is captured in the maxim that reliability is a necessary but not a sufficient condition for validity (e.g., Nunnally, 1978). Understanding the limits that sample size and reliability place on expected outcomes is central to good research design.

Although these relations are well-known to experienced researchers and are captured by statistical formulas, the concepts are often difficult for students to grasp. How small a sample is "too small?" When is a measure too unreliable? Answering these questions requires a firm understanding of the functional relation of study outcome to sample size and reliability. In my undergraduate research design course, I have found it useful to demonstrate these relations with a computer program that visually displays the influences of sample size and reliability on study outcome. The program generates random samples from populations defined by the user. Consequently, it can be used to demonstrate the variability in sample statistics that arises from different sample sizes, the variability in sample correlations that arises from different sample sizes, and the impact of reliability on sample correlations. The program allows the student to explore more fully the relations of sample size and reliability to study outcome and to appreciate the relations in a way that is not immediately apparent from examining a statistical formula.

Program Description

The program has two options. In the first option, the program generates a single sample at a time. The user specifies the population mean and variance for two variables (X and Y), the population correlation between the two variables (ρ_{xy}), the reliabilities for those variables (r_{xx} and r_{yy}), and the sample size (N). The computer then generates a random sample of N pairs of independent uniform random variables on the interval 0 to 1 (generated by the GW-BASIC internal random number generator). The Box-Muller procedure (Box & Muller, 1958) is used to transform these values into pairs of independent standard normal deviates. One standard normal deviate is arbitrarily designated as the true score for variable X (Z_x), whereas the remaining standard normal deviate is designated as an error component (Z_e). True scores for Y are then generated by the equation: $Z_y = \rho_{xy}Z_x + (1 - \rho_{xy})^{1/2}Z_e$. The resulting distributions of Z_x and Z_y (i.e., true scores) have a population correlation of ρ_{xy}. For each member of each sample of Z_x and Z_y values, an additional standard normal deviate (Z_2) is generated to create the random error component reflecting the influence of unreliability. *Reliability* is defined (as in classical measurement theory; e.g., Nunnally, 1978) as the ratio of true score variance (σ_t^2) to the sum of true score variance and error variance (σ_e^2): $r_{xx} = \sigma_t^2/(\sigma_t^2 + \sigma_e^2)$. *True score variance* is defined as 1 because standard normal deviates are used.

Reliability is defined by the user. Thus, the constant (C) by which the random error component (Z_2) must be multiplied to produce the error variance can be calculated as $(1/r_{xx} - 1)^{1/2}$. The new sample estimates, containing the proper proportions of true score and random variability, are calculated (e.g., for X) as $z_x = Z_x + CZ_2$. All that remains is to transform these estimates so that the sample distribution has the defined population mean and variance. That is accomplished by the following transformation (for X): $X = z_x(\sigma_x^2/[1 + C^2])^{1/2} + \mu_x$.

The population parameters and sample statistics are printed on the screen. A subsequent screen provides a scatterplot of the relation between X and Y, the regression line that best fits the scatterplot, and the frequency distributions for X and Y. Repeated runs of this program option can test the effect of different sample sizes and reliability combinations on the sample statistics and sample correlation.

The second program option demonstrates the relation of reliability to validity. For this option, the user provides the sample size and the population correlation. The program then generates 55 sample correlations for reliabilities ranging from 0 to 1 for variables X and Y. A plot of these correlations demonstrates how the obtained correlation approaches zero when the reliability of either X or Y approaches zero and converges on the population correlation only when both reliabilities approach 1. In addition, the influence of sample size on estimation is apparent because the plot of obtained correlations more clearly shows the functional relation between reliability and validity for larger samples.

Time to run the program varies with the machine. On an IBM-compatible running at 10 MHz with an 80286 processor and an 80287 math coprocessor, the program required 10 s to generate and plot a sample of 10 responses using the first option. Generating and plotting a sample of 100 responses required 346 s. Using the second option, the program required 54 s to generate and plot the correlations for a sample size of 10 and 471 s to generate and plot the correlations for a sample size of 100. The second option requires more time because the program estimates 55 separate correlations.

Hardware Requirements

The graphic displays Created by the program require 640 × 350 pixel resolution (enhanced resolution graphics). The program, written in GW-BASIC, requires 14k of memory. Additional memory is required for allocation of arrays to hold sampled responses. The additional memory required can be approximated by the following formula: Memory = $16N + 450$, where N is the sample size.

Program Availability

A listing of the program (338 lines) will be sent on request. Alternatively, a copy of the program is available upon receipt of a properly formatted disk and self-addressed, stamped mailer.

Classroom Use

I use the program in a classroom exercise to demonstrate the impact of reliability on the correlations between variables and thus the impact of reliability on inferences drawn from study outcomes. The students are enrolled in the undergraduate research design course required for our psychology major. They have completed an introductory statistics course as a prerequisite. Accordingly, the students are familiar with basic statistical terminology, and they recognize that common statistical procedures (e.g., t test and bivariate correlation) are related. Consequently, they readily recognize that, although the computer exercise focuses on correlations, the principles extend to other statistical procedures on which inferences are based.

I preface the exercise with a brief introduction to reliability, emphasizing the role of error in research design and inference. The first part of the exercise demonstrates the impact of reliability on the correlation between two variables. Students are given two questions to guide their efforts: (a) How does reliability affect the obtained correlation between two variables?, and (b) How does reliability affect the prediction of one variable from another? Students use the first program option and are instructed to keep the sample size constant at 100 (so estimates are reasonably stable) and to keep the means and variances constant at a chosen level. They are also told to try different values for the population correlation, to use different values for the reliabilities of X and Y, and to compare the scatterplots that result from the different combinations. Students are encouraged to keep a log of their findings for easier comparison. Students typically arrive at the conclusion that as the reliability of either X or Y decreases, the known population correlation is underestimated. They also recognize that decreasing reliability increases the scatter around the regression line, making large errors of prediction more likely. In sum, they conclude that error in the measures can introduce error into the inferences.

The second part of the exercise demonstrates more formally the actual relation between reliability and validity. Students are reminded that validation in the research design sense depends on uncovering relations between variables. For example, they are told that one way to validate a new measure of anxiety is to correlate it with an established measure of anxiety. The exercise requires students to derive a rule describing the relation between reliability and validity when validity is defined as the ability to estimate a known relation between two variables. Students are told to try different population correlations and to assume that the different combinations of X reliability and Y reliability (generated by the program) represent different studies trying to uncover the relation between X and Y. Students are guided by the following questions: (a) What happens to the accuracy of r_{xy} as r_{xx} approaches zero?, (b) What happens to the accuracy of r_{xy} as r_{yy} approaches zero?, and (c) What does this say about the role of reliability in the ability to detect a relation between X and Y? Typically, students are able to state a simple rule that resembles closely the lesson objective: Reliability is a necessary condition for validity. They also recognize that the relation between reliability and validity is a monotonic one, suggesting that some reliability is better than none.

Finally, I ask students to repeat this exercise but to try different sample sizes. They are asked to determine if the effect of reliability depends on sample size. They conclude that it does not, but that small samples create their own problems by making population estimates more variable and thus making inferences less certain.

I follow the exercise with a more formal lecture on the relation between reliability and validity, including a discussion of the formula relating the two: $r_{xy} = \rho_{xy}(r_{xx}r_{yy})^{1/2}$. I also emphasize that reliability, although a necessary condition for validity, is not a sufficient condition. This point serves as a useful introduction to the topic of validity. The exercise helps to emphasize the importance of reliability in research inference and of reducing error in research design.

References

Box, G. E. P., & Muller, M. A. (1958). A note on the generation of random normal deviates. *Annals of Mathematical Statistics, 29,* 610–613.

Neale, J. M., & Liebert, R. M. (1986). *Science and behavior: An introduction to methods of research* (3rd ed.). Englewood Cliffs, NJ: Prentice-Hall.

Nunnally, J. C. (1978). *Psychometric theory.* New York: McGraw-Hill.

Note

I thank Bernard Beins and two anonymous reviewers for their comments on an earlier version of this article.

3. Examining Statistical Tests

Because he discovered that many students had difficulty understanding the complex correlations and interactions between variables that typify many statistical procedures, David Johnson at John Brown University developed a technique for introducing analysis of variance in a concrete fashion. Perhaps your students could also acquire an intuitive understanding of the concepts of between- and within-groups variance and their relationship to each other.

Jeffrey Rasmussen from Indiana University-Purdue University at Indianapolis designed a multimedia-interactive program for teaching analysis of variance (ANOVA) designs. The program tests students' understanding of independent groups and repeated measures variables, as well as the source and degrees of freedom in ANOVA source tables. Although developed for graduate students, the technique can be applied to teaching undergraduates.

To provide individual students with simulated data and analysis capacity for the one-way between subjects design, John Walsh from Fordham University developed an SAS program. The program produces an ASCII data file that students can analyze by calculator or by many statistical software packages. The article includes the SAS program for readers who want to use the technique.

Leslie Cake and Roy Hostetter from Sir Wilfred Grenfell College at Memorial University of Newfoundland describe a BASIC program that creates unique data sets for six analysis of variance research designs. The authors also describe the use of the program and provide samples of student and instructor output. Use of the program can reduce the instructor's time required for grading unique exercises and encourage students to work independently.

John Walsh from Fordham University developed a SYSTAT macro that generates information from available data in published literature to compute analysis of variance and post hoc analyses. Instructors can also use the technique to illustrate concepts involved in computing power for an experiment.

To demonstrate the difference between main effects and interactions in factorial designs, Michael Strube and Miriam Goldstein from Washington University describe a QuickBASIC program. The program guides students through construction of data patterns corresponding to different combinations of main effects and the interaction in a 2 x 2 design. Program feedback provides tailored guidance to help students produce the requested patterns of means. Statistics teachers can also use the program in combination with traditional lecture on factorial designs to develop student skill in recognizing main effects and interactions from graphical displays.

In her survey of 18 introductory statistics textbooks, Jane Buck at Delaware State College found that few texts contained material about tests for differences between group variances. The author provides two reasons to test for heterogeneity of variance when conducting t tests and the analysis of variance, as well as testing hypotheses about differences between variances as the result of experimental treatment. How familiar are your students with these concepts?

Roberto Refinetti from College of William & Mary described the use of a personal computer to conduct a classroom demonstration of the effects of violations of assumptions of analysis of variance (ANOVA) on the probability of Type I error. The demonstration's rationale is that if many data sets of randomly selected numbers are submitted to ANOVA, then the frequency distribution of empirical F values should approximate the probability density curve of the F statistic for the specified degrees of freedom. An objective for this technique is to illustrate the consequences of failing to meet ANOVA assumptions; violations of the assumptions of normality and homogeneity of variances have a measurable but small effect on the probability of Type I error, especially when all groups are the same size.

Miriam Goldstein and Michael Strube from Washington University described two QuickBASIC programs for classroom use. The programs provide students direct experience with interpreting correlation scatterplots and highlight factors that influence the size of a Pearson correlation coefficient. In one program, students estimated the size of the correlation in nine randomly generated scatterplots and received feedback about accuracy. In the second program, students plotted correlations of a certain size or type (e.g., curvilinear) and received feedback about the size of the Pearson correlation coefficient in their plots. Readers are advised that this technique is used with students who have completed statistics and are enrolled in a research methods course.

To help students at the University of Tennessee (Knoxville) understand that increases in σ may lead to an increase, decrease, or no change in r, Schuyler Huck, Paul Wright, and Soohee Park devised a simple classroom exercise. Using standard decks of playing cards, students generated hypothetical data on two well-known variables (IQ and GPA). Once analyzed, the data illustrated that changes in score variability influenced r in different ways, depending on the reason why σ_x (or σ_y) increases or decreases.

An Intuitive Approach to Teaching Analysis of Variance

David E. Johnson
John Brown University

Instructors of introductory statistics know that students approach their course with considerable anxiety (Dillon, 1982; Hastings, 1982). Many students complain about the mathematical nature of the course and their inadequate preparation for it.

Evidence also suggests that a significant number of students in the introductory statistics course may operate at a concrete–operational level of thought, as defined by Piaget (1952). Some researchers have estimated that up to 50% of the adult population functions at this level (Kuhn, Langer, Kohlberg, & Haan, 1977; McKinnon & Renner, 1971). Others have demonstrated that it is common for college students to operate at a concrete level or to be transitional between concrete and formal levels of cognitive development. (Allen, Walker, Schroeder, & Johnson, 1987). According to Piaget, persons at the formal–operational level are capable of abstract thought and reasoning. They can understand hypothetical situations, combine information from several sources, and comprehend correlations and interactions between variables. These capabilities are necessary for understanding the problems students encounter in their first statistics course.

Students who function at a concrete–operational level are unprepared to comprehend the fundamental operations required for complete understanding of basic statistical concepts. The anxiety that students experience may aggravate this situation by causing them to narrow their attention to fewer details of these statistical concepts (Easterbrook, 1959). Instructors could use an effective, concrete demonstration to communicate some of these complex statistical concepts to their students.

The ANOVA appears to be one of those procedures that requires a concrete presentation. A technique I use for teaching ANOVA involves manipulating between- and within-groups variance and observing the resulting changes in the ANOVA summary table. A description of that technique follows.

Method

My introduction to ANOVA is fairly standard: Students are informed of the reasons for using ANOVA (as compared to the more familiar t test for independent groups), the concepts of between- and within-groups variance are wintroduced, the computational techniques for obtaining the F ratio for a one-way ANOVA are explained, and the conceptual relationship of between- and within-groups variance is described.

At that point, I describe a hypothetical experiment in which three independent groups of subjects (labeled A1, A2, and A3, with each group containing five subjects) are exposed to one of three levels of an independent variable. The range of possible responses on the dependent variable is 0 through 4. Students are then given a data set that contains scores for the 15 subjects.

In the initial data set, the values are identical (i.e., each subject recorded a value of 1). The students recognize that this outcome is highly unlikely. They also realize that there is no variability in the data. One of two methods can then be used to continue the presentation. In the first approach, a copy of the data and the outline of an ANOVA summary table are presented on a screen using an overhead projector. The computations are then completed for the students. Another approach involves projecting the data and the completed summary table. This approach takes less time but does not expose students to the actual computational procedures. Regardless of the method used, students observe that the absence of between- and within-groups variability leads to mean squares of 0 in the summary table.

Students are then given a second data set which is identical to the first with one notable exception: Between-groups variance is introduced by increasing all five values in Group A3 to 3. The between-groups variance now indicates the possible effect of the independent variable manipulation. It is obvious to the students that Group A3 is different from the other two groups (mean square A = 6.65); however, there is no within-groups variability (mean square S/A = 0).

Students are given a third data set that incorporates within-groups variance into Group A1 (see Table 1). This data set contains the same amount of between-groups variance as the previous one (i.e., the means are unchanged). Students are encouraged to compare the results of the second and third data sets and to observe the absence of

Table 1. Data Set Number 2

	A1	A2	A3
	0	1	3
	1	1	3
	1	1	3
	1	1	3
	2	1	3
Group Mean	1	1	3

Summary of ANOVA

Source	Sum of Squares	df	Mean Square	F
A	13.3	2	6.65	39.12
S/A	2.0	12	.17	

change in the between-subjects values represented by the mean square of 6.65 for both data sets. They are encouraged to notice how the introduction of dissimilar scores into Group A1 increased the value of the mean square for within-groups variance. The students are asked to note the value of the F ratio, which is 39.12 in this case.

Subsequently, students are given a fourth data set, which differs from the previous one in only one way: Additional within-groups variance has been added by changing the values in Group A2 to march those in Group A1. The students' attention is directed to the fact that the means for each group are identical to those in the previous data set. The computed values reveal that, compared to the previous data set, the between-groups mean square remains unchanged, but the within-groups mean square is larger. As a result, the F ratio is smaller.

At this point, students begin to understand the relationship of between- and within-groups variance and how this relationship affects the magnitude of the F ratio. To reinforce this emerging understanding, a final data set is presented. This data set continues the trend of the previous two data sets in which additional within-groups variance is introduced while the group means remain unchanged. One value in Group A3 is reduced by 1 and another value is increased by 1, thereby maintaining a mean of 3 for that group. Again, students are told to note the unchanged between-groups mean square and the increased within-groups mean square, as compared to the previous data set. As a result, the F ratio is smaller.

The final step in the presentation depends on the class in which it is used. In a statistics class where limited information about research design is presented, I briefly review the procedure and determine the level of students' understanding. Discussion of the functional relationship between the F and t statistics (e.g., $F = t^2$) is useful.

In a research methods course, however, I spend additional time discussing topics that directly relate to the nature of ANOVA and its relationship to practical aspects of experimental procedure and design. The significance of previously discussed issues, such as the importance of controlling sources of variance and developing strong independent variable manipulations, is reinforced.

Results and Discussion

Students in a research design course ($N = 10$) were asked to rate the usefulness of this technique in facilitating their understanding of ANOVA. The ratings were made on a 7-point scale ranging from *not at all* (1) *to considerable* (7). Students were also asked to indicate if they would recommend using this technique in future classes. The mean rating for the usefulness of the technique was positive, but not overwhelmingly so ($M = 4.9$, $SD = 1.85$). When asked whether the technique should be used in future classes, however, 9 out of 10 students answered yes. Because of the variability in their usefulness ratings, students were asked to comment on the procedure. Several students indicated that they believed the procedure is very useful, but that they had doubts as to whether their understanding of ANOVA would ever be "considerable." Apparently, some of the students confused the assessment of usefulness of the procedure with an estimation of their eventual understanding of ANOVA.

I believe that this technique is useful, especially for students who operate at a preformal level of thought. Systematic manipulation of a small range of numerical values seems to alleviate the math anxiety that some students experience. The technique is particularly helpful for students who are intimidated by the dynamic relationship of between- and within-groups variance in determining the F ratio.

References

Allen, J. L., Walker, L. D., Schroeder, D. A., & Johnson, D. E. (1987). Attributions and attribution-behavior relations: The effect of level of cognitive development. *Journal of Personality and Social Psychology, 52,* 1099–1109.

Dillon, K. M. (1982). Statisticophobia. *Teaching of Psychology, 9,* 117.

Easterbrook, J. A. (1959). The effect of emotion on cue utilization and the organization of behavior. *Psychological Review, 66,* 183–201.

Hastings, M. W. (1982). Statistics: Challenge for students and the professor. *Teaching of Psychology, 9,* 221–222.

Kuhn, D., Langer, J., Kohlberg, L., & Haan, N. F. (1977). The development of formal operations in logical and moral judgment. *Genetic Psychology Monograph, 95,* 97–288.

McKinnon, J. W., & Renner, J. W. (1971). Are colleges concerned with intellectual development? *American Journal of Personality, 39,* 1047–1052.

Piaget, J. (1952). *The origins of intelligence in children.* New York: Harcourt, Brace. (Original work published 1936)

Note

I thank Joseph Palladino and four anonymous reviewers for their helpful comments on an earlier draft of this article.

ANOVA MultiMedia: A Program for Teaching ANOVA Designs

Jeffrey Lee Rasmussen
Indiana University-Purdue University at Indianapolis

Analysis of variance (ANOVA) designs are commonly used in psychological research and commonly taught in graduate and undergraduate quantitative psychology courses. In this article, I describe an interactive multimedia program for teaching ANOVA designs.

Program Description

ANOVA MultiMedia is an interactive program that I wrote using the IconAuthor software (AimTech Corporation, 1993). The program incorporates colorful graphics and artwork, short animations, scrollable text boxes, dragable icons, and immediate feedback to test students' understanding of ANOVA designs. The program consists of an introductory screen followed by 10 story problems for which the student indicates (a) whether the variables are independent groups or repeated measures variables, (b) entries in the source column, and (c) degrees of freedom values.

Introductory Screen

The introductory screen provides general information about the program and how to drag the icons. The program also briefly discusses the two types of variables found in an ANOVA design—independent groups or between variables and repeated measures or within variables—and the resultant three types of ANOVA designs—independent groups designs (IGDs), repeated measures designs (RMDs), and mixed IGDs/RMDs. The software provides examples of the types of variables and designs.

The program also informs the student to enter the independent variables in alphabetic order. For example, for a design with sex and age as the variables, the age variable

must be entered first in the source table. This constraint simplifies the program's feedback capabilities.

ANOVA Designs

The program then presents 10 ANOVA designs. There are two examples each of a one-way IGD, two-way IGD, Subjects × Trials RMD, Subjects × Condition × Trials RMD, and Subjects/IGD × mixed RMD. For each design, students interact with three screens.

The first screen gives the story problem and asks the student to decide if the independent variables are independent groups or repeated measures variables. The problem appears in a story problem box that the student can scroll to read. For example, for one problem, students are presented with this story problem: "A comparative psychologist investigates dominance behavior in geese. In one condition, the geese are domesticated; in the other condition, the geese are wild. A total of 10 geese are studied."

Initially, a geese icon is in a variables box below the story problem box. The student uses a mouse to click on the geese icon and drag it to either the independent groups box or the repeated measures box. If the icon is dropped in the correct box, the score is increased by 10 points; if the icon is dropped in the incorrect box, the score is decreased by 3 points and a buzzer sounds. The scoring system gives more points for a correct answer than are subtracted for an incorrect one, to put more emphasis on rewarding correct answers than on punishing incorrect ones. When finished, the student clicks on the Done button to advance to the next screen.

The student moves the icons on the next screen to their appropriate locations in the source table. Using the geese example, there is an icon for the geese, the error term, and the total term of a one-way ANOVA. There are also three blank source boxes. The student drags the three icons to the appropriate source boxes. The score is updated again if the student has correctly placed the icons.

The second screen assists students in determining the correct design. For example, the one-way ANOVA has three icons that are to be dropped in three locations, so the student does not have to figure out how many terms a one-way ANOVA has. Although this structure may be helpful pedagogically, further written assignments could be given to ensure that students can determine correct ANOVA designs without such clues.

The last screen requires the student to indicate the correct degrees of freedom for the design by dragging number icons to their appropriate location in degrees of freedom boxes. The source values are always the correct ones; that is, students' mistakes on the previous screen do not appear on the current screen. For this screen, unlike the previous screen, there are distracter icons, so that the correct degrees of freedom cannot be determined solely by process of elimination.

For the one-way design, the three icons for the source and degrees of freedom fit on the screen easily. For more complex designs, there are more entries for the source and degrees of freedom columns. The icons appear full size in the box under the story problem, but they shrink when the student clicks on them. The one-way design presents static graphic images. Other designs present brief cartoon animations (e.g., a man walking) or video (e.g., a quantitative psychologist being metamorphosed into a cat).

System Requirements

The program was written and successfully executed under Windows 3.1 on a Gateway 2000 4DX2-66V computer. (The relevant specifications include an Intel 486 processor, 16MB RAM, 424MB hard disk, 2X CD-ROM, and a 2MB graphics card.) Given the number of possible configurations of RAM, spin speed of CD-ROM, and size of graphics cards, it was not feasible to evaluate minimal configurations for the program. Because the ANOVA MultiMedia program is more than 40MB, it is only portable via CD-ROM.

Program Use

Students reviewing for their doctoral comprehensive exams and students in a graduate-level quantitative psychology course have used the program, and their informal evaluation has been very positive. The program is intended for individual or small-group use, but it could be used in a lecture format if it were projected to a large screen or presented via television monitor over a computer to television link. Students have taken about 1 hr to complete the program, although the time will vary greatly depending on a student's knowledge of ANOVA.

Availability

The program is available free of charge. A processing fee payable to the author's Psychology Department to cover the cost of producing the CD-ROM and a signed registration agreement are required. The cost of the CD-ROM will depend on the number of requests for the software. If few requests are made, they will be provided via in-house CD-ROM duplication at a higher cost (about $100 to $150). If many requests are made, the CD-ROM can be mass-produced by creating a single glass master at a cost of about $1,000 and a per disk price of about $2.00. Orders will be held for several months to determine which method will be used. For more information, write to the author.

Copyright Information

Reference

AimTech Corporation. (1993). *IconAuthor* [Computer program]. Nashua, NH: Author. (Available from AimTech Corporation, 20 Trafalgar Square, Nashua, NH 03063)

One-Way Between Subjects Design: Simulated Data and Analysis Using SAS

John F. Walsh
Fordham University

In teaching a course in statistics and experimental design, I find that giving students realistic data sets facilitates the integration of statistical analysis and interpretation. Providing each student with unique data is a further instructional refinement, but computing solutions for each individual set is burdensome. The program, CLSSANOV, written in BASE SAS, Version 6.07 (SAS Institute, 1990), creates data and computes answers.

The goal of enhancing statistical instruction by using simulated data sets can be achieved with other software packages, such as SYSTAT (Wilkinson, 1990) and SPSS-X (SPSS, 1988). A modest level of familiarity with any of the standard statistical software packages is adequate for implementing the capabilities of the program. Programming the simulation in BASE SAS was direct because of the flexibility of the language and the ease of using SAS statistical procedures.

The one-way design is a manageable context for introducing students to contrasts, post hoc tests, and trend analysis. Obtaining simulated data for more complex designs, such as covariance, factorial, and repeated measures, is described by Walsh (1992). These designs were programmed using FORTRAN and several proprietary subroutines from the International Mathematical and Statistical Library (IMSL, 1989).

Table 1 lists the SAS program that produces individual ASCII data sets and a summary table for the one-way analysis of variance design for each discrete data set. A student's name appears on the data set and on the summary table, facilitating the correction and assessment of a student's work.

As shown in Table 1, the program generates 35 different data sets. Names of the students are stored in a separate file, names.doc, which is read as the first executable statement in the program. The program in Table 1 generates data for an experiment with five levels and 10 subjects per level. The instructor sets the number of levels of the independent variable (IV), the number of subjects in each group, and the means and standard deviations for each level. The instructor can also craft problems involving heterogeneity of variance.

The numerical specifications that shape the designs are entered using the CARDS specification and are processed as part of the program. The three lines of data, following the CARDS statement in Table 1, specify the parameters of the program that produces the data. The data are entered in list format, which requires a blank space between each value. Line 1 gives the number of students in the class (35 in this example) and the number of subjects in each group of the analysis (10 in this instance). The next two input lines are the values for the means of the five groups and their standard deviations. The SAS function RANNOR produces $N(0,1)$ values that are rescaled according to the values given in Lines 2 and 3 following the CARDS statement. The initial seed for the random number generator arises from the computer's clock. Data for different problems are generated by modifying the last two lines following the CARDS statement (i.e., the values for the means and standard deviations).

Changing the number of values of the IV requires altering several lines in the program. Comment statements in the program identify these lines. Table 2 illustrates the changes to simulate a design having eight levels of the IV with 15 subjects per group, 60 students in the class, and unequal standard deviations. The instructor makes the modifications listed in Table 2 using the editor supplied with the computer system or with a word-processing program in which the file is saved as a text or ASCII file.

On the VAX computer system at Fordham University, each student copies the computer file from the Course Directory to his or her individual directory of files. Then students print the contents of the file. Because the data file is written in ASCII, it can be read by any statistical software package that reads external files. The data file can be written to a diskette and analyzed on a personal computer. Alternatively, using the printed listing, students can perform analyses with calculators.

A description of an experiment prepared by the instructor accompanies the data set given to each student. Students are asked to test and interpret several hypotheses. One example concerns a drug study involving depressed pa-

Table 1. Listing of SAS Program

```
* student names are in the file names.doc.;
* solutions are in the file anova.dat;
filename in 'names.doc';
filename out 'anova.dat';
data anova;
if _n_=1 then do;
infile in;
* names are in list format and have a length of 8;
* change 35 to whatever number of students you have;
length names1-names35 $ 8;
input names1-names35 $;
end;
else;
infile cards n=3;
length name $ 8.;
* nc=number of copies (students) ns=number of subjects;
* m1-m5 represent the means of the levels;
* s1-s5 represent the sds of the levels;
input nc ns / m1-m5 /s1-s5;
file out;
* modify to the number of levels being used.
array sx{5} s1-s5;
array mx{5} m1-m5;
* change to the number of students in the class;
array nx{35} names1-names35;
do id=1 to nc;
put nx{id};
* assignment statement creates name as a variable;
name=nx{id};
* modify to the number of levels being used;
do iv=1 to 5;
do j=1 to ns;
dv=mx{iv} + int(sx{iv}*rannor(0));
output;
* modify to fit the size of the output values
put iv 1. +1 j 2. +1 dv 2.;
end;
end;
end;
keep name id j iv dv;
CARDS;
35 10
50 54 57 52 53
5 5 5 5 5
;
* sorting by name permits the analysis to be done;
* in layers;
proc sort data-anova;
by name;
proc glm data=anova;
class iv;
model dv=iv;
* #byvar permits the student name to be added;
title 'data set for #byvar(name)';
by name;
* insert statements reflecting questions asked;
means iv / tukey cldiff;
contrast 'ques a' iv 4 -1 -1 -1 -1;
contrast 'ques b' iv 0 -1 -1  1  1;
contrast 'ques c' iv -2 -1 0 1 -2;
run;
```

Table 2. Listing of Program Lines for Design Modification

```
length names1-names60 $ 8;
input names1-names60 $;
input nc ns /m1-m8 /s1-s8;
array sx{8} s1-s8;
array mx{8} m1-m8;
array nx{60} names1-names60;
do iv =1 to 8;
CARDS;
60 15
90 94 98 100 102 106 108 110
10 12 12 16 16 12 12 10
;
```

tive? Is there a difference between lower and higher dosage levels? Is there a trend for performance to improve as the dosage level increases? These hypotheses are evaluated by contrast statements. In addition, students are asked to compute a post hoc pairwise test if the global hypothesis of no difference among the set of means is rejected.

Class discussion of comparisons among means includes the Bonferroni, Newman-Keuls, Scheffé, and Tukey procedures. In Table 1, the Tukey test is used, but SAS supports a range of simultaneous and stage post hoc pairwise techniques. Replacement of the Tukey approach by one of the other supported methods is direct. Using an editor, the instructor simply substitutes the name of the selected test for Tukey in the program listing.

The written report provides the opportunity to integrate concepts from statistics and experimental design. Students develop an introduction from the literature that enables them to interpret and discuss their results.

Because this course precedes the experimental laboratory courses in our curriculum at Fordham University, writing a report allows students to begin to learn APA format. Feedback from students indicates that the simulation experience provides skills that are helpful in the experimental laboratory courses.

References

IMSL, Inc. (1989). *International mathematical and statistical library* (3rd ed.). Houston. TX: Author.

SAS Institute, Inc. (1990). *SAS language* (Version 6). Cary, NC: Author.

SPSS, Inc. (1988). *SPSS-X user's guide* (3rd ed.). Chicago: Author.

Walsh, J. F. (1992). Multivariate normal data: A tool for instruction. *Teaching of Psychology, 19,* 188–189.

Wilkinson, L. (1990). *SYSTAT: A system for statistics* (Version 5). Evanston, IL: SYSTAT, Inc.

tients. The experiment has five levels: placebo and four active equally spaced dosage levels of a drug. The assignment requires students to test the global hypothesis of equal means and to evaluate three hypotheses: Is the drug effec-

ANOVAGEN: A Data Generation and Analysis of Variance Program for Use in Statistics Courses

Leslie J. Cake
Roy C. Hostetter
Sir Wilfred Grenfell College
Memorial University of Newfoundland

In many statistics courses, students analyze a common set of data. From an instructor's viewpoint, common data sets are easier to construct and mark. A disadvantage is that common data sets may encourage students to focus on obtaining the same statistical values and interpretations (possibly by copying) rather than concentrating on the principles and methods of analyses. Furthermore, common data sets may fail to provide students with a feeling for the variable nature of repeated sampling from a common population—a basic reason for the existence of statistical procedures.

To overcome these difficulties, we (Cake & Hostetter, 1986) devised DATAGEN, a computer program that creates unique student assignments by generating sets of independent or correlated data from population parameters specified by the instructor. DATAGEN also provides the instructor with intermediate quantities and with descriptive and inferential statistics for grading each student's assignment. In this article, we describe an extension of these basic ideas to a similar program. ANOVAGEN is a BASIC program that generates and analyzes unique data for student assignments involving analysis of variance (ANOVA).

Program Description and Use

Before using ANOVAGEN for the first time, the instructor runs a program (CREFILE.bas) that creates a file containing students' names. Alternatively, the instructor may construct this file using an ASCII text editor.

ANOVAGEN presents a menu offering the instructor the choice of generating unique data sets for one of the following six designs:

1. One-factor between
2. Two-factor between
3. Three-factor between
4. One-factor within
5. Two-factor within
6. Two-factor mixed (one between, one within).

The program indicates how the factors should be described in terms of layers, rows, and columns (after Ferguson & Takane, 1989), whether the factors are assumed to be fixed or random, and the appropriate error terms for the factors to be tested.

The instructor then provides an optional title for the assignment, the number of levels for each factor, optional labels for the levels, and means and standard deviations for each level of each factor. This latter stage is critical because a careful choice of means and standard deviations determines the presence or absence of significant main effects and interactions. To obtain significant differences for simple main effects, the instructor can specify large mean differences or small standard deviations (or both) for the critical conditions. To obtain significant interaction effects, appropriate means and standard deviations should be chosen. The instructor can preview, on-screen, the kinds of data samples and ANOVAs that will be generated by choosing the no-printer option. Following the input, the entered information is presented for verification and possible correction. The instructor may also provide text, such as an experimental description and assignment questions, to accompany the data of each student. Table 1 presents a sample instructor input for a one-factor within design.

After instructor input, the program generates and analyzes unique data for each student using the same algorithms for data generation used in DATAGEN (Cake & Hostetter, 1986). Briefly, the central limit theorem is used to obtain normally distributed random numbers from a population with $M = 0$ and $SD = 1$ (for a detailed description of the algorithm, see Hansen, 1985).

For between-subject factors, the data points for each experimental condition are then calculated using the formula:

$$\text{data point} = \text{input mean} + (\text{input standard deviation} \times \text{random number})$$

34

Table 1. Sample Instructor Input for a One-Factor, Within-Subject Design

[The design options are presented followed by a description of how the factors are described and associated assumptions.][a]
"For the 1-FACTOR WITHIN, the WITHIN factor corresponds to COLUMNS, and the Subjects factor corresponds to ROWS.
It is assumed that the Within Factor is fixed and that the Subjects Factor is random (see Ferguson & Takane, 1989, p. 349).
This means that the Subjects factor is not tested and that the correct error term for the WITHIN factor is the Interaction term.
Enter number of rows (Ss)? 20
Enter number of columns (Within factor)? 3"[b]

LABELS
[An optional label assignment can be provided along with labels for the columns (e.g., 0 mg, 25 mg, and 50 mg for the present example).]

ENTER MEANS AND STANDARD DEVIATIONS
[Means and standard deviations are provided for each of the experimental conditions—see below.]
"Correlation for within factor? .7"

Condition	"VERIFY INPUT INFORMATION"		
	n	M	SD
0 mg	20	60	10
25 mg	20	55	10
50 mg	20	50	10

Input correlation = .70
"Check above information and verify. Are above values o.k.—yes or no? yes"

"DESCRIPTIVE TEXT OPTION"
[An experimental description may be provided—see Table 2]

[a] A summary of input is provided in square brackets.
[b] Material within quotation marks appears verbatim.

For within-subject factors, the program generates an initial data point for each subject as just mentioned and calculates each subsequent correlated score using a second random number, the standard error, and the standard prediction equation (see Cake & Hostetter, 1986, for a detailed description). This procedure is represented in the following formula:

$$\text{data point} = \text{predicted score} + (\text{standard error of estimate} \times \text{random number})$$

The resulting association between scores approximates the input correlation value. For both types of factors, the student data for the specified conditions will approximate random samples drawn from populations with the parameters set by the instructor.

The program prints the descriptive text, the student's name, the assignment title, the input text, the labels for the conditions, and the data on a separate page for each student. Table 2 presents a sample output for a one-factor within design for one student.

On a separate page, the program prints various calculations and statistics for that student's data for use in grading. ANOVAGEN prints the total, total squared, sample size,

and mean for various quantities necessary for calculation of the ANOVA. In addition, other printed quantities include $\Sigma\Sigma X$, $(\Sigma\Sigma X)^2$, N, the grand mean, $(\Sigma\Sigma X)^2/N$, and $\Sigma\Sigma X^2$. Finally, the program provides an ANOVA summary table for that student's data. The Appendix presents a sample of instructor's output for the student's data of Table 2.

ANOVAGEN continues to generate and analyze data automatically for all students. In this way, students are provided with their own data, and the instructor is provided with various calculations and an ANOVA for each student. ANOVAGEN also prints the input values and the descriptive text for the instructor's use.

General Comments on Program Use

We have used ANOVAGEN for 2 years with undergraduate statistics classes and noticed several pedagogical benefits for instructors and students. The first advantage to instructors is the relative ease of preparing and grading assignments containing unique data. In preparing an as-

Table 2. Sample Student Output for a One-Factor, Within-Subject Design

Effect of alcohol on typing speed. [Optional Assignment Label]
Data for Leslie Cake:
An experimenter is interested in the effect of alcohol on skilled performance. Twenty skilled typists each receive 3 dosages of alcohol (0 mg placebo control, 25 mg, and 50 mg per 100 ml blood) on three test days. The dosages are presented in a randomized order for each subject with two days separating the administration of each dosage. Thirty minutes after administration of the dosage, typing speed was measured (in words per minute) using a standard typing test. These data are presented below. Calculate the mean and standard deviation for each condition. Calculate the appropriate ANOVA. What would you conclude about the effect that alcohol has on typing speed in particular and skilled performance in general?

	0 mg	25 mg	50 mg
S 1	49	48	35
S 2	60	52	53
S 3	60	56	50
S 4	68	54	47
S 5	66	65	57
S 6	68	66	62
S 7	61	54	56
S 8	62	53	48
S 9	64	51	49
S 10	67	67	58
S 11	58	59	40
S 12	63	41	51
S 13	40	29	37
S 14	77	72	56
S 15	59	56	51
S 16	68	80	42
S 17	59	55	44
S 18	52	43	44
S 19	64	55	50
S 20	86	77	76

signment the instructor can use the preview facility to fine-tune the kind of results that will be obtained in terms of significant and nonsignificant effects. When grading, the instructor need not repeatedly calculate tedious analyses for each student's data. Furthermore, the various quantities and ANOVA provided by the program facilitate the detection of the exact source of student errors during grading.

A second advantage for the instructor is the possibility of demonstrating various statistical concepts related to the ANOVA. For example, an instructor can demonstrate the importance of variability by providing each student with two data sets with similar means but different variances, resulting in significant and nonsignificant main effects. The concept of interaction can be illustrated by providing each student with two data sets; one set will result in a significant interaction and the other set will result in a nonsignificant interaction. Students can be asked to identify why an interaction does and does not occur. Finally, an instructor can demonstrate the increased sensitivity of within-subject designs as compared to between-subject designs by providing students with two data sets containing similar means and variances for the experimental conditions. Careful choice of means and variance can result in a significant effect occurring in the within-subject case but not in the between-subject case.

For the instructor, using ANOVAGEN can be more time consuming than assigning standard, common exercises from a textbook. This extra effort is offset by students achieving an improved understanding of and facility with the ANOVA.

Students' must perform their calculations independently, although they may collaborate on correct calculational procedures and other aspects of ANOVA. Use of ANOVAGEN appears to improve students' comprehension of the fundamental principles and concepts of ANOVA.

Other Uses of ANOVAGEN

Other possible uses of ANOVAGEN include using the program in courses other than statistics. For example, an instructor of introductory psychology can generate and analyze simulated data in class to introduce students to statistics. An instructor can use ANOVAGEN to present students with simulated data for research methods courses and for laboratory projects, thereby eliminating the time required to collect data. The program can provide common data for examinations, and the instructor can derive a grading key from the output. Finally, slight modification of the program allows ANOVAs to be calculated for actual experimental data.

Concluding Comments

Programs similar to ANOVAGEN exist. For example, DATASIM is a powerful statistical software package that generates and analyses simulated data for assignments and has a number of other uses (Bradley, 1989). However, we believe that ANOVAGEN provides some unique advantages for instructors who are looking for a basic software package for beginning statistics courses. First, the program is simple to use (no manual is required). Second, by providing intermediate values such as $\Sigma\Sigma X$ and $\Sigma\Sigma X^2$, ANOVAGEN permits the isolation of the exact source of the student error and is, therefore, a very useful tool for instruction and grading. Finally, we offer copies of ANOVAGEN free to interested instructors on request.

References

Bradley, D. R. (1989). Computer simulation with DATA-SIM. *Behavior Research Methods, Instruments, & Computers, 21,* 99–112.

Cake, L. J., & Hostetter, R. C. (1986). DATAGEN: A BASIC program for generating and analyzing data for use in statistics courses. *Teaching of Psychology, 13,* 210–212.

Ferguson, G. A., & Takane, Y. (1989). *Statistical analysis in psychology and education* (6th ed.). New York: McGraw-Hill.

Hansen, A. G. (1985, October). Simulating the normal distribution. *Byte,* pp. 137–138.

Notes

1. The ANOVAGEN program was written in standard Microsoft BASIC and can be used on IBM and compatible microcomputers running either GW-BASIC or BASICA.
2. We thank Daniel Stewart for helpful comments on the program, Patricia O'Toole foe editorial assistance, and Sharon Watton for program testing.
3. Leslie J. Cake thanks the Cave Hill campus of the University of the West Indies for providing space and facilities during the preparation of part of this article.

Data for Leslie Cake:
PRINTING TOTALS, TOTALS², SAMPLE SIZES, AND MEANS
Rows correspond to Subjects.
Columns is a Within Factor.
Conditions are: 0 mg, 25 mg, 50 mg

Source	Total	Totals²	n	M
S 1	132	17424	3	44
S 2	165	27225	3	55
S 3	166	27556	3	55.33
S 4	169	28561	3	56.33
S 5	188	35344	3	62.67
S 6	196	38416	3	65.33
S 7	171	29241	3	57
S 8	163	26569	3	54.33
S 9	164	26896	3	54.67
S 10	192	36864	3	64
S 11	157	24649	3	52.33
S 12	155	24025	3	51.67
S 13	106	11236	3	35.33
S 14	205	42025	3	68.33
S 15	166	27556	3	55.33
S 16	190	36100	3	63.33
S 17	158	24964	3	52.67
S 18	139	19321	3	46.33
S 19	169	28561	3	56.33
S 20	239	57121	3	79.67

Σ (Subj. Totals²) = 589654
Σ (Subj. Totals²) $\times$ (1/3) = 196551.4

(continued)

Source	Total	Totals²	n	M
0 mg	1251	1565001	20	62.55
25 mg	1133	1283689	20	56.65
50 mg	1006	1012036	20	50.30

Σ (Column Totals²) = 3860726
Σ (Column Totals²) $\times$ (1/20) = 193036.3

Grand Total = 3390   Grand Total² = 1.14921E + 07
Total N = 60
Grand Mean = 56.5   Grand Total²/Total N = 191535
Σ (individual $\times$ values²) = 199266

Source	ANOVA Summary Table			
	SS	df	MS	F
Rows (Ss)	5016.344	19	264.018	
Columns	1501.297	2	750.648	23.50844
Ss × Columns (Error term)	1213.359	38	31.9310	
Total	7731	59		

Using Summary Statistics as Data in ANOVA: A SYSTAT Macro

John F. Walsh
Fordham University

In a variety of instructional and research settings, the only data available to the reader about an experiment are the summary descriptive measures—the number of subjects in the treatments and the treatment means and standard deviations. From these descriptive measures, it is impossible for the reader to make inferential statements about differences among the conditions of the experiment.

A technique is available that generates data from the descriptive measures sufficient to compute an ANOVA (Fisher, 1951). In implementing this technique on a computer, the software needs to support two options: an option to weigh cases within its ANOVA routine and the capability to write cases or records to an internal file. The SYSTAT program (SYSTAT, 1990) for the microcomputer and the SAS system (SAS Institute, 1985) for the mainframe can implement the technique.

For each line of summary data that describes a condition in the experiment, two pseudo data points, x1 and x2 with weights are developed (Larson & Wartenberg. 1991). Specifically, the relationships, x1 = mean (x) + sqrt (var(x)/n) and x2 = n* mean(x) – (n – 1) *x1, are used. The derivation of the two relations is included in Larson and Wartenberg (1991). The technique handles both equal and unequal group sample sizes. Use of the procedure assumes that the researcher has determined that the data can be analyzed appropriately by ANOVA.

From a processing perspective, the task is to generate the two appropriate pseudo records or cases from each record of the inputted data values and then perform an ANOVA using a software package. In this article, I illustrate the SYSTAT (SYSTAT, 1990) technique, a widely used statistical software package for microcomputers (Fridlund, 1990). SYSTAT has extensive routines for analyzing ANOVA designs. Also, most student applications will probably be implemented at this level.

Within SYSTAT, the input data file containing the summary measures is read within the macro module, and additional data lines are generated and written to a new SYSTAT data file. This new file is analyzed by the MGLH module. MGLH is the name of the SYSTAT routine that analyzes multivariate and univariate linear statistical models.

The macro code appears in Table 1 and is contained in the batch command file, ANOVA.CMD. A *batch command file* is a file that contains all the instructions to be executed by the operating system. It is used in lieu of the user typing the individual commands on a terminal. SYSTAT denotes command files with the three-letter extension CMD. The command file is an ASCII text file that can be written with any word processor. Statements on Lines 50 and 120 produce the values used in the computation.

To illustrate the procedure for a completely randomized design, data from Kirk (1982, p. 140) are used. Table 2 lists the summary input values that are stored in a SYSTAT file,

Table 1. Code for the Macro ANOVA.CMD

```
10 %read
20 %let x1=0
30 %let y=0
40 %let freq=0
50 %let x1=xbar + %sqr(std*2/n)
60 %let y=x1
70 %let freq=n−1
80 %write
90 %let x2=0
100 %let y=0
110 %let freq=0
120 %let x2=n*xbar −(n−1)*x1
130 %let y=x2
140 %let freq=1
150 %write
160 %if eof then %goto 180
170 %goto 10
180 %stop
```

Table 2. Summary Input Data for a One-Way ANOVA

Group	n	M	SD
1	8	2.75	1.48
2	8	3.50	.9258
3	8	6.25	1.0351
4	8	9.00	1.3093

Note. These data are from *Experimental Design: Procedures for the Behavioral Sciences* (2nd ed., p. 140) by R. Kirk, 1982, Belmont, CA: Wadsworth. Copyright 1982 by Brooks/Cole. Adapted by permission.

Table 3. Commands to Produce the ANOVA From Summary Input Data

```
(From within the macro module)
use anova (SYSTAT file containing the input data)
save anovax
submit anova (text file containing the macro instructions)
run
new
MGLH
use anovax
category group (use variable name for group(s))
anova y (pseudo variable created in the macro)
weight freq
estimate
Analysis of Variance
```

SOURCE	SUM-OF-SQUARES	DF	MEAN SQUARE	F
GROUP	194.500	3	64.833	44.458
ERROR	40.832	28	1.458	

ANOVA.SYS, and read by the macro. The names used with the SYSTAT editor were group, n, xbar, and std. These are the variable names used in the macro. Table 3 displays the complete sequence of commands to produce the ANOVA table from the input data.

To summarize, the input data—group designation, group sample size, mean, and standard deviation—are placed into a SYSTAT file, ANOVA.SYS, using SYSTAT's edit module. This file is read from within the macro module by the file, ANOVA.CMD, which generates and writes to a save file, ANOVAX.SYS, the two pseudo data points and weights for each line of input data. The MGLH module analyzes the values in the file ANOVAX.SYS to produce an ANOVA. The procedure—generation of pseudo data points and weights and macro implementation—can be used to read and analyze summary cell data for factorial designs as well.

The macro procedure should be a valuable tool to students and researchers who want to explore additional relations among the results of published studies when the raw data are not available. For example, after computing the summary ANOVA, students can formulate new hypotheses among the treatment means and test them using contrast statements or other analytic procedures.

I have used the technique in an ANOVA classroom exercise to illustrate the interrelations among the concepts involved in computing power for an experiment. Students design an experiment in a content area of their choosing. They specify the summary information (i.e., number of subjects and treatment means and standard deviations) that should produce an experimental design having power of .80. Emphasis is placed on using independent and dependent variables that have a basis in the literature and should have some external validity. In providing summary information, the student needs to consider the interrelations among the concepts of effect size, variability, and sample size. I have found it useful to explore the relations among these concepts iteratively. For example, if effect size and power are fixed, then various combinations of sample size and variability can be investigated by the student. Because decisions about effect size and variability are grounded in literature-based independent and dependent variables, students develop a realistic appreciation of the trade-offs involved. In particular, implications of the small to modest effects usually found in psychology on sample sizes are strongly conveyed.

References

Fisher, R. A. (1951). *The design of experiments* (6th ed.). Edinburgh: Oliver & Boyd.

Fridlund, A. J. (1990, December 24). SYSTAT 5.0: A review. *Info World*, pp. 46–47.

Larson, D., & Wartenberg, C. (1991). Using the ANOVA procedure with summary statistics as input. *Proceedings of the 16th annual SAS Users Group International.* Cary, NC: SAS Institute, Inc.

Kirk, R. (1982). *Experimental design: Procedures for the behavioral sciences* (2nd ed.). Belmont, CA: Wadsworth.

SAS Institute, Inc. (1985). *SAS user's guide: Basics, Version 5 Edition.* Cary, NC: Author.

SYSTAT, Inc. (1990). *SYSTAT version 5.01.* Evanston, IL: Author.

A Computer Program That Demonstrates the Difference Between Main Effects and Interactions

Michael J. Strube
Miriam D. Goldstein
Washington University

The distinction between main effects and interactions is crucial to understanding the advantages of factorial designs (e.g., Cozby, 1993; Elmes, Kantowitz, & Roediger, 1992; Leary, 1991; Neale & Liebert, 1986). Accordingly, instruction in the distinction between main effects and interactions is an important part of most undergraduate research methods courses. Although most students can grasp the basic "it depends" interpretation of interactions, the deeper understanding required for interpreting research results is often lacking, particularly the ability to identify main effects and interactions from graphical displays. We have found that this understanding is facilitated by having students construct data patterns that contain different combinations of main effects and interactions. We have developed an interactive computer program that guides students through a series of data-construction problems that highlight the graphical representation of different combinations of main effects and interactions. The program runs with minimum supervision but should be preceded by a traditional unit on factorial designs, including definitions of main effects and interactions. Understanding of basic statistical inference (e.g., statistical significance, Type I and Type II errors) is also assumed and may need to be reviewed if students are to benefit optimally from the analysis of variance (ANOVA) component of the program.

Program Description

The program, written in QuickBASIC, first presents a brief overview of main effects and interactions. Examples highlight the basic meaning of the two types of effects. Next, the program describes the problem format (i.e., a 2 × 2 design) and explains how data patterns are constructed. Data patterns are generated by changing the height of four bars in a bar graph. Levels of Factor A are represented by two pairs of bars on the right and left sides of the graph; levels of Factor B are represented by different colored bars within each pair. Pressing the U and D keys allows the student to change the height (up or down) of the current bar. Pressing the R and L keys allows the student to move to the next bar to the right or left. When the bar heights are in the desired position, pressing the Enter key causes the program to generate a simulated data set ($N = 80$) based on the data pattern. An ANOVA is conducted, and the results are presented next to the graph. The ANOVA part of the program reminds students of the importance of sample size, effect size, and Type I and Type II errors. The constructed data pattern represents the population from which the sample data are generated; the sample results will deviate from the population expectations in the expected random ways. For example, a correct pattern of means may not produce the desired pattern of significance due to small sample size (Type II errors). This result can occur if the constructed pattern of means correctly represents the desired effects, but the constructed differences are quite small so that random variability obscures them. Likewise, an incorrect pattern of means can produce the desired pattern of significance due to Type I errors. This outcome can occur if a null effect is correctly constructed, but the generation of the data set produces a non-null result by chance.

A practice problem follows the instructions and allows the student to become familiar with the use of the direction keys. The program then guides the student through eight data-construction problems that represent all possible configurations of effects in the 2×2 design: (a) no significant effects, (b) significant A main effect, (c) significant B main effect, (d) significant A and B main effects, (e) significant $A \times B$ interaction, (f) significant A main effect and $A \times B$ interaction, (g) significant B main effect and $A \times B$ interaction, and (h) all effects significant. Each problem begins with instructions for the effect(s) to be produced (e.g., "Design an outcome pattern that contains a Gender [Factor A] main effect and a Gender $\times$ Age [Factor A $\times$ Factor B] interaction but not an Age [Factor B] main effect"). Following the student-generated pattern, the program provides feedback that is sensitive to the pattern of means in relation to the obtained pattern of significance. If the student-generated pattern of means is incorrect, the program provides tailored feedback designed to guide the student to the correct solution. If an unwanted effect is significant, the program describes how to eliminate that effect. If a desired effect is not significant, the program indicates how to create it. When the correct pattern of means is generated but the effect magnitude is not sufficient to produce a correct pattern of significance (i.e., a Type II error has been made), the program indicates that the pattern of means is correct but that the effects need to be enhanced. Correct patterns of significance that represent Type I errors are also identified. After three unsuccessful trials, the program provides an ideal example that fits the desired pattern. The ideal pattern also is shown following correct performance to reinforce the pattern and to demonstrate that more than one data pattern is acceptable. The program concludes with a simple self-test, with feedback, on the basic principles for interpreting main effects and interactions. No additional construction problems are presented as part of this self-test, but the program can be repeated for additional practice.

Hardware Requirements

The graphic display created by the program requires 640 $\times$ 350 pixel resolution (enhanced resolution graphics). The program, written in QuickBASIC, requires 32K of memory. Program response to user key presses for graph construction is instantaneous. Generation of each simulated data set takes less than 1 s on a 33MHz 80486DX IBM-compatible computer. Slightly slower generation times can be expected on 80286 and 80386 machines.

Program Availability

A listing of the program (682 lines) will be sent on request. Alternatively, a copy of the program is available upon receipt of a property formatted disk and self-addressed, stamped mailer.

References

Coky, P. C. (1993). *Methods in behavioral research* (5th ed.). Mountain View, CA: Mayfield.

Elmes, D. G., Kantowitz, B. H., & Roediger, H. L., III. (1992). *Research methods in psychology* (4th ed.). New York: West.

Leary, M. R. (1991). *Introduction to behavioral research methods.* Belmont, CA: Wadsworth.

Neale, J. M., & Liebert, R. M. (1986). *Science and behavior: An introduction to methods of research* (3rd ed.). Englewood Cliffs, NJ: Prentice Hall.

On Testing for Variance Effects

Jane L. Buck
Delaware State College

There are at least two reasons to test for differences between variances. The first, as almost all introductory statistics textbooks point out, is that homogeneity of variance within groups is an assumption of both the *t* test and the ANOVA (Runyon & Haber, 1988; Welkowitz, Ewen, & Cohen, 1988). When sample sizes are equal, both the test and the ANOVA are relatively robust with respect to minor violations of the assumption of homogeneity of variance. However, when sample sizes are unequal, neither the *t* test nor the ANOVA is necessarily robust. It is, therefore, prudent to test for heterogeneity of variance. A statistically significant difference between within-group variances indicates that the more heterogenous group has more extreme scores at the high and low ends of the distribution, which is evidence of a dual effect of the experimental treatment (Runyon & Haber, 1988). This finding might be worthy of further investigation, whether or not there is a statistically significant difference between means.

A second, less frequently mentioned reason to test for differences between variances is that a number of research problems lend themselves to planned comparisons of variances (Landauer, Harris, & Pocock, 1982; O'Brien, 1981). Landauer et al. (1982) cited data from questionnaires in which two groups of subjects were asked to judge the severity of 20 different criminal offenses. They pointed out that despite a total lack of significant differences between means, the variability of the two groups differed significantly in several instances. For example, subjects who had been convicted of driving under the influence of alcohol proposed a more variable list of penalties for speeding than did a control group; the control group was more variable with respect to proposed penalties for shoplifting and embezzlement.

Block, Efthim, and Burns (1989) stated that a major goal of teaching for mastery is the reduction of variability in achievement between slow and rapid learners. Reuman (1989) compared variances to test the hypothesis that student expectancies concerning mathematics achievement are more variable in heterogeneous than in homogeneous classrooms. He also used tests of variances to establish that the students used in his study were, in fact, different with respect to mathematics achievement.

Landauer et al. (1982) and O'Brien (1981) noted that many psychologists use tests for differences between means almost to the exclusion of tests for differences between variances. Both Landauer et al. (1982) and O'Brien (1981) suggested that variance tests are less intuitive and less robust than are tests for means. Nonetheless, several techniques that are robust with respect to the assumption of bivariate normality have been developed for testing differences in variability (Box, 1953; Brown & Forsythe, 1974; Cohen, 1986; Games, Winkler, & Probert, 1972; Miller, 1968; Sandvik & Olsson, 1982; Scheffé, 1959; Wilcox, 1989).

If Landauer et al. (1982) and O'Brien (1981) were correct in asserting that psychologists tend to ignore variance tests, psychology students are unlikely to encounter frequent mention of these tests in the literature. Also, teachers of psychological statistics are unlikely to emphasize them, particularly if statistics textbooks reflect a relative lack of concern with tests of differences between variances.

Survey of Statistics Textbooks

I examined a nonrandom, accidental sample of 18 statistics textbooks published after 1980. All books included in the sample were publishers' review copies. The frequency distribution of publication years was: 1989—4, 1988—7, 1986—3, 1985—1, 1983—1, 1982—2, and 1981—1.

Only 5 of the 18 textbooks (Comrey, Bott, & Lee, 1989; Ferguson & Takane, 1989; Hinkle, Wiersma, & Jurs, 1988; Mansfield, 1986; Runyon & Haber, 1988) include material on performing variance tests. Note that although all textbooks that include the topic were published after 1985, recency does not guarantee inclusion; 9 of the textbooks that do not include the topic were also published after 1985. In all cases, even when variance effects are discussed, only a few pages are devoted to the topic, compared to several chapters on tests of differences between means. If psychology students are to learn techniques for testing hypotheses about variances, they could use some help from the authors of their textbooks.

References

Block, J. H., Efthim, H. E., & Burns, R. B. (1989). *Building effective mastery learning schools.* New York: Longman.

Box, G. E. O. (1953). Nonnormality and tests on variances. *Biometrika, 40,* 318–335.

Brown, M. B., & Forsythe, A. B. (1974). Robust tests for the equality of variances. *Journal of the American Statistical Association, 69,* 364–367.

Cohen, A. (1986). Comparing variances of correlated variables. *Psychometrika, 51,* 379–391.

Comrey, A. L., Bott, P. A., & Lee, H. L. (1989). *Elementary statistics: A problem-solving approach* (2nd ed.). Dubuque, IA: Brown.

Ferguson, G. A., & Takane, Y. (1989). *Statistical analysis in psychology and education* (6th ed.). New York: McGraw-Hill.

Games, P. A., Winkler, H. R., & Probert, D. A. (1972). Robust tests for homogeneity of variance. *Educational and Psychological Measurement, 32,* 887–909.

Hinkle, D. E., Wiersma, W., & Jurs, S. (1988). *Applied statistics for the behavioral sciences* (2nd ed.). Boston: Houghton Mifflin.

Landauer, A. A., Harris, L. J., & Pocock, D. A. (1982). Intersubject variances as a measure of differences between groups. *International Review of Applied Psychology, 31,* 417–423.

Mansfield, E. (1986). *Basic statistics with applications.* New York: Norton.

Miller, R. G., Jr. (1968). Jackknifing variances. *Annals of Mathematical Statistics, 39,* 567–582.

O'Brien, R. G. (1981). A simple test for variance effects in experimental design. *Psychological Bulletin, 89,* 570–574.

Reuman, D. A. (1989). How social comparison mediates the relation between ability-grouping practices and students' achievement expectancies in mathematics. *Journal of Educational Psychology, 81,* 178–189.

Runyon, R. P., & Haber, A. (1988). *Fundamentals of behavioral statistics* (6th ed.). New York: Random House.

Sandvik, L., & Olsson, B. (1982). A nearly distribution-free test for comparing dispersion in paired samples. *Biometrika, 69,* 484–485.

Scheffé, H. A. (1959). *The analysis of variance.* New York: Wiley.

Welkowitz, J., Ewen, R. B., & Cohen, J. (1988). *Introductory statistics for the behavioral sciences* (Alternate 3rd ed.). New York: Academic.

Wilcox, R. R. (1989). Comparing the variances of dependent groups. *Psychometrika, 54,* 305–315.

Note

I thank Charles L. Brewer and three anonymous reviewers for their helpful comments on an earlier version of this article.

Demonstrating the Consequences of Violations of Assumptions in Between-Subjects Analysis of Variance

Roberto Refinetti
College of William & Mary

Most statistics textbooks for the behavioral sciences state that analysis of variance (ANOVA) has two basic assumptions about the underlying populations: These populations are normally distributed and have equal variances. Although introductory textbooks mention only that ANOVA is quite robust and can tolerate violations of the assumptions (e.g., Aron & Aron, 1994; Ott & Mendenhall, 1990; Weiss, 1993; Witte, 1993), more advanced textbooks explain alternative procedures to be used when the assumptions are seriously violated (e.g., Hays, 1988; Howell, 1992; Kirk, 1982; Maxwell & Delaney, 1990). Absent in textbooks is a demonstration of the consequences of violations. In my experience as a statistics teacher, the absence of such a demonstration leaves students with the impression that violation of assumptions is an esoteric matter that they should not even try to understand. Although the esoterism of this subject may have been true in the past, the evolution of personal computers has made it easy to produce classroom demonstrations of the consequences of violations of assumptions of statistical tests.

In this article, I show how a personal computer can be used to demonstrate the effects of non-normality and heterogeneity of variances on Type I error. For classes in which actual demonstrations are impossible, results reported herein can be used for illustration.

Method

The issue of Type I error can be regarded as a simple problem of sampling distribution. If a simple one-way (between-groups) ANOVA is used to analyze a large number of data sets of randomly selected numbers, the frequency distribution of empirical F values will approximate the probability density curve of the F statistic for the specified degrees of freedom. More precisely, the empirical distribution will approximate the theoretical distribution if the assumptions of the test are respected. Violations of the assumptions will impair the approximation. If the violations do not impair the approximation, then they are not serious violations, and the test is robust.

Procedure

All comparisons reported in this article are based on 1,000 trials using random samples from various populations. Each trial consisted of a one-way ANOVA for three groups with 10 subjects per group, unless otherwise noted. A short Quick Basic program calculated the F values and saved them to a disk file. It took less than 5 min to complete the analysis of each set of 1,000 trials (each with $n = 30$) on a personal computer running at 25MHz.

To test the assumption of normality, I generated six different populations. To generate a normally distributed population of 1 million subjects with a mean of 5 and variance of 1, I used a simple computer routine based on the normal probability density curve. For values of X from 1 to 9 in steps of 0.01, each value of Y was multiplied by 10,000. Figure 1 (top) shows the resulting distribution of values. To investigate the consequences of using a discrete variable, I generated another normally distributed population by using the same procedure in steps of 1.0 (Figure 1, middle). As an instance of a population clearly not normally distributed, I generated a binary population (Figure 1, bottom) to simulate variables of the nominal type (yes/no type). Three populations with uniform (flat) distributions were generated within the ANOVA program using the computer's random number generator. One population was continuous (real numbers with resolution of 0.01), one was discrete (integer

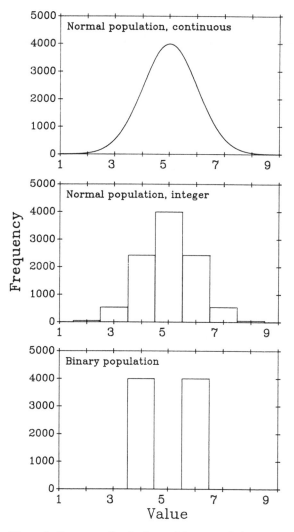

Figure 1. Frequency distributions of three populations used in this study.

numbers), and one was a simulation of ranked data (integer numbers from 1 to 30 without replacement).

To test the assumption of homogeneity of variances, random samples were collected from uniform populations with different variances generated within the ANOVA program. Three different ratios of standard deviations (*tau*) were tested: 1, 5, and 10. All populations in these tests had a uniform distribution with a mean of 5. Tests were conducted for groups of equal size ($n = 10$) or unequal size ($n_1 = 15$, $n_2 = 10$, and $n_3 = 5$).

Software and Hardware

Although I wrote the software specifically for this demonstration, it consisted merely of a calculation algorithm for ι between-subjects ANOVA repeated 1,000 times with υifferent data sets. Statistics teachers may use my software (available on request), write their own software, or prepare a batch file for commercially available statistical packages (e.g., SPSS, SAS, or BMDP). I also wrote my own software to prepare the frequency distributions of F values. Again, others may use my software, write their own, or use a commercially available spreadsheet program (e.g., Lotus, Quattro, or the spreadsheet section of statistical packages). For graphical presentation, I used the Sigmaplot program (Jandel Scientific, San Rafael, CA 94901), but most spreadsheet programs and statistical packages can produce adequate graphs.

Regarding hardware, I used a 486-based microcomputer running at 25 mHz. RAM and hard disk requirements are only those of the programs used for the demonstration. For my own software, there was no need for more than 640K of RAM or more than 10M of hard drive.

Results

The distributions of empirical F values for the normally distributed populations appear in Figure 2. Use of a population of integer numbers instead of real numbers did not seem to affect the distribution of empirical F values, except perhaps at F values below 1.0. Similarly, use of a uniformly distributed population (whether continuous, integer, or integer without replacement) did not substantially affect the distribution of empirical F values (Figure 3, top three panels). Contrarily, use of a binary population resulted in a very irregular distribution of F values (Figure 3, bottom), even though the right tail (which is used for tests of significance) was not drastically affected.

By calculating the cumulative frequency of F values from the right tail up to a total of 5, 10, 25, and 50 values, the cumulative probabilities of .005, .01, .025, and .05 can be estimated and compared to the critical F values found in standard tables (or computed by integration of the probability density curve). As shown in Figure 4 (top), the cumulative probabilities of empirical F values obtained from a normally distributed population closely matched those of theoretical F values. Ranked data (ordinal) and categorical data (binary) produced more variable results. For instance, in a test at the .005 level of significance for binary data, the actual probability of a Type I error would be .01. A much smaller error would occur at the .05 level of significance.

Also shown in Figure 4 (bottom) are results of the tests of homogeneity of variances for groups of the same size (n = 10). When all three groups had the same variance (tau = 1), the distribution of empirical F values closely approximated the distribution of theoretical F values. A good approximation was also obtained when one of the groups had a variance 5 times as large as the other groups (tau = 5) but not when the variances differed by a factor of 10 (tau = 10). For instance, in a test at the .016 level of significance for tau = 10, the actual probability of a Type I error would

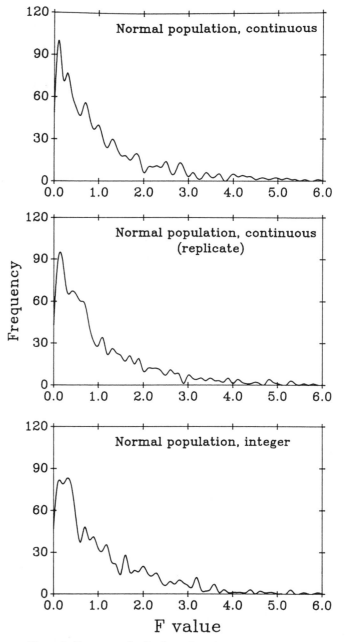

Figure 2. Frequency distributions of empirical F values for 1,000 ANOVAs using samples from three different normal populations.

be .025 (i.e., the F value of 4.83 had a probability of .025 rather than .016). Slightly larger errors were obtained when the groups differed in both size and variance (data not shown).

Discussion

Results are consistent with previous evaluations of the robustness of ANOVA in showing that violations of the assumptions of normality and homogeneity of variances have a measurable but small effect on the probability of Type I error when all groups are of the same size (Glass,

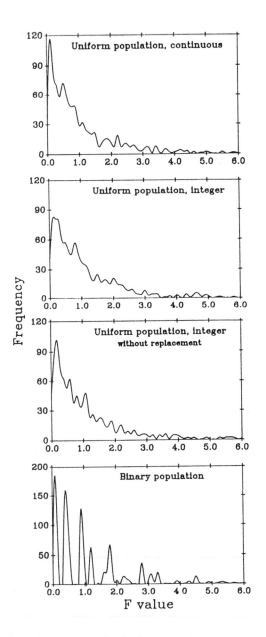

Figure 3. Frequency distributions of empirical F values for 1,000 ANOVAs using samples from four different non-normal populations.

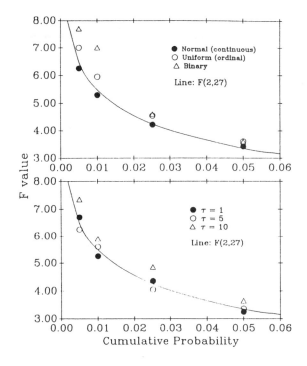

Figure 4. Empirical and theoretical F values for different cumulative probabilities. The top panel shows equal-variance samples with different distributions. The bottom panel shows unequal-variance samples with uniform distribuions. In both panels, the curved line corresponds to the probabilities associated with F values for 2 and 27 degrees of freedom, as found in tables of the F distribution.

tion would be calculated and their frequency distributions shown and discussed.

By experiencing firsthand the consequences of failure to meet the assumptions of ANOVA, students will obtain a deeper understanding of the subject. Also, the empirical construction of sampling distributions involved in this demonstration will provide students with empirical exposure to this concept that many psychology majors fail to grasp.

Peckham, & Sanders, 1972; Wilcox, 1993). Also in agreement with previous evaluations, my results indicate that heterogeneity of variances for groups of unequal size can have a significant effect on the probability of Type I error (in this study, the largest effect was a doubling of the probability). The fact that these empirical results can be obtained within a 50-min class is what makes them noteworthy. I recommend that the data sets be generated before the class and be analyzed in class following a procedure similar to that described in this article. I suggest that the frequency distribution of each data set be shown first. Then, the F values for 1,000 random samples from each popula-

References

Aron, A., & Aron, E. N. (1994). *Statistics for psychology.* Englewood Cliffs, NJ: Prentice Hall.

Glass, G. V., Peckham, P. D., & Sanders, J. R. (1972). Consequences of failure to meet assumptions underlying the analysis of variance and covariance. *Review of Educational Research, 42,* 237–288.

Hays, W. L. (1988). *Statistics* (4th ed.). New York: Holt, Rinehart & Winston.

Howell, D. C. (1992). *Statistical methods for psychology* (3rd ed.). Belmont, CA: Duxbury.

Kirk, R. E. (1982). *Experimental design: Procedures for the behavioral sciences.* Monterey, CA: Brooks/Cole.

Maxwell, S. E., & Delaney, H. D. (1990). *Designing experiments and analyzing data.* Belmont, CA: Wadsworth.

Ott, L., & Mendenhall, W. (1990). *Understanding statistics.* Boston: PWS-Kent.

Weiss, N. A. (1993). *Elementary statistics* (2nd ed.). Reading, MA: Addison-Wesley.

Wilcox, R. (1993). Robustness in ANOVA. In L. K. Edwards (Ed.), *Applied analysis of variance in behavioral science* (pp. 345–374). New York: Dekker.

Witte, R. S. (1993). *Statistics.* Fort Worth, TX: Harcourt Brace.

Understanding Correlations: Two Computer Exercises

Miriam D. Goldstein
Michael J. Strube
Washington University

The concept of *correlation* is one of the building blocks of science. We remind students that correlation does not prove causation, but we acknowledge that the first step in inferring causality is often the detection of a correlation.

When discussing correlations in our undergraduate research design course, we review factors that can affect the size of a correlation. We discuss issues such as truncated or restricted range, applying Pearson's correlation coefficient to curvilinear relations, group contamination, and the presence of outliers in the data. Lecturing is not the most effective way to convince our students of the importance of examining one's data in order to detect some of these factors; our students often lack the statistical background necessary for understanding these issues. To supplement and enhance students' understanding of correlations, we developed two computer programs that allow them a hands-on and "minds-on" experience with correlations, in the spirit of active learning (for a review of active-learning principles, see Mathie et al., 1993). Thus, for example, instead of informing students verbally that an outlier can increase, decrease, or have no effect on the size of the Pearson correlation coefficient, students are required to demonstrate the possible effects of outliers by manipulating a data set.

The computer programs described in this article display the relation between two variables. Moreover, the programs allow students to manipulate this relation and thus explore the effects of some of the problems involved in correlational research on the estimated index of the relation. We designed the programs to provide the two components of good instruction, as identified by Skinner (1989); students receive immediate feedback about their performance, and they receive clear directions about the steps required for task completion.

Program Description

We developed two programs that provide students direct experience with correlations. The first program displays nine randomly generated correlation plots. Each plot contains 20 data points. The correlations in each plot are randomly generated within a given range of correlations; the exact range can be easily modified. Thus, each set of nine correlations will vary. This variation allows for a degree of control over the type and variety of correlations that students encounter, but it does not introduce memory problems over repeated practice. Because the scatterplots do not represent fixed correlations, students cannot simply memorize the size of the correlations. The correlations in the scatterplots range from −1.00 to 1.00 and are programmed so that each set of correlations will include large (i.e., > .80), medium (i.e., .50) and small (i.e., < .20) negative and positive correlations. Students estimate the size of the correlation in each plot. The computer provides the actual size of the correlation after students enter their estimate. At the end, students receive feedback about their performance: They are provided with an average absolute difference score between their estimates and the actual correlations and with the correlation between their estimates and the actual correlations.

The second program requires students to plot scatterplots that produce correlations of certain size and type. The specific sizes and types of correlations can be determined by the instructor (see examples in following sections). The program allows students to plot each data point; once they indicate that they do not wish to add any other points, the program provides them with the Pearson correlation coefficient for their plot. After completing each plot, students may produce a new scatterplot or revise their previous one. If they choose to revise their plot, they can add or delete data points. If they choose to delete data points, they can remove one or several data points, or they can truncate the range of the X or Y variable. This second option allows students to explore the influence of one or several data points on the resulting correlation index without having to reenter the entire set of data.

Both programs are in executable file form and do not require additional software. The programs are simple to use; students interact with the programs by entering numbers of letters as prompted.

Hardware Requirements

The graphic display created by the program requires 640×350 pixel resolution (enhanced resolution graphics). The programs run on any IBM-compatible computer as executable files. The programs require 57k and 47k of memory, respectively.

Program Availability

A listing of the programs (507 lines) will be sent on request. Alternatively, copies of the programs are available upon receipt of a properly formatted disk and self-addressed, stamped mailer. On request, we will also include a worksheet to accompany the second program.

Classroom Use

We use the programs in a classroom exercise to enhance students' understanding of correlations and potential limitations of correlational research. The students are enrolled in an undergraduate research design course and have completed an introductory statistics course. The program could also be used in an introductory level statistics class after coverage of descriptive statistics.

We preface the exercise with a formal lecture on correlational research methods and potential problems in the interpretation of correlation indices. Students use the first program option to estimate correlations from scatterplots and to get a feel for the relations between visual representations of data relations and their numeric counterparts. We encourage students to estimate plots until they have reached a high level of accuracy. To increase student involvement, high levels of accuracy are "rewarded" with a pleasant melody ("Amazing Grace"), whereas low levels of accuracy result in unpleasant decreasing tones.

Students then use the second program option to plot data that produce particular correlations. We provide our students with worksheets that describe the specific correlations they are asked to plot. For example, in the past, we have instructed students to plot (a) perfect positive and negative correlations (i.e., $r = 1.00$ and $r = -1.00$, respectively), (b) a correlation indicating that the variables are not related (i.e., $r = 0$), and (c) correlations within a certain range (e.g., $.4 < r < .6$). When they obtain a scatterplot that produces each correlation, they are asked to draw a rough sketch in a diagram provided in their worksheets.

Once students have mastered these basic relations, we consider more complicated methodological issues, such as the effect of outliers on the correlation. First, students plot a scatter diagram with an obvious outlier. Second, they remove that outlier and note the change in the Pearson correlation coefficient. Finally, students plot diagrams in which the outlier has a specific effect. For example, they are instructed to plot (a) a diagram with an outlier that reduces the size of the correlation and (b) a diagram with an outlier that increases the size of the correlation. This exercise allows students to distinguish among different types of outliers: those that have strong effects on the size and direction of the correlation coefficient and those that have no or little effect on the correlation coefficient.

To illustrate effects of curvilinear relations on the obtained Pearson correlation coefficient, students plot several curvilinear relations and note the size of the correlation coefficient. The major point that students gain from this part of the exercise is that correlation coefficient is an index of only the linear component of the relation.

We also use the program to illustrate the effects of incorrect assumptions about the analyzed data. For example, when examining a correlation between two variables, we assume that the sample we have is representative of the population. We ask students to illustrate the effect of a nonrepresentative sample (i.e., restricted range) on the Pearson correlation coefficient in three ways. They are asked to produce a plot that results in (a) a full-range correlation that is lower than the truncated range correlation, (b) a full-range correlation that is higher than the truncated range correlation, and (c) a full-range correlation that is equal to the truncated range correlation.

We also demonstrate that, when applying the Pearson correlation coefficient, we assume that the association between the two variables is not qualified by a third variable (e.g., a grouping variable). We ask students to demonstrate the following effects of group contamination. First, they produce a plot that results in a forced relation (i.e., no relation is present within each group, but ignoring group membership results in an enhanced relation). Then they produce a plot that results in a hidden or reduced relation (i.e., the relation is present within each group, but ignoring group membership cancels out or reduces the relation).

Once students have completed all required plots, we discuss theoretical and practical implications of the exercise. We emphasize how examining one's data (e.g., looking at scatterplots in correlational research) can help to eliminate or greatly reduce the potential for some of the problems covered in class. Students report that the exercises enhance their understanding of the concepts covered in class. Through repeated use of the first program, students can increase their level of accuracy in estimating correlations.

References

Mathie, V. A., Beins, B., Benjamin, L. T., Jr., Ewing, M. M., Hall, C. C. I., Henderson, B., McAdam, D. W., & Smith, R. A. (1993). Promoting active learning in psychology courses. In T. V. McGovern (Ed.), *Handbook for enhancing undergraduate education in psychology* (pp. 183–214). Washington, DC: American Psychological Association.

Skinner, B. F. (1989). Teaching machines. *Science, 243,* 1535.

Notes

1. Portions of this article were presented at the first annual American Psychological Society Institute on the Teaching of Psychology, Washington, DC, June 1994.
2. We thank Bernard C. Beins and several anonymous reviewers for their helpful comments.

Pearson's r and Spread: A Classroom Demonstration

Schuyler W. Huck
S. Paul Wright
Soohee Park
College of Education
University of Tennessee (Knoxville)

Of the many things that students learn about Pearson's r, one of the most troublesome involves the relation between spread and the magnitude of Pearson's r. The connection between these two concepts is often perplexing because of apparent inconsistencies in what students read (or hear) as their formal academic training unfolds. Over time, students typically confront three seemingly incompatible claims: (a) variability and r are directly related, (b) variability and r are inversely related, and (c) variability and r are unrelated. These claims lead students to wonder how dispersion can be related to Pearson's r in three different ways.

The answer to this question is tied to the meaning of dispersion—or stated differently, why variability is high or low. If the measured spread on X and/or Y is decreased because errors of measurement are reduced, then the correlation between X and Y will increase. If, on the other hand, the variability of X and/or Y is decreased because we focus on a subgroup with restricted range, then the correlation of X and Y will decrease. A third case exists when the metric of X and/or Y is changed by multiplying all observed values by a constant; here, the computed variance changes without a concomitant change in r.

To help students understand that changes in variability affect r in different ways, depending on the reason why the spread of scores has increased or decreased, we developed a simple but powerful exercise. This exercise involves (a) using playing cards to generate hypothetical scores on two well-known variables and (b) computing and comparing various standard deviations and correlation coefficients. As a supplement to textbook discussions and lectures on the topic of Pearson's r, this exercise is easy to conduct and helps students understand the multifaceted relation between spread and r.

Data Generation

Data generation requires approximately 10 min of class time and a standard deck of playing cards for each student. By following an explicit set of instructions, each student generates two sets of self-descriptive (though hypothetical) numbers: true and fallible IQ scores as well as true and fallible grade point averages (GPA).

To generate the IQ and GPA scores, each student takes a deck of 52 cards and divides it into two parts referred to here as HIGH and LOW. The 28 highest cards (7s, 8s, 9s, 10s, Jacks, Queens, and Kings) are assigned to HIGH; the remaining 24 cards (Aces, 2s, 3s, 4s, 5s, and 6s) are assigned to LOW. After forming HIGH and LOW, students shuffle each stack and then place HIGH and LOW face down.

After setting up HIGH and LOW, each student takes the top two cards off HIGH and turns them over to reveal their values. (If selected, a Jack, Queen, or King is valued at 11, 12, or 13, respectively.) These two cards are designated H_1 and H_2.

Once H_1 and H_2 are selected, each student takes the top two LOW cards and turns them over to determine their values. (If selected, an Ace is worth 1 point.) These two cards are designated L_1 and L_2; order of selection is noted. After the values of L_1 and L_2 are recorded, these two cards are returned to LOW, LOW is reshuffled, and then two new cards from LOW are selected as before. The values of this next pair of cards are designated L_3 and L_4; again order of selection is noted. Finally, L_3 and L_4 are returned to LOW, LOW is reshuffled one last time, and then a third pair of cards is selected from LOW. The values of these final two cards are designated L_5 and L_6; again, order of selection is noted.

After two cards from HIGH and six cards from LOW have been selected, students compute their "true" IQ and "true" GPA scores (hereafter referred to as IQ_T and GPA_T) as follows:

$$IQ_T = 5(H_1 + H_2)$$
$$GPA_T = .1(H_1 + H_2) + .08(L_1 - L_2)$$

Students are told that (a) $70 \leq IQ_T \leq 130$ and $1.00 \leq GPA_T \leq 3.00$, (b) IQ_T represents the hypothetical IQ score each of them would earn if given a fully valid intelligence test, and (c) GPA_T represents the hypothetical GPA each of them would have after 4 years of college under the assumption that one's grades are influenced by only two factors: native intelligence and individual decisions to do extra work, to goof off, and so on. (If any student's L_2 is higher than L_1, this means that he or she worked less than average, goofed off more than average, etc.)

After computing IQ_T and GPA_T, students are told that no test is perfectly accurate; test content is sometimes biased, students sometimes select their answers by random guessing, students sometimes take tests when ill or emotionally upset, and so forth. Consequently, "fallible" IQ and "fallible" GPA scores (hereafter referred to as IQ_F and GPA_F)

must be generated to match the realism of actual IQ and GPA scores. The procedure for obtaining these two fallible scores is:

$$IQ_F = IQ_T + 6(L_3 - L_4)$$
$$GPA_F = GPA_T + .2 (L_5 - L_6)$$

The quantities $6(L_3 - L_4)$ and $.2 (L_5 - L_6)$ represent errors of measurement. Once this measurement error is added to the true scores, $40 \leq IQ_F \leq 160$ and $0.00 \leq GPA_F \leq 4.00$.

Before turning to the data analysis, a comment about class size is in order. This exercise works better if many pairs of IQ and GPA scores are produced. Having $N \geq 40$ generally provides sufficient data. If the class size is smaller than 40, each student should generate two (or more) sets of paired IQ and GPA scores.

Data Analysis

After students generate the data, four specific analyses should be performed. These analyses correspond to four sets of questions:

1. Using the data generated by your class, what value does r assume when IQ_T is correlated with GPA_T? How large is the standard deviation for the data collected on each variable?

2. If we introduce measurement error (by looking at the IQ_F and GPA_F scores), how large are the two standard deviations and what value does r assume? Comparing these findings with those of Question 1, what inference can be drawn about the impact of measurement error on standard deviations and on Pearson's r?

3. If we focus on only those cases in which $IQ_T > 100$, how large are the two standard deviations (of IQ_T and of GPA_T) and how large is r when computed on the true scores from this "bright" subgroup? Comparing these findings with those of Question 1, what conclusion can be drawn about the impact of restriction of range on score variability and on Pearson's r?

4. If we double all GPA_F scores to produce a scale that extends from 0 to 8 (rather than 0 to 4), how large will the new GPA standard deviation be? And what value will r assume if computed on IQ_F and the rescaled GPA_F scores? Comparing these findings with those of Question 2, what conclusion can be drawn about the impact of linear data transformations on standard deviations and on r?

By answering the first set of questions, one obtains baseline figures with which subsequent results can be compared. The results obtained by answering the final three sets of questions illustrate that (a) an increase in spread, if brought about by the intrusion of measurement errors, about by restriction in range, causes r to decrease; and (c) a change in σ, if brought about by altering the metric of X and/or Y, has no effect on r.

Expected Results

Because the data generated by students for this exercise involve sampling, one cannot predict with certainty the values that the two standard deviations and the one r will assume in the first, second, or third parts of the data analysis. Nevertheless, the instructor can be confident that the results will allow the desired points to be made. Evidence to support this claim comes from a computer simulation of the full demonstration.

Using SAS/IML, all possible pairs of IQ and GPA scores from the data generation phase of the demonstration were specified, along with their corresponding probability of occurrence. Then this population of values was sampled, with 40 cases extracted randomly. From the resulting pairs of IQ and GPA scores, sample standard deviations and correlations were computed (first using true data, then a second time using fallible scores). These results were then examined to see whether the introduction of measurement errors caused an increase in the IQ and GPA standard deviations and a decrease in the correlation between IQ and GPA.

This first set of 40 sample values also was analyzed to determine the effects of range restriction. To accomplish this objective, cases for which the true IQ was ≤ 100 were deleted, with the remaining cases used as a basis for computing the true standard deviations and the correlation. Results were examined to determine whether the imposed restriction of range caused not only the standard deviations but also the correlation to decrease, as compared with the values computed on the basis of the full 40-person sample.

The full Monte Carlo simulation was based on 1,000 random samples, each analyzed in the same fashion. Outcomes indicated the high probability that results obtained from any group of students will be as desired. For example, when measurement error was introduced, all 1,000 replications were identical in that (a) the computed standard deviation for IQ_F was greater than that for IQ_T, (b) the computed standard deviation for GPA_F was greater than that for GPA_T, and (c) the correlation between IQ_F and GPA_F was lower than the correlation between IQ_T and GPA_T.

The Monte Carlo simulation revealed that this exercise also is highly likely to work well in illustrating the relation between spread and r when the range is restricted. In 975 out of the 1,000 sets of data examined, the correlation between IQ_T and GPA_T was smaller for the "bright" subgroup of the sample than it was for the full sample.

The issue of sampling, of course, has no bearing on the results generated by any group of students to answer Question 4 (i.e., the question dealing with the way a linear transformation of GPA affects spread and r). Here, there is a full guarantee that the variability of the rescaled GPA scores will increase while r changes not a whit.

4. Developing Students' Skills

To assess students' skills and attitudes associated with different approaches to teaching statistics, Mark Ware and Jeffrey Chastain from Creighton University examined classes in which students conducted arithmetic computations with or without computer-assisted statistical analysis. Pre- and postcourse measures consisted of statistical interpretation and selection skills and attitudes toward statistics and computers. Analyses of covariance indicated superior selection and interpretation skills among those who had taken statistics. Students in the computer-assisted statistical analysis group had significantly more favorable attitudes toward statistics than did those in the other groups. Teachers interested in improving students' attitudes toward statistics without a loss of skills may want to try a computer-assisted approach.

In a follow-up study, Mark Ware and Jeffrey Chastain assessed the effectiveness of a teaching strategy emphasizing the use of different statistical tests (i.e., selection skills) in introductory statistics. Analysis of covariance revealed that students in the class emphasizing statistical selection skills achieved significantly higher selection scores than students in the other groups. The techniques reported in this article may interest teachers who are interested in increasing students' facility for choosing appropriate statistical tests.

Richard Rogers from Georgia Southern College described his use of a microcomputer software/textbook package, including computer-generated individualized assignments, in an introductory statistics course. Advantages consisted of producing individual assignments to avoid having one student copying another's work. Moreover, the material facilitated production of problems for examinations that tested students' facility for selecting the appropriate analysis for a particular situation. This article and the previous one provide instructors with a variety of techniques for increasing students' selection skills.

Patricia Oswald from Iona College investigated the benefits of using a personal computer and a projection system to teach undergraduate statistics. The author outlined the method used, and the hardware and software requirements; she also identified four educational objectives. Students reported increased confidence and ability to use computers and solve statistical problems.

Observing that many students in introductory statistics classes committed similar errors in computation and interpretation, Kenneth Melvin and Kristi Huff from the University of Alabama prepared a handout that listed such errors. Use of the handout during classes and examinations elicited favorable student ratings. Students thought the handout reduced errors, and they recommended it for future classes.

If you are looking for ways to reduce common errors, you may want to try this strategy.

Bernard Beins from Ithaca College gave students in four statistics classes different amounts of guidance and instruction in interpretive skills. Students who wrote press releases free of statistical jargon acquired better computational and interpretive skills than did students in a traditional class, but students did not differ in the amount of conceptual knowledge. The technique readily transfers to other courses.

Alverno College students in Paul Smith's Probability and Statistics course wrote assignments that required them to generate and interpret statistics under the guise of a formal professional communication. This format provided opportunities to assess students' understanding of statistical tools and students' writing abilities in a nontechnical context. To be successful at this assignment, students had to demonstrate effective statistical and writing skills. Would you be interested in trying this value-added technique?

Joseph Rossi from the University of Rhode Island had students recompute the values of statistical tests published in journal articles. Undergraduate and graduate students compared the recomputed values to the published results and discovered that about 13% of the results reported as statistically significant were not. The author cautioned against making students mistrust statistical findings; he promoted the exercise as a way to develop a dective-like attitude toward reading journal articles. Using a detective metaphor with statistics classes may also increase students' interest in statistics.

Connie Varnhagen, Sean Drake, and Gary Finley used several components of the Internet to administer the laboratory portion of an intermediate statistics course offered to psychology honors students at the University of Alberta. Using an online questionnaire, the authors evaluated students' perceived effectiveness of using the Internet. Students reported finding the communication components of the Internet laboratory more useful than the information components, perceived few barriers of the system for their learning, and rated the value of the system positively. Are you using the Internet as one tool in teaching statistics?

To promote probabilistic and statistical thinking about important societal issues, Sharon Derry, Joel Levin, and Leona Schauble from the University of Wisconsin-Madison developed a novel statistics course for students who are teachers or are considering a career in teaching. The course was designed to help students use statistical concepts as tools for social reasoning within simulations of real-world problems. Socially sensitive readers will eagerly look forward to evaluative findings about this approach to teaching statistics.

Computer-Assisted Statistical Analysis: A Teaching Innovation?

Mark E. Ware
Jeffrey D. Chastain
Creighton University

Bartz's finding (1981) that 72% of four-year colleges and universities offering a psychology major required at least one course in statistics illustrates the prevalence of statistics as a requirement in the psychology curriculum. The literature on teaching statistics is sparse; Ware and Brewer (1988) reported only 31 articles published in *Teaching of Psychology* (*ToP*) since 1974. Although elaborate models exist for identifying the cognitive skills associated with learning statistics (Forsyth, 1977; Magnello & Spies, 1984), investigators have devoted little attention to students' attitudes toward learning statistics.

Beins (1987) traced the development of computer applications to the teaching of psychology. He examined back issues of *ToP* and *Behavioral Research Methods, Instruments & Computers* (*BRMI&C*). Although not the only forum for information about teaching applications for computers, those journals are the most prominent sources. Results indicate that *ToP* contained no articles on computers until 1978 and that *BRMI&C* averaged fewer than five articles per year before 1980.

Survey research provides an index of computer use in teaching statistics. In a national survey, Castellan (1982) reported that 50% of respondents used computers in statistics and experimental methods and design classes. In another national survey, the use of computers increased to 66% (Couch & Stoloff, 1986) and to 82% in a Virginia survey (Stoloff & Couch, 1987).

Despite increased attention to computer use in statistics classes, only eight articles evaluating strategies for teaching statistics have appeared in *ToP,* and only two evaluated computer-assisted statistical analysis. Tromater (1985) found that when students tried to use statistics in advanced courses their recall was poor, and some students reported that arithmetic computations were distracting and interfered with learning new material. Consequently, he developed a second-level statistics course using SPSS-X. Course objectives included providing students with skills that could be useful in advanced classes and in postgraduate pursuits. Course evaluations indicated that students thought the course objectives had been achieved. Rogers (1987) used a microcomputer software/textbook package in an introductory statistics class. Seventeen of 18 students gave favorable evaluations of microcomputer use. These two authors reported no statistics achievement measures and used no comparison groups.

In an earlier study, Layne and Huck (1981) compared postcourse performance of graduate students in research methods classes. In one class, the instructor presented detailed computational examples and gave students detailed handouts for several statistical procedures. In another section, the same instructor described the same statistical procedures but gave no examples. The groups did not differ in postcourse performance on a test emphasizing skills for interpreting results of statistical tests. The authors concluded that teachers should not spend large amounts of time explaining computational procedures if the course's purpose is to increase interpretive skills. The findings were comforting to the first author (Mark E. Ware) of the study described herein, who experienced considerable anxiety at the prospect that courses involving computer-assisted analysis might result in inferior mastery of statistics, particularly when compared to those taught with the traditional emphasis on derivation of formulas and on computation using a calculator and/or paper and pencil. Layne and Huck (1981) did not report on students' attitudes toward statistics.

The literature contains numerous articles describing individual differences among students taking statistics. Results from research on gender are equivocal. Some evidence indicates that there are gender differences in statistics achievement (Brooks, 1987), and some indicates no differences (Buck, 1985, 1987). In addition, Giambra (1976) reported that students' overall GPA predicted grades in statistics, but the level of previous math (e.g., calculus vs. algebra) did not.

Our study assessed students' skills and attitudes associated with different approaches to teaching statistics. The approaches consisted of classes in which students conducted arithmetic computations with and without the assistance of a computer. Students who had previously taken statistics and those who had not taken statistics constituted comparison groups. Students were also subdivided by gender, GPA, and math competency. Because of inconsistencies in the data or a limited amount of data on the influence of situational and personal factors on skills and attitudes, we made no directional predictions. Finally, we emphasized the influence of situational and personal variables rather than providing a detailed description of the course.

Method

Subjects

Subjects were 120 undergraduates who volunteered to participate in a study of statistical skills during the fall and spring semesters, 1986–87. One group consisted of 55 students from two sections of introductory statistics; they used a mainframe computer for conducting analyses. The same instructor taught both sections. A second group consisted of 41 students from two sections of introductory statistics; they conducted analyses with electronic calculators and/or paper and pencil. Each section was taught by a different instructor, both of whom were different from the instructor for the first group. Instructors taught the course as they chose. Volunteers from several other psychology classes consisted of a third group of 24 students who had not previously taken statistics. One hundred twenty of 139 students completed both the pretest and posttest, reflecting 14% attrition. We conducted several statistical analyses to assess gender differences in attrition and other pretreatment differences among students. Overall, women constituted 58% and men 42% of the sample. Of those who failed to complete the posttest, 53% were women. The results of a chi-square test for independence between gender and those who did or did not complete pre- and posttesting was not significant, $\chi^2(1, N = 139) = 0.23, p < .05.$

A chi-square test for independence between gender and groups revealed no relationship between the two variables, $\chi^2(2, N = 120) = 5.56, p = .062.$ The median GPA for the sample was the interval from 2.95 to 3.14. A Kruskal-Wallis test for differences in self-reported GPAs for students in the three groups revealed no significant differences, $\chi^2(2, N = 118) = 0.35, p = .836.$ There were no differences in self-rated math competency among the groups, $F(2, 117) = 2.47, p = .089.$ Overall, sophomores, juniors, and seniors constituted 18%, 50%, and 32% of the sample, respectively. A chi-square test for independence between year in school and groups revealed no significant difference, $\chi^2(4, N = 119) = 1.89, p = .756.$ The median value for year in school was the same (junior) for all groups. Thus, at the outset of the study, the three groups did not differ with respect to gender, GPA, math competency, or year in school.

Materials

The first author developed an inventory with three parts: (a) self-reported personal characteristics, including the student's gender, GPA, math competency, and year in school; (b) a skills section containing selection and interpretation items; and (c) evaluative items from the Semantic Differential (Osgood, Suci, & Tannenbaum, 1957) that asked students to respond separately to the words *statistics* and *computers.*

Students selected one of nine categories that contained their overall GPA. On a scale for which A = 4.0, the lowest category was less than 2.35, and the highest category was greater than 3.74. The other categories consisted of intervals of .20, (e.g., 2.95 to 3.14). Students rated their math competency using a 9-point scale ranging from *very low* (0) to *moderate* (4 or 5) to *very high* (9).

Initially, there were 10 items each to assess students' statistical selection and interpretation skills. Items assessing selection skill required students to select from four alternatives the appropriate statistical analysis for a given research problem. Items assessing interpretation skill required students to select from four alternatives the appropriate interpretation for a statistical finding. Tables 1 and 2 contain examples used for assessing each skill.

Three faculty colleagues, who routinely teach introductory statistics, evaluated the 20 items for consistency in terminology, clarity, and relevance. Colleagues' recommendations resulted in the elimination of two selection items and the modification in the wording of several other items.

All of us agreed that the final 18 items constituted problems that students should be able to solve after completing the introductory statistics course. Thus, the selection and interpretation measures possessed face and content validity. Moreover, all agreed that success in solving the problems should be independent of students' computer skills.

The first author selected four bipolar items (*good—bad, cruel—kind, clean—dirty,* and *beautiful—ugly*) that loaded .82 or higher on the Semantic Differential's evaluative factor (Osgood, Suci, & Tannenbaum, 1957). Students rated separately the two words, *statistics* and *computers,* on each of the four items. We added each student's ratings on the four items to obtain a total score for attitudes toward statistics and toward computers. A higher score indicated a more favorable attitude.

Calculation of Pearson correlations between precourse selection and interpretation scores and between precourse statistics and computer attitudes produced coefficients of

Table 1. Examples of Selection Items

1. In a study of mother–infant interaction, mothers were classified on the basis of whether or not this was their first child (primiparous vs. multiparous) and on the basis of whether this was a low-birth-weight (LBW) infant or a full-term (FT) infant. The data represent a score on a 12-point interval scale, which was the rating trained observers gave to the quality of the mothers' interactions with their infants. A higher score represents better mother–infant interaction. The investigators hypothesize that there are no differences among the groups.

Primiparous		Multiparous	
LBW	FT	LBW	FT
6	8	7	9
5	7	8	8
5	7	8	9
4	6	9	9
9	7	8	3
6	2	2	10
2	5	1	9
6	8	9	8
5	7	9	7
5	7	8	10

(a) two-factor analysis of variance
(b) Spearman rank order correlation
(c) chi-square test for independence
(d) t test for dependent groups

2. Lesions in the amygdala can reduce certain responses commonly associated with fear (e.g., decreases in heart rate). If fear is really reduced, then it should be more difficult to train an avoidance response in lesioned animals because the aversiveness of the stimulus will be reduced. Assume two groups of rabbits: one group has lesions in the amygdala, and the other is an untreated control group. The following data represent a ranking of the number of trials to learn an avoidance response for each animal.

Group With Lesions   5 7 6 14 15 2 1 3 12 4 13
Control Group   11 19 10 8 16 17 20 18 9

(a) simple analysis of variance
(b) Mann–Whitney U test
(c) Pearson product–moment correlation
(d) t test for dependent groups

Table 2. Examples of Interpretation Items

1. An industrial psychologist conducted a study examining the relation between the IQ score and the productivity of 20 workers. The correlation coefficient was .49. Inspection of a table of critical values revealed a coefficient of .42 at the 5% level and .54 at the 1% level. Which is the appropriate probability value?
(a) $p < .01$
(b) $p > .10$
(c) $p < .05$
(d) $p > .05$

2. An investigator found no significant differences between two groups. The best interpretation is that:
(a) the groups are equal
(b) the investigator failed to reject the null hypothesis
(c) the investigator accepted the null hypothesis
(d) the null and alternative hypotheses were studied systematically

$r = .06$, $p = .533$ and $r = .07$, $p = .419$, respectively. The small degree of relation between the two skill measures and between the two attitude measures suggests that they were assessing different skills and different attitudes.

Procedure

In this study, there were three intact groups. In the first group, the computer-assisted statistical analysis (CASA) group, the instructor had students calculate all statistical analyses using a mainframe computer (UNISYS 1100/70) and the SPSS-X. In the second group, the traditional (TRAD) group, instructors had students calculate statistical analyses using calculators or paper and pencil. The instructors for the CASA and TRAD groups taught a common core of topics for introductory statistics, including measures of central tendency and variability, correlation and regression, z test, t test, analysis of variance, and nonparametric tests. The third group was a comparison group consisting of students who had not taken introductory statistics (NOST).

Analysis and Design

The design of this study was 3×2 factorial design using three groups for types of class (CASA, TRAD, and NOST) and two groups for each of the person variables of gender, GPA, and math competency. In all cases except gender, we formed groups by dividing the students' responses into low and high using the median as the fulcrum value. The four dependent variables were students' scores on the selection and interpretation items and on the measures of their attitudes toward statistics and computers.

The CASA, TRAD, and NOST groups did not differ on the pretest scores for selection, $F(2, 117) = 1.00$, $p = .383$, interpretation, $F(2, 117) = 1.92$, $p = .151$, attitudes toward statistics, $F(2, 117) = 0.41$, $p = .666$, and attitudes toward computers, $F(2, 117) = 0.44$, $p = .644$. We used ANCOVA on the posttest scores with adjusted pretest scores as the covariate. The procedure of using adjusted pretest scores "corrects for the effects of irrelevance as well as measurement error" (Cook & Campbell, 1979, pp. 191–192). We performed separate analyses for type of class and gender, type of class and GPA, and type of class and math competency.

The use of intact groups permits threats to internal validity. An inherent confounding existed between types of class (CASA, TRAD, and NOST), instructor, teaching style, number of class meetings, time of day, and so forth. The influence of instructor variables can be assessed by replicating the study and having instructors teach different types of classes. Random assignment of subjects to groups was impossible. Nevertheless, as pointed out earlier, the groups did not differ at the outset with regard to gender, GPA, math competency, or year in school.

Results

The ANCOVA revealed significant differences in selection and interpretation skills and in attitudes toward statis-

Table 3. Sample Sizes, Means, and Standard Deviations for the Three Types of Class on Each of the Posttest Dependent Variables, as Well as F-Ratios, Degrees of Freedom, and Probability Values From ANCOVA

Dependent Variables	Computer-Assisted Statistical Analysis[a]		Traditional Statistics[b]		No Statistics[c]				
	M	SD	M	SD	M	SD	F	df	p
Selection	3.69	1.71	3.17	1.36	1.71	1.40	4.63	2, 113	.012
Interpretation	5.36	2.24	5.12	1.89	3.29	1.76	12.60	2, 113	.000
Statistics attitudes	14.24	3.43	12.49	3.02	12.50	3.12	8.82	2, 113	.023

[a]$n = 55$. [b]$n = 41$. [c]$n = 24$.

tics between the types of class. We used results from the Tukey HSD multiple comparison test, $p < .05$, to evaluate which groups differed. These results indicated that students in the CASA and TRAD groups obtained higher scores on the selection ($M = 3.69$ and 3.17 vs. 1.71) and interpretation scales ($M = 5.36$ and 5.12 vs. 3.29) than did students in the NOST group, respectively. In addition, students in the CASA group had higher scores on the attitudes toward statistics scale ($M = 14.24$); that is, they evaluated statistics more favorably than did students in TRAD ($M = 12.49$) and NOST groups ($M = 12.50$). There was no difference between the TRAD and NOST groups. Table 3 summarizes the results. There was also no difference in selection scores for the gender variable.

The ANCOVA also revealed that men ($n = 51$) obtained significantly higher scores than women ($n = 69$) on the interpretation scale ($M = 5.59$, $SD = 2.21$ vs. $M = 4.33$, $SD = 1.99$), $F(1, 113) = 8.52$, $p = .004$. There was no significant difference in interpretation scores for types of class; the interaction between types of class and gender was also not significant.

Findings from the ANCOVA for types of class and GPA revealed that students having a lower GPA ($n = 52$) obtained significantly lower scores on the interpretation scale ($M = 4.00$, $SD = 1.98$ vs. $M = 5.73$, $SD = 1.98$) than did those having a higher GPA ($n = 52$), $F(1, 97) = 20.90$, $p < .001$. There was no significant interaction.

The ANCOVA for types of class and math competency revealed no significant differences between those expressing a higher versus lower math competency. There was no significant interaction between types of class and math competency.

Discussion

Our discussion includes sections covering four central issues. The first evaluates the findings regarding group differences in skills and attitudes. The second examines individual differences in skills. The third outlines a proposal for additional research on teaching statistics that takes account of students' cognitive structure. Finally, we sum-

marize the benefits of computer-assisted analysis for teaching statistics.

The superior selection and interpretation scores of those in the CASA and TRAD classes indicate that students who had taken statistics acquired skills that their peers (the NOST class) had not. Because this study used intact groups, we remind readers about the limitations associated with such a design. That the groups did not differ at the outset in gender, GPA, and math competency reduces but does not eliminate our concern about threats to internal validity.

The failure to find differences in skill measures among those with and without computer-assisted statistical analysis allayed the first author's apprehension that computer-assisted statistical analysis might result in inferior performance on selection and interpretation measures. There is no evidence that students suffered a deficit in acquiring skills. Those results are consistent with Layne and Huck's (1981) failure to find differences in interpretation skills between groups given or not given detailed computational examples.

Course evaluations indicated that students in the CASA group thought that they had acquired statistical concepts. All of the students in the CASA group agreed or strongly agreed that they had increased their knowledge and competence in the subject. Students' comments such as, "I liked the involvement with computers"; "It really helped me grasp many concepts, plus helping me with computers in general"; "I would not recommend teaching the course without use of SPSS," suggested that they also learned how to operate a mainframe computer and use SPSS-X procedures. Thus, computer-assisted statistical analysis offers the additional advantage of developing students' computer-related skills.

Additional evidence supporting computer-assisted statistical analysis was the more favorable attitude toward statistics among those in the CASA versus the TRAD and NOST groups. Computer-assisted statistical analysis may promote a more favorable attitude toward statistics and reduce the anxiety that students encounter when taking statistics (Beins, 1985; Dillon, 1982; Hastings, 1982; Jacobs, 1980). However, we offer some caveats about implementing computer-assisted statistical analysis. One caution concerns the danger of replacing the fear of math or statistics with the fear of computers. At the beginning of the course, the first author told students that he assumed that they had no prior experience with computers. We found support for that assumption in the results of a class survey revealing that 38% had no experience with a mainframe computer. Among those who had experience, word processing and/or BASIC constituted most of their activity. In addition, the first author used Dillon's (1982) technique for encouraging students to express anonymously their anxiety about the course. That technique let students know that the instructor was aware of their fears, and it demonstrated that student apprehension about statistics and computers was the rule rather than the exception. The following comments from the students in the CASA group support a conclusion about reducing students' computer anxiety: "Use of the computer was fun and helpful, a necessary part of the course"; "I especially like working with the computer rather than a hand calculator"; "I have no fears about using the computer for other psychology courses."

Another caution about computer-assisted statistical analysis is a concern that some teachers have expressed. They properly pointed out the dangers in students' thinking that results produced from a computer are correct regardless of the appropriateness of the analysis or that a computer analysis can correct flaws in sampling or research design. The mystique of computers increases the risk that results of a computer-assisted statistical analysis might be accepted uncritically. However, our experience suggests that students' failure to recognize that "garbage in" produces "garbage out" is no less a risk when they analyze data by computers, by calculators, or by hand. Our finding of no difference in selection and interpretation skills among those using different computational procedures supports such a conclusion.

The second issue concerns individual differences in interpretation skills. Our findings that men had significantly higher interpretation scores than women is inconsistent with research that found women superior to men in statistics (Brooks, 1987) and research that found no difference between men and women (Buck, 1985, 1987). A Mann-Whitney U test revealed no significant difference in GPA between men and women, $z = .74$, $p = .461$. Thus, there was no evidence that the gender difference in interpretation skills was influenced by GPA. With the dramatic increase in the percentage of female undergraduate and graduate students in psychology (Howard et al., 1986) and because of the central role of statistics in educating psychology students, discovering the conditions that promote effective teaming of statistics regardless of gender could benefit statistics teachers and their students.

Our finding that students with higher GPAs had higher interpretation scores than those with lower GPAs is consistent with Giambra's (1976) report of a significant correlation between GPA and grade in statistics. His finding replicated results from an earlier study (Giambra, 1970) in which he concluded that "success in an undergraduate behavioral statistics course has little to do with a student's past mathematical background, and [it] seems to depend on his overall ability as a student" (p. 367). Our findings extend the scope of the relation between GPA and performance in statistics to include courses taught with computer-assisted analysis. However, computer-assisted statistical analysis is no panacea. The same students who have difficulty in a traditionally taught statistics course appear to have difficulty in a course with computer-assisted analysis.

Our failure to find differences in selection and interpretation skills between students expressing greater or lesser degrees of math competency is compatible with Giambra's (1976) results. He found that students' previous math background did not contribute to their grades in statistics, provided investigators took into account students' overall GPA. Although students' self-ratings of math competency are not synonymous with their math background, we found a moderate and significant Spearman correlation (.49), $p <$ .001, between the two measures. Students who feel incompetent in math are less likely to take math courses. Thus, the failure to find differences was not surprising.

The third issue raised by our results is an observation about the selection and interpretation measures. The percentage of correct interpretation items was consistently higher than that for selection items. In addition, there were more significant differences between groups on interpretation measures. Although the results may reflect the interpretation measure's greater sensitivity, we suspect that they might also reflect teachers' failure to emphasize selection skills. A common practice is to teach statistical tests one at a time. We know of only a handful of introductory statistics teachers who expect students to select appropriate statistical tests for a variety of circumstances. Some might argue that teaching selection skills is not central to a statistics course because students can select the proper statistical test from a book. However, the absence of guidelines for selecting suitable statistical tests can limit the effective use of a book.

What guidelines would be helpful in selecting appropriate statistical tests? Magnello and Spies (1984) assessed students' cognitive structure for various statistical concepts. Their results prompted them to recommend that teachers should facilitate students' learning of statistical concepts by presenting the organizing concepts of scale of measurement and function.

The first author of the study described in this article subsequently taught two classes using a model from Siegel's (1956) nonparametric statistics book, which appeared to meet the guidelines that Magnello and Spies proposed. That model consists of a table having a vertical dimension with rows corresponding to the levels of measurement of the dependent variable. The horizontal dimension identifies columns corresponding to conditions associated with the independent variable. The cells in the resulting matrix identify appropriate statistical tests. The first author adapted that model for use in an introductory statistics course. In addition, he emphasized the selection of appropriate statistical tests on two of four examinations each semester as well as on the final exam. An analysis of data evaluating the effectiveness of those efforts is in progress.

In summary, we concur with Tromater's (1985) observation that computer-assisted statistical analysis can enhance skills that students may apply in other courses and in the world of work; it can also improve students' attitudes toward statistics. These advantages buttress our argument for using this approach in teaching statistics.

References

Bartz, A. E. (1981). The statistics course as a departmental offering and major requirement. *Teaching of Psychology, 8,* 106.

Beins, B. (1985). Teaching the relevance of statistics through consumer-oriented research. *Teaching of Psychology, 12,* 168–169.

Beins, B. C. (1987, August). *The historical pattern of computer use by teachers of psychology in colleges and universities.* Paper presented at the meeting of the American Psychological Association, New York.

Brooks, C. I. (1987). Superiority of women in statistics achievement. *Teaching of Psychology, 14,* 45.

Buck, J. L. (1985). A failure to find gender differences in statistics achievement. *Teaching of Psychology, 12,* 100.

Buck, J. L. (1987). More on superiority of women in statistics achievement: A reply to Brooks. *Teaching of Psychology, 14,* 45–46.

Castellan, N. J. (1982). Computers in psychology: A survey of instructional applications. *Behavioral Research Methods, Instruments & Computers, 14,* 198–202.

Cook, T. D., & Campbell, D. T. (1979). *Quasi-experimentation: Design & analysis issues for field settings.* Boston: Houghton Mifflin.

Couch, J. V., & Stoloff, M. L. (1986, August). *Computer use in psychology: A national survey.* Paper presented at the meeting of the American Psychological Association, Washington, DC.

Dillon, K. M. (1982). Staitisticophobia. *Teaching of Psychology, 9,* 117.

Forsyth, G. A. (1977). A task-first individual-differences approach to designing a statistics and methodology course. *Teaching of Psychology, 4,* 76–78.

Giambra, L. M. (1970). Mathematics background and grade-point average as predictors of course grade in an undergraduate behavioral statistics course. *American Psychologist, 25,* 366–367.

Giambra, L. M. (1976). Mathematical background and grade-point average as predictors of course grade in an undergraduate behavioral statistics course: A replication. *Teaching of Psychology, 3,* 184–185.

Hastings, M. W. (1982). Statistics: Challenge for students and the professor. *Teaching of Psychology, 9,* 221–222.

Howard, A., Pion, G. M., Gottfredson, G. D., Flattau, P. E., Oskamp, S., Pfafflin, S. M., Bray, D. W., & Burstein, A. G. (1986). The changing face of American psychology. *American Psychologist, 41,* 1311–1327.

Jacobs, K. W. (1980). Instructional techniques in the introductory statistics course: The first class meeting. *Teaching of Psychology, 7,* 241–242.

Layne, B. H., & Huck, S. W. (1981). The usefulness of computational examples in statistics courses. *The Journal of General Psychology, 104,* 283–285.

Magnello, M. E., & Spies, C. J. (1984). Using organizing concepts to facilitate the teaching of statistics. *Teaching of Psychology, 11,* 220–223.

Osgood, C. E., Suci, G. J., & Tannenbaum, P. H. (1957). *The measurement of meaning.* Urbana, IL: University of Illinois Press.

Rogers, R. L. (1987). A microcomputer-based statistics course with individualized assignments. *Teaching of Psychology, 14,* 109–111.

Siegel, S, (1956). *Nonparametric statistics for the behavioral sciences.* New York: McGraw-Hill.

Stoloff, M. L., & Couch, J. V. (1987). A survey of computer use by undergraduate psychology departments in Virginia. *Teaching of Psychology, 14,* 92–94.

Tromater, L. J. (1985). Teaching a course in computer-assisted statistical analysis. *Teaching of Psychology, 12,* 225–226.

Ware, M. E., & Brewer, C. L. (1988). *Handbook for teaching statistics and research methods.* Hillsdale, NJ: Lawrence Erlbaum Associates, Inc.

Notes

1. Preparation of this article was supported by a Creighton University Summer Faculty Research Fellowship.
2. We thank Gary Leak, Vic Lupo, and Dan Murphy for their assistance in evaluating the skills items, providing helpful advice, and/or teaching statistics in the traditional manner.

Developing Selection Skills in Introductory Statistics

Mark E. Ware
Jeffrey D. Chastain
Creighton University

Bartz (1981) reported that 72% of 4-year colleges and universities offering psychology majors required at least one course in statistics, but the literature on teaching statistics is sparse. Ware and Brewer (1988) reported only 31 such articles published in *Teaching of Psychology* since 1974; in contrast, they reported 59 articles about teaching research methods.

Widespread use of computers (Castellan, 1982; Couch & Stoloff, 1989; Stoloff & Couch, 1987) minimizes the need for statistics teachers to spend time demonstrating computational procedures. Instructors might better use the available time for teaching students when to use a test, rather than simply teaching computational procedures and statistical tests one after another.

In this study, we assessed the effectiveness of teaching statistics with an emphasis on selection skills. We used the organizing concepts of scale of measurement and function (Magnello & Spies, 1984) because such an approach provides a meaningful way to learn new concepts. In addition, we determined how general academic ability (Giambra, 1976) and gender (Brooks, 1987; Buck, 1985, 1987; Elmore & Vasu, 1980; Feinberg & Halperin, 1978; Ware & Chastain, 1989) affected students' learning when the instructor emphasized selection skills.

Method

Subjects

During a 2-year period, 127 (of 137) students voluntarily completed the pre- and posttest. The 7% attrition was similar for the three groups. Because some students did not complete all items in the inventory, sample sizes vary in later analyses.

The 1986–87, traditional (TRAD) group consisted of 55 students from two sections of introductory statistics; the first author taught the course without emphasizing selection skills. The 1987–88, selection (SELE) group consisted of 48 students from two sections of introductory statistics; the first author taught the course emphasizing selection skills. Volunteers from other psychology classes constituted a comparison (COMP) group of 24 students who had not and were not taking statistics.

The use of intact groups permitted a selection threat to internal validity, but random assignment of subjects to groups was impossible. In addition, variation in emphasis on teaching selection skills (i.e., the treatment groups) was confounded with the year in which the course was taught and the experience of the instructor. However, the instructor was experienced, having taught for more than 20 years and having taught statistics several times. (The Results section contains a more detailed evaluation of the use of intact groups.)

Materials

Our inventory had two parts: (a) self-reported personal characteristics, including students' GPA, gender, and year in school; and (b) a skills section containing selection items. Students completed the inventory during the first week and again during the last week of the semester.

Students selected one of nine intervals that contained their overall GPA. The lowest interval was less than 2.35, and the highest was greater than 3.74. The other categories consisted of intervals of .20 (e.g., 2.95 to 3.14).

Three colleagues, who routinely teach introductory statistics, evaluated an initial pool of 10 selection items for consistency in terminology, clarity, and relevance. We also agreed that the items should illustrate problems that students could answer after completing the introductory statistics course. Items required students to select from among four alternatives the appropriate statistical analysis for a given research problem. The evaluation process produced 8 items possessing face and content validity. The following are abridged illustrations of items previously reported (Ware & Chastain, 1989).

1. In a study of mother-infant interaction, mothers were classified on the basis of whether or not this was their first child and on the basis of whether this was a low-birth weight or a full-term infant. Trained observers rated the quality of the mothers' interactions with their infants. A higher score represents better mother-infant interaction. The investigators hypothesized that there are no differences among the groups.

    (a) two-factor analysis of variance (ANOVA)

    (b) Spearman rank-order correlation

    (c) chi-square test for independence

    (d) t test for dependent groups

2. Lesions in the amygdala can reduce certain responses commonly associated with fear (e.g., decreases in heart rate). If fear is reduced, then it should be more difficult to train an avoidance response in lesioned animals because the aversiveness of the stimulus will be reduced. One group of rabbits has lesions in the amygdala, and the other is an untreated control group. The data are a ranking of the number of trials to learn an avoidance response.

    (a) simple ANOVA

    (b) Mann-Whitney U test

    (c) Pearson product-moment correlation

    (d) t test for dependent groups

Procedure

The three intact groups constituted the treatment variable. The same instructor taught the TRAD and SELE groups a common core of topics for introductory statistics, including measures of central tendency and variability, correlation and regression, z test, t test, ANOVA, and nonparametric tests. The number and type of homework assignments were virtually identical for the two groups.

In the SELE group, the instructor taught the course emphasizing several conditions for selecting statistical tests. The first author developed and distributed a handout, adapted from Siegel (1956), consisting of a table with rows corresponding to the levels of measurement of the dependent variable. The table's columns identified conditions associated with the independent variable, such as the number of groups, whether the groups were independent or dependent, and whether testing for differences or relationships. The table identified a particular statistical test at the intersection of rows and columns. Those conditions constituted two dimensions for selecting a statistical test. These dimensions were similar to the guidelines that Magnello and Spies (1984) derived from factor analysis (i.e., scale of measurement and function) and were used because organizing concepts facilitate the learning of new concepts. In lectures; the instructor repeatedly referred to the handout and emphasized the use of the dimensions on the handout for selecting statistical tests. Finally, on three of five examinations, counting the final exam, the instructor included several multiple-choice questions that required students to select the appropriate statistical test for a particular research problem.

Design and Analysis

The 3×2 factorial design evaluated three treatments (TRAD, SELE, and COMP) and two person variables (GPA and gender). There were separate analyses for treatment groups and GPA and for treatment groups and gender. We formed GPA groups by dividing the students' responses into low and high, using the median as the fulcrum value. The dependent variable was the posttest selection score.

We used analysis of covariance (ANCOVA) of the posttest selection scores with adjusted pretest selection scores as the covariate for all omnibus F tests. Using adjusted pretest scores "corrects for the effects of irrelevance as well as measurement error" (Cook & Campbell, 1979, pp. 191–192), but ANCOVA does not solve the problem of threats to internal validity.

Results

Principal Analyses

The three groups (TRAD, SELE, and COMP) did not differ in pretest selection scores, $F(2, 124) = 1.06, p = .35$. The ANCOVA results, when blocked over GPA, revealed significant differences in selection skills among the treatment groups, $F(2, 120) = 14.67, p < .01$. Results from subsequent Scheffé tests indicated that students in the SELE group ($M = 4.54, SD = 1.64$) obtained higher selection scores ($p < .05$) than did students in the TRAD ($M = 3.69, SD = 1.71$) and COMP groups ($M = 1.71, SD = 1.40$). Students in the TRAD group had significantly higher selection scores ($p < .05$) than did students in the COMP group. Students having higher GPAs obtained significantly higher selection scores ($M = 4.15, SD = 1.91$ vs. $M = 3.10, SD = 1.80$) than did those having lower GPAs, $F(1, 89) = 11.47, p < .01$. There was no significant interaction.

The ANCOVA for treatment groups and gender revealed no reliable differences in selection scores between men and women. There was no interaction between treatment groups and gender.

Threats to Internal Validity

Because the use of intact groups permitted a selection threat, we examined the relationship between the treatment groups and GPA, gender, and year in school. The median GPA for the sample was the interval from 2.95 to 3.14. A Kruskal-Wallis test for differences in self-reported GPAs for students in the three groups revealed no significant differences, $\chi^2(2, N = 126) = .34, p = .85$.

Overall, women constituted 61% and men 39% of the sample. A chi-square test for independence between groups and gender revealed a relationship between the two variables, $\chi^2(2, N = 127) = 7.51, p = .02$. The TRAD group had a lower proportion of women (47%) than did the SELE (69%) and COMP (75%) groups.

Sophomores, juniors, and seniors constituted 26%, 49%, and 25% of the sample, respectively. A chi-square test for independence between groups and year in school revealed a significant difference, $\chi^2(8, N = 122) = 15.45, p < .01$. The SELE group had a higher proportion of sophomores than did the other two groups.

At the outset, a confounding existed between treatment groups and gender and between treatment groups and year in school. Results from studies of gender differences in statistics have been equivocal. When gender differences have been reported, sometimes men (Feinberg & Halperin, 1978; Ware & Chastain, 1989) and sometimes women (Brooks, 1987) have obtained higher scores. Anecdotal evidence indicates that juniors and seniors perform at a higher level in statistics than do freshmen and sophomores. Thus, if the confounding in our study exerted a bias, it favored the TRAD group.

Because Giambra (1970, 1976) found that higher scores in statistics were related to GPA, we were concerned that the confounded variables might be associated with different levels of academic ability among those in the treatment groups. Results of chi-square tests for independence between GPA and groups, $\chi^2(2, N = 96) = .71, p = .70$; GPA and gender, $\chi^2(1, N = 96) = .71, p = .40$; and GPA and year in school, $\chi^2(2, N = 92) = .020, p = .91$, revealed no significant relationships. Thus, the absence of relations between GPA and those three variables reduced but did not eliminate our concern about the confounding threat to internal validity.

Discussion

We found significantly higher selection scores among students taught statistics with an emphasis on selection skills versus those taught statistics without such an emphasis. Moreover, both groups of students taking statistics scored higher than students who had not taken and were not taking statistics. These results extend Ware and Chastain's (1989) findings and suggest that emphasizing selection skills through handouts, lectures, and examinations can increase these skills beyond the levels achieved by conventional methods of teaching statistics. Thus, part of the success of this study might be attributed to the use of a model that is consistent with students' cognitive structure for various statistical concepts (Magnello & Spies, 1984). If one danger of using computers is a greater risk of choosing inappropriate statistical tests and if the acquisition of selection skills is a pertinent objective for an introductory statistics course, then our results suggest that teachers must emphasize selection skills (e.g., through handouts, lectures, and examinations) rather than simply expect students to "get it on their own."

We remind readers to view our results with some caution because of selection threats and confounding. Replication of our study without its design limitations would increase confidence in its results and implications.

Finding that students with higher GPAs scored significantly higher on selection items than those with lower GPAs is consistent with previous research (Giambra, 1970, 1976; Ware & Chastain, 1989). Giambra (1970) concluded that "success in an undergraduate behavioral statistics course has little to do with a student's past mathematical background, and [it] seems to depend on [the person's] overall ability as a student" (p. 367). Research findings appear consistent; students with higher GPAs perform better whether the dependent variable is selection score, interpretation score, or overall score in the course. Discovering cognitive and motivational factors that can increase statistics performance among students with lower GPAs remains a challenge.

Our failure to find gender differences in selection skills is consistent with some studies (Buck, 1985, 1987; Elmore & Vasu, 1980; Ware & Chastain, 1989), but inconsistent with others showing higher interpretation scores for men than women (Ware & Chastain, 1989), higher overall scores in statistics classes for men than women (Feinberg & Halperin, 1978), and higher overall scores for women than men (Brooks, 1987). The inconsistent findings involving gender differences in statistics may depend on the choice of dependent variables and the nature of the demands that different statistics teachers place on selection, interpretation, and other skills. We need additional research to identify conditions that contribute to gender differences in statistics.

Despite its limitations, our study contributes to the sparse literature on teaching statistics. Our findings highlight the importance of emphasizing selection skills if students are to learn them. Ware and Chastain (1989) pointed out that statistical interpretation and computer skills, such as use of a mainframe computer and SPSS-X, are also important. A challenge remains to identify other relevant skills, develop pedagogical strategies, and discover relevant personality variables that facilitate learning in statistics classes.

References

Bartz, A. E. (1981). The statistics course as a departmental offering and major requirement. *Teaching of Psychology, 8,* 106.

Brooks, C. I. (1987). Superiority of women in statistics achievement. *Teaching of Psychology, 14,* 45.

Buck, J. L. (1985). A failure to find gender differences in statistics achievement. *Teaching of Psychology, 12,* 100.

Buck, J. L. (1987). More on superiority of women in statistics achievement: A reply to Brooks. *Teaching of Psychology, 14,* 45–46.

Castellan, N. J. (1982). Computers in psychology: A survey of instructional applications. *Behavior Research Methods, Instruments, & Computers, 14,* 198–202.

Cook, T. D., & Campbell, D. T. (1979). *Quasi-experimentation: Design & analysis issues for field settings.* Boston: Houghton Mifflin.

Couch, J. V., & Stoloff, M. L. (1989). A national survey of microcomputer use by academic psychologists. *Teaching of Psychology, 16,* 145–147.

Elmore, P. B., & Vasu, E. S. (1980). Relationship between selected variables and statistics achievement: Building a theoretical model. *Journal of Educational Psychology, 72,* 457–467.

Feinberg, L. B., & Halperin, S. (1978). Affective and cognitive correlates of course performance in introductory statistics. *Journal of Experimental Education, 46,* 11–18.

Giambra, L. M. (1970). Mathematics background and grade-point average as predictors of course grade in an undergraduate behavioral statistics course. *American Psychologist, 25,* 366–367.

Giambra, L. M. (1976). Mathematical background and grade-point average as predictors of course grade in an undergraduate behavioral statistics course: A replication. *Teaching of Psychology, 3,* 184–185.

Magnolia, M. E., & Spies, C. J. (1984). Using organizing concepts to facilitate the teaching of statistics. *Teaching of Psychology, 11,* 220–223.

Siegel, S. (1956). *Nonparametric statistics for the behavioral sciences.* New York: McGraw-Hill.

Stoloff, M. L., & Couch, J. V. (1987). A survey of computer use by undergraduate psychology departments in Virginia. *Teaching of Psychology, 14,* 92–94.

Ware, M. E., & Brewer, C. L. (1988). *Handbook for teaching statistics and research methods.* Hillsdale, NJ: Lawrence Erlbaum Associates, Inc.

Ware, M. E., & Chastain, J. D. (1989). Computer-assisted statistical analysis: A teaching innovation? *Teaching of Psychology, 16,* 222–227.

Notes

1. A Creighton University Summer Faculty Research Fellowship supported the preparation of this article.
2. We thank Gary Leak, Dan Murphy, and three anonymous reviewers for their helpful comments on an earlier draft of this article.

A Microcomputer-based Statistics Course With Individualized Assignments

Richard L. Rogers
Georgia Southern College

Published surveys of instructional computing in psychology (Butler & Kring, 1984; Castellan, 1982) indicate that computers are most often used in statistics courses. Using computers permits students to spend less time learning and doing computations; hence, more time is available for conceptual understanding and different statistical applications. A valuable by-product of using computers in the statistics course is that students will develop some elementary computer literacy.

A common approach to using computers for instructional purposes is to buy one copy of the software and make it available on a computer network. This approach is necessary when the statistical programs, such as SPSS, require a mainframe (Tromater, 1985). Even if the software will run on microcomputers, the expense involved in providing a copy for each student can be a problem. A network approach works well if the network can handle the demand; if it cannot, the course can be disrupted when the network is down or when students have to wait too long to gain access. I prefer to provide each student with a copy of the software to run on a microcomputer. One important advantage of this approach is that students can do their assignments on the six Apple II microcomputers located in our department where students can usually get help from a graduate assistant or me. Students can also use any of the Apples available to them at other times and places. I also value the greater independence, flexibility, and self-reliance that result from students using stand-alone microcomputers.

Until recently, providing each student with a copy of the software often created economic or ethical problems. At least one textbook/software package is now available at a price comparable to that of a textbook alone (Elzey, 1985). I share here my experiences using this package in an introductory statistics course taught in the psychology department. The class consisted of 18 psychology majors taking my course as a requirement.

Elzey's package falls into Butler and Eamon's (1985) student research category: "programs that may be useful to students who need to analyze research data in lab courses or professionals who need to analyze a small amount of data" (p. 354). The software consists of 19 programs on one diskette. The first two programs, one for univariate data and one for bivariate data, allow students to create data files and save them on disk to be accessed by the statistical programs. The other 17 programs are statistical routines covering the procedures that one would expect to include in an introductory statistics course and more. In addition to basic descriptive statistics, bivariate correlation and regression, t tests, and one-way ANOVA, the package includes multiple regression with two predictors, two-way and repeated measures ANOVA, analysis of covariance, and five nonparametric procedures.

The statistical programs are menu-driven and relatively easy for students to use. The breadth of coverage and the ability to create and access data files increase the package's usefulness for teaching statistics and analyzing data in research-oriented undergraduate courses. On the negative side, the software has some weaknesses. The programs' error-trapping is rather poor. For example, if one tries to do a univariate procedure using a bivariate data file, a common error for inexperienced students, the program displays its computing message indefinitely and will not respond to any further commands; the program must be started over. Another weakness in the current version of the programs is the inability to take advantage of a two-disk system. The user must swap the program disk and the data disk as needed. My students and I discovered a few bugs in the current version of the software. The most troublesome is the reporting of some incorrect probability values. For example, in the two-way ANOVA routine, if the observed value of F is less than 1.00, the program may report an associated p value of less than .001. The publisher's support is an advantage. Halfway through the course I received an update of the

programs and permission to distribute copies to the class members. The publisher also solicited suggestions for enhancements to the programs with the assurance that an enhanced version, supporting a two-disk system, would be available before the fall of 1986.

Weekly assignments consist of a data set and questions about the data to be answered using the statistical routines. Each student received a unique set of data prepared with a program called, *Correlated Samples* (published by HMS Software, P.O. Box 49186, Austin, TX 78765). This program produces random samples from a population defined by the user. The user designates the mean and standard deviation of the population, the sample size, and the correlation between pairs of samples. The program then generates as many pairs of random samples as requested with the data on one page of output and sample statistics (*M, SD,* variance, correlation, and both independent- and correlated-sample t tests) on another page for each sample. I distribute the data and keep the sample statistics to aid in grading the assignments. These individualized assignments help alleviate the problem of a student copying another's work and provide a pedagogical device for the nature of random sampling.

I also use the statistical software to create materials for examinations. Learning to select the right statistical procedure to answer a question about a particular data set is an important aspect of the course. I test the students' ability to do this by presenting several descriptions of research situations and several printouts from the statistical program. The student must select the appropriate printout for each research situation and use it to make statistical decisions and research conclusions. This kind of test item constitutes a major portion of the final exam. It is an in-class exam but students are allowed to use their books and class notes for this part of the final.

Although the software in this package is useful in my course, the textbook is disappointing. The sections of the book dealing with the use of the statistics programs are good, but the book is not as adequate as a source of conceptual understanding and varied applications. Of the approximately 240 pages of text (not including statistical tables, exercises, and solutions to exercises), roughly 75 deal with using the computer programs and the other 165 are devoted to presenting and explaining statistical concepts and procedures. It is not surprising that beginning statistics students derive little understanding from the book, given that the author tries to cover everything from basic descriptive procedures through factorial ANOVA, ANCOVA, and several nonparametric procedures in those 165 pages. I supplement the book with other materials, such as handouts or other books.

It is impossible to compare the performance of students in this class with that of students in previous classes not using the computer materials because the skills assessed and the the evaluation procedures were too different. However, students' performance on the final exam previously described can be reported. Each of 18 students had to select the appropriate statistical procedure for five items. Of the total 90 items attempted, 70 were answered correctly (78%). Nine of the 20 incorrect responses were made by two students who failed the exam. For the students who passed, 86% of these items were answered correctly.

As part of the course evaluation, the class was asked to comment on the use of microcomputers in the course. Seventeen commented positively and one commented negatively. The negative reviewer suggested that being forced to do the calculations by hand would have produced a better understanding of the procedures.

Despite the difficulties caused by the programs' bugs and the textbook's failings, using the package helped to create a good teaching situation by providing each student with a copy of the software and manual as well as the textbook. If the next version of this package eliminates the inaccuracies and the poor error-trapping, it will be a productive tool for teaching statistics.

References

Butler, D. L., & Eamon, D. B. (1985). An evaluation of statistical software for research and instruction. *Behavior Research Methods, Instruments, & Computers, 17,* 352–358.

Butler, D. L., & Kring, A. M. (1984). Survey on present and potential instructional use of computers in psychology. *Behavior & Research Methods, Instruments, & Computers, 16,* 180–182.

Castellan, N. J. (1982). Computers in psychology: A survey of instructional applications. *Behavior Research Methods, Instruments, & Computers, 14,* 198–202.

Elzey, F. E. (1985). *Introductory statistics: A microcomputer approach.* Monterey, CA: Brooks/Cole.

Tromater, L. J. (1985). Teaching a course in computer-assisted statistical analysis. *Teaching of Psychology, 12,* 225–226.

Classroom Use of the Personal Computer to Teach Statistics

Patricia A. Oswald
Iona College

Surveys show that approximately 50% of college-level psychology faculty use computers as one of several pedagogical methods. Faculty teaching statistics courses are the most likely to use computers (Castellan, 1982; Stoloff & Couch, 1987). Many psychology teachers believe that computers are an important component of their courses and that computers facilitate student learning and increase academic achievement (Butler & Kring, 1984; Halcomb et al., 1989; Sexton-Radek, 1993), but Gratz, Volpe, and Kind (1993) noted that there has been little empirical support for this view.

Assessment of student learning is a critical part of any educational endeavor. There has been movement away from relying solely on exams as a way of assessing student learning (Moss et al., 1992). An alternative method involves using computers as a means of assessment. On my campus, faculty are exploring many new techniques for using computers as assessment tools. Two of these initiatives include using computers (a) to help students self-assess in their first year and (b) as part of our scientific and technological literacy program to assist faculty in evaluating students' mastery of laboratory exercises.

In this article, I discuss how using a single personal computer in the classroom enhances student confidence and ability in using computers, and I identify one of the assessment opportunities that this technique provides. I outline the method used, briefly discuss the necessary software and hardware, identify the educational objectives, and analyze the effectiveness of this method.

Method

Subjects

I conducted this research at Iona College. Forty-one undergraduate psychology majors enrolled in two sections of an elementary statistics course constituted the sample. Twenty-one women (51%) and 20 men (49%) participated. The sample included seniors (56%), juniors (37%), and

63

sophomores (7%). The mean age of the students was 20.70 years ($SD = 1.60$). The mean grade point average (GPA) of the students was 2.88 ($SD = 0.50$) on a 4-point scale. All students had taken one computer course before enrolling in basic statistics.

Equipment and Materials

The equipment included an IBM AT personal computer with one hard drive and two external floppy disk drives (3.5 in. and 5.25 in.), a projection pad, an overhead projector, and a projection screen. The cost of the system is approximately $2,500. This equipment, constructed as a mobile unit, could be transported to any classroom in the psychology building.

The statistical software used was MYSTAT (the student version of SYSTAT). Students purchased the *MYSTAT Manual* and software as a package (Harris, 1991). The *MYSTAT Manual* was written to coordinate with the text used, *Introduction to Statistics for the Behavioral and Social Sciences* (Christensen & Stoup, 1991). MYSTAT is a computer program designed for use in introductory statistics courses. It computes descriptive and inferential statistics. I used a questionnaire to evaluate the effectiveness of the classroom techniques investigated. Students responded to five attitude statements about how confident they were that using computers aided their learning. Students responded to these statements using a 9-point scale ranging from 1 (*strongly disagree*) to 9 (*strongly agree*). Table 1 lists the questions on the survey instrument administered to subjects as a pretest and posttest.

Procedure

During the first week of the fall semester, I demonstrated the equipment and introduced the in-class computer problem-solving method to students in both sections of my statistics course. Then, I administered the pretest to students. Students received standard instruction in statistics using lecture, discussion, in-class problem-solving techniques, and homework assignments (approximately 30% of the out-of-class assignments required computer use). The course covered descriptive statistical techniques (e.g., frequency distributions, measures of central tendency, and measures of variability) and inferential techniques (e.g., one- and two-sample *t* tests and one-way and two-way analyses of variance). As I discussed each of the topical areas of the course, I used the computer for in-class problem-solving exercises.

Typically, I began by presenting a research problem. An example of such a problem is the following: An educator thinks there may be a relation between gender and computer usage in second graders. How does she proceed? First, students identified the type of research design appropriate to answer such a question. Second, once students outlined the rudiments of the design and method, I elaborated on the research method. Then, students identified the appropriate statistical procedure to analyze the data.

Next, I provided data and asked an individual student to conduct the computer analysis. The student entered a small data set as part of the demonstration; for a large data set, I provided the data on a disk. Early in the term, I requested volunteers; later, as students became more comfortable with this instructional method, I called on different students. I assisted students throughout the exercise as needed. Assistance varied according to the type of analysis being done. For example, in a simple linear regression, I helped a student identify the slope and intercept values that were then entered in the next MYSTAT command line to continue the analysis. After the student completed the analysis, the entire group joined in to answer the original research question. Each student had the opportunity to use the computer in front of the class a few times during the semester.

I evaluated students' performance on the in-class computer problem-solving exercises on a dichotomous satisfactory-unsatisfactory basis. This activity accounted for 10% of their final grade.

I allocated approximately 20% of class time for in-class computer problem solving each week (about 30 min of a 150-min class). I administered the posttest measure the last week of the semester in December.

Table 1. Means and Standard Deviations for Pretest and Posttest Attitude Statements

Attitude Statement	Pretest M	Pretest SD	Posttest M	Posttest SD
1. In-class computer problem solving helps me understand course material better than in-class computational problem solving.	7.4	1.3	8.2	1.4
2. I am able to use computers effectively to solve statistical problems.	4.9	2.4	6.9	1.4
3. I feel confident when making informal class presentations like those involved in using the computer in class.	5.0	2.4	6.7	1.5
4. Explaining computer analyses and assignments to the other students in class helps me to learn the material better than independent problem solving.	6.3	1.5	7.3	1.5
5. I learn best when the instructor uses the lecture format primarily.	5.8	2.1	3.3	2.0

Note. Students rated these statements on a 9-point scale ranging from 1 (*strongly disagree*) to 9 (*strongly agree*).

Results

Using *t* tests, I compared the pretest and posttest attitude data. The means and standard deviations for the attitude statements are presented in Table 1.

There was a significant increase in student preference for the use of in-class computer problem solving compared to in-class computational problem solving from the pretest to the posttest, $t(37) = 2.176, p < .05$. Students also reported a significant increase in their ability to use computers to solve problems from pretest to posttest, $t(35) = 4.609, p < .0001$.

Students reported an increase from pretest to posttest in the ease with which they were able to present statistical material and computer procedures orally, $t(35) = 3.789, p < .0001$. In the posttest, students also were more likely to agree that explaining various computer analyses to their classmates enhanced their learning of the material, as compared with the pretest, $t(37) = 2.845, p < .01$. Moreover, there was a significant decrease in students' preference for the primary use of the lecture format from the pretest to posttest, $t(35) = 5.247, p < .0001$.

Finally, I compared students in the computer-oriented section with students whose class did not involve in-class computer problem solving (these students did use computers for out-of-class assignments, however). The latter group completed the course 2 years before with the same instructor and the same textbooks. Although intact groups were used for this comparison, no significant differences between the two groups existed in gender composition, year in college when they took statistics, cumulative GPA, or college major. Using 4-point scales, the computer-oriented section course grade mean was 2.90 ($SD = 0.90$), and the comparison section course grade mean was 2.60 ($SD = 1.40$). This difference was not statistically significant, $t < 1.00$.

Discussion

This pedagogical and assessment method allows the instructor to identify students' understanding of the course material specifically as it relates to the computer analysis and to modify later instruction as necessary. Feedback to the instructor and the student is more immediate than homework assignments or exams. That is, the instructor can assess on the spot whether the current concepts and related computer applications are understood by the student doing the demonstration (and through the feedback from the class, the group's understanding as well) and proceed accordingly. I used this method primarily to assess the students' level of understanding of the computer-related material so that I could adjust my teaching. In addition, I used this method as part of my grading of students. The latter is somewhat informal because I evaluated students on a sat-isfactory-unsatisfactory basis only. Moreover, students' performance on the in-class computer problem-solving exercises accounted for only 10% of their course grade. Nonetheless, I believe that this is a useful technique for assessing students. Furthermore, students noted how helpful it was to test themselves immediately on their understanding of the material and the corresponding computer applications.

Several objectives can be realized by using this technique. These objectives include the opportunity to assess: (a) students' ability to formulate psychological concepts (theory) in quantitative terms by having them identify the appropriate design and method to answer a specific research question; (b) students' understanding of specific course content and its application by, for example, having them determine if the results of the analysis are statistically significant and provide an appropriate interpretation; (c) students' ability to use computerized techniques to analyze data statistically (use of computer hardware and software) by having them execute the necessary steps in a particular statistical procedure; and (d) students' oral presentation skills by having them explain the procedures and results to the class. These objectives may be met using a variety of other teaching methods (e.g., separate class periods of lab instruction in computer usage), but my approach meets these objectives in an economical, all-in-one manner.

There are three benefits to using this instructional method, as compared with using computers for out-of-class assignments only or not using computers at all. First, this method is cost-effective because it does not require access to a computer laboratory with 30 personal computers. The system (one personal computer, a projection pad, an overhead projector, and a projection screen) costs approximately $2,500; a computer laboratory costs considerably more.

Second, this method is teaching effective because it allows for ready assessment of student learning that homework assignments, for example, do not. The instructor can observe firsthand students' ability to use the computer to answer statistical questions and can intervene when individual students who are giving demonstrations, or others in the class, are having difficulty.

Third, this method improves students' attitudes about using computers. After participating in computer-learning activities, students report significant changes in their confidence and ability to use computers to solve statistical problems. Their open-ended survey comments suggest that the in-class computer usage was most valuable in this regard; perhaps this was due to the encouragement and support they received. Moreover, this technique helps to prepare students for more advanced statistics and research methods courses and for doing independent research, all of which require computer expertise. Because no reliable difference was observed in course grades between the students who used the computer in the classroom and those who did not, further investigation is necessary to determine if quantitative learning gains will result (i.e., increases in final statistics grades).

This method also sends a valuable implicit message. According to Gray (1993), an implicit message ". . . includes attitudes about the subject under discussion, attitudes about the students, and expectations about what students will do . . ." (p. 69). The implicit message here is that students can do one of the most important tasks in the practice of psychology—use computerized statistical procedures to answer research questions.

In conclusion, using the personal computer in the classroom provides immediate feedback to the teacher and the learner, enhances students' confidence in using computers and learning computer-related course material, is cost-effective, and fosters experiential learning that enlivens the classroom.

References

Butler, D. L., & Kring, D. B. (1984). Survey on present and potential instructional use of computers in psychology. *Behavior Research Methods, Instruments, & Computers, 16,* 180–182.

Castellan, N. J. (1982). Computers in psychology: A survey of instructional applications. *Behavior Research Methods, Instruments, & Computers, 14,* 198–202.

Christensen, L. B., & Stoup, C. M. (1991). *Introduction to statistics for the behavioral and social sciences.* Pacific Grove, CA: Brooks/Cole.

Gratz, Z. S., Volpe, G. D., & Kind, B. M. (1993, March). *Attitudes and achievement in introductory psychological statistics classes: Traditional versus computer supported instruction.* Paper presented at the 7th annual conference on Undergraduate Teaching of Psychology, Ellenville, NY.

Gray, P. (1993). Engaging students' intellects: The immersion approach to critical thinking in psychology instruction. *Teaching of Psychology, 20,* 68–74.

Halcomb, C. G., Chatfield, D. C., Stewart, B. E., Stokes, M. T., Cruse, B. H., & Weimer, J. (1989). A computer-based instructional management system for general psychology. *Teaching of Psychology, 16,* 148–151.

Harris, B. A. (1991). *MYSTAT manual* (2nd ed.). Pacific Grove, CA: Brooks/Cole.

Moss, P. A., Beck, J. S., Ebbs, C., Matson, B., Muchmore, J., Steele, D., Taylor, D., & Herter, R. (1992). Portfolios, accountability, and an interpretive approach to validity. *Educational Measurement: Issues and Practice, 11,* 12–21.

Sexton-Radek, K. (1993). Using computers to teach the role of professional psychologists. *Teaching of Psychology, 20,* 248–249.

Stoloff, M. L., & Couch, J. V. (1987). A survey of computer use by undergraduate psychology departments in Virginia. *Teaching of Psychology, 14,* 92–94.

Notes

1. An earlier version of this article was presented at the Seventh Annual Conference on the Teaching of Undergraduate Psychology: Ideas and Innovations, Ellenville, NY, March 1993.
2. Thanks to Bernard C. Beins, Charles L. Brewer, and the anonymous reviewers who offered many helpful suggestions on previous drafts of this article.

Standard Errors of Statistics Students

Kenneth B. Melvin
Kristi R. Huff
University of Alabama

For psychology students, introductory statistics is often required but rarely desired. Although the first course in statistics is high on the list of courses preferred by graduate schools, many undergraduates face it with trepidation.

Various pedagogical procedures have been used to reduce student "statisticophobia" and increase performance. For example, researchers have studied the use of such techniques as tape-slides (Harding, Riley, & Bligh, 1981), spreadsheets (Lee & Roper, 1986), repeat examinations (Friedman, 1987), computer-assisted instruction (e.g., Ware & Chastain, 1989), and course mastery (Ward, 1984).

After teaching introductory statistics many times, the first author (Kenneth B. Melvin) noticed common errors by students across various textbooks and classes. Communications with other introductory statistics teachers confirmed similar perceptions. However, a cursory examination of several introductory statistics textbooks revealed sparse coverage of such errors.

Thus, it appeared that a handout cautioning students about these common errors may be welcomed and may lead to error reduction. Our article describes the "common errors" handout and an evaluation of it. We also examined 10 recent statistics textbooks to see whether such a handout is redundant.

Common Errors Handout

The common errors handout consists of 21 common errors matched with the appropriate statistic(s). Some examples are:

1. Deleting square root signs during the computation of standard deviations, t tests, and other statistics.
2. Assuming $(\Sigma X)(\Sigma Y) = \Sigma XY$ in computing r.
3. Dropping the constant, 1, during the computation of r_s.
4. Dividing $(0 - E)^2$ by 0 rather than E when computing chi-square.

Errors are listed in order of their appearance in a typical statistics course.

Textbook Treatment of Errors

A handout of this sort is unnecessary if common errors are emphasized in textbooks. Thus, a convenience sample of 10 recent (1982 to 1990) elementary statistics books was thoroughly reviewed to determine how often they mention common errors. Only one common error was discussed in the average (median) text (not necessarily the same error), with a range of 0 to 5 errors. It appears that the handout is not redundant.

Evaluation of the Handout

Forty-eight students enrolled in two sections of Elementary Statistical Methods during 1989 and 1991 provided data. All students were given the handout, to which they could refer during class and examinations. During the last week of the semester, students received a rating scale consisting of three statements designed to evaluate the handout. Each statement was rated on a 5-point scale ranging from *strongly disagree* (1) to *strongly agree* (5). The three statements received favorable ratings, indicating that students appreciated receiving the handout ($M = 4.6$; $SD = .67$), thought it reduced their mistakes ($M = 3.8$; $SD = .88$), and recommended it for future courses ($M = 4.3$; $SD = .86$).

Although we conducted no systematic study of error reduction, our impression is that such errors were reduced.

Summary

We have selected common errors, but our list is not exhaustive, and teachers can tailor it to their liking. In fact, one general check on errors was not included on our list (but given in lecture). This admonition was to ask yourself whether the answer makes any sense. For example, students may turn in answers indicating that rats run 500 mph, IQs = 330, and $r = 17.99$. Such results should automatically prompt a search for the specific errors. A good source for such checks is a text by Spatz and Johnston (1989).

We believe that the common errors handout is well worth the minimal effort involved. Statistics students appreciate small favors, such as receiving our handout. In introductory statistics, as the song says, "Little things mean a lot."

References

Friedman, H. (1987). Repeat examinations in introductory statistics courses. *Teaching of Psychology, 14*, 20–23.

Harding, C. M., Riley, I. S., & Bligh, D. A. (1981). A comparison of two teaching methods in mathematical statistics. *Studies in Higher Education, 6*, 139–146.

Lee, M. P., & Roper, J. B. (1986). Using spreadsheets to teach statistics in psychology. *Bulletin of the British Psychological Society, 39*, 365–367.

Spatz, C., & Johnston, J. O. (1989). *Basic statistics: Tales of distributions* (4th ed.). Monterey, CA: Brooks/Cole.

Ware, M. E., & Chastain, J. D. (1989). Computer-assisted statistical analysis: A teaching innovation? *Teaching of Psychology, 16*, 222–227.

Ward, E. F. (1984). Statistics mastery: A novel approach. *Teaching of Psychology, 11*, 223–225.

Writing Assignments in Statistics Classes Encourage Students to Learn Interpretation

Bernard C. Beins
Ithaca College

The statistics course is ubiquitous in psychology departments (Bartz, 1981). Judging from the attention the course receives in *Teaching of Psychology,* it induces anxiety for many students (Dillon, 1982) and probably always has. Many years ago, Buxton (1956) bemoaned the prospect of "dealing with undergraduates whose palms sweat at the thought of numbers or who are illiterate regarding them" (p. 87).

Statistics teachers still note student difficulties with quantitative concepts (e.g., Spatz, 1991). Nonetheless, many authors have highlighted their successes in teaching statistics (Allen, 1981; Bossley, O'Neill, Parsons, & Lockwood, 1980; Dillbeck, 1983; Magnello & Spies, 1984).

Benjamin (1991) discussed several factors that enhance student learning in large classes. Many of his suggestions generalize to any course, including statistics. His ideas are consistent with research in cognitive psychology that has identified factors leading to successful instruction and learning. Key ingredients include (a) active learning that fosters greater depth of processing (e.g., Craik & Tulving, 1975); (b) organizing related concepts to create a more coherent nomological network (e.g., Bransford & Johnson, 1972); and (c) defining how data, statistics, and interpretations fit into a network of ideas (e.g., Collins & Loftus, 1975).

This article evaluates a technique whose first goal is to maximize the effects of these ingredients as students learn to translate numerical data into words. A second goal is to refine students' writing skills, an objective that many psychology teachers have actively pursued (e.g., Bennett, 1985; Blevins-Knabe, 1987; Nodine, 1990).

Rationale for this approach arose from my observation that students had trouble translating statistical results into nonstatistical terms. That is, students became adept at deciding the fate of the null hypothesis, but they had difficulty writing about concepts that were not directly tied to computations. Consequently, I introduced systematic exercises on data interpretation and an extra-credit system that provided data sets for students to analyze and interpret in press releases for a putatively intelligent but statistically ignorant audience. I hoped that students would better understand statistical concepts and describe their results in coherent prose.

Method

Subjects

Subjects were 21, 39, 27, and 35 students in four successive statistics classes ($N = 122$). All were psychology majors at Ithaca College, generally sophomores and juniors. The percentage of women in the classes ranged from 62% to 76%.

Procedure

In all four classes, students learned the descriptive and inferential statistics commonly covered in an introductory statistics course (i.e., through one-way analysis of variance [ANOVA]). All classes used Howell's (1987) *Statistical Methods for Psychology.* Although each class differed in the specific work performed, all students took about 12 short, open-book, computational quizzes; wrote 4 closed-book, conceptual tests; and completed weekly computational and computer-based homework problems. The final exam always contained a combination of computational, conceptual, and interpretive questions. Writing and verbal skills received increasing emphasis in the first three classes. The structure of the fourth class was the same as that of the second class.

Traditional-emphasis class. In the first class, I required a written conclusion after each computational problem on all tests and homework exercises. This requirement appeared in the instructions at the beginning of each quiz and on each homework assignment, but students received no further guidance. In this respect, the course resembled a traditional statistics course that does not emphasize writing.

Moderate-emphasis class—1. In the second class, students provided the same kind of written conclusions as students in the traditional-emphasis class, but this second group practiced generating conclusions during class meetings. Thus, these students received a moderate amount of training in interpretive skills.

High-emphasis class. In the third class, students received optional extra-credit assignments. For each of five data sets, they performed appropriate statistical analyses to answer a relevant empirical question and typed a one-page press release using no statistical terminology. The intent was for students to describe the results and convey the meaning of the data to a statistically naive reader. Before writing a press release, the class discussed possible ways to organize the information; on the day the assignment was submitted, one or two students described their approach.

Moderate-emphasis class—2. In the fourth class, the extra-credit assignments were omitted, reproducing the structure of the second class.

Writing Assignments

For the writing assignments, students applied their statistical knowledge to topics far removed from theoretical psychology. For example, one problem addressed the question of whether left-handed batters, right-handed batters, or switch hitters achieve different batting averages. Such a problem allows students to generate rival hypotheses to explain any differences. Many students are knowledgeable about and interested in this topic; class discussions provided help for students naive about baseball. Data for this problem were taken from *The Great American Baseball Stat Book* (James, Dewan, & Project Scoresheet, 1987). Other problems involved data printed in the appendix of the text, generated in class, listed in the *Information Please Almanac* (1987), or derived from published research (e.g., Davis, 1987).

Final Exams

The four classes took comparable final exams comprising four computational, six conceptual, and four interpretive components. All tests included the same types of computations on different data sets and posed conceptually similar questions. All students had ample time to complete the test in the allotted 2½ hr.

An ANOVA compared the four classes according to the degree of emphasis on interpretation. The dependent variable was the student's percentage correct for each type of question. Students received some credit for incomplete or partially correct answers.

Data were included for all students in the high-emphasis class, even for those who had not completed writing assignments, because these students still had more extensive experience with interpretation than students in other classes. If these students' scores had been omitted, the means for the high-emphasis group may have been somewhat higher.

The data were analyzed using the multivariate analysis of variance (MANOVA) routine from SPSS-X (SPSS, 1988). Probabilities that appear with the data analysis are exact values from the computerized analysis.

Results

Computational Scores on the Final Exam

Students who received the greatest emphasis on writing and interpretation showed the best computational skills, $F(3, 118) = 3.43$, $p = .019$. The only significant pairwise difference was between the high-emphasis group ($M = 80.9$) and the moderate-emphasis-1 group ($M = 66.2$). As Table 1 indicates, the results show nearly equal means in the traditional-emphasis class and in both moderate-emphasis classes but notably better scores in the high-emphasis class. Thus, writing assignments were associated with higher computational scores.

Conceptual Scores on the Final Exam

Although emphasis on interpretive skills was associated with better computational skills, there were no differences among means on conceptual questions on the final exams, $F < 1$. The low scores presumably reflect difficulty of the material and complexity of the textbook. Fortunately, the emphasis on writing and interpretation seems not to have detracted from students' performance in the conceptual realm.

Interpretive Scores on the Final Exam

Greater experience in writing and interpretation was associated with higher skill level in interpreting statistical results, $F(3, 118) = 7.67$, $p = .0001$. The high-emphasis

Table 1. Mean Percentage Correct on Computational, Conceptual, and Interpretive Segments of Final Exams

Emphasis on Interpretation	Computational Scores	Conceptual Scores	Interpretive Scores	
Traditional	67.6	54.6	41.0	(54.4)
Moderate—1	66.2	54.0	62.8	(61.0)
High	80.9	58.3	79.3	(72.8)
Moderate—2	70.1	54.9	59.7	(61.6)
	(71.2)	(55.4)	(60.7)	

Note. Values in parentheses indicate marginal means.

class had significantly higher scores than did both moderate-emphasis classes, which, in turn, had significantly higher scores than the traditional-emphasis class, according to the Newman-Keuls test ($p < .05$). Thus, the writing program achieved at least one demonstrably ameliorative effect—a greater ability by students to articulate the meaning of their data analyses.

Discussion

The design of this study is quasi-experimental; hence, one must be cautious in assigning a causal role to the intervention of writing and interpretation. Nevertheless, such a conclusion is consistent with the increase in interpretive scores with the introduction of more writing and a subsequent diminution in those scores when the amount of writing decreased.

The relatively poor interpretive performance of students in the traditional-emphasis class is revealing. Even at the time of the final exam, these students either did not understand that interpretation skills are quite important or were simply unable to provide coherent, verbal explanations of the results of their statistical analyses. Students in the traditional-emphasis class apparently developed statistical skills but not perspective about the underlying reason for using statistics. That is, such students may achieve competence in a "cookbook" approach to statistics, but they still fail to recognize the basic reason for using statistics—to help people answer questions.

The high-emphasis group scored reliably higher on the interpretive components of the final exam than did students in the other classes. Apparently, learning to articulate their conclusions also helps students learn that a number derived from a statistical computation only begins the complex process of answering an empirical question using logic, information, and common sense.

Further Applications of Writing to Learn Interpretation

Teachers who use primary sources for their classes have concluded that students also have difficulty articulating the results of studies they read. Poe (1990) recognized this problem and developed a scheme in which students improved their literature reviews through writing. Her approach focused on more technical writing, but the desired outcome was the same—better organization and presentation of empirical information.

Furthermore, writing about primary sources can be a tool for acquiring knowledge in a given content area. Price (1990) initiated a writing program to replace the lecture format in an introductory psychology class and reported that student performance matched that of students in previous courses based on lectures.

Hinkle and Hinkle (1990) also noted potential advantages of writing in content courses and advocated empirical assessment of its efficacy. My results support their tentative findings that writing helps students organize ideas.

I have begun to ask students in my research courses to translate journal articles into jargon-free language for oral presentation. I have not yet evaluated this approach systematically, but students seem to experience the same kind of difficulty understanding published research reports as they do conceptualizing the results of their own data analyses. This approach to writing may inform students about what they do not understand and may foster a more coherent understanding of the relevant concepts.

Finally, I have used a similar approach in my senior seminar by requiring students to make oral presentations of published research. Students are encouraged to make their presentations as informative and interesting as possible and to avoid arcane details. Many students initially had difficulty conveying the meaning of what they read in journals. Students who make the best presentations are those who translate technical details into comprehensible English. Encouraging students to report in nontechnical language may help them overcome the problems of reading and writing mentioned by Poe (1990) and Price (1990).

The major drawback to this approach concerns the time commitment for the students and the instructor. Willingham's (1990) guidelines for improving the effectiveness of feedback illustrate the importance of structuring comments to fit student needs and hint at the time commitment involved. In contrast, Nodine (1987) described ways to enhance student writing with minimal time commitment by students and teachers. Blevins-Knabe (1987) suggested the use of peer critiques in which students benefit from shared interactions in evaluating each other's writing.

Considerable sentiment favors the use of feedback for writing about complicated topics (see McGovern & Hogshead, 1990). Poe (1990) and Price (1990) both concluded that the benefits of a teacher's input outweigh the costs.

My technique can be adapted to courses in any content area. Translating complicated information into everyday English benefits students by actively engaging them in the subject matter. Beyond the classroom, anyone who needs to understand quantitative information will appreciate the skill of a writer who can express complex ideas clearly.

References

Allen, G. A. (1981). The χ^2 statistic and Weber's law. *Teaching of Psychology, 8,* 179–180.

Bartz, A. E. (1981). The statistics course as a departmental offering and major requirement. *Teaching of Psychology, 8,* 106.

Benjamin, L. T., Jr. (1991). Personalization and active learning in the large introductory psychology class. *Teaching of Psychology, 18,* 68–74.

Bennett, S. M. (1985). Coordinated teaching of psychology and composition: A valuable strategy for students and instructors. *Teaching of Psychology, 12,* 26–27.

Blevins-Knabe, B. (1987). Writing to learn while learning to write. *Teaching of Psychology, 14,* 239–241.

Bossley, M., O'Neill, G., Parsons, C., & Lockwood, J. (1980). Teaching implications of statistical procedures used in current research. *Teaching of Psychology, 7,* 107–108.

Bransford, J. D., & Johnson, M. K. (1972). Contextual prerequisites for understanding: Some investigations of comprehension and recall. *Journal of Verbal Learning and Verbal Behavior, 11,* 717–726.

Buxton, C. E. (1956). Issues in undergraduate education in psychology. *American Psychologist, 11,* 84–95.

Collins, A. M., & Loftus, E. F. (1975). A spreading activation theory of semantic processing. *Psychological Review, 82,* 407–428.

Craik, F. I. M., & Tulving, E. (1975). Depth of processing and the retention of words in episodic memory. *Journal of Experimental Psychology, 104,* 268–294.

Davis, M. (1987). Premature mortality among prominent American authors. *Drugs and Alcohol Dependence, 18,* 133–138.

Dillbeck, M. C. (1983). Teaching statistics in terms of the knower. *Teaching of Psychology, 10,* 18–20.

Dillon, K. M. (1982). Statisticophobia. *Teaching of Psychology, 9,* 117.

Hinkle, S., & Hinkle, A. (1990). An experimental comparison of the effects of focused freewriting and other study strategies on lecture comprehension. *Teaching of Psychology, 17,* 31–35.

Howell, D. C. (1987). *Statistical methods for psychology* (2nd ed.). Boston: Duxbury.

Information please almanac. (1987). Boston: Houghton-Mifflin.

James, B., Dewan, J., & Project Scoresheet. (1987). *The great American baseball stat book.* New York: Ballantine.

Magnello, M. E., & Spies, C. J. (1984). Using organizing concepts to facilitate the teaching of statistics. *Teaching of Psychology, 11,* 220–223.

McGovern, T. V., & Hogshead, D. L. (1990). Learning about writing, thinking about teaching. *Teaching of Psychology, 17,* 5–10.

Nodine, B. F. (1987, February). *Process of teaching and learning in psychology.* Paper presented at the Psychology Curriculum Enhancement Conference, Union, NJ.

Nodine, B. F. (Ed.). (1990). Psychologists teach writing [Special issue]. *Teaching of Psychology, 17*(1).

Poe, R. E. (1990). A strategy for improving literature reviews in psychology courses. *Teaching of Psychology, 17,* 54–55.

Price, D. W. W. (1990). A model for reading and writing about primary sources: The case of introductory psychology. *Teaching of Psychology, 17,* 48–53.

Spatz, C. (1991, October). *Teaching hard-to-understand concepts in statistics: Some techniques.* Paper presented at the Mid-America Conference for Teachers of Psychology, Evansville, IN.

SPSS, Inc. (1988). *SPSS-X user's guide* (3rd ed.). Chicago: Author.

Willingham, D. B. (1990). Effective feedback on written assignments. *Teaching of Psychology, 17,* 10–13.

Notes

1. These results were presented at the annual meeting of the American Psychological Association, San Francisco, August 1991.

2. I thank Charles L. Brewer and three anonymous reviewers for their insightful comments on previous versions of this article.

71

Assessing Writing and Statistical Competence in Probability and Statistics

Paul C. Smith
Alverno College

McGovern and Hogshead (1990) identified four primary objectives for written assignments: assess students, promote student learning, develop student writing skills, and facilitate analytic and creative-thinking and problem-solving skills. The authors expressed concerns about how little writing is done by psychology students. I have an additional concern that students will come to think of writing as something done in the "soft" courses (or "opinion" courses) and not in the methods courses.

Writing assignments in my Probability and Statistics course require students to demonstrate different skills than those more traditionally emphasized in this course. The assignments I use specifically emphasize the selection and critical interpretation skills recognized as those that students are likely to use in the future (Rogers, 1987; Ware & Chastain, 1989).

Assignments

In contrast with many probability and statistics assignments, these open-ended written assignments allow advanced students to demonstrate their deeper understanding while providing struggling students with the clear criteria they need for success. The first assignment asks students to make comparisons between men and women using variables they have selected from a data file. Students are to use cross-tabulation tables, so they must use categorical variables, such as marital status, to make their comparisons. In later assignments, other techniques are added. For example, the second assignment requires students to make comparisons between first- and third-world countries, using both cross-tabulation tables and means (with interval/ratio scale variables).

Assessment of Statistical Skills

Selection

Because students begin with a limited set of statistical tools, they learn to select variables to go with the tools, rather than select the appropriate tools to go with the variables. When the students' stock of techniques is more extensive, I give assignments that require students to select from several techniques to answer their questions. These assignments provide students with a general topic of interest, but students select questions to ask and find the computer commands to generate the statistics they need to answer those questions.

Interpretation

These assignments are given in the guise of a formal communication with a supervisor; therefore, I expect them to communicate well. I am most interested in plain English statements of the results that do not make any unsupported claims but do provide answers to the questions asked in the assignment. I also ask students to make conjectures that go beyond the data. This procedure helps make clear the distinction between reason and observation as ways of knowing, and I point out this distinction in a debriefing after returning the assignment.

Assessment of Writing Skills

Our faculty expect students to demonstrate numerous skills involved in writing. These include establishment of common context, use of clear verbal expression, use of appropriate conventions, use of appropriate support and development, and accurate self-assessment of writing skills.

Establishing Common Context

Asking students to establish context amounts to asking them to provide the reader with the information necessary to judge the reliability of the data sources; this is both good writing and good psychological practice. In these assignments, establishing common context involves telling the reader the purpose of the project, identifying the source of the data, and distinguishing between statements supported by the data and those involving conjecture by the student.

Verbal Expression

When learning to write academically, students tend to migrate unnecessarily to obscure words. We need to make continually clear that good academic writing uses obscure words only when necessary for accuracy and to avoid ambiguity. At this point in the curriculum, students do not know what level of knowledge and interest to expect of the readers of academic journals. These papers are, therefore, directed toward more familiar audiences.

Appropriate Conventions

It is important to remind students that they need to use proper spelling, punctuation, capitalization, sentence structure, and format across the curriculum, whether in writing lab or upper level psychology courses. Furthermore, constructive feedback is essential to producing good writers. A student who has a recurring problem will benefit greatly from feedback pointing out the problem and explaining how to correct it.

Support and Development

The general requirement for this skill is that students provide evidence for their claims. These assignments clearly suggest a source of evidence in the results of the data analyses. Students who write about the differences between men and women in some area without citing the specific numbers from the tables that establish these differences have not grasped the need for support in writing.

Self-Assessment

Self-assessment forces students to attend to the specific criteria by which we will judge their writing, and we hope that students will internalize these criteria and apply them to their writing in all contexts. When students develop this self-assessment ability, they also develop the means for using their skills without our guidance.

Conclusion

This framework for assessment of student writing provides a structured way to use written assignments in probability and statistics courses to both teach and assess students' communication abilities. The assignments emphasize accurate interpretation of the numbers, which is the core skill psychology students will need.

References

McGovern, T. V., & Hogshead, D. L. (1990). Learning about writing, thinking about teaching. *Teaching of Psychology, 17,* 5–10.

Rogers, R. L. (1987). A microcomputer-based statistics course with individualized assignments. *Teaching of Psychology, 14,* 109–111.

Ware, M. E., & Chastain, J. D. (1989). Computer-assisted statistical analysis: A teaching innovation? *Teaching of Psychology, 16,* 222–227.

Note

I thank Jane Halonen for her comments on earlier versions of this article and Russell Brooker for his inspiration and effort in implementing the assignments described herein.

How Often Are Our Statistics Wrong?
A Statistics Class Exercise

Joseph S. Rossi
University of Rhode Island

Several years ago, Rosenthal (1978) published an article with the provocative title, "How Often are Our Numbers Wrong?" The point of his study was to determine the frequency of data recording errors, and the extent to which such errors were likely to be biased in favor of the experimenter's hypothesis. His results were encouraging, because only about 1% of all observations were found to be erroneous. However, about two thirds of the errors were biased in favor of the experimenter's hypothesis. In this article, I describe an out-of-class exercise, similar to one first outlined by Barnwell (1984), for a course in statistics or research methodology that examines a question similar to that posed by Rosenthal: How often are our statistical test results wrong?

Exercise

Students are asked to find examples in the journal literature of one or two statistical tests that have been covered in class. Chi-square, *t* tests, and one-way ANOVA are the most frequently assigned tests, because they are among the most commonly used statistical techniques, and more important, they can be recomputed from summary statistics. The number of tests assigned to each student depends on a variety of factors, such as the level of instruction (graduate or undergraduate) and which techniques have been discussed in class. For undergraduate classes, students are usually permitted to choose either chi-square or *t* tests. For graduate classes, I usually assign both *t* and *F* tests to each student.

Each journal article containing the appropriate statistical test must be checked to verify that sufficient information is reported to enable the student to recompute its value. Raw data are rarely reported, but usually there are sufficient summary data to permit recalculation. For example, recomputation of a chi-square test requires cell frequencies. Independent groups *t* tests and ANOVA require sample sizes, means, and standard deviations for all groups. Correlation coefficients and repeated measures analyses (both *t* and *F*) cannot be included in this exercise, because they cannot be recomputed from summary statistics.

Formulas to recompute chi-square and *t* values from summary data are available in most introductory statistics texts. Formulas for computing *F* ratios from summary statistics are not widely known and must be presented to the class. Gordon (1973) and Rossi (in press) have provided such formulas for one-way ANOVA, and Huck and Malgady (1978) for two-way ANOVA. Not all journal articles provide sufficient summary data to recompute statistical tests. Students were asked to record the number of articles searched that had to be rejected for incomplete reporting of data.

Study 1

For the first study, an undergraduate class was assigned the task of locating and recomputing either a *t* test or a chi-square test. Each student recorded the number of journal articles rejected because of insufficient summary data. When a suitable journal article was located, the student recomputed the value of the statistical test. Degrees of freedom (*df*) were also computed and compared to the author's report.

Results

The number of articles searched and rejected by each student ranged from 1 to 50 (median = 8). Sufficient summary data appeared to be more frequently available for chi-squares tests (median rejections = 4.5) than for *t* tests (median rejections = 10). This difference was significant by the Wilcoxon rank-sum test, $p < .05$.

Several students inadvertently selected the same journal articles for analysis. When duplicates were omitted, the number of *t* tests selected for recomputation was 12; the number of chi-square tests was 9. (One student selected and recomputed results based on a one-way ANOVA. This test will be included among the *t*-test results.) Discrepancies between the value of the test statistic reported by the author and the value recomputed by the student were apparent for 3 of the *t* tests (25%) and 2 of the chi-square tests (22.2%). In all, 5 of 21 test values (23.8%) appeared to be inaccurate. No specific criterion (e.g., percentage of discrepancy) was given to students to aid their classification of a result as "in error" or "not in error." However, I checked all student computations, and none of the five discrepancies could be attributed to only minor deviations, which are inevitable due to the rounding of values in reported summary statistics.

Table 1 shows the reported and recomputed values, as well as the percentage of discrepancy,[1] for each of the five statistical tests. The average discrepancy was 23.5% (median = 23.3%). Percentage of discrepancy was also determined for all remaining statistical tests reported in the five journal articles containing the inaccurate results. Average discrepancy for these "nondiscrepant" results was 1.5% (median = 1.3%). Thus, all five discrepancies appeared substantial. In addition, there was one incorrectly reported *df* for a *t* test (reported *df* = 10; recomputed *df* = 5).

Study 2

My original purpose in developing this exercise was to point out to students that the statistical tests taught in class really are used by professional scientists. In addition, I wanted to demonstrate that, using relatively simple computations, the students would be able to achieve the same results as obtained by the authors. At first, I expected only a very small error rate (cf. Rosenthal, 1978). Because the results of the first study yielded a much greater error rate than assumed, I planned a more elaborate exercise for a graduate class in statistics. Each student was instructed to recompute the value of a *t* test and of a one-way ANOVA *F* test. The number of rejected articles was again recorded, as were the reported and recomputed test values and degrees of freedom. Some additional data were also tabulated: the percentage of discrepancy (see Footnote 1) between the author's value and the recomputed results, and the significance levels attained by the reported statistical test results and by the recomputed test results.

---

[1]Percentage of discrepancy was computed using the following formula:

$$100 \times \frac{|A - R|}{R}$$

where A is the value of the test statistic reported by the author, and R is the recomputed value. Thus, it is a measure of the extent to which the published value is discrepant from the recomputed value.

Table 1. Discrepant Test Results for Study 1

Test	Reported Value	Recomputed Value	% Discrepancy
χ^2	2.223	2.904	23.5
χ^2	41.5	48.2	13.9
t	1.25	1.63	23.3
t	2.27	2.95	23.1
F	3.91	5.88	33.5

Results

The number of articles rejected for insufficient data was much lower for the graduate class (range = 0 to 13; median = 2) than for the undergraduate class in Study 1. Rejections for *t* tests (median = 1) and for *F* tests (median = 3) did not differ significantly.

The much lower rejection rate for the graduate class was not unexpected. Graduate student search strategies should be more efficient than those of undergraduates, many of whom may be dealing with the journal literature for the first time. In addition, my experience with the first class led me to recommend some journals and to discourage others. For example, APA journals were not recommended, because complete summary data often appear to be missing in APA journal reports (standard deviations are frequently not reported). *Psychological Reports, Perceptual and Motor Skills,* and several other journals were recommended because the editorial policy seems to encourage complete reporting of summary data. Furthermore, these journals include a large number of articles in each issue, often running no more than two or three pages in length, and with a decidedly empirical (rather than theoretical) basis, resulting in relatively simple statistical analyses. Such journals are thus well-suited for this exercise, especially for undergraduates. Nevertheless, 14 different journals were selected by students in Study 2.

A total of 46 statistical tests were examined (23 *t* tests and 23 *F* tests). Discrepancies between reported and recomputed values of less than 5%—about what might be expected as a result of rounding errors—were obtained for less than 60% of the tests. Discrepancies greater than 20% occurred for almost 25% of the statistical tests, and discrepancies greater than 50% were obtained for about 7% of the statistical tests (see Table 2). Table 3 displays the reported and recomputed values of the statistical tests for which discrepancies greater than 30% were obtained. Errors were almost three times as likely to favor the experimenter's hypothesis than not.

Approximately 13% of the tests published as "significant," *p* < .05, were not significant, *p* > .05, after recomputation. Table 4 shows the reported and recomputed values as well as the percentage of discrepancy for these statistical tests. The discrepancies are quite low for two of the tests, because the reported values are very near the critical (.05) values. Note, however, that for one of the two, even the

Table 2. Cumulative Frequency Distribution of Discrepant Results

Discrepancy	% of Tests
≤ 5%	56.5
> 5%	43.5
> 10%	30.4
> 20%	23.9
> 30%	15.2
> 40%	13.0
> 50%	6.5
>100%	4.3

Table 3. Discrepancies Greater Than 30%

Test	Reported Value	Recomputed Value	% Discrepancy
t	7.66	5.89	30.1
F	1.01	0.72	40.3
t	1.80	3.05	41.0
t	1.70	1.20	41.7
F	4.25	9.47	55.1
F	46.85	21.62	116.7
t	1.70	0.39	335.9

Table 4. Tests Incorrectly Reported as "Significant"

Test (df)	Critical Value	Reported Value	Recomputed Value	% Discrepancy
$t(21)$	2.08	2.07	2.03	2.0
$F(3, 67)$	2.75	2.78	2.67	4.1
$t(22)$	2.07	2.19	1.73	26.6
$t(25)$	2.06	1.70	1.20	41.7
$t(25)$	2.06	1.70	0.39	335.9

Table 5. Incorrectly Reported df for Study 2

Test	Reported df	Recomputed df
F	7, 80	7, 40
F	3, 188	3, 88
F	2, 66	2, 69
F	3, 76	3, 67

reported value was not significant, because it did not exceed the critical value! And for the second "low discrepancy" test, the degrees of freedom were also incorrectly reported. In all, there were four cases of incorrectly reported *df,* all for *F* tests. These are displayed in Table 5.

General Discussion

The results of these two exercises are surprising and worrisome. Results are consistent with those reported by Rosenthal (1978) concerning the proportion of errors that favor the author's hypothesis, but frequency of errors seems to be much greater than reported by Rosenthal. Of course, the context of Rosenthal's study was different. Nevertheless, the frequency of errors in the reporting of statistical test results requires further explanation.

The most optimistic possibility is that some students deliberately sought out instances of discrepant results. Although both classes were explicitly asked not to do this, the possibility cannot be ruled out. Because students in Study 2 turned in copies of their journal articles with their reports, a check of sorts is possible. I analyzed all of the remaining statistical tests in the selected articles, a total of 114 additional tests. Results were not quite as extreme as for the student-selected tests, but in general, the essential character of the results remained the same.

A second possibility is that the reported summary statistics (*M*s and *SD*s) are in error, and not the reported test values. The situation is essentially indeterminate in this respect, and at any rate, it would not be much of a consola-

tion if it were the summary statistics that were incorrectly reported. A third possibility—typographical errors—seems implausible, and would again not be saying much for the journal editorial and review process, nor for the author's responsibility to proofread the galleys.

The impact of these results on students is hard to overestimate. The point of the exercise is to emphasize the need for the student to evaluate critically even the numbers that appear in a journal article. Students may be accustomed to evaluating logical arguments in journal articles, especially by the time they are graduate students. Unfortunately, the data that appear in such articles often seem to be authoritative to students: "It's hard to argue with the numbers." This exercise is extremely successful in dispelling such attitudes.

One cautionary note is in order, however. It is important for the instructor to guard against the establishment of overly critical student attitudes. The goal of the exercise is not to make students mistrust statistical arguments in general, but to generate a detective-like attitude toward reading journal articles. "Statistician as sleuth" would be a good description of my intentions for this exercise.

Therefore, it is important to plan carefully the presentation of the collective results of the exercise to the class. I have found it useful to present the exercise in the context of more general methodological techniques, such as meta-analysis or secondary data analysis. Unfortunately, these are relatively advanced topics that are more appropriate for graduate-level courses. Furthermore, discussion of these issues is not yet common in most methods and statistics textbooks, though reasonably priced paperbound editions on these topics have begun to appear, especially for meta-analysis (Cooper, 1984; Fienberg, Martin, & Straf, 1985; Hunter, Schmidt, & Jackson, 1982; Jacob, 1984; Kielcolt & Nathan, 1985; Light & Pillemer, 1984; Rosenthal, 1984; Wolf, 1986).

For undergraduate classes, the results of the exercise may be described in connection with the general problem of conducting a thorough literature review (i.e., verifying the statistical computations in a journal article should be a routine part of conducting a literature review). It is convenient to present this material toward the end of the semester, because it then leads naturally to a discussion of the literature reviews the students will conduct as part of their laboratory research projects in our experimental methods course, which most of our undergraduate majors take in the semester immediately following statistics.

Finally, it is worth noting that several students (both graduates and undergraduates) involved in this exercise in my most recent classes have spontaneously offered to continue the work as a more formal research project by systematically examining several journals. This work has now begun and several small grants have been secured to facilitate the project. It is difficult to imagine a more rewarding conclusion to a class project.

References

Barnwell, G. M. (1984). The multiple benefits of a research literature exercise. *Teaching of Statistics in the Health Sciences, 38,* 5–7.

Cooper, H. M. (1984). *The integrative research interview: A systematic approach.* Beverly Hills, CA: Sage.

Fienberg, S. E., Martin, M. E., & Straf, M. L. (Eds.). (1985). *Sharing research data.* Washington, DC: National Academy Press.

Gordon, L. V. (1973). One-way analysis of variance using means and standard deviations. *Educational and Psychological Measurement, 33,* 815–816.

Huck, S. W., & Malgady, R. G. (1978). Two-way analysis of variance using means and standard deviations. *Educational and Psychological Measurement, 38,* 235–237.

Hunter, J. E., Schmidt, F. L., & Jackson, G. B. (1982). *Meta-analysis: Cumulating research findings across studies.* Beverly Hills, CA: Sage.

Jacob, H. (1984). *Using published data: Errors and remedies.* Beverly Hills, CA: Sage.

Kielcolt, K. J., & Nathan, L. E. (1985). *Secondary analysis of survey data.* Beverly Hills, CA: Sage.

Light, R. J., & Pillemer, D. B. (1984). *Summing up: The science of reviewing research.* Cambridge, MA: Harvard University Press.

Rosenthal, R. (1978). How often are our numbers wrong? *American Psychologist, 33,* 1005–1008.

Rosenthal, R. (1984). *Meta-analytic procedures for social research.* Beverly Hills, CA: Sage.

Rossi, J. S. (in press). One-way ANOVA from summary statistics. *Educational and Psychological Measurement.*

Wolf, F. M. (1986). *Meta-analysis: Quantitative methods for research synthesis.* Beverly Hills, CA: Sage.

Notes

1. Portions of this article were presented at the 94th annual convention of the American Psychological Association, Washington, DC, August 1986.
2. Preparation of this article was supported in part by National Cancer Institute Grant CA27821 to James O. Prochaska. I thank the editor and reviewers for helpful suggestions and Terri Hodson and Elaine Taylor for manuscript preparation.

Teaching Statistics With the Internet

Connie K. Varnhagen
Sean M. Drake
Gary Finley
University of Alberta

The Internet is a popular tool for instruction and can be used to provide students with greater access to information (Jones & Schieman, 1995; Pask & Snow, 1995). World Wide Web (WWW) pages on the Internet can be used to archive course information and assignments. More important, by using the Internet as a supplement, student learning is not confined to course materials or library research. Students can access networked information located all over the world through the Internet.

Increased access to information is one important pedagogical benefit of using the Internet to supplement traditional instruction. Another important benefit may relate to levels of communication (Anderson, 1995–96; Bruning, 1995; Hiltz, 1986, 1990; Jones & Schieman, 1995; Pitt, 1996). Increasingly, nontraditional students enroll in university courses. In many cases, these students cannot attend every lecture or discussion group and need support outside of the classroom. Opportunities for increased contact exist with Internet communication; e-mail and newsgroups allow for virtual office hours, which is particularly important for nontraditional students who may have difficulty attending traditional office hours. In addition, students experiencing learning problems are less likely to get caught in erroneous efforts that are a waste of time; instead, there is potential for contact outside of class or office hours. Furthermore, interpersonal communication may be enhanced; relevant discussion can extend beyond class time through the use of mailing lists, newsgroups, WWW boards, chats, e-mail, and similar services. Finally, given that increasing class sizes have forced a decrease in written assignments, students are able to practice writing skills and forms of argument through electronic communication.

To address these potentially beneficial components of information access and communication, we developed an Internet-based statistics laboratory in association with the more traditional lecture and discussion format class in intermediate statistics. The course was open only to psychology honors students. The types of statistical procedures the students learned were directly relevant to the research they were conducting as part of their honors theses. The goals of the laboratory portion of the course were: (a) to learn how to analyze psychological data using a statistical analysis program, (b) to learn how to interpret output in terms of statistical and scientific hypotheses, (c) to practice writing results in American Psychological Association (APA) format (APA, 1994), and (d) to become familiar with the Internet as a tool for psychological research and communication of results.

At the beginning of the term, we introduced the components of the Internet in a 30-min lecture, designed primarily to clarify the omnipresent jargon about the "information superhighway." Students learned about the most common services available on the Internet. With this context established, we demonstrated computer use and distributed a short handout of steps for starting the computers and running various applications. Students then completed separate short tasks to allow practice in accessing the Internet, using e-mail, posting to the newsgroup, and jumping to different applications. The students worked individually or in pairs in the laboratory, and we circulated to offer assistance and answer questions. The next day, a follow-up lecture and question period on networking and the Internet reinforced their new understanding.

The WWW home page integrated the Internet components of the course, including: (a) an online syllabus and course information, (b) online project description and data archive for laboratory assignments, (c) online help for describing data, (d) pointers to other statistics sites to obtain information or help, (e) integrated e-mail to the instructor and graduate teaching assistant (GTA) responsible for the laboratory, (f) an integrated newsgroup for discussion, and (g) an electronic form for submitting assignments. During the last week of classes, we added a pointer to an electronic evaluation survey.

Students met in the computer room for a weekly 2-hr laboratory period. We took a short amount of time at the beginning of the laboratory to discuss previous laboratory assignments, introduce the current laboratory, and discuss any other concerns. Students generally began to work on the assignments during the laboratory period; however, students completed most of the laboratory outside of the scheduled period. It was not uncommon for a student to e-mail the GTA in the middle of the night with a problem and to receive an immediate e-mail reply. In addition, many newsgroup discussions occurred late at night. We were active participants in the newsgroup, posing our own questions, addressing student questions, and prompting student discussion.

One goal of this evaluation was to assess what components of the system students used as well as the perceived usefulness of each component (Anderson & Joerg, 1996). The Internet contains masses of information; do students use this information to learn statistics and report writing? We asked students to rate the usefulness of the Internet for information acquisition and communication as well as the other integrated applications. In addition, we asked students to rate the perceived usefulness of these various components of the laboratory computer system.

We were particularly concerned with students' abilities to access information on the Internet (Bruning, 1995; Hornby & Anderson, 1995–96; Jones & Schieman, 1995). Perhaps students would use the Internet sources only if they had the necessary skills and access. However, there may be numerous barriers to learning. The students had various levels of computer expertise, ranging from complete novices with only minimal word processing experience to experts who were familiar with Internet navigation. We were not sure that the 2-hr introductory session was sufficient to enable novice computer-using students to use all components of the system on their own. The students also varied in terms of their abilities to physically access a computer with Internet capabilities. A few students had computers at home but most had access only to on-campus computers.

Finally, we were interested in students' affective impression of the computer laboratory (Oswald, 1996; Varnhagen & Zumbo, 1990). Attitudes regarding any type of pedagogy may not be directly related to learning but may exert an indirect effect on learning. We did not want to continue to develop a system that students did not perceive as positive and appropriate for their learning.

Method

Students

Sixteen 4th-year honors psychology students (9 women and 7 men) participated in the laboratory. All students were actively engaged in research related to their honors theses and attended the lecture and discussion component of the course.

Evaluation Survey

The electronic evaluation survey included three sets of questions, relating to use and usefulness of various components of the system, perceived barriers to learning, and perceived value of the experience. In addition, it contained questions relating to self-ratings of computer expertise, estimates of use of the system, and ratings of the value of the system in comparison with other components of the course.

The response format for the perceived use and usefulness items consisted of pull-down bars for 5-item Likert scales; use responses ranged from 1 (*never used*) to 5 (*used every day*) and usefulness responses ranged from 1 (*not at all useful*) to 5 (*extremely useful*). The perceived barriers items used a similar pull-down response format, ranging from 1 (*major barrier*) to 5 (*no barrier at all*) and included a *not applicable* option. The perceived value items consisted of anchoring opposite adjectives with five click-boxes for responding between the adjectives.

The evaluation appeared on the class home page during the last week of classes. Students received a common access code and password to view the survey as well as an individual user alias for submitting their own completed form. The access code allowed only authorized individuals to view the survey. The individual user alias allowed only authorized students to submit responses, imposed a limit of one response per student, and ensured anonymity of responses.

Students completed the evaluation during the last 2 weeks of class. We directed the responses to a separate mailbox and did not view them until after the term was completed.

Results

We received 14 responses to the electronic evaluation. Five students rated themselves as "novice" in response to the computer expertise item, 8 students rated themselves as "intermediate", and 1 student rated him or herself as "expert"; we grouped the self-rated expert with the intermediate students for analyses considering expertise. Given the ordinal nature of Likert scales, the small sample size, and the disparate group sizes, we used descriptive and inferential procedures applicable to ordinal measurement scale data.

Median responses to the use and usefulness items appear in Table 1. The results indicate that the course-related communications aspects of the system and the other applications on the system were most frequently used and were perceived as extremely useful. Lower ratings were found for the other components. Most notably, students reported that they used the statistics information available on the WWW only occasionally or infrequently. No differences in use and perceived usefulness of the various components of the system were found as a function of computer expertise.

Spearman rank order correlations between use and perceived usefulness reflected a relation between use and usefulness ratings, ranging from a statistically nonsignificant $r_s(12) = .11$ for the e-mail to the instructor or GTA item (the majority of the responses were "used frequently" and "extremely useful") to $r_s(12) = .71$, $p < .05$, for the newsgroup item. The average correlation between use and perceived usefulness was $M = .40$ and indicated that, in general, when students reported having used a component they also rated the component as useful.

Table 2 shows median ratings of perceived barriers to learning. As shown in the table, students perceived minimal barriers. There was a statistically significant difference relating to computer training as a function of self-rated computer expertise, Mann-Whitney $U = 3$, $p < .05$. Although there was a statistically significant difference, the novice group did not perceive their inadequate training to be much of a barrier. In addition, the novice computer users appeared to be satisfied with training related to the use of the laboratory system.

Students did not have 24-hr access to the computer laboratory until the 2nd week of classes; although the results of the electronic evaluation indicated minimal physical barriers to their learning, students were initially very vocal in their demands to have extensive laboratory access. Their need, in part, stemmed from limited access across campus or at home to a computer with Internet capabilities. In fact, only four students responded to the items regarding barriers related to home computer use. Based on the responses to these items, the one self-rated novice who attempted to connect from home experienced major problems.

Student attitudes were generally quite positive, as shown in Table 3. Although the median rating on the frustration dimension was moderate, students perceived the computer system as extremely good, stimulating, productive, moderately friendly, fun, and moderately timesaving. Statistical analyses revealed no attitude differences as a function of computer expertise.

Students varied greatly in the number of times per week they used the computer system ($M = 5.5$ times, $SD = 3.7$) as well as in the number of hours they spent per week ($M = 7.3$ hr, $SD = 7.5$). There were no statistically significant differences in number of times used or hours spent as a function of computer expertise.

Table 1. Median Responses to the Use and Usefulness Items

Item	Use	Usefulness
Course-related information on the WWW		
Home page on the WWW	4	4
Syllabus on the WWW	3	5
Assignments on the WWW	4	5
Help with describing data on the WWW	3	3
Pointers to other statistics sites on the WWW	2	3
Course-related communication using the WWW		
Submit an assignment form on the WWW	4	5
Newsgroup	4	5
E-mail to or from instructor or GTA	4	5
E-mail to or from students in the class	5	5
Course-related applications on the system		
SYSTAT	4	5
Word processing	4	5
Other information and communication on the WWW		
E-mail to or from people outside the class	5	5
Accessing other WWW sites in the university	3	4
Accessing other WWW sites outside the university	3	4
Accessing other newsgroups	2	4

Note. Ratings for use and usefulness were based on 5-point scales ranging from 1 (*never used*) to 5 (*used every day*) and from 1 (*extremely unuseful*) to 5 (*extremely useful*), respectively. WWW = World Wide Web; GTA = graduate teaching assistant.

Table 2. Median Responses to the Perceived Barriers to Learning Items

Item	Perceived Barrier
Barriers related to ability, experience, required training	
Inadequate training on using the computer in general	
Novices	4
Intermediate–Experts	5
Inadequate training on using the computer system	5
Difficulty in learning to use the computer in general	5
Difficulty in learning to use the computer system	5
Discomfort in using the computer	5
Poor keyboarding skills	5
Getting lost in the World Wide Web pages	4
Difficulty in seeing the value of using the computer system	5
Physical barriers	
Inconvenient access to the laboratory	4
Difficulty in accessing the network in class	5
Slow speed of the computer system in class	4
Difficulty in reading the materials on the screen	5
Barriers related to home computer use	
Hardware difficulties in using the computer system at home	4
Software difficulties in using the computer system at home	4
Difficulty in accessing the network from home	3
Slow speed of the computer system at home	4

Note. Ratings were based on a 5-point scale ranging from 1 (*major barrier*) to 5 (*no barrier at all*).

Table 3. Median Ratings of Perceived Value of Using the Computer System

Anchors		
Left	Right	Median
Extremely good	*Extremely bad*	1.0
Stimulating	*Boring*	1.5
Productive	*Unproductive*	1.0
Easy	*Difficult*	2.0
Great fun	*Unpleasant work*	2.0
Time saving	*Time wasting*	1.5
Not frustrating	*Frustrating*	3.0
Friendly	*Imposing*	2.0
Confusing	*Clear*	3.5
Too much work	*Not too much work*	3.5

Note. Medians reported are based on a 5-point scale located between the two anchors, ranging from 1 (left anchor) to 5 (right anchor).

Discussion

In general, students rated the communications aspects of the Internet more highly than the information aspects. Students also generally perceived minimal barriers to their learning and were quite positive about the use of the Internet-based statistics laboratory. There were few differences as a function of computer expertise. In part, this may have been due to a lack of technological problems; dissatisfaction with computer courses has been related to difficulties with the computer system (Pear & Novak, 1996). Possibly fortuitously, the applications were well integrated and ran smoothly in the Windows environment. Few computer or network crashes occurred.

Both quality of discussion and student writing skills appeared to improve during the term. Initial newsgroup posts had to do with identifying interesting WWW sites or advertising parties. However, as Bruning (1995) also observed, students began to discuss topical issues, such as when to use what statistical technique and how to examine the data before blindly testing some hypothesis. Student writing also improved. Besides working with the GTA on a mastery approach for the results section assignments, students began to "flame" (criticize) each other in the newsgroup for poor grammar, spelling mistakes, and unclear writing style.

One finding of particular interest was that the students did not report accessing all of the information that was available. We had expected students to make extensive use of the online help and pointers to other statistical sites. Possibly the students did not recognize the richness of this resource. Indeed, one comment on the newsgroup late in the term (in response to a question about a particular way to present data visually) was "Someone went to an awful lot of trouble developing online help. Why don't you check out that pointer?"

We experimented with changing the cache settings in the WWW browser used in the laboratory so that we could use the WWW server's access logs to trace an individual student's progress though WWW pages. However, we were unsuccessful in obtaining any reasonable behavioral traces because only first hits on a page can be recorded; multiple hits and jumps to targets on a page are not recorded by the program. Possibly with new monitoring software we will be able to observe actual progress through WWW pages. On the other hand, students appeared to rely more on direct questioning of the GTA and instructor than on other sources of information (including the text, lecture notes, handouts, and the WWW). Our virtual office hours appear to have been the most convenient resource for the students.

Overall, our experiences with offering an Internet-based laboratory course have been positive. The key to our approach appears to have been a well-integrated system, introduction and practice in using the different components of the system, multiple options for communication, and instructor and GTA involvement in communication.

References

American Psychological Association. (1994). *Publication manual of the American Psychological Association* (4th ed.). Washington, DC: Author.

Anderson, M. D. (1995–96). Using computer conferencing and electronic mail to facilitate group projects. *Journal of Educational Technology Systems, 24,* 113–118.

Anderson, T. D., & Joerg, W. B. (1996). Perceived effectiveness of World Wide Web to supplement university level classroom instruction. *Canadian Journal of Educational Communication, 25,* 19–36.

Bruning, S. D. (1995, April). *Classroom exercise that incorporates Internet discussion groups as an integral element in a communication course.* Paper presented at the meeting of the Central States Communication Association, Indianapolis, IN. (ERIC Document Reproduction Service No. ED 385 887)

Hiltz, S. R. (1986). The "virtual classroom": Using computer-mediated communication for university teaching. *Journal of Communication, 36,* 95–104.

Hiltz, S. R. (1990). Evaluating the virtual classroom. In L. M. Harasim (Ed.). *Online education: Perspectives on a new environment* (pp. 133–169). New York: Praeger.

Hornby, P. A., & Anderson, M. A. (1995–96). Putting the student in the driver's seat: A learner-centered, self-paced, computer managed, introductory psychology course. *Journal of Educational Technology Systems, 24,* 173–179.

Jones, T., & Schieman, E. (1995). Learner involvement: A review of the elements of more effective distance education. *Canadian Journal of Educational Communication, 24,* 97–104.

Oswald, P. A. (1996). Classroom use of the personal computer to teach statistics. *Teaching of Psychology, 23,* 124–126.

Pask, J. M., & Snow. C. E. (1995). Undergraduate instruction and the Internet. *Library Trends, 44,* 306–317.

Pear, J. J., & Novak, M. (1996). Computer-aided personalized system of instruction: A program evaluation. *Teaching of Psychology, 23,* 119–123.

Pitt, M. (1996). The use of electronic mail in undergraduate teaching. *British Journal of Educational Technology, 27,* 45–50.

Varnhagen, C. K., & Zumbo, B. D. (1990). CAI as an adjunct to teaching introductory statistics: Affect mediates learning. *Journal of Educational Computing Research, 6,* 29–40.

Notes

1. The authors thank the 1995 Honors class who participated in the study and Dr. Eugene C. Lechelt, Chair, Department of Psychology, who created the psychology department computer laboratory and encouraged the development of this course.
2. The most recent version of the home page is located at: http: //web.psych.ualberta.ca/;slvarn/Psyco_406.html.

Stimulating Statistical Thinking Through Situated Simulations

Sharon Derry
Joel R. Levin
Leona Schauble

Department of Educational Psychology
University of Wisconsin–Madison

A particular disease is known to affect 1% of a given population. A screening test for the disease is 90% accurate; that is, for people who have the disease the test shows a positive reaction 90% of the time, and for people who do not have the disease the test shows a negative reaction 90% of the time. Suppose that an individual who is given the screening test shows a positive reaction. How likely is it that the individual has the disease?

So goes the kind of decision-making problem that has been presented to hundreds of college students and academics over the past 25 years (see, e.g., Shaughnessy, 1992). In fact, and of greater cultural relevance to the spirit of this article, such a problem was also presented to millions of Americans one Sunday morning in 1993 by the intellectually renowned *Parade: The Sunday Newspaper Magazine* celebrity, Marilyn vos Savant. In both the academic and general audiences, we discover an important commonality: Although many have been served such problems, few have solved them. Indeed, most attempters of the problem as stated are astonished to learn that there is less than a 10% chance that the tested individual actually has the disease (probability = .083). In the work we describe herein, we seek to increase the probability of successful solution of such problems both in the classroom and in the world beyond.

Literacy and informed decision making in today's society require the ability to reason statistically. (Shaughnessy, 1992, suggested following the European tradition of using the term *stochastics* to include both probability and statistics. We have chosen instead to use the more familiar term *statistics,* but to use it in the broadest sense to refer to both probability and statistics.) News reports about political polls, AIDS research, genetic testing, the federal deficit, discrimination in employment, Supreme Court decisions, and many other current issues often hinge on complicated arguments involving statistical reasoning. Environmental groups, urban-planning committees, health-care advocates, juries, school boards, and many other community decision-making bodies also must frequently consider statistical

concepts in their debates concerning social and scientific issues. There is good reason, therefore, to be concerned about research findings indicating that many adults in mainstream American society cannot think statistically about important societal issues for which they share decision-making responsibility.

For example, the ability to evaluate evidence (including an understanding of what does or does not constitute acceptable evidential argument) depends on good intuitive understanding of such statistical and methodological C words as *covariation, correlation, conditionality, causation, confounding,* and *control* (e.g., Kuhn, 1991; Kuhn, Amsel, & O'Loughlin, 1988). However, that many people do not understand the concept of evidence was established by Kuhn (1991), who interviewed large samples of adolescents and lay and professional adults, asking them to state and justify their beliefs about various issues. Because substantial percentages of these groups were unable to interpret patterns of covariation or lack of covariation between variables and outcomes, they were unable to develop evidential arguments supporting their beliefs. For example, when asked to justify their opinions about why criminals often return to crime after release from prison, many subjects either developed a plausible story explaining why one fictional person may return to crime (pseudoevidence) or refused to give evidence at all on the grounds that everyone was entitled to their personal opinion.

In other research, Konold (1989) found that college students were unable to reason statistically about the outcomes of specific events, such as meteorological predictions and gambling results. In making event predictions, such as predicting the outcome of a gambling bet, college students often behaved as purely deterministic thinkers, in that they did not see the event in question as a member of a larger probability set. Rather than adopting an aleatory (chance-based) view of the world, these students appeared to base predictions on naive assumptions about the existence of deterministic causal models. Such predictions were viewed as either right or wrong and were sometimes associated with beliefs that experts possess knowledge of causal factors, enabling them to determine for certain what outcomes will occur. The type of reasoning observed can be exemplified by the following belief statement: "The meteorologist said there was an 80% chance of rain today; however, because it did not rain, the meteorologist was wrong."

Other researchers have found many situations in which people do adopt aleatory views of the world, but such reasoning seems to be biased or flawed. Based on studies of how college students and lay and professional adults think, Tversky and Kahneman (1974) argued that typical intuitive statistical reasoning is influenced by deep-seated misconceptions and heuristics that are not in accord with accepted statistical principles. One example is the availability heuristic, which causes highly publicized, easily imagined, or vividly remembered events (e.g., air crashes, fires, and lottery wins) to be regarded as much more probable than they are. Another example is the failure of people, including those with some statistical training, to take into account regression-to-the-mean phenomena when interpreting everyday improvements and declines in performance.

Still another common-reasoning fallacy is the ignoring of base rate and contrapositive data, concepts derived directly from Bayesian probability theory. Using our initiating problem on medical testing as an example, the following illustrates a line of reasoning that takes into account both base rate and contrapositive evidence: If only 1% of our tested sample (projected base rate, assuming random sampling) actually has a disease, a test with 90% accuracy will correctly identify about 90% of the cases in this relatively small affected group. However, because 99% of the tested sample does not have the disease (contrapositive data), a test with 90% accuracy will also give a false positive for 10% of the people in this relatively large healthy group. Applying appropriate conditional probability formulas, one discovers that the probability of a correct diagnosis based solely on the screening test results is very low.

Decision theorists like Tversky and Kahneman (1974) have based much of their work on the assumption that people should be, but often are not, intuitive Bayesians. In contrast, some researchers do not characterize human thinking as flawed just because it does not always operate in accord with accepted statistical criteria. Cohen (1981), for example, argued that untrained intuitions that defy statistical criteria can be adaptive and have enabled us "to maintain the sophisticated institutions of modern civilization" (p. 317). Thus, juries sometimes make good decisions on the basis of intuitions that defy statistical evidence, and AIDS victims may both extend and enhance their lives by denying the probabilities that face them. Cohen suggested that such instances of human reasoning should be studied

as models in their own right because they contain keys to understanding what aspects of quality thinking may not follow statistical theory.

In addition, Cohen (1981) noted that there is no universal statistical viewpoint from which we can derive prescriptions for quality reasoning. Even among expert statisticians there is disagreement about which views of probability should form the basis for statistical reasoning. For example, Shaughnessy (1992) described how three different probability camps—classicist, frequentist, and subjectivist—debate one another as though one of these camps represents "truth." Such debates demonstrate that statistics as a subject matter represents controversial knowledge (e.g., Nicholls & Nelson, 1992), an idea that should influence how statistics is taught. If statistics is controversial subject matter, then it should not be taught as a set of final-form, universally accepted concepts that can be handed down by authority and conveyed to students by teachers and textbooks. At a minimum, statistics courses may inform students about statistical debates. We believe that students could gain even more by actually discovering and participating in such controversies.

Participating in statistical controversy is what scientists do when they conduct research; their work involves selecting statistical tools that are perceived to be appropriate for the problem at hand, using them as a basis for conceptually analyzing that problem and often defending their choices to other scientists. Thus, the sophistication of statistical reasoning within scientific and mathematics communities has advanced steadily since the birth of probability theory in the 16th century (Hacking, 1975; Porter, 1986). By contrast, most adults in the United States seldom apply or debate statistical principles when making decisions or interpreting uncertain world events, although to do so could enhance their decision-making processes and the quality of their lives.

This gap between mainstream and scientific culture can be interpreted from the perspective of Vygotsky (1978), who recognized that a society's mainstream thinking styles are culturally rooted, passing from one generation to another through social interaction. Vygotsky argued that advancing sophistication within scientific communities can serve as a powerful force, promoting evolution of thought processes within the broader culture. However, his argument emphasizes the important idea that scientific forms of thinking can be transmitted to the professional and lay public only to the extent that systems of social interaction allow that transmission to happen. Accepting this viewpoint as a basis for analyzing the role of schools in culture, we now address the question of how schools and universities can serve more effectively as systems for helping students and teachers, as well as lay and professional adults, make a transition from culturally rooted, naive thinking styles toward the more analytical statistical thinking that underlies much scientific reasoning and problem solving.

A Course in Informed Statistical Reasoning

Our approach is to offer an educational psychology course in statistical thinking founded on the belief that education should include forums for the kinds of interaction and debate that are needed to help stimulate cultural evolution of human reasoning and problem solving in an uncertain world. In this course, we will engage students in social, cross-cultural problem solving that requires evidential argument, debate, negotiation, decision making; we will follow this with a systematic examination of the students' own thinking and decision-making processes.

Our offering will differ from typical statistics courses and even from some of the newer, more innovative efforts (e.g., Snell & Finn, 1992) largely by its commitment to focusing on problem situations that possess what we termed *statistical authenticity*. As discussed in more detail later, statistical authenticity can be conceptualized and measured along two dimensions: cultural relevance and social activity. The relevance dimension represents the extent to which the subject matter of statistical reasoning is related to meaningful, real-life problems of importance to society. The activity dimension represents the extent to which learning emerges from active conceptualizing, negotiation, and argumentation.

To accomplish the high degree of statistical authenticity proposed, our course will involve students in simulations of real-world problem situations requiring critical statistical thinking. These situated simulations (or SitSims) and the pedagogical activities surrounding them are designed to serve as instructional vehicles for developing students' statistical reasoning capabilities. The type of pedagogical practice envisioned can be described as creating a community within the classroom that represents a microcosm of a productive problem-solving community within larger society. Such problem-solving communities emerge frequently in real life, both within the working world and outside of it, and often require that people from different cultural and academic backgrounds negotiate difficult problems together. Recent examples from our own Madison, WI, community include town meetings, hearings, and referenda dealing with the issues of a proposed citywide ban on handguns; a proposed smoking ban in all city restaurants; and the cultural, economic, and environmental impact of a proposed multimillion dollar convention complex designed by former resident Frank Lloyd Wright.

Theoretical Grounding

Our approach is based in part on the philosophy of Dewey (1938), who advocated meaningful school activity that extends experiences and practices of the adult world. It is also inspired by the theoretical philosophies of radical constructivism (e.g., von Glasersfeld, 1990), situated cog-

nition (e.g., J. S. Brown, Collins, & Duguid, 1989; Lave & Wenger, 1991), and Vygotsky's (1978) psychology. These viewpoint share in common the idea that educational practice should be based on authentic activity in which students socially negotiate meanings and identities. Although these theories are being widely discussed and debated, few programs have been carefully implemented and evaluated to provide formal tests of these ideas. Thus, our plans for evaluating the course include theory-based analyses of individual and group changes in conceptual knowledge, problem-solving processes, and attitudes.

Societal Impact

Our project represents a vision for education wherein classrooms become minicommunities that simulate and extend productive, motivated communities of practice within larger society (see, e.g., Lesgold, 1992, 1993; Resnick, 1987). Moreover, the course will be advertised and offered to teachers and future teachers as part of a movement to enhance the importance of informed statistical thinking in primary and secondary school curricula. Concerning the limited role of statistics in U.S. schools, Shaughnessy (1992) noted that very few secondary schools offer systematic courses, and elementary and middle schools offer virtually none.

Most current and future teachers do, of course, encounter the idea that they are supposed to teach general problem-solving strategies and higher order thinking skills (HOTS). In fact, teachers and teacher trainees are faced with a cornucopia of curricular materials representing guided general approaches to the teaching of HOTS (e.g., Bransford & Stein, 1993; de Bono, 1973–75; Wales & Nardi, 1984). Nevertheless, developmental psychologists have long been aware (e.g., Inhelder & Piaget, 1958; Kuhn, 1989) that understanding such concepts as *evidence* and *criteria* requires at least intuitive understanding of probability and statistical concepts such as *covariance* and *average* (see, e.g., Ross & Cousins, 1993). Thus, effective instruction in critical thinking is necessarily linked with the provision of adequate grounding in statistical reasoning. Moreover, there is experimental evidence that reasoning ability can be improved through thinking skills training that is grounded in statistics (e.g., Nisbett, Fong, Lehman, & Cheng, 1987).

Conceptualizing Statistical Authenticity

A difficulty with most college statistics courses is that they are separated from real-world problem solving. This approach to schooling is problematic for at least two reasons. First, in this age of information explosion, it is no longer possible for students to acquire from courses most of the foundation knowledge they will require in their adult lives. Thus, programs of instruction must become something more than mere purveyors of foundation knowledge. Second, studies indicate that a substantial proportion of the knowledge required for pursuing one's aims in life should be constructed within the context of everyday practice if it is to be available for later use in those contexts (e.g., Lave, 1991; Lave & Wenger, 1991; Saxe, 1988).

These issues are causing many educators to raise questions about the appropriate goals of instruction for schools and colleges. For instance, instead of asking merely what abstract statistical ideas students need to know and how they should be taught, we are framing our thinking about statistics education somewhat differently. An example follows: How can we design a course in statistical reasoning that will help cultivate productive, motivated member of society who can cross boundaries of discipline and culture while working together to solve socially relevant problems?

Our response is a course that aspires to the highest feasible level of statistical authenticity. In the present context of fostering informed statistical reasoning in a college-level course of study, we focus on two dimensions of statistical authenticity. These two dimensions, cultural relevance and social activity, are useful in characterizing different models of teaching basic concepts in statistical reasoning. In Figure 1, we identify six illustrative instructional approaches (including an idealized one) gleaned from both informal sources (e.g., personal experiences, observations, and discussions) and more formal ones (journal articles, conferences, and workshops). In the more formal category, for example, in addition to the books and journal articles cited here, we borrow from models reported in specialized teaching of statistics journals and sections of journals, as well as teaching of statistics symposia sponsored by various professional organizations.

Before discussing the specifics of Figure 1 and the instructional model that represents the core of our course, we provide the following motivating assumption: Students' propensities and capabilities for statistical reasoning in authentic (real-life) settings can be considerably enhanced through (a) instruction that uses examples, illustrations, analogies, discussions, and demonstrations that are relevant to the cultures to which students belong or hope to belong (cultural relevance); and (b) mentored participation in a social, collaborative problem-solving context, with the aid of such vehicles as group discussion, debate, role-playing, and guided discovery (social activity). The anticipated success of the instructional approach that we are developing hinges on the reasonableness of this assumption. In specific regard to the social activity dimension, however, we offer a disclaimer, for we do not argue that social activity per se enhances the quality of thinking. On the one hand, unsubstantiated emotional argument or undirected social banter are unlikely to enhance statistical reasoning abilities; on the

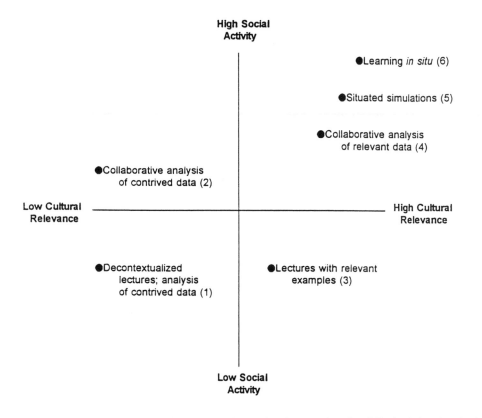

Figure 1. Addressing the problem of statistical authenticity through instructional approaches that differ in their cultural relevance and social activity.

other hand, social activity may involve no overt physical or social behavior at all, but rather strictly mental processing—as when students work to follow a well-reasoned argument, clever proof, or illuminating worked examples presented by classmates or an outside expert (e.g., Sweller & Cooper, 1985).

In the lower left quadrant of Figure 1 appears *decontextualized instruction*—Entry 1. As an exemplar, perhaps, of the least engaging form of statistical instruction, with this approach we find teacher-centered delivery of the rules and recipes for calculating statistics. Due to the culturally irrelevant (or culture-lacking) examples and the social passivity of students (receptivity) that are associated with this traditional professor-providing-a-detached-or-abstract-lecture model, its placement in Figure 1 is low on both dimensions.

Next considered are alternative approaches that subscribe to the notion that student involvement in doing (rather simply receiving) is beneficial, as represented by students working *collaboratively to analyze contrived data*—Entry 2 of Figure 1. In some cases, the effort may be expended in the form of applications of formulas or computerized statistical packages to a set of hypothetical data; in other cases, the activity may consist of deploying HOTS (e.g., conceptualizing the research questions, deciding among competing statistical tests and assessing the validity of those tests' assumptions, and interpreting the statistical outcomes). In both cases, even though the problem content and associated data may be hypothetical or removed from the student's cultural interests, the student is nonetheless more actively interacting with information and others—hence, the higher position of Entry 2 on the social activity dimension.

Moving along the second dimension (cultural relevance) while maintaining a low level of social involvement, we find statistics instruction based on *relevant examples*—Entry 3. Mimicking the didactic lecture style of the traditional anchor entry (Entry 1), the instructor adopting this genre at least bolsters the abstract statistical concepts and procedures being taught with the provision of relevant, meaningful topical content to which the student can personally relate those concepts and procedures.

The best of both worlds—Entries 2 and 3—occurs with *collaborative analysis of relevant data*—Entry 4. Here we discover the combination of active social learning applied to content that is socially relevant, meaningful, or interesting to students. This type of instructional approach, as manifested in various forms and formats, typifies some of the more modern, student-centered, real-world models of introducing statistical concepts and of inducing statistical reasoning through discussion (e.g., Singer & Willett, 1990; Snell & Finn, 1992). In fact, it may be reasonably assumed that this combination is greater than the sum of its parts, which explains why we have positioned Entry 4 at a higher level than either Entry 2 or Entry 3.

From here, we briefly leap to the pinnacle of statistical authenticity in our two-dimensional schematic, which occurs with the idealized Entry 6 in Figure 1, *learning in situ.* This represents the class of contemporary situated cognition models in which instruction takes the form of cognitive apprenticeships that relate directly to job-requisite content knowledge and skill development, as well as to participation in the solution of actual community and societal problems (e.g., Brown, Collins, & Duguid, 1989; Lave & Wenger, 1991). Apprenticeship models of instruction are believed to enhance the usefulness of learned subject matter. In our statistical-reasoning course, we will approximate the real-world, participatory features of learning in situ by engaging students in *situated simulations* (Entry 5) of real-world issues and problems that have less than certain outcomes. However, for the purpose of developing statistical reasoning abilities, SitSims should be instructionally more effective than learning in situ because they will be carefully crafted to provide rich contexts for frequent and extended student engagement with the targeted statistical concepts.

Course Format and Content

The three-credit course will involve four basic types of in-class instructional activity: lecture/demonstrations (20%), simulations (50%), group self-critique sessions (20%), and evaluation (10%). Also, remedial laboratories and help sessions on basic statistical concepts will be offered as needed outside of class. Each format is described next.

Lecture/demonstrations. Only 20% of the course will be presented via a lecture/demonstration format. Each 50-min lecture will cover one or more basic statistical concepts and principles that can be used as tools for reasoning within assigned simulation exercises. In agreement with Davydov (cited in Confry, 1991), we believe that basic concepts should be presented before students engage in social work activity through which in-depth understanding is acquired.

Also, lecture/demonstrations will enable us to explain to students why and how various statistical concepts were invented and how they have evolved. Scholars like Hacking (1975) and Winograd and Flores (1986) have discussed the importance of historical perspective to conceptual understanding. Although traditional statistics courses and materials do not include much about the fascinating history and evolution of statistics, our course will. Part of our preparation for teaching this course will involve researching this history in more depth.

In addition, lectures will cover topics pertaining to ethical issues in statistical decision making, as well as to statistical and methodological concepts that may be needed for specific simulation activities. Some lectures will be presented by guest lecturers who are experts in relevant topics.

Lectures will use what might be dubbed "the Carl Sagan approach to statistical reasoning." That is, presentations will be lively, interesting, and free of mathematical jargon to appeal to students with even weak mathematics backgrounds. They will focus on conceptual explanation, rather than procedures, and will extensively use graphics, relevant examples, analogies, and demonstrations to help students construct appropriate mental models of important ideas and concepts (e.g., Levin, 1982, 1993).

The following is a draft listing of four major areas of emphasis along with sample topics for discussion and demonstration, for the lecture parts of the course.

1. Thinking as argument, the nature of evidence, ways of knowing, scientific forms of thinking, confounding and control, and internal and external validity.
2a. Graphical presentation of data; covariation, correlation, and causation; determinism and causal models; and regression toward the mean.
2b. How to lie with statistics, truth in advertising, and media interpretations of medical research may be hazardous to your health.
3a. Basic probability concepts, the central limit theorem, sampling distributions, and hypothesis testing and estimation.
3b. The perils of polling, medical research revisited, social experimentation.
4a. Conditional probability, Bayesian theory, signal detection theory, and utility theory.
4b. Eyewitness testimony: What you see is not always what you get; and test bias, admissions policies, and hiring practices.

Simulations. About 50% of students' class time will be spent engaged in simulation activities. Eight to 10 different simulation games will be developed, implemented, evaluated, and modified. Although these simulation exercises will vary considerably, they will all incorporate several common elements: (a) a culturally relevant topical theme, (b) specific statistical conceptual goals for students, (c) the requirement of social activity (e.g., debate and negotiation), (d) rules for governing social interaction, (e) the requirement that students cooperatively develop a product or reach a decision, and (f) the requirement that students conduct reflective critiques of their individual- and group-thinking processes.

Here we offer an example of one type of simulation model we plan to explore: role-playing in a problem-solving dilemma. With role-playing, each student adopts a role as a fictional character within a fictional community. During the simulation, roles may be strategically switched among students so that participants will directly experience alternative points of view. To help students construct their fictional identities, each will be supplied with a packet of resource materials containing information on the charac-

ter's educational, family, and career background; personal interests and concerns; and political affiliations and community alliances. Also in each packet will be information about the community culture, including social traditions, governmental structure, and decision-making rules.

In role-playing simulations, the fictional community as a whole is charged with making critical decisions requiring statistical reasoning. For example, the problem may involve making a 50-year plan for power resource management within the community. The SitSims will encourage students to form alliances and working groups; conduct research; and develop presentations, debates, and arguments in the contexts of their community roles. Such discussions and debates will take place within various forums, including newspaper reports, simulated television broadcasts, and town meetings.

Themes for simulation games will be brainstormed and selected with the advice of a community advisory board, described later. Examples of possible SitSim themes are as follows:

a. The relation between television violence and community violence.
b. The fairness of smoking bans.
c. Affirmative action and selection bias in employment.
d. Effects of drug and alcohol abuse on the economy.
e. Mental health care and the plight of the homeless.
f. Crime rates and prison reform.
g. Connections between sunbathing, skin cancer, and the ozone layer.
h. Cases for and against nuclear power.

Critique sessions. An important and innovative component of the instructional method is that students will periodically be asked to step back from each simulation and critically examine their reasoning processes. The purpose of this approach is to facilitate development of students' propensity and ability to reflect on and evaluate their thinking (e.g., A. L. Brown, 1987; Flavell, 1979). We will facilitate this examination of individual and group decision-making processes by videotaping classroom interaction. These videotapes will be examined and discussed during the group self-critique sessions.

Community advisory board. Instructional materials and procedures for the SitSims will be designed in collaboration with a community advisory board representing several different disciplines and lines of work, such as statistics, economics, meteorology, genetics, chemistry, law, medicine, politics, mathematics, and child development.

Concluding Comments

Our cautious optimism about the course we are developing is based on the assumption that the SitSims approach will significantly improve students' abilities to reason critically with statistics about important social issues. We expect that students enrolled in our course will improve their ability to comprehend, develop, and critique evidential arguments in general and statistical arguments in particular. They will improve their ability to read and analyze critically news reports of research. They will develop an ability to make effective persuasive presentations that are enhanced by statistical evidence and graphical presentations of data. They will learn to distinguish between unexamined beliefs and those based on evidence. They will acquire new criteria for judging the quality of evidence and argument observed in presentations and in interactions of social groups. We expect that they will develop an enhanced awareness of and appreciation for quality of thinking, both in themselves and in others. They are also expected to develop greater interest in the thematic topics covered by simulations, as well as greater awareness of and concern for the ethical issues related to those themes. Finally, we anticipate that students who previously have avoided mathematics and have suffered from math anxiety will develop an improved attitude toward statistics and an interest in taking additional courses.

If our expectations about student performance are met, then we will have designed and demonstrated the efficacy of a model for teaching informed statistical reasoning to undergraduates that provides a better alternative to the standard lecture approach. Pronouncing the SitSims approach "successful" at this point is premature, but prognosticating that the approach will achieve some degree of that hoped-for success is well within the realm of probability.

References

Bransford, J. D., & Stein, B. S. (1993). *The ideal problem solver* (2nd ed.). New York: Freeman.

Brown, A. L. (1987). Metacognition, executive control, self-regulation, and other more mysterious mechanisms. In F. Weinert & R. Klewe (Eds.), *Metacognition, motivation and understanding* (pp. 65–116). Hillsdale, NJ: Lawrence Erlbaum Associates, Inc.

Brown, J. S., Collins, A., & Duguid, P. (1989). Debating the situation: A rejoinder to Palincsar and Wineburg. *Educational Researcher, 18*(1), 10–12.

Cohen, L. J. (1981). Can human irrationality be experimentally demonstrated? *The Behavioral and Brain Sciences, 4*, 317–370.

Confry, J. (1991). Steering a course between Vygotsky and Piaget. *Educational Researcher, 20*(8), 28–34.

de Bono, E. (1973–75). *CoRT thinking.* Blandford, Dorset, UK: Director Education Services Limited.

Dewey, J. (1938). *Experience and education.* New York: Collier.

Flavell, J. H. (1979). Metacognition and cognitive monitoring: A new area of psychological inquiry. *American Psychologist, 34*, 906–911.

Hacking, I. (1975). *The emergence of probability.* Cambridge, UK: Cambridge University Press.

Inhelder, B., & Piaget, J. (1958). *The growth of logical thinking from childhood to adolescence.* New York: Basic Books.

Konold, C. (1989). Informal conceptions of probability. *Cognition and Instruction, 6*, 59–98.

Kuhn, D. (1989). Children and adults as intuitive scientists. *Psychological Review, 96*, 674–689.

Kuhn, D. (1991). *The skills of argument.* Cambridge, UK: Cambridge University Press.

Kuhn, D., Amsel, E., & O'Loughlin, M. (1988). *The development of scientific thinking skills.* San Diego: Academic.

Lave, J. (1991). Situating learning in communities of practice. In L. Resnick, J. Levine, & S. Teasley (Eds.), *Perspectives on socially shared cognition* (pp. 63–82). Washington, DC: American Psychological Association.

Lave, J., & Wenger, E. (1991). *Situated learning: Legitimate peripheral participation.* New York: Cambridge University Press.

Lesgold, A. (1992). *Process control for educating a smart work force.* Pittsburgh, PA: University of Pittsburgh, Learning Research and Development Center.

Lesgold, A. (1993). Information technology and the future of education. In S. Lajoie & S. Derry (Eds.), *Computers as cognitive tools* (pp. 369–383). Hillsdale, NJ: Lawrence Erlbaum Associates, Inc.

Levin, J. R. (1982). Modifications of a regression-toward-the-mean demonstration. *Teaching of Psychology, 9*, 237–238.

Levin, J. R. (1993). An improved modification of a regression-toward-the-mean demonstration. *American Statistician, 47*, 24–26.

Nicholls, J. G., & Nelson, J. R. (1992). Students' conceptions of controversial knowledge. *Journal of Educational Psychology, 84*, 224–230.

Nisbett, R. E., Fong, G. T., Lehman, D. R., & Cheng, P. W. (1987). Teaching reasoning. *Science, 198*, 625–631.

Porter, T. M. (1986). *The rise of statistical thinking.* Princeton, NJ: Princeton University Press.

Resnick, L. B. (1987). Learning in school and out. *Educational Researcher, 16*, 13–20.

Ross, J. A., & Cousins, J. B. (1993). Patterns of student growth in reasoning about correlational problems. *Journal of Educational Psychology, 85*, 49–65.

Saxe, G. B. (1988). Candy selling and math learning. *Educational Researcher, 17*, 14–21.

Shaughnessy, J. M. (1992). Research in probability and statistics: Reflections and directions. In D. A. Grouws (Ed.), *Handbook of research on mathematics teaching and learning* (pp. 465–494). Reston, VA: National Council of Teachers of Mathematics.

Singer, J. D., & Willett, J. B. (1990). Improving the teaching of applied statistics: Putting the data back into data analysis. *Journal of the American Statistical Association, 44,* 223–230.

Snell, J. L., & Finn, J. (1992). A course called "chance." *Chance, 5*(3–4), 12–16.

Sweller, J., & Cooper, G. A. (1985). The use of worked examples as a substitute for problem solving in learning algebra. *Cognition and Instruction, 2,* 59–89.

Tversky, A., & Kahneman, D. (1974). Judgments under uncertainty: Heuristics and biases. *Science, 185,* 1124–1131.

von Glasersfeld, E. (1990). An exposition of constructivism: Why some like it radical. *Journal of Research on Mathematics Education Monograph #4.* Reston, VA: National Council of Teachers of Mathematics.

Vygotsky, L. S. (1978). *Mind in society: The development of higher psychological processes.* Edited by M. Cole, V. John-Steiner, S. Scribner, & E. Souberman. Cambridge, MA: Harvard University Press.

Wales, C. E., & Nardi, A. (1984). *Successful decision-making.* Morgantown: West Virginia University, Center for Guided Design.

Winograd, T., & Flores, F. (1986). *Understanding computers and cognition: A new foundation for design.* Norwood, NJ: Ablex.

5. Evaluating Success in Statistics

To evaluate data collection and feedback as a means for teaching basic statistical concepts, Jean Low randomly assigned sections of a human development course at West Texas A&M University to one of three groups. In all three groups, students contributed personal information at the beginning of each class. After each class, the instructor analyzed the information to provide feedback about class frequencies, means, standard deviations, and correlations. Students received this feedback either daily (continuous groups), on an average of twice per month (partial groups), or never (control groups). On an end-of-semester test of statistical concepts, students in the continuous feedback groups scored significantly higher than did students in the other two groups. The continuous feedback format was difficult and time-consuming, but the author believed that its benefits outweighed the difficulties.

To reduce test anxiety and encourage the learning of course material, Herbert Friedman gave students in two sections of statistics at the College of William and Mary the opportunity to offset a poor lecture examination grade by taking a second, equivalent exam. The repeat exam provided immediate reward for using the initial exam as a study guide. Students who took two or three repeat exams had higher final examination grades than those who took fewer repeats. Students responded favorably to the repeat exam procedure, which helped weaker students keep up with the course and was convenient for the instructor to implement.

Mary Hudak and David Anderson used measures of formal operations and learning style to predict success in introductory statistics and computer science courses at Allegheny College. Using a final course grade cutoff of 80% or higher as a criterion for success in the course, the authors reported that discriminant analysis correctly classified 81% of the statistics students and 72% of the computer science students. Success was related to the presence of the ability to act as a formal operator and to the absence of a reliance on the concrete experiences learning style. These findings highlight the need to examine both cognitive maturity and learning style in studies of academic success in these courses.

Anita Meehan, Derrie Hoffert, and Laurence Hoffert from Kutztown University gave several tips for teaching statistics to visually impaired students and provided information about special resources available for them. With appropriate assistance, these students can be held responsible for the same material as sighted students. Suggestions for working with students having other limitations would also be helpful for psychology teachers.

Teaching Basic Statistical Concepts Through Continuous Data Collection and Feedback

Jean M. Low
West Texas A&M University

An understanding of basic statistical concepts is important. Psychology students, as well as students from many other disciplines, must take courses in statistics. Students often approach these courses with no previous knowledge; hence, early exposure to basic statistical concepts could be very helpful. For students who will not be taking statistics courses, an understanding of basic statistical concepts can help them become critical thinkers and educated consumers (Connor-Greene, 1993; Ennis, 1962; Mayer & Goodchild, 1990).

To help students learn basic statistical concepts, I collect classroom data, analyze them, and present the results in the next class. Concepts such as frequencies, normal curves, means, standard deviations, and correlations become a daily part of the class. This technique assumes that learning is improved by repetition of material and use of personally meaningful examples. This article reports an evaluation of this teaching technique.

Procedure

Three sections of an introductory human development course were assigned to either a continuous feedback, a partial feedback, or a control condition. The classes did not differ significantly from each other on age, race, sex, socio-economic status, or college major. In all three classes, I defined and discussed statistical terms during the first week of the semester while presenting the chapter on research methods in human development. For the remainder of the semester, I collected information from the students as a part of each class. I used short verbal surveys to collect most information. For example, I asked the students to write down their age, sex, and a trait that they thought described them. Occasionally, if it could be incorporated into the lecture, I used psychological tests. For instance, during the discussion of stress in early adulthood I had the students complete The Social Readjustment Scale (Holmes & Rahe, 1967). At each data collection, I assured the students that they did not have to contribute data if they did not wish to do so and that all individual data would be kept confidential.

In the continuous feedback condition, the information was analyzed daily and feedback was given during the next class. In the partial feedback condition, feedback was given on an average of twice per month. In the control condition, no feedback was given. I expected that students in the continuous feedback condition would have the best grasp of the statistical concepts by the end of the semester due to continuous repetition of the concepts and the meaningful data used.

To compare students' knowledge of statistics, I gave a brief, unexpected, five-item test at the end of the semester. In the test, students were asked to define and explain in their own words the terms *frequency, normal curve, mean, standard deviation,* and *correlation.* They were told that they should include any information they thought was relevant, and they could use drawings and diagrams if they wished.

A graduate student, who was blind to the three conditions, scored all tests. Each question was assigned a score from 0 to 4; thus, the highest possible score was 20.

Results

A one-way analysis of variance revealed significant differences among the three groups, $F(2, 155) = 28.18, p < .001$. The means and standard deviations were 15.9 ($SD = 3.3$) for the continuous feedback group, 11.3 ($SD = 4.2$) for the partial feedback group, and 10.2 ($SD = 5.1$) for the control group. A Scheffé test indicated that the continuous feedback group did significantly better on the statistical test than did the other two groups, which were not reliably different from each other.

Discussion

The results support the hypothesis that data collection and feedback can be an effective technique for teaching basic statistical concepts. Because the continuous feedback subjects scored significantly higher than the partial feedback subjects, such feedback should be provided in a repetitious manner.

Knowledge of statistical concepts was operationally defined as the scores on an open-ended test given at the end of the semester. Students had been told that the final exam would not be cumulative; so, although they had been tested on statistical terms on the first semester test, they did not expect to be tested on them again and would not have reviewed them from the text. The fact that the continuous feedback group scored the highest on the unexpected test suggests that the students learned the terms during the daily feedback.

Continuous data collection and analysis are difficult and time-consuming for the instructor, but I believe that the benefits to the students outweigh the difficulties. Collecting student data and providing feedback seems meaningful for the students. They are interested in knowing the composition of the class and, when possible, comparing their data to the data presented in the textbook. In an interesting and enjoyable way, they acquire an understanding of statistical terms. This knowledge provides a foundation in later statistics courses, helps them understand and evaluate research reports, and enhances their critical-thinking skills.

References

Connor-Greene, P. A. (1993). From the laboratory to the headlines: Teaching critical evaluation of press reports of research. *Teaching of Psychology, 20,* 167–169.

Ennis, R. H. (1962). A concept of critical thinking. *Harvard Educational Review, 32,* 81–111.

Holmes, T. H., & Rahe, R. H. (1967). The Social Readjustment Rating Scale. *Journal of Psychosomatic Research, 11,* 213.

Mayer, R., & Goodchild, F. (1990). *The critical thinker.* Dubuque, IA: Brown.

Notes

1. I thank Ruth L. Ault and the anonymous reviewers for their helpful comments on previous versions of this article.
2. I thank Bonnie Christensen for daily entry of data throughout an entire semester.
3. Portions of this article were presented at the annual meeting of the Southwestern Psychological Association, Corpus Christi, TX, April 1993.
4. Support was received through a West Texas A&M University President's Teaching Fellowship.

Repeat Examinations in Introductory Statistics Courses

Herbert Friedman
College of William and Mary

A retest policy in introductory psychology courses can have several advantages: reducing test anxiety, clarifying the course evaluation standards, and guiding the relearning of previously tested material (Davidson, House, & Boyd, 1984). These points are even more applicable to courses, such as statistics, in which later topics build on those covered earlier. The retest procedure described in this article was explicitly intended to address two problems: (a) most students find the introductory statistics course anxiety provoking, and (b) less capable students tend to fall increasingly behind as the course progresses.

College exams have limited educational value if the feedback they offer is not used by students. Upon receiving a poor examination grade, the mythical ideal student rushes to the privacy of a dorm room to use the exam as a basis for concentrated review and study. In contrast, the typical student finds that a low grade makes the exam material repellent and that the final examinaation is too distant a threat to lead to current studying. This problem is particularly serious in a statistics course because a student who has not mastered the basic concepts and measures will be greatly hampered in learning subsequent material. The repeat exam system outlined here involves offering students, after each lecture exam is returned and reviewed, the choice of taking a second, equivalent exam that might raise the original grade. The goal is to move students in the direction of the "ideal" by using the initial exams as a source of useful feedback on progress and by having the repeat exams provide immediate reward for needed review.

Some of the elements of the present system have been successfully employed by Ward (1984) with repeated comprehensive final examinations, Foley (1981) with the same test given again as a take-home exam, and Kottke (1985) with a comprehensive makeup exam used to replace the lowest lecture exam grade.

Method

Procedure

There were three 80-min lecture examinations, each consisting of 25 to 35 multiple-choice items (counting for one third of the exam score) and 4 to 6 problems (each made up of individual four-choice items covering calculation and interpretation). One or two brief (one paragraph) essay items were also included as part of the problem section. Test items were taken from the instructor's manual for the course text (Friedman, 1972). An optional weekly laboratory session served for review and the working of practice problems.

The rationale and rules concerning the testing procedure were presented to the students at the first class meeting:

1. To minimize rote learning and to reduce last-minute panic studying, the original exams were given open-book—the students could use their text, workbook, and notes during the exam. The exams were long enough to leave little time to look up answers to the multiple-choice questions. Grading criteria for all exams were determined (before the exams were scored) on the basis of the instructor's experience and expectations. There was no "curving" of grades, students scoring well on the initial exam were not penalized by others improving their grades on the repeat exam.

2. The multiple-choice format facilitated rapid grading of exams, which were returned at the next lecture. At that time, the exam was discussed and the problem section was worked out in detail. The repeat exam was then given at the following lecture period.

3. All students were permitted to take the repeat examinations. In addition, the repeat exam served as a makeup exam if needed (but with a small penalty and no further repeat allowed). Students were not allowed to miss more than one original exam. The three lecture exams together accounted for one half of the course grade and the final exam accounted for the other half.

4. The average of the original and the repeat exam scores entered into the calculation of the course grade so that good performance on the repeat exam would help compensate for a poor initial score. However, any repeat exam that was scored lower than the original was not recorded. This feature encouraged those who did well initially to prepare for and take the repeat exam, assuring them that they would run no risk. It was emphasized that

the primary purpose of the lecture exams was to provide feedback to students rather than to obtain grades.

5. The repeat exams were highly similar to the original exams so that students would concentrate on their earlier mistakes and weaknesses. To avoid the need for retyping the examination, the ditto or xerographic master of the original exam was directly written on and used for the repeat. Numbers in problems and the short essay items were changed, keeping the basic problem context. Most of the multiple-choice questions were left unchanged and the students had to take this portion of the repeat exam with books closed. Errors on this section were multiplied by 1.5 when grading to compensate for the items being familiar. The problem portion of the repeat exam was again open-book and students could refer to the original exam.

6. A comprehensive final examination was open-book, including all lecture exams, but with no repeat option. The final exam counted for half of the course grade to reward students for knowing the material by the end of the course, even if they had to struggle to catch up.

Subjects

A total of 109 students enrolled in two sections of a one-semester course in Elementary Statistics responded to a questionnaire that was added to the final examination. With an additional two sections of the course, a total of 177 students were used for an analysis of examination grades. Most of the students were sophomores planning to major in psychology.

The records of four semesters of the statistics course were examined to select those students who had an average grade of B (typically numerical grades of 82 to 89) on the three initial lecture examinations. This analysis dealt only with students with a B average because a ceiling effect limited improvement for the A students and nearly all C students took at least two repeat exams. Excluded from the sample were students who missed any of the three initial exams or who scored lower on any repeat exam (indicating a lack of studying). In the final sample ($N = 35$), 71% had grades of B on at least two of the three exams. This group was separated into those who took two or three repeat exams and those who took no or one repeat.

Results

The proportion of the questionnaire group taking repeat exams, along with the number of exams repeated, are shown by final course grade in Table 1. Nearly all students took one or more repeat exams and less capable students used the repeat option more frequently.

Comparing the repeat exams to the original exams for all students in the four course sections ($N = 177$), 92% of the repeat exams showed higher grades and the mean number of repeat exams taken was 2.10. The average change from the initial to the repeat exam was an increase of 16.99 points which, after being averaged with the initial grade, resulted in an increase of just over one letter grade for the exam. On the initial exams, 53% of the grades were C or lower. The average score of the exams for which the repeat was taken was 74.40, a minimal C. The general similarity of the repeat exams to the originals, in particular the repetition of much of the multiple-choice portion (one third of the exam), would have made the repeats somewhat easier. However, the problem section, which had the numbers changed, was the bulk of the exam and the major source of errors.

The average scores on the final examination for the two groups of B students are shown in Table 2. The final exam scores for the two to three repeat group were significantly higher than the lecture exam average, $t(18) = 3.66, p < .001$, $rm > .65$ (a correlation-based measure of magnitude of effect–Friedman, 1982). The difference of 4 points was equivalent to half of a letter grade. The increase for the zero to one repeat group was small and not significant, $t(15) = .75$. The difference between the two sets of change scores was statistically significant, $t(33) = 2.17, p < .05, rm > .35$.

The questionnaire responses, summarized in Table 3, were highly positive with all students recommending that the repeat exam procedure be used in the future. All items gave clearcut outcomes except 1.c. and 1.g. on which opinion was evenly divided. Students reported that the procedure reduced anxiety, kept them from falling behind, and led to better learning. Students also reported that they studied as much for the original exams as for the repeats. Added written comments emphasized that the repeat examinations decreased anxiety and helped the students to learn more of the course material.

Table 1. Repeat Examinations Taken as a Function of Final Course Grade

Grade	n	Mean Repeats Taken (Maximum = 3)	% One or More Repeat Exams
A	28	1.42	82
B	51	2.12	96
C	28	2.42	100
D/F	2	2.00	100
Total	109	2.02	93

Table 2. Exam Scores for Students With a B Average on Initial Lecture Exams

Repeat Exams Taken	n	Mean Scores Lecture	Mean Scores Final	Difference
0–1	16	85.31	86.06	0.75
2–3	19	85.26	89.32	4.06

Discussion

Both the analysis of grades and the questionnaire indicated that the goals of the repeat exam procedure were met. Taking repeat exams was associated with improved grades and the system was favorably viewed by students.

The comparison of final exam grades and lecture exam grades clearly showed that the students who took two or three repeat exams improved more on the final exam than did the others. These findings cannot be interpreted unambiguously: either taking the repeat exam directly led to higher final exam grades, or the more motivated students used the repeat exam option. However, in either case the repeat exams provided support for those students who devoted extra effort to mastering the course material.

From the instructor's point of view, teaching was facilitated by reducing the need to push lagging students, thereby allowing the course material to be covered more quickly. The assumption that the repeat exams would both motivate and structure the studying of those students who were falling behind is supported by the higher final examination grades for the repeat exam takers and the high proportion of B and C students taking repeats. The repeat exams also served very well as makeup exams; the slight penalty and loss of the repeat option discouraged missing original exams.

The exam procedure also might have reduced the students' temptation to cheat on exams. The repeat option directly removed the "do or die" element from lecture exams and, with no curving of grades, there was less competitive pressure. In addition, the open-book exams should have minimized rote learning as a factor and reduced the threat to less secure students. Direct evidence on exam-taking behavior is not available because the College of William and Mary has an effective honor code and exams are not proctored. However, the median grade of C on the initial exams indicates that most students worked independently.

Even though half of the questionnaire respondents stated that the repeat exams were as difficult as the original, nearly all of the repeat exam scores were higher. The students' unanimous opinion was that the initial exam was effective as a study guide for the repeat, and these higher scores indicate that studying for and taking the repeat exams was quickly rewarded. The students studying as much for the initial exams as for the repeats shows that the averaging of the initial and repeat grades maintained the value of doing well on the initial exam.

The main disadvantage of this repeat procedure is that it consumed valuable lecture time. If a lecture hour cannot be spared, repeats could be given during a laboratory session or at a special added exam session. Another problem is that repeating multiple-choice items unchanged is not the best procedure. Currently, a word processor makes it practical to change test items to produce new, but equivalent repeat exams. If it is necessary to increase the use of repeat exams by weaker students, those who do poorly on the initial exam could be required to take repeat exams until an acceptable grade is achieved.

In practice, the repeat exam procedure has many of the advantages of the self-paced or Keller (1968) system; it requires little course reorganization and minimal managerial effort. The initial exam provides students with the information they need to decide if taking a repeat exam will be worthwhile, and then serves as an excellent, individually tailored, study guide. This feedback is most important for weaker students who often do not realize, until the original exam is returned, that their grasp of the material is poor.

Table 3. Student Evaluations of the Repeat Exam Procedure

	Percentage		
	Yes	?	No
1. Do you think the present exam system (using repeat exams compared to a nonrepeat system):			
a. improves the student's chances for a higher grade?	91	3	6
b. leads to better learning by the student?	76	13	11
c. requires more work?	47	3	50
d. keeps students from falling behind?	76	9	15
e. decreases anxiety concerning exams?	82	4	14
f. decreases anxiety concerning the course?	79	4	17
g. helps weak students more than good students?	44	20	36
h. provides helpful feedback?	84	10	6
2. Did you study *less* for the initial lecture exam since you could later take the repeat?	% Yes = 12		
	% No = 78		
3. How did the retests compare to the original exams? (7-point scale)	% Easier = 53		
	% Same or Harder = 47		
4. Do you recommend that the retest procedure be used in future courses?	% Yes = 100		
5. How helpful was the initial exam as a study guide for the repeat exam? (7-point scale)	Very Helpful = 72		
	% Moderately to Very Helpful = 100		

Note. N = 109.

References

Davidson, W. B., House, W. J., & Boyd, T. L. (1984). A test-retest policy for introductory psychology courses. *Teaching of Psychology, 11*, 182–184.

Foley, D. P. (1981). Instructional potential of teacher-made tests. *Teaching of Psychology, 8*, 243–244.

Friedman, H. (1972). *Introduction to statistics.* New York: Random House.

Friedman, H. (1982). Simplified determinations of statistical power, magnitude of effect and research sample sizes. *Educational and Psychological Measurement, 42*, 521–526.

Keller, F. S. (1968). "Good-bye, teacher ..." *Journal of Applied Behavior Analysis, 1*, 79–89.

Kottke, J. L. (1985). Using a comprehensive makeup exam to replace a missed exam. *Teaching of Psychology, 12*, 51–52.

Ward, E. F. (1984). Statistics mastery: A novel approach. *Teaching of Psychology, 11*, 223–225.

Note

I thank Deborah Ventis and Patricia Frazier for their valuable comments on early drafts of this article.

Formal Operations and Learning Style Predict Success in Statistics and Computer Science Courses

Mary A. Hudak
David E. Anderson
Allegheny College

One of the most disconcerting aspects of teaching undergraduate courses in statistics and computer science is the appearance of a bimodal distribution of grades. Some students grasp the material with relative ease; others struggle to understand the material, particularly as course concepts become increasingly abstract. Psychologists and computer scientists have addressed this phenomenon (e.g., Hunt & Randhawa, 1973). Many teachers try to design introductory statistics courses to obviate the difficulties of students with lower grades. However, there has been little or no research designed to explain why these students have problems understanding the material. In contrast, with the surge of interest and demand for computer literacy, substantial research has been conducted on variables associated with success in computer science courses. We argue here that the same underlying cognitive abilities are necessary for success in statistics and computer science classes.

Attempts to identify factors related to students' success in college and particularly in computer science courses focus on three descriptive categories of variables—educational background, aptitude, and attitude. Success has typically been defined in terms of course grade. Researched variables include high school or college grade point average, class rank, experience in math or science, ACT or SAT scores, and perceptions of teachers' fairness (e.g., Butcher & Muth, 1985; Campbell & McCabe, 1984; Garrett, 1949; Giambra, 1976; Jones, 1983; Petersen & Howe, 1979). Other research has emphasized cognitive variables such as the advantage produced by critical thinking skills (e.g., Hunt & Randhawa, 1973) or a field-independent cognitive style (Hassell, 1982; Stevens, 1983). For the most part, however, research on student success in college has been more descriptive than explanatory.

A more promising approach is the use of Piagetian theory to explain ability to succeed in science in general (e.g., Chiappetta, 1976) and computer science courses in particular (e.g., Barker & Unger, 1983; Kurtz, 1980). Piaget's (1970) model posits a crucial distinction that may shed light on the differences between successful and unsuccessful student achievement in statistics and computer science courses. This distinction involves the final two stages of development: concrete operations and formal operations. In the concrete operational stage, although elementary logical operations and elementary groupings of classes and relations can be made, thinking is concrete or is at a rudimentary level of abstraction. Hypothetical reasoning is limited because the ability to isolate variables systematically has not been achieved. In contrast, the formal operational stage of development is marked by hypothetical-deductive reasoning. This capacity entails grasping the logic of all possible combinations of items or events, developing a combinatorial system, and unifying operations into a structured whole. Factors can be separated by exclusion, and interpropositional operations are achieved—propositions can be combined by conjunction, disjunction, negation, and implication. Characteristics of the formal operational stage of development have clear connections to abilities required for understanding statistics and computer science.

Piaget (1970) suggested that the ability to function at the formal operational stage evolves over the early adolescent period, from approximately 11 to 15 years of age. However, American adolescents are currently behind this timetable. Data indicate that as many as 50% or more of college students are not formal operators (Higgins-Trenk & Gaite, 1971; Karplus, 1974; Lovell, 1961; McKinnon & Renner, 1971; Tomlinson-Keasey, 1972; Wason, 1968). These findings have been interpreted in two ways. Some (e.g., Martorano, 1977) use such data to question the validity of the formal operational stage in the Piagetian model, suggesting that the criteria for intellectual maturity are too strictly "formal." Others (e.g., Chiappetta, 1976; Forsyth & Bohling, 1986; McKinnon & Renner, 1971; Tomlinson-Keasey, 1976) express alarm, arguing that the use of nonformal operational thinking by college students is increasing, and propose methods for promoting stage advancement or for teaching that is tailored to concrete thinkers.

College teachers often make the incorrect presumption that students have the ability to reason at high levels of abstraction (Arons, 1979). Furthermore, college teachers tend to assume that students can use this ability to reason abstractly in a variety of particular learning situations. However, data suggest that many students who have attained formal operational status do not function reliably in this way (Chiappetta, 1976). Chiappetta offered two possible explanations why some formal operators do not routinely employ abstract conceptualization. It may be that some students are in the early phase of formal operations and are still using strategies from the concrete stage of development, or it may be that they are experiencing an initial inability to use formal operations. He referred to this second phenomenon as a "regression effect" (p. 260).

Success in statistics and computer science courses may require not only formal operational ability but also reliance on a learning style that engages the benefits of this abstract ability. According to Kolb (1976), individuals differ in the way they learn along two dimensions. The first dimension involves an emphasis on concrete experience versus abstract conceptualization; the second dimension involves an emphasis on active experimentation versus reflective observation.

Learning style is important in academic contexts. Keen (1977), for example, suggested that at least 30% of the population possesses a distinct learning style, marked by significant variations in performance and approach over a range of problem-solving tasks. Garvey, Bootman, McGhan, and Meredith (1984) concluded that convergers, who employ abstract conceptualization and active experimentation, are more likely to achieve academic success compared with students of other learning orientations.

Our study was designed to determine if formal operational ability is a key indicator of success in statistics and computer science courses. In addition, we were interested in examining the influence of learning styles that emphasize abstractness over concreteness. Specifically, the ability to act consistently at the formal operations level and a preference for abstract learning were predicted to discriminate successful from unsuccessful students in both statistics and computer science courses.

Method

Subjects

Undergraduate students enrolled in introductory statistics in the psychology department or introduction to computer science served as subjects. Of the 112 eligible students, 101 agreed to participate in the study; complete and usable data were available from 94. Data were collected during four consecutive academic terms. Participation was voluntary and anonymous. All the test material was coded using a five-digit student ID number, and students agreed to allow the course instructors to communicate final course grades to the experimenters using this number.

Measures

Tests were administered at the beginning of each course in group settings outside the classroom. Tests included measures of formal operations and learning style. The three-part Formal Operations Reasoning Test (FORT; Roberge & Flexer, 1982) assessed the level of formal operations. Subscales in this test were designed to assess subjects' level of reasoning for three theoretical components of formal operational thought: combinations, propositional logic, and proportionality. The combinations test involves determining all possible permutations of four double-sided cards. The propositional logic test consists of 16 problems designed to assess if/then propositional ability. The proportionality test consists of eight items designed to assess if/then ratio reasoning ability. The three subscale values are totaled for an overall score of formal operationalism.

Test–retest reliability coefficients of the FORT subtests, using the Kuder–Richardson reliability formula, vary: .80 for combinations, .75 for logic, and .60 for proportionality (Roberge & Flexer, 1982). The validity of the FORT was established by Roberge and Flexer (1982) using both content and construct procedures. The combinations subtest assesses comprehension of the concept (Inhelder & Piaget, 1958). According to Inhelder and Piaget, the proportional logic subtest includes the following items, which require a subject to deduce conclusions for premises drawn from the basic types of logic that define the formal operator: ability to comprehend the binary operations of propositional logic, to distinguish each operator from the others, and to use them to make inferences. The numerical analogy items in the proportionality subtest require a subject to reason with simple equivalences of ratios.

Learning style was evaluated using Kolb's (1971) Learning Style Inventory (LSI), which assesses four learning modes by asking the student to rank order a series of words associated with each learning style. The four modes form two polar opposite dimensions: abstract conceptualization versus concrete experience and active experimentation versus reflective observation. Individuals scoring high on abstract conceptualization function well in learning situations that emphasize theory and systematic analysis. In contrast, individuals scoring high on concrete experience tend to treat each situation as a unique case, rather than to employ theoretical explanations. Individuals scoring high on active experimentation function best when engaged in educational projects or discussions; they tend not to profit from passive learning situations, such as lectures. In contrast, individuals scoring high on reflective observation rely heavily on careful observation in making judgments and prefer learning situations that allow them to take the role of objective observer. Scores on each of these dimensions reflect the extent to which an individual has developed a particular learning strategy. Although these styles have polar opposite characteristics, individual scores are calculated for each of the four modes.

Kolb (1976) reported that split-half reliabilities for the four basic scales for five different samples averaged .75. Test–retest reliability coefficients for four groups over periods ranging from 3 to 7 months varied from .50 to .70; the higher values are associated with the shorter intervals. The validity of the LSI has been evaluated by examining its correlation with personality tests, its relation with preferences for teachers and learning situations, and the relation between learning style and type of career chosen. The data on preferences for teachers and learning situations is especially strong; correlations for individual scales averaged .50 (Kolb, 1976).

Success was measured with grades obtained in the respective courses. Instructors provided final course grades in percentages for students who participated in the study. Other exploratory variables were also included but are not reported here.

Results

Results for statistics and computer science courses were analyzed separately. Data were analyzed using the Rao discriminant analysis procedure because we were interested in differentiating successful from unsuccessful students; we were not interested in distinguishing among levels of success. Experience suggests that students with final grades of C or less in introductory statistics and computer science courses are at considerable risk in subsequent courses in these subjects. Thus, successful students were operationally defined as those who completed introductory statistics or computer science with a grade of at least 80%. Five interval-level scores were entered into the two-group stepwise discriminant analysis: (a) abstract conceptualization, (b) concrete experiencing, (c) active experimentation, (d) reflective observation, and (e) formal operations.

Eighty-one percent of the introductory statistics students were properly classified based on the linear combination of two of the five variables entered: concrete experiencing and formal operations. Concrete experiencing loaded negatively, whereas formal operations loaded positively, suggesting that formal operationalism is advantageous in achieving success but concrete experiencing hinders success; Wilks's lambda = .77, $\chi^2(2) = 10.37$, $p < .01$. Classification results indicate that 84% of the successful statistics students and 75% of the unsuccessful statistics students were correctly classified. The pooled within-group correlation between the canonical discriminant function and formal operations was .69; for concrete experience the correlation was −.68. Stepwise inclusion of the other three variables did not significantly increase the classification rate.

Analysis for the computer science students resulted in 72% overall correct categorization (70% of successful students and 78% of unsuccessful students). As in the analysis with statistics students, concrete experiencing and formal operations contributed to the discriminant function with a positive loading for formal operations (pooled within-groups correlation = .68) and a negative loading for concrete experiencing (pooled within-groups correlation = −.50); Wilks's lambda = .79, $\chi^2(2) = 10.96$, $p < .01$. Like the previous analysis, the other three variables were excluded from the stepwise discriminant function because they did not contribute significantly to the classification process.

Discussion

Results indicate that success in introductory statistics and computer science courses is related to formal operational ability. These findings are consistent with those reported by Barker and Unger (1983) and Kurtz (1980) who found a positive relation between formal operational status and success in computer science coursework. Our results extend previous findings by demonstrating that success in statistics is also predicted by formal operational status. In addition, we found that learning style contributes substantial independent variance to the discrimination between successful and unsuccessful students.

As stated earlier, the LSI (Kolb, 1971) measures on individual's relative emphasis on four learning styles—concrete experience, abstract conceptualization, active experimentation, and reflective observation. Abstract conceptualization was predicted to be the discriminating learning style in this study. The negative loading for concrete experiencing is theoretically consistent with this prediction. Concrete experience is dimensionally opposite to abstract conceptualization. The concrete experience end of the dimension indicates the extent to which an individual emphasizes concreteness over abstractness. The important finding is that the concrete style of learning, marked by lacking the use of theory and inference, is particularly maladaptive in statistics and computer science courses. Although scored separately, abstract conceptualization and concrete experiencing have common negatively related variance ($r = -.47$), as expected from the theory.

These findings emphasize the need to examine students' cognitive maturity and learning style—factors often ignored in research aimed at ascertaining the reasons for academic success at the college level. Our results have important implications for theoretical understanding of the problem and for potential remediation. Although intellectual development probably involves more than formal operational reasoning, as argued by Gilligan and Murphy (1979) and others, our results strongly suggest that formal operations are necessary for the kind of formal educational goals involved in courses like statistics and computer science. Furthermore, because academic skills implicated in formal operations appear to be relevant to many disciplines (Lawson, Nordland, & DeVito, 1975), it is particularly important to recognize the relevance of attainment of this ability for success in academia.

Although lip service has long been given to Piagetian principles in educational planning, little real application of them has been made, especially for the concrete versus formal operational transition. Recently, however, college students advanced to the formal stage of reasoning when the proper teaching methods were employed. Project ADAPT at the University of Nebraska–Lincoln may be the best known, but other efforts also show promise (e.g., Project DORIS and Project SOAR). Fuller (1987) provided a full description of the ADAPT project and a brief description of the others. These models of teaching may also engender changes in learning style by providing the skills that facilitate the abstract conceptualization style and lessen the dependence on concrete experience.

Abundant evidence indicates that substantial numbers of college students have not achieved the formal operational level of cognitive maturity. McKinnon and Renner (1971) reported that 27% of students in their sample were at the lowest concrete operational stage. College teachers can no longer assume that their students are ready for high-level abstraction. More research on how to teach effectively in order to promote cognitive development is needed.

References

Arons, A. B. (1979). Some thoughts on reasoning capacities implicitly expected of college students. In J. Lochhead & J. Clement (Eds.), *Cognitive process instruction: Research on teaching thinking skills* (pp. 209–215). Philadelphia: Franklin Institute Press.

Barker, R. J., & Unger, E. A. (1983). A prediction for success in an introductory programming class based upon abstract reasoning development. *SIGCSE Bulletin, 15,* 154–158.

Butcher, D. F., & Muth, W. A. (1985). Predicting performance in an introductory computer science course. *Communications of the ACM, 28,* 263–268.

Campbell, P. F., & McCabe, G. P. (1984). Predicting the success of freshmen in a computer science major. *Communications of the ACM, 27,* 1108–1113.

Chiappetta, E. L. (1976). A review of Piagetian studies relevant to science instruction at the secondary and college level. *Science Education, 60,* 253–261.

Forsyth, G. A., & Bohling, P. H. (1986, August). A *Piagetian approach to teaching statistics and research methodology.* Paper presented at the meeting of the American Psychological Association, Washington, DC.

Fuller, R. G. (Ed.). (1987). *Piagetian programs in higher education.* Lincoln, NE: University of Nebraska-Lincoln, ADAPT Project.

Garrett, H. F. (1949). A review and interpretation of investigations of factors related to scholastic success in colleges of arts and science and teachers colleges. *Journal of Experimental Education, 18,* 91–138.

Garvey, M., Bootman, J. L., McGhan, W. F., & Meredith, K. (1984). An assessment of learning styles among pharmacy students. *American Journal of Pharmaceutical Education, 48,* 134–140.

Giambra, L. M. (1976). Mathematical background and grade-point average as predictors of course grade in an undergraduate behavioral statistics course: A replication. *Teaching of Psychology, 3,* 184–185.

Gilligan, C., & Murphy, J. M. (1979). Development from adolescence to adulthood: The philosopher and the dilemma of the fact. In D. Kuhn (Ed.), *Intellectual development beyond childhood* (pp. 85–99). San Francisco: Jossey-Bass.

Hassell, J. (1982). Cognitive style and a first course in computer science: A success story. *Association for Educational Data Systems Monitor, 21,,* 33–35.

Higgins-Trenk, A., & Gaite, A. J. H. (1971, September). *Elusiveness of formal operational thought in adolescence.* Paper presented at the meeting of the American Psychological Association, Washington, DC.

Hunt, D., & Randhawa, B. (1973). Relationship between and among cognitive variables and achievement in computational science. *Educational and Psychological Measurement, 33,* 921–928.

Inhelder, B., & Piaget, J. (1958). *The growth of logical thinking from childhood to adolescence.* New York: Basic Books.

Jones, J. L. (1983). Predicting success of programming students. *Collegiate Microcomputer, 1,* 277–280.

Karplus, R. (1974). *Science curriculum improvement study: Teacher's handbook.* Berkeley: Lawrence Hall of Science.

Keen, P. G. (1977). Personality and cognitive style. In J. van Maanen (Ed.), *Organizational careers: Some new perspectives* (pp. 89–105). New York: Wiley.

Kolb, D. A. (1971). *Individual learning styles and the learning process* (Working Paper No. 535-71). Cambridge, MA: MIT Sloan School of Management.

Kolb, D. A. (1976). *Learning style inventory: Technical manual.* Boston: McBer and Company.

Kurtz, B. I. (1980). Investigating the relationship between the development of abstract reasoning and performance in an introductory programming class. *SIGCSE Bulletin, 12,* 110–117.

Lawson, A. E., Nordland, F. H., & DeVito, A. (1975). Relationship of formal reasoning to achievement, aptitudes, and attitudes in preservice teachers. *Journal of Research in Science Teaching, 12,* 423–431.

Lovell, K. A. (1961). A follow-up study of Inhelder and Piaget's growth of logical thinking. *British Journal of Psychology, 52,* 143–153.

Martorano, S. C. (1977). A developmental analysis of performance on Piaget's formal operations tasks. *Developmental Psychology, 13,* 666–672.

McKinnon, J. W., & Renner, J. W. (1971). Are colleges concerned with intellectual development? *American Journal of Physics, 39,* 1047–1052.

Petersen, C. G., & Howe, T. G. (1979). Predicting academic success in introduction to computers. *Association for Educational Data Systems Journal, 12,* 182–192.

Piaget, J. (1970). *Genetic epistemology.* New York: Norton.

Roberge, J. J., & Flexer, B. K. (1982). The Formal Operational Reasoning Test. *The Journal of General Psychology, 106,* 61–67.

Stevens, D. J. (1983). Cognitive processes and success of students in instructional computer courses. *Association for Educational Data Systems Journal, 16,* 228–233.

Tomlinson-Keasey, C. (1972). Formal operations in females from eleven to fifty-four years of age. *Developmental Psychology, 6,* 364.

Tomlinson-Keasey, C. (1976, September). *Can we develop abstract thought (ADAPT) in college freshmen? One year later.* Paper presented at the meeting of the American Psychological Association, Washington, DC.

Wason, P. C. (1968). Reason about a rule. *Quarterly Journal of Experimental Psychology, 20,* 273–281.

Notes

1. This article is based on a paper presented at the meeting of the American Psychological Association, Washington, DC, August 1986.
2. We thank Charles L. Brewer and three anonymous reviewers for helpful comments on an earlier draft of this article.

Strategies and Resources for Teaching Statistics to Visually Impaired Students

Anita M. Meehan
Derrie Hoffert
Laurence C. Hoffert
Kutztown University

The college student population has changed dramatically in the last 2 decades. Not only are more older adults and minorities attending college, but the number of physically disabled students has also increased. This changing student body presents a challenge to instructors as they adapt their ways of teaching to meet diverse student needs. Instructors

99

are often unaware of available resources and services to help disabled students. This was certainly true for the first author when she was called on to teach statistics to visually impaired students. The purpose of this article, which includes the insights of a visually impaired student (the second author), is to help others learn from our experience. We offer some suggestions for teaching statistics to visually impaired students, and we describe agency resources and practical devices that are available. The special equipment we report on is inexpensive and within the budget of most individuals or departments.

Suggestions and Practical Devices

Individual Differences

Visually impaired students are not all alike, and their needs can be vastly different. Some may be totally blind; others have minimal impairment, needing only to have tests and handouts enlarged. Instructors should talk with the student as soon as possible in order to become aware of the degree of impairment and typical coping strategies used by the individual.

Agency Resources

Students themselves are usually aware of existing resources in the local community and can educate the instructor. Most cities or counties have a local braille service that will transcribe course materials for a fee. A major problem is the time required for preparation of these materials, which typically ranges from 6 to 12 weeks. Fortunately, braille versions of z, t, F, and χ^2 tables are available for a minimal charge.[1] Associations for the visually impaired can also provide students with braille typewriters, tape recorders, computers, and talking calculators. The newest of the talking calculators includes a square root key, which should allow the students to perform all calculations required in an introductory statistics course.

Another source of information and assistance is the campus Affirmative Action Office or its equivalent. The first author obtained funds from our campus office to hire statistics tutors who also served as textbook readers and test administrators for blind students enrolled in her course.

Raised Line Drawing Kit

The campus Affirmative Action Office also provided a raised line drawing kit.[2] This is essentially a clipboard made of rubber material. The instructor or tutor places a piece of plastic film on the clipboard and uses a modified ballpoint pen to create a raised imprint. We used this to sketch normal distributions and the location of z scores. Blind students could then feel the imprint to understand what was meant by phrases such as "the area between the mean and z" and "the area beyond z." We also used this to sketch the difference in shape between the normal distribution and the t distribution. If desired, instructors could draw Greek statistical symbols so blind students get a better idea of what the symbols look like.

Verbalization

Because statistics requires frequent chalkboard use for mathematical formulas and sample problems, instructors need to pay special attention to verbalizing what they write and to writing large enough for low-vision students to see clearly. Statistics instructors are generally aware that sighted students often confuse $(\Sigma X)^2$, the square of the summed X scores, with ΣX^2, the sum of squared X scores. Imagine the confusion of a student who cannot see what is written on the board!

Another common pitfall relates to sample statistics versus population parameters. Sighted students can easily see whether the instructor has written the symbol for the sample mean or the population mean or for the sample standard deviation or the population standard deviation. The instructor's verbal description must be precise so the visually impaired student knows which concept is being discussed.

Verbalizing formulas is not an easy task, and confusion will likely arise despite an instructor's best efforts. For example, suppose the teacher describes how to calculate the percent relative frequency of an event. The instructor might describe this as "frequency of the event divided by N times 100." This could be interpreted in two ways, however: $(f/N) \times 100$, which is correct, or $f/(N \times 100)$, which is incorrect. In our experience, formulas are very cumbersome to articulate, and neither the teacher nor the student may be aware at the time that there are two ways to interpret the verbal description. One method for solving this problem is to provide enlarged handouts of the formulas, but this will not work for blind students. Another solution is to check students' notes or have a tutor do so. Having students work through sample problems with a tutor should reveal whether formulas have been misunderstood. Instructors also need to provide a classroom atmosphere that makes students feel comfortable about asking for clarification.

[1]Braille versions of distribution tables can be obtained for 35¢ per page through the National Braille Association, 1290 University Avenue, Rochester, NY 14607, telephone: (617) 473-0900.

[2]A raised line drawing kit is manufactured by Sewell E. P. Corporation, Woodside, NY 11377.

Statistics Software

Many statistics instructors require or encourage the use of computers for data analysis. Computers are used more in statistics and research methods courses than any other courses in the psychology curriculum (Rowland, 1992). Some textbooks even include statistical software as ancillary materials (e.g., Jaccard & Becker, 1990; Sprinthall, 1990). To avoid having visually impaired students miss out on an important component of today's education, we developed a data analysis software called *STATS*. This menu-driven program runs on IBM compatibles and performs most of the basic descriptive and inferential analyses taught in an introductory statistics course.

Although STATS can be used by anyone, four features were added to aid the visually impaired student. First, the display is in 40-character mode. Students who require more magnification can obtain a shareware program called B-POP. This is a 53K memory-resident program that runs on IBM compatibles, and it can magnify text anywhere from 40 to 12 characters per line.[3] Second, STATS allows screen colors to be changed easily so students can determine which color combination best suits their needs. Third, the program includes critical values tables for $z, t, F,$ and χ^2 distributions that are more readable than those found in textbooks. Finally, STATS can print in either large or normal size characters.

Testing

Our experience indicates that severely visually impaired students often prefer to have tests on tape, particularly for multiple-choice questions. This way they can replay the question as often as necessary. They feel uncomfortable asking a tester to repeat questions if the test is being administered orally. Instructors should avoid matching questions because continually replaying questions and response choices is awkward and time-consuming. Visually impaired students find matching questions frustrating, and they easily lose their concentration. Students also prefer to have their own copies of statistical tables, eliminating the need to ask the test administrator for items required from such tables. The STATS program offers enlarged printouts of these tables, and braille tables are available, as mentioned earlier.

Conclusion

Our visually impaired students did the same homework problems, took the same tests, and fulfilled the same course requirements as sighted students, except that blind students were not responsible for plotting graphs or frequency distributions. Most visually impaired students desire to participate fully in all class activities and assignments. With the help of the instructors adaptations and the services and materials described herein, these students can do just that. Also, an awareness of existing resources will make instructors more confident about teaching statistics to visually impaired students.

References

Jaccard, J., & Becker, M. A. (1990). *Statistics for the behavioral sciences* (2nd ed.). Belmont, CA: Wadsworth.

Rowland, D. (1992, January). *Computers within the psychology curriculum: What's possible, what works, and is it worth it?* Paper presented at the 14th National Institute on the Teaching of Psychology, St. Petersburg, FL.

Sprinthall, R. C. (1990). *Basic statistical analysis* (3rd ed.). Englewood Cliffs, NJ: Prentice Hall.

Notes

1. We thank William C. Worrell, Jr., whose statistics programs in BASIC served as a starting point for the development of STATS.
2. We thank Charles L. Brewer and three anonymous reviewers for their helpful comments on this article.

---

[3]B–POP is available for $27 from Hexagon Products, P.O. Box 1295, Park Ridge, IL 60068–1295, telephone: (708) 692-3355. Using CompuServe, the software is available in the IBM Special Needs Forum (Type GO IBMSPEC at the ! prompt).

Section II:
Research Methods

Along with statistics, research methodology undergrids scientific psychology. Courses in research methods challenge teachers and students. We selected articles for this section to help teachers meet some of the challenges by making their courses more meaningful and rewarding for them and their students. The articles contain suggestions for (a) reducing students' fears, (b) evaluating ethical issues, (c) teaching ethics, (d) reviewing the literature, (e) using computers, (f) implementing teaching strategies, (g) demonstrating systematic observation and research design (h) teaching writing and critical thinking, (i) emphasizing accuracy in research, and (j) fostering students' research and presentations. The articles should prompt teachers to reevaluate and improve how they conceptualize and conduct their courses in research methods.

1. Reducing Students' Fears

In a program that incorporates research into the curriculum at all levels, Christiane Brems at the University of Alaska Anchorage developed a method for introducing students to research slowly and carefully. Her approach decreased students' trepidation, and close collaboration of students and faculty in the research process increased enthusiasm and enjoyment for students and teachers.

Evidence suggesting that older left-handed individuals are underrepresented in the general population provided an engaging vehicle for David Johnson to introduce research methods into his courses at John Brown University.

After viewing a graphical representation of this relation, students attempt to explain it. This fetching way of presenting diverse research issues can be used in various courses.

Nigel Barber at Birmingham-Southern College used a participant modeling technique in an introductory psychology class to reduce students' fear of a laboratory rat. Students received a mild level of exposure (holding the rat's transport box) and observed peer volunteers actually handling the animal. Students' fear was reduced without handling the rat, which minimized ethical problems.

Taking the Fear Out of Research: A Gentle Approach to Teaching an Appreciation for Research

Christiane Brems
University of Alaska Anchorage

While teaching an undergraduate research methods course, I became painfully aware of the trepidation with which students approached this class. I decided that introducing students to research must be made more gradual and less intimidating during the first 3 years of college. Then, students may approach their senior research requirements with less apprehension.

This article describes an approach I have used in a psychology department that enrolls over 400 psychology majors and 50 clinical psychology master's degree students. I have used this approach for six semesters, and one other faculty member has adopted it. Two other faculty members have incorporated significant pieces of it, and a fourth is in the process of so doing. Among the four of us, there are now approximately eight classes per year that integrate research. Faculty cannot be required to adopt this approach; hence, not all students in my department are exposed to it. Nevertheless, feedback from those who were exposed has been very positive. One instructor at one of our extended campuses indicated that she has also successfully incorporated research integration.

The first step in the process consists of integrating research at all levels of teaching. How research integration takes place depends on the level of the course, but it best begins in the first year. Integration is possible in all courses that are part of a traditional undergraduate psychology curriculum. For instance, it has been accomplished in Human Development (at the first-year level), Abnormal Psychology (at the sophomore level), Personality Theories (at the junior level), and Psychodynamic Theory (at the senior level). If research is integrated into core courses, psychology majors will be exposed to research early and throughout their training. The more faculty participate, the more exposure students will receive.

First-Year-Level Integration

At this level, the goal is to demystify the research process. First-year students are generally overwhelmed by the concept of research and believe it to be beyond their capabilities. They have visions of scientists working in laboratories full of rats, brewing mysterious potions, and crunching huge rows of numbers. Students need to learn that research is done by ordinary people with ordinary questions about ordinary environments and ordinary human behavior.

The demystification process is best approached in a two-pronged manner: introduce students to research and make students informed consumers of research. The former can be done easily by exposing students to research interests and activities of local faculty and graduate students. Graduate students are preferable as research models at this level because their experience resembles that of the undergraduate student more closely than that of a faculty member. In addition, students can be encouraged to visit the psychology laboratory; meet the assistants (who are rarely much older or more experienced than the students); and observe animals, equipment, or computer simulations.

Introducing students to research as consumers can take place most simply by asking them to read research articles. Although they have to read the entire article, first-year students are required to focus on the introduction section to prevent confusion that method and results sections often induce in neophytes. Reading introductions helps students recognize how authors slowly work their way through relevant literature to develop research questions.

Once students have read and digested a few articles, they can be asked to generate simple research questions. Creative role modeling is conducive to this process. I like to have fun with this approach by asking students to think of a question relevant to the course topic and then helping them reformulate the question into a format that lends itself to research. For instance, students in my Abnormal Psychology course often question the effectiveness of psychotherapy for severe mental illness. As a class, we talk about how a researcher could design a project to measure treatment outcome with such a clinical population. As a clinical psychologist, I enjoy demonstrating through this exercise that research is not limited to experimental psychology.

Sophomore-Level Integration

The demystification process continues at the sophomore level by introducing basic ideas about methodology. Sophomores are asked to read research articles, focusing on the introduction and method sections to get them thinking about how researchers go about answering questions. Students are alerted to basic questions dealing with choice of subjects, comparisons of groups, and instrument options. They read research articles with a fastidious approach so they can write a summary that reviews the question researched and critiques the chosen subjects and instruments.

Trips to the library add a nice component of knowledge to the students' developing research repertoire. They are introduced to *Psychological Abstracts,* computerized search systems, journal stacks, reference guides, and research indexes. The best way to engage students in a basic literature search is to require them to find their own article to review rather than provide the same article for the entire class. Thus, students develop literature search skills and are more interested in what they read for critique.

Junior-Level Integration

More sophistication is required from students at this level, and they are introduced more thoroughly to the intricacies of methodology. Students are asked to read research articles, primarily focusing again on the method section—especially data collection. Article reviews are assigned, with a focus less on interest or clarity and more on the adequacy of data-collection procedures and conclusions drawn from the data.

Basic in-class discussion takes place about threats to internal validity (without necessarily naming the concept) by explaining maturation and history—two of the easiest threats to understand and describe in simple language. Threats to external validity are also discussed (again without necessarily naming the concept) by exaggerating generalizations from a particularly interesting article chosen by the instructor. Newspaper articles covering relevant topics work well for this purpose. In Personality Theories class, for instance, newspaper articles about gender or ethnic differences can be used because they often involve poor sampling and overstate conclusions and generalizability. Often, students have not thought about sampling biases and how they limit generalizability. Their amazement usually motivates them to seek more examples in local papers. They generally bring articles to class, and I gladly allow time to discuss them.

Senior-Level Integration

At the senior level, I require critical consumerism of research and encourage students to conduct their own research. With regard to consumerism, I ask students to review articles in a detailed manner and to comment on all article sections. With regard to the conduct of research, I allow students to substitute a research project for a term paper (usually one or two students will choose this option each semester). I encourage students to choose pertinent research topics that are of interest to them. This research can be carried out in groups or in collaboration with me or another instructor. I do ask that the projects completed with other instructors still be relevant to the course the student is taking from me, which limits collaboration with other faculty somewhat. I help students develop a meaningful research question to investigate. I do not search for perfection here but for a fairly sound study that will convey to students that they can do research. For instance, in my Psychodynamic Theories class, a student's interest in the relation between narcissism and self-esteem led to a creative and complex project through which we developed a procedure for inducing mild narcissistic injuries in subjects (with proper follow-up and debriefing).

If my relationship with students at the senior level takes place in the context of the Research Methods course, I require them to design, conduct, and write up a research project of sufficient quality to be presentable at a regional psychological conference. Some of these projects have been of publishable quality (e.g., Skillman et al., 1992; Wilson, Vercella, Brems, Benning, & Renfro, 1992). In this course particularly, allowing students to develop projects that are of personal interest to them is critically important.

Graduate-Level Integration

At this level, I require students to review articles and conduct research. Reviews at this level are critiques that focus on a body of literature (i.e., assess whether current beliefs and practices in a given area are based on sound research). I require students to conduct research projects individually and to write them up for presentation and publication (e.g., Namyniuk & Brems, 1992; Tucker & Brems, 1993). The publication requirement instills enthusiasm for research like no other task; students are thrilled when they see their name in print.

Interacting With Students About Research

In addition to integrating research into the classroom, instructors can do other things to foster enthusiasm and reduce the fear of research. First, students' interest in research can be piqued by telling them about one's own research. At appropriate times, I talk about my research to help students recognize that research literature develops from many small building blocks, not a few huge studies that answer many questions or are designed to find the truth. Using examples of one's own research brings the process down to earth for the student, makes it seem more relevant to the student, and gives it an applied context. A word of caution: One should never only present one's own work. Otherwise students get bored and suspicious, and they may view the instructor as egotistical.

Telling students about one's own research can also be used as a springboard to invite them to participate in one's own research. I love to invite students to help with my projects (e.g., Brems, Baldwin, & Baxter, 1993), not to exploit them, but to teach them. Ideally, students should not be used as mere data collectors; instead, their involvement should be fairly evenly distributed across all stages of the investigation.

Research teams are another excellent means of interacting with students about research. The research teams I have conducted encouraged students to work on research projects with peers in collaborative efforts. This approach is less threatening because students can share work, exchange information, and capitalize on the individual strengths of project members (e.g., Brems, Baldwin, Davis, & Namyniuk, 1994). I lead such research teams; I do not rule

them. I even let the teams make mistakes, so they can learn from their own experience. For example, during one project, the team decided after some discussion not to match subjects on educational level only to realize later that this variable was indeed an important mediator.

Brown-bag lunches and student clubs help to encourage faculty-student interaction concerning research interests, projects, and findings. Other informal information exchanges about research can involve the development of research can involve the development of research networks that help students learn who does what, where, and when. Mentoring systems through which students can identify instructors and/or other students who share similar interests are equally useful.

Collaborating with students on research is exciting. I enjoy witnessing the awakening of enthusiasm and critical thinking involved in the process. Although research collaboration with students does not always produce a publication, it always includes learning and enjoyment for student and instructor!

References

Brems, C., Baldwin, M., & Baxter, S. (1993). Empirical evaluation of a self-psychologically oriented parent education program. *Family Relations, 42,* 26–30.

Brems, C., Baldwin, M., Davis, L., & Namyniuk, L. (1994). The imposter syndrome as related to teaching evaluations and advising relationships of university faculty members. *Journal of Higher Education, 65,* 183–193.

Namyniuk, L., & Brems, C. (1992, April). *Relationships among narcissism, self-esteem, and empathy as mediated by gender and narcissistic injury.* Paper presented at the annual meeting of the Western Psychological Association, Portland, OR.

Skillman, G., Dabbs, P., Mitchell, M., McGrath, M., Lewis, J., & Brems, C. (1992). Appropriateness of the Draw-A-Person Test for Alaska natives. *Journal of Clinical Psychology, 48,* 561–564.

Tucker, P., & Brems, C. (1993). Variables affecting length of psychiatric inpatient treatment. *Journal of Mental Health Administration, 20,* 57–64.

Wilson, C., Vercella, R., Brems, C., Benning, D., & Renfro, N. (1992). Levels of learned helplessness in abused women. *Women and Therapy, 13,* 53–68.

Notes

1. This article was the outgrowth of an invited lecture about integrating teaching and research presented at the annual Teaching Excellence Conference at the University of Alaska Anchorage.
2. I thank Charles L. Brewer and three anonymous reviewers for their many helpful suggestions on a draft of this article.

A "Handy" Way to Introduce Research Methods

David E. Johnson
John Brown University

Several studies have found that left-handers are under-represented in older age ranges (Coren & Halpern, 1991; Fleminger, Dalton, & Standage, 1977; Halpern & Coren, 1988). Many of these studies reveal relations similar to the one graphically presented in Figure 1, which is adapted from Coren and Halpern (1991).

Coren and Halpern (1991) suggested two possible explanations for this relations. First, left-handers learn to become right-handed due to implicit or explicit environmental pressures. This *modification hypothesis* implies that left-handers convert to being right-handed over time due to the physical and social difficulties encountered living in a right-handed world. For example, most tools, equipment, and common articles (e.g., scissors) require right-handed operation for optimal performance. Conversely, the data might suggest that left-handers have increased mortality rates across the life span that selectively eliminate them from the population (the *elimination hypothesis*).

Coren and Halpern (1991) attempted to determine the viability of these hypotheses by examining data on various topics (e.g., birth stress, environmental risk factors, maturational variables, and immune system variables) and concluded that the elimination hypothesis is more tenable than the modification hypothesis. Left-handers, on average, experienced birth stress more often, experienced higher accident rates, suffered higher rates of immune and autoimmune dysfunction, and died younger as compared with right-handers.

Students find the relation between handedness and mortality intriguing. Because of their interest, I developed a simple classroom activity based on this research that requires students to think about the processes scientists consider when doing research.

Method

The activity requires minimal preparation. Familiarity with the basic core of studies in this area is required. I recommend reading Coren and Halpern (1991) and Porac and Coren (1981) at a minimum. Prepare an overhead transparency (or another method of visual presentation) that contains Figure 1.

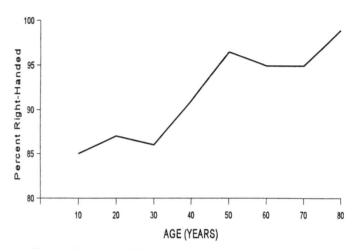

Figure 1. Percentage of right-handers in the population as a function of age. *Note.* From "Left-Handedness: A Marker for Decreased Survival Fitness," by S. Coren and D. F. Halpern, 1991, *Psychological Bulletin, 109,* p. 91. Copyright 1991 by the American Psychological Association, Inc. Adapted with permission.

Typically, I begin the class period by placing Figure 1 on the overhead projector and asking the class the following questions: "What does this graph mean?" "How do you explain it?" "Based on your explanation, how would you decide if your explanation is tenable?" Students organize themselves into groups of five or six to discuss their responses to these questions. Often students' initial response is to express disbelief in the veracity of the data. Spirited discussion results, and students often vigorously disagree about the potential causes of the handedness–mortality relation. Most believe that the data are a result of changes from left- to right-handedness.

After 15 to 20 min of discussion, the groups report the results of their discussion to the entire class. During the group reports, I note responses that address factors requiring further treatment in the discussion with the whole class. Afterward, I summarize and discuss the importance of the issues raised during the class discussion.

I usually implement this activity during the first week of classes because textbooks often present introductory material on research methods in the first chapters. I use the activity in various courses, such as Honors General Psychology, Research Methods, and Behavioral Neuroscience. In research methods or physiological psychology courses, reading some core articles to facilitate discussion of more advanced topics in future class periods can be instructive for students.

Results and Discussion

Many benefits result from this exercise. First, students practice reading and interpreting a line graph (Figure 1), an important skill for understanding research reports.

Second, at least some students recognize the fact that Figure 1 can be interpreted in at least two ways (i.e., modification vs. elimination). I emphasize that these two explanations form a dichotomy that is similar to the nature versus nurture debate that runs through much of psychology. The modification hypothesis focuses more on environmental variables; the elimination hypothesis centers more on biological variables, some of which have genetic origins.

Third, some students realize that acceptance of the modification or elimination explanation depends on how the data in Figure 1 were collected. Essentially, they realize that a cross-sectional methodology may yield a different result from a longitudinal design. Usually, this realization is based on the possibility that subjects born 50 to 80 years ago made the sinistral to dextral change due to more intense social pressures as compared with younger subjects. In upper division courses, I present Coren and Halpern's (1991) data and rationale for discounting this explanation.

Fourth, students always ask, "Who is left-handed?" They point out that some people do some things left-handed and other things right-handed. This observation highlights the need for operational definitions of variables. We discuss ways to operationalize the handedness variable, and I present some definitions used in the literature. For example, Peters and Perry (1991) defined left-handers as those who used the left hand to write, whereas Halpern and Coren (1988) assigned left-handedness to baseball players in their study if the players batted and pitched with the left hand.

Fifth, students mention some of the same variables that Coren and Halpern (1991) tested. For example, almost every class suggests the possibility of increased accident rates for left-handers, genetic variables, and prenatal variables.

Finally, some authors disagree with Coren and Halpern's (1991) conclusion that elimination is the better explanation for this relation (e.g., Dellatolas et al., 1991; Fudin, Renninger, Lembessis, & Hirshon, 1993; Harris, 1993a, 1993b; Hugdahl, Satz, Mitrushina, & Miller, 1993; Peters & Perry, 1991). In research methods classes, we discuss disagreements among researchers that are based on different methodologies or statistical analyses. Introduction to scholarly debate can be accomplished by having students read some of the published replies to these criticisms (e.g., Coren & Halpern, 1993; Halpern & Coren, 1993).

In my most recent Honors General Psychology course, I asked students ($N = 25$) if they believed the activity should be used in future classes. Twenty-four of the 25 students answered in the affirmative.

In summary, this activity can be used in various courses. Students find the topic interesting, and it provides an engaging way to present diverse research issues.

References

Coren, S., & Halpern, D. F. (1991). Left-handedness: A marker for decreased survival fitness. *Psychological Bulletin, 109,* 90–106.

Coren, S., & Halpern, D. F. (1993). A replay of the baseball data. *Perceptual & Motor Skills, 76,* 403–406.

Dellatolas, G., Tubert, P., Castresana, A., Mesbah, M., Giallonardo, T., Lazaratou, H., & Lellouch, J. (1991). Age and cohort effects in adult handedness. *Neuropsychologia, 29,* 255–261.

Fleminger, J. J., Dalton, R., & Standage, K. F. (1977). Age as a factor in the handedness of adults. *Neuropsychologia, 15,* 471–473.

Fudin, R., Renninger, L., Lembessis, E., & Hirshon, J. (1993). Sinistrality and reduced longevity: Reichler's 1979 data on baseball players do not indicate a relationship. *Perceptual & Motor Skills, 76,* 171–182.

Halpern, D. F., & Coren, S. (1988). Do right-handers live longer? *Nature, 333,* 213.

Halpern, D. F., & Coren, S. (1993). Left-handedness and life span: A reply to Harris. *Psychological Bulletin, 114,* 235–241.

Harris, L. J. (1993a). Do left-handers die sooner than right-handers? Commentary on Coren and Halpern's (1991) "Left-handedness: A marker for decreased survival fitness." *Psychological Bulletin, 114,* 203–234.

Harris, L. J. (1993b). Left-handedness and life span: Reply to Halpern and Coren. *Psychological Bulletin, 114,* 242–247.

Hugdahl, K., Satz, P., Mitrushina, M., & Miller, E. N. (1993). Left-handedness and old age: Do left-handers die earlier? *Neuropsychologia, 31,* 325–333.

Peters, M., & Perry, R. (1991). No link between left-handedness and maternal age and no elevated accident rate in left-handers. *Neuropsychologia, 29,* 1257–1259.

Porac, C., & Coren, S. (1981). *Lateral preferences and human behavior.* New York: Springer-Verlag.

Note

A version of this article was presented at the annual meeting of the American Psychological Association, Los Angeles, August 1994.

Reducing Fear of the Laboratory Rat: A Participant Modeling Approach

Nigel Barber
Birmingham-Southern College

The first day of attending a rat laboratory can be a harrowing experience for the student who is even slightly fearful of rats. One solution to this problem may involve preexposing students to the rat in a comparatively nonthreatening classroom situation. Hughes (1990) described a classroom demonstration of phobia treatment in which an expert and peer models handled a snake. Students enjoyed the demonstration and found it valuable, but only a small number of students participated. Because fear reduction was not measured, it is not clear that the modeling procedure was effective. This article describes a modeling procedure for fear reduction to be used with an entire class. A pretest-posttest design allowed fear reduction to be quantified and the relative effectiveness of two levels of exposure (either petting the rat or merely handling its transparent transport box) to be evaluated. Sex differences in initial fear levels and in fear reduction were also examined.

Participant modeling is a clinical procedure for treating phobias. The client is exposed directly to a phobic object in the presence of a therapist; for example, a snake phobic approaches the snake and eventually handles it. This procedure is considerably more effective than symbolic modeling in which the client merely observes an expert handling the snake apparently because direct exposure induces a sense of mastery over the situation (Bandura, Blanchard, & Ritter, 1969). Thus, I predicted that students who were exposed to the rat would show reduced fear and that those who petted the rat would show greater fear reduction than those who merely handled its transport box.

Method

Subjects

Students in two sections of an introductory psychology course served as subjects ($N = 56$, half were men).

Apparatus

The rat was an adult male Long-Evans hooded rat. It was presented in a small, transparent animal transport cage ($22 \times 14 \times 14$ cm) available from large department stores. The cage floor was covered with wood chips to a 2-cm depth. A small door in the ceiling of the cage allowed the rat to be caught. The rat was thoroughly habituated to being handled and carried in the transport cage. Band-Aids and hydrogen peroxide were available (out of sight of the students) in case the rat bit someone, but these were not needed. Plastic gloves were offered to the volunteers, but none used them. Two copies of the Fear of Rats Scale (FRS; see Table 1) were used for each subject. These were identical except that the pretest was labeled *A* and the posttest was labeled *B*.

Procedure

The entire demonstration lasted about 30 min. Subjects were informed of their right to decline participation in any of the subsequent activities. They were instructed to complete the FRS. The students scored their own FRS by summing their ratings of the 10 items; then they turned the paper over. The rat, which had been out of sight, was then revealed in its transport cage. Instructions were as follows:

> We now want to test your insight about rats. I want you to assess the age of the rat in days and write it on the back of your FRS. In order that everyone has a good chance to look at the rat, I want you to pass it around the room.

Table 1. Items on the Fear of Rats Scale

1. Allow a lab rat to climb up your shirt.
2. Catch a lab rat with your bare hand.
3. Touch a lab rat's cage when the rat is inside it.
4. Walk up to where a lab rat's cage is in reach.
5. Walk into a room in which lab rats are housed in cages.
6. Allow a lab rat to rest on your sleeve.
7. Allow a lab rat to crawl around your bare neck.
8. Touch a lab rat with a gloved hand.
9. Open a cage and look at a lab rat.
10. Allow a lab rat to rest on your bare arm.

Note. Students rated the likelihood that they would perform each action on a 7-point scale ranging from *very likely* (1) to *very unlikely* (7).

When the rat had been passed to all participants, further instructions were given:

Now I need the assistance of five volunteers to assess the friendliness of the rat. In order to do this, it is necessary to put your hand into the transport cage and pet the animal. Gloves are available for this purpose, if you wish to use them. If you wish to volunteer, please raise your hand.

Characteristics of a model, such as perceived similarity, are important in determining the model's effectiveness. Because half the subjects were women who were less likely to volunteer, any woman who volunteered was selected. The remaining volunteers were selected at random from men with raised hands. Standing behind the instructor's desk, each volunteer petted the rat in full view of the class until deciding on the animal's level of friendliness. Volunteers then returned to their own desks and wrote the word *volunteer* on the back of their FRS scale. They then rated the rat's friendliness on a 7-point scale ranging from *not friendly at all* (1) to *extremely friendly* (7). Students then took and scored the FRS again.

The instructor described participant modeling and informed subjects that the true purpose of the demonstration was to assess whether exposure to the rat would reduce their fear of rats. Students were asked to subtract the posttest FRS score from the pretest score. By a show of hands, most students indicated that their fear had been reduced by exposure to the rat. Data sheets were then collected so that scoring could be checked and statistical analyses conducted.

Results

Fear was significantly reduced for nonvolunteers in both class sections. One section's mean FRS score dropped from 38.76 (pretest) to 29.64 (posttest), $t(24) = 4.52, p < .001$. In the other section, the mean FRS dropped from 38.55 to 34.00, $t(20) = 3.64, p < .005$.

Volunteers had lower initial fear ($M = 29.45$) than nonvolunteers ($M = 38.66$), $t(54) = 1.66, p = .05$, one-tail test. Comparison of the difference scores (pretest − posttest) revealed that volunteers had a larger reduction in fear ($M = 13.09$) than nonvolunteers ($M = 7.09$), $t(54) = 1.89, p < .05$, one-tail test. This effect could have been due to the fact that volunteers had lower initial fear and were mostly men. When initial fear level and subject sex were controlled in a regression analysis, volunteer status still had a significant effect on difference scores, $t(62) = 2.69, p = .01$. Of the 56 subjects, 2 had a negative difference score, 12 had a difference of 0, and 42 had a positive difference score.

There was a large sex difference on pretest FRS scores: $M = 28.25$ and $M = 45.46$ for men and women, respectively, $t(54) = 4.44, p < .001$. The sexes did not differ, however, in the magnitude of fear reduction, $M = 6.29$ and $M = 10.25$ for men and women, respectively, $t(54) = 1.55, p > .05$. The posttest score for women ($M = 35.21$) was also significantly higher than for men ($M = 21.96$), $t(54) = 3.19, p < .01$.

Validating the FRS

I predicted that students who had almost completed a Learning class with a weekly 1.5-hr rat lab should score lower on the FRS than students without such experience. This prediction was tested by comparing 31 biology and psychology majors (9 men and 22 women) enrolled in a Learning course to the 56 Introductory Psychology students (28 men, 28 women). Using a two-way analysis of variance to control for the differing sex composition of the groups, the Learning students had significantly lower FRS scores ($M = 22.10$) than the Introductory Psychology students' pretest scores ($M = 36.86$), $F(1, 83) = 27.26, p < .001$; and men ($M = 25.50$) scored lower than women ($M = 36.17$), $F(1, 83) = 21.18, p < .001$. The interaction between sex and group was not significant.

Discussion

Even a mild level of exposure to a feared object, such as handling the container in which a rat is housed, can reduce fear in an appropriate social setting. This fact makes fear reduction a nontraumatic and safe procedure for classroom demonstrations. Nevertheless, results of this study suggest that the amount of fear reduction depends on the level of exposure. Volunteers experienced significantly more fear reduction, despite their initially lower scores on the FRS, than nonvolunteers. Although the groups were not initially equal in FRS scores or in sexual composition, regression analysis indicated that these variables were not responsible for the difference in outcome. (However, volunteers may differ from nonvolunteers in other ways that may confound the result.) This demonstration can thus be varied to suit the needs of individual instructors. For example, the whole class could be exposed to the milder or to the stronger manipulation; a random half could be exposed to each condition; or, as reported here, a few peer models could handle the rat.

In addition to participant modeling, symbolic modeling was also involved in the present procedure because subjects who did not handle the rat observed others doing so. Thus, we cannot say whether the observed fear reduction was due to participation, symbolic modeling, or a combination of both.

The FRS appears to be a valid instrument because scores for students with extensive experience in handling rats were lower than for introductory psychology students. Floor and ceiling effects can occur, but these are unlikely to spoil a classroom demonstration. On the first administration, one subject (of 56) scored the maximum (70), and two scored the minimum (10).

The demonstration takes about 30 min, leaving time for extensive discussion. Good topics include the evolutionary functions of fear, volunteer biases in research, sex differences in emotional responses, and the ethical issues concerning potentially traumatic research or classroom demonstrations (Harcum & Friedman, 1991).

The demonstration could backfire and increase students' fear of rats (e.g., if a volunteer were to get bitten). However, this problem is less likely to occur in the classroom than in the early sessions of a rat lab in which frightened and inexperienced students may mishandle a rat while attempting to catch it. The benefits of this demonstration to students in a rat lab seem to outweigh its potential costs. A similar argument can be made for its use in an introductory psychology course. The data presented herein suggest that students' fear can be reduced without handling the rat, which minimizes ethical problems.

References

Bandura, A., Blanchard, E. B., & Ritter, B. (1969). Relative efficacy of demonstration and modeling approaches for inducing behavioral, affective, and attitudinal changes. *Journal of Personality and Social Psychology, 13,* 173–199.

Harcum, E. R., & Friedman, H. (1991). Students' ethics ratings of demonstrations in introductory psychology. *Teaching of Psychology, 18,* 215–218.

Hughes, D. (1990). Participant modeling as a classroom activity. *Teaching of Psychology, 17,* 238–240.

Note

I thank Ruth L. Ault and the anonymous reviewers for their helpful comments on a draft of this article.

James Korn from Saint Louis University discussed the research situation from the perspective of student participants. Participants may assume different roles, varying in the nature of their compliance, as good, faithful, apprehensive, or bad subjects. Rights and responsibilities of research participants are described, and the role of assertive subjects is suggested. The author recommends a collaborative model to increase educational benefits of research participation.

In three experiments, James Korn from Saint Louis University and Kathleen Hogan from Iowa State University studied effects of course credit and money on general psychology students' willingness to participate in hypothetical experiments varying in degree of aversiveness. Willingness to participate was greater with larger incentives (in two experiments) and less for more aversive treatments (in all experiments). The authors emphasize the teachers' role in providing appropriate information for research participants.

Kitty Klein and Brian Cheuvront at North Carolina State University studied subject pool contamination in three experiments that investigated aspects of confidentiality and disclosure by student research participants. Their results suggest that failure to heed requests for confidentiality may be a serious and widespread problem in college subject pools. Researchers who require naive participants should ascertain their subjects' prior knowledge of the experimental tasks and procedures.

James Nimmer and Mitchell Handelsman investigated students' attitudes toward psychology and psychological research at the University of Colorado at Denver. Introductory psychology students in sections with either a semivoluntary or a mandatory research participation requirement completed attitude surveys at the beginning and the end of their course. Students in the semivoluntary policy condition reported more positive attitudes toward the learning value of experiments and toward psychology than did students in the mandatory policy condition. Across both policy conditions, ratings changed over time: Attitudes toward the learning value of experiments became less positive, but attitudes toward experiments themselves became more positive. The authors mention implications of their findings for structuring an ethical research participation policy.

Students' Roles, Rights, and Responsibilities as Research Participants

James H. Korn
Saint Louis University

College students provide most of the data obtained in psychological research with human participants. Recent surveys of studies in personality and social psychology show that more than 70% of the studies use college students as participants (Korn & Bram, 1987; Sears, 1986). The proportions are even higher (about 90%) in the areas of cognition and perception (Korn & Bram, 1987). These figures represent hundreds of thousands of hours of effort by college students.

In exchange for this effort, students receive low wages or dubious educational benefits. It is often difficult, however, to determine exactly what researchers provide as an incentive for participation. Whether students are paid with money or course credit, most authors do not specify the amounts of either kind of incentive.

Only a moderate degree of cynicism is required to characterize psychology as a science based on the contributions of a captive population with little power. Students are used to advance our knowledge, although the value of that knowledge has been questioned (Carlson, 1971; Sears, 1986). They also provide the means for obtaining master's and doctoral degrees and advancing faculty careers.

When people participate in research, psychologists often call them subjects, which means that they are the objects of the investigation. The word *subjects* has other connotations; it symbolizes the general student role from the perspective of the researcher. These are a few of the definitions of subject found in *The Compact Edition of the Oxford English Dictionary* (1971):

One who is bound to a superior by an obligation to pay allegiance, service or tribute; ... a dependent, subordinate; an inferior.

A person ... in the control or under the dominion of another; one who owes obedience to another.

... a person or thing toward which action or influence is directed, or that is the recipient of some treatment.

In an experiment, the subject is treated as an object to be manipulated, but continues to be a person who may be bored, shocked, deceived, or made to feel stupid or anxious. The ethical practice of informed consent is supposed to provide protection from unwanted discomfort by allowing people the freedom to choose whether to participate in research. That freedom is limited when one's grade in psychology is at risk or when the researcher decides that deception is acceptable.

The purpose of this article is to clarify the reality of the research situation from the point of view of the student participant. First, I describe the various roles that students might assume as research participants. Then, based on generally accepted ethical principles, I discuss the rights of participants. Finally, assuming that most psychological research is worthwhile, I discuss the responsibilities of research participants.

Roles of Research Participants

A role is a set of attitudes and behaviors that we adopt in specific situations (e.g., student and teacher roles in classrooms). The psychology experiment is a social situation in which people play roles. Orne (1962) presented one of the first discussions of the social psychology of the psychology experiment. He introduced the idea of the *good subject* whose role is to discover and validate the experimental hypothesis (i.e., to provide whatever the experimenter wants). Because experimenters are not always clear about what they want (they do not reveal their hypotheses), Orne suggested that subjects will use all available cues in the situation to guide their behavior. He called these cues "demand characteristics" (p. 779). The role of the good subject is to do what the experiment demands.

Orne demonstrated the power of the experimental situation by asking subjects to perform this task: Given a sheet of paper filled with rows of random numbers, add each adjacent pair of numbers. This required 224 additions per page. Each subject was given a stack of 2,000 pages. After finishing the additions on each page, subjects were told to tear up the page and do another one. Orne reported,

somewhat to our amazement, subjects tended to persist in the task for several hours with relatively little sign of overt

hostility.... When asked about the tasks, subjects would invariably attribute considerable meaning to their performance, viewing it as an endurance task or the like. (p. 777)

The good subject searches for meaning and purpose even in a situation intended to be meaningless.

Orne's article had a great impact on methodology in psychological research. Investigators recognized that it is important to be aware of, and perhaps to control for, demand characteristics. In social psychology, one now reads about *manipulation checks*. But there is another way to read Orne's article. Put yourself in the place of the subject sitting for hours adding random numbers and then destroying the results. How would you feel? I would get tired. My hand would hurt. I would be angry but would hold it inside, perhaps fearing the professor's disapproval. What would you have learned from this experience? I would have learned to distrust psychologists. The good subject is a sucker.

The *faithful subject* is a variant on the role of good subject (Fillenbaum, 1966). Perhaps less concerned with discovering the experimenter's hypothesis, the faithful subject carefully follows instructions, even though aware that the experiment may involve deception. Fillenbaum showed that subjects who had been deceived before did not perform differently in a learning study from subjects who had not been deceived in a previous experiment. The faithful subject is suspicious but does not act on those suspicions.

A third role is that of the *apprehensive subject* who approaches the situation concerned about performing well and is a bit anxious about what will happen (Adair, 1973). This person knows that this situation is not simply an experiment, but a *psychology* experiment. It may be a test of ability or personality in which deep thoughts may be revealed. The apprehensive subject performs as well as possible and tries to maintain self-esteem. The person playing this role wants to look good.

Last, and probably least common, is the role of *bad subject*. A negative attitude may lead some people to attempt to ruin an experiment by responding in a random or apathetic manner (Adair, 1973). This reaction might occur more often when students are required to participate in research that appears trivial, makes the participant feel uncomfortable, is at an inconvenient time or place, or when the experimenter is aloof or discourteous.

Argyris (cited in Adair, 1973, p. 32) compared research subjects to the low-level employee in a large organization. When students are required to participate in research in which they are never personally involved, they may cooperate to fulfill the requirement. However, they also show higher rates of absenteeism and cheating; in general, their behavior is minimally acceptable to the investigator.

The extent to which participants adopt these roles is unknown. Many experimenters try to design situations that conceal their hypothesis and that are at least mildly interesting for most participants. In such cases, participants are likely to assume a cooperative role.

Cooperation is not always reasonable, however. It is not reasonable to sit and work on a meaningless task for hours, nor is it reasonable to be injected with an unknown substance (Marshall & Zimbardo, 1979), or to be subjected to the violent imagery of rape (Bond & Mosher, 1986). Questionable research occurs often enough (Adair, Dushenko, & Lindsay, 1985) to suggest another role for research participants, the *assertive subject*. Questionable research is that which many people would avoid if given a free choice. For example, most people would rather not be injected with anything for nontherapeutic reasons. The assertive subject is aware of research participants' rights and is willing to exercise those rights.

Rights of Research Participants

The list of participants' rights presented in this section is related to the American Psychological Association's (APA) ethical principles (Committee for the Protection of Human Participants in Research, 1982). For example, the second item on my list and part F of APA Principle 9 both concern participants' freedom to withdraw from research. The critical difference between my list and the APA principles concerns the application of different general ethical principles from moral philosophy (Beauchamp & Childress, 1983).

The APA principles focus on the duties of the investigator and are based largely on the general ethical principle of beneficence (i.e., avoiding harm and providing benefits). The investigator is given the responsibility to decide what is harmful or beneficial for the participants and for what participants should be told, including whether to tell them the truth. The list that I developed and present here focuses on participants and is based on the general ethical principle of autonomy (i.e., freedom to choose and act). Research participants should decide for themselves what is harmful or beneficial.

1. Participants should know the general purpose of the study and what they will be expected to do. Beyond this, they should be told everything a reasonable person would want to know in order to decide whether to participate.

This is the concept of *informed consent*. The statement includes the reasonable person standard for determining what participants have a right to know. This is one standard used in the courts to determine whether informed consent has been obtained (Faden & Beauchamp, 1986). For example, participants should know whether any pain or discomfort, physical or psychological, is involved in a study. If someone agrees to receive an injection, a reasonable person would want to know the true effects of the drug, possible side effects, and how long the effects might last. The principle of informed consent is often violated, especially in studies involving deception. People who are fully informed cannot be deceived.

2. Participants have the right to withdraw from a study at any time after beginning participation in the research. A participant who chooses to withdraw has the right to receive whatever benefits were promised.

A person who agrees to participate in research has the responsibility to go to the research setting for instructions. Typically, students agree to participate after hearing or reading a description of the research in class. It may be difficult, however, to understand the nature of the research before actual participation begins. Participants may begin to feel uncomfortable or may have been misinformed about the study; whatever the reason, they have the right to withdraw. It takes a truly assertive person to exercise this right to withdraw because of the demand characteristics of the situation and the perceived power of the experimenter.

The nature of the agreement between experimenter and participant is not always clear and the obligations of the parties are rarely specified, although the APA ethical principles encourage clear agreements. In the absence of specified conditions, participants have a right to expect payment or credit for making an honest effort to participate. They also have a right to whatever benefits were promised if they were misinformed or if they misunderstood the conditions of participation. Capricious dropping out should not be rewarded, but that would be difficult to prove.

3. Participants should expect to receive benefits that outweigh the costs or risks involved. To achieve the educational benefit, participants have the right to ask questions and to receive clear, honest answers. When participants do not receive what was promised, they have the right to remove their data from the study.

At a minimum, participants should receive whatever course credit or money they were promised. Experimenters often claim educational benefits from research participation, an allegation typically supported by their colleagues who teach the introductory psychology course. An explanation of the study and of each participant's role in it should be given at the time of participation; a summary of the results should be available later. As in other learning situations, students will learn more if they ask questions. They have the right to expect clear and honest answers. Participants should realize that they are not without power in the research situation. When one party to an agreement (the experimenter) does not fulfill the agreement (e.g., by providing an educational experience), the other party (the participant) is no longer obligated. Research participants own the facts of their lives, including data provided in research.

4. Participants have the right to expect that anything done or said during their participation in a study will remain anonymous and confidential, unless they specifically agree to give up this right.

Anonymous means that one's name is never associated with the data that are provided. *Confidential* means that the data for individual participants are not reported, even without names, unless explicit permission has been given. This applies, of course, to published reports. It should also extend to casual conversations and classroom discussions.

My connotation of confidentiality is broader than others. Diener and Crandall (1978), for example, said that confidentiality means, "not disclosing the respondents' identity in any report" (p. 67) when participants' names can be associated with their data. This more limited definition does not discourage the use of thinly disguised case studies, potentially embarrassing quotations, reports of unusual behavior, or the necessity for extending confidentiality to casual coffee room conversations.

5. Participants have the right to decline to participate in any study and may not be coerced into research. When learning about research is a course requirement, an equivalent alternative to participation should be available.

Students may not be forced to participate in any specific study or in research of any kind. This right is violated whenever research participation is a course requirement. In a review of journal articles published in a sample of APA journals in 1985, research participation was said to be a course requirement in 17% of the studies (Korn & Bram, 1987). Students should always be provided with some alternative activity that is equivalent in time and effort.

Coercion is unethical. Requiring participation is coercive if *require* means that a student's grade would be withheld or lowered. Offering extra credit for participation is not coercion but may be manipulation, "intentional and successful influence of a person by noncoercively altering the actual choices available to a person or by nonpersuasively altering the person's perceptions of those choices" (Faden & Beauchamp, 1986, p. 261). If 10 points of extra credit might change a student's grade from B to A, the student's perception of choice is likely to be influenced. Instructors who aid investigators by offering course credit may wish to reconsider this practice.

6. Participants have a right to know when they have been deceived in a study and why the deception was used. If the deception seems unreasonable, participants have the right to withhold their data.

Research involving deception limits the autonomy of participants (Baumrind, 1985). When participants have been deceived, they should know why the investigator thought deception was necessary. They may not be convinced by the researcher, or may resent having been the victim of a lie, or may have been insulted or embarrassed. If so, they have the right to ask that their data not be used.

The APA ethical principles encourage investigators to consider alternative procedures before using deception. Students may learn something interesting if they ask researchers to describe the alternatives that were considered. This may be the first time the researcher has thought about alternatives because deception is so often a standard procedure.

7. When any of these rights is violated or participants object to anything about a study, they have the right and the responsibility to inform the appropriate university officials, including the chairpersons of the Psychology Department and the Institutional Review Board.

There are several steps subjects can take if they think their rights have been violated or they are concerned about the research in which they have participated. First, they should contact the experimenter to clarify the situation. If the experimenter is a student, participants may also want to know how to reach the faculty member supervising the research.

If satisfactory responses are not obtained, the next step is to contact the chairperson of the department in which the research was conducted. Serious problems should come to the attention of the Institutional Review Board (IRB). Every organization that does any research sponsored by the federal government must have an IRB. The IRB must approve almost all research using human participants in that university, not just research by faculty members under a federal grant. Research found to be unethical can be stopped. Drawing attention to ethical violations is a responsibility, as well as a right, because other students may be harmed by the research and a student's university may lose federal support for worthwhile research.

This last step is extreme. It would take a lot of time and most students would probably consider a violation of one of their rights as merely one more abuse of power that must be accepted in order to obtain a grade and a degree. The list of rights presented here is not likely to be used as the basis for a Supreme Court case, but it might help to increase the awareness of participants' rights for subjects and researchers.

Responsibilities of Research Participants

Researchers also have rights and subjects should respect those rights and appreciate the responsibilities of research participation. This list of responsibilities is based on the assumption that the researcher wants to provide a useful educational experience and will honor the participant's rights.

1. Participants have the responsibility to listen carefully to the experimenter and ask questions in order to understand the research.

A person cannot give informed consent without understanding what the research involves. There often will be two opportunities to gain this understanding: (a) when the experimenter solicits participants, usually in the classroom;

and (b) when students go to the laboratory or other research setting where they are told more about the study and are given their instructions for participation. Understanding the research by asking questions is essential if students wish to perform well in the study (i.e., cooperate), receive the maximum educational benefit from participation, and avoid unpleasant experiences.

2. Be on time for the research appointment.

Researchers often work on tight schedules; disrupting a schedule may inconvenience the researcher and other participants. Being on time implies that subjects will show up when they agree to participate. Researchers appreciate being informed when someone must cancel an appointment.

3. Participants should take the research seriously and cooperate with the experimenter.

Although the research may seem unimportant or the task may not make sense, participants can expect the experimenter to explain it later. This item asks that participants be good subjects. An important difference is that, as assertive subjects, they do not cooperate mindlessly, but with knowledge of their rights. Assertive subjects trust the researcher, but know what can be done if that trust is broken.

4. When the study has been completed, participants share the responsibility for understanding what happened.

Participants should ask questions that help to clarify the situation and enable them to learn more about the topic and method of research. Participants are different from subjects because participants contribute to the research by providing insights about the experience. Good researchers want to do more than collect data; they want to understand people. Participants can be of great help by telling the researcher anything they think might be of interest.

If the experience was interesting and educational, participants should thank the researcher. This is good psychology, as well as a matter of courtesy. It reinforces the experimenter's behavior and shows that students value good education and research.

5. Participants have the responsibility for honoring the researcher's request that they not discuss the study with anyone else who might be a participant.

Confidentiality works both ways.

This list of participants' responsibilities is confined to the immediate relationship with researchers. Kimble (1987) pointed out that participants have broader responsibilities. He sees research participation as an opportunity to help solve world problems ("the hour you spend . . . serving as a subject in an experiment may be the finest hour you spend that day," p. 268) and contribute to knowledge ("you owe future generations of students the same benefit that you have received from earlier ones," p. 268). Researchers who benefit from such an inspirational introduction must surely feel obligated to conduct only relevant research and to provide participants with a significant educational experience.

Kimble's statement shows that teachers of psychology have an important place in this process. Teachers can lend credibility and add clarity to statements of rights and responsibilities. Their position is critical; teachers are the gatekeepers of the research labor pool, ensure the provision of benefits to participants, and may be called on to act as mediators in disputes concerning rights. This responsibility bears careful consideration.

These statements of rights and responsibilities seem to be necessary, given the contractual nature of the relationship between experimenter and subject (Carlson, 1971). This relationship can be compared to those of employer and employee or buyer and seller. Contracts recognize the rights and responsibilities of the participants.

Toward Collaboration

There is another model of the researcher-participant relationship, which has been described several times but rarely implemented. Jourard (1967) suggested that we:

> change the status of the subject from that of an anonymous object of our study to that of a . . . collaborator in our enterprise. We can let him tell the story of his experience in our studies in a variety of idioms. We can let him show what our stimuli have meant to him . . . invite him to reveal his being. . . . We can show him how we have recorded his responses and tell him what we think they mean. We can ask him to examine and then authenticate or revise our recorded version of the meaning of his experience. . . . (p. 113)

Carlson (1971) also suggested a collaborative model, which assumes that:

> subjects and settings are chosen for their intrinsic relevance to the problem at hand . . . the basic motive for research participation must be the subject's intrinsic involvement in exploring his own experience . . . [and] that subject and investigator have their different kinds of expertise which are united by a common belief in the possibility and value of clarification of experience through research participation. [A collaborative model] demands more candor and more thought on the part of the investigator in posing research problems, in engaging appropriate subjects, and in interpreting the nature of the experience; it demands more involvement from the subject, and offers the important reward of having his experience taken seriously. (p. 216)

One role in this collaborative relationship could be that of:

> the involved subject. . . . He would no longer be an outsider who is manipulated and coerced but would be asked to assist the experimenter in a partnership in which he not only provided behavioral data but indicated . . . the presence of extraneous influences. (Adair, 1973, p. 94)

The investigator's role would also change to one of greater involvement by, for example, explaining why the topic of the research is intellectually and personally interesting.

This collaborative model is reasonable only if we accept the assumptions on which it is based. It works if researchers want to understand human thought, feeling, and behavior. It is a burden for those who want to gather lots of data that can be quickly analyzed on a computer and submitted for publication as soon as possible to a journal that has page limitations and will not permit summaries of what participants think. The collaborative model works for students who have a strong desire to learn about the human mind and understand the experience of living. It is a burden for those who need a better grade so they can get into medical school, who will do anything for a buck, or who have been forced to play a game they do not understand for reasons that never are made clear.

There are limits to collaboration. It would take time to develop this relationship with every research participant; we must learn to be open to strangers in new situations. Also, people vary in their ability to observe their own functioning accurately. To what degree can honesty and accuracy be achieved? That would be an excellent topic for collaborative research.

Although individual students rarely are allowed to take the role of involved subject, it is possible for students as a group to collaborate with researchers as a group. Members of Psi Chi could play an important role by meeting with the faculty, especially those doing research, to discuss the rights and responsibilities of research participants. Students could try to understand the perspective of the researcher while maintaining their assertiveness with respect to their own rights. Their goal would be to increase the educational benefits of research participation within the traditional contractual model. Beyond this, students must take responsibility for their own learning by trying to find a professor with whom to develop a collaborative research relationship.

References

Adair, J. G. (1973). *The human subject: The social psychology of the psychological experiment.* Boston: Little, Brown.

Adair, J. G., Dushenko, T. W., & Lindsay, R. C. L. (1985). Ethical regulations and their impact on research practice. *American Psychologist, 40,* 59–72.

Baumrind, D. (1985). Research using intentional deception: Ethical issues revisited. *American Psychologist, 40,* 165–174.

Beauchamp, T. L., & Childress, J. F. (1983). *Principles of biomedical ethics* (2nd ed.). New York: Oxford University Press.

Bond, S. D., & Mosher, D. L. (1986). Guided imagery of rape: Fantasy, reality, and the willing victim myth. *Journal of Sex Research, 22,* 162–183.

Carlson, R. (1971). Where is the person in personality research? *Psychological Bulletin, 75,* 203–219.

Committee for the Protection of Human Participants in Research. (1982). *Ethical principles in the conduct of research with human participants* (rev. ed.). Washington, DC: American Psychological Association.

The compact edition of the Oxford English dictionary. (1971). Oxford, England: Oxford University Press.

Diener, E., & Crandall, R. (1978). *Ethics in social and behavioral research.* Chicago: University of Chicago Press.

Faden, R. R., & Beauchamp, T. L. (1986). *A history and theory of informed consent.* New York: Oxford University Press.

Fillenbaum, S. (1966). Prior deception and subsequent experimental performance: The "faithful" subject. *Journal of Personality and Social Psychology, 4,* 532–537.

Jourard, S. M. (1967). Experimenter-subject dialogue: A paradigm for a humanistic science of psychology. In J. F. T. Bugental (Ed.), *Challenges of humanistic psychology* (pp. 109–116). New York: McGraw-Hill.

Kimble, G. A. (1987). The scientific value of undergraduate research participation. *American Psychologist, 42,* 267–268.

Korn, J. H., & Bram, D. R. (1987). *What is missing from method sections of APA journal articles?* Unpublished manuscript.

Marshall, G. D., & Zimbardo, P. G. (1979). Affective consequences of inadequately explained physiological arousal. *Journal of Personality and Social Psychology, 37,* 970–988.

Orne, M. T. (1962). On the social psychology of the psychological experiment: With particular reference to demand characteristics and their implications. *American Psychologist, 17,* 776–783.

Sears, D. O. (1986). College sophomores in the laboratory: Influences of a narrow data base on psychology's view of human nature. *Journal of Personality and Social Psychology, 51,* 515–530.

Notes

1. An earlier version of this article was presented as a Psi Chi distinguished lecture at the 1987 Midwestern Psychological Association convention in Chicago.

2. David Munz and Joan Oliver provided helpful comments on an earlier draft of this article. Many other colleagues helped me develop the list of rights and responsibilities. I thank all of them for their collaboration.

Effect of Incentives and Aversiveness of Treatment on Willingness to Participate in Research

James H. Korn
Saint Louis University

Kathleen Hogan
Iowa State University

Many teachers of introductory psychology and other under-graduate courses serve as gatekeepers for psychological research. They allow experimenters to recruit subjects from their classes and may encourage participation by offering course credit. Their students often agree to take part in studies using aversive treatments involving discomfort that most people would choose to avoid. Perhaps students participate to benefit society, but other variables also are likely to influence their decision.

One of these variables is the incentive provided by the experimenter or the course instructor. A student may agree to experience some discomfort to earn money or for course credit that may lead to a higher grade. Our research investigated the effect of various incentives on college students' willingness to volunteer for experiments involving aversive procedures.

We report three experiments. In each experiment, students read a description of a hypothetical study and reported how willing they would be to participate in that study if they had the opportunity. These descriptions of aversive procedures were based on published articles. Experiment 1 described the administration of a drug by injection (based on Marshall & Zimbardo, 1979) or in capsule form (based on Cooper, Zanna, & Taves, 1978). Experiment 2 described an ambiguous procedure—negative ions in the air (based on Baron, 1987). Our third study compared the injection and ion procedures and confirmed the effect of incentives found in Experiment 2.

Experiment 1

In our first experiment, we studied the effects of two levels of two kinds of incentive (money and course credit) on willingness to participate in one of three studies. Two of these studies described an aversive treatment that involved the administration of a drug; the third study description concerned nonaversive memory.

Method

Participants. Participants were 223 students from two general psychology classes; students in both classes received extra course credit for participating. In one class, the credit was 1 point out of 150 possible points for the course; in the other class, the credit was 1 point out of 400. This was the extra credit actually given to participants in Experiment 1. The participants were informed that they would not actually receive the other incentives associated with the hypothetical opportunities for research participation described in the following procedure.

Procedure. We used a randomized, 3 × 5 (Summaries of a Hypothetical Study × Incentives) factorial design. All testing took place at the beginning of a regular class session. The purpose of the research was explained and students were told to return a blank questionnaire if they did not wish to participate. Materials had been placed in random order before distribution. Each student was given 1 of 15 descriptions. The first two paragraphs were the same for all descriptions:

> The purpose of this study is to find out whether students will agree to take part in certain kinds of psychology experiments. We also are interested in some of the conditions that influence your willingness to participate.

> On the next page you will be asked about your willingness to participate in an experiment, if you had the opportunity to do so. This experiment is not now being conducted at [this] university, but try to respond as though this actually was an opportunity for you to take part in the experiment.

One of three experimental procedures was then described:

> Control: A typical memory experiment involving nonsense syllables was described.

Capsule: This is an experiment on memory processes. Specifically, it concerns the effects of various drugs on a person's short-term memory. The drugs are perfectly safe and have been approved for use by the University Medical Review Board. You will be given a capsule which contains your drug. The capsule may be taken with water. You may experience these symptoms: dryness of the throat, slight headache, and some slight coolness in toes and fingers. (The memory task was then described as in the control condition.)

Injection (same as the previous description, except for the fourth and fifth sentences): Your drug will be given by injection. A physician will give the injection under the skin of your upper right arm.

The final paragraph described one of the five incentives that would be provided for participation:

Voluntary: The experiment would take about one hour to complete. Your participation is voluntary.

$2.00: The experiment would take about one hour to complete. If you could participate, as a reward for your participation you would receive two dollars ($2.00).

$10.00 (same as above, except the amount was 10 dollars).

3 Points: The experiment would take about one hour to complete. If you could participate, as a reward for your participation you would receive one percent (1%) of the total possible points on which your grade in General Psychology is based. In other words, if the total possible points for your grade is 300, you would have 3 points added to your grade *after* the grade cut-offs have been determined.

15 Points (same as above, except the amount was 5% or 15 points out of 300).

Students then rated their willingness to participate. The rating scale ranged from *definitely would not participate* (1) to *definitely would participate* (7). Students also were asked, "What questions or comments do you have about the experiment described on the previous page?" Debriefing took place later in the semester when the first author returned to these classes, reported the results of this experiment, and answered questions.

Results

Analysis of variance (ANOVA) showed a significant effect for Type of Experiment, $F(2, 208) = 25.12$, $p < .001$, but not for Incentive or the interaction of these two factors. The mean ratings for the three types of experiment were: control, 5.17; capsule, 4.07; and injection, 3.31. Tukey's HSD tests showed that all differences between these means were significant ($p < .01$). The more aversive the treatment, the less willing students would be to participate.

Experiment 2

Our second experiment had two purposes. First, we wanted to find out whether willingness to participate in research is affected by uncertainty about the nature of the treatment. We used a hypothetical research situation based on a study of the effects of negative ions on impression formation (Baron, 1987). Baron exposed research participants to increased negative ions while they formed impressions of another person. The ion study presented a situation in which participants might not know whether the treatment was aversive or benign.

The second purpose of this study was to provide a further test of the effects of incentives. Perhaps incentives are more effective in ambiguous situations.

Method

Participants. Participants were 173 students from a general psychology class. They were given ½ of a credit point (out of 150 total points) to be added to their class grade for participating.

Procedure. The distribution of questionnaires and general oral instructions to students were the same as described for Experiment 1. The first two paragraphs of the questionnaire were also the same.

The students were divided into two groups. One group received a description of an experiment about how people form first impressions of others. In addition to this description, the other group read the following, also adapted from Baron's (1987) procedure section:

The effect of negative ions on your impressions of the other person also will be studied. There will be a machine in the room with you which will increase the amount of negative ions in the air. Electrodes will be attached to your legs, above your ankles, for purposes of electrical grounding. This is necessary to ensure the effectiveness of the negative ions. Your blood pressure will also be measured.

Next, all descriptions contained a paragraph concerning the incentive for participating. The participants were offered one of three rewards: $10.00, 1% of the total possible points to be added to their class grade, or 5% of the total possible points. No incentive was mentioned for a fourth group (volunteers).

After reading the description of the hypothetical experiment, students rated their willingness to participate in the study on the same scale used in Experiment 1. A space was provided for questions or comments.

Two days later, the students were asked to complete a follow-up questionnaire. They were (a) provided with a copy of the paragraph describing the increase of negative ions and the electrical grounding, (b) asked if they knew what negative ions were, and (c) instructed to explain them briefly. Next they rated whether they thought that negative ions could help or harm them on a scale ranging from *definitely help* (1) to *definitely harm* (5). Then they were asked the same questions about electrical grounding and given the same rating scales. After students completed this questionnaire, the first author reported the results of Experiment 1, discussed this research in more detail, and answered questions. There was no other debriefing.

Results

An ANOVA yielded significant main effects for Incentive, $F(3, 165) = 8.19, p < .001$, and for Type of Experiment, $F(1, 65) = 4.72, p < .05$. The interaction was not significant.

The mean rating for the impression-formation only condition was 5.79: for the negative ion condition it was 5.41. Although most students (85%) were willing to participate in either study, they were less willing to participate when the study involved the additional condition of negative ions with electrical grounding.

The means for the four incentive conditions were: voluntary, 5.14; $10, 6.04; 1% of grade, 5.05; and 5% of grade, 5.76. Tukey's HSD tests showed that the means of the $10 and 5% conditions were significantly ($p < .05$) higher than those of the voluntary and 1% conditions. The $10 and 5% and the voluntary and 1% conditions did not differ significantly. Willingness to participate was greater for the larger incentives.

On the follow-up questionnaire, 80% of the students did not know what negative ions are and 77% did not know what electrical grounding is. Students also were asked to rate the helpfulness or harmfulness of ions and grounding, even if they did not know what these things are. Most (71%) of the students thought that negative ions were neither helpful nor harmful, 21% thought that ions probably were harmful, and 8% thought they would be helpful. Many thought that electrical grounding might help (30%) or harm (15%) them; 56% thought it would neither help nor harm. Thus, most students were willing to participate in this study even when they did not understand the treatment and were uncertain about its effects. In fact, the placement of electrodes for grounding is only mildly uncomfortable. Negative ions, however, do have an effect on blood pressure and on mood (Baron, 1987).

Incentive had an effect in this study, whereas it did not in Experiment 1. Students were more willing to participate if offered $10 or 5% of total possible grade points. This difference between experiments may have been due to sampling, time of year, or to the use of different stimulus studies (ions rather than drugs).

Experiment 3

The first purpose of our third experiment was to confirm the effects of incentives on willingness to participate in

research. This variable was statistically reliable in the second experiment but not the first. We also were concerned about the way our participants interpreted the voluntary incentive condition. When points are given for research participation, students may assume that *voluntary* means that if they choose (voluntarily) to participate, they still will get some points. Thus, we added an incentive condition that explicitly defined voluntary as involving no external reward for participation.

The second purpose of this study was to compare students' willingness to participate in the situations included in Experiments 1 and 2. Meeting a stranger, as required in an impression-formation study, may itself be aversive compared to taking part in a study of memory. We expected that being injected with a drug would again be the most aversive condition, regardless of whether it was given as part of a memory or an impression-formation experiment.

Method

Participants. Participants were 249 students from two general psychology classes. Students in both classes received extra course credit for participating. In one class, the credit was 1 point out of 150 possible points for the course; in the other class, the credit was 1 point out of 400.

Procedure. The distribution of questionnaires and general oral instructions were the same as described for Experiments 1 and 2. The first two paragraphs of the questionnaire again were the same.

Students were randomly assigned to 1 of 16 groups in a 4 × 4 (Experiment Descriptions × Incentives) design. The four experiment descriptions were memory only (as in Experiment 1), impression formation only (as in Experiment 2), memory with a drug given by injection (as in Experiment 1), and impression formation with a drug given by injection—a new condition. This latter condition combined the drug-injection description from Experiment 1 with the impression-formation description from Experiment 2.

Three of the incentive conditions were the same as in the first two experiments: voluntary, 3 points (1%), and 15 points (5%). In the fourth condition, participants read this statement before making their rating on the same 7-point scale: "Would you agree to participate in this experiment on a voluntary basis? (You would *not* receive course credit or money as a reward for participating.)"

Later in the semester, a summary of the results of this experiment was given to the course instructors, who reported these results to their students.

Results

An ANOVA yielded significant main effects for Incentive, $F(3, 228) = 8.08, p < .001$, and for Type of Experiment,

$F(1, 228) = 21.32$, $p < .001$. The interaction was not significant.

The mean ratings for the four experimental conditions were: memory only, 5.19; impression formation only, 5.19; memory with drug, 3.55; and impression formation with drug, 3.72. Tukey's HSD tests showed that the means for the two drug conditions were significantly different from the two nondrug means ($p < .01$ in each case). Differences between the two drug means and between the two nondrug means were not statistically reliable. Students were equally willing to participate in the nondrug conditions, but most students would not participate in the conditions involving the injection of a drug.

Mean ratings for the four incentive conditions were: voluntary (as in Experiments 1 and 2), 3.95; explicit voluntary, 3.84; 3 points, 4.92; and 15 points, 4.87. Tukey's HSD test showed no significant difference between the two voluntary means. Apparently, there was no need to be concerned that participants misinterpreted the word *voluntary* in the previous two experiments. The credit-point means did not differ significantly from each other, but both were significantly higher than the two voluntary means (Tukey's HSD tests, $p < .01$), providing support for the finding in Experiment 2 that offering credit increases willingness to participate. The two credit-point means did not differ significantly.

General Discussion

These three experiments show that the potential aversiveness of an experimental treatment has a strong effect on willingness to participate in research. The incentive that is offered also has an effect, although not as powerful or consistent. Incentives increase willingness to participate, but there were no significant differences related to kind of incentive (course credit or money). The Incentive × Type of Experiment interaction was not significant in any of our studies.

We selected a range of incentives that we thought would be large enough to produce an effect, but realistic enough to be plausible. An extremely large incentive (e.g., 50% of the grade or $1,000) might have been effective but would not be realistic. Nevertheless, some students' comments indicated that the incentives that they read about would have created some pressure: "Considering my grade in psychology, I could really use the points" (3 points). "Any experiment that has an incentive of 15 points can pull anyone into taking the test." "Students who were on the verge of failing or in between grades would feel pressure to participate . . . I don't think that's right."

Students are less willing to participate in research as the aversiveness of the treatment increases. Although this is not a surprising finding, it has both methodological and ethical implications. The studies on which our stimulus materials were based (Cooper et al., 1978; Marshall & Zimbardo, 1979) do not report refusals to participate. Assuming that students in those studies would have similar concerns to those of students in our psychology classes, one would expect a substantial number of refusals, which would restrict the participant population to students who are willing to swallow or be injected with an unknown drug that produces unpleasant symptoms.

Another possibility is that participants in these previous studies (and other studies using deception) did not know what to expect. They were not given enough information, and consent was not truly informed. Had they known more about the actual treatment, some students may have refused to participate. We believe that an important function of the psychology teacher is to help make students aware of their rights and responsibilities in research (Korn, 1988). Teachers can encourage students to ask reasonable questions (e.g., What is the drug?). They also can provide support that will help students resist the strong demands of the experimental situation and withdraw from the experiment if their questions are not answered or the procedures are not what they expected.

References

Baron, R. A. (1987). Effects of negative ions on interpersonal attraction: Evidence for intensification. *Journal of Personality and Social Psychology, 52*, 547–553.

Cooper, J., Zanna, M. P., & Taves, P. A. (1978). Arousal as a necessary condition for attitude change following induced compliance. *Journal of Personality and Social Psychology, 36*, 1101–1106.

Korn, J. H. (1988). Students' roles, rights, and responsibilities as research participants. *Teaching of Psychology, 15*, 74–78.

Marshall, G. D., & Zimbardo, P. G. (1979). Affective consequences of inadequately explained physiological arousal. *Journal of Personality and Social Psychology, 37*, 970–988.

Note

We gratefully acknowledge the assistance of Deborah Carlin and James Winkelmann in data collection and analysis and D. Gene Davenport who provided advice concerning the design of these studies.

The Subject-Experimenter Contract: A Reexamination of Subject Pool Contamination

Kitty Klein
Brian Cheuvront
North Carolina State University

In recent years, we have seen a renewed concern that undergraduate students enjoy an ethical and educational experience when they participate in psychological experiments. Britton (1987) expressed concern that the direct educational benefits of serving as a research participant are sufficient to justify the costs to the individuals involved. Kimble (1987) and Korn (1988) outlined the educational benefits students should expect. They emphasized that research participants have a right to a discussion of the topic of interest, an explanation of the procedures followed, and a summary of the results. Nonetheless, Coulter (1986) reported that a substantial number of her undergraduates considered their research participation as "boring, irrelevant, and a waste of time" (p. 317). She urged experimenters to prepare debriefings that will educate, rather than simply dismiss, student subjects.

Another side of this ethical coin has received little discussion. With the exception of Korn's (1988) list of participant responsibilities, the rights of the experimenter are rarely addressed. One of these rights, the participant's responsibility to honor the researcher's request not to discuss the study with anyone else who might be a participant, was the impetus for our article. The problem is essentially one of subject pool contamination. Revealing information about an experimental procedure or outcome may affect the willingness of other students to volunteer for a particular experiment and may alter their behavior if they do participate. As Marans (1988) noted, leaked information has the potential to threaten the internal validity of our results.

Subject pool contamination has received some empirical attention, albeit very little. Evidence appears mixed on the severity of the problem. After using a deception procedure, Aronson (1966) employed an extensive debriefing that described how an experimental participant who is aware of the hypothesis could lead researchers to publish erroneous results. All nine of his subjects admitted to a confederate that they had participated in the study, but none revealed its true nature. Two subjects provided a false cover story.

Diener, Matthews, and Smith (1972) also reported low rates of subject pool contamination. They found that, in a class of 440 nonsubjects, only 11 had knowledge of a deceptive experiment in which 52 of their classmates had participated.

Other researchers have reported alarming rates of disclosure. Wuebben's (1967) subjects participated in a persuasion experiment in which fear of an unknown disease was induced. A debriefing, which explained the importance of not discussing their participation, was given to the subjects after the first experimental session. All subjects were asked to nod their head to indicate that they would comply with the researcher's request not to talk to anyone regarding the details of the experiment. When they returned for the second part of the experiment 1 week later, subjects were questioned about their compliance with the experimenter's request. Sixty-four percent admitted talking to at least one other person about the experiment.

Student subjects appear willing to admit that they possess prior knowledge. In a study using the Taffel verbal conditioning procedure, Farrow, Lohss, Farrow, and Taub (1975) reported that 24% of their subjects acknowledged having prior information about the experiment.

Lichtenstein (1970) also found high rates of contamination in a study that directly measured disclosure, as opposed to relying on self-reports. When subjects were approached by a confederate identified as a future subject, no one disclosed information. When the confederate was identified as a nonsubject, 21% disclosed information. After an interval from 1 day to 2 weeks, 79% disclosed information to a telephone interviewer's request for information.

Given the evidence that subject pool contamination occurs, one must ask whether subjects' behavior is affected by prior knowledge of the procedures, particularly when deception is not an issue. Levy (1967) studied the effects of prior awareness on performance in a Taffel verbal conditioning task. Subjects given full disclosure by a confederate just before participation performed better than those not informed, but speed of learning was not affected.

Horka and Farrow (1970) studied the behavior of elementary school children who could win 50¢ for responding correctly to an embedded figures problem. Twenty-eight percent of the subjects tested in the afternoon sessions were correct, compared to 13% of those tested in the morning. The authors concluded that intersubject communication accounted for this difference in performance.

From these studies, three conclusions seem warranted. First, rates of reported or actual disclosure vary considerably and appear to be related to type of debriefing, delay following the experiment, and whether or not the discloser believes the target is a potential subject. The effects of other factors on disclosure, such as liking for the experiment, have not been investigated. Second, prior knowledge of experimental procedure affects performance even when deception is not an issue. Third, although disclosure rates may be high, only a small proportion of subjects are affected by the leakage. In institutions with small subject pools, however, the problem may be more severe than in large institutions in which multiple sections of the introductory course supply potential participants.

Taken together, these earlier studies suggest that contamination occurs and that results may be tainted. Our experiments investigated several variables that might affect undergraduates' willingness to comply with an experimenter's request not to discuss their participation. In the first experiment, we examined the relation between beliefs about the scientific value of participation, general evaluation of the experience, and likelihood of disclosure. In the second experiment, we asked half the participants in a laboratory experiment to sign a pledge to keep the experimenter's confidence. In the third experiment, we telephoned these same participants to see whether the passage of time or promises of anonymity would affect disclosure.

Experiment 1

Method

Sixty-five introductory psychology students volunteered to participate in the experiment, for which they received 1/2 hr of experimental credit. Students in the course have the option of writing a 3-page review of a recent journal article or serving as subjects for a total of 3 hr. Subjects read brief descriptions of two different studies. The first study used a Scholastic Aptitude Test (SAT) type task presented on a computer. The second study was a perceptuomotor tracking task. Only the procedures were described; no rationale for the studies was presented. Both descriptions concluded with a statement that the experimenter requested that participants not discuss the experiment with others "because the results might be affected if other psychology students who might participate in the study found out what it was about." Following each scenario were six questions asking: (a) how much the respondent would enjoy participating in such a study, (b) whether the respondent thought the experimenter would find anything interesting, (c) the importance of complying with the request for confidentiality, (d) the likelihood the respondent would talk about the experiment with another student in the subject pool, (e) the likelihood the respondent would talk about the experiment with another student not in the pool, and (f) whether the respondent would expect to learn anything from participating. Each question was followed by a 7-point response scale ranging from *not at all likely* (1) to *extremely likely* (7).

Results and Discussion

A 2 × 6 (Items × Scenario) analysis of variance (ANOVA) was performed. There were, of course, differences in responses to the items, $F(5, 315) = 34.51, p < .001$, but the only other significant effect was the Scenario ;ts Item interaction, $F(5, 315) = 3.36, p < .005$. Inspection of the means indicated that students believed they would enjoy participating in the SAT study ($M = 3.8$) less than in the tracking task study ($M = 4.4$). Consistent with Britton's (1987) findings, the means on the items measuring the value of the studies did not indicate negative evaluations. The mean response to the question of whether the experimenter might discover something interesting was 4.4 for the SAT and 4.7 for the tracking task. For the issue of whether the participants would learn anything, the mean for the SAT was 3.9 and 3.6 for the tracking task. Students perceived the importance of confidentiality ($M = 5.9$ for the SAT; $M = 5.7$ for the tracking task), but indicated some likelihood ($M = 2.4$ for the SAT; $M = 2.7$ for the tracking task) that they would talk to another student who was in the subject pool. The likelihood of talking to a student not in the subject pool was greater ($M = 4.2$ for the SAT; $M = 4.1$ for the tracking task).

To determine the relation among the items, we conducted separate principal component factor analyses for each scenario. In both cases, two factors emerged. The evaluative items (enjoyment, learning opportunity, and likelihood of scientific discovery) loaded together on Factor 1 in both analyses; all had factor loadings greater than .75. Both of the likelihood of talking items appeared together on Factor 2, with loadings in excess of .80. The item assessing views of the importance of complying with the experimenter's request showed weaker loadings on the first factor (.55 and .56) and low, negative loadings on the second (−.11 and −.19). This factor pattern indicated that the evaluative items and the likelihood of talking items were not correlated.

The results of our first experiment suggest that evaluative judgments concerning the merits of an experiment are unrelated to whether or not subjects believe that honoring an experimenter's request for confidentiality is important. Furthermore, there is no relation between the latter belief and likelihood of revealing information to others. In general, respondents indicated a fairly positive evaluation of the research scenarios but high likelihoods of not honoring an experimenter's request for confidentiality.

Experiment 2

In this experiment, we observed actual disclosure behavior as contrasted with students' self-reports. All our subjects served initially in either the SAT computer study or the perceptuomotor tracking task. Subsequently, a confederate made a direct request for information. We also wanted to determine if signing an agreement would inhibit disclosure. Walsh and Stillman (1974) found less disclosure when subjects were sworn to secrecy but Diener, Kelem, Beaman, and Fraser (cited in Diener et al., 1972) did not.

Method

Twenty-eight students enrolled in the introductory psychology course, who had not served in our first role-playing experiment, participated in the second. These students were selected from a group of 102 participants described in our first experiment. The 28 subjects (13 men and 15 women) were selected because they were scheduled for the SAT/tracking experiment at a time when one of our two confederates was available.

As part of the debriefing, we asked all subjects not to discuss their experiences with anyone else, particularly others who might be future participants (i.e., other introductory psychology students). In addition, 12 of the subjects were asked to sign an agreement stating that they understood the request and agreed to comply. Three different experimenters conducted the debriefings. They were counterbalanced across the two experimental conditions.

After the debriefing, the subject was asked to sit on a bench outside the experimental room while the experimenter went to the psychology office to get the form the subject needed to verify participation. A female confederate was already seated on the bench when the subject arrived. After the experimenter left, the confederate told the subject that she was a student in an introductory psychology course who had not participated in any experiments and wanted to know what it was like to be in one. She asked the subjects to describe the experiment they had just left. The amount each subject disclosed was rated on a 3-point scale ranging from *no disclosure* (0) to *full disclosure* (2) by the confederate and the first author, both of whom were blind as to whether or not the subject had signed a pledge not to talk. Interrater reliability, using gamma, was .899.

Results and Discussion

We were surprised to discover that more than one third of our subjects revealed something to the confederate, even though the experimenter was in the adjacent office and was expected to return at any moment. In two instances, the experimenter stood by while the subject finished a disclosure to the confederate. We were also chagrined when a student not scheduled as one of our subjects entered the SAT experiment with the question, "Is this the experiment where I sign the paper promising not to talk?"

Of the 12 subjects who signed an agreement, 11 refused to reveal any information to the confederate and 1 subject gave some disclosure, but no one provided detailed information. In this condition, we witnessed our only fabrication: One student told the confederate she would be wired to a machine and "shocked like hell." Of the 16 subjects asked to honor the experimenter's request for nondisclosure but not asked to sign an agreement, 7 gave no disclosure, 3 gave partial disclosure, and 6 gave detailed disclosure to the confederate. To ensure adequate expected values, we collapsed the full- and partial-disclosure cells and performed a chi-square test, which indicated that signing the agreement inhibited subsequent disclosure, $\chi^2(1, N = 28) = 6.86$ $p < .01$. Our actual disclosure rate 5 min after the debriefing and not more than 50 ft from the experimenter came as a surprise. Thirty-nine percent of our subjects disclosed information to a self-identified subject who was shopping for experimental credits.

Experiment 3

Although signing an agreement appeared to increase compliance in the short run, we were concerned about its effectiveness over a longer period. We were also interested in how much disclosure would occur when respondents knew such information had the potential to contaminate the entire subject pool.

Method

Two to 3 weeks after participating in the second experiment, 10 of the signers and 10 of the nonsigners were telephoned by a female research assistant blind to the experimental conditions. The caller introduced herself as an undergraduate psychology major who was writing an article on the research experiences of students enrolled in introductory psychology. The article would appear in the student newspaper during the same semester in which the students had served as subjects.

For each experiment in which they had participated, the subjects were asked what they had been required to do, what they thought the researcher was trying to figure out, and whether they thought the experiment was a worthwhile experience. Half the subjects were told that their responses would be anonymous, and half were asked to verify their name so that they could be quoted in the article. The degree of detail that subjects disclosed was rated on a 5-point scale ranging from *no disclosure* (0) to *full disclosure* (4).

At the conclusion of the third experiment, we sent all subjects who had participated in our second experiment a postcard stating:

> Following your participation in an experiment in 635 Poe Hall, you were approached, and in some cases telephoned, by one of our research assistants who asked you to describe your research experiences. The purpose of these inquiries was to evaluate the effectiveness of our debriefing techniques. As in the experiments themselves, your responses cannot be linked to you as an individual. We thank you for your cooperation.

We also provided the name and telephone number of the supervising faculty member.

Results and Discussion

No subject was able to give a coherent explanation of the researcher's goals. The most common response was to "see how we would do on those kinds of problems." All the subjects believed the experiment had been worthwhile, although one said "worthwhile for the experimenter, but not for me." Seventeen of the 20 subjects described the procedure to varying extents. Four indicated that they were asked not to discuss their participation but "guessed it was alright now." Students who were guaranteed anonymity revealed more ($M = 2.27$) than did those whose names were verified ($M = 1.00$), $t(18) = 2.39$, $p < .05$. Signing or not signing an agreement in the actual experiment had no effect on disclosure. Magnitude of initial disclosure to the confederate did not predict magnitude of disclosure in the telephone interview. As in Experiment 1, evaluation of the experience was unrelated to disclosure.

General Discussion

Our results paint a pessimistic picture of how undergraduates honor the clause of our research contract that holds them responsible for not discussing the details of their participation with anyone who might later serve as a subject. In our first study, 22% of the role-players indicated that they would probably not honor the experimenter's request not to discuss the procedure with a potential subject. In the second experiment, 39% of our subjects gave at least some disclosure to a confederate. In the third experiment, after a 2-week interval, 85% of these participants disclosed information that could contaminate the entire subject pool. These rates are particularly alarming, given that our subjects revealed information to a stranger. Even more disclosure might occur with friends or classmates. The student

who asked about the nondisclosure pledge presumably had received such information.

We identified several factors that seem to affect disclosure rates. Asking subjects to sign a pledge decreased immediate but not later disclosure to a confederate. Promising students anonymity increased disclosure rates, suggesting an awareness that such disclosure might have damaging effects. Neither liking for the research nor a belief that it was important was related to compliance with the experimenter's request for confidentiality.

Does this research suggest any improvements in debriefing that might decrease the frequency of disclosure? Asking participants to sign an agreement reduced disclosure to a potential subject in the short run, but this commitment had no effect on later willingness to contaminate the entire pool. Perhaps providing more information about the tasks would have proved effective. The tasks used in Experiment 2 involved no deception, and the studies' rationales were described at length. Nevertheless, none of our subjects was able, 2 weeks later, to describe the researcher's goals. If we had used a more extensive debriefing, subjects may have felt a greater stake in the outcome and been less revealing when questionned. Using the collaborative model that Korn (1988) described might decrease intersubject communication.

Our findings regarding the ability of introductory psychology instructors to minimize subject pool contamination are discouraging. Results of our first study suggest that appreciation of the potential scientific contribution of undergraduates, as Kimble (1987) suggested, is unrelated to honoring a request not to disclose, although such an emphasis may improve overall attitudes toward the research experience.

A final issue concerns our own adherence to the contract. Experiments 2 and 3 involved deception by the confederate. We argue that there were no realistic alternatives for studying the extent to which subjects reveal information about their research experiences. Results of Experiment 1, in which students role-played the same tasks we used in Experiment 2, indicate that they underestimated the amount of disclosure that actually occurred. Our own ethical difficulty arose in trying to settle on the language to use on the postcard. We took care not to suggest that students had violated their promises.

In conclusion, our experiments suggest that subject pool contamination is a problem. Researchers whose work requires naive participants need to ascertain the extent of their subjects' prior knowledge of the experimental tasks and procedures.

References

Aronson, E. (1966). Avoidance of intersubject communication. *Psychological Reports, 19,* 238.

Britton, B. K. (1987). Comment on Coulter and Daniel. *American Psychologist, 42,* 268–269.

Coulter, X. (1986). Academic value of research participation by undergraduates. *American Psychologist, 41,* 317.

Diener, E., Matthews, R., & Smith, R. (1972). Leakage of experimental information to potential future subjects by debriefed subjects. *Journal of Experimental Research in Personality, 6,* 264–267.

Farrow, J. M., Lohss, W. E., Farrow, B. J., & Taub, S. (1975). Intersubject communication as a contaminating factor in verbal conditioning. *Perceptual and Motor Skills, 40,* 975–982.

Horka, S. T., & Farrow, B. J. (1970). A methodological note on intersubject communication as a contaminating factor in psychological experiments. *Journal of Experimental Child Psychology, 10,* 363–366.

Kimble, G. A. (1987). The scientific value of undergraduate research participation. *American Psychologist, 42,* 267–268.

Korn, J. H. (1988). Students' roles, rights, and responsibilities as research participants. *Teaching of Psychology, 15,* 74–78.

Levy, L. H. (1967). Awareness, learning, and the beneficient subject as expert witness. *Journal of Personality and Social Psychology, 6,* 365–370.

Lichtenstein, E. (1970). Please don't talk to anyone about this experiment: Disclosure of deception by debriefed subjects. *Psychological Reports, 26,* 485–486.

Marans, D. G. (1988). Addressing research practitioner and subject needs: A debriefing-disclosure procedure. *American Psychologist, 43,* 826–827.

Walsh, W. B., & Stillman, S. M. (1974). Disclosure of deception by debriefed subjects. *Journal of Counseling and Clinical Psychology, 21,* 315–319.

Wuebben, P. L. (1967). Honesty of subjects and birth order. *Journal of Personality and Social Psychology, 5,* 350–352.

Note

We thank Kim Toussignant, Gabie Smith, and Stella Anderson who helped collect and analyze these data.

Effects of Subject Pool Policy on Student Attitudes Toward Psychology and Psychological Research

James G. Nimmer
Mitchell M. Handelsman
University of Colorado at Denver

In many behavioral sciences, and particularly in psychology, students are used as subjects in experiments. Approximately 74% of the graduate psychology deparments in the U.S. create human subject pools (Sieber & Saks, 1989) to facilitate research in psychology. This raises an ethical imperative for departments to act responsibly in the treatment of human subjects.

The literature offers general prescriptions for the ethical treatment of subjects (e.g., American Psychological Association [APA], 1990; Diener & Crandall, 1978; Kimmel, 1981; Schuler, 1982), and some authors have examined specific issues related to human participation in psychological experiments, such as deception (Baron, 1981; Baumrind, 1979; Gross & Fleming, 1982; Holmes & Bennet, 1974), debriefing and desensitizing (Holmes, 1976a,

1976b), and informed consent (Berscheid, Baron, Dermer, & Libman, 1973; Epstein, Suedfeld, & Silverstein, 1973; Loftus & Fries, 1979). However, whether or not and how students should be recruited to participate in experiments has received little empirical attention.

Psychology departments vary considerably in their policies concerning research participation (Sieber & Saks, 1989). For example, some programs mandate student participation to fulfill course requirements; others offer the experience on a purely voluntary basis. Some departments use barter systems in which students receive money or extra credit in exchange for their participation. These differences may have implications for the ethical treatment of human subjects.

When is requiring student research participation ethical? On one hand, mandating participation may be viewed as coercive by definition. As such, it would be difficult to justify any harm that may occur either to students or to the profession. On the other hand, some may argue that because there is virtually no harm in participating in research and that learning can take place as a result of serving as a subject, participation can be mandated in an ethical way. In this regard, the APA Committee for the Protection of Human Participants in Research (1982) recommended that an ethical participation requirement include providing nonaversive alternatives (e.g., viewing films on the research process) and telling students about the course research requirements in advance.

Psychologists themselves are split on the issue of forced participation. In a recent survey of 482 APA members, Tabachnick, Keith-Spiegel, and Pope (1991) found that 53% believed "having students be research subjects as part of a course requirement" (p. 513) was either unquestionably ethical or ethical. On the other hand, 35% believed that it was either never or rarely ethical to mandate participation. One potential source of harm that may bear on the ethicality of research participation is a possible negative reaction to psychology and research as a result of the type of policy to which students are exposed.

The literature on research requirement policies has been primarily descriptive (e.g., Britton, 1979; Leak, 1981; Miller, 1981; Sieber & Saks, 1989). For example, Leak (1981) examined subjects' reactions to a semivoluntary research requirement policy (i.e., subjects received extra credit for their participation) and found that subjects viewed their research participation positively. Britton (1979) examined the effects of a four-experiment mandatory requirement on student perceptions of experiments as an educational experience and found that the mean rating was positive.

The descriptive nature of the previous research precludes inferences about the effects of various requirement policies on student attitudes toward psychology and psychological research. Our study was designed to assess the effects of two research participation policies on student attitudes toward psychology and psychological research. One policy allowed students to volunteer in exchange for extra credit toward their course grade; the other policy required students to participate.

We predicted that student attitudes toward psychology and psychological research would be more positive when students had the freedom to decide whether or not to participate in experiments than when they are forced to participate. Students may feel used or manipulated by being required to participate in research and thus experience reactance (Brehm, 1966, 1972). As a result, they may attempt to restore their freedom by verbally devaluing psychology (Shaw & Costanzo, 1982).

If reactance occurs, would it be manifested when students are informed of the policy or after they engage in the prescribed behaviors? To answer this question, we assessed student attitudes at the beginning and at the end of the semester.

Method

Participants

Participants were 139 undergraduates enrolled in introductory psychology courses for the spring semester of 1989 and 150 students enrolled in introductory psychology courses for the spring semester of 1990. Their means ages were 24.35 ($SD = 7.27$) and 22.74 ($SD = 6.27$) for 1989 and 1990, respectively. For the 1989 sample, 40.7% of the students were men; for the 1990 sample, 50.1% were men.

Design and Manipulation

The quasi-experimental design most closely resembled an untreated control group design with a pretest and a posttest (Cook & Campbell, 1979). In 1989, student participation in research was semivoluntary, and students received extra credit toward their course grade for participating. Students in the 1990 sample were required to participate in two psychological studies. After meeting the research requirement, students could volunteer to participate in additional experiments and earn extra credit toward their course grade.

During the first week of the semester, the policy (either semivoluntary or mandatory participation) was explained to all students enrolled in the three sections. Later that week, students completed a questionnaire that assessed their attitudes toward psychology and psychological research. At this time, students were told they would complete the same questionnaire at the end of the semester. Fourteen weeks later, the week before final exams, the questionnaire was readministered.

Questionnaire

Demographic information. Demographic data were collected on age, gender, grade point average (GPA), status (part-time or full-time), and class level (freshman, sophomore, junior, or senior).

Attitude information. The attitude questionnaire asked participants to indicate the extent of their agreement with 16 questions about psychology and psychological research. The survey used a 6-point scale ranging from *strongly disagree* (1) to *strongly agree* (6). To reduce the number of comparisons and protect the Type I error rate, a factor analysis was conducted on the 281 completed responses to the survey. The use of maximum likelihood to extract the factors and varimax rotation to interpret them produced three factors. Eight items pertained to the Attitudes Toward Psychological Experiments factor (e.g., "I feel good about the idea of participating in experiments"); three items related to the Attitudes Toward Psychology factor (e.g., "I value the information psychology has to offer"), and two items assessed the Learning Value of Participating in Experiments factor (e.g., "Participating in experiments is a valuable way to learn"). Cronbach's coefficient alpha reliability estimates for the three factors were .86, .85, and .78, respectively. The remaining items did not have a factor loading exceeding .40 and, therefore, were not included in subsequent analyses.

Results

Participants in the semivoluntary and mandatory conditions took part in an average of 3.07 and 3.24 studies, respectively (90.6% of the students participated in at least one experiment). A t test revealed that this difference was not statistically significant.

We predicted that, compared to students in the semivoluntary condition, students in the mandatory condition would evaluate psychology and psychological research less positively. Table 1 presents the means and standard deviations of the three factors extracted from the factor analysis (i.e., Attitudes Toward Psychological Experiments, Attitudes Toward Psychology, and Learning Value of Participating in Experiments) by time (beginning of the semester vs. end of the semester) and by type of policy (mandatory vs. semivoluntary).

To assess differences among the means presented in Table 1, 2×2 analyses of variance (ANOVAs) were conducted on the three attitude measures, with the between-subject variable of policy (semivoluntary vs. mandatory) and the with-in-subject variable of time (administration at Time 1 vs. Time 2).

The first ANOVA examined differences in attitudes toward psychological experiments. The only significant result was a main effect for Time of measurement, $F(1, 269) = 20.03, p < .001$; student attitudes toward psychological experiments were more positive at the end ($M = 4.91; SD = .72$) than at the beginning of the semester ($M = 4.74; SD = .74$). There was also a trend ($p = .13$) for attitudes to be more positive under the semivoluntary policy ($M = 4.89; SD = .65$) than under the mandatory policy ($M = 4.76; SD = 81$).

An ANOVA of student attitudes toward psychology yielded a main effect for the policy manipulation, $F(1, 278) = 6.64, p = .01$, as well as a Policy × Time interaction, $F(1, 278) = 4.51, p = .03$. Students had more positive attitudes toward psychology when participation in research was semivoluntary ($M = 5.16; SD = .67$) than when it was mandatory ($M = 4.93; SD = .90$). However, the interaction qualifies this interpretation. Post hoc Tukey tests showed that the difference between policy groups was significant at the beginning of the semester, $t(278) = 3.41, p = .02$, but not at the end of the semester. A dependent t test also showed that attitudes became less positive between Time 1 and Time 2 under the semivoluntary policy, $t(134) = 2.42, p = .03$, but not under the mandatory policy.

An ANOVA of attitudes toward the learning value of participating in experiments yielded a main effect for the policy manipulation. $F(1, 277) = 5.17, p = .02$, and a main effect for the time of measurement, $F(1, 277) = 31.12, p < .001$. Students in the semivoluntary policy condition felt that the learning value of participating in experiments was greater ($M = 4.62; SD = .95$) than did students in the mandatory policy condition ($M = 4.38; SD = 1.01$). In addition, participants were more positive about the learning value of experiments at the beginning of the semester ($M = 4.66; SD = .88$) than at the end ($M = 4.33; SD = 1.08$).

Discussion

Consistent with reactance theory, we predicted that requiring students to participate in research would have negative effects on their attitudes toward psychology and research. Our hypothesis received some support. On all three measures, attitudes were more positive under the semivoluntary than under the mandatory policies, although this was true only at the beginning of the semester for attitudes toward psychology and only as a trend for attitudes toward psychological experiments.

Because the effects of mandatory participation on student attitudes were not large, a mandatory policy may have only a minimal effect on student attitudes and, therefore, may not present a risk of harm to individuals or to psychology. Two arguments can be raised in response. First, our study may not have tapped other effects of the policy, such as the probability of taking additional psychology courses,

Table 1. Cell Means and Standard Deviations of Student Attitudes by Experimental Conditions

Attitude Measure	Semivoluntary Participation		Mandatory Participation	
	Time 1	Time 2	Time 1	Time 2
Toward experiments				
M	4.81	4.97	4.68	4.85
SD	.68	.62	.79	.82
n	130	141	130	141
Toward psychology				
M	5.23	5.08	4.91	4.94
SD	.58	.76	.88	.93
n	134	146	134	146
Learning value of experiments				
M	4.83	4.40	4.50	4.26
SD	.80	1.10	.95	1.07
n	133	146	133	146

Note. The scale ranged from *strongly disagree* (1) to *strongly agree* (6), with higher numbers representing more positive attitudes.

or emotional reactions. Second, our mandatory policy included the requirement to participate in only two studies, and the average student participated in three. If students had been required to participate in more experiments, as is the case at many schools, the effect may have been more pronounced. Simply put, not much reactance may have been created by mandating participation in two experiments.

Effects of the time variable present a mixed picture. Attitudes toward psychological experiments became more positive as a result of participation. Participation, regardless of policy, may help students appreciate experimentation itself. Perhaps students' naive fears of being hooked up to electrodes or being treated rudely were proven false. In this sense, proponents of subject pools can argue that participation may reduce unfounded beliefs about research.

At the same time, judgments of the learning value of experiments became less positive after participation. Students may have had an overly optimistic view of what they would learn. Students participated in only three experiments, on the average, and may simply not have learned enough. Another possibility is that experimenters may not have provided enough information to participants to make the experience worthwhile. Finally, because the study took place over 2 years, the differences between the two groups could be due to variation in the teaching of the courses or the experiments being conducted.

Our tentative conclusion is that participation has some educational value for students, and it could have even more if greater effort were placed on making experiments better learning experiences for participants. As part of our own policy, experimenters are required not only to debrief subjects but also to provide a one-page feedback sheet with information about the general area being investigated, along with one or two references that students can look up if they are interested.

Despite methodological limitations, our study provides some empirical evidence on the question of how to structure an ethical research participation policy. Future studies should assess the effects on attitudes of participating in more experiments and the effects of different types of policies. As more data are collected, a clearer picture of the ethical issues involved in research participation can be obtained.

References

American Psychological Association. (1990). Ethical principles of psychologists (Amended June 2, 1989). *American Psychologist, 45,* 390–395.

American Psychological Association. Committee for the Protection of Human Participants in Research. (1982). *Ethical principles in the conduct of research with human participants.* Washington, DC: Author.

Baron, R. A. (1981). The "costs of deception" revisited: An openly optimistic rejoinder. *IRB: A review of Human Subjects Research, 3,* 8–10.

Baumrind, D. (1979). The costs of deception. *IRB: A Review of Human Subjects Research, 1,* 1–4.

Berscheid, E., Baron, R. A., Dermer, M., & Libman, M. (1973). Anticipating informed consent: An empirical approach. *American Psychologist, 28,* 913–925.

Brehm, J. W. (1966). *A theory of psychological reactance.* New York: Academic.

Brehm, J. W. (1972). *Response to loss of freedom: A theory of psychological reactance.* Morristown, NJ: General Learning Press.

Britton, B. K. (1979). Ethical and educational aspects of participating as a subject in psychology experiments. *Teaching of Psychology, 6,* 195–198.

Cook, T. D., & Campbell, D. T. (1979). *Quasi-experimentation: Design and analysis issues for field settings.* Boston: Houghton Mifflin.

Diener, E., & Crandall, R. (1978). *Ethics in social and behavioral research.* Chicago: University of Chicago Press.

Epstein, Y. M., Suedfeld, P., & Silverstein, S. J. (1973). The experimental contract: Subjects' expectations of and reactions to some behaviors of experimenters. *American Psychologist, 28,* 212–221.

Gross, A. E., & Fleming, I. (1982). Twenty years of deception in social psychology. *Personality and Social Psychology Bulletin, 8,* 402–408.

Holmes, D. S. (1976a). Debriefing after psychological experiments: I. Effectiveness of post-deception dehoaxing. *American Psychologist, 31,* 858–867.

Holmes, D. S. (1976b). Debriefing after psychological experiments: II. Effectiveness of post-experimental desensitizing. *American Psychologist, 31,* 868–875.

Holmes, D. S., & Bennet, D. H. (1974). Experiments to answer questions raised by the use of deception in psychological research. *Journal of Personality and Social Psychology, 29,* 358–367.

Kimmel, A. J. (1981). *Ethics of human subject research.* San Francisco: Jossey-Bass.

Leak, G. K. (1981). Student perception of coercion and value from participation in psychological research. *Teaching of Psychology, 8,* 147–149.

Loftus, E. F., & Fries, J. F. (1979). Informed consent may be hazardous to health. *Science, 204,* 11.

Miller, A. (1981). A survey of introductory psychology subject pool practices among leading universities. *Teaching of Psychology, 8,* 211–213.

Schuler, H. (1982). *Ethical problems in psychological research.* New York: Academic.

Shaw, M. E., & Costanzo, P. R. (1982). *Theories of social psychology.* New York: McGraw-Hill.

Sieber, J. E., & Saks, M. J. (1989). A census of subject pool characteristics and policies. *American Psychologist, 44,* 1053–1061.

Tabachnick, B. G., Keith-Spiegel, P., & Pope, K. S. (1991). Ethics of teaching: Beliefs and behaviors of psychologists as educators. *American Psychologist, 46,* 506–515.

Notes

1. Preparation of this article was supported in part by a Junior Faculty Development Grant awarded to James G. Nimmer by the University of Colorado at Denver.
2. We gratefully acknowledge the insightful comments of Charles L. Brewer and three anonymous reviewers on an earlier version of this article.

Mark McMinn from George Fox College designed a case-study simulation to aid instructors teaching ethics in psychology. Two cases involving ethical decisions in psychology are included with the computer program. The first case deals with confidentiality in clinical psychology; the second case concerns ethics in planning, conducting, and reporting research. The program is generic and allows instructors to write their own text files.

Bernard Beins generated the Barnum effect to teach students at Ithaca College about the ethics of deception in research and the feelings of subjects who are deceived. Students in research methods classes received feedback about a bogus personality inventory and rated the perceived validity of the interpretations. Seniors were more skeptical than juniors and sophomores. This technique is an engaging and effective way to help students learn firsthand about the costs and benefits of research.

Deciding not to conduct a study because it involves deception or invasion of privacy is as much an act to be evaluated on ethical grounds as is conducting such a study. Robert Rosnow from Temple University designed a classroom exercise to demonstrate that the ethical evaluation of a study can be considered from several standpoints. He used role-play and discussion to sharpen critical thinking and develop an appreciation of the nuances of research ethics.

David Strohmetz and Anne Skleder evaluated the effectiveness of Rosnow's role-play exercise (see the preceding article) in their undergraduate research methods classes at Temple University. Results indicated that the technique can be a valuable tool for sensitizing students to the complex factors involved in judging the ethics of research.

Carl Kallgren and Robert Tauber from Penn State Erie surveyed 53 undergraduate researchers whose projects had received formal approval by an institutional review board (IRB). Students indicated that they had learned more by going through the IRB process, produced a better product, viewed instructor feedback more positively, saw the instructor as more of an ally, treated their research more seriously, and were sensitized to ethical issues. The authors recommend the IRB process for all undergraduate research.

Recognizing the growing controversy over the ethics of using animals in research, Harold Herzog from Western Carolina University reviewed two prominent philosophical justifications for animal liberation and described an exercise that facilitates class discussion of animal research issues. Students simulated participation on an institutional animal care committee and decided whether a series of hypothetical experiments would be allowed. Students reported that the technique increased their awareness about the complexity of making ethical decisions.

Ethics Case-Study Simulation: A Generic Tool for Psychology Teachers

Mark R. McMinn
George Fox College

Psychologists frequently face difficult ethical issues; hence, the teaching of ethics is an important component of graduate and undergraduate psychology education. Keith-Spiegel and Koocher (1985) noted that the American Psychological Association spends more money on ethics-related matters than any other professional organization.

Case studies are frequently used in teaching ethics. Similarly, many ethics books in psychology are liberally sprinkled with case-study illustrations. Using case studies to teach ethics has several advantages. First, case studies are interesting, increasing the salience of the principles being taught. Second, case studies are practical, illustrating to students how the principles are applied in real-life situations. Third, case studies are realistic. Many of the situations we teach students are similar to situations they will encounter in years to come. Specific attention to those issues during students' education will presumably allow them to make wiser decisions as professionals. Finally, case studies powerfully illustrate the difficulty of certain ethical decisions: They help students confront the absence of clear right and wrong answers in some situations.

But if case studies are presented quickly, without adequate exploration and discussion, they can be counterproductive. For example, the ethical issues might easily appear prescriptive to students. Students might begin to think that every case is addressed with a specific principle and not recognize the need for creative problem solving in ethical decision making. Memorizing the "Ethical Principles of Psychologists" (1981) is not the same as learning to be ethical. The process of ethical decision making might easily be overlooked with excessive use of poorly developed case studies.

An excellent alternative is to teach ethics by trial-and-error rather than by prescription. By having students take tentative positions on issues before revealing more information, a simulation of ethical decision making can occur in the classroom. But trial-and-error teaching cannot be done on an individual basis in most settings because graduate students in clinical programs learn by dealing with troubled clients. Appropriate ethical decisions are expected by supervisors without employing trial-and-error methods.

The advantages of in-depth case studies and trial-and-error learning can be combined with computer simulation. Students can see the effects of their choices, understand the importance of process in making decisions, and recognize the kinds of practical dilemmas they may experience.

The case-study simulation program described here was developed to address the need for interactive case studies that allow for trial-and-error learning. The program is written for IBM or compatible personal computers. It requires one disk drive and 128K of random access memory. All students are first presented with the same information; additional information varies depending on choices made by the student. The text is organized as a decision tree with a series of dichotomous choices. Based on their choice, students are presented one of two second-level screens. Based on their choice on the second-level screen, they select one of four third-level screens, and so on. There are five levels altogether, with the fifth level showing one of the 16 possible case outcomes and not requiring a decision by the student. Students can go backward in the decision tree and change their minds on previous decisions, giving the program the capacity to answer "what if" questions the student may have.

Ethics instructors recognize that what a student decides is often less important than why the student comes to that conclusion. After each decision in the simulation, students are asked why that response was chosen. Their reasons are input to a data file that can later be accessed by the instructor. Each reason in the data file is preceded by numbers identifying which screen and decision the reason is justifying. This allows the instructor to evaluate moral reasoning from a developmental, a consequential, or a deontological perspective. Moreover, it provides an excellent starting point for classroom discussions on moral development and ethical decision making. Classroom discussions can also focus on how difficult it is to make ethical decisions before knowing what will happen after decisions are made.

Following the fifth-level screen (i.e., case outcome), students are evaluated based on the 10 "Ethical Principles of Psychologists" (1981). This is a subjective evaluation based on the opinions of the instructor preparing the case study, but the evaluation and the principles used can be tailored by the user.

Two cases related to ethical decision making in psychology are included with this program. The first case, THE SECRET, deals with confidentiality in clinical psychology. The second case, A SHOCKING STORY, concerns ethics in the planning, execution, and reporting of research.

The program is written as a generic tool, allowing others to write text files to be used with this software. An accompanying manual instructs others how to write their own cases. With my supervision, students prepare case studies in a psychology ethics class for upper-division undergraduates. It allows them to anticipate ethical dilemmas and probable effects of certain decisions. Because of the developmental level of undergraduates, I do not use the case studies they develop with other students. Nonetheless, having them prepare the case-study texts provides many hours of profitable, small-group discussion on ethical issues and allows students to anticipate the consequences of certain actions in psychology.

I have found the software to be very useful in teaching ethics. Students are intrigued by case studies, and they enjoy the simulation assignment. Because I have a record of the reasons students give for making certain decisions, I can stimulate fascinating discussions on the moral bases for different ethical decisions. Most students do not perform well on their first trials with the simulation. This gives them a healthy respect for the difficulty of many ethical decisions.

References

Ethical principles of psychologists. (1981). *American Psychologist, 36*, 633–638.

Keith-Spiegel, P., & Koocher, G. P. (1985). *Ethics in psychology: Professional standards and cases.* New York: Random House.

Notes

1. This work was supported by a Pew Foundation Grant for "Ethics Across the Curriculum" administered by the Christian College Consortium.
2. Readers who request the case-study simulation program and manual should send $5.00 to cover cost of duplication and postage.
3. I would appreciate receiving any case study texts that others develop for the software.

Using the Barnum Effect to Teach About Ethics and Deception in Research

Bernard C. Beins
Ithaca College

Psychologists are intensely interested in establishing ethical guidelines that help direct their professional relationships. The American Psychological Association exerts ongoing efforts to revise its guidelines (e.g., "APA Continues to Refine," 1992), and a growing corpus of relevant articles and publications exists (e.g., Tabachnick, Keith-Spiegel, & Pope, 1991).

Although professionals are acutely aware of the importance of this issue, students do not systematically learn about it at more than a cursory level (Korn, 1984). Fortunately, individual instructors have recognized the traditional gap in teaching ethics. McMinn (1988) developed a computerized approach to ethical decision making; Rosnow (1990) described an approach involving role-playing, discussion, and debate.

The approach to teaching ethics described here puts students in the role of the deceived in a classroom project. There are two main students why lectures and discussions about the ethics of deceit need to be supplemented by a more direct demonstration.

First, Milgram (1963) found that people are not very accurate in predicting how subjects will react when confronted with an ethically ambiguous situation. If people cannot reliably predict subjects' behavior, perhaps students might think that they know how a deceived subject would feel, but the actual experience may be much more compelling.

Second, students may not empathize initially with research subjects who are deceived. For example, student researchers who participated in some conformity studies (Beins & Porter, 1989) showed no distress about using deception in the research (the Institutional Review Board that approved the research also showed no distress). Similarly, Harcum and Friedman (1991), who expressed reservations about the ethics of using some fairly common classroom demonstrations, noted that about 93% of their subjects accepted deception as part of a legitimate research design.

The vehicle for creating this teaching activity is the *Barnum effect,* in which individuals are gulled into believing invalid results of psychological tests. This effect was originally used to teach students about testing (Forer, 1949); as a phenomenon, it is well documented (e.g., Baillargeon & Danis, 1984; Furnham & Schofield, 1987; Holmes, Buchannan, Dungan, & Reed, 1986). It can also introduce students to the pitfall of blind acceptance of test results (Palladino, 1991).

The goals of the activity described herein are to foster an appreciation of the feelings of research subjects who are lied to and an awareness of the need to avoid deception when possible. This approach complements those used by McMinn (1988) and Rosnow (1990). The demonstration combines an initial discussion of crucial ethical issues that I take from Reynolds (1982), a firsthand account of being deceived, and a final discussion.

Generating the Barnum Effect

Procedure

Students in a research methods class participated in the project as part of the course requirement. There were 28 women and 11 men; 10 were sophomores, 23 were juniors, and 6 were seniors.

Students completed a 20-item bogus personality inventory, the Quacksalber Personality Inventory for Normal Populations (Beins, 1987). They subsequently received interpretations that were identical for all students. All feedback statements were intended to be neutral or mildly positive.

One class ($n = 19$) completed the test with a version designed for Apple II computers; feedback was provided immediately. The second class ($n = 20$) took a version printed on paper and responded on a computer scoring sheet. A confederate of the teacher left the room and returned about 10 min later with printouts that had been prepared in advance with each student's name written across the top. There was no obvious reason to expect the two groups to differ in their reactions; a comparison between the two would only indicate how robust the effect might be.

Both groups then completed a form designed to access the perceived validity of the test. One question asked how well students thought the feedback described themselves. Students responded using a scale ranging from *this is the real me* (1) to *this is not like me* (10). In addition, they indicated how useful the test would be in five situations: personal adjustment, employment screening, assessment of honesty, identification of a person's minor problems, and identification of a person's major problems. Students responded using a scale ranging from *very useful* (1) to *not very useful* (10).

Assessing the Barnum Effect

Students were predictably accepting of the test results as descriptive of themselves. The mean rating was 3.6. This represented a significant departure from a neutral value of 5.5, $t(38) = 6.24$, $p < .001$. However, students felt that the test would not be particularly effective in assessing personal adjustment, employee honesty and stability, or major or minor emotional problems. Thus, students did not blindly accept the test as being a universally valid instrument.

To test the robustness of the effect, a 2 (Medium: Computer vs. Paper) × 2 (Sex) × 3 (Year in School) analysis of variance was conducted on the acceptance ratings. Only the main effect of year was significant, $F(2, 36) = 5.09$, $p = .011$. Sophomores ($M = 3.00$) and juniors ($M = 3.43$) did not differ reliably, but they were significantly less skeptical than seniors ($M = 5.67$). The small number of seniors renders the difference between them and the sophomores and juniors somewhat suspect. I have tried to generate acceptance of the results of the Quacksalber inventory for other seniors and for graduate students without much success. Even so, these students experience the deceit, their skepticism in the results of the test notwithstanding.

Generating Postdemonstration Discussion

Students discussed their feelings when I told them that they had been deceived. Their initial reaction to the deceit was to feel gullible and stupid. In general, they were mildly distressed at first. I also noted what seemed to be nervous laughter from several students during the initial stages of the discussion.

Discussion focused on the fact that they had taken the Quacksalber inventory seriously, on their feelings about being deceived, and on the idea that their reactions to being deceived were common. I also pointed out that if they used deception in research, their subjects would feel the same way. Finally, I used this situation to illustrate the importance of debriefing.

During the next class meeting, they wrote answers to questions about the suitability of this exercise to illustrate relevant points about deception in research and whether this demonstration should be repeated in future classes. We spent nearly an entire class period discussing what they had written. I made it clear that I would consider their responses seriously before deciding whether to repeat this activity with another class. I pointed out that deception was as much a problem in the classroom as in the context of experimental research.

Assessing Student Reactions to the Deception

Of the 31 students who commented anonymously about whether this demonstration was effective in teaching about both the Barnum effect and deception, 30 students responded affirmatively. Their comments generally asserted that the costs of doing the demonstration (failure to acquire prior informed consent, invasion of their privacy in asking questions about their likes and dislikes, and lying to them about the nature of the test) were outweighed by the benefits of learning that deception is not free of cost and of knowing firsthand how subjects feel when lied to. Other notable and potentially serious effects of this exercise are that students may question the instructor's credibility, they may think that psychological research is without validity or integrity, and they may develop negative feelings about psychological research. None of these unwanted eventualities emerged.

The sole dissenter suggested that it was not worth making students feel stupid and that the point about deception in research could be made simply by giving facts and examples. Several students noted that some students may be distressed (e.g., freshmen who lacked confidence in themselves) and that I should be aware of this. We had not discussed the question of individual differences regarding negative reactions, but some students spontaneously mentioned it.

Discussion

This project seems to have been effective on two levels. On one hand, the students became acquainted with the Barnum effect. More important, they also seemed quite touched at the personal level by the experience. It was clear to me that they did not enjoy the trickery when it was inflicted on them. On the other hand, they agreed that it provided a compelling message. The class discussion was tinged with a sense of empathy with research subjects who are deceived. The degree to which students objected to the procedure was as low as that reported elsewhere (Britton, Richardson, Smith, & Hamilton, 1983; Harcum & Friedman, 1991): Students may have felt some distress, but it was mild and short-lived.

The students also learned that, in some cases, deception can be tolerated. For example, in my classes, the students agreed that I should not regularly lie to them; however, the mild and short-lived discomfort about knowing that they had been lied to served to teach them an important lesson about deception in research. Thus, they asserted that the project was worth repeating with subsequent classes.

This demonstration has several advantages. It teaches about deception in the context of a social psychology phenomenon. It is more accessible than Forer's (1949) original demonstration of the Barnum effect, which was based on his Diagnostic Interest Blank and some astrological personality descriptions. This version is also quicker than Forer's, which extended over a period of 1 week. Also, the Quacksalber inventory provides the same kind of feedback Forer provided, although the personality descriptions used here are more neutral.

Furthermore, when the computer version is used, no responses are actually recorded, thus ensuring confidentiality. (The computerized version is available only for Apple II computers, but is written in BASIC, so it should be easily convertible to GW BASIC for IBM-type computers.)

The project seems amenable either to computerized or paper application. Men and women reacted in the same way, both in generating the effect and in their responses to deception. Seniors seemed more skeptical of the feedback (as did master's level students in education in a similar situation). Even when students failed to accept the output as descriptive of themselves, they still seemed to have accepted the test as legitimate. This demonstration seems robust and pedagogically useful for a wide range of students.

References

APA continues to refine its ethics code. (1992, May). *APA Monitor*, pp. 38–42.

Baillargeon, J., & Danis, C. (1984). Barnum meets the computer: A critical test. *Journal of Personality Assessment, 48*, 415–419.

Beins, B. C. (1987). Psychological testing and interpretation. In V. P. Makosky, L. G. Whittemore, & A. M. Rogers (Eds.), *Activities handbook for the teaching of psychology* (Vol. 2, pp. 266–274). Washington, DC: American Psychological Association.

Beins, B. C., & Porter, J. W. (1989). A ratio scale measurement of conformity. *Educational and Psychological Measurement, 49*, 75–80.

Britton, B. K., Richardson, D., Smith, S. S., & Hamilton, T. (1983). Ethical aspects of participating in psychology experiments: Effects of anonymity on evaluation, and complaints of distressed subjects. *Teaching of Psychology, 10*, 146–149.

Forer, B. R. (1949). The fallacy of personal validation: A classroom demonstration of testing. *Journal of Abnormal and Social Psychology, 44*, 118–123.

Furnham, A., & Schofield, S. (1987). Accepting personality test feedback: A review of the Barnum effect. *Current Psychological Research & Reviews, 6*, 162–178.

Harcum, E. R., & Friedman, H. (1991). Students' ethics ratings of demonstrations in introductory psychology. *Teaching of Psychology, 18*, 215–218.

Holmes, C. B., Buchannan, J. A., Dungan, D. S., & Reed, T. (1986). The Barnum effect in Luscher color test interpretation. *Journal of Clinical Psychology, 2*, 186–190.

Korn, J. H. (1984). Coverage of research ethics in introductory and social psychology textbooks. *Teaching of Psychology, 11*, 146–149.

McMinn, M. R. (1988). Ethics case-study simulation: A generic tool for psychology teachers. *Teaching of Psychology, 15*, 100–101.

Milgram, S. (1963). Behavioral study of obedience. *Journal of Abnormal and Social Psychology, 67*, 371–378.

Palladino, J. J. (1991, August). *The BRPI–The Blatantly Ridiculous Personality Inventory*. Paper presented at the annual convention of the American Psychological Association, San Francisco.

Reynolds, P. D. (1982). *Ethics and social science research*. Englewood Cliffs, NJ: Prentice-Hall.

Rosnow, R. L. (1990). Teaching research ethics through role-play and discussion. *Teaching of Psychology, 17*, 179–181.

Tabachnick, B. G., Keith-Spiegel, P., & Pope, K. S. (1991). Ethics of teaching: Beliefs and behaviors of psychologists as educators. *American Psychologist, 46*, 506–515.

Note

I thank Ruth Ault for her comments on a previous draft of this article.

Teaching Research Ethics Through Role-Play and Discussion

Ralph L. Rosnow
Temple University

When lecturing on research ethics, instructors tend to consider only the costs and benefits of conducting particular studies, as if from the perspective of an institutional review board (IRB). Seldom is due consideration given to the ethical implications of the failure to conduct ethically ambiguous studies that might reduce violence, prejudice, mental illness, and so forth. The failure to conduct such a study because it involves deception or invasion of privacy, however is as much an act to be evaluated on ethical grounds as is the act of conducting a study (Rosenthal & Rosnow, 1984). This idea is important to communicate to psychology students, because it teaches that there is more than one vantage point from which the ethical evaluation of a study can be made. This article describes a classroom exercise that, through role-play and discussion, leads students to develop an appreciation of the subtleties of research ethics.

The technique considers at least three vantage points. The first is that of the research discipline itself, as represented by the ethical principles of the American Psychological Association (1982). A second frame of reference is that of the community in which the research is being sanctioned (e.g., the class in which the person is a student or an IRB). The third is the point of view of the individual investigator (e.g., the student-researcher), who may not have thought much about his or her own ethical assumptions and biases.

This article proceeds in two parts. First, I suggest some readings and ideas to stimulate discussion. The discussion, which takes place either before the role-play (i.e., to set the stage) or afterward (i.e., to tie things together), is intended to provide a real-world context for the students. Next, I describe the role-play technique, which I have condensed into a five-step exercise. In this exercise, students defend a position they have recently attacked by role-playing an author who is defending the value of a study. This exercise helps sharpen critical thinking and reduces the initial tendencies of many students to "play it safe" by eschewing any study that appears to involve deception or intervention. The technique can be modified to fit scheduling constraints or larger classes.

Readings and Discussion

If the exercise is to be part of a research methods class, the textbook will usually contain relevant material. For graduate and advanced undergraduate students, such material can be supplemented by outside readings (e.g., Doob, 1987; Kelman, 1968; Kimmel, 1981, 1988; Schuler, 1982; Sieber, 1982; Smith, 1969), chosen with the course objectives in mind. Because some students tend to approach such readings uncritically, it is helpful to provide a background to focus their attention. For example, students could be assigned to read selected chapters in Miller's (1986) book on Stanley Milgram's classic studies. The ethics of Milgram's research were widely debated; this debate is captured in an absorbing way in Miller's book.

A comparison between the ethical dilemmas faced by Milgram and those faced by action researchers can be made by using the quality-of-work-life experiment that was conducted in 1973 at the Rushton Mining Company in Pennsylvania (Blumberg & Pringle, 1983). Developed on the basis of earlier research in the United Kingdom, the purpose of this project was to improve employee skills, safety, and job satisfaction, which raised the level of performance and as a result, company earnings. After months of research preparation, volunteers were sought for a work group that would have direct responsibility for production in one section of the mining operations. After exhaustive training in safety laws, good mining practices, and job safety analysis, the volunteers were paid at the top rate as the highest skilled job classification on that section and left to coordinate their own activities. They became enthusiastic proponents of "our way of working." Other workers (i.e., those in the control condition), however, expressed resentment and anger at the volunteers' haughtiness. The resulting negativity in the atmosphere surrounding the experiment led the investigators to end it abruptly.

137

Action research can frequently have its own set of ethical problems, quite apart from the ones encountered by Milgram in his laboratory research. There was no deception in this study, but there is the problem of "fairness" because a sizable number of workers (nonvolunteers) did not receive the benefits enjoyed by those in the experimental group. By analogy, the ethical cost of using placebo control subjects in biomedical research could be examined, because they also fail to receive the benefits (if any) received by the experimental group. What if instead of receiving a placebo, the controls received the best available usual or common treatment to serve as a comparison with the effects of the experimental treatment?

Still other ethical risks may be incurred in participant-observer research. For example, what about the moral cost that is possible simply in the reporting of results (cf. Johnson, 1982)? What if, despite the author's use of pseudonyms, some persons or communities can be identified (or can identify themselves) in the publication? Would those that are identifiable be vulnerable to embarrassment or to unwanted publicity? On the other hand, what is the social and scientific cost of not publishing the findings (i.e., not disseminating research results)?

Deception, fairness, and the invasion of privacy also come into play outside the research situation. Broome (1984) discussed the ethical issue of fairness in selecting people for chronic hemodialysis, a medical procedure that can save the life of a person whose kidneys have failed. The procedure is expensive, and in many communities there are not enough facilities to treat everyone who could benefit, yet without treatment a patient quickly dies. How should candidates for hemodialysis be selected? The inventor of hemodialysis was said to have used the following guidelines to select people: under 40 years old, free from cardiovascular disease, pillars of the community, contributors to the community's economics, married, and attends church. Is this ethical and fair? Another procedure would be randomness. Broome noted that selecting people randomly—such as using a lottery to choose conscripts to fight in a war—is justified as the "fairest" procedure, because everyone has an equal chance at being selected for life or death. But suppose conscripts for the military were not selected randomly, but on the grounds of who was the biggest and strongest. Which procedure is more ethical—randomness or selection on the grounds of who is more likely to survive?

These are the kinds of ideas and questions that instructors might pose to stimulate discussion. Students need to understand that research is not conducted in isolation from the surrounding community. For example, when researchers study prejudice, mental illness, or AIDS, they are touching on highly charged social problems. Even when they study topics that appear to be neutral (e.g., marriage and the family, the genetics of intelligence, or learning behavior), they must realize the implications for others.

Thus, it is important to understand that psychological research forces investigators to "tread on thin moral ice" (Atwell, 1981, p. 89).

The Role-Play Exercise

Step 1 is to familiarize the class with the "Ten Commandments" of the APA's ethical recommendations (American Psychological Association, 1982, pp. 5–7). The ethical standards were developed to check the possible tendency of some researchers to be carried away by the judged importance of doing the research. The class might, therefore, be asked to think about the possibility that there are ethical boundaries that should not be crossed, as put forth in the APA code. Then each student peruses the past year's issues of any primary research journal of interest. The assignment is to find an article that reports a research study that the student personally feels used an "unethical" manipulation or other "reprehensible" procedure. The student is instructed to read the article carefully and thoroughly, to be prepared if called on in class to give a detailed report and be able to answer questions about it, and to turn in a brief paper that focuses on the ethics of the study. The sampling bias in this assignment would seem implicit, inasmuch as the students are reading only studies that supposedly have passed ethical scrutiny. Students have an uncanny ability, however, to ferret out ethically ambiguous studies, even in recent APA journal articles.

Step 2 is to have the students give oral reports of the results of their assignment for the entire class. I then pose questions regarding potentially troublesome aspects of the procedure (e.g., invasion of privacy, deception, use of confederates, or concealed observation). The objective of the questions is to draw the group as a "community" into the discussion.

In Step 3, after all the studies have been discussed, the class examines them from a different perspective. Instead of acting as critics, the students role-play the author of the study and defend their study in the face of criticisms by the rest of the group. If the most articulate and confident students begin this phase, they can provide a good example for the students who follow.

Step 4 is to have each person in the group evaluate the studies on their moral or ethical cost and their theoretical or practical utility. Taking each study in turn, the students evaluate the moral or ethical cost on a 101-point scale ranging from *no ethical or moral cost* (0) to *the highest ethical or moral cost* (100). Students evaluate the studies individually, based not on how they think that others in the group will vote but on their own personal perspective. Next, students evaluate each study's utility on a 101-point scale ranging from *no theoretical or practical utility* (0) to *the highest theoretical or practical utility* (100). I then draw two matrices on the blackboard, one for the "cost of doing" and the other for the "utility of doing" ratings. The students' names begin the rows, and one- or two-word descriptors of the studies head the columns. While the group copies down the results, I calculate the row and column means and the grand mean and insert this information. The results tell the students at a glance whether they were tough or easy relative to one another (row means), to the group as a whole (grand mean), and to the collective perception of each study. I also point out outliers and clusters of ratings and ask the students to speculate on their implications.

Step 5 concludes the exercise. Using Figure 1 (Rosenthal & Rosnow, 1984), I then develop the idea that the decision-plane model on the left represents the costs and utilities of doing research. Studies falling at A are not carried out, studies falling at D are carried out, and studies falling at B–C cannot be determined. Results in the previous matrices (Step 4) can be used to illustrate the various possibilities. The model represents the way that most IRBs seemingly operate, but this "IRB" (the class)—through role-play in Step 3—also thought about (but did not rate) the other side of the ethical equation, the costs (and utilities) of not doing research (represented by the model on the right). I point out the ethical value of considering both models to arrive at a balanced analysis of the costs and utilities of doing and not doing a study. Examples from the previous role-play are used to underscore the idea that ethical decision making calls for such a balancing of considerations, even though it makes the decision process more complex. Note that IRBs review research proposals, not research results, but we had knowledge of the results. Did it make a difference in the ratings, and what are the implications?

If the class is large and there are section meetings in which the students are divided into small groups, then it is better to run the exercise in the latter context. Small groups establish a tone that makes it easier for students to be less inhibited and to throw themselves into the exercise. Student

reactions have been consistently positive. Making social comparisons is intrinsically motivating, thus adding to the appeal of the exercise. The exercise provides students with a way of looking to others for information while looking within themselves to cope with their uncertainties.

References

American Psychological Association. (1982). *Ethical principles in the conduct of research with human participants.* Washington, DC: Author.

Atwell, J. E. (1981). Human rights in human subjects research. In A. J. Kimmel (Ed.), *Ethics of human subject research* (pp. 81–90). San Francisco: Jossey-Bass.

Blumberg, M., & Pringle, C. D. (1983). How control groups can cause loss of control in action research: The case of Rushton coal mine. *Journal of Applied Behavioral Science, 19,* 409–425.

Broome, J. (1984). Selecting people randomly. *Ethics, 95,* 38–55.

Doob, L. W. (1987). *Slightly beyond skepticism: Social science and the search for morality.* New Haven: Yale University Press.

Johnson, C. G. (1982). Risks in the publication of fieldwork. In J. E. Sieber (Ed.), *The ethics of social research: Fieldwork, regulation, and publication* (Vol. 1, pp. 71–91). New York: Springer-Verlag.

Kelman, H. C. (1968). *A time to speak: On human values and social research.* San Francisco: Jossey-Bass.

Kimmel, A. J. (Ed.). (1981). *Ethics of human subject research.* San Francisco: Jossey-Bass.

Kimmel, A. J. (1988). *Ethics and values in applied social research.* Beverly Hills: Sage.

Miller, A. G. (1986). *The obedience experiments: A case study of controversy in social science.* New York: Praeger.

Rosenthal, R., & Rosnow, R. L. (1984). Applying Hamlet's question to the ethical conduct of research: A conceptual addendum. *American Psychologist, 39,* 561–563.

Schuler, H. (1982). *Ethical problems in psychological research.* New York: Academic.

Sieber, J. E. (Ed.). (1982). *The ethics of social research* (Vol. 1 & Vol. 2). New York: Springer-Verlag.

Smith, M. B. (1969). *Social psychology and human values.* Chicago: Aldine.

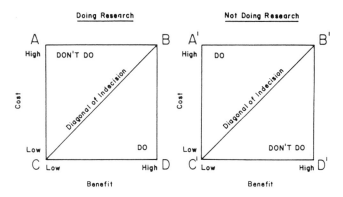

Figure 1. Decision planes representing the costs and utilities of doing and not doing research. *Note.* From "Applying Hamlet's Question to the Ethical Conduct of Research: A Conceptual Addendum" by Robert Rosenthal and Ralph L. Rosnow, 1984, *American Psychologist, 39,* p. 562. Copyright 1984 by the American Psychological Association, Inc. Adapted by permission.

Notes

1. Preparation of this article was supported by Temple University through the Bolton Endowment and an NIH Biomedical Research Support Grant.
2. I thank Robert Rosenthal, Joseph Palladino, and three anonymous reviewers for their helpful comments on a draft of this article.

The Use of Role-Play in Teaching Research Ethics: A Validation Study

David B. Strohmetz
Anne A. Skleder
Temple University

Rosnow (1990) argued that, in order to make students aware of the ethical complexities of psychological research, the moral or ethical costs and benefits of doing research might be evaluated in a role-play context. He described a classroom exercise designed to teach students the necessity of viewing the importance of both cost and benefit considerations in the evaluation of research studies. We incorporated this procedure into our lectures on research ethics and evaluated its effectiveness using questionnaires administered before and after the study.

Following Rosnow's suggestion, the procedure begins with a lecture on research ethics based on the ethical principles of the American Psychological Association (1981). The discussion includes a consideration of why proposed research must be evaluated in terms of the ethical costs and benefits of doing the study as well as the costs and benefits of not doing the study. Students are then given a homework assignment to find a recently published study that they consider to be unethical. They are told to read the study carefully and to be prepared to present it during the next class.

During the next class, students present their studies in a discussion led by the instructor. Afterward, they are asked to rate the cost and utility (benefit) of each study. Students are then asked to role-play a "devil's advocate" and defend the scientific value of their "unethical" study before the rest of the class. Following this role-play, each student rerates the cost and the utility of the studies. Finally, the reevaluations are discussed to uncover how and why cost and utility ratings may have changed as a result of the students advocating studies that they originally viewed as unethical.

How effective is this role-play exercise in communicating the ethical complexity of psychological research? We were able to compare the changes in the cost and utility ratings from classes that used the role-play activity with similar ratings from a class that heard the lecture on research ethics but did not use the role-play activity. We predicted that participating in the role-play exercise would increase students' perceptions of the utility of their "unethi-cal" studies. Similarly, we hypothesized that ratings of the perceived ethical costs of these studies would be lower after the role-play. Finally, we predicted that the magnitude of any obtained effects would be larger in these six classes than in the comparison class, which did not use the role-play exercise.

Method

Subjects

Students in both the role-play and nonrole-play classes were junior and senior psychology majors enrolled in a required research methods course. Six classes incorporated the role-play exercise into the lecture on research ethics; a seventh class had the same research ethics lecture and unethical article assignment but did not use the role-play exercise. Each of the authors taught two of these classes; the remaining two role-play classes and the nonrole-play class were taught by three other instructors. Approximately 18 students were enrolled in each class.

Procedure

We used the role-play exercise as described earlier, with one modification. Because of class size and time constraints, only a limited number of the students' "unethical" studies were selected for the role-play. The number of studies selected was left to the instructor's discretion, so the number of rated articles was inconsistent among the classes, ranging from 5 to 11 studies. Before engaging in the role-play, each class rated the cost and utility of the selected studies on a scale ranging from *no cost or utility* (0) to *highest cost or utility* (100).

After this first set of ratings, we asked each student who had initially critiqued one of the selected articles to imagine himself or herself as the article's primary author or researcher. The rest of the class role-played a peer review board that called upon the student to defend the ethics of his or her study. After the selected articles were defended, students rerated the perceived cost and utility of the articles on the same scale.

The instructor in the comparison class followed the same procedure except that he did not conduct the role-play segment after the initial set of ratings. Instead, the instructor turned to another research topic. After about 30 min, the instructor again asked the students to rate the perceived cost and utility of the selected articles. The changes in cost and utility ratings for each class provided the basis for our analyses.

Results and Discussion

Correlated t tests were computed to evaluate whether there were significant changes in the cost and utility ratings from Time 1 to Time 2. Because each class rated different articles, we treated each class separately in our analyses. We used meta-analytic procedures (Rosenthal, 1984) to compare and contrast the results from each of the classes.

The direction of the changes in utility ratings for all the role-play groups was consistent with our prediction (see Table 1). The magnitude of the effect varied slightly among instructors, with effect sizes (calculated as a Pearson r) ranging from .33 to .75. For the nonrole-play class, the change in the perceived utility ratings was not significant and in the opposite direction of that in the role-play classes.

A meta-analytic comparison revealed that the utility results from the role-play classes were homogeneous with regard to significance levels, $\chi^2(5) = 3.30, p = .65$, and effect sizes, $\chi^2(5) = 4.55, p = .47$. Combining the significance levels for the role-play classes' utility ratings yielded a Z score of 6.05, $p < .0000001$. We calculated that it would take an additional 76 nonsignificant studies to achieve such an effect, thereby suggesting that our combined significance level was not due to sampling bias (Rosenthal, 1984; Rosenthal & Rosnow, 1991). Combining the effect sizes for

the role-play classes resulted in an average effect size of .57 for the change in utility ratings, which is considered to be a large magnitude of effect in psychology (Cohen, 1977).

The results for the utility change ratings were homogeneous among the role-play classes. Therefore, significance levels and effect sizes were contrasted between the role-play and nonrole-play classes. Both the contrasts for significance levels, $Z = 3.089, p = .001$, and effect sizes, $Z = 3.264, p = .0006$, suggest that the role-play exercise affected students' utility ratings.

The separate class results for changes in the perceived cost ratings were also in the expected direction (see Table 2). However, none of Instructor B's results were statistically significant. Instructors A, C, and D's results were homogeneous for significance levels, $\chi^2(3) = 4.17, p = .24$, and effect sizes, $\chi^2(3) = 3.95, p = .27$. They were significantly different from Instructor B's significance levels, $Z = 3.75, p = .0001$, and effect sizes, $Z = 3.74, p = .0001$.

We have no single explanation for this result, but note that Instructor B's cost results were not significantly different from the nonrole-play class. Clearly, the role-play exercise had little impact on student reevaluations of the studies in Instructor B's classes, whereas the other role-play classes differed from the nonrole-play class with respect to significance levels, $Z = 3.83, p = .0001$, and effect sizes, $Z = 4.10, p = .00002$. If we consider Instructor B as an outlier for the purposes of this analysis, then the average effect size for Instructors A, C, and D was .72. For these classes, the role-play exercise produced the hypothesized significant effect on cost ratings.

We thought of two plausible explanations for why Instructor B's changes in cost ratings were significantly different from the other role-play classes. First, Instructor B may have placed less emphasis on defending the perceived costs of the studies during the role-play part of the exercise than the other instructors. As a result, there would be little reason for Instructor B's students to change their initial cost ratings.

Another plausible explanation stems from a consideration of the number of studies discussed by each class. Both

Table 1. Changes in Utility Ratings

Class	Utility Change[a]	Correlated t Test[b]	r
Instructor A			
Semester 1	10.76	$t(15) = 3.31, p = .002$	.65
Semester 2	4.22	$t(21) = 1.61, p = .06$	.33
Instructor B			
Semester 1	8.02	$t(15) = 2.75, p = .007$	.58
Semester 2	8.34	$t(15) = 4.43, p = .0002$	.75
Instructor C	7.37	$t(18) = 3.54, p = .001$	.64
Instructor D	3.13	$t(14) = 1.58, p = .069$	.40
No role-play[c]	-1.18	$t(18) = -.89, p = .39$[d]	-.20

[a]Mean change, Time 2 minus Time 1. [b]One-tailed p-values for role-play groups. [c]The utility ratings for one student were incomplete. [d]Two-tailed p-value.

Table 2. Changes in Cost Ratings

Class	Cost Change[a]	Correlated t Test[b]	r
Instructor A			
Semester 1	-8.98	$t(15) = 5.11, p = .0001$	.80
Semester 2	-6.91	$t(21) = 6.91, p = .00001$	.83
Instructor B			
Semester 1	-.22	$t(15) = .05, p = .50$	.01
Semester 2	-.85	$t(15) = .35, p = .40$	.09
Instructor C	-5.63	$t(18) = 3.08, p = .003$	.59
Instructor D	-8.67	$t(14) = 2.60, p = .011$	.57
No role-play	1.14	$t(19) = -.85, p = .41$[c]	-.19

[a]Mean change, Time 2 minus Time 1. [b]One-tailed p-values for role-play groups. [c]Two-tailed p-value.

of Instructor B's classes discussed approximately five more articles than did the other role-play classes. Perhaps Instructor B's students rated too many articles and were unable to concentrate on both the cost and utility issues for each study. Instructor B's students may have focused on the utility issue because it was a new concept introduced during the previous lecture. Anecdotal evidence seems to support this latter interpretation. In written evaluations of the exercise, Instructor B's students were more likely to suggest that they "needed more time for each study" and that there were "too many studies to consider."

This argument could be extended to explain at least the change in cost results for the nonrole-play class, because this class rated approximately the same number of articles as did Instructor B's classes. However, closer examination of Table 2 reveals that the mean cost ratings from Time 1 to Time 2 for the nonrole-play class appeared to increase, which is in the opposite direction of that of the role-play classes, including Instructor B's classes. Such a pattern suggests that this class may have been evaluating the articles differently than were the role-play classes.

Nevertheless, our results generally support the effectiveness of Rosnow's (1990) exercise in sensitizing students to the complexity of research ethics. However, instructors should be aware of the constraints that class size and time limitations may create when selecting articles for the exercise. The question that future researchers may want to address is whether the role-play has a lasting impact on students' treatment of ethical issues in research.

References

American Psychological Association. (1981). Ethical principles of psychologists (revised). *American Psychologist, 36,* 633–688.

Cohen, J. (1977). *Statistical power analysis for the behavioral sciences* (2nd ed.). New York: Academic.

Rosenthal, R. (1984). *Meta-analytic procedures for social research.* Beverly Hills: Sage.

Rosenthal, R., & Rosnow, R. L. (1991). *Essentials of behavioral research: Methods and data analysis* (2nd ed.). New York: McGraw-Hill.

Rosnow, R. L. (1990). Teaching research ethics through role-play and discussion. *Teaching of Psychology, 17,* 179–181.

Note

This research was supported by Temple University fellowships awarded to both authors. We thank Dixon Bramblett, Richard Shifman, and Donna Shires for assistance in data collection; our students for participating in this study; and Ralph L. Rosnow and the anonymous reviewers for their helpful comments on earlier drafts of this article.

Undergraduate Research and the Institutional Review Board: A Mismatch or Happy Marriage?

Carl A. Kallgren
Robert T. Tauber
Penn State Erie

Controls on research with humans have been instituted at most universities and colleges during the last 3 decades (Adair, Lindsay, & Carlopio, 1983; Grisso et al., 1991; Stanley, Sieber, & Melton, 1987). (See Grisso et al., for a history of ethical standards and review processes.) Proposed research with human subjects is submitted to an ethics review board, typically referred to as the Institutional Review Board (IRB). The IRB reviews the proposal for potential physiological, psychological, ethical, and legal violations of subject welfare and rights.

Despite this broad movement to protect the welfare of research subjects, including the establishment of IRBs, some undergraduate research with human subjects is not subjected to IRB scrutiny (E. Baldwin, Science Directorate,

American Psychological Association, personal communication, March 6, 1991). The purpose of this article is to elucidate arguments for ethics review of undergraduate research and to provide evidence for the educational consequences of IRB review of this research.

There appear to be two reasons for this surprising omission. First, much undergraduate research is conducted at small colleges that do not have IRBs. Only institutions that have federally funded research are legally required to have research with human subjects reviewed by an IRB (Office for Protection from Research Risks, 1983/1989), and many small colleges do not have federally funded research.[1] Second, some undergraduate research escapes IRB scrutiny based on the false premise that, because undergraduate research is primarily educationally motivated, IRB review is not required. Educators with whom we spoke indicated that they believe "it's just student research" and thus is not thought of as "real" research. Logically, educators may assume that student research would not need to be subjected to a "real" review.

Indeed, federal IRB guidelines exempt research that is conducted as a normal part of the educational process (Office for Protection from Research Risks, 1983/1989, Sec. 46.101). However, Section 46.101 only exempts research for which data can be collected as part of the normal, day-to-day educational process, such as anonymous course evaluations, course performance measures, or attendance records. Section 46.101 does not imply that a review is unnecessary if research is educationally motivated or a student is conducting the research. Such an assumption is untenable. Nonetheless, these assumptions appear to be the rationale invoked by some for not having undergraduate research reviewed by an IRB.

Because the number of psychology majors is increasing for the first time in more than 1 decade (McGovern, Furumoto, Halpern, Kimble, & McKeachie, 1991), and because research experience continues to be very important for graduate school admission in psychology (APA, 1992), the number of undergraduate psychology research projects will increase. Four basic arguments for having this undergraduate research reviewed by an IRB are as follows: to protect subject welfare, to protect instructors both ethically and legally, to enhance the public reputation of psychological research, and to enrich the educational experience of student researchers.

---

[1]A survey of the members of APA's Division Two (Teaching of Psychology) indicated that 29% of the responding schools did not have an IRB. Of these,

> 17% reported their department had no mechanism for ensuring ethical research, 52% indicated informal consultation was their mechanism, 21% had a formal written departmental research ethics policy, and 10% indicated "other" (e.g., their department was in the process of developing a written policy). (APA Division Two, 1993)

Subject Welfare

Subjects are at risk when student researchers are at the helm. Student researchers are less able to anticipate what may be an ethical problem; or, if a problem arises, they may not notice the problem. Furthermore, if they notice a problem, they may not respond as effectively or quickly as an experienced researcher.

Quality and Quantity of Supervision

Adequate supervision is less likely to be a problem when an undergraduate assists a faculty member or graduate student or when an undergraduate conducts an independent project under the close guidance of a faculty member.

Even a competent professional occasionally needs to adjust research procedures on the basis of recommendations from the IRB. Adjustment in research procedures is not surprising, given that investigators are not always knowledgeable about specific requirements designed to protect human subjects (Tymchuk & Thompson, 1986) and that psychologists hold diverse attitudes concerning ethical issues in research (Hamsher & Reznikoff, 1967; Kimmel, 1991).

Ethical and Legal Responsibilities

Another advantage of using the IRB for student research is that the instructor's ethical and legal responsibilities are much more likely to be shared by the university or college should the need arise. Without the use of the IRB, the instructor has greater ethical and legal exposure.

Ethical or legal problems are not always easily predicted. For example, while supervising undergraduates conducting research, Carl A. Kallgren (the first author) had reason to praise the IRB's review of undergraduate research and the ethical and legal security it provides. Two students were studying negative attitudes toward homosexuals by the elderly. They designed a study that was carefully refined and simplified while preparing their IRB proposal so as to minimize the chances of a problem occurring, given the potentially sensitive nature of the topic for the target population. Unfortunately, one man became convinced that the students and their instructor/supervisor were agents of Satan, and he erroneously thought the researchers had somehow determined that he was a homosexual and had communicated this to him and others in the nursing home through the debriefing letter sent to participants. He became extremely distraught—to the point that nursing home personnel were worried about his health. After many contacts with the nursing home by the undergraduates' supervisor, the undergraduate researchers themselves, and the IRB (including telephone conversations, letters, and a visit to the man), all signs indicated the issue had been resolved. Sadly, the nursing home informed us several months later that the man was moving to another nursing home because he believed his personal reputation at the home had been irrevocably ruined.

Public Reputation of Psychological Research

Ensuring that undergraduate research fully meets all ethical guidelines (APA, 1990; "Draft of APA Ethics Code," 1991) may contribute to a more positive attitude toward psychological research by many individuals. Undergraduate researchers may form a more positive attitude toward psychological research if they know from experience that research ethics are taken seriously. In turn, they may convey this attitude to others. In addition, if we assume that undergraduate researchers who have gone through the IRB process will be more thorough in their actions to protect subjects in their experiments, then subjects in their experiments may have a more positive impression of psychological research. The ranks of future policy makers, who will influence the fate of psychological research, will likely include individuals whose attitudes toward psychological research will be based on one or more of the aforementioned types of direct or indirect contact with undergraduate research.

Educational Implications

Although we were strongly committed to having undergraduate research reviewed by the IRB for all of the reasons already indicated, we were particularly concerned about the educational consequences of this decision. When we turned to the literature for guidance, we found none. Even an article on the teaching of ethics, which in other respects was comprehensive, omitted any discussion of using the IRB for undergraduate research as a natural vehicle for teaching ethics (Matthews, 1991).

Our initial reaction was that the IRB process would be an educational liability. Students could find the process intrusive, and it would slow them down. Moreover, we thought students may experience reactance (Brehm & Brehm, 1981) or overjustification (Deci, 1980) and become flippant, resentful, or blasé about ethical issues and research in general.

Upon further consideration, however, we thought there would be numerous educational benefits to the IRB process especially if the instructor approached the process in a positive light. The IRB may, in fact, draw students and instructor closer as they faced this hurdle together. Going through the process may educate and sensitize students to the ethical issues involved in conducting research with humans. We also thought our budding researchers may hold their research in higher esteem if a group of outside professionals passed judgment on it. On a more practical level, we thought using the IRB process would be educationally useful because it is a normal part of doing research. Thus, we thought we would be shirking our educational responsibility if we did not prepare our students for this essential ingredient of conducting research.

To assess undergraduates' perceptions of these and other issues concerning the educational impact of subjecting student research to the IRB process, we administered a questionnaire to students after they had handed in the final write-up of their own research in an advanced psychology course.

Method

Subjects

Juniors and seniors enrolled in a 400-level Advanced Research Methods in Psychology course, required of all BS and BA psychology majors, completed the survey. A large portion of this course consists of students conducting their empirical research individually or in small groups. Before taking this course, students are required to have taken Introductory Psychology, Introductory Statistics, and Beginning Research Methods in Psychology.

Voluntary participation was solicited from 55 students during three semesters (ns = 13, 25, and 17) taught by two instructors, one of whom was Carl A. Kallgren (the first author). One student declined to participate, one dropped the course for personal reasons, and one did not fill out the second page of the survey. Seven students had deferred grades in the course; all completed the course during the semester immediately following the one in which they had registered, and all completed the survey. Thus, data were obtained from 53 subjects for the first five questions, and from 52 subjects for the remaining six questions.

Procedure

Students submitted the official IRB forms at midsemester. After obtaining IRB approval, students collected and analyzed their data and wrote their final research reports. After submitting these final reports to the instructor, students filled out a two-page, anonymous questionnaire. Students were assured that the completed surveys would not be examined until course grades had been assigned.

Questionnaire

The questionnaire consisted of a brief introduction and 11 questions concerning the students' reactions to going through the IRB process. The half-page introduction to the survey stated that the psychology program was interested in students' reactions to the ethics review process. The introduction also noted that, "The points addressed in the

IRB review (e.g., rationale for conducting the study, informed consent, risk to subjects, etc.) would have to be addressed as part of doing original student research even if the IRB process were not required."

Responses to Questions 1 through 9 were indicated on a 9-point scale ranging from –4 (*very strongly negatively affected*) to 4 (*very strongly positively affected*), except as noted. The questions read:

1. Did the IRB process and the fact that others in the university would pass judgment on your work affect how seriously you approached your research?
2. Did the IRB write-up affect the quality of your research?
3. Did the IRB write-up affect the quality of your final write-up?
4. Did the IRB process affect how negatively or positively you saw feedback from your professor?
5. Did the IRB process affect how much you saw your professor as an ally in the research process?
6. Did the IRB process change how important you consider ethical issues, such as the potential risk of subject participation in research? (*extremely less important, extremely more important*)
7. Did the IRB process change the speed with which you finished your research? (*slowed down greatly, sped up greatly*)
8. Given that you will have to go through the IRB process or a similar process with future research you conduct (as a student and as a professional), how educational was going through the process?
9. Overall, how useful was going through the process? (*extremely useless, extremely useful*)
10. Identify two words that best describe how you felt when you first learned of the IRB requirement. (free response)
11. Identify two words that best describe how you felt when you received IRB approval. (free response)

Qualitative Response Rating

Qualitative responses to Questions 10 and 11 were combined into one alphabetized list and rated by two independent raters. Thus, raters were unaware of whether a word was an initial reaction or a later reaction. Raters were instructed to rate the words as positive, negative, or neutral, depending on the overall reaction the word conveyed. Words listed more than once were coded only once by each rater, and that rating was used for each instance of the word when final percentages were calculated. For the three instances in which students listed two words that clearly were intended to go together (*really mad, thank god,* and *oh dearie*), the two words were listed together for the raters. Overall, 112 unique words were rated, 26 of which were listed more than once, for a total of 88 words listed as initial reactions and 94 words listed as later reactions. Interrater agreement was 76.8% (86/112). For the 26 instances in which raters disagreed, 25 involved a neutral rating by one of the raters. Disagreements were resolved by discussion.

Results

Initial Reaction

The initial reaction by students to the requirement that undergraduate psychology majors must have student research projects using human subjects reviewed by the IRB was predictable—consternation and frustration. When asked to identify two words that best described how they felt when they first learned about the IRB requirement, students responded with such words as *intimidated, exasperated; surprised, aggravated;* and *scared, frustrated.* Indeed, 65.9% of the words were rated negatively, and only 10.2% were rated positively.

However, we thought students would see numerous educational advantages to the process once they had been through it. To test students' reactions to the IRB process, responses to the questions were analyzed with single sample two-tailed *t* tests with the population means assumed to be the midpoints of the scales (0). One-way analyses of variance (ANOVAs) were conducted to determine the consistency of responses across semesters for each question and are reported when differences were found.

Seriousness of Research

Writing a proposal for the IRB and having this external, professional board pass judgment on their work encouraged students to view their research seriously, $t(52) = 7.62, p < .001$ ($M = 1.56, SD = 1.51$). Our students, all of whom submitted their proposals to the IRB, not only took their proposal writing but also their entire research projects quite seriously. Apparently, going through the IRB process added to the students' perception that they had conducted real research.

Quality of Research and Writing

Students thought they improved the quality of their research, $t(52) = 5.90, p < .001$ ($M = 1.36, SD = 1.68$), and sharpened the writing in their final write-ups, $t(52) = 4.95, p < .001$ ($M = 1.04, SD = 1.52$), as a consequence of the IRB review process even though they knew the IRB would never see their final write-ups.

Perceptions of Instructor

Instructor feedback. The students, all of whom were required to have their research approved by the IRB, perceived instructor feedback constructively, $t(52) = 3.34,$

$p < .01$ ($M = .80$, $SD = 1.72$). Students may have viewed instructor feedback constructively because they perceived the instructor to be working with them toward the common goal of gaining IRB approval. When the instructor offered a criticism of a student's proposal that would require more work, the instructor may not have been perceived as requiring this primarily for the student to obtain a good grade in the course; instead, the instructor may have been seen as helping the student gain IRB approval. Thus, the student may have been more inclined to view instructor feedback as being helpful.

Instructor as ally. Students perceived the instructor as an ally, $t(52) = 5.03$, $p < .001$ ($M = 1.30$, $SD = 1.89$). In effect, students and instructors were drawn together by the common goal of submitting quality proposals that would be judged favorably by an impartial panel.

There was a difference across semesters in how much the instructor was seen as an ally, $F(2, 50) = 7.53$, $p = .0015$ ($Ms = 2.85$, $.95$, and $.59$ for semesters 1, 2, and 3, respectively). Post hoc comparisons indicated that semester 1 was significantly different from semester 2, as well as semester 3 (Tukey's Bs, $ps < .05$). Students in semester 1 may have viewed the instructor as a greater ally because they were aware that the IRB requirement was new for the course and wanted more support from the instructor.

Importance of Ethics

Consistent with our expectations, students reported a strong appreciation of the importance of ethical issues in conducting research, $t(51) = 7.45$, $p < .001$ ($M = 1.69$, $SD = 1.64$). We were initially concerned that students may experience reactance or overjustification because they were required to submit a proposal for external review, and they would become less concerned about ethical issues. Clearly, this was not the case; having student research proposals reviewed by an IRB was a powerful educational tool in the important domain of research ethics.

Length of Time to Do Research

The students' IRB forms must be sent to a different office where they are formally reviewed. Not surprising, students thought using the IRB process slowed them down in their research, $t(51) = 2.801$, $p < .01$ ($M = -1.00$, $SD = 2.57$).

Overall Evaluation

Overall, we thought it was useful to have students use the IRB review process. Students also thought the IRB review process was useful, $t(52) = 6.59$, $p < .001$ ($M = 1.71$, $SD = 1.87$). When asked how educational they thought the process was, given that they would have to go through a similar process for any future research they may conduct, students thought the process was very educational, $t(52) = 7.85$, $p < .001$ ($M = 2.85$, $SD = 1.23$).

Students had an unexpectedly strong positive reaction when their research was officially approved by the IRB. When asked to identify two words that best described how they felt when they received IRB approval, students responded with such words as *great, accomplished; relieved, excited;* and *happy, proud.* In stark contrast to the strongly negative reactions students reported when they first learned of the IRB requirement, 88.3% of the words used to describe their reaction upon IRB approval were rated positively, and only 3.2% were rated negatively (8.5% were rated as neutral).

Discussion

Our initial reasons for subjecting undergraduate research to the IRB process were not educational. Rather, we required the IRB process for student research because of concern for subject welfare, to protect instructors ethically and legally in these litigious times, and to enhance the reputation of psychological research. Indeed, initially we thought the process would be an educational liability because it would turn students away from research. Upon reflection, we thought it could be turned to educational advantage if approached in an appropriate fashion.

Our approach to the IRB process was simply to inform students that the IRB was a requirement with which all researchers had to work and the instructors would be the students' allies in navigating the IRB process. The instructors presented the IRB as an externally imposed hurdle for researchers, but IRB bashing and viewing the IRB as a common enemy were kept to a minimum.

To what extent adopting this posture influenced student researchers' views of the IRB and its educational implications is unclear. It is possible that using the IRB process without the aforementioned attitudinal proscription would have similar effects to those obtained in the present survey. Contrarily, not adopting the recommended approach to the IRB may have implications for students' views of the instructor as an ally as well as students' views of instructor feedback. If an instructor communicated an overall negative view of the IRB process (e.g., "The IRB process is unwarranted meddling in the internal affairs of science by society"), it is highly likely that students would be negatively influenced in terms of their views of research, ethics, and how the IRB process affected their educational experience.

The measures of the broad educational benefits of using the IRB process for undergraduate research were consistently positive. This consistency suggests that many important educational benefits of using the IRB process can reasonably be expected to generalize to other institutional settings when the IRB process is instituted. Specifically, students may be expected to learn more, produce a better product, treat their research more seriously, and, most important, be sensitized to ethical issues and be more careful to protect subject welfare.

Although our results concerning the broad educational benefits of using the IRB process for undergraduate research are highly consistent across three semesters, with two different instructors, the lack of a comparison group and the self-report nature of the measures temper the strength of the conclusions and their generality. However, several points should be considered in evaluating the obtained consistent effects of the IRB process on undergraduate education. First, we repeatedly stressed to all undergraduate researchers that they had complete anonymity in filling out the questionnaire. Second, the questions were very specific in content to induce students to reflect carefully on their research experience while they responded. Every question also included explicit reference to the review process. Third, the instructions for the questionnaire clearly stated that reactions to the effects of the IRB process were being solicited, and it was explicitly stated that the points addressed in the IRB review "would have to be addressed as part of doing original student research even if the IRB process were not required."

We recommend that undergraduate research be subjected to some sort of external ethics review based on the many benefits discussed in this article. At universities and colleges that already have IRBs or similar review panels, we recommend using them for undergraduate research. For the many smaller educational institutions that do not have an IRB or similar ethics review board, we recommend setting one up.

To obtain the educational benefits of such a procedure, a review board composed of three or more faculty should be adequate, as long as (a) the board and each proposal are treated seriously; (b) students submit complete proposals using a standardized format covering all important issues (e.g., rationale for the study, sample and procedure description, informed consent, debriefing, risk assessment, procedures for dealing with risk, and alternative procedures considered); and (c) students receive written notification of approval, request for modification or clarification, or disapproval. We suggest following federal guidelines for determining the appropriate level of review for each proposal (Office for Protection from Research Risks, 1983/1989).

In placing our research within a broader context, we are making what we hope is a valid assumption that, on average, research approved by an IRB will better protect the welfare of subjects than research not approved by an IRB. If this is not the case, the entire review process must be reevaluated. As Kimmel (1991) noted, empirical evidence suggests that IRBs and their individual members vary in their judgments of what is ethical as well as the reasons for their decisions (Ceci, Peters, & Plotkin, 1985; Eaton, 1983;

Goldman & Katz, 1982). Others have provided evidence of potential biases introduced by ethical constraints on subject recruitment (Wicker, 1968), subject retention (e.g., Trice & Ogden, 1987), the use of deception (Christensen, 1988), and informed consent referring to risk and deception (Finney, 1987). More research is needed to evaluate the reliability and validity of IRB decisions and the impact of these decisions and other ethical constraints on cumulative knowledge garnered from empirical research.

Despite these important concerns, in general we see the IRB process and undergraduate research as a happy marriage; we strongly recommend using it. The marriage may not always be harmonious, but it can enhance the educational experience of undergraduate researchers.

References

Adair, J. G., Lindsay, R. C. L., & Carlopio, J. (1983). Social artifact research and ethical regulations: Their impact on the teaching of experimental methods. *Teaching of Psychology, 10,* 159–162.

American Psychological Association. (1990). Ethical principles of psychologists (amended June 2, 1989). *American Psychologist, 45,* 390–395.

American Psychological Association. (1992). *Graduate study in psychology and associated fields.* Washington, DC: Author.

American Psychological Association Division Two. (1993). *Committee on Ethics in Teaching and Academic Life, Annual Report 1992–1993.* Unpublished manuscript.

Brehm, S., & Brehm, J. W. (1981). *Psychological reactance: A theory of freedom and control.* New York: Academic.

Ceci, S. J., Peters, D., & Plotkin, J. (1985). Human subjects review, personal values, and the regulation of social science research. *American Psychologist, 40,* 994–1002.

Christensen, L. (1988). Deception in psychological research: When is its use justified? *Personality and Social Psychology Bulletin, 14,* 664–675.

Deci, E. L. (1980). *The psychology of self-determination.* Lexington, MA: Lexington Books.

Draft of APA ethics code published. (1991, June). *APA Monitor,* 30–35.

Eaton, W. O. (1983). The reliability of ethical reviews: Some initial empirical findings. *Canadian Psychologist, 24,* 14–18.

Finney, P. D. (1987). When consent information refers to risk and deception: Implications for social research. *Journal of Social Behavior and Personality, 2,* 37–48.

Goldman, J., & Katz, M. D. (1982). Inconsistency and institutional review boards. *Journal of the American Medical Association, 248,* 197–202.

Grisso, T., Baldwin, E., Blanck, P. D., Rotheram-Borus, M. J., Schooler, N. R., & Thompson, T. (1991). Standards in research: APA's mechanism for monitoring the challenges. *American Psychologist, 46,* 758–766.

Hamsher, J. H., & Reznikoff, M. (1967). Ethical standards in psychological research and graduate training: A study of attitudes within the profession. *Proceedings of the 75th Annual Convention of the American Psychological Association, 2,* 203–204.

Kimmel, A. J. (1991). Predictable biases in the ethical decision making of American psychologists. *American Psychologist, 46,* 786–788.

Matthews, J. R. (1991). The teaching of ethnics and the ethics of teaching. *Teaching of Psychology, 18,* 80–85.

McGovern, T. V., Furumoto, L., Halpern, D. F., Kimble, G. A., & McKeachie, W. J. (1991). Liberal education, study in depth, and the arts and sciences major—Psychology. *American Psychologist, 46,* 598–605.

Office for Protection from Research Risks. (1989). *OPRR reports: Protection of human subjects. Code of federal regulations, public welfare (Title 45), protection of human subjects (Part 46).* Washington, DC: U.S. National Institutes of Health. (Original work published 1983)

Stanley, B., Sieber, J. E., & Melton, G. B. (1987). Empirical studies of ethical issues in research: A research agenda. *American Psychologist, 42,* 735–741.

Trice, A. D., & Ogden, E. P. (1987). Informed consent: IX. Effects of the withdrawal clause in longitudinal research. *Perceptual and Motor Skills, 65,* 135–138.

Tymchuk, A. J., & Thompson, J. H. (1986). Academic senate members' knowledge of federal requirements for the protection of human subjects in research. *Psychological Reports, 59,* 323–328.

Wicker, A. W. (1968). Requirements for protecting privacy of human subjects: Some implications for generalization of research findings. *American Psychologist, 23,* 70–72.

Notes

1. A preliminary report based on the results of data for semester 1 was presented at the Twelfth Annual National Institute on the Teaching of Psychology, St. Petersburg Beach, FL, January 1989. A more extensive report of this research was presented at the Third Annual Convention of the American Psychological Society, Washington, DC, June 1991.

2. We acknowledge with gratitude the comments of Wendy Gouldthorpe Eidenmuller, Michael A. Ichiyama, Marilyn Livosky, and the anonymous reviewers. We also thank Carolyn I. Spies and Rod L. Troester for their expert assistance in rating the open-ended responses.

Discussing Animal Rights and Animal Research in the Classroom

Harold A. Herzog
Western Carolina University

Since Singer's influential book *Animal Liberation* was published in 1975, public concern over the ethical treatment of animals has increased dramatically. Animal rights groups have criticized a variety of human uses of animals, including sport hunting, rodeos, intensive agricultural practices, consumption of animal flesh, and the wearing of furs. The use of animals in behavioral and biomedical research, however, has become the primary focus of public attention in recent years. Experimental psychology has been singled out as particularly offensive by animal rights activists who consider much behavioral research frivolous and cruel. For example, Rollin (1981) called experimental psychology, "the field most consistently guilty of mindless activity that results in great suffering" (p. 124).

Although psychologists have responded to such criticisms (e.g., Feeney, 1987; N. E. Miller, 1985), the animal rights movement has had a significant effect on animal research. In addition, teachers of psychology courses are being confronted with students who question the ethics and validity of behavioral research using animals (Gallup & Beckstead, 1988). There are three reasons why discussion of animal rights is relevant to students taking psychology

148

courses. First, students should be aware of political and social issues related to psychology that affect their lives. In this context, the animal rights controversy joins other social issues, such as the effects of day care, television violence, and pornography, as topics relevant to psychology courses. Second, the animal rights issue raises questions that are basic to psychological inquiry: What are the essential differences between humans and other animals? Can animals think? What psychological factors influence judgments about what constitutes moral behavior? Finally, the use of animals in laboratory courses has come under special criticism (e.g., Regan, 1983). Many animal liberationists believe that the routine dissection of animals in biology laboratories and the equivalent use of animals in psychology courses (e.g., physiological psychology students learning stereotaxic surgery on rats) are particularly onerous practices.

Although the animal rights movement affects research and teaching, few psychologists are informed about its intellectual underpinnings. Animal activists are often dismissed as intellectual lightweights whose arguments are based on emotional responses to pictures of kittens with electrodes in their skulls. Although this stereotype is accurate in some cases, there are also some first-rate philosophers behind the movement whose arguments are quite rigorous. This article briefly reviews two major philosophical positions used by animal activists in their arguments against the scientific use of animals and then describes a classroom exercise that stimulates discussion about this debate.

Philosophical Positions

The animal defense movement is divided into two groups. *Reformers* admit the necessity of using animals in biomedical research but want to eliminate as much suffering as possible. The more radical faction, *animal liberators,* view animal research as immoral in almost all cases and want to abolish it. It is not the purpose of this article to review all of the philosophical positions on animal rights. Interested readers should consult sources such as H. B. Miller and Williams (1983) for representative statements. Rather, I briefly summarize two of the most influential perspectives used by animal rights activists in their argument against using animals in research.

The Utilitarian Argument

The utilitarian argument is most clearly presented by the Australian philosopher, Peter Singer. In *Animal Liberation,* Singer (1975) effectively invoked emotional appeal and a consistent ethical philosophy to argue the case for abolishing animal research. The *principle of equality* (or *equal consideration of interests*) is the crux of Singer's argument. It holds that all sentient creatures (he draws the "line" at the phylogenetic level of oysters) have the same stake in their own existence ("interests"). Singer argued that this principle leads to the conclusion that there is no basis for elevating the interests of one species, *Homo sapiens,* above any other. Differences in intelligence, race, and gender are not valid criteria to exploit other humans; to Singer, a creature's species is equally irrelevant. He claimed that "From an ethical point of view, we all stand on an equal footing—whether we stand on two feet, or four, or none at all" (Singer, 1985, p. 6). The only relevant moral criterion for discrimination for or against a species is the capacity to suffer. Singer argued that, by definition, all sentient animals have the capacity to suffer and, therefore, are the subject of equal moral consideration. He claimed that to elevate the human species above all others on the basis of criteria other than suffering is arbitrary and a form of *speciesism.* Singer defined this term as "a prejudice or attitude of bias toward the interest of members of one's own species and against those of members of another species" (p. 7). He believed that speciesism is as illogical and morally repugnant as racism or sexism. Note that Singer would permit research with animals in some circumstances, but only if it is so important that we would also consider conducting the experiments using human subjects.

The Rights Argument

The rights argument is forcefully argued by Regan (1983, 1985) and Rollin (1981). Rights positions typically take the form that at least some creatures have certain fundamental rights (e.g., the right to moral consideration and the right not to be harmed). The question then becomes, Who is entitled to hold rights? Many philosophers restrict rights holders to beings that meet certain criteria, such as language, self-consciousness, or the ability to enter into reciprocal contractual obligations that they believe would eliminate nonhuman animals. There are several problems, however, that confront such philosophical positions. One problem concerns the moral status of humans who do not meet the criteria (i.e., the severely retarded, infants, and the insane). A second problem is how to deal with animals that appear to meet some of the criteria (e.g., members of large-brained species such as some primates, cetaceans, etc.)?

Animal rights theorists broaden the criteria so that animals are included as rights holders. To Regan (1983, 1985), the fundamental criterion for having rights is "inherent value." He argued that sentient creatures, including humans, have inherent value in equal measure and thus are entitled to certain fundamental rights, including the right to be treated with respect and the right not to be harmed. For Regan, there are a number of reasons for abolishing research with animals, even research that will directly benefit humans. First and foremost, science treats animals as renewable resources rather than as "subjects of a life"—creatures with inherent value—thus violating what he called the "respect principle." In addition, he argued for the "worst off principle"—that the rights view does not permit the sacrifice of an innocent few even though such sacrifice may benefit many more individuals. For Regan, there is no justification for any animal research; the fact that the experiments could benefit hundreds of thousands of human lives is morally irrelevant.

Comparisons and Comments

There are clear differences between advocates of the utilitarian and rights positions as to why animal research is immoral. Singer suggested that there are philosophical problems with arguments based on the proposition that animals have rights, and Regan insisted that the utilitarian position is fatally flawed. There are, however, commonalties in the two positions. The most important is that Regan and Singer ended at about the same place, even though they took quite different paths. The logical extension of both arguments leads to vegetarianism, and both would eliminate research with animals as it is now conducted. In addition, the two positions are based on the notion that fundamental similarities between humans and other species are ethically significant (i.e., all sentient creatures have "interests") but that differences between humans and other species (i.e., language and greater intelligence) are morally irrelevant. Finally, both positions view speciesism as deplorable and the animal liberation movement as the logical extension of other social movements, such as civil rights and women's movements.

It is not my purpose to critique these views. The interested reader will want to consult sources such as Fox (1985), Frey (1980, 1983), and Narveson (1983) for critiques of the animal liberation philosophers. It is safe to say that most Americans would disagree with one of the basic tenets of activists, that human life per se is not more important than that of other species. If it were possible to transplant an organ from a healthy sheep into a dying infant, most of us would readily approve of the operation; Singer and Regan would not.

Though one may disagree with their thinking, philosophers, such as Regan and Singer, have raised some troubling issues that can be addressed in psychology courses. The following exercise was designed to facilitate discussion of the ethics of animal research in the classroom.

Discussing the Animal Research Controversy

The exercise described here is designed to facilitate thinking on these issues by having students make decisions about whether a series of hypothetical research and educational projects should be conducted. It is appropriate in a wide variety of courses, including general psychology, experimental psychology, animal behavior, and physi-

ological psychology. It would also be useful in biology and bioethics courses.

Method

Institutions receiving federal funds for scientific research must have a standing Animal Care and Use Committee (ACUC) to review and approve all animal research conducted at the institution. In the exercise, students role-play participation on an ACUC. I divide the class into groups of between five and seven students. If class time permits, each group must make a decision on each of four research proposals. Otherwise, each group can discuss and make a decision about one of the proposals and present their decision and rationale to the class. The proposals are based on actual experiments or situations, and they are designed to exemplify different factors related to making ethical decisions. I remind students that the purpose of the exercise is to generate discussion and critical thinking. Thus, groups should be encouraged to reach a consensus rather than simply take a straw poll on each proposal.

Instructions to Students

Your group is the Animal Care Committee for your university. It is the committee's responsibility to evaluate and either approve or reject research proposals submitted by faculty members who want to use animals for research or instructional purposes in psychology, biology, or medicine. The proposals describe the experiments, including the goals and potential benefits of the research as well as any discomfort or injury that they may cause the animal subjects. You must either approve the research or deny permission for the experiments. It is not your job to suggest improvements on technical aspects of the projects, such as the experimental design. You should make your decision based on the information given in the proposal.

Proposals

Case 1. Professor King is a psychobiologist working on the frontiers of a new and exciting research area of neuroscience, brain grafting. Research has shown that neural tissue can be removed from the brains of monkey fetuses and implanted into the brains of monkeys that have suffered brain damage. The neurons seem to make the proper connections and are sometimes effective in improving performance in brain-damaged animals. These experiments offer important animal models for human degenerative diseases such as Parkinson's and Alzheimer's. Dr. King wants to transplant tissue from fetal monkey brains into the entorhinal cortex of adult monkeys; this is the area of the human brain that is involved with Alzheimer's disease.

The experiment will use 20 adult rhesus monkeys. First, the monkeys will be subjected to ablation surgery in the entorhinal cortex. This procedure will involve anesthetizing the animals, opening their skulls, and making lesions using a surgical instrument. After they recover, the monkeys will be tested on a learning task to make sure their memory is impaired. Three months later, half of the animals will be given transplant surgery. Tissue taken from the cortex of monkey fetuses will be implanted into the area of the brain damage. Control animals will be subjected to sham surgery, and all animals will be allowed to recover for 2 months. They will then learn a task to test the hypothesis that the animals having brain grafts will show better memory than the control group.

Dr. King argues that this research is in the exploratory stages and can only be done using animals. She further states that by the year 2000 about 2 million Americans will have Alzheimer's disease and that her research could lead to a treatment for the devastating memory loss that Alzheimer's victims suffer.

Case 2. Dr. Fine is a developmental psychobiologist. His research concerns the genetic control of complex behaviors. One of the major debates in his field concerns how behavior develops when an animal has no opportunity to learn a response. He hypothesizes that the complex grooming sequence of mice might be a behavior pattern that is built into the brain at birth, even though it is not expressed until weeks later. To investigate whether the motor patterns involved in grooming are acquired or innate, he wants to raise animals with no opportunity to learn the response. Rearing animals in social isolation is insufficient because the mice could teach themselves the response. Certain random movements could accidentally result in the removal of debris. These would then be repeated and could be coordinated into the complex sequence that would appear to be instinctive but would actually be learned. To show that the behaviors are truly innate, he needs to demonstrate that animals raised with no opportunity to perform any grooming-like movements make the proper movements when they are old enough to exhibit the behavior.

Dr. Fine proposes to conduct the experiment on 10 newborn mice. As soon at the animals are born, they will be anesthestized and their front limbs amputated. This procedure will ensure that they will not be reinforced for making random grooming movements that remove debris from their bodies. The mice will then be returned to their mothers. The animals will be observed on a regular schedule using standard observation techniques. Limb movements will be filmed and analyzed. If grooming is a learned behavior, then the mice should not make grooming movements with their stumps as the movements will not remove dirt. If, however, grooming movements are innately organized in the brain, then the animals should eventually show grooming-like movement with the stumps.

In his proposal, Dr. Fine notes that experimental results cannot be directly applied to human behavior. He argues, however, that the experiment will shed light on an important theoretical debate in the field of developmental psychobiology. He also stresses that the amputations are painless and the animals will be well treated after the operation.

Case 3. Your university includes a college of veterinary medicine. In the past, the veterinary students have practiced surgical techniques on dogs procured from a local animal shelter. However, there have been some objections to this practice, and the veterinary school wants the approval of your committee to continue this practice. They make the following points.

1. Almost all of these animals will eventually be killed at the animal shelter. It is wasteful of life to breed animals for the vet school when there is an ample supply of animals that are going to be killed anyway, either because their owners do not want them or they are homeless.
2. It costs at least 10 times as much to raise purebred animals for research purposes; this money could be better used to fund research that would benefit many animals.
3. Research with dogs from animal shelters and the practice surgeries will, in the long run, aid the lives of animals by training veterinarians and producing treatments for diseases that afflict animals.

A local group of animal welfare activists has urged your committee to deny the veterinary school's request. They argue that the majority of these animals are lost or stolen pets, and it is tragic to think that the dog you have grown to love will wind up on a surgical table or in an experiment. Furthermore, they claim that as people become aware that animals taken to shelters may end up in research laboratories, they will stop using the shelters. Finally, the activists point out that in countries such as England, veterinary students do not perform practice surgery; they learn surgical techniques in an extensive apprenticeship.

Case 4. The Psychology Department is requesting permission from your committee to use 10 rats per semester for demonstration experiments in a physiological psychology course. The students will work in groups of three; each group will be given a rat. The students will first perform surgery on the rats. Each animal will be anethestized. Following standard surgical procedures, an incision will be made in the scalp and two holes drilled in the animal's skull. Electrodes will be lowered into the brain to create lesions on each side. The animals will then be allowed to recover. Several weeks later, the effects of destroying this part of the animal's brain will be tested in a shuttle avoidance task in which the animals will learn when to cross over an electrified grid.

151

The instructor acknowledges that the procedure is a common demonstration and that no new scientific information will be gained from the experiment. He argues, however, that students taking a course in physiological psychology must have the opportunity to engage in small animal surgery and to see firsthand the effects of brain lesions.

Notes to the Instructor

Case 1 forces consideration of whether injury to another species, which is fairly closely related to humans, is justified if the results will be applicable to human beings. Case 2 asks students to think about the use of animals in pure research in which there is no direct connection to future human application. Based on a study of Fentress (1973), this case offers an excellent opportunity for the instructor to discuss the importance of pure research in the progress of science. Incidentally, in the Fentress experiment, amputated mice exhibited "remarkably normal" grooming movements with their stumps, demonstrating that the movements were innate. Case 3 involves the use of pound animals in research and is one of the more controversial issues in biomedical and veterinary research. Several state legislatures have passed laws banning the use of pound-seizure animals for biomedical research or student surgeries in veterinary schools. (See Giannelli, 1988, for a discussion of this issue from an activist viewpoint.) The use of animals in student laboratories (Case 4) has been singled out by animal welfare groups as being particularly unnecessary. They argue that videotapes and computer simulations are adequate substitutes for live animals in classroom behavioral studies and dissections.

Numerous modifications can be made with these scenarios to tailor them to the needs of particular topics or courses. For example, Case 1 could be changed so that some groups are given the case using monkeys as subjects and some are given the same case using rats. This would lead to a discussion of factors that come into play in making ethical decisions (e.g., why might it be acceptable to use rodents in the study but not primates?). Other cases could be added for different courses. Thus, a proposal in which an ethologist wants to confront mice with snakes to study antipredator behavior (Herzog, 1988) could be included for a course in animal behavior.

Student Responses

I have used this exercise with 150 students in five classes. After the exercise, each student was asked to write an anonymous evaluation of the exercise and indicate whether it should be used in the future. The responses were extremely positive; except for two of the students, the remainder recommended that I continue using the exercise.

The following statements were typical: "I feel that this was a valuable experience as part of my psychology class, and it was beneficial in developing my thoughts on this topic. I had never really considered such issues," and "I believe this exercise was valuable to the students in the class because it made us think about which is more important—an animal's life or a human life."

Discussion

The Christian writer C. S. Lewis (1988) stated, "It is the rarest thing in the world to hear a rational discussion of vivisection" (p. 160). These exercises are designed to elevate discussion of one of the most controversial topics in science to a rational forum. However, attitudes about the appropriate use of animals in research are not only a function of logic. Judgments about animals are influenced by many factors, such as their physiognomic similarity to humans, their "cuteness" and perceived intelligence, and the labels we assign them (Burghardt & Herzog, 1980; Herzog, 1988). In addition to raising sensitivity about an important ethical issue, these exercises promote discussions of how moral judgments are made.

The animal rights movement will continue to grow in numbers and visibility. The goal of many animal rights activists is the abolition of animal research. As Regan (1988) proclaimed, "It is not bigger cages we want, but empty cages. Anything less than total victory will not satisfy us!" (p. 12). Psychologists must be prepared to confront this challenge in their roles as scientists and teachers. Inevitably, there will be disagreements within the profession. Some will side with the animal rights faction and become active in organizations like Psychologists for the Ethical Treatment of Animals; others will support the rights of researchers to use animal subjects. Increasingly, psychology teachers will be confronted by activist students who demand justification for research practices they find disagreeable. (I can also envision pressures on authors and publishers of introductory psychology textbooks to reduce or eliminate coverage of controversial experiments, such as Harlow's studies of social deprivation in monkeys and Seligman's learned helplessness research.) The issue of animal rights is philosophically and psychologically complex. It is mired in a milieu of rationality, emotion, convention, ethical intuition, and self-interest. We owe it to ourselves and our students to become familiar with both sides of this issue so that more light than heat will emerge from the debate.

References

Burghardt, G. M., & Herzog, H. A., Jr. (1980). Beyond conspecifics: Is "Brer Rabbit" our brother? *BioScience, 30,* 763–767.

Feeney, D. M. (1987). Human rights and animal welfare. *American Psychologist, 42,* 593–599.

Fentress, J. C. (1973). Development of grooming in mice with amputated forelimbs. *Science, 179,* 704–705.

Fox, M. A. (1985). *The case for animal experimentation.* Berkeley: University of California.

Frey, R. (1980). *Interests and rights: The case against animal rights.* Oxford, England: Clarendon.

Frey, R. (1983). On why we would do better to jettison moral rights. In H. B. Miller & W. H. Williams (Eds.), *Ethics and animals* (pp. 285–301). Clifton, NJ: Humana.

Gallup, G. G., Jr., & Beckstead, J. W. (1988). Attitudes toward animal research. *American Psychologist, 44,* 474–475.

Giannelli, M. A. (1988, Fall). Shelter animals as research models: Scientific anachronism, social ignominy. *PsyETA Bulletin,* pp. 6–12.

Herzog, H. A., Jr. (1988). The moral status of mice. *American Psychologist, 43,* 473–474.

Lewis, C. S. (1988). A case for abolition. In A. Linzey & T. Regan (Eds.), *Animals and Christianity: A book of readings* (pp. 160–164). New York: Crossroad. (Original work published 1947)

Miller, H. B., & Williams, W. H. (Eds.). (1983). *Ethics and animals.* Clifton, NJ: Humana.

Miller, N. E. (1985). The value of behavioral research on animals. *American Psychologist, 40,* 423–440.

Narveson, J. (1983). Animal rights revisited. In H. B. Miller & W. H. Williams (Eds.), *Ethics and animals* (pp. 45–59). Clifton, NJ: Humana.

Regan, T. (1983). *The case for animal rights.* Berkeley: University of California.

Regan, T. (1985). The case for animal rights. In P. Singer (Ed.), *In defense of animals* (pp. 13–26). Oxford, England: Basil Blackwell.

Regan, T. (1988, September/October). The torch of reason, the sword of justice. *The Animal's Voice Magazine,* pp. 12–17.

Rollin, B. E. (1981). *Animal rights and human morality.* New York: Prometheus.

Singer, P. (1975). *Animal liberation.* New York: Avon.

Singer, P. (1985). Prologue: Ethics and the new animal liberation movement. In P. Singer (Ed.), *In defense of animals* (pp. 1–10). Oxford, England: Basil Blackwell.

Note

My thanks to Mary Jean Herzog, Sandra Skinner, Glen Erikson, Gordon Burghardt, and Lisa Finley for helpful comments on a draft of this article and my treatment of the animal rights movement and to my students at Western Carolina University and Warren Wilson College for discussing and evaluating the exercises.

4. Reviewing the Literature

Students majoring in psychology need the skills to locate and use scholarly literature. After learning that the American Psychological Association had no guidelines for instruction in literature and information retrieval, Joyce Merriam, Ross LaBaugh, and Nancy Butterfield, professional librarians and members of the Standards Task Force of the New England Bibliographic Instruction Committee, developed guidelines for library instruction in psychology. Their recommendations are useful for psychology programs wishing to improve library instruction.

Lynn Cameron (librarian) and James Hart (psychologist) at James Madison University measured student competence in using PsycLIT, related student attitudes toward PsycLIT to level of skill, and examined student preferences for various methods of PsycLIT instruction. Data were from The Library Skills Test for Psychology Majors. Almost 90% of the 145 seniors who took the test reported that they had used PsycLIT, and 83% made competent or exceptionally competent scores. Students rated a workshop taught by a librarian as the most useful of six instructional methods.

Higher levels of PsycLIT performance were related to attitudes of lower anxiety and greater confidence about using PsycLIT.

Because users often do not fully understand indexing techniques and system protocols, retrieval results via PsycLIT can be inconsistent. Kathleen Joswich, a librarian at Western Illinois University, suggests useful ways to make PsycLIT searches more effective and efficient for students and faculty members.

Retta Poe devised a series of presentations and exercises to help students improve their literature review papers in an abnormal psychology course at Western Kentucky University. The sequential writing assignments included focused free writing, summarizing an essay, summarizing a journal article—Part 1, summarizing a journal article—Part 2, integrating findings from two studies, and preparing a reference list in the proper style and format. Although time-consuming, this approach was evaluated favorably by students and teachers.

Library Instruction for Psychology Majors: Minimum Training Guidelines

Joyce Merriam
University Library
University of Massachusetts, Amherst

Ross T. LaBaugh
Library
Southeastern Massachusetts University

Nancy E. Butterfield
Mason Library
Keene State College

In 1988, the Standards Task Force of the New England Bibliographic Instruction Committee identified and collected guidelines for instruction in literature and information retrieval published by professional associations. The American Chemical Society (ACS, 1983) guidelines for instruction in chemical information retrieval for chemistry majors sparked our interest. The ACS guidelines recognize that the literature in the field is increasing in complexity and volume and state that "students can no longer acquire skills in information retrieval without *some formal instruction*" [italics added] (ACS, 1983, p. 13). An appendix to the ACS guidelines contains specific recommendations concerning course content, identifies levels of ability desired, and suggests ways to develop library skills.

The Standards Task Force wrote to several major professional associations to inquire about the existence of similar guidelines for other fields and received responses from 14. Most, including the APA, reported that they were unaware of any formal guidelines published by their associations.

The Standards Task Force accepted the results of this survey as a challenge to develop its own guidelines for library instruction in specific disciplines, beginning with psychology. We wanted to share the guidelines with others interested in developing higher levels of competence in library use among undergraduate and graduate students.

Concerns and Objectives

We conducted a literature review to identify issues concerning library instruction in psychology. This review identified several issues that underscored a need for guidelines. First, psychology faculty have been vague regarding students' specific knowledge about using libraries and sources of psychological literature (Thaxton, 1985). Second, although faculty expected students to be able to use the library well, they did not agree on which skills are important for students (Olivetti, 1979). Third, because of the information explosion, we must prepare students to be self-educating by teaching them how to locate, evaluate, and use information from diverse sources (Makosky, 1990).

Previous reports described methodologies used by individual librarians and teaching faculty to introduce students to the literature search (Gardner, 1977; Schilling, 1983). Mathews (1978) and Parr (1978) described techniques for familiarizing students with basic, relevant resources and their location in the library. Parr (1988) and Feinberg, Drews, and Eynman (1981) presented evidence that training undergraduates in online information retrieval can reinforce traditional bibliographical skills and improve attitudes toward the library and the literature search process. Baxter (1986) emphasized the need for teaching faculty and librarians to engage in more cooperative strategies for alleviating problems students have in developing information-seeking skills.

Recommended Action

The guidelines prepared by the Standards Task Force contain an organized listing that responds to training objectives and concerns mentioned earlier. We believe that minimum training guidelines will give needed impetus to the development of meaningful library instruction programs on college campuses, especially when backed by professional associations. The Standards Task Force encourages *Teaching of Psychology* (*ToP*) readers to respond to these guidelines.

Our guidelines do not reflect the official position of the APA. However, the Standards Task Force intends to continue pursuing contacts within the APA, hoping to obtain official endorsement of a set of guidelines. We also think that faculty and curriculum committees on individual campuses will find the guidelines helpful in developing strategies for library instruction.

Minimum Training Guidelines

Students majoring in psychology should acquire the basic, practical skills needed to locate and use the literature of the field effectively and confidently. To acquire that competence, coursework should include instruction and guided practice in: (a) locating known sources, (b) conducting a literature search, (c) making effective use of resources once they are found, and (d) developing an increased awareness of information resources in psychology and related disciplines. A long-term goal of such instruction should be to prepare students to use library/information resources independently (i.e., to meet personal needs for locating and using information throughout life).

Basic Skills

1. To locate known sources, students should be able to:
   a. Ascertain whether known books, journals, or audiovisual materials are available in the home library, the format in which they are available (print, fiche, or film), and where they are located (e.g., be able to work from a reference list to retrieve sources).
   b. Follow procedures for obtaining materials not available in the home library (e.g., through interlibrary loan or other arrangements).
2. To conduct a literature search, students should be able to:
   a. Define their research topic. Understand the broader and narrower aspects of the topic and focus on a specific issue.
   b. Determine whether the problem has been addressed previously, by whom, and what the results were. Identify books and articles on the topic using appropriate catalogs and indexes (e.g., *Psychological Abstracts,* other relevant indexes and abstracting services, and the card or online catalog).
   c. Understand the use of controlled vocabulary. Know how to find the terms indexers use to describe the topic (e.g., by using the *Thesaurus of Psychological Index Terms* and the *Library of Congress List of Subject Headings*).
   d. Use abstracts as an aid to identify pertinent articles.

e. Understand the purposes served by using a classification system to label and shelve materials about particular aspects of topics (e.g., the Library of Congress system). Recognize advantages and disadvantages of using the system to facilitate browsing as a search method.

f. Use bibliographical references to expand a search.

g. Understand the concept of citation indexing. (When there is access to *Social Sciences Citation Index* and *Science Citation Index,* students should use them.)

h. Understand the basic concepts of computerized literature searching, know about its availability on campus, and understand its value and appropriate use. Know about the availability of data bases relevant to psychology (e.g., when there is access to *Psychological Abstracts* online [PsycINFO] or on CD-ROM [PsycLIT], students should see a demonstration of its use).

i. Identify ways of keeping current on a subject.

j. Interact effectively with reference librarians and instructors to learn about other ways to retrieve specific kinds of information.

3. To make effective use of resources once they are found, students should be able to:

a. Identify ways of evaluating materials (e.g., be able to locate reviews of books, tests, etc.; consider date of publication, possible biases of the author, etc.).

b. Distinguish between scholarly and popular treatment of topics in the literature (e.g., recognize the publication's intended audience and purpose).

c. Write and cite in the format and style of the *Publication Manual of the American Psychological Association* (3rd ed.), the approved style manual for publication/writing in psychology.

d. Demonstrate ethical behavior in using library resources (e.g., respect library policies and property, document use of all sources, etc.).

4. To develop an increased awareness of information resources in psychology and related disciplines, students should be able to:

a. Use indexes and abstracting services relevant to the student's area of concentration (e.g., indexes to management literature relevant to industrial/organizational psychology, to educational literature relevant to educational psychology, etc.).

b. Use other types of standard reference materials (e.g., specialized field-related bibliographies; encyclopedias, handbooks, and dictionaries; statistical compilations; directories of names, addresses, and biographical information; indexes to book reviews; guides to tests and measures; indexes to government information, etc.). In addition, students should:

c. Be aware of state-of-the-art developments in electronic information storage, retrieval, and document delivery, and their implications for the field (e.g., speedier access to some types of information).

d. Be aware of the role of professional associations in providing services relating to literature and information retrieval (e.g., conferences, publications, and computerized services).

Implementation of Library Instruction

1. Instruction can be achieved in the following ways:

a. Through integration in psychology courses when assignments require library work.

b. Through some formal instruction in information retrieval skills. Instruction programs may take a variety of forms—printed, computer-assisted, or audiovisual guides and course-related sessions ranging from 1-hr presentations to meet objectives of a particular assignment—to more thorough treatment of topics and skills in a full-semester course in research methods.

c. Through student interaction with reference librarians on an individual basis for work on special needs.

d. Through student use of appropriate handbooks that expand on information typically presented in library skills sessions (e.g., *Library Use: A Handbook for Psychology;* Reed & Baxter, 1983). (A revised version of this handbook is expected late in 1991.)

2. Faculty communication with library staff is critical:

a. Advance planning and communication with appropriate library staff is essential to ensure availability of needed material and appropriate controls over its use (e.g., communication with collection development, reserve, reference and/or library instruction staff may be necessary, depending on the nature and quantity of materials needed and faculty expectations about how the materials will be used).

b. Objectives of library-related assignments should be made clear to students and to the reference staff who will be on duty to help students learn to make effective use of the library and its resources (e.g., faculty should send a written copy of the assignment and its objectives to the reference staff if students may not know how to find all of the information they need).

c. Faculty interested in arranging for course-related library instruction for their classes should make arrangements for this service with the librarian who coordinates the library instruction program in the home library, with sufficient lead time for necessary preparation and planning.

References

American Chemical Society, Committee on Professional Training. (1983). *Undergraduate professional education in chemistry: Guidelines and evaluation procedures,* with *chemical information retrieval appendix.* Washington, DC: American Chemical Society.

Baxter, P. M. (1986). The benefits of in-class bibliographic instruction. *Teaching of Psychology, 13,* 40–41.

Feinberg, R. A., Drews, D., & Eynman, D. (1981). Positive side effects of online information retrieval. *Teaching of Psychology, 8,* 51–52.

Gardner, L. E. (1977). A relatively painless method of introduction to the psychological literature search. *Teaching of Psychology, 4,* 89–91.

Makosky, V. P. (1990). Teaching psychology in the information age. In J. Hartley & W. J. McKeachie (Eds.), *Teaching psychology: A handbook* (pp. 15–18). Hillsdale, NJ: Lawrence Erlbaum Associates, Inc.

Mathews, J. B. (1978). "Hunting" for psychological literature: A methodology for the introductory research course. *Teaching of Psychology, 5,* 100–101.

Olivetti, L. J. (1979). Utilizing natural structure of the research literature in psychology as a model for bibliographic instruction. *Behavioral & Social Sciences Librarian, 1,* 43–46.

Parr, V. H. (1978). Course-related library instruction for psychology students. *Teaching of Psychology, 5,* 101–102.

Parr, V. H. (1988). Online information retrieval and the undergraduate. In M. E. Ware & C. L. Brewer (Eds.), *Handbook for teaching statistics and research methods* (pp. 117–118). Hillsdale, NJ: Lawrence Erlbaum Associates, Inc.

Reed, J. G., & Baxter, P. M. (1983). *Library use: A handbook for psychology.* Washington, DC: American Psychological Association.

Schilling, K. L. (1983). Teaching psychological issues in context: A library exercise. *Teaching of Psychology, 10,* 57.

Thaxton, L. (1985). Dissemination and use of information by psychology faculty and graduate students: Implications for bibliographic instruction. *Research Strategies, 3,* 116–124.

Note

The authors are members of the Standards Task Force of the New England Bibliographic Instruction Committee (NEBIC), a special interest group of the Association of College and Research Libraries (ACRL; a division of the American Library Association) New England Chapter. NEBIC's primary functions are to facilitate the sharing of information, techniques, and materials developed to support bibliographic instruction (i.e., user education) programs and to improve the quality of instruction and orientation programs in academic libraries in New England. Specifically, through smaller task forces, NEBIC maintains and promotes a circulating collection of bibliographic instruction materials; schedules bibliographic instruction workshops and seminars for New England area librarians; and pursues other special projects, such as that of the current Standards Task Force responsible for this article.

Assessment of PsycLIT Competence, Attitudes, and Instructional Methods

Lynn Cameron
Carrier Library

James Hart
James Madison University

Psychologists (e.g., Mathews, 1978) are interested in teaching bibliographic and library research strategies to their undergraduates. A number of researchers have argued that this teaching is done best by psychology faculty and librarians working together to develop cooperative strategies (Baxter, 1986; MacGregor & McInnis, 1977; Parr, 1978). With the widespread availability of computers, interest has shifted from teaching manual searching strategies to teaching electronic information retrieval strategies (Feinberg, Drews, & Eynman, 1981; Lewis, 1986; Parr, 1979; Piotrowski & Perdue, 1986).

PsycLIT is a comprehensive software package, and students require instruction in order to take full advantage of its capabilities. Librarians have employed a number of instructional strategies to teach students how to use PsycLIT (Lynn & Bacsanyi, 1989), but there is little empirical evidence about which strategies are most effective.

Student attitudes toward PsycLIT, such as anxiety and confidence, may also affect their ability to search the data base effectively. Many studies have been conducted on attitudes toward computers. Positive attitudes, such as confidence and liking of computers, contribute to better computer performance (Munger & Loyd, 1989). With regard to compact disk data bases, Steffey and Meyer (1989) found library patrons liked CD-ROM workstations, and patrons with prior experience with computers felt the data bases were easy to use. In a study by Schultz and Salomon (1990), college students were "overwhelmingly pleased with CD-ROM" (p. 56). The students thought the CD-ROMs were easy to use, preferred them to print indexes, and felt satisfied with their search results. Even students with little computer experience expressed preference for CD-ROM over print indexes, such as *Psychological Abstracts*. Despite patron reports that PsycLIT was easy to use, Lynn and Bacsanyi (1989) reported that more than 50% of the users they surveyed obtained assistance from library staff and only 16% thought formal instruction was unnecessary. The library staff at James Madison University have also observed that untrained students who use PsycLIT act confused and frustrated and frequently ask for assistance.

Several studies examined the importance of providing instruction for CD-ROMs. Instruction in the use of CD-ROM data bases "is both necessary and desired by the public," particularly if users are to take full advantage of the power of CD-ROM technology (Lynn & Bacsanyi, 1989, p. 21). To search CD-ROMs successfully, users must receive instruction in basic research strategies as well as skills specific to CD-ROM, such as the mechanics of CD-ROM systems, an understanding of the data base and what it contains, the relation of data bases to other tools, the format of a record, Boolean logic, evaluating results, and altering the search strategy when necessary (Nipp, 1991).

We found only one study that provided quantitative data on the effectiveness of the various instructional strategies for CD-ROMs. Bostian and Robbins (1990) examined the effects of handouts, a formal lecture, and a live demonstration. After subjects performed assigned searches, the experimenters evaluated their search strategies using established criteria for success. Subjects exposed to the live demonstration performed better than did students who received other methods of instruction.

Although studies have been conducted on attitudes toward computers, experience with computers, instructional methods for teaching computers, and preference for CD-ROM data bases over print indexes, little empirical research has measured level of competence in using CD-ROMs, such as PsycLIT, and how competence relates to attitudes. Our study addressed the following questions:

1. How competent are senior psychology majors in the conceptual skills necessary to use PsycLIT?
2. What are students' attitudes toward PsycLIT?
3. What instructional methods do students rate most useful in learning how to use PsycLIT?
4. What is the relation between student attitudes toward PsycLIT and competence in using it?

The library and the psychology department at James Madison University have a long-standing and cooperative program of library instruction for psychology majors. A librarian assigned to the psychology department as a liaison provides instruction in research strategies and sources in the field to all majors when they are enrolled in experimental psychology, a required course usually taken at the sophomore level. In addition, a number of faculty request instruction for other psychology courses that have assignments requiring library use. PsycLIT is included in all such course-related instruction.

To measure whether psychology majors are learning the crucial library skills, the library and the faculty worked together to assess senior majors' knowledge of psychology sources and search strategies. We hoped that the assessment would provide evidence that the instruction program is effective or show how it might be improved.

Method

As a first step, the psychology faculty and the liaison librarian wrote objectives for the assessment. These objectives dealt with the sources and strategies a psychology major should know, with a strong emphasis on facility with PsycLIT. The librarian then constructed a 60-item instrument, Library Skills Test for Psychology Majors, to measure these objectives.

Materials

An important objective of the assessment is to measure student competence in knowledge of concepts necessary to search PsycLIT, attitudes toward PsycLIT, and usefulness of various methods of PsycLIT instruction. The assessment instrument includes 26 questions relating to PsycLIT. Three questions concern attitudes toward PsycLIT, 6 survey the usefulness of various types of PsycLIT instruction, and 17 are objective questions that measure PsycLIT knowledge.

The 17-item knowledge test focuses on understanding the data base, knowing its components, and the conceptual skills required to identify a successful search strategy, rather than on the mechanics of PsycLIT. The test includes 8 general questions about PsycLIT, 3 questions on using the *Thesaurus of Psychological Index Terms* (referred to hereafter as the *Thesaurus*), and 6 questions on developing a search strategy using Boolean operators.

Procedure

Skills testing. Before the test was administered, the librarian outlined expectations regarding how well the students should perform on the PsycLIT knowledge test—on both the total test and its three subtests—in order to be considered competent PsycLIT users. The designation *competent* is defined as knowledge required to use PsycLIT effectively. These competency standards are summarized in Table 1.

The Library Skills Test for Psychology Majors was administered on a university-wide Assessment Day. The library skills test was a part of a more extensive assessment of senior psychology majors. One hundred forty-five (85%) of the psychology majors took the test. The purpose of the test was explained to the students, and they were assured that their responses would be anonymous and confidential. We used Cronbach's alpha to estimate the internal consistency of the entire Library Skills Test for Psychology Majors and the PsycLIT subtest; alpha values were .84 and .71, respectively. Thus, the test and subtest appear to be internally consistent measures.

Modes of instruction. The library offers several forms of instruction for PsycLIT, including a 1-hr workshop, a self-paced interactive workbook, individual assistance by a librarian, and printed handouts. The workshop, which is a combination of lecture, active involvement, and a demonstration of PsycLIT, focuses on use of the *Thesaurus* and the development of a search strategy using Boolean operators. The workbook covers much of the same material as the workshop. The workbook gives the student hands-on experience, which is not usually obtained during the workshop, and takes less staff time. The handout deals mainly with the mechanics of how to do a PsycLIT search. Indi-

vidual assistance by a librarian is provided at the request of students who are preparing for or conducting a PsycLIT search. In addition to these methods of instruction offered by the library, students also learn to use PsycLIT by trial and error and by help from their friends.

Results

Level of Competence on PsycLIT

The percentages of students demonstrating competency on PsycLIT at the various levels for the total test and for the subtests are presented in Table 2.

These data confirm that students are not only using PsycLIT, but they are using it well. Of the students who took the test, 88.8% reported that they had used PsycLIT, and 82.9% were either competent or exceptionally competent users as measured by the total score.

Performance was weakest on the *Thesaurus* subtest, with only 43.2% of the students scoring competent or exceptionally competent. The highest performance on the subtests was on the search strategy section, on which students selected key concepts for a search and combined these concepts using the appropriate Boolean operators. Seventy-four percent of the students were judged exceptionally competent, a much higher percentage than anticipated.

Usefulness of Instructional Methods

Students were asked to indicate whether they had used a form of PsycLIT instruction. Those who had used a particular form were asked to rate its usefulness. These results are shown in Table 3.

The most commonly used types of PsycLIT instruction were trial and error and the workshop. The least used type of instruction was the *PsycLIT Workbook,* with only 29.3% having completed it.

The types of instruction students reported to be most useful were the workshop, assistance from a librarian, and trial and error. The *PsycLIT Workbook* was considered to be less useful than the other methods, although 53.7% of those who completed it considered it useful.

Table 1. Competency Standards for PsycLIT: Number of Questions

Level of Competence	Total	Subtests		
		General	*Thesaurus*	Search Strategy
Exceptionally competent	15–17	7–8	3	5–6
Competent	11–14	5–6	2	4
Minimally competent	9–10	3–4	1	3
Incompetent	0–8	0–2	0	0–2

Table 2. Demonstrated Competency on PsycLIT

Level of Competence	% of Students Demonstrating Competency			
	Total	Subtests		
		General	*Thesaurus*	Search Strategy
Exceptionally competent	23.3	48.6	18.5	74.0
Competent	59.6	37.7	24.7	8.9
Minimally competent	10.3	10.2	44.5	11.0
Incompetent	6.8	3.5	12.3	6.1

Table 3. Usefulness of Various Types of PsycLIT Instruction

Type of Instruction	% Who Used	% Useful or Very Useful (Rated by Those Who Used it)
Workshop by a librarian	76.4	81.3
PsycLIT workbook	29.3	53.7
Printed handouts	66.4	69.5
Help from classmates	63.9	67.3
Assistance from a librarian	64.5	81.3
Trial and error	85.8	81.0

Attitudes Toward PsycLIT Use

In addition to measuring student performance on the skills test and rating different ways of learning to use PsycLIT, the assessment measured attitudes related to PsycLIT use. Students were asked to rate their level of confidence and anxiety about using PsycLIT.

Although some library users feel intimidated by new technology, these senior psychology majors reported low anxiety about using PsycLIT. Of the students tested, 37% reported feeling no anxiety at all, 28% were not very anxious, 20% were somewhat anxious, 10% were anxious, and 5% were very anxious. The correlation between PsycLIT knowledge and anxiety is significant, $r(135) = .23$, $p < .01$. Because a rating of 1 indicated maximum anxiety, a greater knowledge of PsycLIT is associated with less anxiety.

Students also reported a high level of confidence in using PsycLIT, with 22.2% feeling very confident, 34.1% confident, 23.7% somewhat confident, 5.6% not very confident, and 4.4% not at all confident. The correlation between knowledge of PsycLIT and ratings of confidence was significant, $r(135) = .32$, $p < .01$. A high level of skill shown on PsycLIT corresponds with a high degree of confidence.

Students were also asked to report the number of psychology courses in which they were required to use the library to complete their assignments. This rating was correlated with performance on PsycLIT, $r(133) = .38$, $p < .01$, indicating that the more students used the library to complete assignments for psychology courses, the better they scored on the PsycLIT test.

When asked whether they preferred PsycLIT or the printed index (*Psychological Abstracts*), students showed a strong preference for PsycLIT, with 79.1% preferring it to the printed index. Obviously, the new library technology is being well received by these senior psychology majors.

Discussion

An assessment of the PsycLIT skills of 145 senior psychology majors showed that the majority of the students understood the data base and what it contains and had mastered the concepts necessary to use PsycLIT effectively. These students performed particularly well on the sections dealing with Boolean logic and on general questions about PsycLIT. The consensus of the library staff was that students working at the PsycLIT workstation frequently appeared to have difficulty grasping the concepts of Boolean logic and had misconceptions about what the data base contains. Thus, their high level of performance was unexpected. Perhaps librarians formed these impressions by observing untrained PsycLIT users, many of whom might have been freshmen or sophomores. The psychology majors we tested were seniors experienced in the use of PsycLIT, and at least 75% of these students had received formal training.

Students performed poorly on the section relating to use of the *Thesaurus*. By using the controlled vocabulary listed in the *Thesaurus*, PsycLIT searchers commonly retrieve a greater number of relevant citations than they do when searching free text. For example, a search for the free text term *physical growth* retrieves only 42 citations, whereas a search for the descriptor *physical development* retrieves 427 citations. Most students knew they should use the *Thesaurus* when preparing for a search; however, most missed the questions that require them to identify appropriate descriptors.

In addition to performing well on the knowledge test, students felt very positive toward PsycLIT. These data show a clear relation between better performance and attitudes of greater confidence and lower anxiety. This finding is consistent with earlier research by Munger and Loyd (1989). Our results are also consistent with previous findings on positive attitudes and computer experience (Cohen & Waugh, 1989; Loyd & Gressard, 1984). Students expressed a strong preference for PsycLIT over printed indexes like *Psychological Abstracts*. This finding corresponds to studies by Schultz and Salomon (1990) and Lynn and Bacsanyi (1989), who also found that students expressed a strong preference for CD-ROMs over printed indexes. These results indicate that students are adapting to the new CD-ROM technology, both in attitude and actual performance.

With regard to preference for various methods of PsycLIT instruction, all six methods were rated as useful by students, but the workshop was the preferred method of instruction.

Bostian and Robbins (1990) found a live demonstration to be more effective than a formal lecture or handouts. The 1-hr workshop in our study consisted of three components: a lecture, exercises that require active participation, and a live demonstration using a microcomputer and an LCD panel. Further study is needed to determine whether the combination of components of the workshop contributed to its high ratings of usefulness or whether one component, perhaps the live demonstration, is the most popular component.

The handout was rated more useful than the self-paced *PsycLIT Workbook* but less useful than the workshop. The workbook, which was developed as a substitute for the workshop, was considered by the students to be the least useful method of instruction, although 53.7% of those who used it considered it to be useful. Assistance from classmates and trial and error were also rated as being useful.

The knowledge test used in our study focuses on the conceptual skills, rather than the mechanical skills students must master to use PsycLIT effectively. Further work is needed to determine how well students understand the use of the function keys, how to show and print results, and generally how to operate the PsycLIT software. In our study, students rated the usefulness of methods of instruction they experienced, with a number of students using more than one method. A better way to evaluate the effectiveness of various instructional methods would be to randomly assign students to one of the instructional conditions and then to compare the PsycLIT knowledge scores of students using various methods.

References

Baxter, P. M. (1986). The benefits of in-class bibliographic instruction. *Teaching of Psychology, 13,* 40–41.

Bostian, R., & Robbins, A. (1990). Effective instruction for searching CD-ROM indexes. *Laserdisk Professional, 3*(1), 14–17.

Cohen, B. A., & Waugh, G. W. (1989). Assessing computer anxiety. *Psychological Reports, 65,* 735–738.

Feinberg, R. A., Drews, D., & Eynman, D. (1981). Positive side effects on online information retrieval. *Teaching of Psychology, 8,* 51–52.

Lewis, L. K. (1986). Bibliographic computerized searching in psychology. *Teaching of Psychology, 13,* 38–40.

Loyd, B. H., & Gressard, C. (1984). The effects of sex, age, and computer experience on computer attitudes. *AEDS Journal, 18*(2), 67–77.

Lynn, P., & Bacsanyi, K. (1989). CD-ROMs: Instructional methods and user reactions. *Reference Services Review, 17*(2), 17–25.

MacGregor, J., & McInnis, R. G. (1977). Integrating classroom instruction and library research: The cognitive functions of bibliographic network structures. *Journal of Higher Education, 48,* 17–38.

Mathews, J. B. (1978). "Hunting" for psychological literature: A methodology for the introductory research course. *Teaching of Psychology, 5,* 100–101.

Munger, G. F., & Lloyd, B. H. (1989). Gender and attitudes toward computers and calculators: Their relationship to math performance. *Journal of Educational Computing Research, 5,* 167–177.

Nipp, D. (1991). Back to basics: Integrating CD-ROM instruction with standard user education. *Research Strategies, 9,* 41–47.

Parr, V. H. (1978). Course-related library instruction for psychology students. *Teaching of Psychology, 5,* 101–102.

Parr, V. H. (1979). Online information retrieval and the undergraduate. *Teaching of Psychology, 6,* 61–62.

Piotrowski, C., & Perdue, B. (1986). On-line literature retrieval: An alternative research strategy. *Teaching of Psychology, 13,* 153–154.

Schultz, K., & Salomon, K. (1990, February 1). End users respond to CD-ROM. *Library Journal,* pp. 56–57.

Steffey, R. J., & Meyer, N. (1989). Evaluating user success and satisfaction with CD-ROM. *Laserdisk Professional, 2*(5), 35–45.

Note

We thank Donna Sundre for assisting with the statistical analysis.

Getting the Most From PsycLIT: Recommendations for Searching

Kathleen E. Joswick
University Library
Western Illinois University

PsycLIT, the optical disc version of *Psychological Abstracts,* has enhanced the useful qualities that have distinguished the hard copy version. Comprehensiveness of the indexing and of the abstracts has been maintained, but the number of ways to locate and sort the data has been greatly increased. Dramatic as the improvements are, however, researchers frequently either misuse or use only minimally those features of the data base that are most impressive. Worse yet, the easy access and vast recall often disguise inadequate searches, leaving patrons unaware of what PsycLIT could have provided.

Articles on straightforward topics can be located quickly via PsycLIT even by an untrained user. To improve consistency and comprehensiveness, however, advanced researchers need a deeper understanding of the principles by which the information is organized and accessed. This article explains the distinction between keyword and controlled vocabularies in the data base, the principles used for indexing information, and the syntax required for constructing the most effective search strategies. PsycLIT itself provides helpful information in its GUIDE and HELP screens, so this information is not repeated here. This article supplements the on-screen aids by explaining some of the procedural and conceptual skills needed for maximum search effectiveness.

Problems

The worst consequence of ineffective searching on an electronic data base is the failure to locate all the relevant material. Because what is not asked for is never seen, researchers confidently believe that they have unearthed all the pertinent articles, not realizing that a different search strategy would have identified additional records. Studies have shown that 30% to 50% of all users miss pertinent data (Sewell & Teitelbaum, 1986). Kirby and Miller (1985) reported that patrons who were happy with results they obtained without assistance were dismayed to discover that additional important articles were uncovered when their topic was searched by an expert. Sewell and Teitelbaum (1986) related that over half of the searchers in their study admitted that librarian-performed searches were of a higher quality than their own searches. Nash and Wilson (1991) found that although 64% of students searching CD-ROMs were satisfied with their search results, only 5% of the references retrieved were useful for their research. Fewer than half the searchers used basic features like the connector *and* to link together concepts, and less than one third used the connector *or* to search synonymous terms (Sewell & Teitelbaum, 1986).

Solutions

Know Your Data Base

No data base includes everything or even everything in one subject area. As comprehensive as the APA data base is, unique relevant citations can be located in a number of other data bases as well (Piotrowski & Perdue, 1986). An effective researcher must be familiar with the scope of the data base consulted and be willing to consult other sources when necessary.

Psychological Abstracts (paper), PsycINFO (the on-line data base), and PsycLIT (CD-ROM) are not identical. The American Psychological Association has published *Psychological Abstracts* since 1927, but PsycINFO and PsycLIT go back only to 1967 and 1974, respectively. *Psychological Abstracts* and PsycINFO are updated monthly; PsycLIT is updated quarterly. Only PsycINFO and PsycLIT continue to provide access to non-English language publications; *Psychological Abstracts* discontinued them in 1988. *Psychological Abstracts* began to index books and book chapters in 1992. PsycLIT also began indexing books in 1992, but it includes publications retrospectively to 1987. PsycINFO does not include books. PsycLIT does not index the technical reports included in the other two products; of the three, only PsycINFO indexes

162

dissertations in the field. *Psychological Abstracts* indexes articles only under the descriptors identified as major descriptors (a maximum of five descriptors can be identified as major), whereas PsycLIT and PsycINFO index articles using up to 15 different descriptors. As a result of this limitation, *Psychological Abstracts* can no longer be searched using subject headings referring to developmental stages (i.e., adolescence, adult, etc.) or animal terms (i.e., rats, cats, etc.) as the other versions can.

In *Psychological Abstracts,* an individual article can be located only by the author's name or by the main descriptors assigned to the article. But with PsycLIT and PsycINFO, every word in the record can be used to access that record. Retrieval potential is multiplied hundreds of times over, but greater precision is required for effective searching.

In the electronic sources, every article's record is divided into sections called fields, and each field is identified by a two-letter abbreviation. Searches can be limited to one field or to groups of fields for greater search precision. Because a list of fields and their abbreviations can be found in PsycLIT's GUIDE (Function Key 3), they are not repeated here. However, knowledge of the field abbreviations and how to use them is essential to searching electronic sources. For example, typing in *violence in de* (*de* is the abbreviation for the descriptor field) will limit retrieval to records in which the word *violence* appears in the descriptor or subject heading field, not anywhere in the record. Adding *and English in la* (*la* is the field abbreviation for the language of the document) to a search statement will eliminate all publications in foreign languages. Using the string *not social-work in jn* (*jn* is the field abbreviation for the journal field) will delete records from a journal the researcher has already examined.

Understand the Difference Between Keyword and Controlled Vocabulary

Understanding the difference between keyword and controlled vocabulary is essential in formulating and executing effective searches. The variation in retrieval is dramatic, as shown in the following example:

No.	Records	Request
#1	10,224	*achievement*
#2	6,851	*achievement in de*
#3	601	*achievement-in de*

Line 1 lists the number of times the word *achievement* was located as a keyword, that is, the number of records in which the term appeared in any part of the record: title field, abstract field, descriptor field, or key phrase field. This technique results in the highest retrieval, but it yields the most irrelevant records.

Line 2 represents all the records in which the word *achievement* appears in the descriptor field (*de* is the field label for the descriptor or subject heading field. The limiter *in de* requests that the word or phrase be retrieved only when it appears in the descriptor field). *Achievement in de* (with no hyphen) recalls records with descriptors of *academic achievement, achievement potential, mathematics achievement, need achievement, Stanford Achievement Test,* and so on, as well as records with the single-word descriptor *achievement*. This is a broad search, but it is not as broad as the keyword search.

Line 3, with the hyphen next to the word followed by the limiter *in de,* indicates the number of records for which *achievement* was the single-word descriptor assigned to the article by the APA indexer. The hyphen after a single-word descriptor or between words in a multiword descriptor phrase signals the computer to retrieve only records in which that word or phrase appears in that identical form. This search is the most precise.

Words and phrases from the descriptor field constitute APA's controlled vocabulary. *Thesaurus of Psychological Index Terms* (1990) is the complete list of the controlled vocabulary terms used by indexers to describe articles' contents. It is composed of about 4,500 descriptor terms, each falling into a hierarchical structure of broader and narrower terms. New terms are regularly added to the thesaurus, thereby allowing the indexing to keep pace with changes in the vocabulary. Searching with a descriptor from the thesaurus helps to weed out irrelevant records that may mention the word but do not focus on the concept. Using a descriptor also helps to eliminate unintended uses of the word. Searching for *adoption,* for example, displays articles not only about the adoption of children but also about the adoption of computers, the adoption of business uniforms, and even the adoption of chicken farming techniques. Searching *adoption-child in de* eliminates all the records that do not deal with the adoption of children.

As valuable as it is to search with descriptor terms, it is advantageous at times to use keyword searching. Sometimes, a keyword or phrase is so invariably used to convey a meaning that it focuses the search more than a descriptor. *Soap opera* and *midlife crisis* are good examples of common language terms that consistently refer to the same phenomenon and are, therefore, reliable search terms. Keywords can also be used as a shortcut to identifying relevant descriptors. A searcher could type in any natural language term and, by examining the first few records, quickly locate the most useful descriptor for the topic. Typing in *gender,* for example, as a keyword term retrieves thousands of records. Looking at the first few identifies *human-sex-differences* as the most appropriate descriptor for the concept.

Sometimes a precise descriptor does not exist for the topic being researched. Combining keyword and controlled vocabulary terms will often identify records that are appropriate to a topic. For example, typing in *serial killers* recalls only two records. Using the narrowest descriptor (*homicide-in de*) locates over 500 articles related to murder of all types, not just to murders committed by serial killers. Combining the controlled vocabulary term and a keyword (*homicide-in de and serial*) reduces the 500 records on homicide to those that also contained the word *serial* somewhere in the record. Records that use *serial* in some other context, such as *serial recall, serial discrimination,* and *serial searching,* are eliminated. Combining the keyword and the descriptor picks up seven additional articles that discuss serial killers but do not use those exact words next to each other.

Understand Indexing Techniques

The essential principle of indexing is that only the most specific descriptor available is used to define the contents of the document. Every article is indexed to the level of specificity of the document. Broader terms from the same hierarchy are not used: This is a simple idea but one that foils many search strategies. An indexer would assign the descriptor *mass-media* to an article dealing with television, radio, and film together but would assign the descriptor *television* to an article considering television alone. *Mass-media in de,* therefore, will not retrieve articles only about television. *Narcotic-drugs in de* will not yield articles about heroin alone, even though heroin is obviously a narcotic drug. Typing *animal-parental-behavior in de* retrieves 267 articles. Searching the narrower term *animal-maternal-behavior* retrieves 532 articles, only 19 of which were found in the search of *animal-parental-behavior.* Failing to request records that treat narrower aspects of a topic will result in a search that will miss many relevant articles.

PsycLIT's on-line thesaurus helps in constructing searches that include narrower aspects of the topic. By pressing THESAURUS (F9) and typing in a descriptor, first a permuted list and then a term detail screen will be displayed. The permuted list is a register of all the descriptors that contain a particular word. When searching the thesaurus for *size discrimination,* for example, the permuted display lists all the terms that include the word *size* (*size constancy, body size, brain size, family size,* and *size discrimination*). Selecting *Term Detail* from the menu displays the relational hierarchy in which the selected term falls: broader terms, narrower terms, and related terms. For example, the thesaurus lists the narrower terms *marital conflict* and *marital satisfaction* under the descriptor *marital relations.* A comprehensive search should include all three terms, connected by the operator *or,* typed in as (*marital-relations or marital-conflict or marital-satisfaction*) *in de. Marital-relations in de* searched alone would not include records dealing with marital conflict alone. *Term Detail* also identifies when the term was first introduced into the thesaurus, what term (if any) preceded it, and what common terms are not used to identify this concept.

The *Explode Term* option appears on the menu when a *Term Detail* is viewed in the thesaurus. When a searcher selects this *explode* option, the descriptor term plus all the narrower terms from the same hierarchy are grouped as a set and transferred to the FIND screen. This feature saves the time involved in rekeying terms and greatly improves retrieval by searching for all the narrower descriptors at once.

A related term may also be of interest to a researcher and may need to be included in a search. *Eye-contact* is a related term that might be included in a search of the concept *body-language,* for example. Related terms can be identified in the thesaurus but will not be included by using the *Explode Term* feature. Terms from outside the narrower or broader hierarchy must be keyed in individually, connected with *or.*

Designing an Effective Search Strategy

Translating the research topic from a sentence or a question into two or three key concepts is an essential step in formulating an effective search. This task requires the ability to break the topic down into its major components and to express those components as concisely as possible. Once the main concepts are identified, descriptors for each concept should be located. Envisioning the process as a search worksheet may help to conceptualize the technique. Writing the appropriate descriptors out in columns and filling in the terms under Concept 1, Concept 2, and so forth will group synonymous or related terms. Descriptors selected for Concept 1 are then keyed in, connected by the word *or,* to create a set of records. The same steps are repeated with Concept 2. The sets are then combined with the connector *and,* resulting in a group of records, each one containing the requested concepts (but not every requested term). The following is an example.

In looking for information on cultural variations in the way people experience pain, two key concepts were identified: pain and cultural variations. Descriptors were located in the thesaurus to define the topics. *Pain-, chronic-pain, back-pain, pain-perception, headache-, psychogenic-pain,* and *pain-thresholds* are terms describing the first concept. For the second concept, cultural variations, the descriptors *racial-and-ethnic-attitudes, racial-and-ethnic-differences,* and *cross-cultural-differences* were found. Figure 1 illustrates a completed search worksheet for this topic. Keying in (*pain- or chronic-pain or back-pain or pain-perception or pain-thresholds or headache- or psychogenic-pain*) *in de* retrieves a set of 2,441 records. Keying in the cultural variations descriptors, complete with hyphens, combined with *or,* retrieves a total of 4,901 records. When the set created by the pain terms is combined with the set created by the cultural terms using the *and* connector, 18 records are located. This final set can be limited to articles in English with limit statement *and English in la.* The FIND screen is illustrated in Figure 2. The thousands of records located by searching all the terms are reduced to 17 records.

In contrast, typing in *pain and cultural variations* as keywords retrieves only one record, illustrating how much would have been missed without a planned strategy. Searching two descriptors only (*pain-in de and cross-cultural-differences in de*) retrieves only five records, again missing important articles.

Use System Features to Narrow or Broaden Searches

Electronic features can broaden or narrow a search in many ways. I have already discussed some of these techniques. Making use of the operator *and* can narrow searches by requiring that several terms appear within the same record. The operator *or,* stringing together synonyms or equivalent concepts, can broaden a search. In addition, *not* can be used to eliminate terms or concepts; for example, *student-personnel-services not school-counseling.*

Searches can be limited by age, gender, species, using limit fields, or combining terms with appropriate descriptors. Using the limit field for age group (ag) can limit searches to four broad human age groups: child (birth through age 12), adolescent (13–17 years), adult (ages 18 and over), and elderly (ages 65 and over); for example, *infectious-disorders in de and child in ag.* More specific age limits can be designated by combining the subject with a narrower descriptor (e.g., *infectious-disorders in de and infants-in de,* or *infectious-disorders in de and neonates-in de*). Searches can be limited to either human or animal

research with the limit field for population (po: e.g., *social-environments in de and animal in po*).

Some descriptors describe the form of the document. If the document is a literature review, longitudinal study, meta-analysis, bibliography, and so on, the indexer mandatorily assigns a form descriptor, so these can be used to limit a search (e.g., *exercise-in de and literature-review in de*).

Truncation can broaden searches. The truncation symbol (*) functions as a wild card, allowing all permutations on a root word to be recalled. *Librar*,* for example, retrieves records with the words *libraries, library, librarian, librarians,* and so forth. The imprudent placement of the truncation symbol, however, can result in a deluge of irrelevant records. Typing *inter** retrieves over 90,000 records containing such unrelated words as *interview, interaction, interest, intervention, interface,* and *intermediate.*

The index is an alphabetical list of every word or hyphenated phrase in the data base, and it can be especially useful when searching for a person's name. Selecting INDEX (F5) and typing in the last name of the author allows the searcher to scroll through variant forms of authors' names, identifying differences in name format or spelling. Appropriate names are then grouped as a set and searched without retyping. The index feature, for example, identifies 22 articles written by fulker-david-w, but it also clearly displays an additional 10 articles by fulker-d-w that were not included in the 22 previous articles. Without the index feature, they could easily have been overlooked.

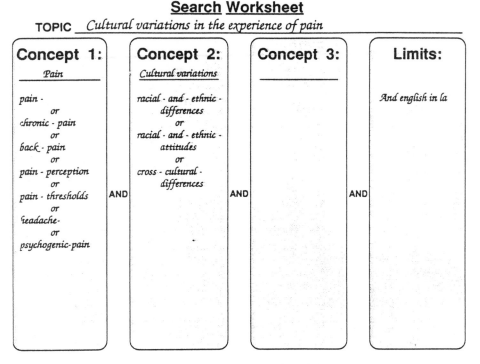

Figure 1. A completed search worksheet.

No.	Records	Request
#1:	804	PAIN-
#2:	694	CHRONIC-PAIN
#3:	233	BACK-PAIN
#4:	640	PAIN-PERCEPTION
#5:	147	PAIN-THRESHOLDS
#6:	235	HEADACHE-
#7:	63	PSYCHOGENIC-PAIN
#8:	2441	(PAIN- or CHRONIC-PAIN or BACK-PAIN or PAIN-PERCEPTION or PAIN-THRESHOLDS or HEADACHE- or PSYCHOGENIC-PAIN) in DE
#9:	1922	RACIAL-AND-ETHNIC-DIFFERENCES
#10:	262	RACIAL-AND-ETHNIC-ATTITUDES
#11:	2873	CROSS-CULTURAL-DIFFERENCES
#12:	4901	(RACIAL-AND-ETHNICS DIFFERENCES or RACIAL-AND-ETHNIC-ATTITUDES or CROSS-CULTURAL-DIFFERENCES) in DE
#13:	18	#8 AND #12
#14:	205135	LA=ENGLISH
#15:	17	#13 AND LA=ENGLISH

FIND:

Figure 2. PsycLIT FIND screen for the sample search.

Occasionally Disregard These Suggestions

There are times when throwing out all the rules and turning to PsycLIT with a simple, spontaneous plea for assistance pays off. A student searched traditional sources to find information on a phenomenon she had heard her aunts describe: witches sitting on them as they slept, preventing them from moving or crying out but allowing them to see and hear what was happening around them. She hunted through books on superstitions, indexes to folklore, and encyclopedias on the supernatural to no avail. Typing in *sleep and witch* in PsycLIT, the student retrieved one record that described the same phenomenon her family members had experienced. Identifying it as a form of sleep paralysis, she was immediately able to locate other descriptions and definitions. Sometimes disregarding the protocols can still retrieve the perfect record.

Remember to Use the Expertise of Librarians

Few users will deny the advantages of searching for the information they need, immediately, by themselves. Eliminating intermediaries and exploring the literature directly is one of the great benefits of CD-ROM searching over on-line data base searching. Self-help guides designed to improve system use are irreplaceable in improving the results of direct patron searches. But no self-help guide can substitute for consultation with a professional. Librarians are familiar with the intricacies of data bases and are trained in search construction, limiting techniques, and indexing principles. The most effective searchers are those who are willing to consult the experts when problems or questions arise. Together, librarians and behavioral scientists can ensure that published research in psychology will be studied more thoroughly and more easily.

References

Kirby, M., & Miller, N. (1985). Medline searching on BRS Colleague: Search success of untrained end users in a medical school and hospital. In *National Online Meeting. Proceedings—1985* (pp. 255–263). Medford, NJ: Leaned Information.

Nash, S., & Wilson, M. (1991). Value-added bibliographic instruction: Teaching students to find the right citations. *RSR: Reference Services Review, 19,* 87–92.

Piotrowski, C., & Perdue, B. (1986). On-line literature retrieval: An alternative research strategy. *Teaching of Psychology 13,* 153–154.

Sewell, W., & Teitelbaum, S. (1986). Observations of end-user online searching behavior over eleven years. *Journal of the American Society for Information Science, 37,* 234–245.

Thesaurus of psychological index terms (6th ed.). (1990). Washington, DC: American Psychological Association.

A Strategy for Improving Literature Reviews in Psychology Courses

Retta E. Poe
Western Kentucky University

As a means of teaching undergraduates in an abnormal psychology class to write scholarly literature review papers, I developed a series of presentations and exercises to address typical student difficulties in completing such an assignment. First, I prepared several minilectures to clarify the nature of the assignment, which was to write a review of the scholarly literature on a topic relevant to the course (using a minimum of 10 data-based articles published within the preceding 10 years). I devoted portions of several class periods to discussing the following issues: What a scholarly literature review is, how to distinguish between scholarly sources and popular press periodicals, the nature of the library search process, how to use abstracting services, appropriate use of quoted material, how to reference studies in APA style, what constitutes plagiarism, and how to write an abstract for a journal article. In preparing my discussion of these topics, I relied on material presented in Rosnow and Rosnow (1986); Maimon, Belcher, Hearn, Nodine, and O'Connor (1981); and the *Publication Manual of the American Psychological Association* (3rd ed.; APA, 1983).

To teach students to formulate a topic, summarize articles, and integrate findings from several sources, I designed a series of overlapping writing assignments intended to shape the major skills needed in writing a literature review. I did not grade any of the writing assignments leading up to the final paper. Instead, students were able to get "free" feedback (i.e., with no effect on their course grades) simply by turning in assignments as requested. Although completion of the assignments was optional, nearly all students turned in each assignment.

The sequence of writing assignments was as follows.

1. Focused freewriting. Because Maimon et al. (1981) and Schor and Summerfield (1986) recommended focused freewriting as a way to begin writing, I asked students to write one paragraph on each of three topics they might be interested in researching for the paper assignment. Each paragraph was to include a description of the topic, why the student was interested in that topic, and how the student expected to benefit from researching that topic.

2. Summarization of an essay. At the beginning of a class period, students wrote summaries of a short essay (fewer than 1,000 words) I had photocopied from a readings book. The article I selected was an argumentative essay on a nontechnical topic unrelated to abnormal psychology. After discussing the qualities of good and bad summaries and providing examples of both (cf. Maimon et al., 1981, pp. 102–107), I asked students to write a one-paragraph summary of the key points of the essay. I then gave them a summary I had written of the same essay and offered students suggestions for evaluating the quality of their own summaries. In particular, I asked them to note whether they had identified the main points as well as the author's conclusions and to check their summaries for plagiarism.

3. Summarization of a journal article–Part 1. I selected a journal article on an abnormal psychology topic, removed the author abstract, and assigned students the task of writing an abstract following APA guidelines. The journal article chosen was a brief report of an investigation using terminology, procedures, and statistics easily understood by undergraduates. After the students had completed their abstracts, they were given the author abstract for comparison. They also exchanged papers with other class members, who were instructed to give feedback on whether the student had included all the required information in the abstract.

4. Summarization of a journal article–Part 2. Students wrote abstracts of a second journal article on the same topic as the first journal article. Again, the author abstract was removed before photocopying and was provided to students for comparison after they had written their own abstracts. This time, however, I gave students written feedback on the thoroughness of their abstracts as well as on each writer's strengths and weaknesses in grammar and composition.

5. Integrating findings of two studies. Each student wrote a comparison/contrast essay of about 350 words regarding the purpose, methodology, and findings of the two studies for which they had written summaries. In addition to providing students with written feedback on their essays, I gave them a comparison/contrast essay I had written on the same two studies.

6. <u>Preparing a reference list.</u> The final assignment was to submit a one-sentence description of the student's research topic along with a list of 10 references suitable for the paper assignment. I marked these for departures from APA style and also commented on the adequacy of the topic selected (too general, too specific, etc.).

Evaluation

I used two sources of informal information to evaluate the success of the writing projects: student feedback on course evaluations and quality of research papers (compared to the previous semester when no specific help with the writing process was provided).

About 60% of the students specifically commented on the writing component of the course. Most respondents indicated that they had found the writing exercises helpful and that they appreciated having had the opportunity to acquire writing skills without any penalty on their grades. The only negative comments concerned the extra time required to write the summaries and essays.

Because I received better papers, I was satisfied that the extra effort invested was justified. Compared to the previous semester, twice as many students received As, and no student's paper earned less than a C (vs. 13% Ds and Fs in the preceding semester). Moreover, I have repeated the shaping procedure in my senior-level psychology of women course. I received a greater number of high-quality papers compared to previous semesters when I made the same research paper assignment but did not help students with the writing process.

Conclusions

Although the intervention described is clearly time-consuming to implement, it offers as compensation the potential to have a noticeable impact on students' writing skills. With minor modifications, the multifaceted strategy used here to teach writing of literature review papers could be used to teach students to write other kinds of papers. Students will benefit from this effort by acquiring skills that will likely transfer to other courses, and instructors will benefit by reducing the frustration they often feel when evaluating students' writing. Perhaps most important of all, the writing assignment described here helps students to accomplish one of the goals of any psychology course: to learn about psychology writing and reading.

References

American Psychological Association. (1983). *Publication manual of the American Psychological Association* (3rd ed.). Washington, DC: Author.

Maimon, E. P., Belcher, G. L., Hearn, G. W., Nodine, B. F., & O'Connor, F. W. (1981). *Writing in the arts and sciences.* Boston: Little, Brown.

Rosnow, R. L., & Rosnow, M. (1986). *Writing papers in psychology: A student guide.* Belmont, CA: Wadsworth.

Schor, S., & Summerfield, J. (1986). *The Random House guide to writing* (3rd ed.). New York: Random House.

Note

Development of the techniques described in this article was supported by a 1986 grant from the Hendrix-Murphy Foundation while the author was a faculty member at Hendrix College, Conway, AR.

168

5. Using Computers

Paula Goolkasian describes an early microcomputer-based laboratory for the undergraduate research methods course at The University of North Carolina at Charlotte. She used six Apple II microcomputers in a teaching laboratory that enabled students to get firsthand experience with various techniques. The author mentions hardware and software requirements, highlights advantages of using a microcomputer lab for instruction, and stresses the need for a part-time programmer.

Blaine Peden from the University of Wisconsin-Eau Claire outlines an approach that incorporates Apple II microcomputers into the entire research process as he works individually with advanced undergraduates. The strategy involves everything from developing researchable hypotheses to preparing manuscripts for presentation or publication. The author highlights pedagogical and practical advantages of this technique.

Undergraduates in Robert Rittle's research design course at Indiana University of Pennsylvania learned to program microcomputers for controlling experimental tasks. The training used a database management system with a full programming language (dBASE III Plus). The author illustrates how this general approach can be used in various psychology courses.

A Microcomputer-Based Lab for Psychology Instruction

Paula Goolkasian
The University of North Carolina at Charlotte

This article describes the experiences of our department in establishing and using a computer-based lab for instruction in psychology. Our goal was to provide hands-on experience in psychological research for our required sophomore-level course in Research Methodology.

Our experience in teaching this course using traditional laboratory methods was often frustrating because of the continual struggle to find resources. Over the past 5 years we have averaged 75 students per semester in three sections of the course. Our inventory of equipment assigned to the instructional lab included such standard pieces of equipment as a 2-channel tachistoscope, a 2-channel polygraph, several reaction-time devices, a slide projector, a tape recorder, a videotape unit, several memory drums, finger mazes, and pursuit rotors. All this equipment was only partially sufficient to service the needs of the students. To equip the lab with enough materials to support student projects each semester would have required a sizable one-time investment as well as yearly expenditures to keep the equipment maintained and up-to-date.

Moreover, the use of a traditional psychology lab required a considerable investment of instructor time, and there was a feeling of dissatisfaction among the instructors that the traditional student projects were not representative of contemporary psychology. Memory drums, finger mazes, and pursuit rotors have long since been replaced in research labs by computers. The students were being presented with an outdated view of psychological research and limited practical experiences in the lab.

For all these reasons, funds were sought to develop a microcomputer lab for research methodology. Six Apple II microcomputers were used to establish a teaching lab where students could experience firsthand a broad variety of laboratory techniques. Computer-based labs for psychology instruction have been used successfully at a number of institutions (Benedict & Butts, 1981; Eckerman, 1981; Levy, 1980; Posner & Osgood, 1980). Although we needed funding from a grant (National Science Foundation Instructional Scientific Equipment Program) to acquire the initial hardware, the continuing costs of the lab could be paid through our departmental budgets.

There are some specific hardware and software requirements that are needed to support an instructional lab. First of all, the physical layout of our microcomputer laboratory is a six-room suite. The Apples in each of the small (10' × 6') rooms are configured as stand-alone stations. They include: an Apple II 64K microcomputer, two disk drives, a color monitor, thunderclock, joystick, a printer with graphics capabilities, and a micromodem. The layout was designed to provide the student with the opportunity to conduct research. Printers were needed to provide a hard copy of the raw data from the lab exercises and the results of statistical tests. The thunderclock has made it easy for our programmers to write lab projects that involve reaction times or that try to simulate tachistoscopic control of stimulus presentation rates. The micromodem allows the Apple to be used as an intelligent terminal to the campus mainframe. When analyzing large data sets, some faculty members prefer to store their data on Apple diskettes and upload the files to the campus mainframe to be analyzed with such commonly used programs as SAS or SPSS.

A major factor in the successful implementation of our lab was the availability of Apple software for use in psychology labs. We were able to take advantage of "ready to run" software that had been developed at other institutions.

Three kinds of software programs are used: (a) lab exercises that allow students to conduct experimentation, (b) canned programs for statistical analysis, and (c) computer-assisted instruction (CAI) lessons which offer repeated practice with conceptually difficult material. Table 1 lists the software in our library.

Programs in the first category were acquired primarily through Conduit. We use these programs to give students experience with contemporary psychological phenomena as well as practice using specific designs. For example, the span-of-attention exercise from the Levy package is used in my class to demonstrate a two-group design. Students are randomly assigned to one of two treatment condition and they collect data on themselves during the lab. A lab

Table 1. A Listing of Instructional Software for a Research Methodology Laboratory

A.   Lab Exercises

Levy Program "Lab in Cognition and Perception" (Conduit)
Keenan and Keller "Computer Lab in Memory and Cognition" (Conduit)
Gregory and Poffel "Start: Stimulus and Response Tools for Experiments in Memory, Learning, Cognition, and Perception" (Conduit)
Release from PI (Belmore, 1983)
M.T.S.: An adaptable microcomputer-based testing system (Foree, Eckerman, & Elliott, 1984)
Apple Pascal Tester (University of Denver) (Poltrock & Foltz, 1982)

B.   Data Analysis Programs

Statistical programs for the Apple II microcomputer (Steinmetz, Romano, & Patterson, 1981)
Stepwise Multiple Regression (Gorman & Primavera, 1981)
Descriptive Statistics (Conduit)
Exploratory Data Analysis (Conduit)

C.   Computer-Assisted Instruction Lessons

Power (Fazio & Backler, 1983)
Interactions (Fazio & Backler, 1983)
Sampling (Fazio & Backler, 1983)
Experimental vs. Correlational Research (Spivey, 1983)
Graphing Data (Spivey, 1983)
Statmaster (Levy, Froming, & Belcher, 1983)

assistant records the raw data from each student, and then distributes the class data so that they can be analyzed using the statistical test appropriate for the design under discussion. The class meets as a group to discuss the result and conclusions of the study. Following each lab exercise the students write a lab report. It is possible to complete a lab project within a 2-hour lab period. In my class 4 or 5 lab projects are run per semester each demonstrating a different design. In each case the students use the microcomputer as their personal lab assistant to present the stimuli and record responses which they later add to data from the other students and analyze with appropriate statistical tests.

The Apple Pascal Tester (Poltrock & Foltz, 1982) and the Microcomputer-based Testing System (Foree, Eckerman, & Elliott, 1984) are particularly useful for independent research projects. The programs allow the user to construct an experiment, present stimuli, and record responses. Although students must be familiar with the Pascal Editor and Filer, they do not have to know how to program in Pascal to construct an experiment. These programs have been used by several of our seniors to conduct independent research projects and by a few faculty members for research projects.

Several programs in our department software library are used for data analysis. The program that has been the most valuable for instruction is entitled "Statistical programs for the Apple II microcomputer" (Steinmetz, Romano, & Patterson, 1981). This is a menu-driven program that allows students to conduct statistical tests on data inputed at the keyboard. It is user friendly and students do not need much explanation on how to use a variety of statistical procedures which range from descriptive statistics to split-plot ANOVAs. We also have a program that calculates a stepwise multiple regression (Gorman & Primavera, 1981), and a few others from Conduit entitled "Descriptive Statistics" and "Exploratory Data Analysis." Through the use of these programs students can practice with data analysis without the hassle that typically comes with use of a campus mainframe.

The third category of programs are lessons that provide extensive practice with topics such as interactions, sampling theory, power, and so on. These lessons are used for remedial work by students who find the topics under study hard to conceptualize. My students always find that factorial interactions are difficult to understand. Working through the CAI exercise on "Interactions," which mixes graphical and textual presentation of the topic, has helped students achieve mastery of the concept.

To summarize, there are several advantages in using a microcomputer lab for instruction. It takes the hassle out of preparations for the lab for both the student and the instructor. Time pressure is no longer a factor because all of the time consuming aspects of research projects such as equipment setup, stimulus preparation, and scoring data have been minimized through the use of microcomputers. Also, the frustration due to lack of equipment has been removed because the micro is such a versatile instrument that it can replace such standard lab instruments as T-scopes, reaction timers, pursuit rotor devices, finger mazes, and so forth.

The only hidden cost with this lab is the need to hire a part-time programmer. We have been fortunate in getting instructional programs at minimal costs from other psychology departments, but many of these programs needed some alteration. In some cases the programs had to be tailored to the Apple configuration in our labs, and in others the programs had serious problems that had to be "bulletproofed" before we could use them in the labs. A software programmer is a necessity. We have been satisfied with the help that we have received from junior and senior computer science students who work at reasonable rates to get practical experience with the Apples.

References

Belmore, S. M. (1983). Release from PI: Comparisons of traditional and computer modules in an experimental psychology laboratory. *Behavior Research Methods and Instrumentation, 15,* 191–194.

Benedict, J. O., & Butts, B. D. (1981). Computer simulation or real experimentation: Is one better for teaching experimental design? *Teaching of Psychology, 8,* 35–37.

Eamon, D. B. (1980). Labsim: A data-driven simulation program for instruction in research design and statistics. *Behavior Research Methods and Instrumentation, 12,* 160–164.

Eckerman, D. A. (1981). Developing a laboratory course using Pascal on the Apple II. *Behavior Research Methods and Instrumentation, 13,* 204–208.

Fazio, R. H., & Backler, M. H. (1983). The use of computer lessons in a social psychology research methods course. *Behavior Research Methods and Instrumentation, 15,* 135–137.

Foree, D. D., Eckerman, D. A., & Elliott, S. L. (1984). M. T. S.: An adaptable microcomputer-based testing system. *Behavior Research Methods, Instruments, & Computers, 16,* 223–229.

Gorman, B. S., & Primavera, L. H. (1981). Basic backstep: A simple backward selection multiple-regression program for minicomputers and microcomputers. *Behavior Research Methods and Instrumentation, 13,* 703.

Levy, C. M. (1980). Getting an on-line departmental teaching laboratory on-line. *Behavior Research Methods and Instrumentation, 12,* 111–113.

Levy, C. M., Froming, W. J., & Belcher, M. (1983). *Statmaster.* Boston: Little, Brown.

Poltrock, S. E., & Foltz, G. S. (1982). An experimental laboratory system for the Apple II microcomputer. *Behavior Research Methods and Instrumentation, 14,* 103–108.

Posner, M. I., & Osgood, G. W. (1980). Computers in the training of inquiry. *Behavior Research Methods and Instrumentation, 12,* 87–95.

Spivey, J. E. (1983). Software development for computer-assisted instruction in experimental psychology. *Behavior Research Methods and Instrumentation, 15,* 183–186.

Steinmetz, J. E., Romano, A. G., & Patterson, M. M. (1981). Statistical programs for the Apple II microcomputer. *Behavior Research Methods and Instrumentation, 13,* 702.

West, R. F. (1983). Data-editing basic programs for creating, modifying, and combining Apple II disk files. *Behavior Research Methods and Instrumentation, 15,* 387–388.

Note

The microcomputer lab was developed with the financial support of a grant from the National Science Foundation (ISEP) program SER #8162645.

Learning About Microcomputers and Research

Blaine F. Peden
University of Wisconsin–Eau Claire

In regard to psychologists' use of computers for instruction, interest is growing and resistance is diminishing (Butler, 1986). Bare (1982), Goolkasian (1985), and Hovancik (1986) described innovative uses for microcomputers in undergraduate laboratory courses. All three articles described the use of computers for data collection and analysis. Only Goolkasian discussed using the computer for instruction, although there are other uses for computers in teaching, such as computer-assisted instruction, modeling, and simulation (e.g., Atnip, 1985; Collyer, 1984).

This article outlines an approach that integrates the microcomputer into the entire research process. The method evolved over a period of several years as I worked individually with advanced undergraduates on research for presentation and publication. Nonetheless, this article should provide ideas and impetus for the classroom teacher by illustrating uses for the microcomputer throughout the research process–from the development of researchable hypotheses to the preparation of a manuscript for submission. In this process, students: (a) learn organizational skills, (b) acquire creative problem-solving and forecasting skills, (c) learn to think logically, and (d) develop and refine analytical and writing skills. Students also acquire knowledge about how to structure and program experiments and an appreciation for hardware and software.

Each semester one to three undergraduates begin work in my operant conditioning laboratory. They remain for one to four semesters, starting as assistants and later becoming collaborators. We conduct experiments dealing with conditioning and learning (e.g., Peden & Liddell, 1983), foraging and feeding (e.g., Peden & Rohe, 1984), and cognition and memory. We present the results at undergraduate research conferences or professional meetings, and sometimes they are published.

A typical student entering my laboratory has completed courses in statistics and research methods and has expressed an interest in performing research and attending graduate school. Although highly motivated, these students have little experience with research or microcomputers. My primary concern is to further their goals by involving them in research. This article discusses (a) student use of the Apple II microcomputer before, during, and after an experiment; and (b) some advantages of learning about microcomputers, in particular, and of conducting research, in general.

Prior to an experiment, students read pertinent articles to develop the background and expertise required to understand or generate testable hypotheses for a particular experiment. Although my lab is not now equipped to search on-line data bases for new references (Lewis, 1986), students use the microcomputer to organize previously obtained references from articles, books, and chapters on a specific topic. For example, it is possible to use a file card box for references, but the microcomputer with a specialized data base for references entitled, "Quick Search Librarian" (Interactive Microware), is better than a file card box (Collyer, 1984). This program uses a separate diskette for each different data base rather than different file card boxes. It also permits entering and editing all references in a particular data base, searching and sorting references according to key words, and printing a reference list. Students quickly learn to appreciate such an organizational boon, and experience with this data base prompts them to identify and use other, more generalized data-base programs for academic and personal applications.

Students working on questions about foraging and feeding soon encounter quantitative models. A second application of the microcomputer prior to an experiment involves the use of spreadsheets to perform "What-If" simulations. For example, we use an inexpensive and simple spreadsheet "Magical JR" (Main Street Publishing). This program allows us to compute a variety of hypothetical cost/benefit functions in order to select appropriate parameters for a new experiment, and to compare predictions for different quantitative models. Such activity develops problem-solving and forecasting skills that are applicable in many situations. Proficient students sometimes learn to use more advanced spreadsheets such as Visi-Calc.

In combination with ancillary hardware, students use the microcomputer during an experiment to present stimuli, such as lights and tones, and to record responses by pigeons and rats working in an experimental chamber. In my lab, each Apple II microcomputer is connected to one, two, or four different experimental chambers by a MED Associates interface that makes it easy to present stimuli, record responses, and time events. According to students, conducting an experiment with a microcomputer markedly enhances their appreciation for hardware and software.

All programs controlling our experiments are written in APPLESOFT, a version of interpreted BASIC. We use several Beagle Brothers diskettes containing "utility programs" that facilitate writing and editing an APPLESOFT program. They are: (a) "ProntoDOS," which minimizes the time required to load a program into memory and to save a program to a diskette; (b) "Global Program Line Editor" (GPLE), which provides quick and efficient means to correct errors in lines of code; (c) "Double-Take," which requires just a few keystrokes to perform various functions, such as listing the program, cataloging a disk, appending files, renumbering a program, and clearing the screen; and (d) "D-Code," which promptly identifies an error upon entering a line. This function is helpful to student programmers because it identifies statements with typographical errors and illegal commands immediately rather than later during program execution.

"D-Code" also contains a program called COMPACT that eliminates reminders (REM statements) and compresses a program into fewer lines of code. Although it is easier to understand and modify a documented program with many REM statements, a "compacted" (as compared to a fully documented) version of the program executes more rapidly during an experiment. A substantial increment in the speed of execution can also be demonstrated for "compiled" rather than "interpreted" programs. Two familiar and easily used compilers for APPLESOFT programs are the "Einstein" compiler (Einstein Corporation) and "The APPLESOFT Compiler or TASC" (Microsoft). In brief, the fastest program is one that is both compacted and compiled.

All students use the microcomputer to conduct an experiment; however, only the more advanced students and I actually write APPLESOFT programs for an experiment. We are, of course, more interested in conducting experiments than in computer programming per se. Students with majors or minors in computer science typically must learn to program in BASIC because their training begins with PASCAL. Students who have taken only an introductory computing course possess rudimentary programming skills in BASIC. In either case, it is useful for students to improve their programming skills. The computer science students learn a new language and respond enthusiastically to the opportunity to program in a real-time as opposed to a batch mode. A modicum of programming experience helps computer novices understand how the previously described utilities help to overcome the tiresome aspects of writing an APPLESOFT program. The students also learn how long it takes to write a program. Moreover, some programming experience helps computer novices understand the need to write logically organized, or structured, programs, and to document programs thoroughly–ideas well-entrenched for more sophisticated programmers. To this end, our programs contain many subroutines, each of which performs one function and includes many REM statements.

Learning about structured programs with internal documentation provides at least three benefits to students. One advantage is that new students can study previous programs and quickly learn the commands required to time events, activate outputs (e.g., lights), and measure inputs (e.g., responses). This experience helps a student to feel more confident about programming an experiment, and to appreciate hardware and software. A second advantage is that the experimenter must use organizational skills to specify each step in the sequence of experimental events before trying to write a program. Attempting to write a program prematurely often reveals logical and procedural problems, whereas the careful planning required to write a program for an experiment may suggest parametric manipulations and variations in the procedure that might not otherwise be obvious. A third advantage of this approach is that a subroutine solving a particular problem may be "transported" from one experiment to another, thereby decreasing the amount of time required for programming from experiment to experiment. For example, a subroutine we named "Activate the Peripheral Devices" provides instructions to the student experimenter about the order in which different peripheral devices, such as the MED Associates interface and the power supply, should be activated. This structured and documented subroutine is easily "transported" from a program for rats to one for pigeons by using "Double-Take" (Beagle Brothers) to append files. In sum, students learn to program experiments, understand procedures, and transfer solutions for one experiment to another. The extent to which an individual student's sophistication grows varies directly as a function of time spent in the lab and the number of projects completed.

After an experiment, the primary goal for the student is to write a report that is correct in form and content. At this point in the research process, the microcomputer is an invaluable tool for statistical analysis, data plotting, and word processing.

My students use statistical programs such as "Key Stat" (Oakleaf Systems) or the "Introductory Statistics Software Package" (Addison-Wesley) for simple statistical analysis and the "HSD Statistics" (Human Systems Dynamics) programs for complex analysis. Easy-to-use statistics programs make a student more willing to analyze data and to perform different analyses on a set of data. Programs such as "Scientific Plotter" (Interactive

Microware) or "Alphachart" and "Curve Plotter" (Spectral Graphics Software) make it easy to plot data. These programs encourage a student to consider alternative ways to represent the data.

Finally, all students learn to use "Applewriter II or IIe," a word processor, to prepare successive drafts of their laboratory reports. Word processing encourages students to revise manuscripts. Students are more willing to explore problem-solving strategies for writing, such as generating and organizing ideas, and editing for style and organization (Flower, 1981), when using a word processor than when writing by hand or typing. An outline processor (Rogers, 1986) is another program that will promote student use of problem-solving strategies for writing initial drafts of a paper. Ultimately, I favor use of "Manuscript Manager" (Pergamon Press), perhaps the word processor of choice because it is specifically designed for preparing manuscripts according to the APA style manual. Once students approach a final draft, they use "The Sensible Speller" (Sensible Software) to eliminate misspelled words and typographical errors.

In conclusion, a crucial component to the success of this endeavor is individualized instruction during one or more semesters (see also, Atnip, 1985, for a similar emphasis). This component is more important than either the particular microcomputer or the programs used, because programs comparable to those I have described are available for other machines as well.

Undergraduates working in my lab become skilled in only some of the microcomputer applications to which they are exposed—in large part, by choice. Students tell me that how much they learn about a particular application depends largely on the availability of the microcomputer and the software, and on personal needs. For example, in comparison to the university microcomputer lab, in which pertinent software is unavailable and computer access is limited, students have virtually unlimited access to the software and microcomputers in my lab, except during the hours reserved for experiments. This opportunity allows students to exploit some applications and to explore others according to their needs and interests.

Student use of the microcomputer before, during, and after an experiment produces benefits from learning about microcomputers and from conducting research. Undergraduates working with microcomputers in my laboratory derive, to varying degrees, several benefits, which help them to compete in graduate programs or the job world. With respect to learning about computers and computer applications, students: (a) learn creative problem-solving and forecasting skills, (b) learn organizational skills, (c) develop an appreciation for hardware and software, (d) learn to think logically and to write structured programs for real-time experiments, and (e) improve their analytical and writing skills. Students also gain laboratory experience and have an opportunity to present their experiments at under-

graduate research conferences. Students report that these experiences foster self-discipline, responsibility, social skills, a spirit of cooperation, self-confidence, and a sense of personal achievement.

The ideas expressed in this article should also be useful for teachers who use microcomputers in laboratory courses. For example, students exposed to data-base and spreadsheet applications will develop their own uses for these tools, especially as simple and easy-to-use programs become increasingly available in the public domain or at low cost. In a similar fashion, students learn quickly that expertise in using hardware and software programming aids is valuable in academic and applied settings. Finally, experience with outline processors, word processors, and spelling checkers helps students improve the quality of their writing, another important skill in academic and job settings.

References

Atnip, G. W. (1985). Teaching the use of computers: A case study. *Teaching of Psychology, 12,* 171–172.

Bare, J. K. (1982). Microcomputers in the introductory laboratory. *Teaching of Psychology, 9,* 236–237.

Butler, D. L. (1986). Interests in and barriers to using computers in instruction. *Teaching of Psychology, 13,* 20–23.

Collyer, C. E. (1984). Using computers in the teaching of psychology: Five things that seem to work. *Teaching of Psychology, 11,* 206–209.

Flower, L. (1981). *Problem-solving strategies for writing.* New York: Harcourt Brace Jovanovich.

Goolkasian, P. (1985). A microcomputer-based lab for psychology instruction. *Teaching of Psychology, 12,* 223–225.

Hovancik, J. R. (1986). Using microcomputers in the undergraduate laboratory. *Teaching of Psychology, 13,* 94–96.

Lewis, L. K. (1986). Bibliographic computerized searching in psychology. *Teaching of Psychology, 13,* 38–40.

Peden, B. F., & Liddell, B. (1983, May). *The paws that refresh: A preliminary attempt to condition self-grooming and other-grooming by rats.* Paper presented at the meeting of the Association for Behavior Analysis, Milwaukee, WI.

Peden, B. F., & Rohe, M. S. (1984). Effects of search cost on foraging and feeding: A three-component chain analysis. *Journal of the Experimental Analysis of Behavior, 42,* 211–221.

Rogers, R. L. (1986). Preparing course materials with an outline processor. *Teaching of Psychology, 13,* 154–155.

Notes

1. This article is based on a paper presented as part of a symposium, *Preparing Psychology Majors for Careers in Business: Teaching Computer Skills and Applications,* conducted at the meeting of the Midwestern Psychological Association in Chicago, IL, May 2–4, 1985.

2. Preparation of this article was supported in part by the University of Wisconsin–Eau Claire Faculty Sabbatical Leave Program and by a supplement to National Science Foundation Grant No. 84-11445 to William Timberlake at Indiana University, Bloomington.

3. I thank Allen Keniston and several anonymous reviewers for their comments on an earlier draft of this article.

Computer Literacy in the Psychology Curriculum: Teaching a Database Language for Control of Experiments

Robert H. Rittle
Indiana University of Pennsylvania

Computer literacy, a major goal in current university curricula, can be achieved in various ways. The strategy at my university is to incorporate computer training into the students' academic majors. Thus, our psychology curriculum was expected to address the computer skills needed by psychologists and to do so in the broader context of preparing students for a computer-oriented society.

One approach to meeting this departmental goal was to have students program microcomputers to control experimental tasks. Teaching students to program computers for research is not a new idea (Cozby, 1984; Peden, 1987). Previous suggestions, however, focused on the use of traditional programming languages such as BASIC. This article advocates the Structured Query Language (SQL), which introduces students to the general concept of database management.

Database management is a common application for psychologists; 31% of psychology departments reported the use of database systems (Stoloff & Couch, 1987). My experience in applied research indicates a frequent need among social agencies for database applications such as client tracking. Another database application for a social scientist involves monitoring the supply and demand of workers with given types of vocational training (Rittle, 1987, 1989).

This article describes a plan to teach database concepts in a research design class and to meet the specific need of programming computers for research purposes. The article presents exercises that progress from simple examples of computer programming to tasks used in actual experiments. A mail survey is reported in which students judged the relative importance of this topic in their research design course.

Method

Subjects

The subjects were 12 undergraduates who completed the course, Research Design and Analysis II, during the spring semester of 1989. The course was required for psychology majors and was the second in a two-course sequence I taught.

Materials

The SQL was chosen for several reasons. The computer commands that constitute SQL can be used with a choice of commercial database packages (e.g., the dBASE series from Ashton-Tate, 1986, or the Clipper series from Nantucket Corporation, 12555 West Jefferson Boulevard, Suite 300, Los Angeles, CA 90066). The basic commands needed to begin programming in SQL can be learned with relative ease by nonspecialists. The language enables one to create interactive, user-friendly screens as needed for an experimental task. The SQL is a complete programming language that offers the option of compiled programs to increase processing speed (Rubel, 1987).

To use a program written in SQL, one must have access to appropriate types of computer software and hardware. The most common choice of database software and the one used in this study is dBASE III Plus (Ashton-Tate, 1986). The cost of the database software generally ranges from $300 to $500, depending on available discounts. Reading assignments on dBASE can be drawn from a variety of textbooks (e.g., Byers & Prague, 1989; Chou, 1985).

To use dBASE III Plus (or an anticipated upgrade, dBASE IV), one must have access to the family of microcomputers commonly called the IBM/XT series or IBM compatibles. Students in my study used a microcomputer laboratory containing four Zenith Model ZDE-1211 computers with a hard drive and monochrome monitor.

Procedure

The subjects were generally unfamiliar with microcomputers and needed preliminary training on the computer's disk operating system (DOS). A 15-min exercise was used to introduce the DOS commands, which select a particular directory on the computer's disk drive and display, copy, or delete computer files (Norton, 1985).

Three class periods of 60 min each were devoted to the topic of programming a microcomputer to control experimental tasks. To keep within this time constraint, the exercises did not require original programming by the students. Rather, the students first ran a program written by the instructor and then modified the program to implement a desired change.

In one of the initial exercises, students ran a program for which they entered two numbers into the computer and received the sum of the numbers. The assignment sheet illustrated additional commands needed to incorporate this sequence into a loop, making it possible to calculate a series of sums. Students made the programming changes on a floppy disk and then completed test runs of the program. The goal of this exercise was to teach the concept of controlling a long series of trials by including a short set of commands in a repetitive loop.

In a later exercise, students ran a program that might be applicable in a social psychology experiment. The computer presented two numbers on the screen and instructed the subject to enter either the sum or the difference. The computer tallied the number of correct responses entered by the subject and displayed that tally along with the "top score earned by previous subjects." After running this program, students modified the dBASE code to create a more competitive version of the task. One requirement was to increase the top score as displayed by the computer. A second requirement was to program the computer to display a "nasty" message if subjects gave the wrong response. To illustrate the relative simplicity of the dBASE language, the program code for this exercise is given in Table 1.

Additional exercises involved a reaction-time task and a paired-associates task. To avoid the need for special peripheral

devices, such as a clock card, the programs were written so that elapsed times were measured by counters embedded in a DO WHILE loop. When the paired-associates task was given as an exercise, students altered the program to double the intertrial interval. They also modified the accompanying database file to change the pairs of words presented by the computer.

The final example of a computer-controlled task was designed for a class experiment. The computer was programmed to present six-letter stimulus words. The experimental task was to enter new words, using only the letters in the stimulus word. All students were trained to execute the program, but only students who chose to use it for their independent project actually modified the program code. For different independent projects, the task was customized to measure the response latency (in a study of drive level), to measure commonality of the subjects' responses, or to give predetermined feedback that subjects were highly creative.

Survey of Student Attitudes Toward the dBASE Unit

A survey was mailed in mid-July to the home addresses of the 12 students. The survey listed in chronological order

Table 1. dBASE Code for a Laboratory Task

```
* dBASE program named MATH.PRG
SET TALK OFF
TALLY = 0
CLEAR
@06,10 SAY 'YOUR            BEST'
@07,10 SAY 'SCORE           SCORE'
@08,10 SAY '----------      ----------'
@09,10 SAY '     0             102  '
* Open database file MATH.DBF (to read que & ans)
USE A:MATH.DBF
*Repeat DO loop until user does Not want to continue
STORE 'Y' TO FLAG
DO WHILE FLAG = 'Y'
@10,00 CLEAR
STORE SPACE(5) TO MYANSWER
@12,00 SAY 'THE NEXT QUESTION IS: ' + MATH_QUE
@12,40 GET MYANSWER
READ
IF MYANSWER = MATH_ANS
TALLY = TALLY + 1
ELSE
@16,00 SAY 'WRONG!! CORRECT ANSWER IS ' + MATH_ANS
WAIT
ENDIF
* Display current score; skip to next que in data file
@09,04 SAY TALLY
IF .NOT. EOF( )
SKIP
ELSE
GOTO TOP
ENDIF
@20,00 SAY 'Do you want another question (Y/N)?'
@20,37 GET FLAG PICTURE 'YN'
READ
ENDDO
SET TALK ON
```

the 10 units covered in the course. Subjects were asked to rank each unit from 1 to 10, with a rank of 1 indicating the unit most valuable "for a new psychologist like yourself." The units are listed in Table 2. To reduce demand characteristics, the survey was mailed under the sponsorship of the department's Undergraduate Committee; it was not connected to the instructor of the course.

Results

Surveys were returned by 7 of the 12 students. Table 2 shows the median rank for each unit, as calculated from the seven individual ranks. The target unit, using dBASE to program special tasks on a microcomputer, received a median rank of 5. Comparing the median rank across units, two of the units were perceived by students as being more important than the unit on dBASE. Four of the units were perceived as being less important.

Discussion

The survey responses indicate that the new unit, programming microcomputers to control experiments, was recognized as an important topic by students in a research design course. This finding confirms the result from an earlier class in which the dBASE unit was pilot tested. The 12 students from the pilot test completed a Likert scale immediately after the unit, rating its importance on a scale ranging from *much more important than other topics* (1) to *same importance* (5) to *much less important* (9). The mean rating was 5.2.

The training exercises were designed to introduce broad concepts, not to produce skilled programmers. Students modified existing programs rather than writing programs of their own. The programs were carefully structured to increase the likelihood that students would be successful in their modifications. This approach appeared important because roughly one half of the students expressed anxiety about the use of computers while completing the exercises. For the more anxious students, the instructor's primary goal was simply to increase confidence in using the hardware (IBM-compatible microcomputers) and the software (database management systems) that are prevalent in social and government agencies.

Various psychology courses could incorporate database training. A human learning class might complete exercises like those discussed here. A social psychology class could develop a database system to analyze survey data. A practicum class in clinical psychology could generate reports using a client tracking system developed by the instructor. If applications such as this were adopted by a group of faculty members, then the overall psychology curriculum would provide a broad introduction to the use of computers for database management.

References

Ashton-Tate. (1986). *Programming with dBASE III Plus.* Torrance, CA: Author.

Byers, R. A., & Prague, C. N. (1989). *Everyman's database primer, featuring dBASE IV.* Torrance, CA: Ashton-Tate.

Chou, G. T. (1985). *dBASE III handbook.* Indianapolis, IN: Cue Corp.

Cozby, P. C. (1984). *Using computers in the behavioral sciences.* Palo Alto, CA: Mayfield.

Norton, P. (1985). *PC-DOS: Introduction to high-performance computing.* Bowie, MD: Brady.

Peden, B. F. (1987). Learning about microcomputers and research. *Teaching of Psychology, 14,* 217–219.

Rittle, R. H. (1987). *Civilian training inventory for the U.S. Naval Reserve: System documentation.* Washington, DC: National Occupational Information Coordinating Committee.

Rittle, R. H. (1989). *An occupational information system for the Pacific Northwest: System documentation.* Salem, OR: Oregon Occupational Information Coordinating Committee.

Rubel, M. C. (1987). Benchmarking dBASE III Plus compilers. *BYTE, 12*(10), 277–281.

Stoloff, M. L., & Couch, J. V. (1987). A survey of computer use by undergraduate psychology departments in Virginia. *Teaching of Psychology, 14,* 92–94.

Notes

1. I thank Mary Lou Zanich, Gordon Thornton, and Loretta Rittle, for their valuable comments on a draft of this article.

2. The computer exercises completed by students are available from the author for the cost of duplication and mailing; include with your request a $5.00 check payable to the IUP Institute for Research and Community Service. The material includes student worksheets and a 5.25-in. floppy disk containing the corresponding computer programs. The programs must be used on an IBM/XT or compatible microcomputer, in conjunction with commercial software such as dBASE III Plus.

Table 2. Median Rank of Importance for 10 Course Units

Rank	Topic
1	Two-factor, mixed designs
8	Quasi-experimental methods
2	BMDP for statistical tests on a mainframe computer
5	dBASE to program special tasks on a microcomputer
5	Survey research
5	Three-factor designs
7	Nonexperimental designs
9	Chi-square tests
5	Single subject designs
6	Making sense of research (bias, meta-analysis)

6. Implementing Teaching Strategies

A simple stay-switch probability game demonstrates the importance of empirically testing our beliefs. Based on intuition, most of Art Kohn's undergraduate participants at North Carolina Central University believed that a *stay* strategy leads to a higher percentage of winning, and most faculty participants believed that *staying* and *switching* yielded equal probabilities of winning. A simple in-class demonstration proved that switching wins twice as often as staying, suggesting the importance of empirically validating our beliefs. A follow-up questionnaire indicated that participating in this experiment may increase students' trust in the empirical method.

John Bates at Georgia Southern University told his introductory psychology students that he had telepathic powers and demonstrated these "psychic" abilities by transmitting images into the minds of students and a confederate. Students generated alternative hypotheses to account for the observed phenomena and suggested ways to test their hypotheses. This article describes how to perform the psychic acts and outlines the hypothesis-testing activity. The demonstration encourages greater scientific skepticism and promotes enthusiastic class participation.

At the University of Richmond, James Polyson and Kenneth Blick interpreted a basketball game as a psychology experiment to teach students about scientific methodology. Their analogical approach compared aspects of a basketball game with important concepts used in planning and conducting an experiment, including the hypothesis, independent variables, dependent variables, operational definitions, and control. This activity probably works best for basketball fans.

Kerry Chamberlain from Massey University in New Zealand describes his use of topical laboratory projects that are relevant to course content and that meet various objectives. An appropriate core article from the published literature serves as the basis for each project, which entails full or partial replication of an experiment from the core article. The author mentions several advantages and limitations of this unusual approach.

A method for improving performance in laboratory courses is described by David Carroll from the University of Wisconsin–Superior. Students worked in small groups in which each person made a unique contribution to a research project. The technique encourages cooperation, and evaluations suggest that students liked the approach and that it enhanced their academic performance. Advantages and potential problems are mentioned.

Donald McBurney from the University of Pittsburgh used the problem method, sometimes called the case-study method, in teaching research techniques to undergraduates. Problems are assigned in advance, students use course material to solve each problem, and solutions are discussed in class. The approach emphasizes problem-solving and critical-thinking skills, and students find the method challenging and interesting.

Thomas Wilson from Bellarmine College and Douglas Hershey from George Mason University designed an unusual classroom activity for students in a research methods course. Students identify and evaluate their own procedural knowledge of the research process, generate scripts from their event-based mental representation of the process, and compare their own scripts to one from expert psychologists. Students consider the activity to be interesting and useful.

After a minute of study, William Marmie's students at the University of Colorado, Boulder recalled more features of a dime than of an unstudied penny. This demonstration illustrates the subjective nature of scientific judgment, the value of statistics in data management, and the rationale for including the method and results sections in a scientific paper. Also, it illustrates the principle that details of an object or event are difficult to remember unless they are studied intentionally.

Richard May and Michael Hunter at the University of Victoria found widespread confusion about random sampling and random assignment to different treatment groups among psychology undergraduates, graduates, and faculty. The authors attribute this confusion to a bias in psychologists' training, and they recommend more coverage of both procedures.

For his research methods students at the University of Utah, Bryan Gibson devised a game based on the TV show Jeopardy. The format involves students in study sessions and helps them organize course material. Students said that the game was educational and entertaining.

Defying Intuition: Demonstrating the Importance of the Empirical Technique

Art Kohn
North Carolina Central University

In about 350 BC, Aristotle argued that the speed with which an object falls to earth is directly proportional to its weight (i.e., that heavier objects would fall to earth faster than lighter ones). Aristotle was wrong. But owing to the sheer force of his rhetoric, his axiom remained unchallenged for more than 2,000 years. Indeed, it was not until the Renaissance that Galileo performed his famous experiment proving gravity works with equal force on all objects. This refutation of Aristotelian physics shook the intellectual community of the time because it highlighted the limits of human intuition and emphasized the importance of inductive reasoning. This insight, in turn, helped to usher in the era of empirical exploration.

The following classroom demonstration, which is based on a puzzle that appeared in *Parade* magazine, dramatically illustrates both the limitations of intuitive judgments and the power of empirical investigation. The activity takes about 15 min of class time, and the only materials required are three identical envelopes and a $1 bill. I conduct this activity on the first day of my introductory and experimental psychology courses to set an empirical tone for the semester.

The Demonstration

The demonstration consists of three parts: presenting the probability puzzle, polling the class's intuitive judgments about the optimum solution to the puzzle, and conducting an experiment to test the accuracy of these intuitive judgments. To begin, tell your students that you plan to present a simple probability question involving three choices. Place the $1 bill into one envelope, seal all three envelopes, and then shuffle them so that no one, yourself included, knows which one contains the $1 bill. (You may want to put some folded paper into each envelope so that the students cannot see or feel the bill through the envelope.)

Now ask a volunteer to select an envelope, promising that the person will be able to keep the $1 bill if she or he guesses correctly. After the volunteer selects the envelope, announce that you plan to reveal that one of the unchosen envelopes is empty. Examine the contents of the two unchosen envelopes and, with a bit of fanfare, reveal to the class that one of them does not contain the $1 bill. (Indeed, at least one remaining envelope must be empty.) Finally, holding up the remaining unchosen envelope, present the class with the critical question: "As you can see, the volunteer and I each have an envelope. However, at this time I will offer the volunteer a chance to switch with me. In your opinion, for the greatest chance of winning, should the volunteer stay with the initial choice or switch to my envelope?"

Following the discussion, poll the class's opinions. In my sections, typically 50% to 60% of the students favor staying, 20% to 30% favor switching, and 10% to 20% argue that, in terms of probability, it makes no difference whether the volunteer stays or switches.

Point out to the class that they are basing their opinions on intuition rather than on empirical data. Invite them to test their intuitive beliefs by conducting an experiment that will identify the best strategy.

Instruct the students to pair up, with one member acting as the experimenter and the other as the subject. Each experimenter should make a data sheet by labeling four columns "Correct Answer," "Subject's Choice," "Stay/Switch," and "Win/Lose" and by numbering the rows 1 to 20. Finally, the experimenters should fill in the correct-answer cells with a random assortment of the letters *A, B,* and *C*.

To conduct the experiment, each experimenter simply imitates the procedure I used with the class volunteer. The experimenter should (a) prompt the subject to guess either *A, B,* or *C;* (b) reveal that one of the unchosen options is incorrect; and (c) offer the subject the option of switching to the other unchosen option. On Trial 1, for example, if the correct answer is *A* and the subject chooses *C,* then the experimenter would inform the subject that *B* is an incorrect choice and offer the subject a chance to switch to *A.* On Trial 2, if the correct answer is *A* and the subject chooses *A,* then the experimenter would reveal that *B* (or *C*) is incorrect and offer the subject the chance to switch. For each of the 20 trials, the experimenter should record the subject's initial choice, whether the subject switched, and whether the subject ultimately selected the right choice. After everyone has completed the procedure, experimenters calculate the number of times that switching led to a win and the number of times that staying led to a win. Finally, the instructor should combine the results for the entire class and draw a graph comparing the percentage of wins that result from switching and from staying.

Evaluation

I evaluated this demonstration in three ways. First, I asked 140 undergraduates and 73 university faculty members which strategy they thought was most likely to result in winning. Each subject read a 150-word summary of the situation and then circled one of the following responses: "Your chances are best if you stay with your initial choice," "Your chances are best if you switch to the other choice," or "It will not matter whether you stay or switch; your chances of winning will be the same."

Fifty-five percent of the undergraduates believed that staying provided the greatest chance of winning, whereas 66% of the faculty believed that staying and switching yielded the same chance of winning. Only 28% of the undergraduates and 7% of the faculty believed that switching envelopes provided the best chance of winning.

Second, I conducted the in-class experiment with 84 introductory psychology students. I tallied the number of times the 42 subjects chose to stay or switch and the consequences of each choice.

Subjects significantly preferred the staying strategy, staying on 60% of the trials (binomial test, $N = 840$), $p < .001$. Although the subject preferred to stay, switching actually resulted in a significantly greater proportion of wins, $\chi^2(1, N = 840) = 95.9, p < .001$. Subjects won in 69% of the trials when they switched, whereas they won in only 34% of the trails when they stayed. I recently replicated this study with as few as 6 subjects, so the demonstration should work for all class sizes.

Finally, I asked all the students to complete the Trust in Research Survey (Kohn, in press) that measures reliance on intuition versus empirical investigation. The questionnaire consists of 10 questions such as "Your religion tells you that an event occurred, but research clearly shows that it did not happen. What will you base your opinion on?" and "You need to buy a reliable car, and your intuition tells you to buy *Brand X*. However, all the research shows that *Brand Z* is better. How will you decide which car to buy?" For each question, the subjects rated whether they would base their actions on *intuition only* (1) to *research only* (9). The students filled out the Trust in Research Survey along with several other unrelated surveys. Half the students filled out

the survey immediately before participating in the demonstration, and half of them completed it 2 hr afterward.

Results of the Trust in Research Survey indicate that students who participated in the demonstration had higher trust in the empirical technique than students before the demonstration; however, this effect did not reach statistical significance. The mean for students who took the survey before the demonstration was 4.5, whereas the mean for those who took it afterward was 6.1, $t(166) = 1.53, p < .1$.

Discussion

This activity provides a dramatic example of the limitations of intuitive judgments and the importance of empirical testing. Although the puzzle is simple, involving only three possible answers, most subjects fail to solve it; ironically, subjects with doctorates err more often than undergraduates.

After the demonstration, you may want to explain the mathematical rationale for these counterintuitive results. In this explanation, the critical premise is that the instructor's act of eliminating an unchosen envelope does not affect the chances that the student's envelope is a winner. To illustrate this, I begin with an analogous, realistic situation. I tell my class to imagine that four teams have qualified for an upcoming Final Four basketball tournament. In the first round, Kentucky is scheduled to play Duke and Indiana is scheduled to play UCLA. Given equal quality of the teams, the chances that Kentucky, for example, will win the tournament are one in four. However, assume that the Indiana team decides to withdraw from the tournament. How will this affect Kentucky's chances? In fact, the odds of Kentucky winning do not change at all. Indiana was outside Kentucky's qualifying bracket in the first round, so Kentucky still must win two games. As a result, the chances that Kentucky will win the tournament remain one in four. For UCLA, however, the chances of winning improve to one in two. A betting person should shift from backing Kentucky to backing UCLA.

This situation is analogous to the three envelope problem. The initial probability that the instructor has the $1 bill is two chances in three, and the initial probability that the student has the $1 bill is one chance in three. Importantly, once the student selects an envelope, that envelope becomes a set that is entirely independent of the instructor's set; in effect, the envelope is placed into a separate qualifying bracket. Thus, when the instructor acts as an omniscient agent and eliminates a certain loser from within his or her set that act in no way affects the probabilities that the student's set contains the winner. The chances that the instructor has the winner remain two out of three; the chances that the student has the winner remain one out of three. As a result, the student is better off switching envelopes.

Consider a different situation, however, in which the student selects envelope *A* and then accidently peeks into envelope C and realizes that it is empty. Should the student switch from A to B? The answer is no because, under these conditions, A was not segregated into a separate category; the student's insight simply eliminated an option from the set A, B, and C. Thus, the student's insight leaves two alternatives with equal probabilities of being correct. This latter situation is analogous to a student guessing A on a three-item multiple-choice exam. If the student later realizes that answer C is certainly wrong, the student gains no advantage by switching from A to B.

Your students might appreciate knowing that when mathematicians were confronted with an analogous puzzle, their intuition misled them as well. In 1990, a similar question was submitted to Marilyn vos Savant, a newspaper columnist who, according to the *Guinness Book of World Records,* has the world's highest IQ. When Ms. vos Savant answered (correctly) that switching provided the greatest chance of winning, she received a storm of protests from mathematicians around the country. See Posner (1991) for an interesting history of this controversy.

Following the discussion, you can again ask your volunteer whether he or she wants to stay with the original choice or switch to the remaining envelope. About 90% of the time, my volunteers seem convinced by the data and switch envelopes. However, if your experience is like mine, some of your students (and even some of your colleagues) will continue to insist that switching envelopes does not increase their chances of winning. Under these conditions, your only option may be to encourage them to conduct the experiment on their own, and then you may want to remind them that truth is not obliged to be consistent with intuition.

References

Kohn, A., (in press). *Communicating psychology: An instructor's resource guide to accompany Kalat's Introduction to Psychology* (3rd ed.). Belmont, CA: Wadsworth.

Posner, G. P. (1991). Nation's mathematicians guilty of 'innumeracy.' *Skeptical Inquirer, 15,* 342–345.

Note

I thank the students in Experimental Psychology and in History and Systems at North Carolina Central University for their assistance with this study. I also thank Wendy Kohn, Richard Burke, Jim Kalat, Ruth Ault, and anonymous reviewers for their help in improving this article.

Teaching Hypothesis Testing by Debunking a Demonstration of Telepathy

John A. Bates
*Department of Educational Foundations & Curriculum
Georgia Southern University*

Many postsecondary educators are concerned about the rising tide of pseudoscientific, fundamentally anti-intellectual belief among otherwise well educated Americans. Bates (1987) reported that nearly half of a large sample of teacher education students believed that the full moon causes violent behavior. Feder (1986) found that more than one third of the students at a northeastern state university believed that ghosts are real. Miller (1987) conducted a national survey indicating that nearly two fifths of college graduates believe that the earth has been visited by aliens from other planets.

Educators combat student misbeliefs by debunking pseudoscientific claims specific to their own disciplines (e.g., Eve & Harrold, 1986; Harrold & Eve, 1986; Hoffmaster, 1986). These efforts have met with modest success: Some have demonstrated increased factual knowledge about reality without much corresponding decrease in pseudoscientific beliefs (Harrold & Eve, 1986); others have reported significant gains in scientific skepticism, but only for students with a neutral position on pseudoscientific claims (Banziger, 1983). Only a few reported attempts (notably, Gray, 1984) have demonstrated significant long-term changes in students' beliefs across a broad range of paranormal and irrational claims.

The classroom exercise described here holds some promise as a technique to debunk a specific pseudoscientific claim and to promote critical, scientific inquiry into psychological phenomena in general. An important goal of this exercise was to capture and hold students' attention. As Hoffmaster (1986) noted, "one of the driest subjects on earth to try to teach is the scientific method" (p. 432). The key to this goal, I believed, was to be found in the application of some basic principles of psychological arousal theory and of stage magic.

Format of the Activity

The Students

The activity was conducted in two different classrooms of introductory psychology. Both classrooms included about 35 students, all first-semester freshmen, about two thirds of whom were women.

The Lesson

All aspects of the activity were identical for both classrooms and proceeded in four stages.

Introductory information. The first 30 min of a class meeting was used to discuss some basic concepts of science. Initial consideration was given to the scientific belief in a physical reality that is independent of any observer. Special emphasis was given to the formulation of empirical hypotheses, in contrast to other sorts of answers to questions. Finally, it was pointed out that scientific hypotheses must be stated in such a way that evidence could be obtained to demonstrate that they are false, if they really are false. The lecture component of the presentation concluded with the assertion that all scientific endeavors, including scientific psychology, are not attempts to establish absolute truth, but rather are attempts to expose and eliminate false claims about the nature of reality.

Demonstration of psychic ability. After completing the lecture component, I announced that I had discovered a talent for transferring my thoughts telepathically into the minds of other people. I offered to demonstrate my talent, but said that it was not yet refined, so I could not guarantee that everyone would receive exactly the right thought.

I told the class that I would think of a two-digit number from 1 to 50, such that both numbers would be odd and different from each other. As examples, I told them that the number could not be something like 11, but that 15 would be okay. After a moment, I wrote a number on my tablet, drew a line through it, wrote another, and commented that the second number seemed to be a better choice. Next, I stared at the number and announced that I was transmitting it to the class. Each student was to write down the first number that came to mind and that fit my description.

As soon as all students had written a number, I asked if any of them had chosen 37. To their surprise, about one third of the students had thought of that number. I looked disappointed, then asked whether any had chosen 35. I showed them my tablet and explained that I had written 35 first, then crossed it out. Some of the class thus might have picked up the wrong signal. I asked how many of them had thought of either 35 or 37, and more than half the class raised their hands.

I suggested that numbers do not always work for everyone; sometimes, a picture is better. Therefore, I told them that I would think of two simple geometric shapes, one inside the other. At this point, I drew something quickly on the tablet, grumbled about being sloppy, tore off the page, and drew something else. I informed the class that I was sending the image of the two shapes, and I asked them to draw what first came to their minds. After a moment, I held up the tablet for all to see the shapes of a triangle completely circumscribed by a circle. Again, about one third of the class indicated that they had drawn the same picture.

I asked whether any had drawn a circle inside a triangle, explaining that the images sometimes become reversed in the transmission. Another third raised their hands. I then showed them the drawing that I had rejected—one of a square not fully surrounded by a circle—and asked if anyone inadvertently had picked up a stray signal of it. Several more hands went up. Then, one student volunteered that she had put a triangle inside a square. I asked whether anyone else had received parts of both signals. By now, nearly everyone had raised a hand.

Finally, I told them we had with us a guest who shared with me an almost perfect psychic link. The guest, another member of my department, was introduced. I explained that our special mental relationship was best demonstrated by a simple playing-card guessing game. A volunteer shuffled a standard deck of cards and dealt three rows of five cards each, face up, on the table at the front of the room. My partner faced the back of the room, and I asked one of the students to point to one of the cards. When the student did, my partner turned around, and I proceeded to point to an apparently random sequence of the cards, saying after each, "Is it this one?" or "Is it that one?" Each time I did not point to the target card, my partner replied negatively. When, after five or six repetitions of this procedure, I finally pointed at the target, my partner quickly responded affirmatively.

Small-group generation of hypotheses. Several repetitions yielded successful detection of the target card. Students who were still skeptical of my ability were challenged to develop a more parsimonious account of what they had observed. Students organized into groups of three or four and tried to produce at least two different testable hypotheses that could answer the question, "How did he do that?"

Hypothesis testing/revision. At the beginning of the next class meeting, students again organized into their groups, and a single, one-page worksheet requiring several categories of responses was distributed to each group. Students first were asked to summarize their observations of the psychic phenomena, to generate at least two alternative empirical hypotheses to account for their observations, and to design a test that could falsify each hypothesis. Thirty min were allotted for this part of the activity.

Next, my colleague and I made ourselves available for hypothesis testing. The groups took turns specifying a set of conditions under which the playing card "thought transfer" should occur. To ensure all groups sufficient time to test their hypotheses, I informed the class that if I knew it would be impossible to perform the transfer under a given set of conditions, then I would tell them so, rather than taking the time to demonstrate it.

The most common hypotheses involved either some prearranged number of cards to which I would point before reaching the target card or some mathematical formula involving the numerical values of the target and other cards. These were quickly rejected when the groups discovered that they could specify when in a sequence I should point to the target, and my colleague still would be able to identify it. The next most common hypotheses involved where on a card my finger was when I pointed to it. These were rejected when I varied the part touched or when I was not permitted to touch the card, which had no effect on the outcome.

Once all groups had tested both hypotheses once, they were given the opportunity either to retest what seemed to be the better of the two or to test a modified or new hypothesis. Most groups rejected all versions of numerical or positional hypotheses and focused on the modification of what I said to my partner or the tone or volume of my voice.

Within about 20 min, one or two groups were certain that they had determined the correct explanation for the phenomena, so I invited one of the members to take the place of my partner to see if the outcome could be duplicated. It was to their considerable delight, as well as to the consternation of some of their classmates, when these students were able to identify the target card.

Hypothesis testing, revision, and retesting continued until 15 min remained in the class period. Time was provided for the completion of the worksheet, including discussions of test outcomes, modifications of hypotheses, and final conclusions regarding my "special ability." As the students turned in their assignments and filed out, many of them looked at me with knowing smiles, some appeared less than sure of themselves, but nearly all were commenting to each other about what had occurred, using words like *falsified, replicate,* and *empirical.*

Postscript: How the Psychic Deeds Were Done

There were three components to the psychic demonstration, all supposedly involving the transference of thoughts from one mind into one or more other minds. The first two—transference of a number and transference of a shape—are illusions commonly performed by stage mentalists like Kreskin and may be thought of as the hook to capture student attention. Procedures for performing these feats are discussed in detail by Marks and Kammann (1980) in their critical analysis of claims of psychic ability.

Number transference and shape transference rely on poorly understood but documented and reliable population stereotypes in the construction of various categories of thought. As you recall, the demonstration involved the mental transference of a two-digit number between 1 and 50, such that both digits were odd and different from each other. Generally, few people realize that the qualifications placed on number selection have severely reduced the possible choices. There are only eight numbers that satisfy all the criteria: 13, 15, 17, 19, 31, 35, 37, and 39. Furthermore, the instructions were clarified by adding that the number could not be 11, but that something like 15 would be acceptable. Using 15 as an example of an acceptable target guarantees that virtually no one will select it, thus reducing the number of likely choices to seven. Marks and Kammann (1980) found that about 33% of a sample of adults think of 37 as the target number and that another 25% select 35. Thus, by claiming to have chosen first one then the other of these numbers as I was performing the thought transference, I was able to include nearly 60% of the class in my set of successes.

Most college students probably could discover that the limited number of possible targets made the outcome far less dramatic than it first appeared. It is important, therefore, to move on immediately to another, different demonstration of psychic ability—the transfer of an image of two simple geometric shapes, one inside the other. Population stereotypes for shape selection are as strong as those for number selection. Marks and Kammann reported that 33% will draw a combination of a triangle and a circle, 25% will draw a combination of a square and a circle, and 11% will combine triangle with square. With a little showmanship, I demonstrated to about 70% of my students that I had indeed transferred my thoughts into their minds.

The central component of the entire demonstration was the card-selection routine that my colleague and I enacted. To perform this illusion, cards are arranged randomly in three rows; the number of cards in each row is irrelevant. The confederate for this task needs only to remember that the top and bottom rows will be the *this* rows and the middle row will be the *that* row. If the "mentalist" points to a card and uses the correct adjective for that row of cards, then it is not the target card. The mentalist is pointing to the target only when the incorrect modifier is used.

For example, assume that the target card was in the middle row. I might point successively to cards in the top row, the middle row, and the bottom row, before pointing to the target. I would ask, "Is it *this* one?," "Is it *that* one?," and "Is it *this* one?," respectively. My partner would respond, with varying degrees of apparent certainty, that none of those was the target. Finally, I would point to the target and ask, "Is it *this* one?" My partner quickly would be able to respond correctly.

This routine has several advantages as an event for which students must generate empirical hypotheses. First, it is easy to do: My colleague only had about 1 min of instruction before we entered the classroom for our performance, and he never made a mistake. Second, very few students are likely to be familiar with it. Third, the trick behind the event seems to be obvious but it is not. The unexpected difficulty that students experience in trying to explain what they have observed tends to arouse and maintain their curiosity. Most important, for its use in a classroom, the demonstration and its underlying causes are empirical events. Students can directly manipulate the variables of the demonstration and observe a variety of outcomes. Hypotheses can be tested quickly, modified, or rejected, without special equipment or training. Best of all, when students uncover the solution to their problem and are able to replicate the event as evidence of their success, they experience the same sort of satisfaction felt by scientific psychologists in their systematic study of human behavior.

An important goal of this activity is to capture student attention. I have been teaching undergraduate students the basic principles of science for about 12 years and do not recall ever having achieved the enthusiastic class participation that is maintained throughout the demonstration of my psychic powers. Whether this enthusiasm is due entirely to the mode of presentation of the lesson or to some combination of environmental and student factors, I cannot say. My experience suggests that incorporating novel, surprising, and varied (i.e., psychologically arousing) stimuli is essential if students are going to pay attention to the abstract concepts and philosophical issues central to scientific inquiry. This lesson incorporates such stimuli and captures student attention.

References

Banziger, G. (1983). Normalizing the paranormal: Short-term and long-term change in belief in the paranormal among older learners during a short course. *Teaching of Psychology, 10,* 212–214.

Bates, J. A. (1987). Degrees of scientific literacy and intellectualism among students in a college of education. *The Foundations Monthly Newsletter, 4,* 7–9.

Eve, R. A., & Harrold, F. B. (1986). Creationism, cult archaeology, and other pseudoscientific beliefs: A study of college students. *Youth and Society, 17,* 396–421.

Feder, K. L. (1986). The challenge of pseudoscience. *Journal of College Science Teaching, 26,* 180–186.

Gray, T. (1984). University course reduces belief in paranormal. *The Skeptical Inquirer, 8,* 247–251.

Harrold, F. B., & Eve, R. A. (1986). Noah's ark and ancient astronauts: Pseudoscientific beliefs about the past among a sample of college students. *The Skeptical Inquirer, 11,* 61–75.

Hoffmaster, S. (1986). Pseudoscience: Teaching by counterexample. *Journal of College Science Teaching, 26,* 432–436.

Marks, D., & Kammann, R. (1980). *The psychology of the psychic.* Buffalo: Prometheus Books.

Miller, J. D. (1987, June). The scientifically illiterate. *American Demographics,* pp. 26–31.

Note

I thank Leigh Culpepper for his help in preparing this article.

Basketball Game as Psychology Experiment

James A. Polyson
Kenneth A. Blick
University of Richmond

Helping students understand basic concepts in experimental method can be quite a challenge for the introductory psychology teacher. Some students find the topic difficult or boring, leading one teacher (Gleitman, 1984) to recommend covering methodology only where it is necessary in order to understand some other topic. Even if one agrees with Gleitman, that still leaves a lot of methodology to be taught in introductory psychology.

It has been suggested (Vandervert, 1980) that the learning of psychological concepts is facilitated when the material is presented in relation to topics that are meaningful to students. One strategy for making psychological knowledge more relevant to students' real-world interests has been the use of popular culture in the classroom (Hughes, 1984; Polyson, 1983; Solomon, 1979). Using a similar approach, we have found that it is possible to introduce new methodological concepts and illustrate previously defined concepts using a basketball game.

It should first be noted that using basketball examples might be more effective at a school with a high level of enthusiasm for the intercollegiate basketball program. Such was the case at the University of Richmond this past season. The Spiders had their best season ever, winning two games in the NCAA tournament before losing to perennial power Indiana. Basketball was a popular topic of conversation on campus, and it was during such a discussion that the present authors discovered their mutual interest in using basketball to illustrate basic experimental method.

A basketball game can be construed as a psychology experiment. For example:

Hypothesis. A basketball game is the testing of a hypothesis regarding which of two teams is "better" in the wide array of mental ad psychomotor skills called basketball. Some observers, such as a loyal fan or bettor, would predict a winner. That is a one-tailed hypothesis. An impartial observer, such as a TV commentator, might decline to say which team will win, thus making a two-tailed hypothesis.

Independent Variable. The independent variable is simply the two teams, the groups that are being compared. The experimenter in psychology often tries to compose the two groups in a random fashion so they are as equal as possible at the outset. Random assignment is impossible in basketball, although the pro draft is an attempt to introduce some "fairness" into the team selection process at that level.

Dependent Variable. The behavior that is being compared must be defined in a measurable way. The measure of skill in a basketball game is the number of points scored; the "better" team is the one scoring higher on that measure. That is the operational definition. We must also define "higher." How much higher? When psychologists compare the scores of two or more groups, they use statistical analysis to decide what difference is necessary in order to say that the outcome was not just luck or chance. In basketball, the necessary difference is 1 point, except for some neighborhood pick-up games in which a team must win by 2 points.

Control. The basic reason a basketball game is an experiment and not just a "guess" is that the designers of the game have attempted to minimize any explanations for the game's outcome other than basketball skill (''to keep the losers from making excuses," as one student put it after our big upset win over Auburn). That is why the number of players on the court is kept even and irrelevant skills such as judo are ruled out by calling fouls. The home court advantage can be ruled out by doing the experiment twice in a home-and-away series (replication). A loose rim provides no advantage for either team because the teams switch goals at halftime (counterbalanced design). This is essentially what a psychology experiment attempts to do: Define the relevant variables and control for as many irrelevant ones as possible. For example, basketball did not adopt the 12-foot goal proposed during the dominant college career of Lew Alcindor (now Kareem Jabbar), presumably because it was decided that a player's height is relevant to the game and should not be counteracted with that rule.

These and other basketball examples were presented during lecture in three introductory classes and one experimental psychology class. In the introductory classes, the lecture and discussion were presented in conjunction with a 30-minute film, "Methodology: The Psychologist and the Experiment" (produced by McGraw-Hill), and in both courses the same concepts were brought up throughout the semester whenever a topic involved experimental research.

Unfortunately, we have no direct evidence for the effectiveness of the basketball analogy as a learning device. However, we were impressed by the quality of class discussion generated by the basketball lecture. (For instance, how would you design a rule in basketball to eliminate coaching as an influence on the outcome?) Also, in the second author's experimental psychology course, there was a final exam question asking students to illustrate experimental concepts using another sport of their choice. Students chose a variety of team and individual sports and most of their answers were thoughtful and well-written. It is possible that any unifying theme around which students can organize a number of related concepts could be helpful in promoting students' understanding of those concepts. Perhaps the basketball analogy just caught their attention.

Sort of like a good slam dunk.

References

Gleitman, H. (1984). Introducing psychology. *American Psychologist, 39,* 421–427.

Hughes, R. L. (1984). Teaching concepts of personal adjustment using popular music. *Teaching of Psychology, 11,* 115.

Polyson, J. A. (1983). Student essays about TV characters: A tool for understanding personality theories. *Teaching of Psychology, 10,* 103–105.

Solomon, P. R. (1979). Science and television commercials: Adding relevance to the research methodology course. *Teaching of Psychology, 6,* 26–30.

Vandervert, L. R. (1980). Operational definitions made simple, lasting, and useful. *Teaching of Psychology, 7,* 57–59.

Devising Relevant and Topical Undergraduate Laboratory Projects: The Core Article Approach

Kerry Chamberlain
Massey University

The value of research experience in the undergraduate curriculum is widely recognized (Edwards, 1981; Palladino, Carsrud, Hulicka, & Benjamin, 1982; VandeCreek & Fleischer, 1984), and various approaches can be taken to provide this experience (e.g., Carroll, 1986; Chamberlain, 1986; Kerber, 1983; Palladino et al., 1982). The most common approach is probably the class laboratory project, which achieves several purpose, ranging from giving students research experience to developing their abilities in statistical analyses.

Several innovative procedures for laboratory assignments have been proposed. Lutsky (1986) outlined a procedure based on the analysis of data sets. Carroll (1986) described a jigsaw approach; students work in small groups and each is responsible for one aspect of the project. Suter and Frank (1986) used classical experiments from the journals as the basis for projects.

This articles outlines an approach to devising laboratory projects that are topical and relevant to the course content and meet a variety of course objectives. The approach is based on choosing a core article that provides the framework for the research project in terms of scope, method, and reporting. It differs from Suter and Frank's procedure by using recent rather than classical research articles and by having students go beyond critical reading of the article to replication of the research. Because the core article defines the research systematically, projects can be readily generated by the instructor and more easily completed by individual students.

Aims

In my second-year undergraduate course on cognition, I had several aims for my laboratory projects. First, I wanted to have the projects well integrated with the course text. Second, I wanted students to read beyond the text and to use and reference original reports in journal article format.

186

I wanted these articles to be manageable, appropriate for the undergraduate level, and current. Third, I wanted students to function as experimenters rather than as subjects and to collect their own data from "real" subjects rather than their classmates. This data collection needed to be held to manageable proportions to ensure that it was achievable and interesting rather than tedious and time-consuming. Fourth, I wanted to provide opportunities for students to develop their skills at reporting research in APA format. I also wanted to restrict the literature review and data analysis in order to sustain the students' focus on accurate and concise communication. Finally, to avoid the problems of laboratory project reports being passed on from year to year, I wanted to have projects that were easy to generate so that they could be changed annually.

Procedures

Although these aims may appear to be difficult to achieve simultaneously, in practice they were not. The central requirement was to choose a core article as the basis for each project. The core article determined the dimensions of the research and defined the scope of the reports.

Core articles were identified by scanning the course text and recent journals for possibilities, with the constraint that each had to be relevant to a central theme taught in the course, up-to-date, and suitable in length and complexity of design and analysis. Ideal core articles were typically 5 to 7 pages, reported one or two experiments, and warranted at least a brief discussion in the text. Copies of each core article, provided in conformity with current copyright legislation, were issued to students along with the materials and specific requirements for each project.

Each project was organized as a full or partial replication of an experiment in the core article. Procedural details for the research, such as list lengths, number of trials, and stimulus presentation times, were kept as close to the original as possible. Stimulus materials were taken from the core article where possible or generated under the same constraints otherwise. All students in the course completed the same projects but collected data individually. Following data collection, class meetings were held to discuss the research issues arising from each project.

Each student was required to collect data from 4 to 10 subjects, depending on how extensive the procedure was and how many conditions the research design contained. To make the analysis more viable, additional data were provided. Students added their own data and analyzed the total data set. Statistical analyses were limited to techniques already in the students' repertoires, because the course did not include teaching statistical procedures. The provision of additional data also served to ensure that students usually obtained significant results in the

direction of the original research and avoided the problem of ambiguous nonsignificant results, which frequently afflicts the group laboratory class. Further, providing data meant that the success of the project did not depend entirely on the students' skills as experimenters. On the other hand, poor data collection skills could usually be identified by comparing results obtained by other class members. Sources for the additional data were either a subset taken directly from data reported in the core article or hypothetical data generated from the summary statistics given in the core article.

A report of the research in standard APA format was required. Reference sources for the report were limited to the core article and the course text, ensuring that the reports were focused and relevant.

Outcomes

I have been using this approach for 4 years and find it to have several benefits. Although the approach has not been formally evaluated, informal student feedback is positive. The use of a core article produces assignments that are focused specifically. As a result, students report being very clear about the scope of the task and what is expected of them in conducting and reporting their research. Because students are required to collect their data individually, they must rely on their own resources. They comment favorably on the opportunity to conduct research with real subjects and the freedom to complete the laboratory work in their own time. The personal responsibility associated with this approach appears to be highly valued.

From the instructor's viewpoint, the approach produces projects that are relevant to the course content. Studies described briefly in the text can be brought to life when the original material is used as a core article and for a laboratory project. Use of research literature is enhanced, as students must read and understand core articles in detail in order to conduct their projects successfully. Making copies of core articles available ensures ready access to the required material and avoids competition for library resources. Because students find assignments to have a clear and manageable scope and high relevance, compliance with requirements is high. Class laboratory times, scheduled following data collection for each project, provide useful discussion sessions on research issues arising out of the projects. Because students have conducted the research at this point, the discussions are relevant to their experience and provide pertinent learning situations. Finally, the approach allows projects to be developed and changed readily to maintain a topical content and to accommodate course changes, such as the adoption of a new text.

Projects organized on this basis do have some limitations, however. Because the background reading is quite narrowly defined, students gain only limited skills in organizing a body of literature and reporting it in an introduction section. The limited reference set also makes it difficult to develop an in-depth discussion section. Because references are readily available, students need not engage in library search or journal browsing for relevant materials. Suitable core articles are difficult to locate in some areas. Problems also arise when sophisticated equipment is required (e.g., to measure precise reaction times or to control the brief presentation of stimuli).

As with any approach to laboratory project design, this one is a compromise between an ideal and what can be achieved realistically. Certain limitations can be overcome by using other types of assignments to supplement this approach. The advantages of the core article approach outweigh its limitations and help to achieve the course aims just outlined. The approach works well, is highly accepted by students, and should be valuable for other teachers who have similar goals for the laboratory project. Although reported here as part of a cognitive psychology course, the approach should generalize readily to other courses in which laboratory projects are required.

References

Carroll, D. W. (1986). Use of the jigsaw technique in laboratory and discussion classes. *Teaching of Psychology, 13,* 208–210.

Chamberlain, K. (1986). Teaching the practical research course. *Teaching of Psychology, 13,* 204–208.

Edwards, J. D. (1981). A conceptual framework for a core program in psychology. *Teaching of Psychology, 8,* 3–7.

Kerber, K. W. (1983). Beyond experimentation: Research projects for a laboratory course in psychology. *Teaching of Psychology, 10,* 236–239.

Lutsky, N. (1986). Undergraduate research experience through the analysis of data sets in psychology courses. *Teaching of Psychology, 13,* 119–122.

Palladino, J. J., Carsrud, A. L., Hulicka, I. M., & Benjamin, L. T., Jr. (1982). Undergraduate research in psychology: Assessment and directions. *Teaching of Psychology, 9,* 71–74.

Suter, W. N., & Frank, P. (1986). Using scholarly journals in undergraduate experimental methodology courses. *Teaching of Psychology, 13,* 219–221.

VandeCreek, L., & Fleischer, M. (1984). The role of practicum in the undergraduate psychology curriculum. *Teaching of Psychology, 11,* 9–14.

Use of the Jigsaw Technique in Laboratory and Discussion Classes

David W. Carroll
University of Wisconsin–Superior

Although undergraduate courses in research design are invaluable for giving students a perspective on how research is done, many students find such classes difficult. Many are more interested in the nonresearch aspects of psychology, and even those who see its importance are sometimes afraid of a class that requires them to develop, perform, and report an original study.

For 8 years I have taught a one-credit, upper-division, laboratory course in the psychology of learning and memory. Each student is required to carry out a sample experiment provided by the instructor and then develop, perform, and report an original experiment. During the first 4 years

of teaching this course, I noticed several distressing trends, including:

1. Approximately one third of the students failed to complete the course in a single quarter.
2. Those who did complete the work on time often chose simple topics and finished them in a perfunctory fashion.
3. Nearly all of the students regarded the course as more than one credit of work.
4. Student evaluations were generally poor.

In the last 4 years, I have been using an adaptation of the "jigsaw classroom" (Aronson & Bridgeman, 1981) as a means of teaching this course. This technique is designed to encourage cooperation by making individuals dependent on each other in pursuit of a common goal. Each person is assigned or chooses one piece of a larger task, and group members depend on each individual to complete the assigned function. Aronson and Bridgeman found that positive changes occurred in group members' attitudes toward one another. My more immediate concern was with the potential of this structure to enable students to tackle more substantial challenges and complete them in a single term.

Method

The jigsaw technique is first introduced in the sample experiment, in which the class replicates a published study. The assumption is that the group process can be learned in the sample experiment and then applied to the subsequent original experiment. In the sample experiment, students are assigned to one of four tasks (construction of study materials, construction of test materials, randomization of study and test lists, and writing instructions). They spend 3 weeks developing the materials, performing the study, and then discussing it.

Each student is then required to develop a proposal for an independent experiment. The goal of the proposal assignment is to get students to think through an idea to the point of presenting it to the entire group. After the students present their ideas, they are given the options of (a) choosing one idea for a group project, (b) combining or consolidating ideas into a group project, or (c) doing an individual project. Ideas are presented one week, with decisions due the next week.

Students who select a group project sign a contract that specifies the members of the group (maximum: four), the tasks each person will perform (for example, pilot study, instructions, running subjects, statistical analysis), and the division of labor in the writing of the final report (introduction, method, and so on). Those who do a group project are given the further option of writing a group report or writing separate reports. If a group report is chosen, all group members receive the same grade on the report (which is the major but not the total basis for the course grade). Decisions regarding the various aspects of the contract are placed at different parts of the term: Students must form groups by the 5th week, but have until the 6th week to divide the tasks, and until the 9th week to decide on writing assignments. This schedule gives them time to learn more about the work habits of group members and make more informed decisions about how much to entrust their course grade to another person.

Results

There are three sources of evidence of the effectiveness of the jigsaw approach: student evaluations of the class, the percentage of students who complete the course in a single term, and subjective impressions of the choices students make for projects.

Student evaluations are available for the last 3 of the 4 years the jigsaw approach has been in effect, and they indicate a positive student response. Student evaluation was assessed by a 13-item form. Each item was rated on a 5-point scale ranging from a highly negative response (1) to a highly favorable response (5). The means of the individual item means were 4.19, 4.04, and 4.41, respectively, for the last 3 years. Individual items included the knowledge gained from the course (4.12), the fairness of the grading system (4.19), and the degree of intellectual motivation in the class (4.63). On the negative side, comments on the evaluation form revealed that students still regarded the course as more than one credit of work.

The question of whether students were better able to complete coursework in a single term was examined by comparing course records for the 4 years before and the 4 years after the introduction of the jigsaw approach. Of the 55 students who took the course prior to the jigsaw approach, 35 (64%) completed the course, 16 (29%) took incompletes, and 4 (7%) dropped the course or received an F; comparable numbers over the last 4 years were 40 out of 46 (87%), 1 (2%), and 5 (11%).

Whether or not students tackle more challenging assignments is difficult to say, but there are some indications that this is the case. There is much evidence of serial revision throughout the term whereas students in the earlier years, partly due to time pressure, tended to pursue the first idea that came to them. There has been an increase in studies of children as opposed to college students, despite the additional difficulties in securing child participation. Moreover, there has been an increase in students' commitment to their research. For example, one group chose to do a study on mice even though our school has no animal laboratory. The students bought the animals, secured a room, and continued their work the next term as an independent study project. Further evidence of such commitment has been the increased participation in student research conferences.

Discussion

Some of the most significant advantages of this technique relate to the attitudes of students. They seemed to be convinced of the usefulness of the approach. In addition to learning about research design, they learned some valuable lessons in how to organize a complex task and how to structure an interpersonally ambiguous situation. They also seemed to be having more fun.

Some care, however, must be taken in how the technique is presented and used. There is some potential for resentment toward individuals perceived as not doing their share of the work. The structure of the course (allowing students to choose the jigsaw approach, and giving them time to make important decisions) helps to alleviate some of these concerns, but it does not eliminate them. Ultimately, students must decide how much they trust one another. One year, two different groups had to decide on writing assignments at a time when one member of each group was absent without explanation. I encouraged each group to wait as long as possible to allow the student to rejoin the group, but told them it was ultimately their decision. Both waited and, in one case, the missing group member returned after a brief absence to help finish the project successfully. In the other case, the student remained missing for too long, and the other three members reluctantly decided to write the report on their own, forcing the fourth student to do a great deal of work near the end of the term. The jigsaw technique thus forces students to do some hard thinking about their judgments of their peers and to take responsibility for their decisions.

Though I have used this technique in only this one course, it might work very well in discussion and seminar classes. It is an excellent motivational device and has the pedagogical value of calling on the distinctive backgrounds, experiences, and abilities of different students. To sum up, the technique enables students to learn course material efficiently, while dealing with social situations that contribute to their overall education.

Reference

Aronson, E., & Bridgeman, D. (1981). Jigsaw groups and the desegregated classroom: In pursuit of common goals. In E. M. Hetherington & R. D. Parke (Eds.), *Contemporary readings in child psychology* (2nd ed., pp. 339–345). New York: McGraw-Hill.

The Problem Method of Teaching Research Methods

Donald H. McBurney
University of Pittsburgh

The purpose of this article is to describe a technique of teaching research methods that I have used successfully for many years in an undergraduate course. For some time, I had believed that trying to teach research methods in a lecture was often like trying to teach someone to ride a bicycle without a bike. When I became aware that business schools routinely use problems in teaching principles of management to master's of business administration students, it occurred to me that the method could be used to teach research methods; so I began to use it in my class and my research methods texts (McBurney, 1990, 1994).

Although the problem method is widely used in teaching law and business courses, it does not seem to be used much in psychology. Exceptions are found in areas such as abnormal and clinical psychology, in which individual cases are used to illustrate particular diagnoses, and industrial/organizational psychology, in which applications of principles discussed in the literature are illustrated. I am unaware of any literature on the use of problems in teaching research methods.

Definition of the Problem Method

The *problem method* should be distinguished from the *case study method*. The case study method was introduced by Christopher Columbus Langdell when he became dean of Harvard Law School in 1870 (Moskovitz, 1992). Langdell replaced the lecture method with a Socratic analysis of particular cases from the law. The case study method is still used today to teach first-year students the fundamentals of the law.

In second- and third-year law courses, the problem method is used instead. Whereas the case study method analyzes particular cases to identify facts and principles, the problem method requires students to find their own solution to the problem presented (Ogden, 1984).

It is a source of confusion that the business literature uses the term *case study* to refer to what the law literature calls the *problem method*. In deference to the distinction made in the law literature, I use *problem method* henceforth in this article to refer to the method I am describing.

Characteristics of the Problem Method

There are three characteristics of the problem method: "1) assignment of problem statements for solution; 2) use of course or other materials to solve problems; and 3) discussion of solutions in class" (Ogden, 1984, p. 655). There are many variations among problems. Problems can be as short as a paragraph that illustrate a particular issue in a law course; in business school courses, however, they are generally many pages long and include much financial and other data. Generally, the problem does not have a single correct answer, so students must weigh alternatives and defend their choices. Some instructors assign problems to the whole class for open discussion, whereas others make them the responsibility of a subgroup of students. Furthermore, the instructor's role can vary from presenting the whole problem as an example to serving as a discussion facilitator (Dooley & Skinner, 1977).

It is risky to claim to know how the problem method differs from the typical classroom discussion techniques because there may be as many discussion methods as there are instructors. Nevertheless, the problem method focuses attention on the design of an end product and requires students to make choices among competing alternatives and justify those choices. In my experience as a student and instructor, the problem method is distinctive in its emphasis on a practical solution to a problem that is posed. The solution of the problem that is arrived at provides closure in a way that the usual discussion methods may not.

Furthermore, class discussions too often are perceived by the students as a digression from the real material in the course (i.e., what will be covered on the test)—namely, the lecture. I have seen students put down their pens, ostentatiously fall asleep, or walk out when the instructor initiates a discussion. By contrast, my students know that the problems are an integral part of the course. Those students who have been assigned the particular problem under discussion (considered next) have a personal interest in discovering how close their solution came to the one arrived at in class. All students know that they will be tested on their grasp of the concepts discussed in the problems.

Why the Problem Method Is Applicable to Research Methods

Designing research is an example of a classic ill-defined task. Frequently, the problem is not clearly stated, the theory being tested may be poorly developed, and the expected results are not well constrained. Moreover, there are many different choices to be made, many of which interact with each other. As a result, no two researchers may design a particular study the same way, and there is no one perfect design. Although this reality is well known to researchers, it is difficult to convey to students who are used to memorizing three claims of so-and-so's theory, four lines of evidence in favor of it, five objections to it, and six alternative theories. Students tend to become anxious and sometimes dispirited when an instructor refuses to tell them the right answer. The problem method is designed to teach students that there is no one right answer.

Perry (1970) found that college students tend to progress through a series of stages of intellectual development during their college years. Initially, they see the world in terms of polar opposites, including right and wrong answers. Next, they perceive that there is diversity of opinion. Later, they perceive knowledge as contextual. Perry found nine stages of development, culminating in moral relativism and commitment to a personal style. One could question whether Perry's emphasis on relativism is as cogent in science as it is in the humanities. Nevertheless, he captured the reactions of many students to the ambiguities involved in designing research.

Furthermore, the problem method is an excellent vehicle for teaching critical thinking. The concept of critical thinking is quite broad, and the literature is extremely heterogeneous. The National Research Council's Committee on Mathematics, Science, and Technology Education (Resnick, 1987) listed the following characteristics of higher order thinking: It is nonalgorithmic; complex; entails uncertainty; has multiple solutions; involves nuanced judgment; and requires the application of multiple criteria, self-regulation, imposition of meaning, and effort. Each of these is well illustrated by the process of research design, and each is required in solving a problem.

Kurfiss (1988) listed eight teaching practices that support critical thinking. Five of them are exemplified by the problem method: The instructor and students serve as resources in developing critical-thinking skills; problems serve as the point of entry to the subject and as a source of motivation; the course is assignment-centered, with an emphasis on using content rather than acquiring it; students are required to formulate and justify their ideas in writing; students collaborate in their problem solving.

The Problem Method in a Research Methods Course

My class generally enrolls about 120 students. I have used problems as a way of summarizing and illustrating material from the lectures. About every fourth class period is devoted to a problem that requires students to make use of principles discussed in a chapter of the book. The problem is handed out 1 or 2 weeks in advance; all of the students are expected to study it, but a subset is also required to turn in a written analysis at the beginning of the class period in which it is to be discussed. Students are encouraged, but not required, to work in pairs. Many of them choose to work in pairs. The written analysis is to be 3 to 5 pages long and contain a summary of the problem; a suggested solution, with justification for the selected alternatives; and reasons for rejecting alternatives. In this way, all students should be familiar with the problem, but a certain number can be counted on to provide the bulk of the discussion.

How the Problem Is Presented in Class

I usually start the class discussion by briefly summarizing the facts of the case for the benefit of those who may not have prepared. Then, I emphasize that I am not as interested in the particular solution as I am in the reasoning that went into it. My role is to pose questions, draw out incomplete answers, probe inconsistencies, and so forth. The discussion of a typical case takes up most of a 50-min class period.

How the Students Respond to the Method

I wish I could say that the students are enthusiastic about the problem method. The truth is that I have received very few spontaneous comments about it over the years. Students do not seem to comment on it in the course evaluation. One problem, however, that did elicit spontaneous comments from the students involved research ethics. I assigned several students the task of playing the role of various individuals in a fairly complicated case of alleged violation of research integrity. Students found this very engaging and realistic. Not all problems lend themselves to this format, however.

To obtain some systematic data on student reactions, I administered a questionnaire in class that requested opinions on how much the problems contributed to learning the course material, how interesting they were, whether they forced students to think through things they had not yet thought about, whether problems should be continued as a part of the course, and whether they helped students learn things they would not have learned from a lecture. In a nutshell, the results fell close to neutral on all items. They reported spending about 4 hr on their problem.

In retrospect, such a questionnaire may not be particularly informative about how the problem method furthers the goals of the course. It may be more useful to compare their performance on tests of the material in the course or their grades in later courses to that of students who did not experience the method. These measures would, of course,

require appropriate controls, which would present considerable design problems of their own.

It is fair to conclude that the students find the problem method about as acceptable as the rest of the course, which they regard as quite challenging but rate favorably overall. I believe that students at the undergraduate level are not used to this method of teaching and find it somewhat anxiety provoking. Students pose many questions on how to solve the problems before they are due. They seem to be somewhat uncomfortable with ambiguity, as Perry (1970) predicted. Because most students in the course are sophomores, the majority of them are probably in the early stages of their journey from bipolar to contextualized thinking that Perry documented.

My own impression is that students learn to deal with some of the complexities of research design by working on these problems. Together with lectures and laboratory, the problem method helps students obtain a realistic introduction to research methods in a wide variety of situations. This fulfills one of the recommendations of the National Research Council's Committee (Resnick, 1987) that teaching of critical thinking should be embedded within the curriculum of the discipline. I recommend the problem method to instructors who wish to take a problem-solving or critical-thinking approach to teaching research methods.

References

Dooley, A. R., & Skinner, W. (1977). Casing case methods. *Academy of Management Review, 2,* 277–289.

Kurfiss, J. G. (1988). *Critical thinking: Theory, research, practice, and possibilities* (ASHE-ERIC Higher Education Report No. 2). Washington, DC: Association for the Study of Higher Education.

McBurney, D. H. (1990). *Experimental psychology* (2nd ed.). Belmont, CA: Wadsworth.

McBurney, D. H. (1994). *Research methods* (3rd ed.). Belmont, CA: Brooks/Cole.

Moskovitz, M. (1992). Beyond the case method: It's time to teach with problems. *Journal of Legal Education, 42,* 241–270.

Ogden, G. L. (1984). The problem method in legal education. *Journal of Legal Education, 34,* 654–673.

Perry, W. G., Jr. (1970). *Forms of intellectual and ethical development in the college years: A scheme.* New York: Holt, Rinehart & Winston.

Resnick, L. (1987). *Education and learning to think.* Washington, DC: National Academy Press.

Note

I thank John Grant and Edward Symons for helpful suggestions and Richard Moreland, Peter Moshein, and two anonymous reviewers for comments on a draft of this article.

The Research Methods Script

Thomas L. Wilson
Bellarmine College

Douglas A. Hershey
George Mason University

Scripts are mental representations of the ordered actions and events that take place in commonly experienced situations (Abelson, 1981; Bower, Black, & Turner, 1979). Studies of expertise in knowledge-rich domains have identified scripts as part of the knowledge used to solve complex problems (Hershey, Morath, & Walsh, 1991; Hershey, Walsh, Read, & Chulef, 1990). According to these authors, a problem-solving script specifies the optimal information to consider and the sequence of actions to take in a particular problem-solving context. Hershey, Wilson, and Mitchell-Copeland (in press) investigated psychologists' procedural knowledge of scientific problem solving in the context of psychological research. Thõ discovered that, in contrast to undergraduate students of psychology, career psychologists possess reliable and readily available *psychological research scripts* that represent their knowledge of the sequential steps involved in the research process. Results indicated that development of the research script is a negatively accelerated function of experience and training in psychological research, with the greatest developmental change taking place during undergraduate education.

The class activity described in this article is based on script theory and takes advantage of students' preexisting knowledge of the scientific method. Students generate their own research methods script by following standard procedures of script generation and analysis found in the literature (e.g., Bower et al., 1979). Then, students compare and discuss their scripts, evaluating them in relation to the composite script of the class and a composite script of experienced psychology professors. Students receive a sound overview of topics typically discussed in a research methods course and a structural foundation on which to build new knowledge. The activity also allows students to participate as subjects in an informal experiment, analyze their findings, and discover their own baseline knowledge of the psychological research process.

Research Methods Scripts as Mental Representations

Scripts represent event knowledge that is readily accessible from long-term memory, making scripts a powerful way to organize and recall information. Script events are sequenced in a particular order and are organized hierarchically in memory so that basic-level events are grouped under goal categories at a higher level (Bower et al., 1979). The research methods script is no exception. According to Hershey et al. (in press), expert psychologists typically organize events in the research script into four higher order goal categories: formulate ideas, collect data, analyze data, and report findings. These authors found that experts agreed on the research activities generated and on the basic level of specificity of those activities (e.g., read literature, obtain subjects, and collect data). Experts did not mention lower level activities (e.g., turn on computer and go to work). The scripts students generate about the research process are likewise organized around a common set of events and are usually written with a specific level of abstraction. Thus, becoming aware of the research methods script can be helpful for students because it organizes their knowledge of the various research procedures they are learning.

The Class Activity

Script Generation

Sometime within the first 2 weeks of a research methods course, we ask students to participate in an activity to discover what they already know about the psychological research process. Following the procedures and instructions used by Hershey et al. (in press), we give them a response sheet with the phrases, "Get idea for project" printed near the top of the page and "Publish the research paper" printed near the bottom. Then, students are given the following instructions:

> List about 20 actions, steps, or stages that characterize the process psychologists go through when working on a research problem. As you list these research activities, focus on the *typical* actions that a researcher would engage in while carrying out a *typical* psychological research project. List only activities that take place between the anchor events *Get idea for project* and *Publish the research paper,* and try to list the activities in their appropriate order.

Students usually complete this task in less than 10 min. Although students and experts usually generate only 10 to 16 events under these instructions, asking for about 20 appears sufficient to elicit an exhaustive recall and, consequently, a variety of events from all students in the group.

Next, we ask students to examine their lists while presenting a brief introduction to the script concept (Abelson, 1981) to focus them on the structural features of scripts that enhance their organization of knowledge. Explaining the central features of scripts (nothing more than we have presented in this introduction) provides students with an immediate link between the event-generation process they just completed and the notion that such event-based knowledge is organized in their own long-term memory. A treatment of script theory beyond the typical information found in an introductory psychology textbook is not necessary for instructors to follow the procedures presented herein and the evaluation portion of the activity mentioned later.

Students are instructed to draw lines between items on their ordered list to group the activities into higher order categories and to generate a name for each category. Students rarely have questions or problems in completing these tasks; they generate and divide their lists with ease. The entire procedure to this point takes about 20 min, and the evaluation stage that follows can vary in time according to the instructor's preference. We take 20 to 30 min for the following evaluation stage.

Script Evaluation

After students generate their research scripts, we assign them to small groups of two to four students to compare their event lists. As a first step in script evaluation, students can learn about several features of their research methods script by responding to the following questions:

1. Did you have any difficulty generating script events, or did they come easily to mind?
2. Scripts are organized around a common set of events at a particular level of specificity. In comparison to other students, how many events did you list? How many of the events in your script were also in the lists of other students? What kinds of events did you list?

3. Are the events in your script listed in a logical order? Are they listed in the same order as similar events in other students' scripts?
4. How many goal categories were in your script? Did the names you used for your categories correspond to the typical category names?

In the next part of the activity, students are asked to share their event lists with the class. A master list of all unique events along with their frequency of mention can be compiled on the chalkboard or an overhead projector. Help students sequence events in a logical order to create a composite script for the class. (In our classes, we draw a line through those events mentioned by fewer than 20% of the students to highlight research activities of greatest significance to them.) After a brief class discussion of the composite script, the instructor can present a composite script from experts in psychology (see Table 1) alongside the class script for direct comparison. An evaluation of students' scripted knowledge of the research process continues with the following questions:

5. How closely does the class script compare to the expert script? How many high-consensus and low-consensus activities are in each script?
6. Does the class as a whole already possess a good deal of knowledge about the research process?
7. Look at your own script. How does it compare to the expert script? How does it compare to the class script? Given that scripts provide a structure that helps us comprehend new information, how might you use the script concept to increase and monitor your own understanding of the research methods you will learn about this semester?

Class Discussion

Upon identification of the class composite script, students are pleased to recognize that their collective knowledge is, in many respects, similar to that of experts. They are usually surprised by both the similarity among their individual scripts, the class composite script, the expert script, and the subtle differences in the way we each conceptualize psychological research. By answering the questions in the activity, students are challenged to think critically about the research process. The classroom situation gives the instructor an opportunity to help students improve their understanding of the research process before misconceptions can hinder their further learning of methodological details. Students should be reminded that they are in the course to begin to assimilate the more detailed knowledge that experts possess. In this regard, an individual's script represents a good foundation for building new knowledge from the course. Hershey et al. (in press) found

Table 1. Composite Psychological Research Script From 49 Psychology Professors

(anchor) Get idea for project
READ LITERATURE ON TOPIC
Discuss idea with colleagues
Conceptualize project
Determine appropriate subject population
Formulate Hypotheses
DESIGN EXPERIMENTAL METHODS
Obtain available materials and measures
Construct experimental materials and measures
Obtain research assistants
Pilot Test Procedures and Measures
Refine experiment based on pilot results
Obtain Subjects
DATA COLLECTION
Code and organize data
DATA ANALYSIS
Determine if hypotheses were supported
Make a conference or brown-bag presentation
Conduct final literature review
WRITE DRAFT OF PAPER
Get feedback on paper
Revise draft of paper
Submit Paper for Publication
Make post-review revisions
(anchor) Publish the research paper

Note. Following Hershey et al. (in press), high-consensus events (mentioned by ≥ 60% of professors) are shown in capital letters, moderate-consensus events (mentioned by 40% to 59% of professors) are shown in upper and lower case, and low-consensus events (mentioned by 20% to 39% of professors) are shown in italics.

that undergraduates already have a working knowledge of the higher order goal categories within the research process. These authors referred to this higher level of knowledge as the *research metascript* and suggested that it is a mental framework on which students develop more detailed knowledge of the research process.

Students find the expert script interesting in its simplicity and coherence. Learning opportunities from discussion of the expert script seem limited only by one's imagination. For example, students may ask the meaning of such activities as a brown-bag presentation or pilot research (events often left out of students' scripts; see Table 1). The instructor could then discuss what it is like to go to graduate school by noting that experts present brown-bag talks, conduct pilot studies, obtain research assistants, and so on. Or the instructor may elect to focus students on specific course concepts. For example, students can be encouraged to take note of any event in the expert script that they did not have in their own script, so that they can gain more understanding of those particular research activities.

Finally, the research script activity may be useful in other ways. For example, it can illustrate the structure of mental representations and, for those with an interest in metacognitive awareness, it can demonstrate how to monitor one's own understanding in a problem-solving domain. We have used the activity to assess changes in students' knowledge of the research process from the beginning to the end of our methods courses. The activity is also suitable for introductory courses as a review of concepts in scientific psychology and basic research methodology.

Evaluation and Conclusion

In one undergraduate research methods course, the activity was administered during the second week and then referred to regularly throughout the course. On the last day of class, 31 students completed a survey that included eight questions about the script activity. The mean ratings given by students on a scale ranging from 1 (*not at all*) to 5 (*very often*) were as follows: (a) I thought about the research methods script on occasions other than the day of the activity ($M = 3.94$), (b) I specifically studied class material related to research events that I left out of my original script ($M = 3.35$), (c) I created study questions from the expert script to assess my understanding of course material ($M = 2.03$), (d) I felt like the research methods script was helping me organize my understanding of the research process ($M = 4.19$), and (e) I took time to memorize the expert script to organize my thinking for class exams and projects ($M = 3.10$). Mean ratings on a scale ranging from 1 (*strongly disagree*) to 5 (*strongly agree*) were as follows: (a) Knowing about my own research methods script was useful in this class ($M = 4.35$), (b) The research script activity was interesting ($M = 4.13$), and (c) I believe my research methods script is more like the expert script now that the class is over ($M = 4.55$).

From these data, we conclude that students perceive the research script activity as interesting and useful. Students who generated and evaluated scripts used the activity more for the general organizational information it provided than as an active study strategy; thus, students may not use their scripts in novel ways without some direction by the instructor. Nevertheless, students tended to reflect on their scripts throughout the course, and they could gauge their learning by comparing their scripts to the expert script. To obtain comparative data on the development of students' scripts, 17 students from a different methods class generated scripts and constructed a composite script at the beginning and end of the term. Results demonstrated that agreement on events between the class composite script and the expert script increased by 37% during the term. It appears that the utility of the script activity for increased learning is promising.

Student comments during one term included: "I did not know there was so much to doing research before you actually collect the data"; "Now that I have done my own study" (a course requirement), "I will never leave 'code data' out of my script again!"; and the inevitable, "I memorized the expert script because I thought you would test us on it." One student wrote in the margin of her survey, "Showed me what I needed to learn from the start." The survey results, comparative data, and comments indicate that the research methods script activity is a worthwhile experience. The activity reinforces and enhances students' organization and understanding of the procedures involved in psychological research. It also allows students to identify areas in which they need further study.

References

Abelson, R. P. (1981). Psychological status of the script concept. *American Psychologist, 36,* 715–729.

Bower, G. H., Black, J. B., & Turner, T. J. (1979). Scripts in memory for text. *Cognitive Psychology, 11,* 177–220.

Hershey, D. A., Morath, R., & Walsh, D. A. (1991, November). The use of scripts to solve financial planning problems. In C. Berg (Chair), *Age differences in cognitive strategies.* Symposium conducted at the meeting of the Gerontological Society of America, San Francisco.

Hershey, D. A., Walsh, D. A., Read, S. J., & Chulef, A. S. (1990). The effects of expertise on financial problem solving: Evidence for goal-directed problem solving scripts. *Organizational Behavior and Human Decision Performance, 46,* 77–101.

Hershey, D. A., Wilson, T. L., & Mitchell-Copeland, J. (in press). Conceptions of the psychological research process: Script variation as a function of training and experience. *Current Psychology.*

Using an Everyday Memory Task to Introduce the Method and Results Sections of a Scientific Paper

William R. Marmie
University of Colorado, Boulder

Nickerson and Adams's (1979) task of recognizing a U.S. penny among a set of counterfeits, which vary only in the placement of features, is often described in introductory cognitive psychology textbooks to demonstrate the failure to store details encountered in an everyday context in memory (e.g., Bourne, Dominowski, Loftus, & Healy, 1986; Medin & Ross, 1992; Reed, 1992). The task has also been suggested for use as a classroom demonstration showing the consequences of lack of attention (Shimamura, 1984). Marmie, Rully, and Healy (1993) showed that subjects, when asked to draw the features of a familiar U.S. penny without any external cues, did quite poorly; in contrast, if they studied an unfamiliar Mercury dime for only 1 min, they recalled the features of the dime better than those of the penny. This finding is counter-intuitive because people see a U.S. penny almost every day but cannot remember its features. Marmie et al. concluded that memory for details of everyday objects is poor unless subjects use intentional mnemonic strategies. The empirical work of Marmie et al., designed to highlight the role of intentional study in remembering details, can be extended as a classroom demonstration and can also be used effectively to introduce the method and results sections of a scientific paper. The present demonstration illustrates the important role of intentional study in memory and is enjoyable for

students. In addition, as opposed to simply recalling the penny alone, students will feel less ignorant about not remembering what an everyday object looks like after they have studied and recalled the dime.

I use the demonstration in an introductory course in cognitive psychology. Generally, the class contains upper level undergraduates with one course in statistics. The demonstration is manageable for a class of up to 20 students. Ideally, coin presentation order should be counterbalanced, but the demonstration demands that the penny be recalled before the dime in order to leave students feeling good about their memory abilities. At the beginning of the class, I give each student a piece of paper with two 4-in. (10.16 cm) circles on it. I tell the students that this is an everyday memory demonstration, and I ask them to draw the front and back of a U.S. penny from memory. I inform them they will have 2 min to draw it, and I emphasize that they should write out all of the words on the penny and that they are not being tested on their artistic ability. Students react by laughing and groaning.

Before I collect the drawings, students write the last four digits of their student number on the sheet. Next, I distribute to each student a second drawing sheet and an envelope containing a single Mercury dime (see Figure 1). This out-of-mint dime has the advantage of being a coin most

Figure 1. The four faces of the Mercury dime and the U.S. penny.

students have never seen before. I purchase the dimes at a local coin shop for 50¢ each. I tell students that they will have 1 min to study the dime and 2 min to recall it in the same manner as the penny. After 1 min, I instruct students to return the dimes to the envelopes. Then I repeat the recall instructions I used for the penny.

I return each student's penny drawing and distribute score sheets. The score sheet lists each of the nine features shared by both coins: (a) the head figure, (b) the tail figure, (c) the phrase "In God We Trust," (d) the phrase "E Pluribus Unum," (e) the word *Liberty,* (f) the phrase "United States of America," (g) the phrase "One Dime" or "One Cent," (h) the date stamp, and (i) the mint stamp. Students generally feel somewhat self-conscious about their drawings. Class discussion relieves this anxiety. The Latin phrase "E Pluribus Unum" is often humorously rendered (e.g., "In Plubius Obium"). The class decides whether to score a feature as correct if it is included or if it is both included and correctly placed on the coin face. Keep in mind that if students decide to adopt the latter policy, the difference between the number of correctly recalled features for the penny and the dime is pronounced. Students raise many questions (e.g., "Should we count the head as correctly positioned if it is facing the wrong direction?," "Is a dome on the Lincoln memorial acceptable?," or "Is '*In* Pluribus Unum' acceptable for '*E* Pluribus Unum?'").

Students remember the studied coin much better than the unstudied coin. This effect is often dramatic as well as robust. I ask the students to count the total number of features they both included and correctly positioned, and I write these totals on the front board. On average, my students have remembered 2.7 features from the penny and 7.6 features from the dime. I have never seen a student who has recalled more features of the penny than of the dime. Next, I ask students whether there appears to be an overall difference between memory for the dime and penny. I point out that some of the memory differences between coins are large and some are small. To introduce the concept of a *t* test I ask them, "How can we tell if, overall, these differences are significant?"

The demonstration allows me to make the following three points:

1. Scientific judgments are always subjective. The class needed to decide on the rules for counting a feature as correct or incorrect. Would the difference in memory for the dime and the penny have been significant with a more lenient criterion? The answer is yes (see Marmie et al., 1993). Should students have scored their own drawings or someone else's? I use these questions to emphasize the point that, without a method section, readers would have no idea how a researcher measured the dependent variables and that a researcher's conclusions would be difficult to evaluate.

2. Statistics provide a way of condensing data into a manageable description of the findings. They also allow researchers to estimate the probability that obtained differences are simply due to chance.

3. Details of an object or event are often hard to remember unless they are intentionally studied. In the demonstration, 1 min of study was enough to make memory for an unfamiliar coin better than memory for a familiar coin. I contrast this finding with the priming effect in which it is not even necessary to consciously attend to something in order for it to be remembered. In priming studies involving word fragment completion, previous exposure to a word significantly helps subjects complete word fragments (see Schoen, 1988, for an effective demonstration of this point).

I close my class by assigning students to write the method and results sections of the demonstration. I distribute a description of the procedure (written as short facts) with step-by-step instructions for conducting a *t* test. They copy the data from the board before leaving the classroom.

Student Evaluations

At the end of the class period, students anonymously responded to a four-item questionnaire. It was apparent that most students enjoyed this demonstration from the high degree of participation in the discussions. Pooling data across two classes, I found that on a 5-point scale ranging from *not at all* (1) to *very well* (5), 38 University of

Colorado students gave a mean rating of 3.47 ($SD = 1.04$) to the question of how well the demonstration illustrated the importance of a method section in a scientific paper. On the same scale, students gave a mean rating of 3.95 ($SD = .82$) to the question of how well the importance of a statistical analysis was illustrated by the demonstration. To determine whether students felt differently about their memory abilities from the penny to the dime, I first asked "Did you feel good about your memory ability after recalling the penny?" On a 5-point scale ranging from *not at all* (1) to *very much* (5), students reported feeling slightly below the neutral value ($M = 2.43$, $SD = 1.09$). Second, they responded to the question, "Did you feel better about your memory ability after recalling the dime?," on a 5-point scale ranging from *no* (1) to *yes* (5). Students reported feeling well above the neutral value ($M = 4.27$, $SD = 1.04$). A t test was conducted comparing the means of the last two values. The mean for the dime was significantly higher than the mean for the penny, suggesting that students are left feeling good about their memory abilities after the demonstration, $t(36) = 7.33$, $p < .01$.

This demonstration is effective because many bright students in an introductory cognitive psychology course feel somewhat daunted after repeated demonstrations of their average memory, problem-solving, and decision-making abilities. This demonstration has the added benefit, over and above the standard procedure of simply recalling a U.S. penny, of showing students the importance of intentional study. Everyday objects may be familiar but, without intentional study, they are not memorable. Students are not left feeling ignorant about their knowledge of everyday objects but rather feeling knowledgeable about the importance of intentional study.

References

Bourne, L. E., Dominowski, R. L., Loftus, E. F., & Healy, A. F. (1986). *Cognitive processes* (2nd ed.). Englewood Cliffs, NJ: Prentice-Hall.

Marmie, W. R., Rully, G. R., & Healy, A. F. (1993). On the long-term retention of studied and unstudied U.S. coins. In *The Proceedings of the Fifteenth Annual Conference of the Cognitive Science Society* (pp. 687–692). Hillsdale, NJ: Lawrence Erlbaum Associates, Inc.

Medin, D. L., & Ross, B. H. (1992). *Cognitive psychology*. Ft. Worth, TX: Harcourt Brace.

Nickerson, R. S., & Adams, M. J. (1979). Long-term memory for a common object. *Cognitive Psychology, 11*, 287–307.

Reed, S. K. (1992). *Cognition: Theory and applications* (3rd ed.). Pacific Grove, CA: Brooks/Cole.

Schoen, L. M. (1988). The word fragment completion effect: A computer-assisted classroom exercise. *Teaching of Psychology, 15*, 95–97.

Shimamura, A. P. (1984). A guide for teaching mnemonic skills. *Teaching of Psychology, 11*, 162–166.

Note

I thank Walter Kintsch and Alice Healy for comments on a draft of this article.

Interpreting Students' Interpretations of Research

Richard B. May
Michael A. Hunter
University of Victoria

Students' answers to examination questions in statistics and research methods courses frequently indicate confusion concerning interrelationships among research methods, statistical analysis, and interpretation of results. Although they may have learned a theoretical principle, such as that random sampling facilitates the ability to generalize results beyond specific samples, they frequently apply this principle when it is not appropriate (Mook, 1983).

Consider the following question: Why did the researcher randomly assign subjects to the two treatment conditions? Here is one representative student answer: "The random assignment was done in order to generalize the results as much as possible so the sample would be representative of a defined population." In general, students appear to acknowledge a link between randomness and generalizability, but they overextend their interpretation to include both random sampling and random assignment.

We would expect more experienced psychologists to be less likely than undergraduates to make this kind of error. Ostrom (1984), however, reported that as a journal editor he encountered several instances in which both authors and reviewers inappropriately focused on external validity. They made arguments about generality when the purpose and method of a study were directed toward testing a theoretical process about what can happen rather than what generally happens.

To shed further light on this issue, we asked samples of undergraduates, graduates, and faculty two multiple-choice questions dealing with the implications of random sampling and random assignment. The questions, each with the same options, were as follows:

Question 1–Random sampling of subjects from a specified population of interest facilitates:
Question 2–Random assignment of subjects to groups receiving different treatments facilitates:
(A) generality interpretations of results.
(B) cause-effect interpretations of results.
(C) both A and B, but A more than B.
(D) both A and B, but B more than A.
(E) both A and B equally.

The best available answer to Question 1 is alternative A and the best available answer to Question 2 is alternative B.

The 64 subjects were 18 faculty and 46 students. All students were enrolled in an upper level course in statistics for psychology majors and had taken at least one previous statistics course (mode = 2). Eighteen were graduate students, and 28 were fourth-year undergraduates. Most faculty were tenured, had their PhD for a median of 17 years, and had a median of 17 publications. Students were surveyed during a regular meeting of their statistics class. Faculty were seen individually in their offices by a research assistant who waited for them to respond to the questions.

On the random sampling question, 48 of the 64 subjects (75%) correctly indicated that random sampling facilitates generality interpretation, and this percentage was approximately the same in each group. In striking contrast, on the random assignment question only 17 of 64 (27%) correctly linked random assignment specifically to causal interpretation. Again, both students and faculty showed similar results. Perhaps surprisingly, only 7 of 18 faculty (39%) correctly answered the question.[1]

Thus, although the role of random sampling in the interpretation of results appears to be understood, the role of random assignment is less clear. In particular, random assignment does not seem to be well differentiated from random sampling; it is often misperceived as at least partly related to generality inference.

---

[1] A detailed breakdown of the data is available from May (first author).

We believe that students and faculty alike confuse the role of random assignment in the interpretation of results, because both groups have been exposed to the same biased training. Specifically, their statistics education focused almost exclusively on the normal curve model, which emphasizes random sampling and generality inference. The fact that psychological research more often involves random assignment than random sampling typically receives only cursory attention in statistics courses, and when it is mentioned, alternative statistical techniques for analyzing randomly assigned groups are not discussed. Instead, normal curve statistics are applied regardless of which type of random process is used to collect data. A reasonable consequence of this practice is that students are misled into accepting the idea that both random sampling and random assignment facilitate generalizability.

Kempthorne (1979) argued that mathematical statisticians have done applied researchers a disservice by implying that there is a single statistical model, the normal curve model. Attempting to encompass all types of investigation in a single model "has led to the pooling of different types of investigation that have strongly different logical natures, to the detriment of applied statistics" (p. 124). Kempthorne pointed out that research can be divided into categories (e.g., surveys and experiments) and each category has different methods and inferential goals. Attention to Kempthorne's distinctions can elucidate the place of random sampling and random assignment in research and help minimize errors in the interpretation of results.

The goal of survey research typically is parameter estimation. Thus, most surveys attempt to obtain random samples from some well-defined population, and when successful, valid generality inference is possible using the normal curve model and associated statistics (e.g., t and F).

In contrast to surveys, the goal of experiments is to delineate causal links between variables and, more often than not, this goal is pursued with convenience samples (see Mook, 1983). Thus, nonrandom samples are used in most experiments, but care is taken to randomly assign experimental units during the execution of the study. For example, subjects are randomly assigned to different treatments or the order of presenting stimuli to subjects is randomly determined. In this context, data analyses that assume the normal curve model would be inappropriate or at least superfluous. Not only is parameter estimation biased without random sampling, it is not even desired in typical experiments. Moreover, the goal of testing hypotheses about relative group performance cannot be validly accomplished from a normal curve perspective. The independence assumption fundamental to deriving meaningful probability values from theoretical sampling distributions is violated with nonrandom samples, and normal curve statistics are not robust to this violation. As Hays (1973) stated: "[The] assumption of random sampling is not to be taken lightly.... Unless this assumption is at least reasonable, the probability results of inferential methods mean very little and these [normal curve] methods might as well be omitted" (p. 197).

A model that is appropriate for testing hypotheses in comparative experiments has been developed (e.g., Edgington, 1987; Fisher, 1935; Pitman, 1938). This model is based on probabilities derived from all possible permutations or randomizations of the obtained sample of data. Probabilities are attained from the frequency of the obtained and more extreme arrangements of scores across groups relative to all possible arrangements of the same scores.[2] No reference to parameters is made, and none of the normal model assumptions are required, other than independence, which is met through random assignment. The model is ideally suited for experimental research because, as long as random assignment has occurred, valid causal inference is possible regardless of how the sample was selected. Moreover, it is virtually impossible to teach the random assignment model without explicating the link between random assignment and causal inference.

Forsyth and Bohling (1986) and Bohling and Forsyth (1987) proposed teaching the random assignment model before the normal model. They suggested that many college students have difficulty grasping the level of abstraction required to understand the normal model. In contrast, the primary requirement for understanding the random assignment model and its associated tests (called *randomization tests*) is the concrete ability of listing possible arrangements of the data at hand. For small data sets, this relatively easy task can illustrate the principles of hypothesis testing without reference to parameter estimation, properties of theoretical sampling distributions, and other normal model concepts.

We concur with Forsyth and Bohling's suggestions and see additional reasons for implementing them. First, the random assignment model provides a useful vehicle for translating probability concepts into hypothesis testing concepts. Too often students do not understand what combinations, permutations, and probability values derived by tossing coins have to do with random sampling, the central limit theorem, and probabilities derived from the density functions of theoretical sampling distributions. The random assignment model allows students to derive probability distributions by hand, using procedures like combinations and permutations, while learning the fundamentals of hypothesis testing such as rejection region, one-tailed versus two-tailed tests, and Type I and Type II errors. In the end, they might be better prepared for the normal curve approach to hypothesis testing.

A second advantage of teaching the random assignment model is that it provides a rationale (helpful to both students and teachers) for using the normal curve in the absence of random sampling. The rationale is that, in many instances, certainly those covered in most introductory statistics courses, normal curve tests provide a good estimate of the probability values that would have been obtained if randomization tests been used (e.g., Boik, 1987). Of course, in using a normal curve test to estimate the results of a randomization test, one must adjust the nature of the null and alternative hypotheses accordingly and orient interpretation toward causality rather than generality. But that serves to emphasize the third, and what we consider to be the most important, reason for teaching the random assignment model along with the normal curve model. Students who learn both models will have a better chance of correctly discriminating the conditions of causal versus generality inference.

References

Bohling, P. H., & Forsyth, G. A. (1987). Statistical significance: Concrete operational activities. In V. P. Makosky, L. G. Whittemore, & A. M. Rogers (Eds.), *Activities handbook for the teaching of psychology* (Vol. 2, pp. 213–221). Washington, DC: American Psychological Association.

Boik, R. J. (1987). The Fisher-Pitman permutation test: A non-robust alternative to the normal theory F when variances are heterogeneous. *British Journal of Mathematical and Statistical Psychology, 40*, 26–42.

Edgington, R. S. (1987). *Randomization tests* (2nd ed.). New York: Dekker.

Fisher, R. A. (1935). *The design and analysis of experiments.* Edinburgh: Oliver and Boyd.

Forsyth, G. A., & Bohling, P. H. (1986, August). *A Piagetian approach to teaching statistics and research methodology.* Paper presented at the annual convention of the American Psychological Association, Washington, DC.

Hays, W. L. (1973). *Statistics* (3rd ed.). New York: Holt, Rinehart & Winston.

Kempthorne, O. (1979). Sampling inference, experimental inference, and observation inference. *Sankhya: The Indian Journal of Statistics, 40*, 115–145.

Mook, D. G. (1983). In defense of external invalidity. *American Psychologist, 38*, 379–387.

Ostrom, T. M. (1984). The role of external invalidity in editorial decisions. *American Psychologist, 39*, 324.

Pitman, E. J. G. (1938). Significance tests which may be applied to samples from any populations. III. The analysis of variance tests. *Biometrika, 29*, 322–335.

Siegel, S., & Castellan, N. J., Jr. (1988). *Nonparametric statistics for the behavioral sciences* (2nd ed.). New York: McGraw-Hill.

---

[2]An elementary illustration of the procedure is given in Siegel and Castellan (1988, pp. 151–155.)

Research Methods Jeopardy: A Tool for Involving Students and Organizing the Study Session

Bryan Gibson
University of Utah

The research methods course is viewed by most psychology instructors as an important core course because it introduces students to the scientific method and how it is used to advance psychological knowledge. However, many students consider course completion a mere formality that is necessary for enrollment in more "interesting" courses. Thus, it is sometimes more difficult to involve students in this course as compared with upper level content courses in psychology.

One area in which students' involvement may be lacking is in the typical pretest study session. In many cases, these sessions consist of simple question-and-answer periods that are of little benefit to a majority of students. However, Aamodt (1982a, 1982b) demonstrated that study sessions do help students perform better on exams, particularly when the study session organizes the material, rather than simply giving students an opportunity to ask questions.

In an attempt to get students involved in and excited about a pretest study session and to provide a format for organizing the class material, I devised a game based on the TV game show Jeopardy. Students were assigned to one of three teams a week before the game and were told that members of the winning team would be awarded an extra point on the exam. To prepare for the game, I identified six categories that ranged from general topics, such as "the scientific method," to specific topics, such as "reliability," and devised five questions for each of the six categories. The easiest question in each category was assigned a value of 100 points, with each subsequent question increasing by 100 points.

To begin play, the teams are randomly ordered, and a member of the first team chooses a category and point value. The instructor reads the selected statement, and the student must respond with the correct question (in true Jeopardy format). For example, an item in the "ethics" category might be: "The right to be informed of all information that might influence a decision to participate in a research project." The correct response to this statement would be "What is informed consent?" If a correct response is given, the next player on that team selects a category and

point value. When a student responds incorrectly, the second team has an opportunity to "steal" the points by providing the correct response. When attempting to steal, team members are allowed to discuss potential responses. If members of that team successfully steal the question, they are allowed to choose a category and point value. If they are unsuccessful, the third team may attempt to steal. If the third team is unable to answer correctly, Team 2 will then choose the next category and point value. If no one is able to provide the correct response, the instructor explains the answer and tries to stimulate discussion about the item.

A "daily double" is hidden among the items on the Jeopardy board. The student who chooses this item decides (with input from teammates) how many team points to wager. This item is presented to the student privately. If the student responds incorrectly, the wagered points are removed from that team's score, and the next team can choose an amount to wager without knowing what the item is.

After the last item on the Jeopardy board is completed, a topic for the final Jeopardy question is revealed. Team members decide how many points to wager, the final Jeopardy item is presented, and each team discusses potential responses and writes its response on a sheet of paper. Each team reveals its answer, and points are added or subtracted to determine the winning team.

My goal was to create an entertaining and competitive procedure that would actively involve all students and highlight the current course material. Anecdotal reports from students indicate that these goals were achieved. Several students reported that the advanced notice made them study harder than they normally would have. In addition, students displayed much team spirit through hearty congratulations for a correct response and words of encouragement for an incorrect response. Finally, when asked whether a second Jeopardy game should be planned before the next test, students were enthusiastic in their support.

The game also seemed to provide an organization of the material for students. By selecting six major topics, the instructor provided an overarching framework to help students organize their study. Students who were unable to answer questions in a given category could then focus their study on that topic. Although the nature of the game does not provide a review of the more complex theoretical concepts covered, these issues can be dealt with through writing and research critiquing assignments presented at other points in the course. In summary, research methods Jeopardy stimulated enthusiasm in the topic and helped students identify where to focus their study for the exam.

References

Aamodt, M. G. (1982a). A closer look at the study session. *Teaching of Psychology, 9,* 234–235.

Aamodt, M. G. (1982b). The effect of the study session on test performance. *Teaching of Psychology, 9,* 118–120.

7. Demonstrating Systematic Observation and Research Design

Dwight Krehbiel and Paul Lewis from Bethel College stress the importance of observational methodology and describe a program that focuses on this approach. They point out specific advantages of systematic observation and describe pertinent lab exercises designed to show students how subdisciplines of psychology can be integrated.

Recognizing a lack of emphasis on naturalistic observation, Harold Herzog from Western Carolina University describes exercises designed to provide students experience in quantifying behaviors observed in a small mouse colony. These techniques can be applied in numerous courses and with almost any species, including humans.

Since Oskar Pfungst exposed the "thinking horse" as an unwitting fraud, Clever Hans has been used to illustrate various concepts in experimental psychology. Michael Marshall and David Linden at West Liberty State College replicated the Clever Hans effect by training a rat to bar press in response to a signal that was surreptitiously controlled by the instructor. This demonstration stimulated student interest and critical thinking.

Miriam Goldstein and Michael Strube from Washington University and Roy Hopkins from St. Mary's College of Maryland developed a classroom demonstration of observer bias. Students were led to expect that response time of a subject's performance on a motor task would decrease across three trials, because of alcohol consumption. The subject (a trained confederate who drank a nonalcoholic beverage) displayed consistent behavior and performance across trials, but students reported a trend that was consistent with their expec-tancy. The demonstration had a strong and memorable effect on students.

James Carr from the University of Nevada and John Austin from Western Michigan Unviersity provide a brief overview of single-subject designs and describe a demonstration for teaching these designs to undergraduate psychology majors. Using a reversal design, students collected repeated measures of their own behavior, and they graphed and visually interpreted their data.

Using the Howard-Dolman depth perception apparatus, Dominic Zerbolio and James Walker at the University of Missouri–St. Louis devised an exercise that facilitates exposition of a factorial design and addresses perceptual problems experienced in everyday life. The exercise illustrates the nature of an interaction and the necessity of additional analyses of simple main effects.

William Stallings from Georgia State University had graduate students design and conduct an experiment to evaluate effects of fertilizers on the growth of radish seedlings. The goal of this project is to provide practice in making design decisions, collecting and analyzing data, and writing results. Informal evaluations suggested that the technique is a promising one for teaching experimental design.

Mark Vernoy from Palomar College developed a Stroop-type experiment that demonstrated an interaction effect in a factorial design. Data for several semesters of an experimental psychology laboratory course indicate a consistent main effect and a significant interaction. The computer program that executes this experiment is described and explanations for the interaction are mentioned.

An Observational Emphasis in Undergraduate Psychology Laboratories

Dwight Krehbiel
Paul T. Lewis
Bethel College

Systematic observation is a versatile set of measurement methods that deserves greater emphasis in undergraduate research methods instruction. These methods can be used in both experimental and quasi-experimental designs. They are useful in many domains of psychology and are already widely used in, for example, child development (Kave & Fogel, 1980), personality (Shweder, 1975), emotion (Ekman & Friesen, 1978), and social interactions (Duncan & Fiske, 1977).

The importance of observational methodology in psychology can be seen in the classic work of Barker (1963) as well as in more recent instructional innovations (Hoshmand, 1985; Zeren & Makosky, 1986). Hogan (1991) argued that these methods should be stressed more strongly in liberal arts undergraduate psychology programs because they help students succeed in a variety of occupations. That students may benefit from this approach is also suggested by Boice's (1983) review indicating that observational skills can be improved by training. The availability of a convenient introductory textbook of observational methods (Martin & Bateson, 1986) facilitates this emphasis in instruction.

The greatest advantage of observational methods is their usefulness in demonstrating important scientific principles and concepts. Observational methods provide students a means of validating self-reports, much as we compare people's actions with their words in everyday life. These methods also help students appreciate the dynamic nature of psychological events through repeated observations and consideration of the question of when to observe. Other approaches often do not examine behavioral changes because measurements are taken at only one time.

Observational methods allow clarification of operational definitions. Students understand in a concrete way how technology (e.g., camcorder, lighting, VCR, and film type) and use of technology (e.g., where and for how long to point the camera) interrelate with the behavior observed (e.g., a smile or a kick) to produce an operational definition of that behavior. Understanding operational definitions facilitates exploration of reliability issues, especially through the study of inter- and intraobserver reliability. For example, students become aware of how individual differences in camera operation can reduce interobserver reliability.

Observational methods also permit analysis of a phenomenon at a range of levels from the molar (e.g., being aggressive) to the molecular (e.g., making physical contact), depending on the breadth of the behavioral categories used. Development of behavioral categories helps students appreciate the distinction between observation and interpretation as they search to define categories clearly enough to achieve acceptable levels of reliability. Students thus come to appreciate the interdependence of interobserver reliability and operational definitions, as well as the interrelated nature of the concepts and principles of the scientific method as a whole.

Instruction in observational methods provides an interesting context in which to discuss ethical issues. This fact is especially noteworthy in laboratory exercises involving hidden observers (either in person or via a camcorder) behind the one-way vision screen. For example, students become aware of the subtle trade-offs between treating subjects honestly versus providing the occasion for honest (i.e., unbiased) behaving.

Finally, learning to use videotaping equipment and computerized event recorders allows students to master technologies that are widely used in psychology laboratories. Fortunately, this equipment is now modestly priced, and its widespread use in undergraduate laboratories is feasible.

In the remainder of this article, we briefly review the components of observational methodology used in our courses and describe pertinent laboratory exercises. Like most behavioral methodologies, the observational approach involves data collection and data analysis. We discuss each in turn.

Data Collection

Preparation of Videotapes

Students learn techniques of camcorder use (lighting, movement, close-ups, etc.) and the importance of hypotheses in choosing which individual(s) and behavior(s) to record. They also learn the circumstances under which a more exploratory scan-sampling approach (Martin & Bateson, 1986) might be used to gain a simple appreciation of behaviors occurring in a population.

Split-Screen Recording of Both Members of a Dyad

Students learn the techniques of closed television circuit camera placement and VCR use and come to appreciate the dynamic nature of behavior in the subtle moment-to-moment interactions in a dyad. These interactions can be seen when each member of a dyad is videotaped with a separate camera (thus allowing a frontal view of face and body), but the images are displayed side by side on the monitor by virtue of a split-screen board inside one of the cameras.

Establishment and Refinement of Measurable Indices

Students learn to categorize behavior, do preliminary interrater reliability checks, and refine category definitions and observational procedures to obtain reliable behavioral measures. The development of acceptable interrater reliability helps demonstrate how to conduct an experiment with objectivity, thereby minimizing bias and enhancing the likelihood of replication. Introducing such principles concretely increases the probability that students will be guided by them in their later research projects.

Computer-Based Coding of Observational Data

Students learn to use IBM-compatible laptop computers (Eventlog software and CONDUIT, available from the University of Iowa) to encode the occurrence of their chosen behavioral categories by assigning each to a key (as many as there are in the keyboard); data are saved in a form that can be readily subjected to statistical analysis. Through this process, students learn to distinguish continuous recording from various forms of time sampling and to realize their respective advantages and disadvantages.

Data Analysis

Data reduction and editing are also done by computer. Eventlog computes frequencies and durations of single or combined behaviors. Eventlog files are edited with a word processor or spreadsheet so that they can be read by a statistical package (e.g., SYSTAT; Wilkinson, 1990) for calculation of reliability and descriptive and inferential statistics.

Reliability statistics, such as Cohen's kappa or Pearson's correlation coefficient, are computed. Kappa shows the degree to which a rate of agreement is significantly different from what might be obtained by chance (Hollenbeck, 1978). It can be used at more specific levels of analysis (e.g., those related to errors of omission and commission). Pearson correlations can be used at more general levels of analysis (cumulative durations or frequencies for entire sessions). The various descriptive and inferential statistics on groups and conditions are computed, and summary graphs are created.

Laboratory Exercises

Emotion and Motivation

One of the principal laboratory exercises for this course involves videotaping posed facial expressions and recording psychophysiological data during expressions. Students study and practice judgments on still photographs illustrating facial expressions for different emotions (Ekman & Friesen, 1975). They also learn some of the main categories of facial movement from the Facial Action Coding System (FACS) that are relevant to emotion (Ekman & Friesen, 1978). Finally, they partially replicate an experiment by Ekman, Levenson, and Friesen (1983) on autonomic changes during various posed facial expressions. Primary goals are to familiarize students with the principles underlying the FACS for measuring facial behavior, approaches to integrating behavioral observation and psychophysiology, and problems of demand characteristics in such experiments.

Developmental Psychology

Taking advantage of a nearby preschool, students videotape children playing. Students work out preliminary observation schedules, view the videotapes several times, and make refinements. They construct a set of final behavioral categories, subcategories, measurable indices, and associated definitions and examples, along with the actual observation schedule (or checklist). They translate this schedule into a computerized form by assigning individual behaviors to individual keys in Eventlog on a laptop computer and use the schedule to quantify observations of the videotape. They take interrater reliability estimates and reduce and analyze the data. Students see how behavior unfolds in time; that is, they see how different behaviors in the same person interact and how each person's behavior influences and is influenced by others' behavior.

In another exercise using two cameras and a split-screen board, the instructor and students make videotapes of two different mother-infant dyads at two times (about 3 months and 15 months). The mother is asked simply to get the attention of her baby and relate to him or her as she normally does (Kaye & Fogel, 1980). With the aid of a simplified version of Kaye and Fogel's (1980) coding schema, students categorize and analyze a videotape, frame by frame, at several levels: how mothers attempt to shape their childrens' utterances by imposed adult conversation frameworks; how infants differ in their desire to interact; and especially how the facial expressions, physical gestures, and verbal and nonverbal utterances of infant and mother are subtly intertwined. Comparisons of mother-infant interaction are made when infants are 3 months old and 15 months old. The students come to appreciate the nature of mother-infant interactions at various levels of analysis, as well as how these interactions change over time.

Social Psychology

In an experiment on conversation turn-taking (Duncan & Fiske, 1977), students create videotapes of two people having a conversation. They analyze verbal and nonverbal behavior with a truncated version of the coding scheme proposed by Duncan and Fiske. Cues making up the turn-yielding signal (e.g., head shift, inhalation, gesticulation, etc.), along with back-channel behaviors (e.g., vocalizations, etc.), are recorded and analyzed. Some students also focus on the relations among speaking, gestures, and self-adaptors. Students see how the seemingly "natural" event of conversation is made possible by a series of interlocking behaviors across the two conversants.

Concluding Comments

Although we prefer to use observational methodology and instrumentation to help integrate our set of upper level psychology laboratories, they can also be taught and emphasized in a single experimental or research methods course or in a course with content especially suited to such measurements (e.g., a course in animal behavior). Our emphasis on systematic observation in teaching research methods has been as illuminating for us as our students. Both student and instructor gain greatly from the discipline of observing behavior in an unbiased way.

References

Barker, R. G. (Ed.). (1963). *The stream of behavior: Explorations of its structure and content.* New York: Appleton-Century-Crofts.

Boice, R. (1983). Observational skills. *Psychological Bulletin, 93,* 3–29.

Duncan, S., Jr., & Fiske, D. W. (1977). *Face-to-face interaction: Research, methods, and theory.* Hillsdale, NJ: Lawrence Erlbaum Associates, Inc.

Ekman, P., & Friesen, W. V. (1975). *Unmasking the face.* Englewood Cliffs, NJ: Prentice-Hall.

Ekman, P., & Friesen, W. V. (1978). *Facial action coding system: Investigator's guide, Part 2.* Palo Alto, CA: Consulting Psychologists Press.

Ekman, P., Levenson, R. W., & Friesen, W. V. (1983). Autonomic nervous system activity distinguishes among emotions. *Science, 221,* 1208–1210.

Hogan, P. M. (1991). Vocational preparation within a liberal arts framework: Suggested directions for undergraduate psychology programs. *Teaching of Psychology, 18,* 148–153.

Hollenbeck, A. R. (1978). Problems of reliability in observational research. In G. P. Sackett (Ed.), *Observing behavior: Vol. 2. Data collection and analysis methods* (pp. 79–98). Baltimore: University Park Press.

Hoshmand, L. L. S. T. (1985). Module on observation methods: A perspective on the teaching of inquiry. *Teaching of Psychology, 12,* 132–136.

Kaye, K., & Fogel, A. (1980). The temporal structure of face-to-face communication between mothers and infants. *Developmental Psychology, 16,* 454–464.

Martin, P., & Bateson, P. (1986). *Measuring behaviour: An introductory guide.* Cambridge, England: Cambridge University Press.

Shweder, R. A. (1975). How relevant is an individual difference theory of personality? *Journal of Personality, 43,* 455–484.

Wilkinson, L. (1990). *SYSTAT: A system of statistics.* Evanston, IL: SYSTAT, Inc.

Zeren, A. S., & Makosky, V. P. (1986). Teaching observational methods: Time sampling, event sampling, and trait rating techniques. *Teaching of Psychology, 13,* 80–82.

Notes

1. Preparation of this article was supported in part by the National Science Foundation's Instrumentation and Laboratory Improvement Program through Grant USE-905167.
2. Authors' names are listed in alphabetical order because contributions were equal.

Naturalistic Observation of Behavior: A Model System Using Mice in a Colony

Harold A. Herzog, Jr.
Western Carolina University

Among the ethologists' contributions to psychology is the development of methods that allow quantitative analysis of naturally occurring behaviors. As a result, ethology has emerged from its descriptive, natural history phase to become a quantitative science. Even though naturalistic observation can be applied to a wide variety of research problems and requires little equipment, it is typically neglected in undergraduate research methods courses. The exercises described herein were developed to give students experience with naturalistic observation, using mice as subjects. The exercises also offer students an opportunity to work with animals in an ethically sensitive

206

fashion at a time when many psychology departments are eliminating animal colonies because of pressures from animal welfare groups and government regulators.

Mice are ideal animals for these exercises, although other small mammals, such as gerbils, can be substituted. They are readily available from pet shops or from colleagues in biology departments. Mice come in a variety of colors and patterns, which makes for easy identification of individual animals. (If they are available only in white, a dab of hair dye can be used to mark individuals.) Because mice almost never bite and have an interesting repertoire of behaviors, even students who do not like working with larger animals, such as rats, enjoy observing them.

Preparation

Mouse colonies can be made from 10-gallon aquaria with cedar chips for bedding and wire mesh tops. The animals should have soft paper or other materials available for building nests. They can also be provided with objects to climb on or hide in. Between three and five mice should be placed in each aquarium. The use of mixed-sex groups leads to a greater variety of behavior patterns, but can also lead to population problems in 3 to 4 weeks.

Although the techniques are explained during class, students come into the laboratory on their own time to make observations. Observations are made by pairs of students who work as a team throughout the exercise. So that they can experience the widest possible range of behaviors, students are encouraged to observe the animals at several different times a day.

Techniques of Naturalistic Observation

Constructing an Ethogram

The students first spend 1 hr or so simply observing a group of mice. They are instructed to look for, and make notes on, patterns of behavior. This "field note stage" is sometimes referred to as *ad libitum sampling* and is particularly useful in the initial stages of naturalistic observation. A list of the behavior patterns is then constructed. This catalog is called an *ethogram* and forms the basis of a behavioral coding system. Each recurring behavior pattern is given a one- or two-word name, an abbreviation, and a brief description. The exercises are based on the category system, and it is important that students in each pair agree on the categories and have a clear understanding of what constitutes the specific behavior in each category. The ethograms are discussed in class, and I emphasize the importance of avoiding anthropomorphic interpretations of behavior and of specifying the difference between functional and descriptive categories.

Ideally, ethograms should be exhaustive and mutually exclusive; all behaviors a mouse normally exhibits should be included on the list, and the animal's observed behavior should fall into only one category. In reality, these goals can be obtained only by many hours of careful observation. However, even the first short observation period typically generates an ethogram containing between 15 and 25 of the most common mouse behaviors. Students are encouraged to include a miscellaneous category for new behaviors that they will inevitably encounter.

Quantification of Streams of Behavior

Once each pair of students has developed a category system, they can use it to quantify streams of behavior in a number of ways. The advantages and disadvantages of various techniques are discussed in several sources (e.g., Altmann, 1974; Hutt & Hutt, 1974; Lehner, 1979; Martin & Bateson, 1986). The students typically practice two methods, instantaneous sampling and focal animal sampling.

Instantaneous sample. In instantaneous sampling, observations are made of ongoing behaviors at precise intervals. For example, samplings made every 15 sec for 15 min will yield 60 observations. The technique requires that students in each pair prepare checklists based on their ethogram categories. The checklist we use is a matrix with 60 observation periods numbered across the top (several pages may be needed) and the behavioral categories listed along the left side. Each pair also needs a timer to signal exactly when the observations are to be made. Although a mechanical timer that produces a tone at preset intervals can be used, a tape recorder is quite adequate. Simply make a tape with either an audible signal or the word *observe* at regular intervals (e.g., 15 sec).

It is important that the students in each pair make simultaneous, independent observations on the same animal, because their data will be used to calculate interrater reliabilities. During the observation period, students independently check the category best describing what that animal is doing when the signal occurs. Care must be exercised to ensure that the check is placed in the column representing the appropriate observation interval. At the end of the period, each student should have a single check in each of the 60 columns. They then count the number of times each behavior was scored. By dividing these numbers by 60, they can calculate the percentage of intervals in which each behavior was observed. This measure estimates the relative amount of time the animal spent performing the various behaviors during the observation period.

Students may then evaluate their observational skills by calculating interrater reliability as estimated by percent agreement. Interrater reliabilities of over 90% are normally interpreted as indicating an acceptable level of agreement, but in this exercise, they often vary widely. The reliabilities obtained depend on several factors, including the number of categories, how well they are defined and understood, and the activity level of the animals when they are observed.

Focal animal sampling. Focal animal sampling involves recording all the ongoing behaviors of individual animals. Data can be used to make a variety of comparisons, such as behavioral differences between sex and age. This method can also be used to generate information amenable to the analysis of behavioral sequences. Students again work in pairs, with one student initially designated observer and the other recorder. Using the ethogram categories, the observer dictates the behavior patterns the animal performs sequentially. After 50 behaviors have been dictated, the observer and recorder change roles for another 50 behavior changes.

The list of 100 behaviors can now be analyzed in a number of ways. The simplest way is to count the relative frequencies of various behavior patterns. Data gathered using this method can also be used for sequence analysis in which the stream of behavior is divided into units consisting of an initial behavior and a following behavior. These units can be entered into a matrix, and transition probabilities can be calculated. After all pairs of behaviors have been entered in the matrix, it is easy to calculate the relative frequencies of the various behaviors. More important, the students also see that patterns emerge; some behaviors frequently follow each other, but others rarely do.

Take, for example, a chain of behaviors in which a mouse engages sequentially in the following behaviors: scratch–sniff–rear up–scratch. This chain contains three pairs of behaviors (scratch–sniff, sniff–rear up, rear up–sniff). These two-behavior units are then entered into a transition matrix. The ethogram categories are listed across the top and along the left side of the matrix. The left-side categories are designated initial behaviors, and the categories across the top are subsequent behaviors. Tally marks for the pairs of behaviors are placed in the matrix as follows: The first pair of behaviors, scratch–sniff, is scored by placing a tally mark in the box that has scratch as the initial behavior and sniff as the subsequent behavior. Sniff now becomes the initial behavior for the next pair (sniff–rear up), which is entered in the matrix with sniff as the initial behavior and rear up as the subsequent behavior. Rear up now becomes the initial behavior for the unit rear up–scratch.

Discussion

These exercises provide students with opportunities to learn how naturally occurring behaviors can be subjected to quantitative analysis. I use them as required labs (graded on a satisfactory/unsatisfactory basis) in courses in experimental psychology and animal behavior. However, they are also appropriate for courses in social or developmental psychology. Course evaluations and informal discussions with students indicate that most of them find the exercises interesting and enlightening. Many students report being surprised at the patterns that emerge as they begin to quantify the animals' behavior.

These techniques can be applied to virtually any species that can be unobtrusively observed, including our own. Indeed, the instructor may want to include an investigation of humans as an exercise. For example, a coding system of the book-carrying behavior of college students can be quickly constructed, and students can be sent out on campus with a checklist of the categories to look for sex differences in book-carrying modes (Hanaway & Burghardt, 1976; Jenni & Jenni, 1976). Sex differences will inevitably be found, and a lively discussion of possible reasons for this result will likely ensue.

References

Altmann, J. (1974). Observational study of behavior: Sampling methods. *Behavior, 49,* 227–265.

Hanaway, T. P., & Burghardt, G. M. (1976). The development of sexually dimorphic book-carrying behavior. *Bulletin of the Psychonomic Society, 7,* 276–280.

Hutt, S. J., & Hutt, C. (1974). *Direct observation and measurement of behavior.* Springfield, IL: Charles C Thomas.

Jenni, D. A., & Jenni, M. A. (1976). Carrying behavior in humans: Analysis of sex differences. *Science, 194,* 859–860.

Lehner, P. N. (1979). *Handbook of ethological methods.* New York: Garland STPM Press.

Martin, P., & Bateson, P. (1986). *Measuring behaviour: An introductory guide.* Cambridge, England: Cambridge University Press.

Note

I thank Gordon Burghardt, Mary Jean Herzog, and Jerry Baumgartner for their comments on this article.

Simulating Clever Hans in the Classroom

Michael J. Marshall
David R. Linden
West Liberty State College

The case of Clever Hans, the apparently sapient horse, marks a famous success in the annals of behavioral science and provides much fodder for illustrating psychological concepts. Early in this century, a German mathematics teacher toured Europe and amazed the public with a horse that could correctly tap out the answers to algebra problems, indicate the time of day, and even spell German words using a code that converted numbers to letters. Many "experts" of the day believed Clever Hans provided clear evidence that an animal was capable of human intelligence, especially because Hans responded correctly even when questioned by others in the absence of his master. Only when the psychologist, Oskar Pfungst (1911), systematically manipulated the conditions under which Clever Hans performed was the "thinking horse" exposed as an unwitting fraud. After much careful testing, Pfungst found that Hans simply responded to a subtle visual cue. Questioners invariably tilted their heads toward the horse when he had reached the correct number of taps, a signal that Hans used to stop tapping.

Because students find this story inherently interesting, psychology instructors have effectively used it to illustrate concepts such as systematic manipulation, hypothesis testing, uncontrolled conditions, experimenter effects, parsimony, falsifiability, and the dangers of relying on testimonial evidence (Kalat, 1993; Sebeok & Rosenthal, 1981; Stanovich, 1992). We believed the Clever Hans effect would have a more powerful impact on students if we could replicate it in class using a live animal.

This article describes and evaluates a demonstration in which the instructor covertly signals a rat to press a bar, giving the impression that it responded correctly to yes or no questions posed by students. A purist may call this demonstration a *Clever Hans-like effect* because it uses an auditory rather than a visual cue, and the experimenter intentionally rather than inadvertently cues the animal. We believe the demonstration aids in learning experimental design concepts and stimulates students' critical thinking and scientific skepticism.

Method

Subjects

The human subjects were 21 women and 16 men enrolled in an introductory psychology class. The demonstration subject was a female, Long-Evans hooded rat that was 4 months old when operant discrimination training began. The animal was housed in an individual cage with water available continuously and was reduced to 80% to 85% of free feeding weight for training and demonstrations.

Apparatus

A Lafayette Instruments Co. Student Operant Conditioning System was used. The operant chamber had clear plexiglass side walls and lid and a metal lever centered in the front wall. A motorized pellet dispenser delivered 45-mg Noyes pellets to a reinforcement cup at the right of the lever. The jewel light above the lever was disconnected so that the switch on the handheld unit, which normally illuminated it, could be used to activate an interval timer. A bar press could activate the pellet dispenser only during the 4-s interval set on this timer.

The terms *YES* and *NO* were cut into separate 8- × 12-cm pieces of black construction paper backed by white paper. These signs were taped to the top of the system control console. Each could be illuminated from behind by a 6W-115 VAC light bulb. A bar press during the 4-s interval illuminated the bulb behind the YES sign and reset the timer. If the interval elapsed without a bar press, the NO sign was illuminated.

During the classroom demonstrations, the operant chamber was placed on the instructor's desk and the control console, with the YES and NO signs attached, sat on top of a cart 2.5 m from the desk. The hand control unit was given to a student volunteer who was instructed to turn on the switch to initiate a trial when the rat was to answer a question.

During training, the auditory stimulus was presented from a Lafayette Precision Signal Generator (Model ANL-916) to an 8 w speaker set outside the front or side of the operant chamber. During demonstrations, the auditory signal was presented from an electronic dog whistle, called a Dazzer (made by K-II Enterprises, $24.95), that was concealed on a belt beneath the instructor's jacket. Both of these instruments produced a 22,000-Hz signal of 80 db against a background of 60 db to 65 db, measured inside the operant chamber.

Procedure

In the training phase, the rat was shaped to approach and press the lever for continuous reinforcement. After a response pattern was established, discrimination training was instituted with continuous reinforcement during the auditory signal and no reinforcement when the signal was absent. The signal was set at 1,000 Hz during the first two sessions of discrimination training so that the trainers could hear it. As discriminative responding emerged, the signal was changed to 22,000 Hz, and training continued until the animal responded only during the signal. The procedure was then changed so that the first response after signal onset was reinforced and terminated the signal. The duration of the signal was then reduced until the animal responded consistently within 4 s of signal onset. Although the rat's performance was almost perfect within 10 sessions, training was continued with refresher sessions, so that the behavior was well established and would not be disrupted by distracting events during the classroom demonstrations that were conducted 4 and 6 months later.

The demonstration took place after the students learned major concepts in research methods and experimental design at the introductory level through the assigned reading (Morris, 1993) and a lecture. The instructor told the students that psychologists used selective breeding and these research methods to breed and train rats to be as intelligent as humans. Students' denunciations were met with an offer by the instructor to "prove" it was true with a rat that was brought into the classroom in a Skinner box. The class was told that the rat, named Hanzel, would be able to answer correctly almost any yes or no question that anyone in the class posed by pressing the bar to indicate an answer of yes and refraining from bar pressing to indicate an answer of no. Just after each question was asked, a student volunteer flipped the switch on the hand control unit, which activated the 4-s timer. In response to a question such as "Is the moon made out of cheese?," the instructor did not trigger the ultrasonic signal, the rat did not bar press, and the NO sign was illuminated after a 4-s delay. In response to such questions as "Is 5 the square root of 25?," the instructor covertly activated the ultrasonic tone with a surreptitious push of the wrist against the on button of the Dazzer. This tone signaled the rat to bar press, which illuminated the YES sign. (The YES and NO signs were used only for theatrical purposes. The demonstration could be performed just as easily by saying that a bar press means yes and no bar press means no.)

After demonstrating that the rat could indeed answer correctly almost any question posed to it, the students were polled to find out who was and who was not convinced that the rat had superior intelligence. The class was divided about evenly. The instructor then guided the ensuing discussion to determine which half of the class was right by assessing the evidence through the use of critical thinking. In turn, students were challenged to try to ascertain the validity of the instructor's claims by suggesting some more parsimonious explanations and checking them with testable (falsifiable) hypotheses. After awhile, the class reasoned that they could systematically manipulate the situation to assess the validity of the instructor's claims. They tested the hypothesis "The instructor is providing visual cues to the rat" by having the instructor stand out of view of the rat for a set of trials. Eventually, they figured out that the instructor was the source of the rat's sapient performance by having the instructor leave the room. After the class identified the successful experimental manipulation, the instructor related the story of Clever Hans. The instructor guided a discussion to generalize the principle of the Clever Hans effect to thinking critically about testimonial evidence provided in relevant media reports of psychological findings.

Evaluation

After the exercise, 37 students completed a 7-item questionnaire evaluating their experience on a scale ranging from *strongly disagree* (1) to *strongly agree* (5). Student responses indicated that the exercise was very interesting ($M = 4.81$, $SD = .39$), worthwhile ($M = 4.54$, $SD = .55$), and a positive experience ($M = 4.51$, $SD = .64$). They also indicated that this activity helped them better understand the concepts in experimental design ($M = 4.46$, $SD = .39$), improved their ability to think critically ($M = 4.16$, $SD = .72$), enabled them to understand better how the methods of psychology can be helpful in solving real problems ($M = 4.35$, $SD = .67$), and should be used in future classes ($M = 4.84$, $SD = .37$).

Informally, students commented that they especially liked this exercise because (a) the live animal captivated their attention, (b) the challenge to prove the rat did not have human intelligence motivated them to think critically about the situation and apply their knowledge of research methods, and (c) active involvement in an actual event was more fun than discussing it in the abstract (Benjamin, 1991). Hanzel also created a minor sensation on campus; students from all over campus came to the animal lab and requested to see Hanzel. We have had requests from nonpsychology instructors to show the demonstration to their classes, including requests for Hanzel to perform for middle school students and a class from a neighboring college.

Discussion

This exercise is appropriate for any psychology class that requires students to learn about experimental research methods. In particular, the experimental concepts of systematic manipulation, hypothesis testing, uncontrolled conditions, experimenter effects, parsimony, falsifiability, and the danger of relying on testimonial evidence can be discussed in relation to this demonstration. The instructor's original claim that psychologists could create rats with human intelligence was testimonial evidence. The students were then able to test and disconfirm this claim by generating their own falsifiable hypotheses and systematically manipulating the variables under controlled conditions to develop the more parsimonious explanation—that the rat's performance was due to experimenter effects.

In addition, this demonstration can be used as a critical-thinking exercise to help students acquire the skills necessary to assess the validity of psychological events reported in the media. Teaching critical thinking with this type of demonstration is superior to the traditional method of teaching critical thinking (i.e., as a general formula of abstractly learned steps) because students become engaged in finding an implicitly generated solution to a problem rather than studying critical thinking per se (Gray, 1983). Students initially challenge the instructor to prove that the rat is sapient, and then the instructor puts the shoe on the other foot by challenging the students to prove it is not. The switching nature of these roles nicely incorporates an active learning approach (Benjamin, 1991).

The media are replete with news reports that cry out as targets to which students can generalize this lesson. For example, a *Time* magazine cover asked, "Can Animals Think?" (Linden, 1993). Inside was a story about animals, such as chimpanzees and dolphins, that seem to use language to communicate with their trainers. Also, there are the omnipresent stories of psychic readings and paranormal communication. Other types of relevant news items are

usually reported as psychological breakthroughs. A recent example involves the use of facilitated communication for profoundly retarded, autistic children who suddenly show literacy by typing on a computer with the aid of a human facilitator, whose role is to lightly support their hands over the keyboard (Wheeler, Jacobson, Paglieri, & Schwartz, 1993). Could this be just a modern equivalent of the Clever Hans effect? To the degree that this type of exercise can help students assess more critically the validity of these types of real-world claims, its value extends beyond learning the subject matter.

References

Benjamin, L. T., Jr. (1991). Personalization and active learning in the large introductory psychology class. *Teaching of Psychology, 18,* 68–74.

Gray, P. (1993). Engaging students' intellects: The immersion approach to critical thinking in psychology instruction. *Teaching of Psychology, 20,* 68–74.

Kalat, J. W. (1993). *Introduction to psychology* (3rd ed.). Pacific Grove, CA: Brooks/Cole.

Linden, E. (1993, March 22). Can animals think? *Time,* pp. 54–61.

Morris, C. G. (1993). *Psychology: An introduction.* Englewood Cliffs, NJ: Prentice-Hall.

Pfungst, O. (1911). *Clever Hans.* New York: Holt.

Sebeok, T. A., & Rosenthal, R. (1981). *The Clever Hans phenomenon: Communication with horses, whales, apes, and people.* New York: The New York Academy of Sciences.

Stanovich, K. E. (1992). *How to think straight about psychology* (3rd ed.). New York: HarperCollins.

Wheeler, D. L., Jacobson, J. W., Paglieri, R. A., & Schwartz, A. A. (1993). An experimental assessment of facilitated communication. *Mental Retardation, 31,* 49–60.

Note

We thank three anonymous reviewers for their insightful comments on a draft of this article.

"The Eye of the Beholder": A Classroom Demonstration of Observer Bias

Miriam D. Goldstein
Washington University

J. Roy Hopkins
St. Mary's College of Maryland

Michael J. Strube
Washington University

Human beings are neither objective nor accurate processors of information: We often see what we want or expect to see and tend to remember information that is consistent with our schemas or expectations (Mischel, Ebbesen, & Zeiss, 1976; Snyder & Swann, 1978; Snyder & Uranowitz, 1978). In other words, prior theories or hypotheses have a strong impact on the processing of new information.

Biases in human perception have important implications for scientific research. The researcher, being human, is not immune to such bias. Indeed, extensive research has demonstrated that hypotheses held by researchers can have a strong influence on the obtained data (Anderson, 1983; Rosenthal, 1963; Rosenthal & Rosnow, 1969). Thus, it is not surprising that issues of experimenter bias and observer fallacies are often highlighted in psychology courses of all levels (see Aronson, Ellsworth, Carlsmith, & Gonzales, 1990; Neale & Liebert, 1986).

We created a demonstration in which students experienced directly the powerful effects of observer bias. We led students to believe that they would be monitoring the self-report accuracy of a subject (actually a trained confederate) who was expected to display a decrease in performance across trials due to alcohol consumption. Students reported a trend that was consistent with the expectancy yet was not present in the behavior observed; the confederate actually drank apple juice and displayed consistent behavior across trials.

Format of the Demonstration

Participants and Procedure

Students in an experimental psychology class were led to believe that they would observe a demonstration of subject response bias. We explained that researchers such as Nisbett and Wilson (1977) suggested that self-report is often inaccurate, thus rendering the validity of measures based on self-report questionable. We told students that a subject would be unable to report accurately an obvious decrement in performance due to alcohol consumption. In other words, we suggested that students would be more objective than the subject, or less likely to display a bias, in reporting the subject's level of performance.

After being told that she was about to participate in a study of motor coordination, the subject (a trained confederate) engaged in three trials of a mirror-tracing task (see Mednick, 1964). In this task, subjects must trace within the outline of a double-lined star with only a mirror's reflection to guide them. The subject was instructed to trace the pattern with a pencil while looking only at the mirror, not directly at her hand or the pattern. The subject used her right hand and traced clockwise. At the beginning of each trial, the subject placed the point of her pencil between the boundaries of the figure at an indicated starting point. When signalled by the experimenter, she began tracing the figure as rapidly as possible, trying not to go out of the boundary lines. At first, this task is very difficult. With practice, however, one becomes able to fill in the star quite easily (Mednick, 1964). To assure consistent performance across trials, the confederate was trained before the demonstration to maintain a constant rate and constant number of errors (i.e., number of times she crossed the outline of the star). Despite such training, slight performance changes could occur in the actual demonstration. Moreover, one runs the risk that the tracings will vary in a consistent manner (e.g., become worse across trials). Thus, it is advisable to obtain quality ratings of the tracings from objective judges after the demonstration. Another limitation of this variation is

212

that our confederates had a difficult time keeping their performance consistent while following a verbal and non-verbal script.

To avoid these difficulties, we have also run the demonstration with pretraced stars so that the confederate needs only to concentrate on time to complete the task. All three stars are identical. To assure that the tracings are not obviously identical, each tracing is rotated clockwise (i.e., the master tracing is copied onto the other forms at a different angle). Students do not suspect that the tracings are not actually completed during the demonstration (their view of pencil-paper contact is obstructed). However, to reduce potential suspicion, we invite students to attempt the tracing task, using blank forms pulled from a drawer (this procedure also serves to illustrate the difficulty of the task). The pretraced forms are located at the bottom of the pile of forms and, with a little sleight of hand, can be easily placed on the apparatus during the demonstration.

We provided our confederate with a detailed script for her behavior. Once she began to trace, she counted silently for 20 s, remarked "okay," counted another 20 s, smiled, counted another 20 s, and remarked "This isn't easy" (during Trial 1), "This is hard" (during Trial 2), and "This is difficult" (during Trial 3). She then counted another 20 s, laughed, counted another 20 s, and announced that she was finished. The confederate's performance on each trial was inconspicuously timed to assure equivalent performance time across trials.

Before each trial, the confederate consumed what students believed was a mixture of rum and cola. To reduce possible suspicion and increase realism, the drinks were prepared in class, using a can of cola, a shot glass, and a rum bottle actually containing apple juice. After each trial, the traced star was passed around for students to see. Students were then given a questionnaire that asked them to "rate the effect of the alcohol on the subject's speech and behavior" and to "rate the effect of alcohol on the subject's performance." Students were provided with a 10-point scale ranging from *no effect* (1) to *strong effect* (10) and were instructed to circle the number that corresponded to their answers. Students were instructed not to put their names on the questionnaires. The answer sheets were collected after each trial. The confederate completed what students believed to be similar ratings; presumably, her answers were to be used to assess the accuracy of her self-reports. Actually, the confederate circled random responses.

In order to give the "alcohol" time to take effect, the confederate was given a 15-min break after each trial. During this time, we proceeded with class activities.

After the final trial and collection of all answer sheets, we revealed that in this demonstration we expected the students, not the subject, to exhibit bias. We explained that the subject was in fact a trained confederate and that she had not consumed alcohol. We also told the students that

we planned to analyze their answers to see whether they had indeed displayed an observer bias. We described what pattern of results would offer support for a bias and what pattern would offer support for objective rating. During the next class period, which focused on experimenter and subject biases, we presented the results described in the following section.

Results

Overview

In this section, we present empirical evaluation of two variations of the demonstration that we have used in past years. In the first variation (hereafter Demonstration 1), the confederate is actually performing the tracing task. We recommend using Demonstration 1 if the students will have a clear view of the tracing apparatus. In the second variation of the demonstration (hereafter Demonstration 2), the tracings are objectively identical.

Demonstration 1

The confederate's performance times for the three trials were highly consistent (Trial 1 = 1.46 min, Trial 2 = 1.39 min, and Trial 3 = 1.41 min). Students' ratings of the effects of alcohol on the confederate's speech, behavior, and performance were analyzed using a repeated measures analysis of variance (ANOVA). Significant linear trends were found for speech and behavior ($M_1 = 1.29$, $M_2 = 1.60$, and $M_3 = 3.00$), $F(1, 13) = 10.95$, $p < .006$; and for performance ($M_1 = 1.43$, $M_2 = 2.14$, and $M_3 = 4.07$), $F(1, 13) = 18.91$, $p < .001$. Thus, students rated the effect of alcohol as increasing across the trials for speech, behavior, and performance.

Demonstration 2

We ran this variation in two sections of an experimental psychology class. Because the results did not differ across sections, the following results refer to both sections combined.

The confederate's performance times for the three trials were highly consistent (Trial 1 = 2.18 min, Trial 2 = 2.20 min, and Trial 3 = 2.17 min). Students' ratings of the effects of alcohol on the confederate's speech, behavior, and performance were analyzed using a repeated measures ANOVA. Significant linear trends were found for speech and behavior ($M_1 = 1.50$, $M_2 = 2.69$, and $M_3 = 2.85$), $F(1, 26) = 19.90$, $p < .001$; and for performance ($M_1 = 2.30$, $M_2 = 3.30$, and $M_3 = 4.70$), $F(1, 26) = 19.89$, $p < .001$. As in Demonstration 1, students rated the effect of alcohol as increasing across the trials for speech, behavior, and performance.

Following the discussion, students completed an anonymous questionnaire reporting whether they personally succumbed to observer bias and whether they thought the deception involved in the demonstration was justified. The purpose of this questionnaire was twofold. First, it allowed us to assure that students were not upset or anxious about being deceived. Second, it allowed us to examine whether students were convinced that they individually succumbed to the observer bias. We think that the responses to these questions revealed that the demonstration was effective. In a recent class, 25 of 27 students agreed that their expectations influenced their observations, and all students thought that the deception was justified. One student wrote: "Although we can learn through lecture that we are all biased, you just *proved* it to us. You couldn't have done that without deception." Another student commented: "I'm glad I was fooled. I'll scrutinize and think more when I plan an experiment. I want to avoid these flaws."

Discussion

Both variations of our demonstration allow students to experience personally the powerful effects of prior expectations on perception. Results verify that our demonstrations are effective in producing an observer bias.

This demonstration is an excellent tool to use in both experimental and introductory psychology classes. Although bias in information processing is a well-established finding, we believe that students were more appreciative of this effect after they experienced it personally. The demonstration has led easily into a discussion of both experimenter and subject biases and other experimentation issues, such as reliability and validity of measures. For example, we pointed out that students served as the measurement instrument in this demonstration. They were to observe and record a subject's behavior and performance. Were their measurements valid? Probably not: The students' measurement of the confederate's behavior and performance was biased by their expectations and thus did not reflect the actual behavior and performance. It follows that their recordings were not a valid measure of the confederate's behavior, because they did not measure what they set out to measure. Similarly, to the extent that the students' bias reflects random and, thus, nonreplicable variance, the students' measurements were not reliable. The effects of expectations on perception outside of the lab (e.g., stereotypes) can also be discussed.

Students have eagerly shared their thoughts about why they fell prey to the bias, often providing specific examples of neutral behaviors that they had processed in an expectation-consistent manner. For example, one student commented that, during the final trial, he had thought that a smile indicated "tipsiness." Similarly, a student noted that she now realized that a comment made by the confederate during the last trial ("this is difficult") was not different from a comment made in an earlier trial ("this is hard"). At the time of the demonstration, however, she had thought that the comment in the last trial indicated greater difficulty in performance, which she had attributed to the alcohol consumption.

Students also remarked on how they actively distorted their reports. One student commented that, even when she thought there was no difference in performance, she rationalized that there must be a difference. She ignored certain things that the subject did at times but noticed and exaggerated their meaning at other times. Such comments can be used to illustrate the difference between demand characteristics (i.e., subjects report what they think the experimenter wants to hear) and observer bias (subjects see what they expect to see), both of which contribute to explaining the results of our demonstration. Another student noted that he watched for signs, such as blinking, that he thought were characteristic of someone under the influence. One student had an interesting insight into one possible source of observer biases. She said "Don't you think it would be dangerous for us all not to think that her behavior was influenced at least a little bit by the alcohol?" Her intriguing question led to a discussion of whether biases and heuristics (or cognitive shortcuts) are indeed errors (see Funder, 1987).

Although we have demonstrated that students succumbed to observer bias and that they can articulate the reasons why they thought they did so, another important issue is whether our students actually learned from the demonstration. We addressed this question in two ways. First, at the beginning of the semester, we provided students with a manuscript containing numerous methodological problems and APA-style violations. Embedded in the manuscript was an example of a potential observer bias. Students handed in a list of detected methodological problems and APA-style violations several times throughout the semester to demonstrate their progressive mastery of course material and to hone their ability to evaluate research critically. Students handed in their lists for the first time before the demonstration and for the second time 2 weeks after the demonstration. None of the students detected the observer bias before the class demonstration, but seven (22%) did after the class demonstration.

Because the manuscript described earlier was fairly long and complex, we sought other ways to demonstrate that students had learned the concept of observer bias. In an exam that followed the class demonstration by 3 weeks, we presented students with a brief description of a hypothetical study and instructed them to identify its major problems. One of the major problems involved a potential observer bias. Eleven students (35%) detected the bias. The seven students who detected bias in the manuscript also detected bias in the exam.

In summary, our demonstration provides students with a lively and memorable introduction to observer biases. Students' personal involvement in the demonstration should improve learning.

References

Anderson, C. A. (1983). Abstract and concrete data in the perseverance of social theories: When weak data lead to unshakable beliefs. *Journal of Experimental Social Psychology, 19,* 93–108.

Aronson, E., Ellsworth, P. C., Carlsmith, J. M., & Gonzales, M. H. (1990). *Methods of research in social psychology.* New York: McGraw-Hill.

Funder, D. (1987). Errors and mistakes: Evaluating the accuracy of social judgment. *Psychological Bulletin, 101,* 75–90.

Mednick, S. A. (1964). *Learning.* Englewood Cliffs, NJ: Prentice-Hall.

Mischel, W., Ebbesen, E. B., & Zeiss, A. M. (1976). Determinants of selective memory about the self. *Journal of Consulting and Clinical Psychology, 44,* 92–103.

Neale, J. M., & Liebert, R. M. (1986). *Science and behavior: An introduction to methods of research.* Englewood Cliffs, NJ: Prentice-Hall.

Nisbett, R. E., & Wilson, T. (1977). Telling more than we can know: Verbal reports on mental processes. *Psychological Review, 84,* 231–259.

Rosenthal, R. (1963). On the social psychology of the psychological experiment: The experimenter's hypothesis as unintended determinant of experimental results. *American Scientist, 51,* 268–283.

Rosenthal, R., & Rosnow, R. L. (Eds.). (1969). *Artifact in behavioral research.* New York: Academic.

Snyder, M., & Swann, W. B. (1978). Hypothesis-testing processes in social interaction. *Journal of Personality and Social Psychology, 36,* 1202–1212.

Snyder, M., & Uranowitz, S. W. (1978). Reconstructing the past: Some cognitive consequences of person perception. *Journal of Personality and Social Psychology, 36,* 941–950.

Note

We thank Tammy Hershey and David Stotz for their contributions to this project and Saera Khan for her superb performance as the confederate in Demonstration 2. We also thank Ruth L. Ault and several anonymous reviewers for their helpful comments on a draft of this article.

A Classroom Demonstration of Single-Subject Research Designs

James E. Carr
University of Nevada

John Austin
Western Michigan University

When conducting experimental research, social scientists most often use group designs to assess behavior change (Kantowitz, Roediger, & Elmes, 1994). Likewise, psychology classes and textbooks in experimental design focus almost exclusively on group research. An alternative to the analysis of group data is the single-subject design (Baer, Wolf, & Risley, 1968; Krishef, 1991). A group design often requires many subjects to achieve adequate power and identify statistically significant differences between group means. Alternatively, a single-subject design can require only one subject and is often useful when large numbers of subjects sharing similar features are unavailable. Whereas group designs identify statistical differences between or within two or more groups of subjects, single-subject research exercises its power through examining changes in subjects' responding over time across experimental conditions. For instance, a reversal design demonstrates experimental control by repeatedly presenting and withdrawing a treatment (i.e., independent variable). When an effective treatment is repeatedly presented and withdrawn, responding should change accordingly. In this procedure, rather than using statistical tests of significance, the data are graphed and visually inspected for substantial change across conditions (e.g., from baseline to treatment).

Researchers have used single-subject designs to study various phenomena, including disruptive and learning behavior in school settings (e.g., Birnbrauer, Wolf, Kidder, & Tague, 1965), recycling and littering in community settings (e.g., Austin, Hatfield, Grindle, & Bailey, 1993), occupational safety (e.g., Austin, Kessler, Riccobono, & Bailey, 1996), work productivity and quality (e.g., Gowen & Jennings, 1990), clinical disorders (e.g., Carr & Bailey, 1996; Knox, Albano, & Barlow, 1996), and the habilitation and treatment of individuals with developmental disabilities (e.g., Vollmer, Marcus, & Ringdahl, 1995).

There are many variations of single-subject designs, including multiple baseline, multiple probe, withdrawal, changing criteria, multielement (or alternating treatments), and reversal designs (Cooper, Heron, & Heward, 1987; Iwata et al., 1989). Because the reversal design is the most widely used and often provides the most compelling and believable results, this demonstration focuses on the use of the reversal design to evaluate intrasubject changes.

Sometimes referred to as the baseline-treatment-reversal design (i.e., A-B-A or return to baseline), the reversal design demonstrates the functional control, or causal status, of the independent variable or variables by showing an obvious on-off relation between the independent and dependent variables. This relation is sometimes referred to as a "water-faucet" effect because presentation of the independent variable turns "on" the behavior (i.e., the dependent variable changes in the expected direction) and removal of the independent variable turns "off" the behavior (i.e., the dependent variable returns to approximately baseline level).

The purpose of this demonstration is to teach undergraduate psychology students about single-subject methodology by having them collect repeated measures of their own behavior during the three phases of a reversal design.

Method

Begin by presenting your class with adequate information, via lecture or otherwise, on the theory and applications of single-subject methodology (including the graphing of behavioral data). Once students understand the basic concepts (e.g., baseline and reversal) and techniques (e.g., line graphs) involved, the demonstration can begin. Instruct students that the demonstration will require them to engage in physical exercise for 15 separate 20-s periods. Any student who is unable to exercise or is uncomfortable about exercising should be allowed to use another student's data for the final analysis. Inform students that they will be using a reversal design to study the effects of physical exercise on their pulse rate. In addition, they will take repeated measures of their pulse rate to ensure that the difference between conditions is not artifactual. Provide them with a data sheet that has five spaces for data (five per condition).

Ensure that all students can adequately record their own pulse. The pulse can be obtained by placing the index and middle fingers of the left hand over the carotid artery in the neck (on the right side) or over the right side of the right wrist (palm up). After students practice taking their own pulse, you can provide them with the details of the demonstration.

The independent variable is 20 s of exercise (jumping jacks). The dependent variable is frequency of pulse beats during a 1-min interval. During the baseline condition, students should be cued to start recording their pulse. You should have a stopwatch to time the intervals. After 1 min has passed, have students record the number of pulse beats for that interval on their data sheets. This number represents the first baseline data point. Have students repeat this recording process for another 4 min, yielding a total of five baseline data points.

During the treatment phase of the demonstration, instruct students to stand up and begin jumping jacks for 20 s. After the exercise period, have them sit down and record their pulse for 1 min. After 1 min, have them record the number of pulse beats on their data sheets. This number represents the first treatment data point. Instruct students to repeat this exercise-recording process four more times, yielding a total of five treatment data points. For the reversal condition, have students repeat the baseline procedure until they have obtained five data points.

Finally, instruct each student to make a line graph of all 15 data points, including vertical lines separating the three conditions. Graphing may be facilitated by providing a graph sheet with preprinted axes. After students graph the data, have them raise their hands if the exercise increased their pulse rate. Next, have students raise their hands if there was no change or if they experienced a decrease in heart rate. Most students should have experienced an increase in pulse rate as a result of the exercise. You can use this discussion time to share some of the finer points of single-subject methodology. For example, you may discuss how this independent-dependent variable relation could be tested with a multiple-baseline design using delayed exercise start times for some students. In addition, you can discuss how the aforementioned other single-subject designs can be used to study this relation and others. Another possible avenue of discussion is the utility of repeated measures in data analysis and their assistance in locating extraneous sources of variability and reducing the probability of making Type I errors.

Results

We conducted the demonstration with 14 students in an undergraduate psychology laboratory in research methodology. Students had previously heard a lecture on single-subject designs. All graphs showed substantial changes in pulse rate as a result of the exercise as well as a successful reversal. Figure 1 illustrates representative graphs from three students.

Student Opinions and Evaluations

We solicited student opinions about the utility of the demonstration immediately after completing it. There were no negative comments about the demonstration. Comments included the following: "I thought it worked rather well. It was hands-on, and you could actually see the changes." "It was a great way to demonstrate the A-B-A design." "Over-

all, I thought the lab was very informative." "I thought the lab was useful. It made the concept of single-subject design more clear, and made the class more interesting." "I think it was a good idea because it took something that we could easily manipulate and measure." "I think that the single-subject design involving exercise was a great idea in reflecting the reversal design. Results were quick, obvious, and understandable."

Discussion

Tell the class that the demonstration covered only the most rudimentary aspects of single-subject methodology. Another crucial point is that, although the demonstration conditions were changed after five trials, single-subject methodology is based on the foundation that conditions be changed only when data are stable and do not exhibit linear trends that may confound the interpretation of subsequent data. The demonstration could be improved by using a phase-change criterion to illustrate steady-state responding before experimental conditions are changed. Furthermore, the methodological rigor of this procedure could be enhanced through the use of interobserver agreement measures for the dependent variable (see Carr, Taylor, & Austin, 1995).

This simple demonstration can be helpful in teaching students about single-subject designs because it provides opportunities to study their own behavior during different experimental conditions. The students collect, graph, and visually interpret their own data, which allows them to perform many of the practical behaviors necessary in using single-subject designs. The demonstration can be completed in less than 30 min and should be a useful addition to instruction on experimental research methods.

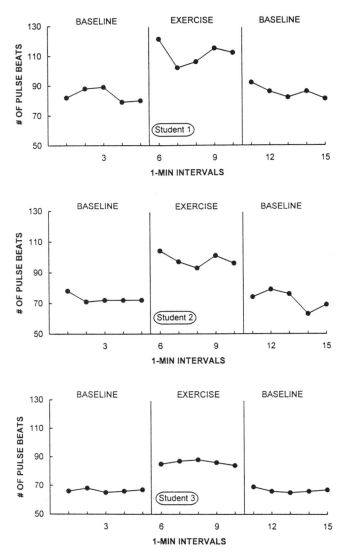

Figure 1. Representative line graphs of pulse-rate data from three students.

References

Austin, J., Hatfield, D. B., Grindle, A. C., & Bailey, J. S. (1993). Increasing recycling in office environments: The effects of specific, informative cues. *Journal of Applied Behavior Analysis, 26,* 247–253.

Austin, J., Kessler, M. L., Riccobono, J. E., & Bailey, J. S. (1996). Improving roofing performance and safety using incentives and feedback. *Journal of Organizational Behavior Management, 16,* 49–75.

Baer, D. M., Wolf, M. M., & Risley, T. R. (1968). Some current dimensions of applied behavior analysis. *Journal of Applied Behavior Analysis, 1,* 91–97.

Birnbrauer, J. S., Wolf, M. M., Kidder, J. D., & Tague, C. E. (1965). Modifying the classroom behavior of pupils with token reinforcement. *Journal of Experimental Child Psychology, 2,* 219–235.

Carr, J. E., & Bailey, J. S. (1996). A brief behavior therapy protocol for Tourette Syndrome. *Journal of Behavior Therapy and Experimental Psychiatry, 27*, 33–40.

Carr, J. E., Taylor, S. L., & Austin, J. (1995). A classroom demonstration of self-monitoring, reactivity, and interobserver agreement. *The Behavior Analyst, 18*, 141–146.

Cooper, J. O., Heron, T. E., & Heward, W. L. (1987). *Applied behavior analysis.* Columbus, OH: Merrill.

Gowen, C. R., III, & Jennings, S. A. (1990). The effects of changes in participation and group size on gainsharing success: A case study. *Journal of Organizational Behavior Management, 11*, 147–169.

Iwata, B. A., Bailey, J. S., Fuqua, R. W., Neef, N. A., Page, T. J., & Reid, D. H. (Eds.). (1989). *Methodological and conceptual issues in applied behavior analysis.* Lawrence, KS: The Society for the Experimental Analysis of Behavior.

Kantowitz, B. H., Roediger, H. L., III, & Elmes, D. G. (1994). *Experimental psychology: Understanding psychological research* (5th ed.). St. Paul, MN: West.

Knox, L. S., Albano, A. M., & Barlow, D. H. (1996). Parental involvement in the treatment of childhood obsessive-compulsive disorder: A multiple-baseline examination incorporating parents. *Behavior Therapy, 27*, 93–114.

Krishef, C. H. (1991). *Fundamental approaches to single subject design and analysis.* Malabar, FL: Krieger.

Vollmer, T. R., Marcus, B. A., & Ringdahl, J. E. (1995). Noncontingent escape as treatment for self-injurious behavior maintained by negative reinforcement. *Journal of Applied Behavior Analysis, 28*, 15–26.

Note

We thank Charles L. Brewer and three anonymous reviewers for their extremely helpful comments on a draft of this article.

Factorial Design: Binocular and Monocular Depth Perception in Vertical and Horizontal Stimuli

Dominic J. Zerbolio, Jr.
James T. Walker
University of Missouri–St. Louis

Factorial designs represent one of our most useful and powerful research tools. Yet the major advantage of factorial designs over simpler designs (i.e., the ability to detect interactions between variables) is also what makes them difficult to teach, because interactions are not always intuitively obvious to students. Teaching students to understand the nature and interpretation of an interaction can be greatly facilitated by an exercise, as long as it reliably produces an interaction, and the results are readily and obviously interpretable. We have tried to manipulate many variables factorially during our collective 4 decades of teaching. None of these efforts was completely satisfactory until recently, when we discovered an exercise that meets these requirements. In addition, this exercise requires minimum equipment and makes a substantive point about a real-world perceptual problem.

The equipment required is some form of the Howard-Dolman depth perception apparatus (Howard, 1919a, 1919b; the Howard-Dolman depth perception apparatus was supplied by Lafayette Instrument Company, P.O. Box 5729, Sagamore Parkway, Lafayette, IN 47903) and masks or goggles to restrict viewing to one eye. The usual application of the Howard-Dolman apparatus requires the subject to adjust two vertical rods in the third dimension so that they appear equidistant from the observer. The dependent variable measure is the separation between the two rods, measured along the subject's line of sight. The average error is typically much smaller when rods are viewed binocularly than when viewed monocularly. If the apparatus is laid on its side, the rod orientation becomes horizontal (see Figure 1); in this orientation, Howard (1919b) found that the average errors for binocular and monocular viewing did not differ.

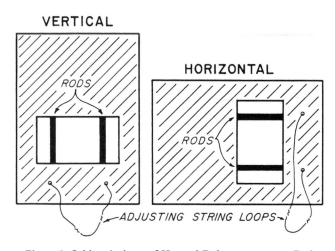

VERTICAL

HORIZONTAL

RODS

RODS

—ADJUSTING STRING LOOPS—

Figure 1. Subjects' views of Howard-Dolman apparatus. Rods are adjusted to appear equidistant in depth using loops of string. A pointer indicates the adjustment error on a scale hidden from the subject. Extraneous cues are reduced by diffused white back-lighting.

Orienting the apparatus horizontally or vertically allows a factorial combination of Rod Orientation and Viewing Condition. We expected and found little or no difference between monocular and binocular viewing conditions with the rods in the horizontal orientation, but a substantial superiority of binocular over monocular with the rods in the vertical orientation (i.e., a Viewing Condition × Rod Orientation interaction). The example we report used an independent-groups procedure, but the design lends itself just as well to a repeated-measures design, assuming the instructor wishes to grapple with the problems associated with teaching interactions and repeated measures simultaneously.

Method

Subjects

Thirty subjects participated as a class requirement in an undergraduate research methods course.

Apparatus

The apparatus (see Figure 1) was adjusted by means of a string looped around the back of a chair. Subjects were allowed to use only one hand in making adjustments in order to minimize kinesthetic cues.

Procedure

The experiment used a 2 × 2 independent-groups factorial design. The factors were Viewing Condition (binocular and monocular) and Rod Orientation (vertical and horizontal). Using a table of random numbers, we assigned each of 30 students to one of the four experimental conditions with the constraint that the number of subjects per cell was to be as nearly equal as possible. The dependent variable for each subject was the mean separation between the rods in 10 adjustment trials.

In two of the groups, the largest scores were so deviant that questions were raised regarding whether the subjects were following instructions in adjusting the apparatus or whether the student-experimenters were recording the data accurately. In the interest of reducing error variance, these two scores were discarded.

The apparatus was located approximately 5.5 m from the subject. At the beginning of each trial, the rods were positioned at their extreme departure from equidistance, 20 cm apart. The rod nearest to the subject (left or right in the vertical orientation and top or bottom in the horizontal orientation) was determined randomly using a Gellerman series. The student-experimenter blocked the subject's view of the apparatus with his or her body during the initial positioning of the rods before each trial. In monocular viewing, each subject used the dominant eye, as determined by a measure of sighting dominance.

Results and Discussion

The mean separations for all four groups appear in Figure 2. The main effect of Viewing Condition was significant, $F(1, 24) = 4.91, p < .05$. The effect of Rod Orientation approached significance, $F(1, 24) = 3.77, p < .10$, and there was a significant interaction between these factors, $F(1, 24) = 9.59, p < .01$. Because the main effects are not interpretable when an interaction is present, simple main effects for Viewing Conditions at each Rod Orientation were calculated. With the rods oriented vertically, binocular viewing was significantly superior to monocular viewing, $F(1, 24) = 14.11, p < .001$. With the rods oriented horizontally, no difference between binocular and monocular viewing was observed, $F < 1$. These results are clearly illustrated in Figure 2.

The results allowed us to demonstrate the problem of interpreting a main effect in the presence of an interaction and readily led our students to see the necessity of partitioning the data into simple main effects. Figure 2 was particularly helpful in this respect. In this context, the question of whether binocular or monocular vision is better clearly depends on the horizontal or vertical orientation of the target stimuli.

This exercise greatly facilitates the exposition of a factorial design, and it relates to some perceptual problems in the real world. Horizontally extended stimuli, such as wires, are difficult to localize in depth because they provide little or no binocular disparity. Thus, line workers, tree trimmers,

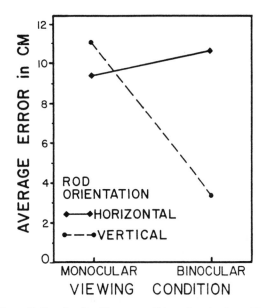

Figure 2. Results. Smallest mean (binocular viewing with vertically oriented rods) differs significantly from all other means, $p < .01$, which do not differ from each other.

and construction workers moving equipment near power lines are at great risk, as accidents frequently occur in such situations. Airplane pilots flying near wires are also at risk, as Howard (1919b) pointed out long ago. Our exercise serves the dual purpose of explicating a factorial design and providing a substantive basis for understanding a real-world perceptual problem.

References

Howard, H. J. (1919a). A six meter stereoscope. *American Journal of Ophthalmology, 2,* 849–853.
Howard, H. J. (1919b). A test for the judgment of distance. *American Journal of Ophthalmology, 2,* 656–675.

Return to Our Roots: Raising Radishes to Teach Experimental Design

William M. Stallings
Georgia State University

Alternative ways of teaching applied statistics have been described in journals such as the *American Statistician* (e.g., Hogg, 1972; Tanner, 1985), *Chance* (Joiner, 1988), *Teaching of Psychology* (Hettich, 1974), and the *Journal of the Royal Statistical Society Series A* (Jowett & Davies, 1960). This literature emphasizes the importance of having students work with real data. For example, Singer and Willett (1990) argued that "real data sets provide a more meaningful and effective vehicle for the teaching of applied statistics" than do synthetic data, no matter their numerical tractability (p. 223). Perhaps ideally, students should pursue their own research interests, collecting data from studies they design and conduct (see Jowett & Davies, 1960; Tanner, 1985).

Teachers of psychological and educational statistics are concerned that some students can complete the assigned computational exercises without understanding the purpose of the computations. For example, one of my students correctly computed a two-way analysis of variance (ANOVA) but could not distinguish between the number of levels in a factor and the number of independent variables. This incident illustrates the limitations of textbook exercises.

Although students could replicate classic experiments or design and complete simple studies of their own, both options are time-consuming. In addition, one now has to comply with institutional guidelines for research participants. Fortunately, many of these problems can be avoided. Students can work with real data by conducting simple agricultural experiments, what I call "returning to our roots." After all, as Lovie (1979) noted, "the first practical application of analysis of variance (ANOVA) was on the

220

effects of manure on the rotation of potato crops (Fisher & Mackenzie, 1923)" (p. 151).

The last three times I taught our second course in statistics, an ANOVA-based course using Keppel (1991), I required each student to collect and analyze data from a gardening experiment. Students assess the effect of growth accelerators on radish seedlings that they grow at their homes.

Typically, students enrolled in the course are working toward advanced degrees or certification in education or nursing; they tend to be mature women who are employed. Our students live off campus. Except for the nurses, they tend to have weak science and mathematics backgrounds.

Equipment

The inexpensive equipment consists of plastic ice cube trays or egg cartons, potting soil, fine gravel, mechanical drawing dividers (for measuring the heights of the seedlings), a ruler, radish seeds (or any other fast-germinating vegetable seeds), several jars with lids, and one or more growth accelerators (e.g., Miraclegro® or RA-PID GRO®).

Procedure

Instructions for the procedure and analysis are given in Table 1. Students decide whether to compare different growth accelerators (qualitatively different levels) or different amounts of the same growth accelerator (quantitatively different levels). Other issues that each student considers are experimental mortality, unequal sample sizes, unit of analysis, number of comparison groups, and choice of dependent variables. Most students use seedling height, but germination rate and length of tap root are possible also.

Students have reported that seeds germinate in 3 to 5 days. Most students obtain usable measurements at intervals of 5 to 7 days. I allow several days for students to obtain the equipment and set up the experiment. Two weeks has been a sufficient time for analysis and write-up. Hence, students can complete the project in 5 to 6 weeks.

As an illustration of a typical student project, one student grew three sets of 10 seedlings each with treatments of water and no accelerator, two drops of accelerator, or four drops of accelerator. After 4 weeks, the mean growths were 1.50, 2.74, and 2.96 in., respectively. A completely randomized ANOVA on these data yielded a significant difference, $F(2, 27) = 7.41$, $p < .01$. To obtain equal sample sizes, which is not a requirement of the completely randomized design but helpful in other analyses, students often have thinned seedlings immediately after germination.

Table 1. Instructions for Project: Procedure and Analysis

Procedure

1. Prepare three ice cube trays or egg cartons. To facilitate drainage, punch small holes in the bottom of each tray or carton. Then add gravel, and fill with potting soil.
2. In each mold or receptacle, plant three to four seeds about 1/4 in. deep. Soak seeds in water for 15 min before planting to promote germination.
3. Use the jars to mix and store the various concentrations or brands of growth accelerators.
4. Administer the treatment, either different types of growth accelerators or different concentrations of the same growth accelerator (e.g., no drops, one drop, and two drops).
5. Except for the application of the experimental treatment, treat all containers alike.
6. After germination (3 to 5 days), make three sets of measurements at equally spaced intervals (5 to 7 days).

Analysis

1. Write your report in a fashion similar to writing the Method, Results, and Discussion sections of a journal article.
2. Under Results, present the outcomes in words, graphs or tables, and statistics (both descriptive and inferential). For each data-gathering period, construct a graph showing the mean height of the seedlings plotted against levels of the independent variable.
3. For the final data-gathering period, compute a completely randomized ANOVA, omega squared, and (if you find statistical significance) Scheffé and other post hoc comparisons. If your experiment involved quantitatively different levels and if you obtained statistical significance, analyze the data for trends.
4. Optional analyses (beyond minimal expectations) could include computing a repeated measures design, making a priori comparisons, and estimating post hoc power.

Evaluation

Anecdotal evidence of students' positive reactions to the radish project comes from seven written comments appended to project reports and course evaluations. Examples include the following:

"The radish experiment . . . seemed to tie up many of the principles and techniques we learned in class."

"My classmates seemed unanimously enthusiastic about the project."

"The concept of experimental learning is an excellent one and very useful in helping students to grasp abstract concepts such as ANOVA. The requirements . . . were not too costly or time-consuming."

To further evaluate this project, I conducted a content analysis of 31 student reports. I examined the various statistical and design features that students used or could have used, and I judged the appropriateness of their decisions. For example, a post hoc trend analysis following a nonsignificant omnibus F was an inappropriate application;

Table 2. Frequency of Design and Statistical Treatment Decisions

Topic	Appropriate		Inappropriate	
	Application	Nonapplication	Application	Nonapplication
Design selection	29		2	
Post hoc comparisons	15	8	6	2
Effect size/omega squared	23			8
Trend analysis	12	11	3	5
Interpretation of significance	29		2	
Graphs	22		2	7

Note. Thirty-one student reports were analyzed. Each report is listed only once in each row but may appear more than once in each column.

a failure to follow up a significant omnibus *F* with a post hoc test was an inappropriate nonapplication. By contrast, not following up a nonsignificant omnibus *F* was an appropriate nonapplication. The content analysis is summarized in Table 2.

The data suggest that, overall, students made appropriate decisions. However, post hoc analyses of means and trends were troublesome. Graphing also appears to have been a problem. This may be attributed to students' weak science and mathematics backgrounds. Only seven students went beyond the minimal statistical requirements. Given Keppel's (1991) emphasis on planned comparisons, it is disturbing that only two students even attempted an a priori test. None considered low power due to small sample size as an explanation for not obtaining statistical significance. Four students reported problems with experimental control (e.g., "The cat walked on the trays"). Still, most met the minimal expectations.

Conclusion

Overall, I am satisfied with the results of the radish project, but I plan several changes. I will provide a more detailed handout of instructions (including suggested schedules); encourage and reward use of more complex designs, associated ancillary tests, and tests of model assumptions; and append a project evaluation to the anonymous course/instructor evaluation.

All of my students have completed this project in an 11-week academic quarter. Nearly all informally agreed that the project made vivid the concepts of experimental design and ANOVA. During class discussion, some reported that the project was fun and even became a topic of family conversation. In my experience, raising radishes is a successful teaching technique.

References

Fisher, R. A., & Mackenzie, W. A. (1923). Studies in crop rotation. II: The manurial responses of different potato varieties. *Journal of Agricultural Science, 13,* 311–320.

Hettich, P. (1974). The student as data generator. *Teaching of Psychology, 1,* 35–36.

Hogg, R. V. (1972). On statistical education. *American Statistician, 39,* 168–175.

Joiner, B. L. (1988). Let's change how we teach statistics. *Chance, 1,* 53–54.

Jowett, G. H., & Davies, H. M. (1960). Practical experimentation as a teaching method in statistics. *Journal of the Royal Statistical Society Series A, 123,* 11–35.

Keppel, G. (1991). *Design and analysis: A researcher's handbook* (3rd ed.). Englewood Cliffs, NJ: Prentice Hall.

Lovie, A. D. (1979). The analysis of variance in experimental psychology: 1934–1945. *British Journal of Mathematical and Statistical Psychology, 32,* 151–178.

Singer, J. D., & Willett, J. B. (1990). Improving the teaching of applied statistics: Putting the data back into data analysis. *American Statistician, 44,* 223–230.

Tanner, M. A. (1985). The use of investigations in the introductory statistics course. *American Statistician, 39,* 306–310.

Note

I thank Ruth L. Ault and three anonymous reviewers for comments on earlier drafts of this article.

A Computerized Stroop Experiment That Demonstrates the Interaction in a 2 × 3 Factorial Design

Mark W. Vernoy
Palomar College

This article describes a computerized Stroop experiment used to demonstrate the concept of interaction in a factorial experiment conducted by students in my research methods course. The course is a lower division, one-semester introduction to psychological research methods and experimental design with a required 3-hr laboratory. During the first 6 weeks of the laboratory, students run three predesigned experiments of increasing complexity. The first experiment is a simple bilevel design, the second is a multilevel design, and the third is a factorial design. The purpose of this last exercise is to give students some feel for the interaction when they are interpreting the results from a factorial experiment. I designed a computerized experiment that consistently produces an interaction that is interesting and fairly easy to explain. I briefly describe the experiment, the computer program that generates the stimuli, and the results gathered in six classes during the last 3 years.

In the original version of the Stroop (1935) task, subjects were shown words printed in colored ink and were instructed to name the color of ink as quickly as possible. The word on a given trial was the name of a color that was the same as the color of ink in which the word was printed (the congruent condition), the name of a color that was different from the color of ink in which the word was printed (the conflicting condition), or the name of something not related to the color of ink (the neutral condition). Subjects took longer to name the ink color in the conflicting condition (e.g., the word *blue* printed in red ink) than to name the ink color in the congruent condition (the word *blue* printed in blue ink). Interest in the Stroop effect has persisted, even though the original experiment was published many years ago.

Stroop-type effects can be demonstrated with colors, pictures, geometric shapes, and even with words in different languages. (See MacLeod, 1991, for an extensive review.) It is even possible to separate the elements (e.g., the color and the word) and still achieve the Stroop effect. For example, Dyer and Severance (1973) reported that color naming was delayed when a color bar was preceded by a 50-ms flash of a conflicting color name in black ink. In addition, Kahneman and Chajczyk (1983) showed that presenting a word above or below a color bar can affect the naming of the color of the bar. When they presented a congruent color word, the naming of the bar was facilitated, but when the color word was conflicting, the naming of the color bar was inhibited. Goolkasian (1981) demonstrated that the Stroop effect depends on the retinal location of the target. She found that foveal targets showed more facilitation or inhibition than peripheral targets.

In my experiment, students investigated the effect of the spatial placement of distractor words, either conflicting or congruent, on the reaction time for naming a color bar. I hypothesized that (a) reaction time will be longer when subjects are presented with a conflicting color word than with a congruent color word, and (b) reaction time will vary with the spatial placement of the color word—above, on, or below the color bar.

Method

The Experiment

Each semester, approximately 50 Introduction to Psychology students participated in a computerized version of the Stroop effect using a procedure similar to Kahneman and Chajczyk's (1983). The design of the experiment was a within-subjects 2 × 3 factorial. The first independent variable involved whether the color word and the color bar were congruent or conflicting. The second independent variable was placement of the color word—above, on, or below the color bar (see Figure 1).

Each subject was seated in front of an IBM-PC compatible computer (80286) with an EGA color monitor. The experimenter sat behind the monitor with the keyboard in front, facing the subject, so that the experimenter could not see the stimuli presented on the monitor. Using four colors, the computer presented the six different conditions in two blocks of 24 trials each. Each subject was instructed to say the color of the bar as quickly and as accurately as possible. As soon as the subject said each color, the experimenter hit

RED

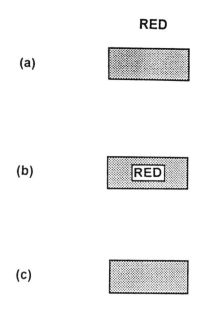

(a)

(b) RED

(c)

RED

Figure 1. Examples of the three different types of spatial location used in the experiment: (a) The color word is above the color bar, (b) the color word is on the color bar, and (c) the color word is below the color bar.

the space bar on the keyboard. The computer measured the reaction time for each trial and computed and printed the mean reaction times for each of the six conditions.

The Computer Program

The computer program that runs the Stroop experiment is written in Microsoft® Quick Basic 4.0 for the IBM PC and compatible computers. It requires a minimum of 640 K memory, a color EGA display card, and a color EGA monitor. Most EGA color monitors do a fairly good job of displaying the colors red, green, and blue, but finding a fourth color is sometimes a problem. This program has two different versions: one with yellow as the fourth color and another with brown as the fourth color. (The instructor can choose the version that looks best on a particular computer.) The computer controls the entire experiment; it presents the stimuli and measures and displays the reaction times.

The program begins by asking the name of the experimenter. After the experimenter types his or her name and hits Enter, the experiment begins. The program instructs the subject that the task is to say the color of the bar as quickly and as accurately as possible. Then the program begins to display the stimuli. Because this is a 2 × 3 experiment with four different colors, there are 24 possible combinations of the three attributes of the stimulus (Red, Blue, Green, or Yellow × Conflicting or Congruent × Above, On, or Below). These 24 combinations are displayed in a pseudoran-

dom order in two separate blocks. The order is the same for all subjects and was predetermined using a Latin square. Before the experimental blocks, eight practice trials are presented so that both the subject and the experimenter can become familiar with the procedure.

Each trial begins with a + sign as a fixation point in the center of the screen. After a random time interval, between 1 and 3 s, the stimulus pair appears on the screen. The appearance of the stimulus pair starts a timer that stops when the experimenter hits the space bar on the computer keyboard. The computer records the appropriate reaction time and presents the next stimulus pair. After the two blocks of 24 stimulus trials, the computer calculates the means for each condition and presents the option of printing the results. If instructed to do so, the computer displays the results on the monitor and prints them. If the experimenter does not wish to print the results, the computer displays them on the monitor.

Results and Discussion

Reaction times were analyzed using a repeated measures two-way analysis of variance (ANOVA). The main effect of conflicting versus congruent was always significant (in 6 semesters, no F ratio was ever less than 8.00). The main effect of spatial location was significant in 4 of the 6 semesters. The interaction between the two independent variables was always significant (in 6 semesters, no F ratio was ever less than 6.00).

The interaction is the reason for the lack of significance among the various spatial locations. The graphs in Figure 2 indicate why the interaction hides the significance in spatial location. When one views only the line for the conflicting condition, it is clear that there is little difference between the reaction times in the above and below conditions, but the on condition has a much slower reaction time. The line for the congruent condition is a mirror image of the conflicting line. In the congruent condition, the above and below conditions are similar, whereas the reaction time in the on condition is much faster. Thus, the interaction hides the effect of the spatial location of the distractor word: The increase in reaction time for the conflicting on condition cancels the effect of the decrease in reaction time for the congruent on condition.

The graphs help students see that the placement of the word on the color bar enhances any effect of the word on the naming of the color of the bar. If the word on the color bar is congruent, it facilitates the naming of the color of the bar. If the word on the color bar is conflicting, it inhibits the processing of the color of the bar. Placement of the word above or below the bar does not have as strong an effect on the naming of the color of the bar. This interaction is extremely robust and has occurred every time my students

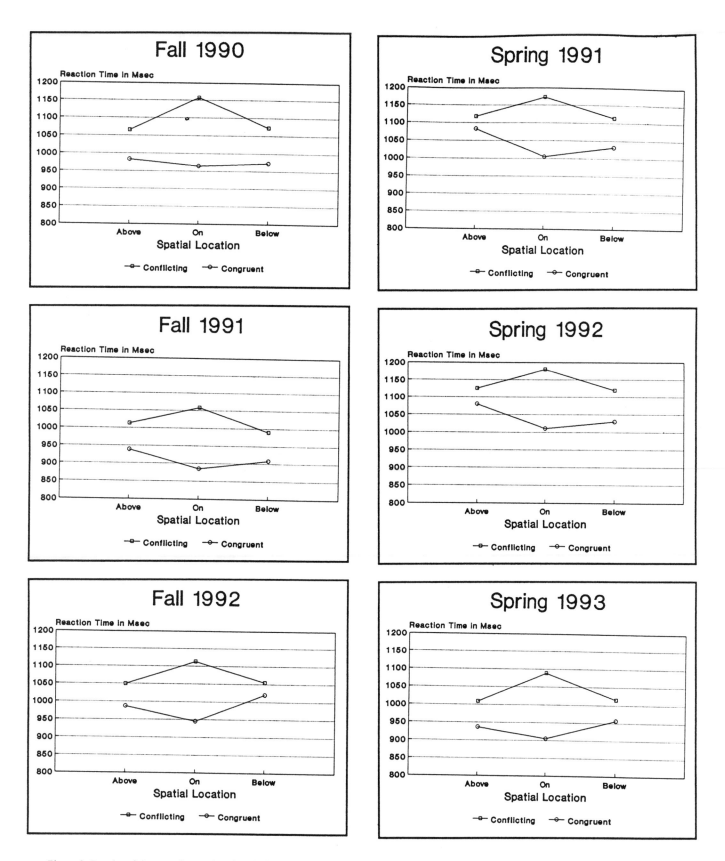

Figure 2. Results of the experiment showing the interaction for the six semesters, beginning with fall 1990 and ending with spring 1993.

have used this computer program to run the experiment, even with sample sizes less than 30.

One feature of the computer program can be seen as an advantage or a disadvantage. This feature involves the fact that the experimenter must hit the space bar to measure the subject's reaction time. This is a disadvantage because the reaction time of the experimenter is added to that of the subject (a voice-actuated timing system would be better), but it is also an advantage because no hardware beyond the computer is required. Also, because all trials for each subject are conducted by the same experimenter using a within-subjects design, the reaction time of the experimenter is not a confounding variable, assuming that it is constant over all trials. Because the experimenter stops the clock, the experimenter must remain attentive throughout the experiment. The only necessary control is that the experimenter sit with the keyboard in a position that allows the experimenter to see and hear the subject but prevents the experimenter from seeing the display screen. Inasmuch as the computer signals the beginning of the practice and the experimental blocks with a beep, there is no need for the experimenter to watch the screen. This procedure also gives the teacher a chance to discuss in class the realities of dealing with the constraints involved in doing psychological research.

Results of this experiment demonstrate a reliable interaction and support the results of the original Stroop (1935) experiment and those of more recent experiments, such as those performed by Goolkasian (1981), Dyer and Severance (1973), and Kahneman and Chajczyk (1983). There-fore, this experiment and computer program can be an effective teaching tool in a laboratory course in research methods or a cognitive psychology course.

References

Dyer, F. N., & Severance, L. J. (1973). Stroop interference with successive presentations of separate incongruent words and colors. *Journal of Experimental Psychology, 98,* 438–439.

Goolkasian, P. (1981). Retinal location and its effect on the processing of target and distractor information. *Journal of Experimental Psychology: Human Perception and Performance, 7,* 1247–1257.

Kahneman, D., & Chajczyk, D. (1983). Tests of the automaticity of reading: Dilution of Stroop effects by color-irrelevant stimuli. *Journal of Experimental Psychology: Human Perception and Performance, 9,* 497–509.

MacLeod, C. M. (1991). Half a century of research on the Stroop effect: An integrative review. *Psychological Bulletin, 109,* 163–203.

Stroop, J. R. (1935). Studies of interference in serial verbal reactions. *Journal of Experimental Psychology, 18,* 643–662.

Note

I thank Bernard C. Beins and three anonymous reviewers for their comments on an earlier draft of this article.

8. Teaching Writing and Critical Thinking

William Addison from Eastern Illinois University describes how a research proposal, used in conjunction with reports based on data collected by students, can be an effective exercise in the experimental psychology course. A combination of the two approaches encourages students to think critically and creatively about the research process and about methodological and ethical issues.

The homework assignment used by Ruth Ault at Davidson College teaches students to organize information from an APA journal article. She distributes the contents of a short journal article in scrambled order and instructs students to unscramble the order of paragraphs and to determine the headings under which the paragraphs are subsumed. This exercise helps students learn about conventional organization and style, and it saves time for the teacher when students later write their own experimental reports.

Dana Dunn emphasized collaborative learning and peer review in his statistics and research methods course at Moravian College. Pairs of students collaborated on the design, data collection, statistical analysis, and writing of an experiment. After a peer review workshop conducted by the instructor, student pairs served as peer reviewers for drafts of the final paper. These reactions aided students in making substantive and stylistic changes for their final papers.

Timothy Lawson from the College of Mount St. Joseph and Randolph Smith from Ouachita Baptist University developed a guide to facilitate preparation of manuscripts in the style and format described in the *Publication Manual of the American Psychological Association* (4th ed.). Their guide will save students and faculty members much time when they format APA pages in WordPerfect.

Richard Hubbard and Kathy Ritchie use the human subjects review process to stimulate students' critical thinking in their experimental psychology courses at Indiana University South Bend. Students integrate existing literature into their proposals and operationally define their methods and measures. They critically analyze their objectives and evaluate potential risks and benefits of their proposals.

The procedure challenges students to present arguments logically to scientific and general audiences.

Joe Hatcher from Ripon College describes his use of fascinating riddles to expose students in introductory and experimental design courses to key points concerning scientific thinking as well as the process and experience of being a scientist. Students liked and learned from this unusual approach, which reminds one of Sherlock Holmes and Dr. Watson.

At Clemson University, Particia Connor-Greene uses creative techniques to teach critical evaluation of scientific research as reported in the popular press. A classroom exercise emphasized the distinction between correlation and causation by having students analyze a newspaper account of a research study. An individual assignment requires students to critique a newspaper or magazine summary of research. Reactions indicated that students enjoyed these activities and became more critical of what they read in the popular press.

Scott VanderStoep from Calvin College and John Shaughnessy from Hope College tested students in Research Methods and in Developmental Psychology courses on methodological and statistical reasoning at the beginning and the end of a term. As expected, reasoning scores of Research Methods students improved more than did scores of Developmental Psychology students. The authors interpreted their results as having encouraging implications, because the data supported the intuitive notion that what we teach has application to everyday life.

At Yeshiva University, Moshe Anisfeld designed a course to train graduate students to read original articles independently and critically. The seminar uses a case-study approach to develop students' data-reading skills and habits. Students learn to pay close attention to the method and results sections of empirical articles from the primary literature and to draw independent conclusions from what they read. In addition, they gain considerable confidence in their critical-reading skills.

Student Research Proposals in the Experimental Psychology Course

William E. Addison
Eastern Illinois University

Teachers of undergraduate courses in statistics and experimental psychology generally agree that students should become directly involved in the research process to enhance their understanding of research design and analysis (Edwards, 1981; Singer & Willett, 1990; Yoder, 1979) as well as to develop their writing and critical-thinking skills (Nadelman, 1990; Snodgrass, 1985). In psychology, this involvement typically occurs in the research methods or experimental psychology course in which students are often required to complete a research project of their own design (Chamberlain, 1986; McGill, 1975).

In addition to improving students' analytical and writing skills, the research project brings together important concepts addressed during the lecture portion of the course. Concepts such as randomization, sampling, operational definitions, and research ethics become more meaningful when students have to apply them to their own research. Because it combines attention to conceptual material with experience in analysis and writing, the research project can be viewed as a capstone experience for the experimental psychology course.

The research project has drawbacks as well as benefits. One limitation associated with student-conducted research is the lack of time needed to design and carry out an even minimally sophisticated project (Carroll, 1986; Forsyth, 1977; Yoder, 1979). With little time available and the typical limitations of equipment and laboratory space, many students conduct simplistic studies from which they gain little knowledge about the principles of behavioral research.

Another problem with student-conducted research is that it is virtually impossible for the instructor to provide adequate supervision of individual projects when each student is involved in a unique study. This limitation is of particular concern when one considers the number of research-based ethical issues that may arise in a moderate-size class.

Several authors have developed techniques designed to address these problems. For example, Carroll (1986) described what he called the *jigsaw technique:* Small groups of students complete a research project to which each member makes a separate contribution. Chamberlain (1988) suggested that recent "core articles" in psychology be used as a basis for student projects (p. 207). Chamberlain's technique involves at least a partial replication of an experiment from a core article. Data collected by individual students are pooled and analyzed by each student in separate research reports.

Another technique that introduces students to the research process and avoids many of the problems associated with the student-conducted research project is the research proposal. This article describes how the research proposal can be combined with data-based research projects to provide students with a comprehensive introduction to the research process.

In my course, students are required to write three APA-style research papers. The first paper is a group project similar to Carroll's (1986) jigsaw technique; the study is based on data collected by the class, and each member of the group is responsible for one of the major sections of the paper (i.e., introduction, method, results, and discussion). Each section contributes 5% to the student's grade in the course. The second paper is an individual report also based on data collected by the entire class, worth 10% of the student's grade. The third paper, worth 20% of the student's grade, is the research proposal, which is due at the end of the semester. For this paper, each student is required to design a study and submit a written proposal in APA style, including all major sections of an APA-style manuscript.

The introduction takes much the same form as it does in a typical research report; it includes a fairly thorough literature review and the specific research issues being addressed by the proposal. The method section describes the subjects, equipment or materials, and procedure that would be used to complete the proposed study. For the results section, I ask students to identify the appropriate statistical tests and include a specific account of the expected results of the analyses. For example, a student who proposes to conduct a two-way analysis of variance is expected to indicate whether a significant interaction is predicted, as well as the specific nature of the interaction. The discussion section focuses on the consistency of the expected findings with previous research, potential confounds, ethical considerations, and directions for further research.

The research proposal has most of the advantages of the student-conducted research project without the drawbacks that result from limitations of time, equipment, and space. For example, critical thinking involves problem solving and hypothesis testing (Baron, 1988; Halpern, 1989; Neimark, 1987), and these processes are important components of both research projects and research proposals. However, because the research proposal has fewer practical constraints, students can be creative in selecting topics for their research. I frequently remind students that they can consider various methods and subjects for their proposals and that they can select a topic based on their own interests, regardless of the practical limitations. Students seem to have taken this advice to heart; perhaps as a result, their proposals often seem more mature, both conceptually and methodologically, than the typical, student-conducted project. For example, recent proposals have included the effects of neuroleptics on amphetamine poisoning in rats, social adjustment of children in day-care centers, and the capacity of neonates to imitate adult models. Students have even suggested that they will use a grant from a specific agency to fund their research.

Student proposals tend to be relatively sophisticated on a methodological level. Consequently, the methodological, ethical, and practical issues that students must address in their papers often require much thought. For example, one student, who proposed to study effects of speech style (masculine vs. feminine) and sex of speaker on listeners' perception of the message, had to consider whether subjects may be more likely to pay attention to one speech style than the other. To address this issue, the student synthesized information from research on speech styles as well as from studies of attentional cues in information processing.

Perhaps the main difficulty with this approach is getting the students to think creatively when they select a topic. Because many of our majors are not asked to engage in creative thinking in other psychology courses, they generally need some encouragement in this direction. I periodically remind students that they are not required to conduct the study; therefore, they are not limited to particular methods or subjects. To illustrate what former students have done in this regard, I provide a list of proposal titles from previous classes.

A related problem is that students frequently have difficulty addressing methodological and ethical issues in a study that they have not actually conducted. This problem is not limited to students' research proposals. As Neimark (1987) pointed out, we all have a tendency to engage in context-tied thinking. Neimark suggested that one way to alleviate this tendency is to participate in exercises designed to encourage context-free thinking. By requiring students to engage in "what if" thinking about potential methodo-

logical and ethical issues, the research proposal constitutes just such an exercise.

Critics may argue that because data collection is an essential part of the research process, students who write a research proposal in lieu of conducting a study are not getting a complete, firsthand research experience. For this reason, the research proposal is most effective when used to supplement research assignments based on data collected by students. Under these conditions, the proposal can be an effective way to get the students to think critically and creatively.

References

Baron, J. (1988). *Thinking and deciding.* Cambridge, England: Cambridge University Press.

Carroll, D. W. (1986). Use of the jigsaw technique in laboratory and discussion classes. *Teaching of Psychology, 13,* 208–210.

Chamberlain, K. (1986). Teaching the practical research course. *Teaching of Psychology, 13,* 204–208.

Chamberlain, K. (1988). Devising relevant and topical undergraduate laboratory projects: The core article approach. *Teaching of Psychology, 15,* 207–208.

Edwards, J. D. (1981). A conceptual framework for a core program in psychology. *Teaching of Psychology, 8,* 3–7.

Forsyth, G. A. (1977). A task-first individual-differences approach to designing a statistics and methodology course. *Teaching of Psychology, 4,* 76–78.

Halpern, D. F. (1989). *Thought and knowledge: An introduction to critical thinking* (2nd ed.). Hillsdale, NJ: Lawrence Erlbaum Associates, Inc.

McGill, T. E. (1975). Special projects laboratory in experimental psychology. *Teaching of Psychology, 2,* 169–171.

Nadelman, L. (1990). Learning to think and write as an empirical psychologist: The laboratory course in developmental psychology. *Teaching of Psychology, 17,* 45–48.

Neimark, E. D. (1987). *Adventures in thinking.* San Diego: Harcourt Brace Jovanovich.

Singer, J. D., & Willett, J. B. (1990). Improving the teaching of applied statistics: Putting the data back into data analysis. *American Statistician, 44,* 223–230.

Snodgrass, S. E. (1985). Writing as a tool for teaching social psychology. *Teaching of Psychology, 12,* 91–94.

Yoder, J. (1979). Teaching students to do research. *Teaching of Psychology, 6,* 85–88.

Note

I thank John Best for his comments on a draft of this article.

What Goes Where? An Activity to Teach the Organization of Journal Articles

Ruth L. Ault
Davidson College

When students in research methods or experimental psychology classes write their own research reports in APA style, they often misplace information, such as putting procedural information in the apparatus section or beginning the introduction with the hypothesis and design statement. Although they have access to numerous examples of correctly written articles, the instructions from their textbook, the *Publication Manual of the American Psychological Association* (American Psychological Association, 1983), and inclass lectures on how to write journal articles, their research reports usually contain fundamental mistakes. Because they are attempting the complicated task of creating and organizing prose while trying to learn all the format conventions, I have sought ways to break the task down into smaller components to facilitate initial learning. One homework assignment useful for learning the correct order of information involves distributing the contents of a short journal article in scrambled order, with instructions to unscramble the order of paragraphs and to determine the location of headings under which the paragraphs belong.

The article used should be short enough to be manageable but long enough to have several paragraphs under each heading so that students consider the internal logical order of each section. I recommend looking in journals containing Brief Reports sections, selecting one that describes a single experiment with a minimum of technical jargon. I use 20 of 23 paragraphs from Patterson and Carter (1979), including the abstract (but not title information) and excluding three discussion paragraphs. Using a random number table, I assign each paragraph in the article a letter (*A* to *T*). For example, the abstract might be labeled *R* and the four procedure paragraphs might be *L, Q, E,* and *A*. I then cut, paste, and photocopy the paragraphs in alphabetical order. Students turn in a single sheet of paper numbered 1 to 20 with their choices of a paragraph letter beside each number; they also indicate the placement of headings (Abstract, Method, Subjects, etc.). Alternatively, they could cut and paste the paragraphs to return them to the original order.

Of 21 students in a junior-senior research methods class who did this assignment, none reconstructed the article perfectly, but 3 correctly placed all paragraphs under their proper headings, making errors only in sequencing paragraphs. Nine students placed a single paragraph under the wrong heading, and 6 of them also incorrectly sequenced some paragraphs. The remaining 9 students placed from two to five paragraphs under the wrong headings and misordered paragraphs in zero to four of the seven possible sections.

By diagnosing the errors students make, instructors can determine where additional teaching is needed. For example, half of my students put a discussion paragraph in the introduction, even though the paragraph contained an explanation for one of the results, because it contained a reference citation. In class discussion about the assignment, many students reported having no strategy for organizing the results section, not even putting the overall analysis of variance ahead of the follow-up tests. Such simple, customary writing conventions are not explicitly stated in the *Publication Manual* and, apparently, are not salient enough from reading journal articles to lead students to the general rule.

On the other hand, no student missed the distinctive style and content of the abstract, all but one isolated the one subjects paragraph, and none failed to include all three results paragraphs under that heading, although one third of them included procedural or discussion information there too.

I prefer to grade this assignment on a pass-fail basis for two reasons. First, occasionally paragraphs may reasonably fall into several orders, especially in the apparatus section where no logic compels one piece of equipment to be described before another and in the results section if there are two or more major dependent variables. Second, once a particular paragraph is misplaced, other arrangements for the remaining material then become reasonable. Keeping track of these alternatives complicates the grading if matching an exact pattern is the criterion for a particular grade. On the other hand, it is relatively simple to check for the presence of major headings and to assess whether most paragraphs are located under their proper headings.

My students reported spending 1 to 2 hr on the assignment and generally reacted positively to it. To evaluate the assignment, 19 of the 21 students checked whether each of five statements was applicable. Although only 2 students checked that it "taught new information," 14 checked that it "provided needed practice for information I already knew," and 10 indicated that "I used something I learned on the homework later in the course." Because several students had already taken another research methods course and had done independent research, it was not surprising that 4 indicated the assignment was "busywork" and 5 checked that "the amount of time spent doing [it] was not worth the amount I learned from it."

I spent less than 10 min per student grading the assignment, and I saved a considerable amount of time grading experimental reports because information was more likely to be located in the proper place.

References

American Psychological Association. (1983). *Publication manual of the American Psychological Association* (3rd ed.). Washington, DC: Author.

Patterson, C. J., & Carter, D. B. (1979). Attentional determinants of children's self-control in waiting and working situations. *Child Development, 50,* 272–275.

Note

Portions of this article were presented at the Eastern Conference on Teaching of Psychology, Harrisonburg, VA, October 1989.

Collaborative Writing in a Statistics and Research Methods Course

Dana S. Dunn
Moravian College

Treating writing as a process skill that can be developed—not simply as an outcome-related task–is a dominant theme in contemporary pedagogy on college-level writing (e.g., Elbow & Belanoff, 1989a, 1989b; Nodine, 1990). I (Dunn, 1994) suggested a variety of ways that writing techniques can be incorporated into psychology classes. In this article, I apply collaborative writing and peer review in Statistics and Research Methods of Psychological Inquiry (PS 210). I also discuss student reactions to these techniques and recommend ways to refine their use in the future.

Our PS 210 is an intermediate-level, one-semester course required of all psychology majors. Two sections of the course are taught each semester, and enrollment is limited to 20 students each. The course is divided into two sections—basic descriptive and inferential statistics and elementary research methodology. The material is taught in tandem (i.e., one class is devoted to data analysis, and a subsequent class deals with methods). Students usually complete four examinations and conduct two research projects. The first project is a simple in-class exercise (e.g., survey). The second project, the focus of this article, involves a collaborative experiment.

So that they may teach and learn from one another, pairs of students collaborate on the creation, design, data collection, analysis, and write-up of an experiment. The key to this experience is writing.

The Writing Process

Step 1: Writing a Prospectus

Students select partners and are told that they have a contractual obligation to them. All work is shared equally, and, in successful collaborations, both partners receive the same grade. Unsuccessful collaborations (i.e., one-sided pairings when one partner does most of the work) result in differential grading.

Although a polished laboratory report written in APA style is the desired product of most research methods courses, the collaborative process of creating this outcome may be more important. That is, students identify key variables, search and read relevant literature, and reason through a research idea by working closely with a partner;

the process of shared writing pulls these activities together. After student pairs select a research topic and design, the process I use involves shared prewriting and freewriting (Belanoff, Elbow, & Fontaine, 1991; Wingard, Dunn, & Brown, 1993), outlining, drafting, and revising of a prospectus (essentially the Introduction, Method, and References sections of an APA manuscript). To ensure that students understand the articles they have found for the literature review in the Introduction, I provide them with a worksheet that leads them through empirical journal articles, highlighting key information that should be gleaned from them (Anselmi, Wall, & Zannoni, 1993; see also, Poe, 1990).

Step 2: Drafting the Final Project Paper

After I provide detailed comments on the prospectus (see Dunn, 1994; Elbow, 1993) and a grade, the students collect their data, conduct the appropriate statistical analyses, and begin writing the final project paper. The final paper is based on the collaborative editing and revising of the prospectus, as well as the initial writing of the Results and Discussion sections.

Peer Review

Step 3: Revising and Editing the Final Project Paper

After a draft of the final paper is completed, one entire class session is devoted to a peer review workshop. During this workshop, each pair of students shares copies of the final project draft with at least one other pair of students; thus, all student pairs act as peer reviewers. Students are instructed to make substantive evaluations of the papers they read (i.e., Why is the research interesting? What does it reveal about human behavior?) and to note grammatical errors and deviations from APA style. I coach the students on how to offer specific and constructive feedback on the papers, emphasizing that detailed comments written in the margins in addition to precise verbal comments to authors are the goals of the workshop (see Dunn, 1994; Elbow & Belanoff, 1989a, 1989b; Haaga, 1993; Wingard et al., 1993, for more specific suggestions). These reactions to the penultimate draft of the project paper aid students in making final revisions and editorial changes.

I offer to read the project papers at any stage of the writing process as long as two conditions are met: The draft (or even outline) is relatively complete, and both members of the pair are present to hear my comments. I write comments on the papers as well; experience suggests that, when students hear and later read my comments, an improved paper is likely to result.

Student Reactions to Collaboration

Process Journal

Throughout their collaboration, student writers keep a process journal in which they can reflect on the quality of the effort. Is responsibility for the project being shared? Was more accomplished by two writers than one? After the project paper is complete, each student submits a separate process journal to me, thereby gaining privacy and assurance that any collaborative problems will be noted.

Survey Results

Because a collaborative project in psychology that emphasizes process writing is somewhat unusual—and in the context of an already demanding course, perhaps even stressful—I surveyed student reactions to the exercises. In spring 1994, 25 of the 43 students who comprised the two sections (22 women and 3 men) returned the survey (for a 58% response rate). Generally, their responses were highly favorable. Eighty-eight percent of the respondents indicated that the division of labor in their pair was equal. Fifty-six percent said they liked collaboration, 40% said they preferred to work alone, and 4% were neutral. These survey responses were consistent with what students wrote in their journals. However, when asked if they learned more or less about psychological research by working with another student, 96% indicated that they learned more as a result of collaboration.

Seventy-two percent of the students found the peer review exercise to be helpful. Closer examination of the responses, however, indicated a between-groups difference: On a 5-point scale ranging from *not at all helpful* (1) to *very helpful* (5), traditional-age undergraduates (those 18 to 22 years old) rated peer review as much more helpful ($M = 4.59$) than did older students from our evening program ($M = 3.25$), $t(23) = 3.22$, $p < .002$. Experience with both groups suggests that the evening students tend to have a more mature work ethic; hence, their project papers may have been more polished at the time of the review than were those by students in the day program. Also, the concept of collaboration may be less compatible with the beliefs of older students, who were taught to rely on their own efforts. Indeed, evening students tend to be more competitive than traditional-age students, who may be more accustomed to collaborative exercises due to more recent (i.e., precollegiate) experiences with them.

In open-ended responses, several students remarked that they wished that the peer review had been done before the final draft of the prospectus was due and then again before completion of the final project paper. I will follow this suggestion next time because I believe that it will improve students' writing and make peer review more helpful.

Conclusions

Collaborative writing that focuses on process and peer review is helpful. Collaboration promotes student appreciation of the creation, presentation, and reception of ideas (see also, Dunn & Toedter, 1991). Sharing the work associated with a statistics and methods project also ensures that many details are addressed, potential errors are caught, and careful proofreading—a perennial faculty lament—actually happens. Also, material pertaining to the psychological import of the work is discussed more thoroughly than is the case for single-author papers.

References

Anselmi, D., Wall, B., & Zannoni, D. (1993, November). *Assignments that encourage critical thinking and active learning across the disciplines.* Workshop presented at the third annual conference of the Institute for the Study of Postsecondary Pedagogy: Interdisciplinary Curricula, General Education, and Liberal Learning, New Paltz, NY.

Belanoff, P., Elbow, P., & Fontaine, S. I. (Eds.). (1991). *Nothing begins with n: New investigations of freewriting.* Carbondale and Edwardsville: Southern Illinois University Press.

Dunn, D. S. (1994). Lessons learned from an interdisciplinary writing course: Implications for student writing in psychology. *Teaching of Psychology, 21,* 223–227.

Dunn, D. S., & Toedter, L. J. (1991). The collaborative honors project in psychology: Enhancing student and faculty development. *Teaching of Psychology, 18,* 178–180.

Elbow, P. (1993). Ranking, evaluating, and liking: Sorting out three forms of judgment. *College English, 55,* 187–206.

Elbow, P., & Belanoff, P. (1989a). *A community of writers: A workshop course in writing.* New York: McGraw-Hill.

Elbow, P., & Belanoff, P. (1989b). *Sharing and responding.* New York: Random House.

Haaga, D. A. F. (1993). Peer review of term papers in graduate psychology courses. *Teaching of Psychology, 20,* 28–32.

Nodine, B. F. (Ed.). (1990). Psychologists teach writing [Special issue]. *Teaching of Psychology, 17*(1).

Poe, R. E. (1990). A strategy for improving literature reviews in psychology courses. *Teaching of Psychology, 17,* 54–55.

Wingard, J., Dunn, D. S., & Brown, C. K. (1993, November). *Writing to learn: Learning to write.* Paper presented at the third annual conference of the Institute for the Study of Postsecondary Pedagogy: Interdisciplinary Curricula, General Education, and Liberal Learning, New Paltz, NY.

Notes

1. Portions of this article were presented at the First Annual American Psychological Society Teaching Institute, Washington, DC, June 1994. Preparation of this article was partially funded by the Moravian College Faculty Development and Research Committee.

2. I thank Sarah Dunn, Stacey Zaremba, the reviewers, and Charles L. Brewer for their helpful comments on a draft of this article.

Formatting APA Pages in WordPerfect: An Update

Timothy J. Lawson
College of Mount St. Joseph

Randolph A. Smith
Ouachita Baptist University

Smith (1992) developed a guide to help students use WordPerfect® 5.1 (WordPerfect Corporation, 1989) to format pages in the style specified in the third edition of the *Publication Manual of the American Psychological Association* (*PM;* APA, 1983). As he suggested, students often have problems determining how to translate APA style into the commands necessary to format word-processing documents (e.g., create headers, set margins, set justification,

Table 1. Menu Commands and Keystrokes to Format APA Pages in WordPerfect 5.1 for DOS, 6.0 for DOS, and 6.0 for Windows

Step	5.1 for DOS	6.0 for DOS	6.0 for Windows
		WordPerfect Version	
1	Shift F8 1—Line	Shift F8 1. Line	Layout Line
2	1—Hyphenation No	6. Hyphenation Empty brackets	Hyphenation Empty box
3	6—Line Spacing Type **2**	3. Line Spacing Type 2	Spacing Type 2
4	3—Justification 1 Left	2. Justification Left	Justification Left
5	7—Margins Left 1″ Right 1″	2. Margins 1. Left 1″ 2. Right 1″	Margins Left 1″ Right 1″
6	2—Page 5—Margins Top .67″ Bottom 1″	3. Top .67″ 4. Bottom 1″	Top .67″ Bottom 1″
7	3—Headers 1—Header A 2—Every Page	5. Header/Footer . . . 1. Headers 1. Header A 1. All Pages Create	Header/Footer Header A Create Placement Every Page
8	Alt F6	Alt F6	Alt F7
9	Type your manuscript page header followed by five spaces and the page number code (see Step 10)		
10	Ctrl B	Ctrl P	Number Page Number
11	F7 (twice)	F7	Close
12	Type your document		
13	Shift F7 6—View Document	Shift F7 7. Print Preview	

Note. Read down the column for a particular WordPerfect version, not across columns. The steps are as follows: 1 = format line screen, 2 = turn off hyphenation, 3 = set double spacing, 4 = set left justification, 5 = set left/right margins, 6 = set top/bottom margins with room for manuscript page headers, 7 = set manuscript page headers, 8 = right-justify page headers, 9 = enter page headers (see *PM*, 1994, p. 241, for header information), 10 = format page numbers, 11 = return to document, 12 = see *PM* (1994) for information on parts of a manuscript, and 13 = optional step: print document to screen (unnecessary in WordPerfect 6.0 for Windows).

and prevent splitting words at the ends of lines). These problems and the wide availability of WordPerfect have made Smith's guide useful to students and faculty.

The fourth edition of the *PM* (APA, 1994) and recent versions of WordPerfect—6.0 for DOS (WordPerfect Corporation, 1993) and 6.0 for Windows (WordPerfect Corporation, 1994)—create a need for an updated version of Smith's (1992) guide. Thus, we developed a guide (see Table 1) that can be used with the fourth edition of the *PM* and with several popular versions of WordPerfect.

Although APA designed the fourth edition of the *PM* to facilitate preparation of manuscripts with word processors (APA, 1994), it does not adequately address the aforementioned problems experienced by students. The *PM* addresses manuscript preparation with word processors in general, but it does not cover particular word-processing programs, such as WordPerfect. Moreover, it does not explicitly state that the top margin should be 0.67 inch to leave room for the headers: This requirement must be inferred from the sample paper presented in the fourth chapter. Thus, we believe that this guide will help students

and faculty minimize the amount of time needed to determine how to format APA pages with WordPerfect.

We recommend executing the first six steps, shown in Table 1 and saving them as a document (e.g., TEMPLATE.APA) that can be retrieved and renamed to begin APA-formatted documents. An alternative strategy is to save the first eight steps in a macro (e.g., APA.WPM) that can be retrieved with a few keystrokes.

References

American Psychological Association. (1983). *Publication manual of the American Psychological Association* (3rd ed.). Washington, DC: Author.

American Psychological Association. (1994). *Publication manual of the American Psychological Association* (4th ed.). Washington, DC: Author.

Smith, R. A. (1992). Formatting APA pages in WordPerfect® 5.1. *Teaching of Psychology, 19,* 190–191.

WordPerfect Corporation. (1989). *WordPerfect 5.1* [Computer program]. Orem, UT: Author.

WordPerfect Corporation. (1993). *WordPerfect 6.0* [Computer program]. Orem, UT: Author.

WordPerfect Corporation. (1994). *WordPerfect 6.0 for Windows* [Computer program]. Orem, UT: Author.

Note

We thank Bernard C. Beins and the anonymous reviewers for helpful comments on a draft of this article.

The Human Subjects Review Procedure: An Exercise in Critical Thinking for Undergraduate Experimental Psychology Students

Richard W. Hubbard
Kathy L. Ritchie
Indiana University South Bend

Much critical thinking in psychology focuses on evaluating and analyzing research results used to support arguments made by theorists and researchers (Bell, 1991; Mayer & Goodchild, 1990). Engaging in psychological research also involves the evaluation of the questions posed and methods considered in developing experiments. Although many studies conducted by undergraduates are exempt from a full human subjects review (e.g., classroom exercises), others, particularly those in advanced laboratory classes, require an expedited review. Having all students fill out a human subjects review form provides an excellent opportunity to teach the application of critical-thinking skills, especially as they pertain to the development of ideas and hypotheses. When students consider the questions posed in the review, they can evaluate their research along important dimensions, such as parsimony, logical consistency, and the degree to which hypotheses are testable. Kaplan (1964) stressed pragmatism (i.e., what difference does the hypothesis make if it is supported by data) as being important to reasoning in research. This theme is emphasized in our approach.

Critical thinking about research in our model also involves consideration of exactly what is predicted and what phenomena the researchers are attempting to explain. The human subjects review process requires students to evaluate their proposals in terms of the questions they pose and the potential explanations for significant findings. It also involves an analysis of the linkages among these more broadly based issues and the methodology to be used. As the last step in the development of a proposal, the review process is perfectly timed to provide an opportunity for a full critique of a proposed study in the following ways:

1. Researchers must develop a written description of their proposed research that should be appropriate for a professional group of reviewers who do not have expertise in the area. Thus, students identify the central idea in their research, justify measures to be used, and convey this information in a straightforward fashion. One of the problems many of our students encounter centers on the integration of hypotheses and methods. They tend either to have clearly defined hypotheses, lacking measures that will provide data concerning their predictions, or they have well developed measures but have not arrived at a theoretical base for their study. As they remove jargon and increase the specificity of the procedures in their proposals, they are encouraged to ask "Will the measures provide data that will answer my research question?"

2. Researchers are required to develop an informed consent form and materials, such as debriefing statements, that describe the experiment in detail to a naive audience. By considering the subject's role, students develop an appreciation for the way in which instructions and measures may confuse or offend their study's participants. Methodological confounds, such as confusing response formats, missing data (e.g., subject age or sex), or inadequate instructions, are often identified during this step. The translation of the study's purpose and design into language suitable for psychologically naive subjects requires students to reduce their proposal to a logical explanation of the scientific method: What is the question you are asking, and how will you collect data to answer it?

3. The review involves consideration of the risks and benefits of the proposed research. This requires students to view their study from an ethical perspective and consider

benefits of the study to the subject as well as to society. Again, critical thinking about what difference a significant finding may make is stimulated, further developing a pragmatic perspective.

Specific Questions Addressed in the Classroom

In addition to the general orientation described earlier, a number of specific questions on the review form also lend themselves to critical-thinking exercises. They are as follows:

1. Describe the objectives of the study. This challenges students to identify the aims of their research and describe how the methodology they have selected meets those objectives. Students must ask "What is it I want to find out," and "How will collecting data in this way answer my question?" Such questions are critical to developing a data-based argument.

2. What are the specific characteristics of your subject population, and how will subjects be selected? Students must also consider their projects in terms of criteria related to at-risk populations. The selection process is also examined in relation to possible implied demands to participate. This presents an opportunity to consider certain types of confounding variables for their research. Close consideration of subjects to be used leads to an evaluation of the utility of variables, such as sex and race, in testing hypotheses and to a consideration of how such characteristics may influence the phenomenon to be studied.

3. What are the risks of the study to your participants? The students must examine psychological risk as a concept, including factors such as stress level, fatigue, and the importance of confidentiality. Concerns about the use of deception in research often arise here. Students are also frequently interested in clinical areas, such as sexual abuse, marital discord, or child-rearing practices, that require them to consider the notion of psychological discomfort in subjects. Evaluation of risk also requires a literature review to ascertain whether the proposed methods and procedures have been used in other research without undue harm. This prompts additional criticism and justification of their methodology.

4. What specific measures are to be used? Students must not only identify what is to be measured but how. Validity and reliability estimates are made from a review of the literature, and even apparently simple surveys come under scrutiny. Operational definitions, important concepts in critical thinking, are often further refined during this aspect of the review.

5. What are the potential benefits of your study? In considering this question, students view their study in terms of its contribution to science. Specifically, they must describe how their research will contribute to the literature in the field, the ways in which it extends or builds on existing research, and what benefits this area of study offers for society. Too often, students simply focus on completing the study. This question forces them to justify their research and consider its implications in a broader context.

Classroom Application

We have used the human subjects review process as a critical-thinking exercise at both introductory and advanced levels of undergraduate experimental psychology courses. In both classes, the process of teaching critical thinking using the review is similar. First, material on the steps and procedures used in experimentation are covered in lectures over several classes. This includes areas such as ethics, hypothesis formation and operational definitions, surveys, and observational procedures. When students are ready to begin to develop their experiments, a lecture on the process and questions involved in the human subjects review procedure is presented. Our goal here is to link the review process directly to critical thinking about experimental design. For example, questions on measurements are related to issues concerning operational definitions. We also examine limitations of procedures, such as surveys and observational studies. Material on the costs and benefits to society is introduced, with an emphasis on the pragmatic implications of research (Kaplan, 1964).

Conclusion

The human subjects review process embodies many of the elements of critical thinking. Students integrate existing literature into their proposals and operationally define their methods and measures. They critically analyze their goals and objectives, justify the importance of the study, and evaluate the potential risks and benefits of their proposal. The review challenges students to present arguments logically to scientific and general audiences.

References

Bell, J. (1991). *Evaluating psychological information: Sharpening your critical thinking skills.* Boston: Allyn & Bacon.

Kaplan, A. (1964). *The conduct of inquiry: Methodology for behavioral science.* Scranton, PA: Chandler.

Mayer, R., & Goodchild, F. (1990). *The critical thinker.* Dubuque, IA: Brown.

Using Riddles to Introduce the Process and Experience of Scientific Thinking

Joe W. Hatcher, Jr.
Ripon College

Science has been described as a process of puzzle solving (Kuhn, 1970). The use of riddles described in this article is useful in demonstrating to students, especially those in introductory or experimental design classes, key points concerning scientific thinking as well as the process and experience of being a scientist.

Students are told that they will participate in an exercise involving scientific thinking. They are given the following information.

> You are walking in the desert and find a man lying face down with a pack on his back, dead.
> How did he die?

Students are told that the instructor will respond to any yes/no questions. After several false starts, the class arrives at the correct answer: The man is a parachutist whose chute failed to open. Students are divided into small groups and given the following series of riddles, one at a time, with one member of each group receiving the answer and serving as moderator.

A. A man walks into a bar and asks the bartender for a glass of water. The bartender reaches under the bar, pulls out a large pistol, and points it right in the man's face. The man says "thank you" and turns and walks out of the bar. Why did the man say "thank you"? (He had the hiccups.)

B. A man is at work and wants to go home. However, he will not go home because a man wearing a mask is waiting there for him. What does the first man do for a living? (He's a baseball player standing on third base.)

C. A man is found shot to death in a room with a table, four chairs, and 53 bicycles. Why was he shot? (He was cheating at cards by having an extra ace; there are 52 Bicycle playing cards in a normal deck.)

After the riddles have been solved, I point out that both scientific thinking and riddle solving attempt to make sense of data that may appear contradictory. More specifically, the following lessons in scientific thinking may be derived from solving the riddles.

1. It is often important to view a problem from more than one perspective.

The ability to alter perspective, termed *lateral thinking* by De Bono (1967, 1968, 1985), is fundamental to any science and is demonstrated in the paradigm shifts discussed by Kuhn (1970). From this exercise, students learn that determined questioning from a wrong perspective leads to little or no progress, but once the correct perspective is found, the solution to the riddle is often easily determined.

2. Prior assumptions concerning data are dangerous.

In the parachute riddle, students typically assume that the man is wearing a common backpack, leading to fruitless questioning. Similarly, in viewing scientific data, interpretations can be guided by assumptions to the point of overlooking the unexpected. For this reason, questioning basic assumptions is often productive.

3. Yes/no questions, properly formed, yield highly useful data.

The yes/no questions of the riddles are paralleled in science by the alternative and null hypotheses of the typical experiment. In each case, when precisely formed, the question (or experiment) allows one to choose between two mutually exclusive views.

4. Details that do not fit expected patterns are often of crucial importance.

In the parachute riddle, discovering that there are no footprints around the body is inconsistent with most interpretations of the problem, leading to a swift reappraisal of the situation and usually a quick solution. Similarly, details inconsistent with general assumptions often spur scientific advances.

5. Persistence is a key quality in problem solving.

Students often terminate a promising line of questioning, unaware that the answer is close at hand. Although persistence can lead to the accumulation of mounds of useless data (e.g., alchemy), some degree of persistence is often necessary to solve a problem.

6. By expecting complicated answers, simple ones may be overlooked.

Students often comment that the riddles, although they appear complex, have simple solutions. This observation can be developed in several fruitful directions, such as: (a) discussing the law of parsimony; (b) noting that a conceptually simple approach may account for vast amounts of data (e.g., Darwin's theory of natural selection); and (c) extending the second point to the possibility that we may be able someday to understand behavior from relatively simple principles, a position I find especially interesting (Hatcher, 1987).

7. Science is an enterprise that is frustrating, exciting, and requires considerable courage.

This exercise also serves to introduce students to the "human" side of scientific thought. While solving riddles, students become alternately frustrated and excited, and by exposing their own thought processes to the scrutiny to others, students gain a glimpse of the courage that it takes to subject one's ideas to possible falsification. At the conclusion of the exercise, I note that, whatever the similarities between riddles and the scientific process, there is a crucial difference. Although riddles have solutions that perseverance will discover, science makes no such guarantee; scientists must pursue their goals with no assurance of success, which requires a special kind of commitment.

Three laboratory exercises used in the class were evaluated on 5-point scales by two classes of experimental design students ($N = 40$), on the dimensions of *uninteresting–interesting* ($M = 4.62$ for the present exercise vs. 3.87 for the other two labs combined), *not useful–useful* (4.09 vs. 4.05), and *definitely drop–definitely keep* (4.58 vs. 4.06). Written comments indicate that students often remember the riddles when attempting to solve a difficult experimental design problem and that the riddle exercise is a good icebreaker for the class.

Based on student responses and my observations, I believe that this simple exercise helps students to understand the process and experience of science. The technique may be useful in a variety of classes involving scientific thinking.

References

De Bono, E. (1967). *The five day course in thinking.* New York: Basic Books.

De Bono, E. (1968). *New think: The use of lateral thinking in the generation of new ideas.* New York: Basic Books.

De Bono, E. (1985). *De Bono's thinking course.* New York: Facts on File.

Hatcher, J. W., Jr. (1987). Arguments for the existence of a general theory of behavior. *Behavioral Science, 32,* 179–189.

Kuhn, T. S. (1970). *The structure of scientific revolutions* (2nd ed.). Chicago: University of Chicago Press.

Note

I thank Mark Nussbaum, Robert Wallace, Patricia White, three anonymous reviewers, and the editor for comments and suggestions on earlier drafts of this article.

From the Laboratory to the Headlines: Teaching Critical Evaluation of Press Reports of Research

Patricia A. Connor-Greene
Clemson University

Undergraduate education in psychology should help students understand scientific methodology and improve their critical thinking. These are important skills, given the frequency with which research findings are reported in the mass media. People tend to perceive the press as an objective source of information, despite the fact that subjective decisions determine what is reported (Howitt, 1982). Constrained by space limitations, newspaper and magazine depictions of research findings often omit essential information that would permit the reader to evaluate adequately the strength of the research conclusions. News summaries often distort research findings by sensationalizing the results, minimizing discussion of the research limitations, and confusing correlation with causation (Jacobs & Eccles, 1985).

The distinction between correlation and causation is essential to understanding research methods and statistics (Boneau, 1990). Although a recent analysis indicated that correlational designs are discussed in 87% of introductory psychology textbooks (Hendricks, Marvel, & Barrington, 1990), I often hear upper level students make causal statements when describing correlational studies. The frequency of this error highlights the need to develop teaching strategies that emphasize this important distinction.

The exercise described in this article involves a collaborative, active-learning task in which students use information about the scientific method to analyze a newspaper account of a research study. The technique is designed to increase students' awareness of the distinction between correlation and causation and to encourage them to become critical consumers of research reported in the popular press. I use this exercise in abnormal psychology classes, but it is also appropriate for introductory psychology and other courses that address research methods.

The Class Exercise

Students are given a homework assignment to study the research methods chapter in their textbook and be prepared to discuss these concepts in class. During the next class period, each student is assigned to a small group of 4 or 5 people. One member of each group serves as recorder, and each group member is expected to participate in the small-group discussion. Every student is given a copy of an article from *USA TODAY* titled, "Gay Men Show Cell Distinction" (Snider, 1991; see Appendix) and the following list of questions to be addressed by the group.

1. What conclusion does this article imply? What statements in the article suggest this conclusion?
2. Is this conclusion warranted by the study described? Why or why not?
3. Is the title an accurate summary of the study described? Why or why not?
4. Can this study "prove . . . being gay or lesbian is not a matter of choice," as the task force spokesman suggests? Why or why not?
5. What questions do you have after reading this article?
6. If you had the power to create guidelines for the press's reporting of a research study, what would you recommend?

Class Discussion

After each group addresses these questions (which takes approximately 40 min), the entire class reconvenes to discuss the group responses. At this point, I provide excerpts, via overhead projector, from the original research article published in *Science* (LeVay, 1991) that is the subject of the *USA TODAY* article. Students identify omissions and distortions in the newspaper's account of the original research study. By examining both the newspaper article and the original research report, they can now identify flaws or unanswered questions in the original study and recognize any misrepresentation of the research in the newspaper article.

Usually the small-group responses to the questions are very similar. All groups interpret the newspaper article (Snider, 1991) as implying that male homosexuality is caused by smaller brain cell nuclei. They cite the statements "The debate over the *roots* of homosexuality has been going on a long time, but this finding 'suggests a *biological phenomenon*'" (p. 1D) and "It might explain '*why* male homosexuality is present in most human populations'" (p. 1D) [all italics added] as suggesting causality.

In deciding whether this implication of causality is warranted by the research study as described, students discuss the requirements for a true experimental design. They recognize LeVay's (1991) study as a correlational design because it simply identifies a relation between size of brain cell nuclei and sexual orientation. Discussing alternative interpretations of this association (e.g., sexual orientation could affect size of brain cell nuclei, rather than the reverse; the differences may be caused by a third variable) helps to clarify the seriousness of the error of confusing correlation and causation.

Students note two problems with the title of the newspaper article. First, they think the title suggests that all cells are different in gay men, but the news article refers only to brain cell nuclei. (The difference is actually much more specific than implied in the news article; it is only one area of the anterior hypothalamus.) Second, the title suggests that gay men are the "different" ones, but the article reports gay men's brain cell nuclei to be similar in size to those of women. Consequently, the "different" ones are actually the heterosexual men. Then we discuss the political and social context in which *normal* and *deviant* are defined and how subjectivity and bias can occur in the formulation of research questions and in the interpretation and reporting of findings.

The quote from the news article (Snider, 1991) that the study can "prove . . . being a gay or lesbian is not a matter of choice" (p. 1D) provides an excellent opportunity to discuss the nature of scientific experimentation and the inappropriateness of the term *prove* in science.

Students generate questions after reading the news article (Snider, 1991), setting the stage for discussion of the specifics of LeVay's (1991) study. After obtaining information from LeVay's article, students are able to identify limitations in the study itself. (For example, the heterosexual men were "presumed" to be heterosexual; for all but two of them, there was no available information on sexual orientation; there was no comparison of heterosexual and homosexual women; the actual cause of death can vary greatly among AIDS patients; and the brain cell nuclei differences could be a result of the disease process itself.

Students always ask "How did this study get published? How could a respectable scientist confuse correlation and causation?" At this point, I show them several quotes from LeVay's (1991) article in which he pointed out the speculative and preliminary nature of his research, identified limitations of his study, and emphasized that it is correlational and does not permit causal inferences. Then students see that the *USA TODAY* article (Snider, 1991) sensationalizes LeVay's results and that Snider, not LeVay, confused correlation with causation.

In addition, I show the students the following excerpt from "Is Homosexuality Biological?" (1991), which appeared in the same issue of *Science* as LeVay's (1991) article.

Lest eager believers jump to too many conclusions, LeVay points out that his finding *contains no direct evidence that the difference he has observed actually causes homosexuality.* He and others in the field acknowledge that the paper *needs replication,* since such studies are difficult and somewhat subjective. "Simon is very good; he's extremely well-equipped to make those observations," said one neuroscientist who is familiar with LeVay's work. *"But we ought to put off big speculation until it is confirmed."* (p. 956) [all italics added]

Clearly, speculation was not put off until LeVay's (1991) findings were replicated; the study was widely reported in the print media and on the network news. Nearly all the students in my class had heard or read about this study and were surprised to learn that the research did not address causality. The extensive media coverage, contrasted with the preliminary nature of the research itself, helps students recognize that factors other than scientific merit may determine degree of media attention and that science and the reporting of science are not value-free.

Students generated recommendations for changing the press's approach to reporting scientific research. These recommendations included discussing limitations of studies, improving accuracy of headlines, distinguishing between correlational and experimental studies, providing a full reference citation to enable the reader to locate the original research article, and making the degree of media attention proportional to the scientific strength of the study.

Individual Assignment

After completing the class exercise, students were individually assigned to find a newspaper or magazine summary of research and compare it to the original journal article. Their written critiques assessed the accuracy of the popular press article and discussed important omissions or distortions in the popular press article (e.g., limitations of the study and accuracy of the title).

Because some popular press articles contain serious distortions and others are accurate summaries, this assignment helps students become critical evaluators rather than simply dismissing all popular press articles as flawed. Several weeks are needed for this assignment. Most students reported that although press summaries of research were easy to find, many of these articles failed to include a citation sufficient to locate the original article.

Evaluation and Conclusions

The day after participating in the class exercise, students ($N = 33$) anonymously completed a four-item questionnaire using a scale ranging from *very much so* (1) to *not at all* (5). The items and mean ratings are as follows: (a) This exercise gave me a clearer understanding of correlational research ($M = 1.70$), (b) this exercise will help me evaluate media reports of research more critically in the future ($M = 1.55$), (c) this exercise was interesting ($M = 1.61$), and (d) it was helpful to work in groups for the class exercise ($M = 1.61$). Students' written comments, such as "It gives me a good idea of how to look at articles critically," "newspaper articles need to be examined much more closely than I've done previously," and "this will help me remember the difference between correlational and experimental studies," suggested positive aspects of the exercise. Students were also asked for written comments after completing their individual assignment. Overall, students perceived the assignment as valuable.

The class exercise and individual assignment encourage students to apply information learned in class to their outside experiences (i.e., reading the newspaper), which makes their learning more personally relevant. The exercises help students understand why the popular press is not an appropriate source of information to be used in writing term papers. The fact that the press typically emphasizes results and not methods convinces students that they can properly evaluate the strengths and weaknesses of a study only after examining the original source. Greater awareness of the importance of precision in reporting research methods and findings should encourage students to be more critical of information they read in newspapers, journal articles, and textbooks.

References

Boneau, C. A. (1990). Psychological literacy: A first approximation. *American Psychologist, 45,* 891–900.

Hendricks, B., Marvel, M. K., & Barrington, B. L. (1990). The dimensions of psychological research. *Teaching of Psychology, 17,* 76–82.

Howitt, D. (1982). *Mass media and social problems.* New York: Pergamon.

Is homosexuality biological? (1991). *Science, 253,* 956–957.

Jacobs, J., & Eccles, J. (1985). Gender differences in math ability: The impact of media reports on parents. *Educational Researcher, 14*(3), 20–25.

LeVay, S. (1991). A difference in hypothalamic structure between heterosexual and homosexual men. *Science, 253,* 1034–1037.

Snider, M. (1991, August 30). Gay men show cell distinction. *USA TODAY,* p. 1D.

Note

I thank Charles L. Brewer, Ruth L. Ault, and the anonymous reviewers for their helpful comments.

Appendix

Gay Men Show Cell Distinction
By Mike Snider
USA TODAY

A new study of the brain suggests a biological difference between homosexual and heterosexual men.

The debate over the roots of homosexuality has been going on a long time, but this finding "suggests a biological phenomenon," says neurologist Dennis Landis, Case Western Reserve University, Cleveland, in comments accompanying the study in today's *Science.*

It might explain "why male homosexuality is present in most human populations, despite cultural constraints."

In a study of the brain cells from 41 people, 25 of whom had died from AIDS, certain brain cells of heterosexual men had nuclei that were more than twice as large as those in homosexual men, says researcher Simon LeVay, Salk Institute for Biological Studies.

The difference was apparently not caused by AIDS, because it was constant in a comparison of cells from heterosexual and homosexual male AIDS victims. LeVay also found homosexual men's cells similar in size to women's.

Robert Bray, spokesman for National Gay and Lesbian Task Force, called the study "fascinating."

"If used ethically, (it) can shed light on human sexuality and prove what we've always believed–being a gay or lesbian is not a matter of choice.

"Used unethically, the data could reinforce the political agenda of anti-gay groups that advocate 'curing' or 'repairing' homosexuals–the notion that gay people could be made straight by tweaking a chromosome here or readjusting a cell there."

Note

Taking a Course in Research Methods Improves Reasoning About Real-Life Events

Scott W. VanderStoep
Calvin College

John J. Shaughnessy
Hope College

Teachers get excited when students recognize the relevance of what they are taught to something outside the classroom. We are pleased when students tell us that what they learned in our class helped them with some other aspect of their lives or that our class taught them to think like a psychologist. Likewise, we are disappointed when students simply memorize factual information without reflecting on its relevance or when they fail to see even the most obvious examples of the applicability of course material to new situations.

What students take away from psychology courses will depend on the course. In developmental psychology, for example, students may reflect on their own childhood and how it has made them who they are, they may see how the course material can make them better parents, or they may learn how to deal more effectively with aging parents and grandparents. Each content course in psychology has such real-life applications.

What do students take away from a research methods course? We hope they learn how to conduct psychological research, including the mechanics of experimental design, survey sampling, and data analysis. Beyond learning how to conduct research, however, research methods has the potential for teaching students real-life thinking and reasoning skills that may be useful in various settings.

The ability to reason methodologically and statistically is a domain-general cognitive activity that students can transfer to a variety of contexts (Nisbett, Fong, Lehman, & Cheng, 1987). Furthermore, instruction has been shown to improve students' methodological and statistical reasoning. Specifically, undergraduates who majored in social science disciplines showed greater improvements in methodological and statistical reasoning than either natural science majors or humanities majors (Lehman & Nisbett, 1990). We expected, at least among psychology courses, that research methods would explain a large part of the change in methodological and statistical reasoning. Thus, we tested whether taking a research methods course would improve reasoning more than another undergraduate course, Developmental Psychology.

Method

Participants

Participants were students enrolled in two sections of Research Methods and two sections of Developmental Psychology at Hope College. The two sections of Research Methods were taught by different instructors; the two sections of Developmental Psychology were taught by a third instructor. The second author was the instructor for one of the Research Methods courses. Thirty-one students from the Research Methods classes and 32 students from the Developmental Psychology classes took the pretest and the posttest. Most were traditional-age college students. Most students were women (78%), although no gender differences were found in reasoning scores (see Results). The mean American College Test (ACT) composite score of incoming students at this institution is 24, and the mean high school grade point average is 3.4.

Instrument

Each form of the instrument for measuring reasoning contained seven items; three items involved statistical reasoning, and four items involved methodological reasoning. Two forms were used and were counterbalanced across pretest and posttest. Some of the items were modified versions of those used by Lehman and Nisbett (1990), and others were created for this study. The statistical reasoning questions tested whether students could recognize examples of regression to the mean and the law of large numbers when applied to everyday events. The methodological reasoning items tested whether students recognized concepts such as a spurious causal relation and selection bias. All items were phrased in everyday language with no reference to methodological or statistical concepts. The scenarios were followed by four or five alternatives that might explain the event. Although all responses were plausible explanations, we agreed that one response best illustrated methodological and statistical reasoning. Participants' scores could range from 0 to 7 based on how many correct answers were selected. A question illustrating a spurious causal relation is as follows:

Suppose it were discovered that students who majored in math, engineering, or computer science scored higher on tests measuring "problem-solving" ability at the end of 4 years of college than did students who did not major in these fields. How would you interpret this information?

a. Physical science training has positive effects that improve complex reasoning ability.
b. Math, engineering, and computer science majors have more class assignments that require students to use complex reasoning.
c. Physical science majors may differ on many other things besides problem-solving ability, and they would have scored higher at the beginning of their freshman year as well.
d. It is likely that physical science students will score lower on tests of *verbal* ability.

Answer c demonstrates that the relation between selection of major and future problem-solving skill may not be causal based only on the evidence provided (i.e., no pretest scores).

Procedure

We administered the instrument to students in their classrooms on the second day of the semester and again near the end of the semester. Students were told that the stories were similar to events they might read about in a newspaper or encounter in everyday conversation.

Results

Pretest and posttest means were calculated for the number of correct responses on the seven methodological and statistical reasoning items for the two courses. There were no gender differences, $t(61) = 1.01$, $p = .275$, and no between-instructor differences for the Research Methods instructors, $t(29) = 1.10$, $p = .28$, in methodological and statistical reasoning.

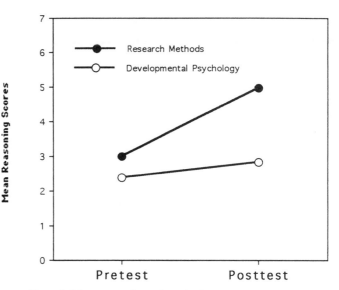

Figure 1. Mean scores for students in the two courses.

The means from the seven-item instrument (see Figure 1) for the Developmental Psychology students were 2.38 at pretest and 2.84 at posttest. The means for the Research Methods students were 3.0 at pretest and 4.97 at posttest.

Using change scores as the dependent variable, Research Methods students showed greater improvement than Developmental Psychology students, $t(61) = 3.62$, $p = .002$. When the four methodological reasoning items were analyzed separately, greater improvement was again found for Research Methods students, $t(61) = 3.02$, $p = .004$. However, the effect was not present when the statistical reasoning items were analyzed separately, $t(61) = 1.52$, $p = .13$, although the change scores were in the same direction. This result suggests that the effect is produced by the change in students' methodological reasoning scores.

Also, we found that the number of psychology courses taken was a significant predictor of posttest methodological and statistical reasoning scores, $ß = .28$, $t(61) = 2.28$, $p = .026$. To assess the relative contribution of the Research Methods course while accounting for the variance explained by the number of courses taken, we conducted an analysis of covariance (ANCOVA). The ANCOVA indicated a significant effect for course, $F(1, 60) = 11.6$, $p = .001$, suggesting that there is an effect of taking Research Methods on reasoning beyond that accounted for by the number of psychology courses taken.

Discussion

Our study extends work by Lehman and Nisbett (1990) on the effects of undergraduate education on student reasoning. Whereas Lehman and Nisbett found long-term effects of certain courses, we found more specifically that a course in methodology can be important in cultivating students' ability to think critically about real-life events.

243

General reasoning skills are important, especially when information is modified and updated very rapidly. For example, a student taking social psychology in 1996 will be learning very different material than a student who took the course in 1970. We do not know what tomorrow's domain-specific knowledge will be or whether what we are teaching today will still be relevant in the future. However, if we can teach students to develop general thinking skills, then the importance and relevance of our courses will be greater. If psychology majors can be taught general skills that they can apply to novel domains, we can better ensure the relevance of what we teach. Students taking research methods classes may not remember the precise definition of a confounding variable or how exactly to design a randomized blocks experiment. However, our results suggest that they may leave with some general skills that they can use while watching the evening news, shopping for automobiles, voting, or deciding whether to adopt a new weight-loss technique that they saw advertised.

As psychology instructors, we have intuitive notions about the usefulness of the skills we teach our students. We talk confidently about the benefits of an undergraduate major in psychology and how "thinking like a psychologist" helps students in many areas of life. Our results suggest that there is value in learning to think like a psychologist. There is more to real-life thinking than is represented by our small set of items, but we are pleased that our intuitions held up to empirical scrutiny.

References

Lehman, D. R., & Nisbett, R. E. (1990). A longitudinal study of the effects of undergraduate training on reasoning. *Developmental Psychology, 26,* 952–960.

Nisbett, R. E., Fong, G. T., Lehman, D. R., & Cheng, P. W. (1987). Teaching reasoning. *Science, 238,* 625–631.

Note

We thank Jim Motiff and Jane Dickie for the use of their classroom time.

A Course to Develop Competence in Critical Reading of Empirical Research in Psychology

Moshe Anisfeld
Yeshiva University

Seven years ago, I introduced a new graduate course entitled, Reading Critically in Child Development. The course has now matured to the point where I believe it is ripe for sharing with others. This article describes the aims and design of the course and discusses its value.

Aims

The course is motivated by a concern about the tendency of many graduate students–and others as well–to accept the conclusions and interpretations of empirical articles at face value without examining the results independently. Typically, the Method and Results sections are read less closely than the Introduction and Discussion sections, and information about the findings tends to be gleaned from the author's verbal summaries rather than the tables and graphs. To correct this situation, I designed a course to train students in critical reading of empirical literature in psychology.

The objective of the course is to help students exercise data-reading skills and develop the attitudes, mental sets, and habits that facilitate independent evaluation of empirical research. The assumption underlying these aims is that the relative neglect of the methodological and data sections of empirical articles is due not so much to the lack of requisite abilities as it is to inappropriate habits and mental sets.

Method and Evaluation

A case-study approach, is used to train students to pay closer attention to the Method and Results sections of empirical articles and to draw independent conclusions from this information. The course is conducted as a seminar in which students are given guidance in practicing the

244

independent, critical approach to reading. The course is divided into an introductory session at the start, an examination session at the end, and student-presentation sessions in between.

Introductory Session and Guidelines for Reading Critically

The introductory session is devoted to: (a) amplification of the guidelines for reading empirical articles critically (presented in Table 1), and (b) a demonstration analysis of an article, including direct examination of the tables, by the instructor. The demonstration uses projection equipment and handouts to allow students to mark copies for review.

Student-Presentation Sessions

In the student-presentation sessions, students summarize and evaluate individual articles that were read by the entire class. The articles are either assigned by the instructor or selected by the students according to the following criteria: (a) the articles represent a particular area or subarea, (b) they are empirical, and (c) they appear in peer-review journals.

In each of the student sessions there are two presentations. The presentations concentrate on the method and results of the articles. To encourage direct and detailed examination of tables and graphs, presenters are urged to use projection equipment. After each presentation, which lasts about 15 to 25 min, an open discussion focuses on aspects of the method and results that were not handled by the presenter or were inadequately grasped. Through the examination of individual articles, students gain a working knowledge of the points shown in Table 1. They also increase their understanding of methodological and statistical matters. When methodological or statistical issues come up during the examination of a particular article, they are either clarified there and then or are set aside for later, more systematic discussion, for which students could prepare by appropriate reading.

In the session following their presentations, presenters submit reviews of their articles, concentrating on a critical summary of the method and results, and an evaluation of the conclusions. The review incorporates relevant points from the class discussion. To ensure that all students, not just the two presenters, read the material for each week, a ½-page abstract, written with the aims of the course in mind, is due every week for each of the two articles.

Test Session

The last session is devoted to an in-class reading and review of a previously unseen article. The article selected should not be too theoretically involved so that students can

Table 1. Guidelines for Reading Empirical Articles Critically

1. Read the Abstract and then direct your attention first to the Method and Results sections to facilitate a view of the findings that is as independent as possible from the author's view. After you have formed your own conclusions, you will be in a stronger position to evaluate the conclusions of the author and to see whether they are influenced by any paticular biases.

2. Whenever possible, schematize on your own the details of the method and results. For instance, if the study compared two groups, you may write down in a table the variables on which they were equated. This will readily reveal any gaps in the matching of the groups. Similarly for the results, organizing them in a table will give a clear, concise view, and will raise issues that may not have otherwise occurred to you. If the results are already presented in tabular form in the article, it may still be valuable to reorganize them in another way that is meaningful to you. The important thing is not to absorb the article passively, but to process it actively. As an active reader, you will more likely recognize the author's biases and not be swept away by them.

3. Look carefully at the results in tables and graphs. Are the results internally consistent? Do they show what the author says that they do? If a particular finding does not "feel right," you may be able to recompute the relevant statistic from the data provided in the article. (On the basis of recalculations, Rossi, 1987, found errors in the statistical values reported in journals.) In addition, by looking independently at the results, you may be able to see things that the author, who was looking for something in particular, did not see. (Thus, new phenomena have emerged in the area of language development, Anisfeld, 1984, pp. 82–84, 107–109, through an independent analysis of published results.)

4. What is the weight of the positive results in the context of the entire picture of the findings? One would have less confidence in the conclusions when only one variable out of several was significant. Examine not only whether a particular effect is significant, but also what its magnitude is. Are the conclusions based on strong or marginal results? Be skeptical about results that are significant at the .05 level in one-tailed tests.

5. Watch out not only for biased interpretations but also for biased analyses of the data. For instance, are the data coded in a way that presupposes the hypothesis that the author set out to test?

6. Distinguish clearly between theoretical constructs and operations used to measure them, and consider whether the operations used are valid for the constructs at hand. Authors often state the results in terms of the theoretical constructs. In order to facilitate an independent evaluation of the results, you must not accept this bias.

7. Try to identify the author's bias and look for possible distortions that are consonant with the bias. A useful approach to seeing the results in a new light is to try to interpret them from the perspective of a bias that differs from the author's bias.

8. The results reported in an article are the final product of several steps of transformation and reduction of the original information obtained from the subjects. To gain an understanding of the inner workings of the study and to discover potential problems, reverse the process and try to determine what information was obtained from the subjects and what kinds of analyses it was subjected to. By engaging in this step-back process, a reader discovered that the means reported in one article reflected not only response quality, as claimed by the authors, but also response quantity.

9. Recognize the distinction between limitations of a study and outright inadequacies. If a study tested only one type of subjects (e.g., fifth graders), this does not make it invalid, it only limits its generalizability.

Table 1. *(Continued)*

---

10. Do not force criticism on an article. Acknowledge a good article when you see one. Recognize the practical limitations of empirical research. Avoid nit-picking, and easy, routine types of criticism (e.g., "Why did they test only X number of subjects?"). Remember that by itself a method is neither good nor bad; it can be evaluated only in relation to questions that it seeks to answer. The most valuable critical analysis relates the results and conclusions to the method. Such an analysis may suggest that the results could have been an artifact of some aspect of the method.
11. Above all, don't be overawed or intimidated by authorities, fancy terms, and statistics. Authors have the advantage of knowledge of their work. But you have the advantage of objectivity, psychological distance, and unbiased common sense. Do not give up these tremendous assets!

---

demonstrate what they have learned in the course without being encumbered by conceptual difficulties. The instructions for the test are that it be patterned on the reviews done by the presenters following their presentations. The students are asked to summarize the main findings in as theoretically neutral a fashion as possible, and to evaluate the research and its conclusions from this objective perspective. The test papers are graded on the extent to which they reflect the methodological sophistication and the active, critical approach to reading practiced in the course. The grades on the test constitute the main ingredient in the students' course grades. The grades given on the abstracts (26 of which are normally submitted by each student) and on the reviews (2 of which are normally submitted by each student) are deemphasized or discounted altogether in the consideration of the course grades to make these papers an instrument of learning, not of evaluation.

Reading Material

Although the course is technique oriented, it is desirable that the participants have a common interest. This is why the course, as I have taught it, is entitled, Reading Critically in Child Development, even though it provides training for reading critically in psychology in general. The material I use as a vehicle for this training is drawn from the field of child development to assure some common interest. Any area of psychology, not just child development, can serve to define a shared focus of interest. It is advisable to narrow the field to provide topical coherence for the course. As a compromise, the instructor can define a specific topic (e.g., the effects of early bilingualism or intelligence) for the first half of the course and be less restrictive in the second half, in order to allow students to work in their individual fields of interest, within the broad area prescribed by the course.

In addition to the concern with assuring commonality of interest and topical coherence, there is another criterion that should be taken into consideration in selecting reading material. The students (and instructor) should feel comfortable with the issues covered in the articles chosen. Lack of confidence about any aspect of the reading can only inhibit a critical stance and stifle self-expression. It is, therefore, desirable that classes be composed of relatively homogeneous groups of students to assure that there would be topics that are familiar to all.

Openness

An obstacle to clear thinking, which is a prerequisite for critical thinking and independent reading, is the tendency to make believe that one understands something that one really does not understand. To help students develop habits of clear thinking, an atmosphere is created in the course that makes it acceptable to acknowledge gaps in one's understanding, as long as there is an effort to identify specifically the issue or concept that requires clarification. The reward system in the course (grading of papers, and open praise and criticism) is the main contributor to the creation of such an intellectually honest atmosphere. On occasion, I have even resorted to public exposure of pretentiousness to impress on students the importance of not "fooling oneself." (One rarely succeeds in fooling others.)

Statistics and Methodology

Although a basic introduction to statistics is a prerequisite for the course, one of the sources of insecurity that students bring to the reading of empirical articles is the feeling of inadequacy (often justified) concerning statistics. To help students overcome this obstacle to active, assertive reading, the instructor should endeavor to show that one can understand what a statistic does without knowing how it does it. For instance, one can readily explain how to read a factor analysis table without involving students in the technicalities of the procedure. Appropriate sources that give intuitive explanations of statistical concepts may be suggested. A suitable treatment of factor analysis, for instance, can be found in Anastasi (1982, pp. 358–365).

A research methods course is not required as background for this course. All graduate students know the basic concepts of research design, and beyond this it is a matter of becoming acquainted with the specialized techniques of each field. In this course, students gain knowledge of specialized techniques by reading research that uses those techniques. As with statistics, it is appropriate to provide students with suggested readings on methodological points that come up in class. If time permits, one could systematically review the research techniques used in the particular field that the course emphasizes. One year, students in my course read Vasta's (1979) book on research methods in child development, and one session was devoted to a discussion of the book. The course can also benefit from Barber's (1976) book on the pitfalls encountered in psychological research. Both books have the advantage of being short and direct.

The Abstracts and Reviews

The abstracts and reviews are returned with comments and grades the week after they are handed in. Timely return makes it possible for students to derive maximum benefit from the feedback. In addition to individual comments, sheets noting points of general interest, especially common deficiencies, are also provided.

The abstracts, originally introduced to ensure that the articles were read by the nonpresenters, turned out to be valuable in their own right. Because the ½-page allotted does not permit the indiscriminate inclusion of "everything," students are forced to weigh the relative importance of different points. Moreover, what is included in the abstract has to be stated at the appropriate level of generality or specificity to facilitate communication. In this way, students learn to write in a coherent, well-proportioned manner.

The Course in Perspective

Every time I teach this course I come away with a feeling of satisfaction. Students do develop the habit of looking carefully at the Method and Results sections. Most important, they gain confidence in their ability to pass judgment on published researchers. In the words of one student: "I came away realizing that researchers are as fallible as anyone else. Just because a paper has been published does not mean that it is sacrosanct." Perhaps, the most convincing indication of the sense of competence students gain is that practically all of them gave an affirmative answer to the question: "Do you feel that you could (with some preparation) teach the skills you have acquired?" The sense of competence that students acquire is properly tempered by a recognition of their limitations. Students realize that to be useful, the approach to reading that they have learned has to be practiced and developed.

An attempt is made to put the course in perspective. It is explained to the students that the one-sided emphasis on method and results was necessary as a corrective to their old habits. Similarly, the suspicious attitude and the "hunting" for author biases were intended to instill a critical attitude. Once students have acquired the data-oriented, critical approach, they have to use it, not for its own sake, but in the service of reaching valid conclusions from research publications. Not every article one reads has to be analyzed as carefully or evaluated as strictly as were the articles read in the course. Many articles published in refereed journals reach well-founded conclusions and are not subject to serious criticism. But, it is always appropriate to read psychological literature in an active, self-confident, analytic, and data-oriented manner. A reader skilled in this mode of reading will be sensitive enough to identify problems in the material read without having to look for them.

One of the most encouraging things about the course is that what students learn transfers to other relevant endeavors. Teachers of other courses have commented to me that they can readily tell the students who have taken this course from those who have not. Students comment that the course helps them to develop not only reading skills but also writing skills and methodological sophistication.

References

Anastasi, A. (1982). *Psychological testing* (5th ed.). New York: Macmillan.

Anisfeld, M. (1984). *Language development from birth to three*. Hillsdale, NJ: Lawrence Erlbaum Associates, Inc.

Barber, T. X. (1976). *Pitfalls in human research: Ten pivotal points*. New York: Pergamon.

Rossi, J. S. (1987). How often are our statistics wrong? A statistics class exercise. *Teaching of Psychology, 14,* 98–101.

Vasta, R. (1979). *Studying children: An introduction to research methods*. New York: Freeman.

Note

This article was improved substantially by the editorial review process and by the reactions of Elizabeth Anisfeld. I am grateful for this help and for the encouragement I received from Dean Morton Berger in the development of the course described here.

Deploring students' casual attitudes about the importance of recording, analyzing, interpreting, and reporting empirical data, Terry Cronan-Hillix at San Diego State University proposed that students in introductory experimental psychology courses should be assigned grades of A or F for the Results sections of laboratory reports. Papers receiving Fs could be resubmitted for reduced grades until they were free of errors. She concluded that we must teach students that accuracy in research is essential if we expect to produce more competent researchers and a more precise science.

Catherine McDonald from the University of California, Berkeley and Keith Peterson from Vanderbilt University supported Cronan-Hillix's concern for accuracy in all aspects of research (see preceding article), but they challenged her assumptions about the nature of the problem and disagreed with her proposed solution. Citing theories of motivation, they suggested that Cronan-Hillix's approach may perpetuate the very attitudes and behaviors that her proposal was intended to change. Rather than being punished, students should document the rationale for their analyses so that the cause of errors can be identified and misunderstanding addressed in a positive way.

In a rejoinder to McDonald and Peterson's comment about her proposal to give As or Fs for the results sections of students' laboratory reports (see the two preceding articles), Cronan-Hillix suggested that the empirical basis for their objections has little relevance. She indicated that evidence for the effectiveness of her approach comes from her own classroom experience. The method works well for her, and she urged other teachers to try it and judge for themselves.

Blaine Peden from the University of Wisconsin–Eau Claire outlined and evaluated a strategy for teaching students to recognize and prepare references for four types of works often cited in research reports. Students' later performance on the Reference section of their research reports earned either an A or F grade, as suggested by Cronan-Hillix (see the three preceding articles). This approach helped students learn to prepare accurate reference lists and sensitized them to other aspects of proper style and format. Also, Peden said that using this technique improved his own referencing skills!

Teaching Students the Importance of Accuracy in Research

Terry Cronan-Hillix

San Diego State University
Navy Personnel Research and Development Center

I conduct research with students at the university and at a research institute. I see students as their teacher and as a consumer of their research training. As a researcher, I expect students to apply research skills learned in the classroom. Nearly all of these students have taken statistics and one or two experimental psychology courses; most are in a master's degree program.

It has been my experience that we are not training research psychologists adequately. For example, students working at the research institute have had to recode data two and three times because random checking revealed many errors. Students often appeared unconcerned and dismissed the errors by saying "Oh, well, I haven't had much experience coding data." Other components of the research were treated with similar casualness.

My current views crystallized while working with one of the "better" graduate students who appeared to be hardworking and wanted to enter a PhD program. He had never published a paper and was interested in working on a project that would produce one. We had a very large data set and worked with him to develop a research question. We told him that he could take the lead by performing statistical analyses, which had been previously discussed, and writing the first draft of the paper. Weekly or semi-weekly meetings to discuss progress revealed that computations were often done incorrectly or inconsistently because he did not include the same subjects in each analysis. He also had many problems writing the paper because he could not organize or express his thoughts well.

These experiences are not unique to me or to my academic institution. A colleague told me about a student who had completed one course in statistics and two experimental psychology courses with laboratories. While preparing to present research at a professional conference, they met to review the results and decide on the method of presentation. The student brought in six F values because the analysis of variance had been run six times on the same data and each time yielded a different value. The student wondered whether all six of the values, or the average of them, should be reported. This student was then a senior and is now enrolled in a graduate program in psychology.

Our failure to demand precision in data handling may also allow students to remain vague about the meaning of statistical concepts. I once talked to a PhD candidate from another university about her dissertation and expressed some reservations about the reliability of her Minnesota Multiphasic Personality Inventory (MMPI) measure. She responded "you mean like test-retest?" I said "yes." Her reply was "Oh, I don't have to worry about that. I'm only giving it once."

These problems indicate that students are often inadequately trained to do research. What must be lacking in their education is the critical lesson that completeness, comprehension, and accuracy in analysis are essential. Errors in doing research are taboo. If students receive grades of B or A—when any part of data entry or analysis is wrong, we are not communicating that research must be done precisely. If we do not stress these points in classes, how can we expect students to know that, in "real" research, they must always be accurate? Maybe the reason that they do not feel a need to be 100% correct is that they are not trying to produce an A+ paper. Perhaps they believe that if their research is a little sloppy, they will simply submit it to a journal that expects C papers.

If this sounds silly to you, consider how many authors are unable to find their raw data for other investigators or have performed inappropriate analyses (Rosenthal, 1978; Rossi, 1987). The attitudes expressed by my students mirror those of some people who have earned their terminal degrees and may lead to errors in our professional literature (Rosenthal, 1978; Rossi, 1987).

How do we stress the importance of being correct? How do we teach students that there is only one correct description of data? One possibility is to assign an A or F grade for the recording and manipulation of research data. Certainly there is variability in the ability to write a strong introduction or discussion. Therefore, there is no absolute right or wrong in these areas. However, there must be an uncompromised correctness in the acquisition and manipulation of data and in statistical analyses. Our professional standards dictate that any paper with a technical error should be given a provisional F and returned to the student.

If the data and analyses are correct, then the student receives an A for the results section, and the instructor, proceeds to review the entire paper and assign an overall grade. This procedure is similar to practices in many English departments. Students who submit papers with imperfect grammar and spelling receive Fs. If grammar and spelling are perfect, then the instructor reviews and grades the paper. Because the scientific enterprise is no less exacting than writing a theme, we must reflect our expectations in our grading.

To avoid complaints about fairness, students submitting papers with errors may accept the F or correct the mistakes and resubmit the paper for regrading. Grades for resubmitted papers should be reduced one letter. We need to communicate to students that careful research is important and not just another academic game. The proposed method of grading would teach students that research is serious business. Students should be told that research can have beneficial or devastating effects for people treated in ways that research conclusions indicate are effective (Fairweather & Davidson, 1986).

To reduce the number of papers with errors, the instructor should model appropriate methods before students do their first project. The instructor could design a simple experiment and have the students observe the data collection, coding, entry, and analysis. During this demonstration, the instructor would enter the data twice and have the computer compare the two entries, or the instructor could enter the data and have a student proofread the data entries and calculations. The instructor could also prepare a short APA-style paper based on the experiment to illustrate the correct methods.

The "colleague swap" (Camplese & Mayo, 1982) could also be used. Students exchange papers, and each student critiques and provides feedback to the one who wrote the paper. Students should be told to demand perfect accuracy.

To summarize, we need to reexamine our current methods of teaching. The "multiple-guess" attitude cannot be applied to the teaching of experimental psychology. Teaching students that research is important and must be done correctly will produce better researchers and a more accurate science.

References

Camplese, D. A., & Mayo, J. A. (1982). How to improve the quality of student writing: The colleague swap. *Teaching of Psychology, 9*, 122–123.

Fairweather, G. W., & Davidson, W. S. (1986). *An introduction to community experimentation: Theory, methods, & practice.* New York: McGraw-Hill.

Rosenthal, R. (1978). How often are our numbers wrong? *American Psychologist, 33*, 1005–1008.

Rossi, J. S. (1987). How often are our statistics wrong? A statistics class exercise. *Teaching of Psychology, 14*, 98–101.

Note

I gratefully acknowledge the assistance of Charles L. Brewer and three anonymous reviewers for their critical review of this manuscript.

Teaching Commitment to Accuracy in Research: Comment on Cronan-Hillix (1988)

Catherine S. McDonald
Department of Educational Psychology
University of California, Berkeley

Keith A. Peterson
Vanderbilt University

Cronan-Hillix (1988) expressed alarm at a perceived lack of concern among students about rigor and accuracy in methodological aspects of psychological research. To promote a more conscientious attitude toward research, Cronan-Hillix proposed giving students in experimental psychology courses failing grades for results sections containing even one error and providing lower grades for corrected and resubmitted papers. Although we support Cronan-Hillix's concern for the importance of accuracy in all aspects of research, we take issue with her assumptions about the nature of the problem and with her proposed solution.

Contradictory Assumptions About the Problem

Cronan-Hillix (1988) attributed the source of students' errors to apathy and carelessness. Her assumption that students are lackadaisical and unconcerned with conducting rigorous research is reflected by her comment that:

> maybe the reason that they [students] do not feel a need to be 100% correct is that they are not trying to produce an A+ paper. Perhaps they believe that if their research is a little sloppy, they will simply submit it to a journal that expects C papers. (p. 206)

Although the concern for accuracy is important, Cronan-Hillix's argument lacks empirical foundation and neglects other reasons for making errors.

Many careless errors students make in research may be caused by a poor understanding of research concepts or inexperience handling data, rather than carelessness or apathy. Given the variety of mistakes students make, attributing all errors to a single cause is an injustice to students (and contributes little to fostering students' learning and interest in a subject). Teaching students the importance of accurate research is essential but should be done in a positive manner.

Contradictory Assumptions About Ways to Improve Accuracy

We distinguish between Cronan-Hillix's performance-oriented approach to instruction and a mastery-oriented approach (Slavin, 1987). In mastery learning, the consequences of failure are reduced. Even after repeated attempts at mastery, students still have the opportunity to achieve a full measure of success and the associated sense of accomplishment (for an example involving college students, see Covington & Omelich, 1981). Cronan-Hillix's approach emphasizes the role of the failing grade as a punisher that rivets the student's attention to the importance of careful thought and accuracy.

Our view is that this punitive form of feedback will not establish commitment to accuracy or a positive attitude toward the learning process, but may instead perpetuate the very attitudes and behaviors Cronan-Hillix hoped to eliminate. Educational theory suggests that an overemphasis on extrinsic motivators, namely grades, creates a classroom climate that undermines intrinsic motivation and focuses students on performance rather than learning (Ames, 1984; Nichols, 1989). Theories of motivation in academic settings, including self-worth (Covington, 1984), control (deCharms, 1972), and intrinsic motivation (Condry & Chambers, 1978), predict the negative effects of fostering performance-oriented motivational states. Learning environments that highlight the importance of external reinforcers, particularly negative ones, foster maladaptive motivational orientations (Nichols, 1989), often leading to task avoidance, higher performance anxiety, cheating, and a weaker understanding of material (Covington, 1984).

Message Conveyed to Students

Cronan-Hillix (1988) perceived that her students were often unconcerned with errors, stating that "we need to communicate to students that careful research is important and not just another academic game" (p. 206), and argued that a failing grade would communicate the wrongness of such an attitude. However, the message actually conveyed may be that "you are being failed because you did not try hard enough or are lazy and careless." Such a message may alienate and demotivate students who have potential to conduct good research. Although we agree with the idea of providing students multiple opportunities to produce a correct product, basing such a method on failure avoidance impedes the learning process.

Cronan-Hillix's approach will not instill a concern for accuracy in research because students are punished for what may be a lack of experience or conceptual misunderstandings of material rather than the lack of a serious attitude toward the research enterprise. As Piaget (cited in Ginsberg & Opper, 1979) noted, mistakes aid the learning process and provide the teacher with valuable information about students' conceptual (mis)understandings of material. In keeping with this view, we believe that the role of the teacher is to help students learn from mistakes and to promote a self-regulatory attitude so that they will be able to identify and correct mistakes. Students will be vigilant about identifying and learning from mistakes only if motivated to do so. Trying to motivate students by threatening failure does not accomplish this goal (Covington & Omelich, 1981; Deci & Ryan, 1986), and once the contingency of grading is removed, neither a commitment to accuracy nor a fostered interest in the importance of rigorous methodology is likely to remain. If Cronan-Hillix's program is effective, it is because students are motivated to avoid failing grades, not because she has instilled a lasting commitment to accuracy. As an alternative, we suggest that students be required to document the reasons for their treatment of data and other analytic decisions so that the causes of errors can be identified.

For many years, repeated calls have been made to develop teaching methods that involve the student in the long-term learning process (Dewey, 1938). In considering options to enhance student performance, teachers should focus on developing more effective methods of instruction to help students understand difficult concepts, use more effective learning strategies, and appreciate the value of accuracy. Cronan-Hillix advocated two methods of noted effectiveness, peer review and teacher modeling. However, as an alternative to her proposal, we suggest that conceptual misunderstandings be addressed in a positive manner so that the anxiety produced by failure will not overshadow the learning process. By doing so, perhaps we can better promote interest, excitement, and commitment to a more accurate science.

References

Ames, C. (1984). Achievement attributions and self-instruction under competitive and individualistic goal structures. *Journal of Educational Psychology, 76,* 478–489.

Condry, J., & Chambers, J. (1978). Intrinsic motivation and the process of learning. In M. R. Lepper & D. Greene (Eds.), *The hidden cost of reward: New perspectives on the psychology of human motivation* (pp. 61–84). Hillsdale, NJ: Lawrence Erlbaum Associates, Inc.

Covington, M. V. (1984). The motive for self-worth. In R. Ames & C. Ames (Eds.), *Research on motivation in education* (Vol. 1, pp. 77–113). New York: Academic.

Covington, M. V., & Omelich, C. L. (1981). As failures mount: Affective and cognitive consequences of ability demotion in the classroom. *Journal of Educational Psychology, 73,* 796–808.

Cronan-Hillix, T. (1988). Teaching students the importance of accuracy in research. *Testing of Psychology, 15,* 205–207.

deCharms, R. (1972). Personal causation training in the schools. *Journal of Applied Social Psychology, 2,* 95–113.

Deci, E. L., & Ryan, R. M. (1986). The dynamics of self-determination in personality development. In R. Schwarzer (Ed.), *Self-regulated cognitions in anxiety and motivation* (pp. 171–194). Hillsdale, NJ: Lawrence Erlbaum Associates, Inc.

Dewey, J. (1938). *Experience and education.* New York: Macmillan.

Ginsburg, H., & Opper, S. (1979). *Piaget's theory of intellectual development.* Englewood Cliffs, NJ: Prentice-Hall.

Nichols, J. G. (1989). *The competitive ethos and democratic education.* Cambridge, MA: Harvard University Press.

Slavin, R. E. (1987). Mastery learning reconsidered. *Review of Educational Research, 57,* 175–213.

Teaching Student the Importance of Accuracy in Research: A Reply to McDonald and Peterson

Terry Cronan-Hillix
San Diego State University

McDonald and Peterson (this issue) challenge my approach to teaching students the importance of accuracy in research (Cronan-Hillix, 1988). Students working on research projects made many of the following errors: simple checks on the accuracy of data coding were not conducted (35 was coded as 3), calculational errors were made (dividing by the wrong number), incorrect data from larger databases were included in analyses (instead of selecting smokers, all people were included), or wrong information was recorded (an individual's age was recorded as number of cigarettes smoked). In a few cases, results seemed to come from another research project. These errors prompted questions about the methods used to teach students that completeness, comprehension, and accuracy in analysis and writing are essential. My solution was to give students an A or F grade for the results section of their research reports.

McDonald and Peterson (this issue) attribute many student errors to a lack of conceptual understanding, and they propose a mastery-oriented approach to teach students that accuracy is important. The merits of the mastery-oriented approach have been examined for more than 2 decades, but its effectiveness remains questionable (see Slavin, 1987). The mastery-oriented approach may be appropriate when the goal is conceptual understanding; however, inaccuracy and carelessness when analyzing data are not conceptual problems. Most errors in my students' reports arise from computation or recording rather than conceptual misunderstanding. Although I value McDonald and Peterson's suggestion that students be required to document the reasons for their treatment of data and other analytic decisions so that the causes of errors can be identified, it does not address the central question: How do we teach our students that precision in research is necessary to maintain the quality of the science and one's own professional reputation?

Assigning As or Fs to papers that contain errors in the results sections may seem harsh. However, if the results are incorrect, the remainder of the report is meaningless. The most brilliant introduction and discussion sections do not compensate for incorrect results. The enduring consequences for science and one's professional reputation completely overshadow the temporary harshness to a student, and my method effectively communicates this point to students.

It is also important to acknowledge that several steps occur before students submit their papers for review: They conduct research, gather data, perform statistical analyses, discuss the analyses and interpretations in class, and receive help if they have difficulty. Only when students submit papers to be graded must the results be correct. Before the due date, I answer questions and offer assistance to students having conceptual problems with statistical procedures. Students receiving an F on their results section may accept the F or correct the mistakes and resubmit the paper for regrading. Resubmitted results sections are reduced only one letter grade. Thus, this procedure should lead to mastery of the lesson I want students to learn.

In three semesters, no student complained that the procedures were unfair; in fact, no student has ever complained about this policy in anonymous evaluations completed at the end of the semester. In discussions about their papers, students receiving an F on their results section said that they were upset with their grade, but did not think that the policy was unfair. Typically, they were upset for being so careless, and their greatest concern has been that my opinion of them might be colored by the incident. All students receiving an F have checked and rechecked their work before turning in additional papers for grading. In three semesters, only 1 of approximately 80 students has resubmitted a paper that still contained a mistake. Many students who made no mistakes have told me that announcing this policy on the first day of class and following through with it made them feel that professionalism was required and that research was serious business.

Last semester, only one student received an F on her results section. She later told me that she went home and cried because she was upset about being so careless. However, she never made another mistake on her results section, and she went on to be one of the top students in the class. I am now very proud to have her as a research team member on one of my projects.

McDonald and Peterson (this issue) claim that my approach lacks empirical foundation, and they cite research to support their viewpoint (Ames, 1984; Covington, 1984; deCharms, 1972; Nichols, 1989). However, the putative support for their view is highly inferential because none of it derives from the context in question: a university laboratory class.

If we allow inferential evidence, then my approach is supported in the learning literature. There is strong support for the belief that behavior can be changed through the appropriate use of reinforcement and punishment principles. Students who have correct results receive As, increasing the likelihood that such research behaviors will be repeated. Students who receive an F are less likely to repeat such unacceptable behaviors in the future. Although great controversy surrounds the use of punishment, there is little controversy about its effectiveness when appropriately delivered (Azrin & Holz, 1966). Punishment is most effective when it is contingent on the targeted behavior and when it is immediately and consistently applied at maximum intensity. The punishment for making an error is clearly defined at the beginning of the semester, consistently applied, given as immediately as possible, and introduced at maximum intensity. It is effective—as it should be.

Whether reinforcement or punishment should be used in training students to be accurate researchers is an empirical question. Some empirical evidence about the effectiveness of my approach comes from my own classroom experience. The method works well for me; I recommend that others try it and judge for themselves.

References

Ames, C. (1984). Achievement attributions and self-instruction under competitive and individualistic goal structures. *Journal of Educational Psychology, 76,* 478–489.

Azrin, N. H., & Holz, W. C. (1966). Punishment. In W. K. Honig (Ed.), *Operant behavior: Areas of research and application* (pp. 380–447). New York: Appleton-Century-Crofts.

Covington, M. V. (1984). The motive for self-worth. In R. Ames & C. Ames (Eds.), *Research on motivation in education* (Vol. 1, pp. 77–113). New York: Academic.

Cronan-Hillix, T. (1988). Teaching students the importance of accuracy in research. *Teaching of Psychology, 15,* 205–207.

deCharms, R. (1972). Personal causation training in the schools. *Journal of Applied Social Psychology, 2,* 95–113.

McDonald, C. S., & Peterson, K. A. (this issue). Teaching commitment to accuracy in research: Comment on Cronan-Hillix (1988). *Teaching of Psychology, 18,* 100–101.

Nichols, J. G. (1989). *The competitive ethos and democratic education.* Cambridge, MA: Harvard University Press.

Slavin, R. E. (1987). Mastery learning reconsidered. *Review of Educational Research, 57,* 175–213.

Teaching the Importance of Accuracy in Preparing References

Blaine F. Peden
University of Wisconsin–Eau Claire

My experience teaching research methods and reviewing manuscripts for *Teaching of Psychology* indicates that correctly citing and referencing works in APA style is a difficult task for inexperienced and veteran authors. Nonetheless, instructors should teach and students should learn precision in preparing reference lists. One reason is that "accurately prepared references help establish your credibility as a careful researcher" (American Psychological Association, 1983, p. 112). Another reason is that inaccurate citations and references produce and perpetuate mistakes and misconceptions (e.g., Griggs, 1988; Soper & Rosenthal, 1988).

This article summarizes and assesses a method for teaching students to identify and list four types of references frequently cited in research reports. Later in the term, students receive a grade of A or F on the reference section of their own research reports (after Cronan-Hillix, 1988). The method improves accuracy in preparing reference lists and seems to increase students' attention to other facets of APA style.

Method

Subjects

Subjects were 63 women and 27 men enrolled in an undergraduate research methods course in the 1989–90 fall or spring semesters.

Materials

A handout summarized the first page of the table from the *Publication Manual of the American Psychological Association* (APA, 1983, p. 118) listing types of work referenced and presented three examples of references for each of four works typically used by students in research reports: journal articles, magazine articles, books, and chapters in an edited book. Other pages in the handout illustrated citations and quotations.

Students' knowledge about references was measured two ways. Three recognition tests each presented five correct references (the four types just mentioned and another type of work, e.g., an unpublished paper or a conference presentation) that students matched with the correct label (e.g., journal article, magazine article . . . none of these). Three production tests each provided information about a journal article, a magazine article, a book, and a chapter in an edited book that students used to prepare a reference list in APA style.

Procedure

Instruction was the same in both semesters. Early in the term, I distributed and discussed the handout. I stressed the importance of correctly citing and referencing works, illustrated the types of works used in research reports, discussed examples of references for the four common sources, demonstrated citations in text, and announced that students would take a multiple-choice recognition test on 3 successive days. At the beginning of the next three classes, students completed a recognition test, exchanged tests for scoring on the basis of 1 point for each correct answer, and then submitted them to me for verification and recording of the grades. On the day of the third recognition test, I dispensed the first production test. Students completed it outside of class, exchanged papers in the next class for grading on the basis of 1 point for each correct reference and one fifth of a point for listing references in the proper order, submitted the papers for verification and recording, and then received another production test. After collecting the third production test, I handed out copies of Cronan-Hillix's (1988) article. In the next period, we briefly discussed the article and the policy of A or F grading for the reference section of their research reports. After further discussion

during the next class, students completed one or two posttest questionnaires.

The evaluation was somewhat different in the two semesters. Although students in both terms completed the same 10-item posttest questionnaire and a two-part follow-up question, students in the spring class also completed a 10-item reference recognition pretest and a 12-item pre- and posttest questionnaire. They completed the recognition pretest and the 12-item pretest questionnaire during the first week of class. Students answered the posttest questionnaires and follow-up question in successive periods after finishing the instructional sequence and before the due date for the first research report.

Results

Recognition Test

Forty-four students in the spring semester completed the 10-item reference recognition pretest. The mean percentage of accurately identified references was 93.2% for magazines, 84.1% for books, 72.7% for chapters in an edited book, and 53.4% for journal articles; overall, the mean score was 75.7% correct. The mean scores on the recognition tests were comparable in the two semesters and justified computing an overall mean score. In order, the grand means on the three recognition tests were 90.4%, 98.6%, and 99.4% correct. Thus, the handout and instruction appeared to improve students' ability to recognize types of references above their baseline level.

Production Test

The mean scores on the three production tests were comparable in the two semesters and also justified computing an overall mean score. In order, the grand means were 33.6%, 65.4%, and 78.9% correct. Errors on the final production test were not distributed equally across the five types of answers. The grand mean percentage of errors on the final test was 44.3% for chapters in an edited book, 34.1% for magazine articles, 12.5% for books, 8.0% for journal articles, and 1.1% for listing references in the correct order. Thus, this technique seemed to help students prepare accurate reference lists, although students' production skills lagged behind their recognition skills.

Student Evaluation

Eighty-six of the 90 students completed the 10-item posttest questionnaire. The virtually identical mean scores in the two terms on a scale ranging from *strong disagreement* (1) to *strong agreement* (5) justified reporting an overall mean score. Students agreed that they learned how to recognize different kinds of references ($M = 4.48$, $SD = .41$) and how to prepare the reference section of a research report ($M = 4.55$, $SD = .55$). Students agreed that the number of tests was appropriate ($M = 3.67$, $SD = .69$), the purpose of the activity became increasingly clear ($M = 4.10$, $SD = .28$), and grading of the recognition and production tests was fair ($M = 3.86$, $SD = .63$). Students endorsed Cronan-Hillix's (1988) contention about their need to learn the importance of accuracy in research ($M = 4.21$, $SD = .58$), agreed that it was equally important for them to learn accuracy in referencing ($M = 4.26$, $SD = .54$), and recommended use of this technique in the future ($M = 4.33$, $SD = .75$). Students agreed that feedback was adequate ($M = 3.72$, $SD = 1.25$), but suggested that making and keeping a copy of the production tests might help them understand and correct their mistakes, especially in the absence of the originals submitted for grading. Opinion was divided on whether it was fair to apply an A or F grading system to the reference section of their research reports ($M = 3.33$, $SD = 1.29$).

The lack of consensus prompted me to assess student opinion on the grading issue in two additional ways. First, 81 of 90 students in the two semesters answered a two-part follow-up question by indicating whether or not and why the system was fair. Sixty-two percent asserted that this procedure was fair and typically explained that they had learned and mastered the skill of preparing accurate reference lists and that errors resulted from carelessness (see Cronan-Hillix, 1988). The remaining 38% argued that the procedure was unfair and typically said that the absolute scale produced distress and ignored effort (see McDonald & Peterson, this issue). The sentiment of these students was that "trying hard" should result in intermediate rather than failing grades. Second, 37 students in the spring completed a 12-item pre- and posttest questionnaire that included a question comparable to one on the 10-item posttest questionnaire. On the most pertinent item (space limitations preclude a report of all the data), students significantly changed their opinion away from *disagreement* (2) on the pretest ($M = 2.21$) toward *neutrality* (3) on the posttest ($M = 2.89$) for a question concerning the fairness of the A or F grading system, $t(37) = 3.25$, $p = .003$. Thus, the two additional measures of student opinion indicate movement toward greater acceptance of an A or F grading system, but students do not unanimously endorse it.

Compared with the first papers in previous semesters, the first research reports seemed to contain fewer citation and reference errors and to conform better to other aspects of APA style.

Discussion

This instructional technique illustrates sound educational principles. The procedure provides repeated practice with feedback to shape accurately prepared reference lists. Moreover, the sequence of events is consistent with the principle that distributed practice is more effective than massed practice.

This technique reveals unexpected problems for students. For example, students learn that journals and magazines require different formats in the reference list, but find it difficult to distinguish between the two. This problem arises and persists because there are no clear criteria that distinguish these two types of periodicals.

This technique benefits students. First, they learn to recognize the format for different kinds of references, an important but often forgotten prerequisite to locating resources by "treeing" backward through the literature. Second, they learn to prepare a reference section for a research report and appear to be more sensitive to other aspects of APA style. Finally, they better appreciate the professional attitude that accuracy is important in conducting and reporting research. These benefits prompt students to endorse this teaching and learning technique; however, they do not unanimously support an A or F grading system.

This technique also benefits instructors. First, an instructor can perform each step in the learning sequence in only a few minutes of class time. Second, an instructor can use the technique to teach other subtleties about preparing a reference list. Third, although instructors spend time producing and administering tests, they can save time during the grading process because students produce stylistically more accurate reports that are more easily and quickly graded. This benefit multiplies during courses that require several research reports.

Coda

Developing and using this technique enhanced my own referencing skills because I had to verify many details about which I thought I was certain, only to learn that I labored under misconceptions. Developing and using this technique promoted my mastery of APA style because students asked more frequent and more challenging questions about APA style than ever before. In my opinion, developing and using this technique increased my awareness and understanding of other aspects of writing beyond referencing (e.g., Gray, 1988; Woodford, 1967), abilities that serve all of us well in our roles as authors, reviewers, and teachers.

References

American Psychological Association. (1983). *Publication manual of the American Psychological Association* (3rd ed.). Washington, DC: Author.

Cronan-Hillix, T. (1988). Teaching students the importance of accuracy in research. *Teaching of Psychology, 15*, 205–207.

Gray, D. J. (1988). Writing across the college curriculum. *Phi Delta Kappan, 69,* 729–733.

Griggs, R. A. (1988). Who is Mrs. Cantlie and why are they doing those terrible things to her homunculi? *Teaching of Psychology, 15,* 105–106.

McDonald, C. S., & Peterson, K. A. (this issue). Teaching commitment to accuracy in research: Comment on Cronan-Hillix (1988). *Teaching of Psychology, 18,* 100–101.

Soper, B., & Rosenthal, G. (1988). The number of neurons in the brain: How we report what we do not know. *Teaching of Psychology, 15,* 153–156.

Woodford, F. P. (1967). Sounder thinking through clearer writing. *Science, 156,* 743–745.

Notes

1. I thank Allen Keniston, Ken McIntire, Mary Meisser, Karen Welch, and three anonymous reviewers for helpful comments on this article.

2. This article exemplifies the teachings of Mitri Shanab and Eliot Hearst. By word and deed, they taught students to strive for perfection in writing research reports, an attitude I try to foster in my students.

3. A preliminary report of these results was presented at the Mid-America Conference for Teachers of Psychology, Evansville, IN, October 1989.

10. Fostering Students' Research and Presentations

Large enrollments and limited resources often preclude requiring all psychology majors to participate in one-on-one research with faculty members. Pamela Gibson, Arnold Kahn, and Virginia Mathie from James Madison University designed two research team models to offer research opportunities for as many students as possible. Model 1 is a single-faculty, single-project team, and Model 2 is a large multifaculty, multiproject team. Students and faculty valued these approaches because they involved students in all aspects of the research enterprise.

Steven Prentice-Dunn and Michael Roberts from the University of Alabama describe an intensive 6-week summer internship designed to strengthen research skills of honor students from the Minority Access to Research Careers Program sponsored by the National Institute of Mental Health. Their approach combined didactic and experiential research components to provide breadth and depth of exposure to research methodology. Interns first participated in faculty-sponsored research and later designed and conducted their own studies. The program, which enriches students and faculty alike, would be valuable for all undergraduates considering advanced study in psychology.

Mary Starke combined a research practicum for 17 undergraduates with the implementation and evaluation of an assertiveness training program for pysically disabled students at Ramapo College. Evidence indicated that undergraduates can function as competent and dedicated research assistants (RAs). A follow-up study 1 year later revealed that most of the RAs were using the skills they had learned or practiced in the project.

Andrew Newcomb and Catherine Bagwell from the University of Richmond describe the laboratory component of their introductory psychology course and a teaching fellows (TFs) program in which undergraduates direct these laboratory experiences. They presented the goals of the course and described its curriculum; discussed goals and operations of the TF program; mentioned the specific responsibilities of the TFs as well as the procedures for selecting, training, and supervising them; and summarized the many advantages of this exemplary program.

Paul Gore and Carmeron Camp describe the use of a poster session as part of their undergraduate experimental design course at New Orleans University. Students demonstrate principles of experimental methodology when they design and conduct their own research using radishes as subjects. Students present their results in a poster session held in a festival atmosphere and open to the entire college community. Students and faculty considered this approach to be effective and enjoyable.

Jerome Rosenberg and Ronald Blount from the University of Alabama describe their department's student research convocation. Undergraduates and graduate students presented their empirical research in a poster session. Submitted research may have been conducted as part of an experimental psychology course requirement, with other students and minimal faculty supervision, or in collaboration with faculty. In addition to being a valuable experience for students, the convocation helped faculty members become more familiar with their colleagues' research.

In-class poster sessions supplanted traditional term papers in Brian Baird's classes at Pacific Lutheran University. He described instructions to students about preparing posters, logistics of planning and conducting poster sessions, and the approach's advantages for students and faculty. Students preferred this approach over conventional term papers; in one survey, 100% of the respondents favored poster sessions.

Andrea Welch and Charles Waehler from The University of Akron surveyed 271 participants attending poster sessions at the 1993 convention of the American Psychological Association in Toronto. Respondents evaluated posters on three dimensions: visual display and organization, demeanor of the presenter, and content. Participants rated visual display as paramount but also considered the other two dimensions to be important. These authors' data provide excellent guidance for anyone preparing and presenting a poster or teaching others to do so.

Undergraduate Research Groups: Two Models

Pamela Reed Gibson
Arnold S. Kahn
Virginia Andreoli Mathie
James Madison University

Undergraduate involvement in research beyond a research methods course is a valuable experience, especially for students interested in graduate school (Kiemiesky, 1984; Purdy, Reinehr, & Swartz, 1989). Purdy et al. found that most experimental and clinical psychology graduate programs rated research experience as a "very important" admissions criterion; most counseling programs rated research as "moderately important." Unfortunately, only a small minority of undergraduates have the opportunity to gain research skills (Baird, 1990; Hartmann, 1990).

A dilemma for faculty members in publish or perish environments is that undergraduate research projects are frequently time-consuming and seldom yield publishable results. Although instructors of research methods courses often try to provide comprehensive research experiences for students (Yoder, 1979), a long-term, out-of-class experience offers students the opportunity to evaluate the strengths and weaknesses of their discipline (Hartmann, 1990) and to experience the advantages, complications, and accountability of the research setting (Kuo, 1987/88; Vittal, Treinen, & Nikuie, 1990). Supervising faculty can also serve as models and mentors for students (Ware & Matthews, 1980).

One solution to this dilemma is to have a research team of undergraduates work on faculty members' projects. Research teams are not new. Beins (1993), Evans, Rintala, Guthrie, and Raines (1981), and Nadelman, Morse, and Hagen (1976) described teams with positive results. In this article, we describe two successful models for incorporating undergraduates into research groups. Depending on the department's staffing needs, these teams may or may not count as part of the faculty member's teaching load.

Faculty research interests are typically announced in the department's semiannual newsletter, and students apply directly to the supervising faculty member. We generally require students to complete statistics and experimental psychology courses before participating in the research groups. We also strive for more than one semester's involvement because the research process is rarely completed in a semester. Students receive course credit for independent readings or independent research.

Model 1: Single-Faculty, Single-Project Team

One of us organized a group in fall 1992 to conduct a regression study to predict hope in those with environmental illness/multiple chemical sensitivity. The team usually has three or four student members.

Each student completes a student learning plan that itemizes the research skills that the student possesses and those skills she or he would like to acquire from participating in the research group. Skills include library research, reviewing and critiquing journal articles, preparing questionnaires, entering data, conducting data analyses, and writing in APA style.

Students begin using the skills they already possess and acquire new skills as they gain confidence. In the regression study, students began by choosing a variable, conducting a literature review on that variable, and helping choose the most appropriate measure for the study. Students reviewed social support, hope, and adjustment to chronic illness.

The group meets once a week for 2 hr and performs tasks as necessary. For example, we discussed basic questionnaire development in one group meeting. In later meetings, students led discussions on specific measures they had critiqued. Students' disagreements about which measure to adopt were instructive, illuminating, and illustrative of the problems that arise in the research process. Students generally appreciated an opportunity to participate in hands-on research in a nonthreatening atmosphere and realized that they had much to offer. Because students are given considerable ownership of the project, they feel responsible for its implementation.

Another goal of the out-of-class research experience was to give students an opportunity to present and publish research. Student coauthors presented conference posters and papers using data from the several dependent variables (hope, social support, and adjustment). Because each student focused on one variable, the research was manageable. Involvement in the larger group allowed students to see how their variables were part of a larger study. The more comprehensive analyses, including the regression model, were more appropriate for faculty publications or for joint authorship with students who remained with the project for a long time. For this model, the maximum size group was four students because one faculty member was responsible for guiding each student from conceptualization to publication.

Benefits of the faculty member's involvement include assisting with library work, aiding on various time-consuming tasks (including coding and data entry), interacting with and teaching students who have a genuine interest in the research process, and consulting and advising students at every stage of the research process. Each student's valuable skills become evident. For example, the faculty member learns to depend on one student for excellent feedback about questionnaire wording and on another for excellent overall planning/troubleshooting ability. We have presented two posters (Cheavens, Gibson, Warren, & Pasquantino, 1993; Gibson, Warren, Pasquantino, & Cheavens, 1993) and three conference papers (Cheavens, Gibson, & Warren, 1994; Gibson, Cheavens, & Warren, 1994; Crowley & Gibson, 1995), submitted two journal papers for review, and written a grant proposal to the Virginia Board for People with Disabilities (unfunded) to expand our research.

Model 2: Large Multifaculty, Multiproject Team

This research team consists of three faculty members and several students involved simultaneously in four research projects on the topic of sexual assault. The structure of this team has evolved over 4 years to accommodate more students.

The first team, two faculty members and two students, started in January 1991 to follow up previously reported differences between acknowledged and unacknowledged rape victims in their scripts of what occurred before, during, and after a typical rape. The team met weekly to review relevant research and discuss new studies. Since fall 1991, 34 other students have participated on the team; the size of the team has ranged from 7 to 12 students.

Initially, all team members worked on all projects, meeting formally once a week for 2 hr to coordinate and plan research activities. For example, in two studies, we obtained handwritten rape scripts from subjects and devoted the weekly meetings to developing a detailed script-coding scheme and coordinating further data collection. Outside of class, students collected the data, coded the scripts, and continued the literature review. Faculty and students worked together on all phases of the research.

As the size of the team and the number of projects grew, we modified the team structure. Students affiliated with one of three project groups, with each group taking primary responsibility for one project. Project groups met once a week, sometimes with a faculty member and sometimes on their own, to work on the details of their project. All team members still had input into all projects through weekly 2-hr team meetings. At these meetings, each group updated the others on its project status, and the entire team made final decisions about procedures, measuring instruments, and other methodological concerns. We also used these meetings to prepare for data collection and analysis and to discuss the results and implications of findings. In addition, students had a chance to see three faculty members discuss research ideas, offer different views, and collaborate on research.

Students presented their research at state (Hinely et al., 1993; Schoka et al., 1993) and regional meetings (Andreoli Mathie et al., 1994; Baker et al., 1992; Chau, Lally, Schmitt, & Stover, 1994; Salimi et al., 1994). One study has been published (Kahn, Andreoli Mathie, & Torgler, 1994), and team members have drafted manuscripts for two other projects. In addition, students have written a grant proposal (not funded) to obtain funding for one project, and they outlined a plan for a longitudinal study. Because working in groups on separate studies led to a lack of team cohesiveness, we now meet twice a week with all team members working on all projects.

One of the requirements for the research team at the end of the 1993 spring semester was to respond to the question, "What skills have you gained from being a part of the team?" Almost all students said participation increased their library, writing, computer, and critical-thinking skills, as well as their ability to speak in front of a group, work effectively in a group, understand research ethics, and work closely with faculty members. They also noted that good research is a tedious and time-consuming endeavor.

Summary

We discussed two models for meeting the research needs of faculty and students. Both models provide undergraduates the opportunity to participate in the full range of research activities–conceptualize, design, collect and analyze data, and write up and present the results at professional meetings. Students reported that these experiences were valuable. Research teams enable faculty to continue their research and serve as mentors to undergraduates while carrying heavy teaching loads. The research team appears to be a useful way to meet the research needs of students and faculty.

References

Andreoli Mathie, V. A., Kahn, A. S., Baker, S., Feria, G., Gregory, C., Heiges, K., Hinely, H., Linn, K., & Scholten, B. (1994, April). *Counterfactual thinking in women's perceptions of their rape experience.* Paper presented at the meeting of the Southeastern Psychological Association, New Orleans, LA.

Baird, L. L. (1990). The undergraduate experience: Commonalities and differences among colleges. *Research in Higher Education, 31,* 271–279.

Baker, S., Beeghly, P., Bradley, K., Feria, G., Hastings, K., Hinely, H., Schoka, E., Stuckey, J., Sullivan, M., Kahn, A., & Andreoli Mathie, V. A. (1992, March). *Rape scripts as determinants of acknowledged vs. unacknowledged rape victims.* Poster presented at the meeting of the Southeastern Psychological Association, Knoxville, TN.

Beins, B. C. (1993, August). *Research team: Bonding, enjoyment, and programmatic research.* Paper presented at the annual meeting of the American Psychological Association, Toronto, Canada.

Chau, L., Lally, C., Schmitt, M., & Stover, K. (1994, April). *Men's perceptions of rape.* Poster presented at the meeting of the Southeastern Psychological Association, New Orleans, LA.

Cheavens, J., Gibson, P. R., & Warren, M. L. (1994, October). *Social support and isolation in persons with multiple chemical sensitivities.* Paper presented at the first annual conference of the Southern Regional Chapter of the Association for Women in Psychology, Hilton Head, SC.

Cheavens, J., Gibson, P. R., Warren, M. L., & Pasquantino, D. (1993, November). *Chemical sensitivities: Patients' views for improved access in a technological society.* Poster presented at the annual conference of the Virginia Women's Studies Association, James Madison University, Harrisonburg, VA.

Crowley, C., & Gibson, P. R. (1995, March). *Disability due to chemical sensitivity: People, controversies, legalities.* Paper presented at the annual meeting of the Southeastern Psychological Association, Savannah, GA.

Evans, R. I., Rintala, D. H., Guthrie, T. J., & Raines, B. E. (1981). Recruiting and training undergraduate psychology research assistants for longitudinal field investigations. *Teaching of Psychology, 8,* 97–100.

Gibson, P. R., Cheavens, J., & Warren, M. L. (1994, May). *Chemical sensitivity/chemical injury: Life impacts.* Paper presented at the meeting of the American Psychological Association, Washington, DC.

Gibson, P. R., Warren, M. L., Pasquantino, D., & Cheavens, J. (1993, November). *Limitations and thwarted goals for persons with chemical sensitivities.* Poster presented at the annual conference of the Virginia Women's Studies Association, James Madison University, Harrisonburg, VA.

Hartmann, D. J. (1990). Undergraduate research experience as preparation for graduate school. *The American Sociologist, 21,* 179–188.

Hinely, H., Baker, S., Beeghly, P., Feria, G., Hartwell, C., Higgins, D., Jacobs, H., McCarthy, A., Schoka, E., & Schuyler, W. (1993, April). *Rape scripts and the unacknowledged rapist.* Paper presented at the meeting of the Virginia Psychological Association, Virginia Beach, VA.

Kahn, A. S., Andreoli Mathie, V. A., & Torgler, C. (1994). Rape scripts and rape acknowledgment. *Psychology of Women Quarterly, 18,* 53–66.

Kierniesky, N. C. (1984). Undergraduate research in small psychology departments. *Teaching of Psychology, 11,* 15–18.

Kuo, S. (1987/88). Research experience for college juniors. *Journal of College Science Teaching, 17,* 209.

Nadelman, L., Morse, W., & Hagen, J. (1976). Developmental research in educational settings. Description of a seminar/practicum. *Teaching of Psychology, 3,* 21–24.

Purdy, J. E., Reinehr, R. C., & Swartz, J. D. (1989). Graduate admissions criteria of leading psychology departments. *American Psychologist, 44,* 960–964.

Salimi, L., Andreoli Mathie, V. A., Kahn, A. S., Beeghly, P., Dolby, L., Hartwell, C., Jacobs, H., & Schor, J. (1994, April). *Sexual assault experiences of international women.* Paper presented at the meeting of the Southeastern Psychological Association, New Orleans, LA.

Schoka, E., Baker, S., Beeghly, P., Feria, G., Hartwell, C., Higgins, D., Hinely, H., Jacobs, H., McCarthy, A., & Schuyler, W. (1993, April). *Effects of relationship and force on acknowledged vs. unacknowledged victims' perception of rape.* Paper presented at the meeting of the Virginia Psychological Association, Virginia Beach, VA.

Vittal, V., Treinen, R., & Nikuie, M. (1990). Research experience for undergraduates at Iowa State University. *IEEE Transactions on Power Systems, 5,* 1420–1423.

Yoder, J. (1979). Teaching students to do research. *Teaching of Psychology, 6,* 85–88.

Ware, M. E., & Matthews, J. R. (1980). Stimulating career exploration and research among undergraduates: A colloquium series. *Teaching of Psychology, 7,* 36–38.

Note

We thank Charles L. Brewer and three anonymous reviewers for their helpful comments on an earlier version of this article.

A Summer Internship in Psychological Research: Preparation of Minority Undergraduates for Graduate Study

Steven Prentice-Dunn
Michael C. Roberts
University of Alabama

The President's Commission on Mental Health (1978) noted the shortage of minority professionals in mental health. Recent studies indicated that nonwhite membership in the American Psychological Association is only about 4% (Russo, Olmedo, Stapp, & Fulcher, 1981) and that ethnic minorities comprise only 4.5% of graduate students in psychology (Taylor, 1977). In response to the imperative for greater ethnic representation, the recruitment and retention of qualified minority students remains a goal often unachieved for psychology graduate departments nationwide (Bernal, Barron, & Leary, 1983). Clearly, methods that increase the number of ethnic minority students deserve careful attention.

Bernal et al. (1983) focused attention on university programs' application materials to facilitate minority admissions. Another focus, however, should be on the background and preparation of students for graduate training. Advice frequently given to all students considering graduate study in psychology is to gain undergraduate research experience (Weber-Levine, 1984). With graduate admissions becoming increasingly competitive, students with research experience often receive more favorable consideration over their counterparts with similar grades, test scores, and practical experiences (Saccuzzo & Schulte, 1978). Once in graduate school, such students are likely to encounter fewer difficulties in conducting both faculty-sponsored research and their own studies–activities that have been shown to promote postgraduate professional development (Rickard, Dinoff, & Fowler, 1970; Rickard & Siegel, 1976).

With the prescription for research exposure becoming standard for admission to graduate study, we expect a concomitant increase in methods and programs for improving research training at the undergraduate level. Currently, attention to undergraduate research training is sparse, although there are increasing exceptions (cf. Kierniesky, 1984). For example, attention has been given to innovations employed to teach research within the traditional class format (Kalat, 1980; Yoder, 1979) as well as to train under-graduate research assistants in applied settings such as mental health (Norcross & Wogan, 1982) and longitudinal field investigations (Evans, Rintala, Guthrie, & Raines, 1981). Interest in undergraduate research conferences has also increased (Carsrud, Palladino, Tanke, Aubrecht, & Huber, 1984). Overall, however, very little effort has been made to facilitate exposure to research. When asked what adjustments to their undergraduate programs were being implemented to ensure that students were more competitive for graduate appointments, only 8% of a national sample of 206 chairpersons responded with more student research requirements (Lunneborg, 1982). Thus, the problem remains "how to train and encourage the brightest students to continue in the field and contribute to the scientific development of the profession" (Palladino, Carsrud, Hulicka, & Benjamin, 1982, p. 71).

The purpose of this article is to describe a summer research internship that we developed to address both the call of Palladino et al. (1982) for ways to encourage capable undergraduates to remain in the discipline and the need for increased minority participation in graduate study in psychology.

The research internship was designed to serve students from colleges and universities conducting Minority Access to Research Careers (MARC) programs. Funded by the National Institute of Mental Health, these MARC programs have two primary objectives (National Institute of Mental Health, 1979):

(a) to increase the number of well-prepared students from institutions with substantial minority enrollment who can compete successfully for entry into Ph.D. programs in disciplines related to alcoholism, drug abuse, and mental health; and

(b) to help develop biobehavioral, psychological, social, and/or public health sciences curricula and research training opportunities in institutions with substantial minority enrollment in order to prepare students for research careers related to alcoholism, drug abuse, and mental health. (p. 2)

MARC programs are restricted to institutions that have student populations with substantial numbers of ethnic minority groups (e.g., Black, Hispanic, American Indian, Asian, and Pacific Islander). Funded institutions (e.g., Tuskegee Institute, Howard University, Jackson State University) typically serve minority student enrollments. Approximately 10 funded programs exist. In addition, similar programs (e.g., Minority Biomedical Research Support: MBRS) are funded in the biomedical research field by the Division of Research Resources of the National Institutes of Health. MARC program institutions select a small number of outstanding juniors and seniors for participation in the 2-year honors program. The institution receives financial support for some faculty and supplies; the MARC students receive a stipend for living expenses, tuition, and fees for the 2 years. During the school sessions, students complete their undergraduate degree requirements with the special honors courses serving as electives. In the summer before their senior year, MARC students obtain hands-on experience as they work intensively with active researchers. MARC-oriented summer programs have been established at several universities (e.g., University of Delaware, University of Vermont) across the country. Our summer internship at the University of Alabama was created to provide the intensive research experience noted earlier.

The underlying philosophy of our 6-week summer internship program was that basic research skills necessary for success in graduate training are best acquired through intensive exposure to and experience with a variety of research topics, methodologies, and scientists. Narrowing the focus of training to one area or one type of method at the undergraduate level was thought to limit the student in later study and work. Although specialization is a necessary feature of graduate research endeavors, we believe that undergraduate research experiences should broaden the student's learning of research principles while instilling in the student an excitement over and respect for the scientific process. Because of this rationale, the summer research internship deliberately juxtaposed didactic and experiential research components with several researchers and topics to provide breadth of exposure while achieving in-depth training in research methodology.

Three faculty members were primarily involved; many other department faculty members and graduate students assisted. Didactic sessions were conducted with very small student-faculty ratios to promote an informal atmosphere in which conversation replaced lectures. In addition, such a structure facilitated the answering of numerous questions posed by MARC students. To supplement instruction on conventional topics such as experimental design, survey design, and research ethics, we gave MARC students sessions on quasi-experimental methods, observation of dyadic interaction, and writing papers according to APA style (American Psychological Association, 1983). The didactics often were conducted in settings outside the classroom.

For example, survey methods were taught at the university facility where statewide opinion polls are conducted. The didactic included direct training in telephone interviewing and, eventually, a few evenings helping conduct an actual survey for the facility. For the component on program evaluation, the students went to a residential treatment facility run by the Psychology Department. Here the research director (a psychology professor) discussed issues of measurement and computer analyses. In addition, several of our colleagues met with the interns to inform them of representative research topics and methodologies used in their own specialties. Among these specialties were child psychology, social psychology, mental retardation, and behavioral medicine.

Consistent with the underlying philosophy of the summer research internship was the belief that a student's close involvement with faculty scientists as mentors is an invaluable way of providing the student with more than just research instruction. The intensive contact also helped the student to gain active experience in ongoing projects. Consequently, we developed a research apprenticeship in which interns initially worked on faculty research through participation in discussions at several research team meetings of professors and graduate students. Among the various research problems were the effects of exercise on the mentally retarded, factors influencing the use of child safety seats in automobiles, deindividuation and aggression, children's medical fears, imitation and social learning, and factors influencing parental interaction with developmentally delayed children.

Working at first on several projects accomplished two goals: Students gained an appreciation for the diversity of research topics investigated by psychologists; students were provided with an array of methodological issues that served as examples of concepts and problems discussed in the didactic sessions. In addition, exposure to several role models allowed the interns to learn what one investigator called the "psychology of becoming a psychologist" (Kalat, 1980). This exposure was accomplished by encouraging the presenting researchers to personalize their research by discussing their undergraduate and graduate careers, the factors in their professional and personal lives that led to their choosing the particular topic under study, and so forth.

Following the apprenticeship model outlined earlier, each student eventually gained sufficient background and skills to conduct an individual project under the supervision of one faculty member. Experience with this approach at a number of institutions has indicated that student involvement of this type leads to greater likelihood of admission to graduate programs and to successful completion of graduate training for research-oriented careers in the behavioral sciences (cf. Rickard & Siegel, 1976).

Before the research internship began, we were asked by the director of one MARC program to use numerous writing assignments to improve students' skills and to enhance their chances for graduate admission and retention. In addition to the teaching sessions on scientific writing and APA style, we assigned writing topics on a daily basis. Early in the program these took the form of brief literature reviews, which required searches through *Psychological Abstracts* and preparation of a summary. Later, faculty members provided written problems that required interns to read a general description of one research area and subsequently to design several studies for possible investigation. In all cases, extensive feedback on content and writing style was given the following day.

As noted earlier, one objective of the summer program was to assist the students in preparation of a specific research proposal and in later implementation of the project. Research topics were chosen by students in consultation with faculty members. Preliminary library searches provided a basic literature review and conceptual approach. As the internship progressed, consequently, more of the students' writing time was spent shaping these individual research projects. The research project process was separated into the four broad phases incorporated by Gant, Dillon, and Malott (1980) into their behavioral system for supervising undergraduate research. These phases were: (a) design generation, (b) project implementation, (c) report writing, and (d) results presentation. Each category provided several opportunities for writing. For example, in the design phase, students submitted a preliminary proposal, a complete proposal, a literature review, and a paper discussing alternate designs, possible confounding variables, and so on. Although all core faculty members were involved with all students, each student was assigned to a primary supervisor. Each assignment was preceded and followed by discussions with the faculty supervisor and other faculty participants.

Because of the brief duration of the summer internship, the students were unable to proceed beyond data collection on their projects. This limitation necessitated the availability of the faculty members during the next semester for consultation on data analysis and report writing. As directors of the internship, we considered this strategy to be an acceptable alternative to our interns' designing simplistic, superficial studies that could be completed within a few weeks. After completing their research, the interns presented their findings at regional professional conferences.

Students enrolled in the summer internship were very busy. They reported 8-hr days without exception and occasional 12- to 14-hr days. Despite the harried pace, students thought the time went quickly because they were exposed to a diversity of people, research topics, and activities. The students reported that the most time-consuming aspects of the internship were the writing assignments. However, both interns and faculty noted a substantial improvement in the students' writing skills over the 6-week period. Another benefit of the program was that interns were able to learn of the individual histories and motivations that led the

faculty researchers to their particular careers and research areas. This personalization of the research process is something to which most students in traditional undergraduate study are seldom exposed.

As directors of the internship, we suggest two improvements to the program. First, more formalized and quantifiable evaluation data must be implemented. Our students unanimously rated their writing of anonymous narratives very positively. We recognize, however, the limitations of testimonials as a comprehensive measure of program effectiveness. In our case, organizing such an extensive program demanded so much of our attention that we were unable to form a more definitive evaluation framework. Future directors may wish to use formal assessments of writing and research skills, comparative rates of graduate school admission for internship participants, and performance in graduate school as outcome measures.

Our second suggestion is that greater exposure of students to researchers who are themselves minority members must be ensured. This might be accomplished in a situation such as ours—neither of us is from an ethnic minority—through a colloquium series in which invited minority speakers with research track records discuss career exploration and research topics. This type of colloquium structure, already implemented in the University of Delaware MARC summer program, was reported successful (Ware & Matthews, 1980). Yet this improvement is made more difficult by the very reason for which the MARC program was initiated–the dearth of minority mental health researchers. Although we recognize that such a feature has a positive impact on MARC students, we firmly believe that it is not a prerequisite for the success of an intensive research program; this conclusion was also reached by our students.

For graduate program directors interested in active recruitment of minority students, the MARC students and their sponsoring institutions provide an outstanding resource. Because of their intensive experience with sophisticated research, these students are prime candidates for graduate study. As faculty members involved in the summer internship, we also found the experience challenging and rewarding. The intensive nature of this experience and the dedicated fresh approach that these students brought to the internship made the summer program all the more enjoyable. We and the students sometimes compared our experiences to a research boot camp. Nonetheless, the format of the internship favorably contrasted with our experiences of working with undergraduates through the more conventional academic routes of directed readings and independent studies conducted on a few-hours-per-week basis.

In conclusion, the summer research internship outlined in this article was designed to instill in minority students research skills that will make them competitive for graduate appointments and that perhaps will engender interest in research careers. It should be remembered that the experiences gained by our interns would be beneficial to all undergraduate students. We encourage our colleagues to develop similar programs that will enrich students and faculty alike.

References

American Psychological Association. (1983). *Publication manual of the American Psychological Association* (3rd ed.). Washington, DC: Author.

Bernal, M. E., Barron, B. M., & Leary, C. G. (1983). Use of application materials for recruitment of ethnic minority students in psychology. *Professional Psychology, 14,* 817–829.

Carsrud, A. L., Palladino, J. J., Tanke, E. D., Aubrecht, L., & Huber, R. J. (1984). Undergraduate psychology research conferences: Goals, policies, and procedures. *Teaching of Psychology, 11,* 141–145.

Evans, R. I., Rintala, D. H., Guthrie, T. J., & Raines, B. E. (1981). Recruiting and training undergraduate psychology research assistants for longitudinal field investigations. *Teaching of Psychology, 8,* 97–100.

Gant, G. D., Dillon, M. J., & Malott, R. W. (1980). A behavioral system for supervising undergraduate research. *Teaching of Psychology, 7,* 89–92.

Kalat, J. W. (1980). Introducing students to research by use of biographical materials in a comparative psychology course. *Teaching of Psychology, 7,* 71–74.

Kierniesky, N. C. (1984). Undergraduate research in small psychology departments. *Teaching of Psychology, 11,* 15–18.

Lunneborg, P. W. (1982). How are changes in graduate admissions affecting the teaching of undergraduate psychology? *Teaching of Psychology, 9,* 140–142.

National Institute of Mental Health. (1979). *Program announcement and guidelines for Minority Access to Research Careers Program.* Washington, DC: Author.

Norcross, J. C., & Wogan, M. (1982). Undergraduates as researchers in mental health settings. *Teaching of Psychology, 9,* 89–91.

Palladino, J. J., Carsrud, A. L., Hulicka, I. M., & Benjamin, L. T., Jr. (1982). Undergraduate research in psychology:

Assessment and directions. *Teaching of Psychology, 9,* 71–74.

President's Commission on Mental Health. (1978). *Report to the President from the President's Commission on Mental Health.* Washington, DC: U.S. Government Printing Office.

Rickard, H. C., Dinoff, M., & Fowler, R. D., Jr. (1970). Research apprenticeships: An experiment in the training of clinical psychologists. *The Clinical Psychologist Newsletter, 23,* 6.

Rickard, H. C., & Siegel, P. S. (1976). Research apprenticeship training for clinical psychologists: A follow-up study. *Professional Psychology, 7,* 359–363.

Russo, N. F., Olmedo, E. L., Stapp, J., & Fulcher, R. (1981). Women and minorities in psychology. *American Psychologist, 36,* 1315–1363.

Saccuzzo, D. P., & Schulte, R. H. (1978). The value of a terminal master's degree for Ph.D. pursuing students in psychology. *American Psychologist, 33,* 862–864.

Taylor, D. A. (1977). *Ethnicity and bicultural considerations in psychology: Meeting the needs of ethnic minorities.* Washington DC: American Psychological Association.

Ware, M. E., & Matthews, J. R. (1980). Stimulating career exploration and research among undergraduates: A colloquium series. *Teaching of Psychology, 7,* 36–38.

Weber-Levine, M. L. (1984, February). Summer placements worth planning well. *APA Monitor* [Undergraduate update], p. 30.

Yoder, J. (1979). Teaching students to do research. *Teaching of Psychology, 6,* 85–88.

Notes

1. The authors gratefully acknowledge the special contributions of Jeri Breiner and Edward A. Konarski to the summer research internship. In addition, we thank several colleagues and graduate students who participated in the program.
2. We thank two anonymous reviewers and the editor for their helpful comments on an earlier version of the manuscript for this article.

A Research Practicum: Undergraduates As Assistants in Psychological Research

Mary C. Starke
Ramapo College

For years psychology educators have stressed the importance of teaching methodology, research design, and statistics in the undergraduate curriculum. In a survey conducted among small liberal arts colleges, Cole and Van Krevelen (1977) found this material to be the most frequently cited as an appropriate requirement for all psychology majors. Two more recent surveys highlight the fact that undergraduate participation in research is becoming increasingly popular as a means of teaching even in colleges that are not research centers. The American Psychological Association's Educational Affairs Office has just completed the first national survey of undergraduate curriculum in 15 years via a 17-page questionnaire mailed to the department heads of 200 two-year and 200 four-year colleges. They report that student research with faculty members can be performed for credit in 55% of the four-year colleges and in 12% of the two-year colleges (Scheirer & Rogers, 1985). Kierniesky (1984) mailed a survey on undergraduate research to 337 liberal arts colleges. In response to the question "How many students do, or participate in, an empirically-based research project each year? (A project that is *not part* of a formal course like Research Methods or Experimental Psychology.)" (p. 16), only 43 of the 262 respondents said "None." Because 84% of the respondents support undergraduate research to some degree, Kierniesky concluded that this research is not restricted to a few elite schools.

Educators favor such research opportunity for undergraduates as it teaches them to think critically and independently, develops an appreciation and understanding for research, teaches research skills, helps them to apply what is learned, and is important for acceptance to graduate school. Graduate students have traditionally served as research assistants in clinical outcome studies where research design dictated that blind observers, raters, and test administrators assist the primary investigator in evaluating program effectiveness. Interest in enhancing the research skills of undergraduates as well as shrinking graduate enrollments have, however, prompted increasing participation by undergraduates in research experiences previously reserved for graduate students and professionals.

A research practicum for undergraduates was used to design, implement, and evaluate an assertiveness training program for physically disabled college students. Research assistants were recruited from two upper level psychology courses. An announcement was made that students would have the opportunity to participate in a psychology research practicum during the following semester. Those students who chose to participate would receive two course credits upon satisfactory completion of the practicum course. Nine students volunteered to participate in the first study, and 8 students served as research assistants in a replication of the project.

Student Training and Supervision

The author met in seminar with the group of research assistants from 3 to 6 hours per week for the first 4 weeks of the semester for a total of 17.5 hours of class time. Topics discussed during these meetings included research hypotheses, the design of the project, assessment (reliability and validity of instruments, behavioral vs. paper-and-pencil tests, self-report vs. observer ratings), assertiveness training (definition and rationale as well as role-playing and training techniques), selected topics in physical disability and rehabilitation, instruction in the use of video equipment, "nuts and bolts" research issues involving subject recruitment and test administration, as well as ethical concerns raised by this type of research. These meetings were structured as brainstorming sessions even in addressing those areas where the author had previously made a decision about direction. For example, in discussing the 2 × 3 repeated measures design (subjects assigned to assertiveness training, discussion-placebo, or waiting-list control groups were tested pre- and postintervention), the author invited assistants to explore the pros and cons of all possible research designs that might have been employed. As many decisions as possible were made cooperatively. Such brainstorming sessions resulted in an active participatory learning experience for the students and also served to promote an enthusiastic team spirit, which carried them through some of the frustrations and the less glamorous chores of implementing applied clinical research. In addition, the students often offered sound and creative suggestions concerning test items or scoring criteria, especially in the assertiveness role-playing practice sessions.

After completing the 4 weeks of training, research assistants contacted disabled undergraduates who had expressed interest in communication effectiveness training and scheduled them for pretesting. Research assistants worked in pairs to videotape and score subjects' role-playing responses to 11 hypothetical situations requiring assertiveness (the Behavioral Observation Scale) as well as to administer 3 paper-and-pencil tests and a demographic information questionnaire. During the week of pretesting, the author met with research assistants as necessary for supervision on an individual basis.

During the subsequent 8 weeks, while the author met weekly with the subjects assigned to the assertiveness training and discussion groups, there was no work for the research assistants. At the end of the subjects' training sessions, the research assistants, still blind to which of the treatment groups a subject had been assigned, were asked to administer the same battery of tests that had been used in the pretest phrase. Working in pairs, the research assistants tested 43 subjects. Each assistant thus acquired 13.5 hr of field experience. Two additional seminar meetings totaling 3 hr served as wrap-up and evaluation of the research experience. A party for research assistants and subjects celebrated the successful completion of the project.

Project Effects

Research assistants anonymously filled out course evaluation forms which were returned to the instructor after grades were submitted for the course. Sixteen of the 17 assistants returned these forms. All respondents indicated that the course increased their knowledge in the areas of research design and implementation. Responses to the question, "Do you feel that you could have learned similar material from another course that is offered at the College?" were "No," "Never," and "Absolutely not!" In response to this question, students cited the integration of theory and practice as well as the hands-on experience of the practicum. They were also enthusiastic about the benefits derived from working with a cohesive group of peers on a cooperative group project. All assistants found the readings and personal experience in assertiveness training helpful. Students were also unanimous in appreciating the opportunity to acquire skills in working with a physically disabled population and to learn the mechanics of operating video recording equipment. All research assistants responded affirmatively to the question, "Do you feel that this course

has helped or will help you in your work or in future vocational/educational pursuits?"

A follow-up of students' activities 1 year after the project revealed that the majority were indeed using skills that they had learned or practiced in the project. Two were enrolled in doctoral programs in psychology; one in a master's level program. There was one participant in each of the following fields: counseling spinal cord injury and rehabilitation patients, training psychiatric clients in assertiveness, conducting a counseling workshop for divorced women, and rehabilitating mentally retarded clients through behavior therapy. Four of the assistants have found the research experience helpful though less directly relevant to their post-baccalaureate positions as head teacher, administrator, supervisor, and first-year law student. These students reported that the organizational, statistical, and assertiveness skills gained from the practicum served them well in their present occupations. Two of these four assistants discussed specific plans to enroll in psychology graduate programs within the next 2 years. The three remaining assistants are completing their senior year at the college.

Substantial benefits were also realized by the disabled students who participated in the project. Subjects who received assertiveness training improved significantly more than discussion group or control group subjects in their social skills and self-perceptions as measured by a number of behavioral and paper-and-pencil instruments (Starke, 1984). In anonymous evaluations of the training, subjects also cited improved quality and frequency of class participation, more self-confidence and higher self-esteem, improved knowledge of self, and enlarged social circle as benefits of the project. The very act of interacting with the research assistants during the pre- and posttesting sessions was beneficial for some of the subjects who had little contact with able-bodied peers outside of their classes. Subjects who participated in the discussion group also improved on various behavioral and self-report measures.

A cost/benefit analysis of the project includes benefits accrued for the psychology literature and for the instructor. In the author's opinion, the undergraduate research assistants demonstrated competence and motivation equal to or greater than that generally ascribed to graduate students. In the course of brainstorming sessions, the assistants offered many helpful suggestions for recruiting subjects, retrieving data, and increasing interrater reliability on the behavioral assessment measures. Training in scoring received during the seminars resulted in interrater reliability scores of .98 on the pretest and .97 on the posttest administrations of the Behavioral Observation Scale. Such high reliability scores for the blind raters, as well as their competence in administering assessment instruments to the subjects, allowed for presentation of the project results in the professional literature. The research team approach supported a close and mutually satisfying work relationship among faculty and students.

Costs for the project were minimal. The undergraduates paid tuition for the course and received course credit. The college provided a small grant to pay for the costs of videotapes and allowed the use of empty classrooms for practicum seminars, subject assessment, and training sessions with subjects.

Discussion and Conclusion

Yoder (1979) has stated that there are many resources for the lecture content on research methods. He reported, however, that the experiential segment of the research course is less documented even though it is probably more influential in meeting the objectives of this course. This article has described both the methodology and the advantages that such a practicum might offer.

A cost/benefit analysis of the project indicates that costs were negligible in view of the benefits to the undergraduates who served as research assistants, to the physically disabled students who served as subjects, to the primary investigator, and to the body of knowledge in the field of psychology. I find myself most heartily in agreement with the 84% of Kierniesky's (1984) respondents who endorse undergraduate research.

References

Cole, D., & Van Krevelen, A. (1977). Psychology departments in small liberal arts colleges: Results of a survey. *Teaching of Psychology, 4,* 163–167.

Kierniesky, N. C. (1984). Undergraduate research in small psychology departments. *Teaching of Psychology, 11,* 15–18.

Scheirer, C. J., & Rogers, A. M. (1985). *The undergraduate psychology curriculum: 1984.* Washington, DC: American Psychological Association.

Starke, M. C. (1984, November). *Assertiveness training: Two studies with physically disabled young adults.* Paper presented at the meeting of the Association for the Advancement of Behavior Therapy, Philadelphia, PA.

Yoder, J. (1979). Teaching students to do research. *Teaching of Psychology, 6,* 85–88.

Note

The author gratefully acknowledges Gordon Bear and Donna Crawley for comments on a draft of this article. The author also thanks the following research assistants for their dedication: Diane Allcroft, Pam Bankert, Danielle Barilla, Marge Brown, Claire Coughlin, Joyce Contrino, Debbie Hoffman, Kathy Kalmar, Judy LaPadula, Lenny Marano, Jackie Melchior, Shirley Parkin, June Roderick, and Frank Scangarella.

Collaborative Learning in an Introduction to Psychological Science Laboratory: Undergraduate Teaching Fellows Teach to Learn

Andrew F. Newcomb
Catherine L. Bagwell
University of Richmond

Doceas ut discas provides an excellent summation of our Introduction to Psychological Science project that places students and an undergraduate teaching fellow (TF) in a demanding collaborative-learning environment, requiring all parties to assume unusual responsibility for their own learning. Translated as "teach to learn" or, more literally, "teach that you may learn," this Latin phrase is thought to be derived from the writings of Saint Ambrose. In the preface to his treatise, *On the Duties of Ecclesiastics,* Saint Ambrose (374 A.D.) questioned his preparation for the priesthood and his ascendance to the see of Milan, and he spoke of his need to learn and teach at the same time. In a similar way, we designed a laboratory curriculum and TFs program that uniquely challenges our ablest majors and actively engages introductory students in psychological science—one of the most liberating of disciplines in the liberal arts (D. L. Cole, 1982).

Since the fall of 1993, the entire department faculty has joined together to implement a new Introduction to Psychological Science course that consists of a 3-hr per week lecture section and a corequisite 2-hr weekly laboratory class. The primary objective of this beginning-level course is to familiarize first- and second-year undergraduates with the questions psychologists raise about human behavior and with the methods used to answer these questions. In both the lecture (up to 144 students per semester) and laboratory (as many as 12 students in each of 12 sections), our fundamental premise is that the most enduring and useful aspects of undergraduate education in psychology lie not in learning the content of the field but in learning how to acquire knowledge. The lecture section is unique because the curriculum is focused on nine themes that correspond to core areas of study in psychological science. Furthermore, all faculty share the responsibility of introducing students to different scientific perspectives by teaching the assumptions and methodologies of their respective subdisciplines (for details of the lecture component, see Allison, 1995).

Although this approach in the lecture section is a drastic departure from the traditional introductory course, the intellectual core of this endeavor rests with the TFs program and the laboratory component. Neither the idea of undergraduates teaching undergraduates nor the requirement of a laboratory in introductory psychology is a new concept. What makes our program unique is the scope of the undergraduates' responsibilities in the laboratory and the magnitude of the laboratory experience itself. We know, for example, that undergraduates are productive leaders of discussion groups (Diamond, 1972; Janssen, 1976), effective in teaching small classes (Harris, 1994; Wortman & Hillis, 1976), and successful in supervising laboratory experiences that demonstrate various psychological phenomena (Goolkasian & Lee, 1988; Kohn & Brill, 1981). In our program, however, the TFs are fully responsible for directing laboratory classes that actively engage introductory students in the scientific methods used in psychology.

In this article, we describe the Introduction to Psychological Science laboratory and the TFs program. First, we consider the goals of the laboratory and describe the curriculum. Next, we examine the goals of the TFs program; the responsibilities of the TFs; and the procedures for TF selection, training, and supervision. Then, we review how similar programs may be established. Once these basics of the laboratory and the TFs program are outlined, we discuss the effectiveness of the experience for the introductory students and the TFs. We conclude with a consideration of the implications of this type of program on quality undergraduate education.

Goals and Objectives

The goal of the Introduction to Psychological Science laboratory is to familiarize students with the various methods psychologists use to ask and answer questions about behavior. The course has six specific objectives: (a) to introduce research issues from a variety of theoretical and empirical perspectives; (b) to offer an active-learning experience with an emphasis on discovery; (c) to teach analytical- and critical-thinking skills necessary to formulate and answer research questions using various scientific methodologies; (d) to enhance communication skills, especially scientific writing; (e) to provide opportunities for interactive learning with more senior peers; and (f) to foster an appreciation of psychology as a science.

The Laboratory Curriculum

Although the laboratory curriculum supports the themes presented in lecture, the laboratory is not specifically integrated into the thematic organization of the lecture class. The primary purpose of the laboratory is to provide introductory students with an intensive and active experience with the methods of inquiry used in psychological science. Students complete primary source readings before each laboratory, actively participate in the laboratory session, and write weekly laboratory reports following the appropriate professional style (American Psychological Association, 1994b). The laboratory sessions are supplemented by a laboratory manual that includes course materials, prelaboratory assignments, and primary source readings (Newcomb, Bagwell, & Wright, 1995).

The 11 laboratory sessions are organized within a conceptual framework that provides for a progression of learning within three specific areas. First, students actively experience and learn about methodologies, assumptions, and research questions within a particular subdiscipline of psychology in each laboratory. Second, computer technology and statistical concepts are presented in a logical sequence that begins with graphing and visual inspection of data and proceeds to descriptive and inferential statistics, correlational analysis, and nonparametric statistics. In this progression, curricular demands increase in difficulty, and knowledge is reinforced and enhanced with each successive laboratory. Third, requirements for the laboratory reports gradually increase as students gain experience using the library, reading and understanding primary source material, and finding theoretical and empirical support for their hypotheses.

Within this conceptual framework, the curriculum is divided into two sections. As shown in Table 1, the first four laboratories provide a foundation in computer skills,

Table 1. Psychological Science Laboratory Curriculum: Content Area, Laboratory Activities, and Skills Developed

Laboratory	Title	Content Area	Laboratory Activities	Skills Developed
1	Freud, Apples, and Science	Free association and the concept of perceptual defense; readings include excerpts from Freud and Jung	Introduction to the scientific method with emphasis on hypothesis development; completion of a perceptual defense experiment and examination of results in the context of hypotheses	Core computer skills and fundamentals of scientific writing
2	Scientific Writing: An Essential Tool for Sharing Knowledge	Effective written communication	Direct instruction and collaborative-learning exercises in scientific writing	Scientific writing and computer graphics
3	Memory, Methodology, and Statistical Madness	Basics of experimental design and principles of descriptive statistics	Completion of two recall experiments and instruction in experimental design and statistics	Understanding of fundamental design and statistical concepts; use of statistical software package
4	More Memory, More Methodology, and More Statistical Madness	Principles of variability and inferential statistics	Completion of levels of processing experiment; instruction in between-subjects analysis of variance	Fundamental conceptual appreciation of inferential statistics and expanded skills with statistical software packages
5	Observation: A Window to Behavior	Observational methodology in the context of developmental psychology	Discussion of the use of coding schemes; application of sampling techniques to code a videotape of two children at play	Understanding and use of observational methodology, including development of own observational coding scheme
6	The Righteous Path to Questionnaire Construction	Questionnaire construction in the context of social psychology	Review and critique of the use of questionnaires in the psychological literature; development of computer-based questionnaire	Appreciation of questionnaire methodology, including use as manipulation checks for independent variables and as measures of dependent variables
7	First Impressions, Lasting Memories	Social cognition and impression formation	Continued exploration of experimental design issues in using questionnaires; discussion of real-world situations versus the psychology laboratory	Program questionnaires on computer
8	Wall Flowers and Social Butterflies	Psychometric properties of psychological tests in the context of personality assessment	Assessment of extroversion and introversion and examination of the relation between personality inventories and behavioral rating measures	Understanding of the concepts of reliability and validity and of correlational analyses
9	Experiencing the Third Dimension	Methodologies of psychophysics	Investigation of the relation between binocular disparity and depth perception with computer-based experiment on magnitude estimation	Enhanced understanding of inferential statistics, including within-subjects analysis of variance
10	The Birds and the Bees and the Rats	Observational methodology in the study of the sexual and maternal behavior of rats	Discussion of the biological origins of behavioral differences between men and women; examination of prenatal and postnatal influences on the display of male sexual behavior and maternal behavior	Increase skills in observational methodology, understand the distinction between nominal and ratio data, and complete a chi-square analysis
11	Visualizing the Mind	Neuroscience and neuronal morphology	Use of computerized microscopy and image analysis to measure the structures of neurons	Appreciation of the importance of computer technology in the field of neuroscience and review of inferential statistics

writing skills, and statistical concepts that form the backbone of the later laboratories. Although these first labs proceed within the context of specific subdisciplines of psychology, they focus on the development of a strong base of skills. In contrast, the last seven laboratories emphasize the methodologies and research questions of specific subdisciplines of psychological science. Our goal in these laboratories is not to offer students simple demonstrations of psychological phenomena or experiments with clear hypotheses and flawless outcomes. Furthermore, we do not

269

ask students to learn the intricacies of statistics. Instead, with guidance and instruction from the TFs, students explore the methodologies of various subdisciplines and gain personal experience with the complexities of designing and evaluating a psychological study.

The final exam for the laboratory component of the course is constructed each semester by the TFs who each write a summary of a research question in a biologically or socially based subdiscipline. Students are given a choice of two questions, and during the in-class exam, they must design a study to explore that question. They propose hypotheses, formulate hypothetical data, and analyze their data using appropriate statistical tests. As the product of this 2-hr exam, students turn in a complete laboratory report in which they have fully defined the problem, developed their hypotheses, described their study, and analyzed and discussed their hypothetical findings. In this way, the final exam requires students to demonstrate their skills at all phases of the research enterprise.

Revisions of the Curriculum

During the four semesters that the laboratory has been offered, we have made three prominent curricular revisions. We initially began each laboratory with a short discussion session centered on a book that addresses important themes in psychology. Student response to this text was negative, and we dropped the discussion groups. During the second semester, we introduced a laboratory devoted to scientific writing. Finally, we edited the student and instructor manuals each semester and completed two extensive end-of-year revisions. We now have a contract with McGraw-Hill to handle copyright issues and to publish the student manual (see Newcomb, Bagwell, & Parker, 1996). In addition, our instructor's manual has been significantly improved and serves as a comprehensive resource for the TFs.

Several other issues remain. Students are concerned with the time frame for returning papers because they turn in a new laboratory report before receiving the previous week's corrected paper. As a result of this delay, students tend to repeat similar mistakes. Possible solutions are a revision of the scoring schedule, which may be too demanding on the TFs, or the option for students to rewrite several of their laboratory reports. Students also believe that the laboratory component should comprise more than 25% of their final grade in the introductory course; we will reapportion the credit level to 35% in future semesters. Furthermore, because most of the introductory students do not plan to major in psychology, many want the option for nonmajors to omit the laboratory component. This change would be contrary to the goals of our general education curriculum; because few students come to college with the intention of majoring in psychology, such a modification may significantly reduce the number of psychology majors.

The Psychology TFs Program

Goals, Objectives, and Responsibilities

The overall goal of the TFs program is to engage introductory students and the TFs in a process of mutual discovery. The specific objectives of the program are to: (a) afford a capstone experience that requires application of previous knowledge and acquisition of new information, (b) strengthen skills in critical thinking and oral defense of diverging viewpoints, (c) emphasize different modes of problem solving and interpreting ideas and data, (d) cultivate an appreciation of intellectual complexity and discovery, and (e) promote the development of a stronger academic community of majors and department faculty.

In achieving these objectives, the TFs have unique and demanding responsibilities. In two-person teams, the TFs direct three laboratory sections per week. They score approximately 30 papers per week, hold 2 office hours each week, and develop and score the final laboratory exam. Finally, the TFs participate in weekly 2-hr supervision sessions. In all, the TFs frequently work as many as 15 hr each week, but they are paid a fixed stipend for working 10 hr per week.

Selection of TFs

The TFs program can encourage our best and brightest students to consider academic careers. Therefore, in designing the selection process, we drew from the results of a retrospective examination of the undergraduate careers of individuals who later went on to become accomplished college teachers (D. L. Cole, 1986). D. L. Cole suggested that identifying the brightest students is an easy task; these are the students who have top grades, complete departmental honors, and receive the best recommendations. However, he proposed that only a subset of these students are best suited to excel in a wide range of teaching situations with a diverse population of student learning styles.

Our selection process is simple. Students submit a statement describing their interest in being a TF, a list of psychology course work and grades, and names of three faculty members who know them well. This information is given to faculty members who provide two or three descriptive phrases for each candidate and rate each applicant's overall potential as a TF. All candidates are then randomly placed in groups of five or six applicants and complete a 1-hr group problem-solving task. The group is asked to design a laboratory experience that promotes introductory psychology students' understanding of scientific inquiry. The faculty supervisor combines his or her evaluation of performance in this group setting with the other data and completes the selection of TFs.

270

What is the outcome of our selection process? Our impression is that we do find our best and brightest students who are, in many ways, like individuals who have become accomplished college teachers (D. L. Cole, 1986). In particular, our inaugural class of TFs consisted of individuals who would be successful in many different endeavors. They have a positive outlook on life, a wealth of interests, the emotional flexibility to gain a balanced perspective about themselves and their academic pursuits, and a genuine concern with self-presentation and effective communication.

Training of TFs

The training program for the TFs begins during the summer when each new TF receives a packet of training materials. The TFs read seven background articles covering the following topics: (a) characteristics of quality undergraduate psychology programs (American Psychological Association, 1994a), (b) goals and objectives of the institution's general education curriculum, (c) ideas about how to start class off on the right foot (Zahorski, 1993), (d) development of effective skills in assessing written work (Larson, 1986; Sommers, 1982; Willingham, 1990), and (e) reasons for establishing high standards for academic performance (W. Cole, 1993). Also in preparation for the formal training sessions, the TFs receive the student manual and lesson plans for the first three laboratories; an outline of the conceptual organization of the laboratories, including the topics and statistical procedures covered in each; three student laboratory papers; and the midsemester and final course evaluations from the previous semester.

After returning to campus, the 2½ days of formal training begins with a team-building dinner. The first morning session is focused on the goals and philosophy of the laboratory within the context of general education requirements. The evaluations of the previous semester are reviewed to capitalize on prior experience. Then, the TFs work together as a team to design a research project, formulate hypothetical data, and use various software packages to analyze the data. In the afternoon session, the course syllabus and logistical issues are reviewed, but the primary focus is on assessment of student work. The originator of our writing-across-the-curriculum and undergraduate writing fellows program works with the TFs to improve their understanding of the assessment of student papers. The TFs also receive training in how to help students effectively use microcomputers for writing and data analysis.

During the second day of training, the TFs work in pairs to teach the first three laboratory classes. Each pair is videotaped, and these taped segments are reviewed and critiqued by the entire group. The objectives are to improve the TFs teaching skills and increase their comfort level with directing the first three laboratories. In addition, the TFs

work with the social science reference librarian to enhance their skills in completing computerized library searches and learn effective ways to help introductory students with information retrieval.

Supervision of TFs

The weekly supervision sessions provide a critical means to support the TFs professional development, and these sessions ensure quality, consistency, and coherence in the curriculum (cf. Wesp, 1992). In the first semester, the faculty member who designed the next laboratory teaches it to the TFs during weekly supervision. This procedure allows the TFs to observe a model of effective pedagogy, ask questions about the laboratory, and engage in collaborative development of alternative ways of accomplishing the objectives of the laboratory. In addition, the primary faculty supervisor meets individually with the TFs during the first semester to explore concerns. The supervision format changes in the second semester when pairs of TFs teach the next laboratory to their peers and the supervising faculty. In this way, the TFs are refreshed in course material, and they have the opportunity to hone their pedagogical skills. An added benefit of faculty supervision is that it fosters a sense of community, and the faculty have a vested interest in the TFs and the introductory students' experiences.

Development of Similar Programs

Development of the laboratory course and TFs program has been a major undertaking, and the establishment of similar programs rests first and foremost in collaborative faculty initiative. All nine of our faculty cooperatively team teach our lecture course, and five faculty are active in the development of the laboratory curriculum. Individual faculty rotate teaching credit for the lecture course over nine semesters, the primary faculty supervisor receives credit equivalent to two ninths of the annual teaching load, and the four supporting faculty direct TF supervision sessions without receiving course credit.

The history of our introductory course provides an important context in which to assess this level of faculty participation. A decade ago, we offered five or six introductory sections each semester that required approximately 17% of our total faculty teaching load. Since then, nominal teaching load has been reduced by 25%, and now we use approximately 6% of our total faculty load to support the introductory course and laboratory. The net gain is equivalent to one faculty member's teaching load for an entire year.

The relatively low expenditure of faculty resources to implement a general education experience of this magnitude was an important factor in our garnering financial support for the project. Furthermore, at an institution whose strategic plan is titled "Engagement in Learning," the laboratory curriculum and TFs program are well matched to institutional strategic goals. Although there were significant expenditures in new facilities, the resulting 13-station Macintosh instructional classroom supports the entire psychology curriculum and is scheduled for direct classroom instruction for more than 40 hr per week. Other one-time expenses included summer support for one faculty member and a student assistant who worked to organize the laboratory curriculum, the student and TF manuals, and the training materials. The ongoing expense for paying each TF is approximately $1,300 per year, and the introductory laboratory itself has a small operating budget of about $500 per year.

In an era of limited resources and increasing class sizes, the initial facility expenditure may be prohibitive, but this expense could be lessened by creating a less elaborate laboratory classroom or possibly retrofitting an existing facility. The ongoing expense of paying TFs could be replaced through the use of course credit (for variations of this approach, see Harris, 1994; Zechmeister & Reich, 1994). As an alternative to adding more sections for introductory courses with larger enrollments, the laboratory curriculum could be reduced and offered to students on alternate weeks thereby doubling potential enrollment. In this way, benefits of the small class size in laboratory sections are maintained. Regardless of implementation strategy, a program such as ours has important implications for personalizing large introductory classes and for providing introductory students with hands-on and minds-on experiences (Benjamin, 1991).

Outcomes of the Psychological Science Laboratory Experience

Outcomes for Introductory Students

To assess students' experience in the Introduction to Psychological Science laboratory, narrative evaluations were completed by all students at midterm and the end of the semester. Four open-ended questions about positive and negative aspects of the laboratory as well as suggestions for improvement were asked each time. Results of the summative evaluations from the first two semesters in which the laboratory was taught were content analyzed and organized around five themes: (a) connection to the lecture class component of the course, (b) hands-on experience with psychology, (c) collaborative learning and skill development, (d) class structure, and (e) demands and expectations of the laboratory.

Connection to the lecture class component of the course. The laboratory was intended to provide a unique opportunity for students to think and behave like psychologists, and

the methodological focus of the lecture class was expected to be augmented by the laboratory experience. Although many students commented about the connections between the lecture class and the laboratory, student evaluations fell on both sides of this issue. Some said that the class and laboratory were not adequately related and wished the connections were more direct (e.g., a laboratory on personality the week personality is discussed in the lecture), whereas others said that the laboratory provided an opportunity to apply methodologies to research questions and reinforced the material covered in the class.

Hands-on experience with psychology. What the students consistently described as hands-on experience can be more formally conceptualized as active learning. There were two specific ways in which students thought they actively engaged in learning about the science of psychology, and these experiences were often described as the best aspects of the laboratory. First, students consistently commented on the value of learning the methodologies of psychological science and the complexities of experimental design. Second, students expressed favor about how computers were incorporated into the laboratory. They were given minimal instruction, but they gained the necessary tools to use computers effectively on their own.

Collaborative learning and skill development. Whether praising or questioning the value of the laboratory experience, most students indicated that the laboratory promoted the development of critical- and analytical-thinking skills. This evaluation was also supported by responses to the standard teaching evaluation question on promotion of critical and analytical thinking: Seventy-two percent of the students gave the highest rating and less than 3% gave the lowest rating across all laboratory sections on a 3-point scale. Furthermore, students believed that their writing skills greatly improved. The most pervasive criticism of the laboratory was the amount of work required, and the weekly laboratory reports bore the brunt of this criticism. Nevertheless, students indicated that, as their writing skills improved, they gained a greater understanding and appreciation for scientific writing. The collaborative learning that characterized the laboratory experience was also highly praised by students. They enjoyed working with the TFs and their classmates in a process of mutual discovery, and they valued the opportunity to help one another learn.

Class structure. Perhaps the most prevalent topic of students' evaluations was their experience with the TFs. Although the feeling was not universal, the vast majority of students had a positive experience with the TFs, who were viewed as more effective and less intimidating than faculty. Many phrases were used to describe the TFs; however, students most frequently commented on their patience and willingness to help, their thoroughness and ease at explaining difficult concepts, and their enthusiasm and desire to help students learn. Furthermore, the laboratory students enjoyed having other students lead them in collaborative discovery and said that, as their peers, the TFs could easily understand them. Other aspects of the laboratory structure that students appreciated were the small class size, the individual attention given to them by their TFs, and the ease of following the laboratory manual.

Demands and expectations of the laboratory. An almost universal comment was that the laboratory was too much work. However, some students added a caveat to their comments about the workload; they thought the laboratory required too much work, but it was challenging and interesting. In particular, they believed they gained a strong knowledge base in the methodologies used in different disciplines, the use of computers, the methods of scientific writing, and the importance of developing critical- and analytical-thinking skills. Hence, we think that the work required in the laboratory class is just about right! Another problem with the laboratory, according to many students, has to do with inconsistencies in the TFs application of scoring standards. As in any course with many sections, teachers of each section will grade slightly differently, and we are not overly concerned with this criticism. In addition, the view that performance in the laboratory is scored too harshly is a misperception. The mean score students received on laboratory reports was 81.4 ($SD = 9.8$), and the average grade for introductory classes across the institution is approximately a B-.

Outcomes for TFs

In addition to the positive outcomes for the introductory students, the laboratory also has important outcomes for the TFs. In the summer following their tenure, the original eight TFs were asked to write a letter about their experience. Although each TF did not necessarily speak to each point, a content analysis of these reflective and candid evaluations revealed five major themes: (a) learning about teaching, (b) collaborative relationships among the TFs, (c) a capstone experience that provided connections across the baccalaureate experience, (d) academic skill development, and (e) personal development.

Learning about teaching. First and foremost, the TFs valued the opportunity to teach and to learn about teaching. Through close supervision and direct experience, TFs learned about different modes of teaching, and their teaching skills in and out of the classroom dramatically improved. Also, TFs were better able to recognize their personal strengths and weaknesses, and they gained insight into what is required to teach effectively. Perhaps the most important outcome of the TF experience was the development of a pedagogical philosophy centered on empowering students with responsibility for their own learning, encouraging collaborative discovery, and promoting the development of a method of inquiry.

These three principles represent the essence of the TFs approach to teaching, but the TF experience was also very satisfying. The TFs described their "passion for teaching" and the personal rewards of teaching, including the moments of "excitement and fulfillment from seeing something click for a student." The rewards of teaching were also evident in learning to cope with the frustrations of students who appeared unmotivated and did not live up to their potential. Finally, for those TFs contemplating a career in academics, their desire to become professors was fostered by the opportunity to gain a quality, closely supervised teaching experience even before entering graduate school.

Collaborative relationships. The TF experience provided a focal point for academic and intellectual pursuits. As a group, the TFs were dedicated to psychology and their introductory laboratories. Their initial training experience brought them together as a team and encouraged them to help and support one another. As the TFs worked more closely as a group, they respected one another, challenged each other's ideas, and worked collaboratively to solve problems. Likewise, the demands of learning to coordinate team teaching were at times challenging, but immensely valuable, aspects of the experience. This combination of unique opportunities provided the TFs with a common experience steeped in intellectual richness and vitality.

A capstone experience. Each TF had considerable psychology course work, and all were involved in independent research. Nevertheless, teaching the introductory laboratories was a valuable capstone experience that supported interconnections among knowledge areas. Just as a primary goal of the Introduction to Psychological Science laboratory is for students to gain an appreciation for the science of psychology and to understand the role of various subdisciplines, a similar and more sophisticated outcome was obtained by the TFs. The TFs imparted this scientific orientation to their students, and they developed a conceptual framework for their own baccalaureate experience.

As part of their teaching responsibilities, the TFs tried to make connections among various subdisciplines of psychology. They worked to make psychological science come alive for their students and to demonstrate how different researchers may ask the same questions but seek to answer these questions in different ways. Within this context, TFs were better able to tie together the seemingly distinct experiences they had in their various psychology classes. Their search for connections among what they had learned transcended the boundaries of psychology because TFs also looked for interconnections with their other classes in the liberal arts.

Academic skill development. A fundamental outcome of the TF experience was the feeling that teaching the introductory labs made the TFs better students. The TFs were better able to integrate their knowledge of psychology and draw connections among subdisciplines. In addition, all TFs wrote of the refinement and development of their academic skills. They were continually called on to explain concepts and answer questions. Consequently, oral communication skills as well as critical thinking skills were enhanced by the TF experience. In addition, teaching an entire laboratory on writing scientific papers and scoring students' weekly laboratory reports raised the TFs awareness of their own strengths and weaknesses in writing.

Also, TFs believed that their experiences made them more active students. TFs realized that their students learned more when they asked questions, posed problems or alternative solutions, or stimulated discussion on a particular issue, and TFs encouraged each other and their peers to do the same in their own classes. Furthermore, the TFs consistently advocated collaborative learning, and they tried to promote that kind of environment in the classes in which they were students. One might suspect that the intense demands on the TFs would detract from their course work. However, just the opposite was the case; every TF did as well or better than the previous year: As a group, they went from a previous 3.41 overall grade point average (GPA) to a 3.87 GPA for the first semester.

Personal development. All TFs also wrote about some aspect of the experience as contributing to their personal growth and development. Although these outcomes differed, each TF mentioned personal development as an important result of the experience. For example, teaching their peers and being completely responsible for the labs fostered a sense of confidence and competence. In addition, the TFs dealt with many students and handled their problems, concerns, and frustrations. They also collaborated to work through difficulties of teaching as a team. Due to these experiences, many TFs said that they became more effectively assertive in interpersonal interactions. Furthermore, the TFs believed that their time-management skills greatly improved. Their position as a TF added 10 or more hr a week to their schedule, but each TF achieved the best GPAs of their college career. A common sentiment among the TFs was that they realized how much time mattered, and they became more effective managers of their time.

Overall, the TFs described their experience as "the best academic experience I had," "extremely helpful," "an extremely rewarding experience, both academically and personally," and "so exciting that I have realized how important becoming a professor is to me." Each of these comments points to the important professional socialization that takes place when undergraduates teach their peers (cf. Harris, 1994). In particular, by participating in the life of the university through the roles of student and teacher, TFs increased their connection to the academic community, and they truly became an integral part of that community through their investment in the psychology department and in the arts and sciences.

Implications for Undergraduate Education

The Introduction of Psychological Science laboratory and the TFs program offer unusual challenges to introductory students and advanced undergraduates. Few faculty would take issue with the high expectations for the introductory students. The nonmajor has a marvelous opportunity for hands-on and minds-on exploration of how psychologists ask and answer questions about behavior. Students planning to major in psychology are provided with an intensive firsthand experience with psychological science. This preparation should have important benefits when these students enroll in more challenging courses in our hierarchical curriculum (Walker, Newcomb, & Hopkins, 1987).

Just as the outcomes for the introductory student are very positive, so too are the outcomes for the TFs. An unanswered question is whether the responsibilities of the TFs are at a level appropriate for high-quality undergraduate education. Some faculty may question the use of undergraduates to teach introductory laboratory sessions. They could point out many reasons why TFs would be less than successful as laboratory instructors—their undergraduate status, their inexperience, and their ignorance of what defines good pedagogy. Nevertheless, our experiences with the TFs belie these notions; in fact, some of these concerns have been transformed into assets. For example, TFs make connections with students that faculty cannot ordinarily make, TFs share their experiences as learners who are growing intellectually and who acknowledge—as all teachers should—that they are closer to the beginning than to the end of such growth, and TFs have a freshness and enthusiasm that is contagious and allows every laboratory student to be energized by their passion for learning. Skeptics may think that we have taken active learning too far, but our experience suggests that everyone comes out a winner.

References

Allison, S. T. (1995). Reconceiving and reconstructing the introductory course in psychology. *The Faculty Exchange, 8,* 14–20.

American Psychological Association. (1994a). *Principles for quality undergraduate psychology programs.* Washington, DC: Author.

American Psychological Association. (1994b). *Publication manual of the American Psychological Association* (4th ed.). Washington, DC: Author.

Benjamin, L. T., Jr. (1991). Personalization and active learning in the large introductory psychology class. *Teaching of Psychology 18,* 68–74.

Cole, D. L. (1982). Psychology as a liberating art. *Teaching of Psychology, 9,* 23–28.

Cole, D. L. (1986). Attracting the best and the brightest to teach psychology. *Teaching of Psychology, 13,* 107–110.

Cole, W. (1993, January 6). By rewarding mediocrity we discourage excellence. *The Chronicle of Higher Education,* pp. B1–B2.

Diamond, M. J. (1972). Improving the undergraduate lecture class by use of student-led discussion groups. *American Psychologist, 27,* 978–981.

Goolkasian, P., & Lee, J. A. (1988). A computerized laboratory for general psychology. *Teaching of Psychology, 15,* 98–100.

Harris, R. J. (1994, June). *Using undergraduates as teachers in a large university psychology class.* Paper presented at the meeting of the American Psychological Society, Washington, DC.

Janssen, P. (1976). With a little help from our friends. *Change, 8,* 50–53.

Kohn, A., & Brill, M. (1981). An introductory demonstration laboratory produced entirely by undergraduates. *Teaching of Psychology, 18,* 133–138.

Larson, R. L. (1986). Making assignments, judging writing, and annotating papers: Some suggestions. In C. W. Bridges (Ed.), *Training the new teacher of college composition* (pp. 109–126). Urbana, IL: National Council of Teachers of English.

Newcomb, A. F., Bagwell, C. L., & Wright, C. L. (Eds.). (1995). *Psychological science laboratory.* New York: McGraw-Hill.

Sommers, N. (1982). Responding to student writing. *College Composition and Communication, 33,* 148–156.

Walker, W. E., Newcomb, A. F., & Hopkins, W. P. (1987). A model for curriculum evaluation and revision in undergraduate psychology programs. *Teaching of Psychology, 14,* 198–202.

Wesp, R. (1992). Conducting introductory psychology activity modules as a requirement in advanced undergraduate courses. *Teaching of Psychology, 19,* 219–220.

Willingham, D. B. (1990). Effective feedback on written assignments. *Teaching of Psychology, 17,* 10–13.

Wortman, C. B., & Hillis, J. W. (1976). Undergraduate-taught "minicourses" in conjunction with an introductory lecture course. *Teaching of Psychology, 3,* 69–72.

Zahorski, K. J. (1993). Planning the first class. *The Teaching Professor, 7*(6), 5.

Zechmeister, E. B., & Reich, J. N. (1994). Teaching undergraduates about teaching undergraduates: A capstone course. *Teaching of Psychology, 21,* 24–28.

Notes

1. Catherine L. Bagwell is now a doctoral student in clinical psychology at Duke University; she was instrumental in developing the teaching fellows program and served as a teaching fellow during the 1993–94 academic year.

2. We thank Michelle Acosta, Cheryl Gaumer, Jennifer Humm, Melanie Morgan, Michele Nahra, Kevin Proudfoot, and Sandy Stevens—all members of the inaugural class of teaching fellows.

3. We also express appreciation to the Department of Psychology faculty, the University of Richmond Program for the Enhancement of Teaching Effectiveness, David Leary, and Zeddie Bowen for their generous support of the teaching fellows program.

A Radical Poster Session

Paul A. Gore, Jr.
Cameron J. Camp
University of New Orleans

Poster sessions have been described as teaching aids for advanced undergraduate seminars (Chute & Bank, 1983) and graduate student/faculty colloquia (Ventis, 1986). Since the spring of 1985, we have used a poster session as an integral part of a sophomore-level course in experimental design; it accounts for 20% of the course grade.

In this course, each student must design and conduct an original experiment and report the results in a poster session entitled "Spring/Fall Radish Festival." The title of the festival is derived from the fact that the subjects in these experiments are radishes. Aside from the long and noble history of radishes in experimental psychology (Lenington, 1979), these plant subjects have much to offer for our purposes. Radishes have a 30- to 40-day growth cycle; hence, in the course of a quarter or semester, almost any experimental design known to psychology (including sequential analyses from developmental psychology) can be executed. Radishes also do best with a spring or fall planting, grow quickly (in case disaster strikes and a fast replication is needed), and their seeds are bought rather than recruited. It is neither surprising nor fortuitous that the statistics of Student and Fisher have their roots in agricultural research.

Most important, the exercise provides students with hands-on experience in applying the principles of experimental design. Because they are working with a different species (indeed, phylum), the students often must be flexible and creative in using operational definitions. For example, two experiments were conducted to test the popularly-held idea that talking to plants influences their growth. One student studied the effects of playing motivational tapes on radish height. As a control measure, she played a tape of mumbling to her comparison group. One student studied the effects of speaking Spanish to her plants, with English being spoken to her control group. Students doing such exercises quickly learn why saline injections or placebos are used as control procedures in more traditional experimental settings.

All posters are required to have an abstract of no more than 300 words, and a listing of hypotheses and operational definitions. In addition, the independent and dependent variables must be clearly listed and defined. Threats to both internal and external validity must be listed, and an explanation of control procedures must be presented. The Results section must include the statistical tests used, as well as tables and charts when appropriate. In drawing conclusions, the students are urged to pay close attention to the question presented in the hypothesis, and the answer as given by the statistical analysis. Finally, a statement about what level of construct was contained in the study must be included (theoretical constructs must be free of mono-method and mono-operational bias, Cook & Campbell, 1979).

The poster session is held in a festival atmosphere, with 1st, 2nd, and 3rd prizes awarded. Students are, however, expected to answer questions presented to them on design decisions, statistics, or other information pertinent to the course. Previous prize winners include studies that examined the effects of the following variables on the growth of radishes: radiation, diazepam with shock, motivational tapes, carbon dioxide enriched atmosphere, and river water versus bottled water. The "Angel of Death" prize for the student suffering the highest level of experimental mortality and the "Square Radish" prize for the most bizarre independent variable are also rewarded.

Students also learn the relationships among statistics, experimental design, and subjects' behavior. Students are required to bring their radishes to the poster session so that the effects of their independent variables can literally be observed. One student reported a highly significant F statistic as a result of comparing the height of two groups when visually the groups were indistinguishable. When forced by the instructor to recalculate the between-groups sum of squares on the spot, the student realized the error of his ways (statistically speaking), and also learned a lesson in the relationship between statistical tests and common sense. The presence of the subjects in this case provided a valuable, concrete lesson in what within-groups and between-groups variance looks like.

Students also are required to bring printouts of data analyses using the SPSS^x MANOVA program. Because many students use more than one dependent measure, they stumble on multivariate statistics included on their printouts, and curiosity leads them to learn more about multivariate analyses. We have found this approach to be a valuable introduction for students. In addition, students learn that interventions can have multiple effects, some positive and some negative. For example, a student who watered plants with milk found that the experimental plants had less root growth but larger leaf size in comparison to a control group of water-watered plants.

Finally, our students develop a sense of pride in their craft from this exercise. This festival is open to the entire college community, is featured in the campus newspaper, and is a topic of conversation for weeks afterward. Previous festival participants return each year to observe the growth of "radish psychology." Demonstrating their expertise in experimental design solidifies the lessons of the course in ways that are highly enjoyable for our students.

References

Chute, D. L., & Bank, B. (1983). Undergraduate seminars: The poster session solution. *Teaching of Psychology, 10,* 99–100.

Cook, T. D., & Campbell, D. T. (1979). *Quasi-experimentation.* Chicago: Rand McNally.

Lenington, S. (1979). Effects of holy water on the growth of radish plants. *Psychological Reports, 45,* 381–382.

Ventis, D. G. (1986). Recycling poster sessions for colloquium series. *Teaching of Psychology, 13,* 222.

Poster Sessions Revisited: A Student Research Convocation

Jerome Rosenberg
Ronald L. Blount
The University of Alabama

Conducting research in psychology is essential for the further development of our field. Training students to engage in research is one of the primary jobs of psychologists in university settings, which is not always an easy task. Research is a complex activity, and shaping is necessary before students are able to behave in a truly independent manner. An important aspect of this shaping process is helping to assure that reinforcers are available for students' research efforts.

Among the most potent reinforcers for research are publications and presentations. However, obtaining these reinforcers requires varying degrees of skill, effort, and luck. The amount of time, effort, and skill required for preparing journal submissions, including possible rewriting and resubmissions, as well as rejections, can be overwhelming to inexperienced students. Also, interesting exploratory data may lack adequate substance for publication. Convention presentations offer a less demanding alternative for presenting research. The acceptance rate for convention submissions is typically higher than for journals, allowing more students to sample the reinforcers. However, many students still appear to be intimidated by the idea of presenting research at national or regional conventions where professionals judge their work and, some appear to believe, their worth. Poster sessions for members of a psychology department are a third possible presentation format. Because acceptance rate at departmental sessions would most likely be high and students would know many of the attendees, departmental poster preparations appear to offer the least demanding avenue for research presentation.

Chute and Bank (1983) advocated the use of departmental poster sessions as a means for undergraduate students taking seminars to present their literature reviews. Ventis (1986) used a departmental poster session as a means for faculty from her department to present their research to students in an informal setting. These posters had previously been presented at other conventions. The Department of Psychology at the University of Alabama recently used a departmental poster session to promote the presentation of empirical research conducted by undergraduate and graduate students. Approximately half of the presenters had never attended a poster session.

Research submitted for the convocation may have been conducted in collaboration with faculty, with other students and limited faculty supervision, or as part of an experimental psychology course requirement. Each project submitted for review included the title, author, and a 300- to 500-word abstract. The student was not required to be the first author, and a faculty coauthor was not necessary. Each submission was reviewed by three faculty members. Acceptance was based on the nature of the problem being investigated, adequacy of the methods and controls, nature of the results, and significance of the conclusions. After a poster was accepted, the student prepared it for presentation with help from a member of the Undergraduate Committee or, if applicable, a faculty coauthor. To stimulate participation, one undergraduate and one graduate student received an award based on the importance of the research, soundness of the design and analysis, and originality and appearance of the presentation. Student award winners were selected by a secret ballot completed by all faculty who attended. The awards included a certificate and a $15.00 copy card for photocopying.

The first convocation, which included presentations by five undergraduate and seven graduate students, was held in the faculty lounge. More than 200 people attended during the 2-hr period. Of those attending, approximately 15 were faculty (out of a department of 20 faculty), 60 were graduate students, and the rest were undergraduate students. A questionnaire was made available for evaluating the convocation, and 31 attendees responded: 9 faculty, 13 graduate students, and 9 undergraduates. The overwhelming response from all three groups was very favorable; more than 90% wanted the program continued on a yearly basis, and all rated the program as "good" or "very good." Although some caution must be exercised when interpreting the responses of only 30 of the 200 attendees, we believe that the other attendees' impressions of the convocation were equally positive. Faculty and presenters indicated that they heard only positive comments about the convocation from those attending. Also, all comments at the next faculty meeting indicated enthusiastic support for future convocations.

Because faculty were frequently coauthors of the presentations (8 of the 12 posters), this convocation also had the benefit of familiarizing faculty and students with faculty members' current research. Since the convocation, two undergraduates and four graduate students had their posters accepted for presentation at regional or national conventions. Although we are unable to determine what the base rate for submissions by our students would have been, several indicated that they were capitalizing on their efforts that went into preparing for our departmental convocation by submitting elsewhere. They also indicated that they felt less intimidated about presenting research at regional or national conventions.

References

Chute, D. L., & Bank, B. (1983). Undergraduate seminars: The poster session solution. *Teaching of Psychology, 10,* 99–100.

Ventis, D. G. (1986). Recycling poster sessions for colloquium series. *Teaching of Psychology, 13,* 222.

In-Class Poster Sessions

Brian N. Baird
Pacific Lutheran University

An unfortunate fact of teaching is that the opportunities for creative, individualized student activity tend to decrease in direct proportion to the number of students in a class. Instructors seeking a way around this dilemma may find in-class poster sessions a practical and rewarding solution.

Poster sessions have been described by Chute and Bank (1983) and in a slightly different form as "fairs" for high school students by Benjamin, Fawl, and Klein (1977). This article presents a more detailed description of how poster sessions can be conducted in classes ranging from small seminars to large introductory sections.

Poster Session Project Description and Requirements

My in-class poster sessions resemble the poster sessions held at professional and scientific conferences. Instead of each student submitting a paper that only the instructor reads, students present projects to their classmates in poster session format. Depending on the class size, we hold poster sessions on sequential days, with a portion of the class simultaneously presenting their posters at various locations in the room while the remaining students circulate to discuss, evaluate, and give feedback. The students then evaluate the projects, with the instructor reserving the right to assign final grades.

During the second week of class, students receive a handout describing the rationale, requirements, and procedures for the poster sessions. In an effort to promote creativity and diversity, poster sessions are not limited to written papers. Instead, I offer the more general requirement that the students present projects. These projects, which I must approve, may be anything from traditional papers or research studies to auditory, video, or other artistic presentations. All projects require some combination of written and visual presentation during the poster sessions. To assist students in understanding the requirements, I place examples of papers, videos, and audio productions from previous students on library reserve. Although most students grasp the nature of the assignment on their own, instructors using this activity for the first time may wish to provide class time to discuss ideas and options for poster sessions. Instructors may also wish to present examples of their own work in poster session format. If students still have difficulty understanding the assignment, the two-stage approach (discussed later) provides opportunities to observe the work of other students and to receive additional feedback and direction.

All projects must meet three criteria that also serve as the bases for grading: (a) extended research beyond the information available from text or lecture materials, (b) critical thinking and analysis of the subject matter, and (c) clear communication of the information and ideas. For the purpose of this assignment, *critical thinking* is defined rather broadly as doing more than just reporting what others have written on a topic. Students are expected to evaluate, synthesize, interpret, and critique information, not just paraphrase. I discuss each of the criteria in the handout and in class.

Three Steps to Developing Posters

A three-step approach to developing posters is helpful. First, early in the semester, students are given a written description of poster project requirements. I then suggest that students explore their textbooks, personal experiences, or other sources to identify topics they would like to pursue. Students are also encouraged to find one or two other students with whom they would like to work on a project. Students must then submit a one-page proposal describing the topic they will address, the methods they will use, any ethical considerations, and the responsibilities of each student in the group.

The one-page descriptions give me a chance to ensure that the proposed projects are within the students' abilities and do not pose significant risks or other ethical concerns. The descriptions also let me brainstorm with students, suggest possible resources or approaches, and help anticipate or iron out problems.

After approving the project proposals, I schedule a date for initial presentation of the projects. During the semester, students present their projects on two occasions. The first presentation is given midway through the semester. This presentation allows students an opportunity to present what they have completed and receive feedback from their peers.

Setting a midsemester presentation date helps reduce the last minute "cramming" guaranteed to accompany assignments that are due at the end of the semester. Of greater importance is the opportunity for students to give and receive feedback. During the first poster session presentation, students' work will be reviewed by half of the other students in the class. Before this session, I instruct students in the value of such feedback and how best to give and receive it. This approach encourages students to learn from one another and to appreciate the value of the process of revision (Baird & Anderson, 1990). A recent student demonstrated this value by placing a sign beside his paper that read, "Tear it up please. I want your suggestions." Encouraging students to share their work and constructive criticism with others establishes a precedent that will serve them well throughout their educational experience.

A third benefit of the initial session is that the opportunity to observe the work of other students encourages project improvement among all participants. In the traditional model of assigned papers, only the instructor sees and evaluates student work. In such situations, students know only what they have produced and have no way to compare or contrast their work with that of their peers. The poster session, on the other hand, provides an opportunity for students to learn from comparison. The midsemester presentation leaves time for improvements.

A final benefit of the poster session and the two-stage presentation is that complaints concerning grades diminish. When students have no opportunity to observe the quality of their peers' work, they do not know why they received a particular grade. Poster sessions do not entirely solve this problem, but many students seem more ready to accept the grade their projects earn. As one student admitted, "When you gave me a C on my project I was mad at first, but then I saw what some of the other students had done and I understood. Now I want to make my final version a lot better."

Following the initial presentation of posters, I schedule the final step in the process for the next to last week of the semester. At this time, students present their revised projects. Presentation during this week allows time to grade and give feedback before the semester ends.

Session Logistics

Because students often choose similar topics, I review the first proposals and schedule presentations on different days to avoid redundancy. After topics are selected and assigned, a printed program describes what will be presented and by whom during the poster sessions. Copies of this program are distributed in advance to build a sense of the importance of the event. I also post the programs so other students or faculty may attend the sessions.

Along with balancing the content of the poster sessions, the instructor must consider the number of posters to be presented and how much time will be available for students to visit each poster. In large introductory classes, I allow the nonpresenters approximately 5 min to visit each poster that day. I also follow this time limit as I circulate among the posters to evaluate and discuss them with the students. If two or three students collaborate on each project, we can review posters for a lecture class of 50 to 60 students in 2 or 3 days. For larger classes, I schedule more presenters on a given day, with the trade-off being less time for interaction or the inability of all the students to visit all of the posters for that day. For smaller, upper division classes, I allow 10 to 15 min for each poster presentation. The added time permits greater discussion of presumably more advanced topics and projects.

Another suggestion is to take a signed, written roll on each day of the poster sessions. Although most students look forward to presenting their own work and attending the other days to view the posters of others, some attend only on the days of their presentations. Such absences are unfair to students who attended the first presentations. Absent students also defeat the goal of having students learn from each others' posters. Making attendance mandatory at all sessions is regrettable but necessary to ensure equal participation.

We hold poster sessions in a classroom where students spread out around the perimeter and display their material either on tables or the wall. Poster sessions require a room that is large enough for students to have at least 5 to 8 ft in which to present their posters, with several feet between adjacent posters.

At the students' request, we recently held poster sessions in the informal, club-like, student union cafeteria. This allowed others outside the class to join the session and circulate among the posters. The response was positive, and other instructors say that they will follow suit with their classes.

Grading

As noted earlier, students participate in grading posters. This approach reduces the grading burden on the instructor and encourages students to evaluate the quality of their own work and that of others. Unfortunately, my experience suggests that when students are asked to grade others they tend to give everyone As. Such generosity is understandable, but it does not require students to consider what "quality work" means, and it is unfair to those students who have clearly produced superior work. To address this problem, give students the grading criteria before they grade any projects. The session program lists these criteria, and students assign each project a grade for each of the three criteria. Students record the grades on the programs and then return the programs anonymously at the end of each session. Even with these measures, the instructor should reserve the right to assign final grades. The instructor may wish to recognize exceptional effort that students might overlook or reduce the grade of mediocre projects that students graded too highly.

One final grading issue concerns the evaluation of collaborative projects. Most students find collaboration instructive and enjoyable. In some instances, however, students complain that they carried all the load while their partners did little or none of the work. With grades assigned on a per project basis, all students connected with the project receive the same grade, although some may not have earned it. I know of no solution that is entirely satisfactory. Asking students to identify their role during the proposal phase, then giving them an opportunity to individually grade their own project, as well as their contribution and that of their partners, may be useful. This approach at least provides a way for students to tell the instructor who in their group they felt earned what grade.

Student Evaluation of Poster Sessions

To assess student reactions to the poster sessions, I prepared a brief evaluation form and distributed it to two introductory psychology sections that participated in the poster sessions. I asked students to complete these forms anonymously and return them as part of the end of semester course evaluation. Abbreviated items from the questionnaire and response frequencies for each item are presented in Table 1.

The overall response to the poster sessions was positive as revealed in Table 1. Students indicated that the poster sessions were a valuable activity and that the main goals of the sessions were achieved. Some students expressed ambivalence about grading other students' papers and having their own work graded by peers. Even in these areas, however, the responses were almost all positive.

The clearest indication of support for poster sessions was seen in response to the last item of the survey. When asked if they would prefer to follow the poster session format or the standard term paper approach, 100% of those who responded to the question favored the poster sessions.

Table 1. Poster Session Evaluation Results

1. Did the poster sessions increase interaction among students and provide exposure to other students' learning styles?

A	B	C	D	E
58%	37%	5%		

2. By viewing other students work, do you feel you were able to gain more information about other topics that interested you?

A	B	C	D	E
73%	25%	2%		

3. The poster sessions involved three steps—the original proposal, the first session, and the final session. Do you feel this was a valuable approach?

A	B	C	D	E
74%	22%	4%		

4. How valuable was it for you to have the opportunity to do something other than a written paper?

A	B	C	D	E
75%	21%	4%		

5. What is your reaction to the process of you grading other posters?

A	B	C	D	E
34%	36%	25%	5%	

6. What is your reaction to having other students grade your work?

A	B	C	D	E
37%	38%	15%	8%	1%

7. Overall, how would you rate the effectiveness of the poster session format?

A	B	C	D	E
63%	33%	4%		

8.[a] What percentage of your course grade do you think the poster session should comprise?

% of Grade	0%	10%	15%	20%	25%	30%	Selected
	3%	43%	28%	17%	4%	1%	4%

9. As a student, would you prefer to follow this format or go back to the term paper approach?

Poster	Term Paper	No Answer
93%	0%	7%

Note. A represents a *very positive* response to an item, C is *neutral,* and E is *very negative. N* = 73.

[a]The top row for this item indicates the percentage of the final grade the students think the posters should comprise. *Selected,* in the top row, means the grade value of the poster sessions would vary and students would choose for themselves how much their poster contributes to their final grade. The bottom row indicates the percentage of students preferring a given grade percentage for the poster sessions.

References

Baird, B. N., & Anderson, D. D. (1990). Writing in psychology. *The Teaching Professor, 4*(3), 5.

Benjamin, L. T., Jr., Fawl, C. T., & Klein, M. (1977). The fair—Experimental psychology for high school students. *American Psychologist, 32,* 1097–1098.

Chute, D. L., & Bank, B. (1983). Undergraduate seminars: The poster session solution. *Teaching of Psychology, 10,* 99–100.

Note

I thank Gayle Robbins for her assistance in developing the activities described in this article.

Preferences About APA Poster Presentations

Andrea A. Welch
Charles A. Waehler
The University of Akron

Poster sessions at APA conventions complement paper sessions and symposia by providing extended opportunities for direct exchanges of professional ideas. Although poster sessions are an integral part of professional conventions, little research has appeared in psychological journals concerning the optimal use of this medium for scientific interchange. Literature from other fields contains a few suggestions on how to conduct poster presentations. Woolsey (1989), for example, described characteristics of poster design that produce maximal visual effect. He advised strict editing to avoid crowding the poster with unnecessary wording, a hierarchical organization wherein typeface decreases in size with greater detail, and an arrangement that eliminates visually distracting angles by aligning text in left-justified columns rather than uncentered blocks.

Instructors have found posters to be effective supplemental-learning tools in undergraduate courses. For instance, Baird (1991) reported that a poster session project was preferred by students over a term paper in his introductory psychology course. Chute and Bank (1983) reported that a poster session was superior to a seminar format in upper level undergraduate courses because it allows students to practice scientific communication without filling many class periods with individual presentations. These authors reported that students appreciated the opportunity to learn directly from each other by observing the work of their peers and receiving feedback on their own work.

Two studies examined the effectiveness of poster presentations. Hirsch and Edelstein (1992) found health education posters to be motivating and interesting to their college students even though the students reported that they did not acquire new information. Horton (1986) noted that more people displayed behavior indicative of attending to a poster (e.g., visual scanning) when the presenter was standing rather than sitting. He referred to this difference as a "trend," however, and did not specify whether it was significant.

Although these reports are helpful in planning a scientific poster, an empirically derived summary of the characteristics that APA convention attendees prefer in a poster presentation would be more relevant for psychologists presenting their work. At present, APA provides presenters with a pamphlet describing the basic layout of posters ("Instructions," 1993). Mention of pictures, typeface, or graphics is not included, and there is no guidance concerning interaction with attendees. Because the effectiveness of posters may hinge on visual and interpersonal characteristics as well as the content of a presentation, review of all these components is needed. We identified characteristics of effective posters by surveying individuals attending the 1993 APA convention. Their responses suggest that certain variables increase understanding of and interest in scientific posters.

Method

Participants

Six hundred sixty individuals attending the Division Two or Division 17 poster sessions at the 1993 APA convention were given a questionnaire and asked to participate in this study. Two hundred seventy-one questionnaires were completed at the convention or returned by mail, for a return rate of 41%. The average age of participants was 37.4 years ($SD = 11.0$ years). One hundred forty-three women (53%) participated. One hundred seventy-five participants (65%) had doctoral degrees, and 61 (23%) had master's degrees. Participants held membership in 41 of the 48 APA divisions. Most commonly identified memberships were Division 17, Counseling Psychology ($n = 58$, 21%); Division 8, Personality and Social Psychology ($n = 36$, 13%); Division 12, Clinical Psychology ($n = 32$, 12%); and Division Two, Teaching of Psychology ($n = 32$, 12%). The average number of conventions attended by these participants was five ($SD = 5.9$), with 29% attending their first. One hundred eighteen participants (43%) presented a poster at the convention. Seventy-two percent of participants spent at least half of their professional time in an academic setting, 20% spent over half of their professional time in an applied setting, and most individuals reported involvement in some combination of these professional pursuits.

Instrument

The Poster Preference Questionnaire was designed specifically for this study. It contains eight Likert-scaled, one multiple-choice, and three short-answer items. Questions pertaining to demographic information were also included.

Results and Discussion

In response to objective items addressing poster appearance, attendees prefer larger than normal print and supplemental graphs and charts. In addition, accessibility to the material and presenter were important, as reflected in the preference for the availability of more than 50 copies of a handout and a notepad for addresses. Respondents were neutral concerning the use of pictures or colored charts and graphs, as well as the dress and positioning of the presenter. Responses to these Likert-type items were comparable across the four largest divisions in our sample, suggesting that these findings may have association-wide applicability.

The multiple-choice item asked what poster presenters engaged in a conversation should do if they notice other individuals looking at their poster from several feet away but not advancing toward it. About half ($n = 130$, 48%) of all respondents would encourage onlookers to join in the conversation with the first attendee, whereas the other half were split, with 27% ($n = 72$) suggesting continuation of the conversation with the first individual without attending to onlookers and 25% ($n = 69$) wrapping up the conversation with the first individual to give others a chance to participate. Although there is a preference for engaging people in an ongoing conversation, these results suggest that there is no one best way of handling this predicament. The optimal method probably depends on subtle situational distinctions.

The three short-answer questions yielded a wide range of responses coalescing around certain themes. We created categories to classify the idiosyncratic responses and developed subcategories for each question. Two scorers who were instructed regarding the assignment of responses to categories had a satisfactory interrater agreement of 87.9%. We reconciled scoring differences.

The first short-answer question asked respondents to "Please list any mannerisms of presenters you have encountered that have particularly distracted you so that you were not able to fully appreciate the merit of their work." About half of the surveys had no response to this question. Most of the responses concerned either interactions between the presenter and attendees (63%) or some aspect of the presenter's unprofessional comportment (28%). The most commonly noted distracting mannerism was involvement of the presenter in conversation unrelated to the poster. Presenters who show an optimal level of interaction are preferred: Overzealous presenters were noted as distract-

ing, as were those who were uninviting or not available for questions. Two other troubling mannerisms were watching the attendee while he or she was reading the poster and having an arrogant attitude. Common criticisms of presenter comportment included blocking visual access to the poster and absence from the poster display area.

The second short-answer question elicited more positive comments as it asked the respondent to "Think about an APA poster that particularly impressed you. What specific factors made that poster stand out for you." Responses were classified into four categories. Visual presentation of the poster was the most commonly endorsed category (41%), with preference given for large print within the body of the report, high-quality graphics, use of color, and a large title. Effectiveness with which the ideas were communicated was the second most commonly endorsed category (37%). Among important communication aspects of the poster were brevity, clarity of writing, supportive graphs and charts, and highlighted main points. Specific aspects of the work, including the personal relevance of the poster to the attendee, was the third most commonly endorsed category (11%). The novelty of the project and the quality of the research were only marginally noted. Presenter characteristics was the fourth category (8%), with a personable, friendly presenter making a positive impression.

The final question invited constructive feedback by asking "What would you like to tell (anonymously) some of the poster presenters that you feel have been particularly weak?" The 363 responses cluster into the three major areas: visual appearance of the poster (55%), poster content (25%), and interpersonal interaction style (10%). The most noted weaknesses were that the print of the poster text was too small and that the presenter did not take the time to make the poster professional and visually pleasing. Posting too many pages was another common criticism.

Comments about poster content were varied. Some respondents suggested that posters tried to present too much information; others commented that not enough information was presented. Others criticized the quality of the research presented, and a few suggested that the presenter "ought to check his (her) work for spelling and grammar." Interpersonal interaction style also received varied comments, with some respondents suggesting that presenters be more available for questions and show more interest in their work. Other concerns included the observation that handouts were not available.

Future investigations evaluating poster impact may be enhanced by using experimental designs that present stimuli that vary according to the dimensions identified in this survey. These designs may also be structured to overcome possible bias wherein comments pertaining to visual aspects may have been encouraged at the expense of research content. In addition, although few differences across divisions were noted, future researchers may consider using stratified random sampling.

APA poster presentations involve a two-step process: initial peer review to select for scientific merit and subsequent public display. Once scientific merit has been determined, packaging and presentation are important. Quality of the research should take precedence over superficial concerns, but a visually pleasing display may be necessary to engage the observer in more than a cursory inspection of posters at APA conventions.

References

Baird, B. N. (1991). In-class poster sessions. *Teaching of Psychology, 18*, 27–29.

Chute, D. L., & Bank, B. (1983). Undergraduate seminars: The poster session solution. *Teaching of Psychology, 10*, 99–100.

Hirsch, R., & Edelstein, M. E. (1992). In the eye of the beholder: Pretesting the effectiveness of health education materials. *Journal of American College Health, 40*, 292–293.

Horton, A. M. (1986). Reinforcement of poster attendance. *The Behavior Therapist, 9*, 198–222.

Instructions for poster presentations. (1993). Washington, DC: American Psychological Association.

Woolsey, J. D. (1989). Combating poster fatigue: How to use visual grammar and analysis to effect better visual communications. *Trends in Neuroscience, 12*, 325–332.

Appendix

Section I: Statistics

1. Generating Data Sets
   Thompson, 1994, *21*, 41–43.
   Walsh, 1993, *20*, 188–190.
   Beins, 1989, *16*, 230–231.
   Walsh, 1992, *19*, 243–244.
   Riniolo, 1997, *24*, 279–282.
2. Illustrating Statistical Concepts
   Pittenger, 1995, *22*, 125–128.
   Weaver, 1992, *19*, 178–179.
   Zerbolio, 1989, *16*, 207–209.
   Strube, 1991, *18*, 113–115.
3. Examining Statistical Tests
   Johnson, 1989, *16*, 67–68.
   Rasmussen, 1996, *23*, 55–56.
   Walsh, 1994, *21*, 53–55.
   Cake & Hostetter, 1992, *19*, 185–188.
   Walsh, 1991, *18*, 249–251.
   Strube & Goldstein, 1995, *22*, 207–208.
   Buck, 1990, *17*, 255–256.
   Refinetti, 1996, *23*, 51–54.
   Goldstein & Strube, 1995, *22*, 205–206.
   Huck, Wright, & Park, 1992, *19*, 45–47.
4. Developing Students' Skills
   Ware & Chastain, 1989, *16*, 222–227.
   Ware & Chastain, 1991, *18*, 219–222.
   Rogers, 1987, *14*, 109–111.
   Oswald, 1996, *23*, 124–126.
   Melvin & Huff, 1992, *19*, 177–178.
   Beins, 1993, *20*, 161–164.
   Smith, 1995, *22*, 49–50.
   Rossi, 1987, *14*, 98–101.
   Varnhagen, Drake, & Finley, 1997, *24*, 275–278.
   Derry, Levin, & Schauble, 1995, *22*, 51–57.
5. Evaluating Success in Statistics
   Low, 1995, *22*, 196–197.
   Friedman, 1987, *14*, 20–23.
   Hudak & Anderson, 1990, *17*, 231–234.
   Meehan, Hoffert, & Hoffert, 1993, *20*, 242–244.

Section II: Research Methods

1. Reducing Students' Fears
   Brems,1994, *21*, 241–243.
   Johnson, 1996, *23*, 168–170.
   Barber, 1994, *21*, 228–230.
2. Evaluating Ethical Issues
   Korn, 1988, *15*, 74–78.
   Korn & Hogan, 1992, *19*, 21–24.
   Klein & Cheuvront, 1990, *17*, 166–169.
   Nimmer & Handelsman, 1992, *19*, 141–144.
3. Teaching Ethics
   McMinn, 1988, *15*, 100–101.
   Beins, 1993, *20*, 33–35.
   Rosnow, 1990, *17*, 179–181.
   Strohmetz & Skleder, 1992, *19*, 106–108.
   Kallgren & Tauber, 1996, *23*, 20–25.
   Herzog, 1990, *17*, 90–94.
4. Reviewing the Literature
   Merriam, LaBaugh, & Butterfield, 1992, *19*, 34–36.
   Cameron & Hart, 1992, *19*, 239–242.
   Joswick, 1994, *21*, 49–53.
   Poe, 1990, *17*, 54–55.
5. Using Computers
   Goolkasian, 1985, *12*, 223–225.
   Peden, 1987, *14*, 217–219.
   Rittle, 1990, *17*, 127–129.
6. Implementing Teaching Strategies
   Kohn, 1992, *19*, 217–219.
   Bates, 1991, *18*, 94–97.
   Polyson & Blick, 1985, *12*, 52–53.
   Chamberlain, 1988, *15*, 207–208.
   Carroll, 1986, *13*, 208–210.
   McBurney, 1995, *22*, 36–38.
   Wilson & Hershey, 1996, *23*, 97–99.
   Marmie, 1994, *21*, 164–166.
   May & Hunter, 1988, *15*, 156–158.
   Gibson, 1991, *18*, 176–177.
7. Demonstrating Systematic Observation and Research Design
   Krehbiel & Lewis, 1994, *21*, 45–48.
   Herzog, 1988, *15*, 200–202.
   Marshall & Linden, 1994, *21*, 230–232.
   Goldstein, Hopkins, & Strube, 1994, *21*, 154–157.
   Carr & Austin, 1997, *24*, 188–190.
   Zerbolio & Walker, 1989, *16*, 65–66.
   Stallings, 1993, *20*, 165–167.
   Vernoy, 1994, *21*, 186–189.
8. Teaching Writing and Critical Thinking
   Addison, 1996, *23*, 237–238.
   Ault, 1991, *18*, 45–46.
   Dunn, 1996, *23*, 38–40.

Lawson & Smith, 1996, *23*, 56–58.

Hubbard & Ritchie, 1995, *22*, 64–65.

Hatcher, 1990, *17*, 123–124.

Connor–Greene, 1993, *20*, 167–169.

VanderStoep & Shaughnessy, 1997, *24*, 122–124.

Anisfeld, 1987, *14*, 224–227.

9. Emphasizing Accuracy in Research

Cronan–Hillix, 1988, *15*, 205–207.

McDonald & Peterson, 1991, *18*, 100–101.

Cronan–Hillix, 1991, *18*, 101–102.

Peden, 1991, *18*, 102–105.

10. Fostering Students' Research and Presentations

Gibson, Kahn, & Mathie, 1996, *23*, 36–38.

Prentice–Dunn & Roberts, 1985, *12*, 142–145.

Starke, 1985, *12*, 158–160.

Newcomb & Bagwell, 1997, *24*, 88–95.

Gore & Camp, 1987, *14*, 243–244.

Rosenberg & Blount, 1988, *15*, 38–39.

Baird, 1991, *18*, 27–29.

Welch & Waehler, 1996, *23*, 42–44.

Subject Index